TOWNSHEND-SMITH ON DISCRIMINATION LAW: TEXT, CASES AND MATERIALS

Second Edition

Michael Connolly

Senior Lecturer in Law,
University of Westminster

Cavendish
Publishing
Limited

London • Sydney • Portland, Oregon

Second edition first published in Great Britain 2004 by
Cavendish Publishing Limited, The Glass House,
Wharton Street, London WC1X 9PX, United Kingdom
Telephone: + 44 (0)20 7278 8000   Facsimile: + 44 (0)20 7278 8080
Email: info@cavendishpublishing.com
Website: www.cavendishpublishing.com

Published in the United States by Cavendish Publishing
c/o International Specialized Book Services,
5824 NE Hassalo Street, Portland,
Oregon 97213-3644, USA

Published in Australia by Cavendish Publishing (Australia) Pty Ltd
45 Beach Street, Coogee, NSW 2034, Australia
Telephone: + 61 (2)9664 0909   Facsimile: +61 (2)9664 5420

British Library Cataloguing in Publication Data
Connolly, Michael
Townshend-Smith's discrimination law: text, cases and materials – 2nd ed
1 Discrimination law – law and legislation – Great Britain
I Title II Townshend-Smith, Richard
344.4'101133

Library of Congress Cataloguing in Publication Data
Data available

ISBN 1-85941-795-7

1 3 5 7 9 10 8 6 4 2

Printed and bound in Great Britain

To Cath

PREFACE

Since the first edition, published in 1998, discrimination law has grown and developed hugely. The growth in discrimination law has been legislative and, for reasons outlined below, it has become exceedingly complicated. In recent years, European directives have been issued covering sex, race, disability, sexual orientation, religion or belief, and age. Among other things, this generation of European directives has introduced a new definition of indirect discrimination, a free-standing definition of harassment and procedural rules on the burden of proof.

The directives covering sex, race and disability have been (or will be) implemented by amending the existing domestic legislation. The problem here is that in some respects, the directives fall short of the existing domestic legislation. For instance, the directives covering sex and disability (but not race) are limited to employment matters, and the definition of 'race' in the Race Directive excludes colour and nationality. Consequently, there are two classes of sex, disability and race discrimination law entwined within the amended legislation. For sex discrimination, some of the amendments came into force in October 2001, whilst others, notably the free-standing definition of sexual harassment, are not due until 2005. The race discrimination amendments came into force on 19 July 2003 and the amendments to the Disability Discrimination Act 1995 are due in force on 1 October 2004.

The Equal Treatment at Work Directive has led to discrete and parallel statutory instruments covering discrimination on the grounds of sexual orientation and religion or belief coming into force on 1 and 2 December 2003. Age discrimination legislation is due to be implemented by 2006.

A further dimension to discrimination law is the European Convention on Human Rights, which is of much greater significance since the Human Rights Act 1998 came into force in October 2000. All courts and tribunals, as well as Parliament, must now observe the Convention, whose rights must be secured without discrimination, although, as of yet, the Convention contains no free-standing article against discrimination. Extracts from all of this legislation (save the domestic versions on age and sexual harassment, which have yet to be published) are included in this edition.

With a legislative 'scheme' this complicated, it is no surprise that there have been calls for a single Equality Act and, perhaps, a single enforcement commission. Proposals and discussions on these issues are included.

There have also been many case law developments since 1998, some positive and some negative. In *Pearce v Governing Body of Mayfield School* (2003), the House of Lords emphasised that the sex discrimination legislation could not be used where the principal discrimination was on the ground of sexual orientation, thus marginalising the Court of Appeal's enlightened and logical decision in *Smith v Gardner-Merchant* (1998) that homophobic taunting could also amount to sex discrimination where the abuse also was gender-specific: for example, 'gay men spread AIDS'. The House of Lords have considered and reconsidered the meaning of victimisation in *Nagarajan v LRT* (1999) and *Chief Constable of West Yorkshire v Khan* (2001). In *R v Secretary of State for Employment ex p Seymour-Smith* (1999 and 2000), the European Court of Justice and the House of Lords had to wrestle with detailed statistics in a case of indirect discrimination, something which is likely to become more common, as it is in the USA, where the law is highly developed.

There has been much case law under the Disability Discrimination Act, exploring the meaning of disability and the particularly technical meaning of disability discrimination. Notable in this context are the enlightening and authoritative judgments of Morison J. Although age discrimination has yet to be outlawed, the Employment Appeal Tribunal explored the possibility of it being actionable where it coincides (as it often will) with sex discrimination in *Harvest Town Circle Ltd v Rutherford* (2001). The new statutory definition of harassment does not cover all cases (see above) and as such some victims of harassment will still have draft their claim as a case of direct discrimination. For these claimants, the House of Lords' judgment in *Pearce* (2003) was a disappointment: the suggestion in *Porcelli v Strathclyde Regional Council* (1986) that gender- (and by implication race-) specific taunting, without more, amounted to discrimination 'went too far' according to Lord Nicholls. Thus, victims of sex- or race-specific harassment will have to show that they were treated less favourably than a comparator, which in many cases will be impossible. The potential of European equal pay law surprised some when the Court of Session in *South Ayrshire Council v Morton* (2002) allowed the claimant, a head teacher, to compare her pay with a male head teacher working for a different local authority, because there was a common salary scale was set by national agreement. However, a limit to this potential was restated by the European Court of Justice in *Lawrence and Others v Regent Office Care* (2002), which held that the difference in pay had to be attributable to a 'single source'. The ECJ continued to take a positive view of affirmative action programmes in *Re Badeck* (2000), whilst the United States Supreme Court ruled on the long-running disputes at the University of Michigan's affirmative action programmes in *Grutter v Bollinger* (2003). In *Vento v Chief Constable of West Yorkshire Police* (2002), the Court of Appeal made a detailed review and offered guidance for damages for injury to feelings in discrimination cases.

The human rights dimension to discrimination has also seen some important case law. The decision of the European Court of Human Rights in *Goodwin v UK* (2002) led the Government to publish a draft Gender Recognition Bill to equalise the status of transsexuals. In 2002, in *Mendoza v Ghaidan* and *A and Others v Secretary of State for the Home Department*, two differently constituted Courts of Appeal ruled on two important discrimination cases brought under the Human Rights Act 1998 and left a strong impression that the Court of Appeal has no common approach to the anti-discrimination principle enshrined in the Act and the Convention. Finally, the complicated relationship between EC law, the European Convention on Human Rights and domestic law was explored, with a practical purpose, by the Court of Appeal in *A v Chief Constable of West Yorkshire* (2002). Extracts from all of these cases are included in this edition.

It may be obvious now that the principal task in preparing this edition was to bring order to chaos. To help understand the new legislative 'scheme', I have changed the structure of the first edition by breaking down the contents into smaller sections, in an attempt to make each topic digestible. I have maintained the discursive content, although this may now straddle several sub-headings. This brings a risk of irritating advanced readers and all I can ask is that you are a little forgiving and appreciate the need for this layout.

The socio-legal section of the first edition required less attention and remains largely the same, except for updated national statistics and in two other respects. There have been two major events affecting race relations in the UK since 1998. The first was the Macpherson Report on the Stephen Lawrence murder investigation. This changed the way British institutions and, indeed, the public thought about race relations, with the phrase 'institutional racism' coming into common usage. Substantial extracts are included. The second event was the terrorist attack on the USA on 11 September 2001. I have included some early research into its effect on race relations in Britain.

I would like to pay tribute to Richard Townshend-Smith, who, I am sad to report, died in early 2002. Not only was he a master of discrimination law, he also had a thorough knowledge of its political and social context. He wrote on the subject from the very early days of Britain's anti-discrimination legislation and contributed to its development. More recently, he created the original edition of this book, which was the first comprehensive work dedicated to discrimination law and its social context.

I would like to thank the marvellous and utterly dependable research assistant, Louisa Hopkins. I should mention Nina Scott, for introducing me, as an undergraduate, to the *Perera* problem and the Living Tree school of statutory interpretation, which were seeds of some my thoughts on discrimination law. I am grateful to those at Cavendish Publishing for their diligence in proof-reading and patience in allowing me to include so many late developments. Naturally, I am solely responsible for any remaining errors and inadequacies. The law is stated as of 19 July 2003, with some minor updates added thereafter. If you have any comments, please email me at connolm@wmin.ac.uk.

Michael Connolly
London
July 2003

ACKNOWLEDGMENTS

Grateful acknowledgment is made to the following persons and organisations for granting permission to reproduce copyright material:

Blackwell Publishing, including extracts from the Journal of Law & Society and the Modern Law Review; Cambridge University Press; Columbia Law Review; Disability Rights Commission; Hart Publishing; Harvard Law Association for extracts from the Harvard Law Review; Institute of Employment Rights, London; John Wiley & Sons Ltd; Journal of Civil Liberties; Kluwer Law International for material from the Common Market Law Review; L Sheridan, E Blaauw, R Gillett and FW Winkel for an unpublished piece of research; Macmillan Publishers; Office for National Statistics; Office for Official Publications of the EC; The Open University Press; Oxford University Press, including extracts from Current Legal Problems, the Oxford Journal of Legal Studies, and the Industrial Law Journal; Pluto Press; Policy Studies Institute, London; Reed Elsevier (UK) Limited trading as LexisNexis UK for extracts from the Equal Opportunities Review; Routledge; Sage Publications Ltd; Steven L Willborn, Dean & Professor of Law, University of Nebraska, Lincoln, Nebraska, USA; Sweet & Maxwell, including extracts from Public Law, European Law Review and the Law Quarterly Review; University of Chicago for an extract from the Journal of Law & Society; University of Minnesota, Law & Inequality: A Journal of Theory and Practice; Wheatsheaf; The Yale Law Journal.

Every effort has been made to trace all the copyright holders but if any have been inadvertently overlooked, the publishers will be pleased to make the necessary arrangements at the first opportunity.

CONTENTS

TABLE OF CASES

TABLE OF STATUTES

TABLE OF STATUTORY INSTRUMENTS

TABLE OF EUROPEAN LEGISLATION

TREATIES AND CONVENTIONS

PART 1

SOCIAL, ECONOMIC AND THEORETICAL BACKGROUND

CHAPTER 1

THE BACKGROUND TO RACE DISCRIMINATION LEGISLATION IN THE UK

This chapter will examine the background to the issues of racial discrimination, racial inequality and consequent legislation in the UK. We will highlight key statistics and the way in which they have been changing and developing in recent years. Consideration will be given to some theories and causes of racism and to racism in practice. Finally, we will examine the history of race discrimination legislation in the UK.

1   THE BRITISH ETHNIC MINORITY POPULATION

The population of the UK is about 60 million.[1] 'In 2000–01, about one person in 14 (7.1%) in Great Britain was from a minority ethnic group.'[2] Of these, about 500,000 (0.8%) were Black Caribbean and 400,000 (0.7%) Black African, contributing to a total black population of 1.3 million (2.2%). About 1 million (1.7%) were Indian, 700,000 (1.2%) Pakistani and 300,000 (0.5%) Bangladeshi. This is based on the following table:[3]

Table 1.4
Population: by ethnic group and age, 2000–01[(1)]

Great Britain		Percentages			
	Under 16	16–34	35–64	65 and over	All ages (=100%) (millions)
White	20	25	39	16	53.0
Black					
Black Caribbean	23	27	40	10	0.5
Black African	33	35	30	2	0.4
Other Black groups	52	29	17	..	0.3
All Black groups	34	30	31	5	1.3
Indian	23	31	38	7	1.0
Pakistani/Bangladeshi					
Pakistani	36	36	24	4	0.7
Bangladeshi	39	36	21	4	0.3
All Pakistani/Bangladeshi	37	36	23	4	0.9
Other groups					
Chinese	19	38	38	4	0.1
None of the above	32	33	32	3	0.7
All other groups[(2)]	30	34	33	3	0.8
All ethnic groups[(3)]	20	26	39	15	57.1

(1)   Population living in private households. Combined quarters: Spring 2000 to Winter 2000–01.
(2)   Includes those of mixed origin.
(3)   Includes those who did not state their ethnic group.
Source: Labour Force Survey, Office for National Statistics.

1   *Social Trends*, 2002, No 32, London: HMSO, Table 1.1, p 28. Estimated in mid-2000. The UK is made up of England, Scotland, Northern Ireland and Wales.
2   *Ibid*, Table 1.4, p 30. Great Britain excludes Northern Ireland.
3   *Ibid*, Table 1.4, p 30.

In general, minority ethnic groups have a younger age structure than the White population, reflecting past immigration and fertility patterns. The 'Other Black' group has the youngest age structure with 52 per cent aged under 16. The Bangledeshi group also has a young age structure, with 39 per cent aged under 16. This was almost double the proportion of the White group. In contrast, the White group had the highest proportion of people aged 65 and over at 16 per cent, compared with 4 per cent of the Pakistani, Bangledeshi and Chinese groups. Progressive aging of the ethnic minority population is anticipated in the future, but changes will be dependent upon fertility levels, mortality rates and future net migration.[4]

It is very important to stress the diversity between the backgrounds and experience of Britain's minority ethnic groups. This manifests itself in numerous ways. First, the pattern of geographical distribution is complex.[5] There may be high levels of local segregation between different ethnic groups and between those whose origins lie in different parts of the Indian subcontinent or the Caribbean. Secondly, there is a distinction of great significance between those groups whose first language is English, that is, those from the West Indies and some Asian groups, and those who had little or no knowledge of English on arrival. Thirdly, those of Afro-Caribbean origin are very likely to come from a notionally Christian background, while Asians are predominantly Muslims, Hindus and Sikhs. The nature of religious affiliation may profoundly affect both relationships between different groups and the ability and willingness of people to embrace what may be seen as a more 'Western' way of life. Fourthly, there may be significant cultural differences between older people, for whom the ideas and values of the land they left may continue to loom large, and younger people, born and brought up entirely in the UK. These and other factors influence the experience of racism and inequality, and may also influence the ability of the law to tackle it in a meaningful way.

Immigration into Great Britain is not simply a recent phenomenon.[6] There was a large influx of Irish people, especially in the 19th century. 'In purely numerical terms the number of Irish immigrants to Britain over the last two centuries has been far in excess of any other immigration.'[7] Yet, this does not imply an absence of racism on the part of the indigenous population. 'Images of the racial or cultural inferiority of the Irish were based not only on particular ideological constructions of the Irish but on a self-definition of Englishness or Anglo-Saxon culture in terms of particular racial and cultural attributes. In later years, such images of the uniqueness and purity of Englishness were to prove equally important in the political debate about black migration and settlement.'[8]

The next main wave of immigration, from the late 19th century onwards, was of Jews. There is also a significant and long-standing history of black communities in Britain, often associated with seaports, such as in Liverpool and Cardiff. 'By the

---

4   *Ibid*, Table 1.4, p 30.
5   'People of Indian and Pakistani origin are characteristically found in nearly all towns [where immigrants have settled], but the population of West Indian origin is not nearly as widespread, being heavily concentrated in London and the West Midlands.' Brown, C, 'Ethnic pluralism in Britain: the demographic and legal background', in Glazer, N and Young, K (eds), *Ethnic Pluralism and Public Policy*, 1986, Aldershot: Gower, pp 34, 38. See also Skellington, R, with Morris, P, *'Race' in Britain Today*, 2nd edn, 1996, London: Sage, pp 52–62.
6   Solomos, J, *Race and Racism in Britain*, 2nd edn, 1993, London: Macmillan, pp 38–51.
7   *Ibid*, p 42.
8   *Ibid*, p 43.

Second World War there was already a long historical experience of political debate and mobilisation around issues of ethnicity, race and religion.'[9]

Brown, C, 'Ethnic pluralism in Britain: the demographic and legal background', in Glazer, N and Young, K (eds), *Ethnic Pluralism and Public Policy,* **1986, Aldershot: Gower, p 34:**

[T]he period of [black] immigration of any scale begins after the Second World War. An initially small migration increased during the 1950s to a substantial flow from the West Indies, India and Pakistan. This peaked sharply in the years before the introduction of immigration control in 1962, and since then there has been an overall downward trend in black immigration ...

[T]here have been substantial changes in the pattern of that immigration. First, the peak period of West Indian immigration was before the first immigration controls: in the 1950s there were migrants from both sending areas, but West Indians predominated. Since then, the position has been reversed, and throughout the 1960s and 1970s migrants from the Indian subcontinent [were] in the majority. Secondly, the earlier stages of the migration were characterised by a predominance of adult males, and these were later to be outnumbered by women and children. More than 90% of New Commonwealth citizens accepted for settlement on arrival in 1979 were women, children or elderly men.

Social Trends, **2002, No 32, London: HMSO, pp 34–35:**

The pattern of people entering and leaving the United Kingdom changed over the twentieth century. There was net loss due to international migration during the first three decades of the twentieth century and again during the 1960's and 1970's. However, since 1983 there has been net migration into the United Kingdom.

Over the period 1996 to 2000, net international migration to the United Kingdom averaged 89 thousand a year [see Table 1.12 below]. This was nearly three and a half times the annual average of the preceding five years. Between 1991–1995 and 1996–2000 the largest increase in migration to the United Kingdom was from the Old Commonwealth, an annual average of 30 thousand, followed by other EU member states with annual increase of 19 thousand ...

There are various reasons why people choose to move in or out of a country. The common reason given by immigrants in the period 1991–1995 was to accompany or join a partner already in the country. Recent figures for the period 1996–2000 show that the most common reason given for migration, by both immigrants and emigrants, was work-related.[10]

---

9   *Ibid,* p 51.
10   *Social Trends,* 2002, No 32, London: HMSO, pp 34–35, Table 1.12. 'New Commonwealth' countries are those that joined freely, typically in the post-WW2 era, in contrast to those countries which gained independence and dominion status long before, such as Canada (1867), Australia (1900) and New Zealand (1907).

Table 1.12

Average international migration[1]: by region of next or last residence, 1991–1995 and 1996–2000

United Kingdom   Thousands

	1991–1995			1996–2000		
	Inflow	Outflow	Balance	Inflow	Outflow	Balance
New Commonwealth	46.5	24.4	22.1	58.5	22.4	36.1
European Union	70.7	61.8	8.9	89.2	72.9	16.3
Old Commonwealth	45.2	50.0	–4.8	75.5	62.3	13.1
United States of America	24.6	30.6	–6.0	29.6	27.6	2.0
Middle East	8.8	10.9	–2.1	11.7	9.5	2.3
Rest of Europe	14.7	11.4	3.3	15.0	13.7	1.3
Rest of America	2.5	4.1	–1.6	4.4	3.3	1.0
Other	25.9	19.7	6.3	37.6	20.7	16.9
All countries	238.9	212.8	26.1	321.5	232.5	89.0

(1) Derived from International Passenger Survey migration estimates only. Excludes migration between the United Kingdom and the Irish Republic. Excludes asylum seekers. International migration estimates.

Source: International Passenger Survey, Office for National Statistics

Jones, T, *Britain's Ethnic Minorities: An Analysis of the Labour Force Survey*, 1996, London: Policy Studies Institute, p 61:

A number of factors led to the migration of people to Britain from its former colonies ... Perhaps the most important was the contrast in terms of economic well being between Britain and many of the countries it had colonised. People were attracted by the prospect of a higher standard of living, and more developed education and health systems. Because of specific labour shortages affecting jobs then considered undesirable in some of the main conurbations, the early immigrants had very good prospects of finding work. Two further developments boosted immigration. First, the partition of India, which created a population of political and religious refugees who had a high incentive to emigrate. Second, from the late 1960s onwards the political persecution of South Asians living and working in East Africa created a new class of migrants ... There is a great deal of evidence that the life chances of [migrants] were powerfully constrained by widespread racial discrimination. They tended to be in the more poorly paid jobs which the indigenous population did not want, and had to live in cheap, low quality housing.

2   RACE AND RACISM

(1)   Immigration and Racism

The social significance of this immigration cannot be understood without some consideration of the concepts of 'race' and 'racism'.

Solomos, J and Back, L, *Racism and Society*, 1996, London: Macmillan, pp 34, 59:

[O]nly in the late 18th century and early 19th century does the term race come to refer to supposedly discrete categories of people defined according to their physical characteristics ... [T]he concept as we understand it today came into being relatively late in the development of modern capitalist societies. Although usages of the term race have been traced somewhat earlier in a number of European languages, the development of racial doctrines and ideologies begins to take shape in the late 18th century, and reached its high point during the 19th and early 20th centuries ...[11]

Although racial ideologies often appeal to primordial notions of kinship and myths of common ethnic origins to support their arguments, it is worth emphasising that the notion that there are races and racial relationships is relatively new ... This means breaking with the view that sees race and racism as transhistorical categories and as unchanging.

The concept of 'race' is thus historically and scientifically problematic.

Skellington, R with Morris, P, *'Race' in Britain Today*, 2nd edn, 1996, London: Sage, p 25:

[T]he ethnic or racial categories used in a census or survey are not fixed or given ... but have to be decided upon and have to be constructed. It is important to note that 'race' and ethnicity are generally conceptualised as interchangeable categories in the various areas of data collection. Indeed the category 'white' is a good example of this, in that it is regarded as a fixed and unchanging category, whereas 'black' is generally broken down into different 'ethnic' groups. The only truly objective category in this

---

11   See Miles, R, *Racism*, 1989, London: Routledge, pp 11–30.

respect is that of legal nationality ... A woman who is a Pakistani national living in Scotland, for example, may think of herself as black or Asian or Muslim or Scottish. A British-born black girl may think of herself as West Indian or black or British or Afro-Caribbean. Probably such people would think of themselves as each of these things at different times and in different situations.

Each country has a separate and unique history in respect of racial issues, thus, the American experience of slavery has a significant and continuing impact upon current argument and opinion. The different histories in the USA and the UK suggest that the drawing of social and legal analogies in the field of race relations and anti-discrimination legislation should be done only with the greatest of care. What is distinctive about British history is the colonial experience which, while in some regards paralleling slavery, was fundamentally different from it. The form colonial racism took related more to an ideology of national, cultural, religious and economic supremacy.

Lester, A and Bindman, G, *Race and Law*, 1972, Harmondsworth: Penguin, p 13:

The opposition to Jewish immigrants – European in physical appearance and culture – might have led us to expect that the ... immigration from Asia and the Caribbean of people with an unfamiliar culture and a different skin colour would meet a strong tide of racial feeling. Still more predictable is this reaction when one recalls the salient chapters of British imperial history: the vast and lucrative trade in African slaves in the 17th and 18th centuries and the encouragement of a brutal system of servitude in the colonies; the replacement of that system by Asian indentured labour in the 19th century; and the creation of rigidly segregated societies, dominated by white settler minorities, in British Africa in this century. In several senses, post-war immigration from the new Commonwealth has transplanted to the old mother country prejudices and patterns of behaviour which could be conveniently ignored or righteously condemned so long as they flourished only within an Empire beyond our shores.

Even if one accepts that there are such things as racial differences, the issues so far as race and racism are concerned focus more on supposed social, cultural and religious differences. Therefore, the experiences of a particular society are far more relevant to racism than they are to gender issues.[12]

(2)   Theories of Racism

In examining the causes of racism and racial inequality in Britain, we will first consider some theories of racism and then examine how such assumptions are translated into practice and operate to the disadvantage of minority ethnic groups. In the following extracts, Solomos explains some tensions between the White majority population and minority groups, whilst Miles explores the State's role in this. Next, in two extracts, Solomon and Back examine the role of imagery and symbolism. Finally, the Macpherson Report explores and defines 'institutional racism'.

---

12 'Critical Race Theory' has informed much of the discussion about racism and racist thought in the USA. That theory builds on the view that racism can be understood only in the light of the particular historical and cultural experience of any particular society. For a helpful introduction to the theory, see Caldwell, V, 'Review of Critical Race Theory: the key writings that formed the movement' (1996) 96 Columbia L Rev 1363.

Solomos, J, *Race and Racism in Britain,* **2nd edn, 1993, London: Macmillan, pp 8–9, 183–85, 193:**

[I]t has long been recognised that, notwithstanding the long history of debates about this category, races do not exist in any scientifically meaningful sense. Yet it is also clear that in many societies people have often acted and continue to act as if race exists as a fixed objective category, and these beliefs are reflected in political discourses and at the level of popular ideas. Common sense conceptions of race have relied on a panoply of classificatory variables such as skin colour, country of origin, religion, nationality and language to define different groups of people ...[13]

[R]acism is broadly defined in the sense that it is used to cover those ideologies and social processes which discriminate against others on the basis of their ... different racial membership. There is little to be gained from seeing racism merely as a signifier for ideas of biological or cultural superiority, since it has become clear in recent years that the focus on attributed biological inferiority is being replaced in contemporary forms of racist discourse by a concern with culture and ethnicity as historically fixed categories ... [R]acism is not a static phenomenon. In societies such as Britain racism is produced and reproduced through political discourse, the media, the educational system and other institutions. Within this wider social context racism becomes an integral element of diverse social issues, such as law and order, crime, the inner cities and urban unrest.[14]

By the 1980s ... the language ... used to describe the politics of race in contemporary Britain had as much to do with a definition of Englishness or Britishness as it did with characteristics of the minority communities themselves ...

[N]ew-right racial discourses increasingly present black people as an 'enemy within' that is undermining the moral and social fabric of society. In both popular and elite discourses about immigration and race, black communities as a whole, or particular groups such as young blacks, are presented as involved in activities which are a threat to social order and political stability. Such ideological constructions do not necessarily have to rely on notions of racial superiority in the narrow sense ...

Commonly held images of black people include assumptions about differences between the culture, attitudes and values of black people compared with the white majority. Additionally the attempts by black people to assert their rights and lay claim to social justice have often been presented in the media as a sign of the failure of the majority communities to adapt to British society, and not as a sign that racial injustice is deeply embedded.

This ... amounts to the claim that the demands of black minorities are not legitimate, that they are in fact the product of attempts to claim special privileges and thus a threat to the majority. Because such claims are presented as coming from groups which are outside the traditions of culture of British political life they are more easily portrayed as a challenge to the values of the majority communities, and by a twist of logic as unjust ...

[O]ne important aspect of contemporary racial ideologies in Britain is the tendency to obscure or deny the meaning and implications of the deployment of race categories. This fits in with the wider tendency (a) to deny the importance of racism in British society and (b) to deny that hostility to the presence of black communities in Britain is a form of racism. According to this line of argument it is only natural that, given the

---

13   Miles, R, *Racism,* 1989, London: Routledge, pp 30–40, 70–71.
14   *Ibid,* pp 41–50.

choice, people should prefer to live with their own kind and not become a multiracial society. Such a wish is not seen as the manifestation of racialist attitudes, but as a natural response to the presence of people of a different cultural and racial background.

Miles, R, *Racism*, 1989, London: Routledge, p 119:

[I]t is now clear that the problematisation of the migrant presence occurred through the signification of both biological and cultural characteristics, and that the working class played an active role in what was a process of racialisation.[15] This process, and the related articulation of racism, was a significant political force before the onset of major economic crisis and it was a form of partially autonomous resistance from below in that it derived from the experience of competition for scarce resources and of localised economic decline ... But ... the British State has been ... an active agent of racialisation by, *inter alia*, passing exclusionary immigration legislation which has institutionalised racism and identifying young people of Caribbean origin as a threat to 'law and order'. In so doing, the economic and political consequences of the crisis of capital accumulation have been expressed in part through the idea of 'race' ...

But this process of racialisation has articulated intimately with nationalism ... [T]he issue is not whether or not people of Asian and Caribbean origin were inferior 'races', but rather one of reconstructing a positive sense of Englishness ...

The representational content ... is classically nationalist, but it is neatly lined, and therefore sustained, by racism. This articulation depends, in part, upon a simultaneous signification of cultural differences and somatic features: the Other is differentiated by skin colour as well as by clothing, diet, language and religion, for example. The presence of the Other is represented as problematic by virtue of, for example, its supposed use of the resources and facilities of 'our own people', its propensity to violence or its stimulation of the 'natural prejudice' of 'our own people' against those whose 'natural home' ... is elsewhere in the world.

Solomos, J and Back, L, *Racism and Society*, 1996, London: Macmillan, pp 210, 216:

[A]lthough at its root racism may involve clear and simple images, it is by no means uniform or without contradictions. Indeed, what is really interesting about racism as a set of ideas and political practices is that it is able to provide images of the 'other' which are simple and unchanging and at the same time to adapt to the changing social and political environment. Thus contemporary racist ideas are able to retain a link with the mystical values of classical racism and to adopt and use cultural and political symbols which are part of contemporary society ... It is precisely this combination of the mystical and the scientific that lies at the heart of the attempts by contemporary racist movements to reinvent their ideas as those which are attempting to protect the cultural and ethnic boundaries of race and nation.

Simplistic and monolithic accounts of racism ... do little to enlighten us as to why it is that in particular social and political contexts millions of people respond to the images, promises and hopes which are at the heart of mass racist movements.

Solomos, J and Back, L, *Racism and Society*, 1996, London: Macmillan, pp 19, 26:

The role of the press and other popular media in shaping social images about racial and ethnic minorities has been a particular focus [of research]. A number of detailed studies have looked at how press coverage of racial questions can help to construct

---

15 See Phizacklea, A and Miles, R, 'The British trade union movement and racism', in Braham, P, Rattansi, A and Skellington, R (eds), *Racism and Anti-Racism: Inequalities, Opportunities and Policies*, 1992, London: Sage, pp 30–45.

images of racial minorities as outsiders and a threat to racial cohesion ... One important example of this was the furore about Salman Rushdie's *The Satanic Verses* and the response of some Muslim political leaders to its publication ... The attempt by some ... to use the affair as a means of political mobilisation received wide coverage in the media and led to a wide-ranging debate about the future of race relations in British society ... Sections of the press used the events ... to question the possibility of a peaceful transition towards a multiracial society. Hostile media coverage of the events surrounding the political mobilisations around the Rushdie affair thus served to reinforce the view that minorities who do not share the dominant political values of British society pose a threat to social stability and cohesion.

In a very real sense the question of how to conceptualise racism has never been purely an academic matter. From its very origins the study of racism has been intimately connected to issues such as the rise of fascism, the holocaust, and the destructive consequences of racist political mobilisations. In this sense the analysis of racism cannot be easily separated from the wider political culture ... Indeed it is clearly the case that the manipulation of racial symbols and the development of racist movements has involved a politicisation of racist signifiers through political discourse and State policies.

This last extract also shows that racism may be reproduced at a national level, such as through the media, as well as through decisions by, say, individual employers (see below, '(3) Racism in Practice', and '(4) The Reproduction of Racism').

The Macpherson Report was a report of the inquiry into the police response to the murder of the black teenager, Stephen Lawrence (see '(4) The Reproduction of Racism' below). In Chapter 6, the Report drew together many explanations of the phrase 'institutional racism' to produce a widely accepted definition. After making the point that overt racism was not at issue in the inquiry, it identifies Lord Scarman's reference to 'unwitting' racism, and to that adds 'unconscious' racism. The Report then refers to American definitions from 1967 and the views of the Black Police Association, which identifies the 'effect' of actions and police 'culture' as areas for attention. Dr Oakley explained how the problem lies not with individual officers, but with the organisation. Secondly, he suggested that the nature of policing will produce institutional racism. This is the strongest argument for positive action to redress the 'natural' consequence of policing. Dr Bowling offered an 'uncritical racism' analysis. Finally, the Report gives its definition and applies it to the facts of the case. (The Report refers to the 'Kent Report', which was the first inquiry into the police conduct of the case.)

The Stephen Lawrence Inquiry, Report of an Inquiry by Sir William Macpherson, advised by Tom Cook, The Right Reverend Dr John Sentamu, Dr Richard Stone. February 1999. Presented to Parliament by the Home Secretary. Cm 4262-I, London: HMSO, (www.official-documents.co.uk/document/cm42/4262/4262.html), Chapter 6:

6.1 A central and vital issue which has permeated our Inquiry has been the issue of racism ... Mr & Mrs Lawrence allege and fervently believe that their colour, culture and ethnic origin, and that of their murdered son, have throughout affected the way in which the case has been dealt with and pursued ...

6.2 The Kent Report *'found no evidence to support the allegation of racist conduct by any Metropolitan Police Officer involved in the investigation of the murder of Stephen Lawrence'* (Kent Report, para 14.28) ... Each of 17 officers interviewed by Kent was baldly asked whether his or her *'judgment and subsequent actions were based on the fact that Stephen was black'*. In some cases Mrs Lawrence's condemnatory words about the lack of first aid [the Inquiry found that this did not contribute to Stephen Lawrence's death] were quoted to the officers. Each officer roundly denied racism or racist conduct. Each officer plainly and genuinely believed that he or she had acted without overt racist bias or discrimination ...

6.3   In this Inquiry we have not heard evidence of overt racism or discrimination, unless it can be said that the use of inappropriate expressions such as 'coloured' or 'negro' fall into that category. The use of such words, which are now well known to be offensive, displays at least insensitivity and lack of training. A number of officers used such terms, and some did not even during their evidence seem to understand that the terms were offensive and should not be used.

6.4   Racism in general terms consists of conduct or words or practices which disadvantage or advantage people because of their colour, culture, or ethnic origin. In its more subtle form it is as damaging as in its overt form.

6.5   We have been concerned with the more subtle and much discussed concept of racism referred to as institutional racism which (in the words of Dr Robin Oakley) can influence police service delivery 'not solely through the deliberate actions of a small number of bigoted individuals, but through a more systematic tendency that could unconsciously influence police performance generally'.

6.6   The phrase 'institutional racism' has been the subject of much debate. We accept that there are dangers in allowing the phrase to be used in order to try to express some overall criticism of the police, or any other organisation, without addressing its meaning. Books and articles on the subject proliferate. We must do our best to express what we mean by those words, although we stress that we will not produce a definition cast in stone, or a final answer to the question. What we hope to do is to set out our standpoint, so that at least our application of the term to the present case can be understood by those who are criticised ...

6.10   Lord Scarman [In his 1981 report *The Brixton Disorders*] (Para 4.63) moreover referred specifically to the dangers of 'racist' stereotyping when he said:

> Racial prejudice does manifest itself occasionally in the behaviour of a few officers on the street. It may be only too easy for some officers, faced with what they must see as the inexorably rising tide of street crime, to lapse into an unthinking assumption that all young black people are potential criminals.

6.11   Such assumptions are still made today. In answer to a question posed to a member of the MPS [Metropolitan Police Service] Black Police Association, Inspector Leroy Logan, he referred to 'what is said in the canteen', citing simply as an example his memory that '... *as a Sergeant I was in the back of a car and a female white officer on seeing a black person driving a very nice car just said "I wonder who he robbed to get that?", and she then realised she was actually voicing an unconscious assumption*' (Part 2, Day 2, p 215). This is a mere example of similar experiences repeatedly given to us during our public meetings ...

6.13   Thus Lord Scarman accepted the existence of what he termed '*unwitting*' or '*unconscious*' racism. To those adjectives can be added a third, namely '*unintentional*'. All three words are familiar in the context of any discussion in this field ...

6.16   The officers questioned by the Kent investigators expressed their indignation at any suggestion of overt racism. The Kent Report in our view however, never dealt satisfactorily with the other evil of unwitting racism, in both talk and action, played out in a variety of ways. The evidence we heard in this Inquiry revealed how unwitting racist discriminatory language and behaviour may arise.

6.17   Unwitting racism can arise because of lack of understanding, ignorance or mistaken beliefs. It can arise from well intentioned but patronising words or actions. It can arise from unfamiliarity with the behaviour or cultural traditions of people or families from minority ethnic communities. It can arise from racist stereotyping of black people as potential criminals or troublemakers. Often this arises out of uncritical self-understanding born out of an inflexible police ethos of the 'traditional' way of doing things. Furthermore such attitudes can thrive in a tightly knit community, so that there can be a collective failure to detect and to outlaw this breed of racism. The police canteen can too easily be its breeding ground.

6.18   As Lord Scarman said (Para 4.97) there can be '... *failure to adjust policies and methods to meet the needs of policing a multi-racial society*'. Such failures can occur simply because police officers may mistakenly believe that it is legitimate to be 'colour blind' in both individual and team response to the management and investigation of racist crimes, and in their relationship generally with people from minority ethnic communities. Such an approach is flawed. A colour blind approach fails to take account of the nature and needs of the person or the people involved, and of the special features which such crimes and their investigation possess. As Mr Dan Crompton, Her Majesty's Inspector of Constabulary (HMIC), helpfully said to us it is no longer enough to believe '*all that is necessary is to treat everyone the same ... it might be said it is about treatment according to need*' (Part 2, Day 2, p 57) ...

6.22   What may be termed collective organisational failure of this kind has come to be labelled by academics and others as institutional racism. This is by no means a new term or concept. In 1967 two black activists, Stokely Carmichael and Charles V Hamilton stated that institutional racism '*originates in the operation of established and respected forces in the society. It relies on the active and pervasive operation of anti-black attitudes and practices. A sense of superior group position prevails: whites are "better" than blacks and therefore blacks should be subordinated to whites. This is a racist attitude and it permeates society on both the individual and institutional level, covertly or overtly*' (*Black Power: the Politics of Liberation in America*, Penguin Books, 1967, pp 20-21).

6.23   Reference to a concept described in a different national and social context over 30 years ago has its dangers; but that concept has been continuously debated and revised since 1968. History shows that 'covert' insidious racism is more difficult to detect. Institutions such as Police Services can operate in a racist way without at once recognising their racism.

6.24   It is vital to stress that neither academic debate nor the evidence presented to us leads us to say or to conclude that an accusation that institutional racism exists in the MPS implies that the policies of the MPS are racist. No such evidence is before us. Indeed the contrary is true. It is in the implementation of policies and in the words and actions of officers acting together that racism may become apparent. Furthermore we say with emphasis that such an accusation does not mean or imply that every police officer is guilty of racism. No such sweeping suggestion can be or should be made ...

6.28   The oral evidence of the three representatives of the MPS Black Police Association was illuminating. It should be read in full, but we highlight two passages from Inspector Paul Wilson's evidence:-

(Part 2, Day 2, p 209):

    The term institutional racism should be understood to refer to the way the institution or the organisation may systematically or repeatedly treat, or tend to treat, people differentially because of their race. So, in effect, we are not talking about the individuals within the service who may be unconscious as to the nature of what they are doing, but it is the net effect of what they do.

(Part 2, Day 2, p 211):

A second source of institutional racism is our culture, our culture within the police service. Much has been said about our culture, the canteen culture, the occupational culture. How and why does that impact on individuals, black individuals on the street? Well, we would say the occupational culture within the police service, given the fact that the majority of police officers are white, tends to be the white experience, the white beliefs, the white values.

Given the fact that these predominantly white officers only meet members of the black community in confrontational situations, they tend to stereotype black people in general. This can lead to all sorts of negative views and assumptions about black people, so we should not underestimate the occupational culture within the police service as being a primary source of institutional racism in the way that we differentially treat black people.

Interestingly I say we because there is no marked difference between black and white in the force essentially. We are all consumed by this occupational culture. Some of us may think we rise above it on some occasions, but, generally speaking, we tend to conform to the norms of this occupational culture, which we say is all powerful in shaping our views and perceptions of a particular community.

We believe that it is essential that the views of these officers should be closely heeded and respected ...

6.31   Dr Robin Oakley has submitted two helpful Notes to our Inquiry:-

For the police service, however, there is an additional dimension which arises from the nature of the policing role. Police work, unlike most other professional activities, has the capacity to bring officers into contact with a skewed cross-section of society, with the well-recognised potential for producing negative stereotypes of particular groups. Such stereotypes become the common currency of the police occupational culture. If the predominantly white staff of the police organisation have their experience of visible minorities largely restricted to interactions with such groups, then negative racial stereotypes will tend to develop accordingly.

In Dr Oakley's view, if the challenges of 'institutional racism' which potentially affect all police officers, are not addressed, this will:-

result in a generalised tendency, particularly where any element of discretion is involved, whereby minorities may receive different and less favourable treatment than the majority. Such differential treatment need be neither conscious nor intentional, and it may be practised routinely by officers whose professionalism is exemplary in all other respects. There is great danger that focusing on overt acts of personal racism by individual officers may deflect attention from the much greater institutional challenge ... of addressing the more subtle and concealed form that organisational-level racism may take. Its most important challenging feature is its predominantly hidden character and its inbuilt pervasiveness within the occupational culture.

He goes on:-

It could be said that institutional racism in this sense is in fact pervasive throughout the culture and institutions of the whole of British society, and is in no way specific to the police service. However, because of the nature of the police role, its impact on society if not addressed in the police organisation may be particularly severe. In the police service, despite the extensive activity designed to address racial and ethnic issues in recent years, the concept of 'institutional racism' has not received the attention it deserves. (Institutional Racism and Police Service Delivery, Dr Robin Oakley's submission to this Inquiry, parts of paras 6, 7, 8, and 11.)

6.32 Dr Oakley in his second Note (17 December 1988) echoes the view of Professor Holdaway who has argued rightly that emotively powerful words such as 'racism' must not be used simply as rhetorical weapons:-

> Such terms need to be given a clear analytic meaning which can demonstrably help illuminate the problem at hand. (Para 1.4.)

> The term institutional racism should be understood to refer to the way institutions may systematically treat or tend to treat people differently in respect of race. The addition of the word 'institutional' therefore identifies the source of the differential treatment; this lies in some sense within the organisation rather than simply with the individuals who represent it. The production of differential treatment is 'institutionalised' in the way the organisation operates. (Para 2.2.)

Towards the end of his Note Dr Oakley says this:-

> What is required in the police service therefore is an occupational culture that is sensitive not just to the experience of the majority but to minority experience also. In short, an enhanced standard of police professionalism to meet the requirements of a multi-ethnic society (Para 5.6.)

6.33 We are also grateful for the contribution to our Inquiry made by Dr Benjamin Bowling:-

> Institutional racism is the process by which people from ethnic minorities are systematically discriminated against by a range of public and private bodies.... However, some discrimination practices are the product of uncritical rather than unconscious racism. That is, practices with a racist outcome are not engaged in without the actor's knowledge; rather, the actor has failed to consider the consequences of his or her actions for people from ethnic minorities ... Violent Racism: Victimisation, Policing and Social Context, July 1998. (Paras 21–22, pp 3–4.)

6.34 Taking all that we have heard and read into account we grapple with the problem. For the purposes of our Inquiry the concept of institutional racism which we apply consists of:

The collective failure of an organisation to provide an appropriate and professional service to people because of their colour, culture, or ethnic origin. It can be seen or detected in processes, attitudes and behaviour which amount to discrimination through unwitting prejudice, ignorance, thoughtlessness and racist stereotyping which disadvantage minority ethnic people.

It persists because of the failure of the organisation openly and adequately to recognise and address its existence and causes by policy, example and leadership. Without recognition and action to eliminate such racism it can prevail as part of the ethos or culture of the organisation. It is a corrosive disease.

6.38 ... Does the condemnation by Mr & Mrs Lawrence of the police and the criminal justice system have validity? We address [the question] upon a fair assessment and judgement of all the facts and circumstances which have been rehearsed before us ...

6.45 Institutional racism is in our view primarily apparent in what we have seen and heard in the following areas:-

(a) in the actual investigation including the family's treatment at the hospital, the initial reaction to the victim and witness Duwayne Brooks, the family liaison, the failure of many officers to recognise Stephen's murder as a purely 'racially motivated' crime, the lack of urgency and commitment in some areas of the investigation.

(b) countrywide in the disparity in 'stop and search figures'. Whilst we acknowledge and recognise the complexity of this issue and in particular the other factors which can be prayed in aid to explain the disparities, such as demographic mix, school exclusions, unemployment, and recording procedures, there remains, in our judgment, a clear core conclusion of racist stereotyping;

(c) countrywide in the significant under-reporting of 'racial incidents' occasioned largely by a lack of confidence in the police and their perceived unwillingness to take such incidents seriously. Again we are conscious of other factors at play, but we find irresistible the conclusion that a core cause of under-reporting is the inadequate response of the Police Service which generates a lack of confidence in victims to report incidents; and

(d) in the identified failure of police training; not a single officer questioned before us in 1998 had received any training of significance in racism awareness and race relations throughout the course of his or her career ...

We hope and believe that the average police officer and average member of the public will accept that we do not suggest that all police officers are racist and will both understand and accept the distinction we draw between overt individual racism and the pernicious and persistent institutional racism which we have described.

6.47 Nor do we say that in its policies the MPS is racist. Nor do we share the fear of those who say that in our finding of institutional racism, in the manner in which we have used that concept, there may be a risk that the moral authority of the MPS may be undermined.

(3)   Racism in Practice

The strength of the next extract is to show how, at a micro level, these attitudes and stereotypes may be translated into real employment decisions. It does not make for comfortable reading, as it suggests how difficult it will be for the law to have an impact on the racial dimension of such decisions.

Jenkins, R, *Racism and Recruitment: Managers, Organisations and Equal Opportunity in the Labour Market,* **1986, Cambridge: CUP, pp 46, 74–78, 92–97, 102–05, 108:**

In making selection decisions, recruiters are attempting to do two things: first, to satisfy themselves that the candidate is capable of carrying out the practices entailed in the ... job in question, and second, to predict whether or not the candidate will integrate smoothly into the managerial procedures and social routines of the employing organisation ... Selection criteria ... can be broadly divided into two categories, the *functionally specific*, such as educational qualifications, training or physique, which relate to job performance and competence, and the *functionally non-specific*, which relate to the organisational context and are much less easy to delineate. [The author refers to these as suitability and acceptability respectively.] ...

[The author shows how the concept of acceptability may be overlaid with conscious or unconscious assumptions which may disadvantage black people.]

[I]t is necessary to have regard to those non-verbal and largely unselfconscious aspects of communication such as facial expression, eye contact, physical proximity and body contact (ie, shaking hands, etc). Psychological research has indicated that these are all significant in determining the outcome of selection interviews ... they are also evaluated in different ways in different cultures. Thus, to take the example of the maintenance of eye contact, a white English recruiter might well interpret an avoidance of direct eye contact by a candidate as indicative of anything from 'shiftiness' to a lack of self-confidence. For many jobseekers with cultural backgrounds deriving from the Indian subcontinent, however, the refusal of eye contact might well be a respectful attempt to avoid being rude. It is only to be expected that, in inter-ethnic selection interviews, non-verbal communicative behaviour may be systematically misinterpreted by both sides of the exchange. This kind of miscommunication is particularly important inasmuch as the evaluation of manner and attitude, appearance, speech style and the ability to 'fit in' are all at stake here, not to mention the manager's 'gut feeling'. Job candidates whose cultural repertoire, and understanding, of non-verbal communicative behaviour is the same as the interviewer's will clearly be at an advantage, albeit an unconscious one ...

Selection decisions which rely heavily on implicit criteria are likely to be more opaque than those involving explicit criteria ... Unsuccessful job applicants in such a situation are not necessarily going to understand the reason for their rejection – which will make it difficult for them to enhance their acceptability in the future – and decisions are going to be difficult for bodies such as Industrial Tribunals to investigate convincingly after the fact. Furthermore ... the implicitness of much selection decision making will, by virtue of the ambiguity and lack of definition of many of these implicit criteria, allow direct, ie, deliberate racist and sexist discrimination, scope to operate with relative impunity ...

The ethnocentrism of many of the components of acceptability is of relevance to the discussion of *indirect* discrimination. None of these criteria are necessarily racially *prejudiced*, nor do they involve the *intent* to discriminate against black workers ... In their unintended consequences, however, there is good reason to suppose that they will systematically place many black jobseekers at a disadvantage ...

[C]riteria such as 'gut feeling', speech style, and the ability to 'fit in', which are both ethnocentric and implicit, are, by virtue of their taken-for-grantedness and lack of definition, extremely elusive ...

One of the most interesting aspects of this material is the relatively low level of definition of the category 'white' or 'English' ... There are, I suspect, two reasons for this. In the first place the notion of 'Englishness' is largely taken for granted; it is a background common-sensical assumption which managers assume that 'everybody knows about'. Second, it is equally the case that one of the pervasive themes of ethnocentric categorisations ... is that 'we're all different, but they're all the same'. This is the proposition which lies at the heart of many ethnic stereotypes. As a result, there is a very real sense in which 'we' don't constitute an ethnic group at all. As a result, it seems likely that there may be a greater predisposition on the part of white managers to regard white job candidates as individuals, as opposed to their black counterparts, who may be more likely to be treated as representatives of a stereotypical category ...

[T]he stereotype might best be regarded as a model of *probability*, not a statement of certainty. Thus, when faced with job candidates of any particular ethnic identity, the manager may choose to discriminate against them simply because he or she feels that there is a degree of *likelihood* that the worst predictions of the stereotype may be fulfilled.

[Having demonstrated the 'racism of acceptability', the author establishes the other side of the coin, which he refers to as 'the acceptability of racism'.]

[A]lthough ... managers may recognise that it is 'wrong' for other managers or workers to resist the recruitment of black workers, their principles do not usually extend to counteracting that resistance. Putting up with racism is definitely the lesser of the two evils, when compared with the organisational and industrial relations problems which moving against it might precipitate.

Clearly there are some managers who do respect the 'customs and habits' of their workforce. It is likely that many more do not, however. For this group of managers, there is a 'right' way of doing things: this is the white, 'British' way. In this profoundly ethnocentric world-view, cultural difference is viewed as alien and distasteful, and racism is merely the upholding of 'normal standards'. Discrimination, by this token, vanishes; in its place one finds people insisting that they are not prejudiced, but simply defending what is 'right and proper', upholding the maintenance of 'acceptable' standards.

There are two related themes ... In the first place, the problem is seen to be created by black workers, not by discrimination or other racist behaviour by managers or other white workers ... Second ... the root of the problem is seen to lie in the prejudice of black workers ... Once again the problem of white racism is not even considered by most of these managers: 'I've got no colour prejudice, of course I've not'. Since there is, therefore, not a problem of this nature, the reaction of black workers becomes defined as irrational and unreasonable.

Even where ... the manager does admit the existence and force of racism, black workers 'often look for prejudices where there aren't any', and, because of this, they 'use their race or their colour against the company'. Thus, in one move, racism is either ignored or underestimated, on the one hand, or defined away as a problem of 'their' making, on the other. Viewed from within this logic, equal opportunities policies, or any other attempts to deal with the problem of racism in the workplace, become unfair and 'lopsided'.

[T]he perception by managers of these problems undoubtedly does have an influence, and possibly a major one, on the selection process. This influence is to the systematic detriment of black workers ... [M]ost of the perceived problems relate in one way or another to the issue of acceptability ... [I]t is equally clear that, to use the word in another context, racism, whether on the part of colleagues, subordinates or self, is acceptable to a great many of these managers. It is ... not a problem so long as the routines of the organisation continue to run smoothly, defined as simply to do with personalities, unrecognised except as a reflection of the unreasonable prejudice of black workers, or, in some cases, positively approved of. There is very little evidence of managers choosing to oppose discrimination or racism on moral or political grounds. Depressing though this conclusion may be, this is perhaps only to be expected, given that managers are paid to manage in the interests of the goals of the organisation, among which is not usually numbered opposition to racism.

[T]he clearest thread which runs through [the research] is the notion that black workers are not British, they are alien. Put very simply, black workers do not belong in Britain in the eyes of these managers, and admission into the UK should not be, nor should it ever have been, theirs by right. A second, and perhaps equally strong theme, is that black migrants are somehow taking without giving, whether it be welfare benefits, health care, or sending home remittances to their families.

It is unlikely that recruiters will either consciously or deliberately relate their stereotypical notions of acceptability to their repertoire of ethnic stereotypes and decide the fate of individual jobseekers accordingly. The process is likely to be more subtle and less obvious than that. The ambiguity of many selection criteria, and the tacit taken-for-grantedness of many of the decisions which are made, do not lead one to have much confidence in the accountability of recruitment.

Cockburn, C, *In the Way of Women: Men's Resistance to Sex Equality in Organisations*, 1991, Basingstoke: Macmillan, pp 174, 182:

The purchase of labour power is ... a purchase for the services of a certain kind of person, someone with a perceived social status (it may be high or low), certain cultural attachments and certain looks, to all of which ethnicity and skin colour are germane. The system of male power which operates in and through major employing organisations in Britain is specifically *white* male power and the culture of management is almost solidly a white monoculture, identifying and excluding other groups ...

What appeared to be appearing in all four organisations [researched] was a split in white intentions. Some, characteristically the equal opportunity officers and a few enlightened senior managers, wanted to encourage black recruitment and promotion. Other white people did not want to see any dilution of the white workforce by black incomers. The deal that was struck between the two white positions and between whites and incoming blacks cohered around the issue of cultural *assimilation*. Non-white ethnic groups would be 'acceptable' if as nearly as possible indistinguishable from the host group. '*If you want equality you must forgo difference.*' It is the same theme we saw invoked in resistance to sex equality and will see again in the case of homosexuals and people with disabilities. It is of course a condition impossible for most members of out-groups to fulfil, even if a minority of individuals is able and willing to adopt protective colouring.

The next extract reports research into *religious* discrimination before and after the terrorist attacks in the USA on 11 September 2001. This research also identifies further examples of covert racism and suggests that an event can cause pre-existing covert racism to surface into overt discrimination.

Sheridan, L, Blaauw, E, Gillett, R and Winkel, FW, 'Discrimination and implicit racism on the basis of religion and ethnicity: effects of the events of September 11th on five religious and seven ethnic groups', unpublished research, University of Leicester:

On September 11th 2001, a series of terrorist attacks were launched against the United States of America. Four aeroplanes were hijacked, two of which were flown into the New York World Trade Center, one into the Pentagon in Washington DC, and the final plane crashed in rural Pennsylvania. The suspected hijackers were believed to have links with al-Qaeda ('the base'), a radical Islamic organisation. Following the September 11th attacks, the USA and the United Kingdom declared 'war on terrorism' and invaded Afghanistan where a prominent al-Qaeda member, Osama Bin Laden, was believed to be located. Over two million Muslims live in the UK, and although the mainstream Muslim community publicly attacked a 'tiny lunatic fringe' who supported the attacks on the US, the media have reported instances of hate mail, verbal abuse and physical assaults on Muslims, as well as the vandalism of mosques. For instance, on September 16th an Afghan taxi driver in London was left paralysed by what police believe to be a racist attack. There have also been reports of attacks on members of other religious groups. For example, the BBC reported that Sikh men in Birmingham and Glasgow had been targeted due to their supposed superficial resemblance to Osama Bin Laden.

This study assesses the impact of the events of September 11 on prejudice and discrimination experienced by five religious and seven ethnic groups in the UK ...

'*Implicit racism experiences*' were measured by 19 items. Participants were asked how often they had experienced these purely on the basis of their race, ethnicity or religion

(i) during a typical year and (ii) since the attacks on the USA. The experiences were based on daily life situations and were designed to reflect the incidence of more covert prejudice, rather than overt racism (and religious discrimination) and included: being treated rudely, being closely observed, not being taken seriously, being treated as if one is stupid, and being asked to speak for one's entire ethnic, racial or religious group ...

The current UK-based work indicates that the events of September 11th 2001 and shortly thereafter have impacted upon levels of both implicit racism and general discrimination. Of the five religious groups assessed, Muslims were found to have not only the greatest risk of being victims of both implicit racism and general discrimination before September 11th, but also the highest increase in experiences of racism and discrimination since the events of that day, and, consequently, the greatest risk of being victims of both implicit racism and general discrimination after September 11th. Sikhs and Hindus also reported increases in experiences of implicit racism post-September 11th, but these increases were not as great as those reported by Muslims. By comparison, Christians and Jews reported a decrease in implicit racism experiences. In terms of ethnic origin, the most at risk groups of the seven examined appear to be Pakistanis and Bangladeshis, supporting findings from 2000 British Crime Survey (Clancy et al, 2001).

Overall, results would suggest that significant world events do impact on racial and religious prejudice and on discriminatory actions, and that religion is more important than ethnicity in indicating which groups are most likely to experience racism and discrimination post-September 11th.

Support was found for the theory of modern racism (McConahay et al, 1981), a covert and disguised expression of prejudice in a post-civil rights 'politically correct' era. In the current work participants reported high levels of negative daily life experiences on the 'implicit racism experiences' scale that they believed were directly related to cultural, racial and religious differences. In addition, the degrees to which the participants were subjected to such experiences were clearly associated with their race or religion. For instance, on the basis of religion Muslims reported experiencing more implicit racism both pre and post-September 11th than did other religious groups, whilst Pakistanis and Bangladeshis reported the highest levels on the basis of ethnicity ...

The present research found that overall, and particularly for Muslims, not only did reports of implicit racism increase, but also that reports of general discriminatory behaviour increased. This suggests that overt racism is practiced in the UK and that religious discrimination exists, and that these were subjected to an increase as a result of major world events. Is it possible that major events such as the September 11th attacks on the USA allow implicit racism or religious discrimination to develop into overt discrimination? Perhaps the September 11th attacks have made patriotism and race a more salient source of identity for many westerners because they feel insecure and under threat, with the effect that all Muslims may now be viewed by some westerners as a possible menace.

These analyses reveal just how difficult it could be for the law alone to bring about a significant reduction in either discrimination or disadvantage.[16] The research in the section below shows that any improvement has been no more than minor.

---

16 We shall see how the law operates to combat these practices in the chapters on substantive law. In the first edition, Richard Townsend-Smith suggested that it was 'unlikely' that the law could achieve a reduction in racism. Respectfully, I leave the question open.

(4)   The Reproduction of Racism

In the last section we saw overt and covert discrimination identified in peoples' behaviour and decision-making. In addition, racial disadvantage is compounded by structures and institutions that operate to the detriment of ethnic minorities. The following extracts examine and identify how such behaviour and decision-making is reproduced.

Solomos, J and Back, L, *Racism and Society*, 1996, London: Macmillan, pp 67–69:

[W]e need to understand forms of racial inequality at levels on which decisions are taken which, consciously or not, either increase or decrease such inequalities. 'It is necessary to understand the workings of social institutions, such as those which socialise children, which channel jobseeking and employee selection so that particular sorts of people end up in particular jobs' ... Such detailed investigations have highlighted the complex processes which have helped to shape racialised inequalities in both an institutional and an everyday context.

Migrants to Britain of the 1950s and 1960s came to find work primarily in those sectors experiencing labour shortages. Workers from the Caribbean, India and Pakistan were recruited for employment in foundries in the Midlands, textile mills in the North, transport industries in major cities, and the health service. In common with migrant workers across Europe, these workers experienced a high degree of exploitation, discrimination and marginalisation in their economic and social lives. Despite the need for their labour, their presence aroused widespread hostility at all levels ... Employers only reluctantly recruited immigrants where there were no white workers to fill the jobs; white workers, through their unions, often made arrangements with their employers about the sorts of work immigrants could have access to ... At this time the preference for white workers was seen to be quite natural and legitimate – immigrant workers were seen as an inferior but necessary labour supply.

Over time these workers remained in a relatively restricted spectrum of occupational area, over-represented in low paid and insecure jobs, working anti-social hours in unhealthy or dangerous environments. Although by the 1970s African-Caribbean and Asian people worked in a broader range of occupations than before, these were still jobs that were 'deemed fit' for ethnic minorities rather than white workers. In 1984 the Policy Studies Institute published a major survey of the state of black people in Britain, covering housing, education and employment, showing that black people are still generally employed below their qualification and skill level, earn less than white workers in comparable job levels, and are still concentrated in the industries they were 25 years earlier.

Miles, R, *Racism*, 1989, London: Routledge, pp 124–25:

[C]ertain economic sectors faced acute shortages of labour, and in conditions of relative full employment, these positions could not be filled from the population within Britain. Thus, structural circumstances defined a demand for labour in certain sectors of the economy, and it was these positions that Caribbean and Asian migrants filled ...

[T]hose present in the labour market are ranked by employers. Where that hierarchy is constructed in such a way that the qualities of individuals are perceived to be representative of a wider collectivity, and if the individual is deemed to possess the criteria that designate membership of that collectivity, the question of suitability may be determined by reference to the perceived qualities of the collectivity rather than to the perceived qualities of the individual applicant. In such circumstances, the processes of inclusion and exclusion are effected by signification and group categorisation. Where such a process is effected by reference to phenotypical characteristics, the recruitment of labour is racialised. That is, the labour market is perceived to include members of different 'races', each of which is seen to possess a different range of skills and abilities which distinguish that group as a supposed 'race'.

Brown, C, 'Same difference: the persistence of racial disadvantage in the British employment market', in Braham, P, Rattansi, A and Skellington, R (eds), *Racism and Anti-Racism: Inequalities, Opportunities and Policies,* **1992, London: Sage, pp 60–63:**

There was no evidence during the 1980s to suggest that the extent of discrimination fell at all. Repeats of the applications trials ... in 1984 and 1985 produced figures for the minimum level of employer discrimination that were no lower than in 1973 and 1974 ... [T]he research ... showed that at least one-third of private employers discriminated against Asian applicants, Afro-Caribbean applicants, or both ...

In addition to ... reports on direct, deliberate discrimination there has been research ... detailing the disadvantage still suffered by ethnic minorities in employment because of both direct and indirect discrimination ...

The lack of substantial improvement in the general position of blacks and Asians within the labour market is all the more disappointing because the past decade has been a period of apparent political breakthrough for Britain's minorities. The number of elected local councillors from the minority communities has risen steeply; race equality became a real issue in local politics in urban areas and, occasionally, a national issue ... the provisions of the Race Relations Act 1976 have facilitated 'positive action' by employers on race equality; and some large employers – particularly in the public sector – have openly paid a good deal of attention to reviewing policy and practice to eliminate direct and indirect discrimination. The small progress that has taken place has therefore involved an enormous expenditure of effort by ethnic minority organisations and by others campaigning and working alongside them ...

The patterns of employment among blacks and Asians are shifting, and there is now greater diversity among them than before. Examples of success in business, in the professions and in politics are now easier to point to; in particular, business and commerce seems to have reached a 'critical mass' within some sections of the Asian communities, sufficient to sustain its own growth and to insulate itself partially against discrimination. But these achievements have been in spite of the general experience of hostility, stereotyping and exclusion, and they should not blind us to the other realities of minority employment. Considering the years that have passed and the work that has been put in, the surprising fact is not that some people have hewn a niche in the business world or become professionally qualified, but that so few have been allowed to succeed ... [P]rogress has been most evident where the acceptance, endorsement and help of white employers has been least required: in self-employment and in the professions. Even the contrast between business and the professions is illuminating in this respect. Although entry to the professions has been achieved by many ... progress within them has been restricted because it relies on the decision making of white superiors ...

Prospects for the future cannot be expected to rest on this circumvention of racial discrimination. It is unrealistic to expect the whole black and Asian population to develop strategies of dealing with racism by avoiding it. We therefore have to turn to the reduction of discrimination as a priority for public policy. As a nation we have to confront the fact that racial hostility underlies the persistence of racial discrimination, and that it is unlikely to wither with time ... In the absence of any vigorous action from central government, the chances of any real reduction in the extent of racism and discrimination are slim.

The Macpherson Report: What follows is a description of the murder, the police response and the Inquiry's findings (which illustrate the reproduction of racism).

The Stephen Lawrence Inquiry, Report of an Inquiry by Sir William Macpherson, advised by Tom Cook, The Right Reverend Dr John Sentamu, Dr Richard Stone. February 1999. Presented to Parliament by the Home Secretary. Cm 4262-I, London: HMSO
www.official-documents.co.uk/document/cm42/4262/4262.htm).

1.1   ... The whole incident which led to his murder probably lasted no more than 15–20 seconds ... Stephen Lawrence had been with his friend Duwayne Brooks during the afternoon of 22 April. They were on their way home when they came at around 22:30 to the bus stop in Well Hall Road ... Stephen went to see if a bus was coming, and reached a position almost in the centre of the mouth of Dickson Road. Mr Brooks was part of the way between Dickson Road and the roundabout when he saw the group of five or six white youths who were responsible for Stephen's death on the opposite side of the road ... Mr Brooks called out to ask if Stephen saw the bus coming. One of the youths must have heard something said, since he called out *'what, what nigger?'*. With that the group came quickly across the road and literally engulfed Stephen. During this time one or more of the group stabbed Stephen twice. [Mr Brooks] then turned and ran and called out to Stephen to run and to follow him ... The group of white murderers then disappeared down Dickson Road ... Mr Brooks ran across the road in the direction of Shooters Hill, and he was followed by ... Stephen Lawrence, who managed somehow to get to his feet and to run over 100 yards to the point where he fell ... Stephen had been stabbed to a depth of about five inches on both sides of the front of his body to the chest and arm. Both stab wounds severed axillary arteries, and blood must literally have been pumping out of and into his body as he ran up the road to join his friend ... The medical evidence indicates that Stephen was dead before he was removed by the ambulance men some time later. The amount of blood which had been lost would have made it probable that Stephen died where he fell on the pavement, and probably within a short time of his fall ...

1.10   What followed has ultimately led to this public Inquiry ...

46.1   The conclusions to be drawn from all the evidence in connection with the investigation of Stephen Lawrence's racist murder are clear. There is no doubt but that there were fundamental errors. The investigation was marred by a combination of professional incompetence, institutional racism and a failure of leadership by senior officers ...

46.26 At its most stark the case against the police was that racism infected the MPS [Metropolitan Police Service] and that the catalogue of errors could only be accounted for by something more than incompetence. If corruption and collusion did not play its part then, say the critics, the case must have been thrown or at least slowed down because officers approached the murder of a black man less energetically than if the victim had been white and the murderers black. An example of this approach was that posed by Mr Panton, the

barrister acting for Greenwich Council, who argued that if the colour of the
victim and the attackers was reversed the police would have acted differently:

> In my submission history suggests that the police would have probably swamped the
> estate that night and they would remain there, probably for the next however long it
> took, to ensure that if the culprits were on that estate something would be done
> about the situation.

46.27 We understand why this view is held. We have examined with anxiety and care
all the evidence and have heeded all the arguments both ways. We do believe,
[see section (3) above] that institutional racism is apparent in those areas
described. But we do not accept that it was universally the cause of the failure of
this investigation ...

46.28 Next we identify those areas which were affected by racism remembering
always that that emotive word covers the whole range of such conduct. In this
case we do not believe that discrimination or disadvantage was overt. There was
unwitting racism in the following fields:

i   Inspector Groves' insensitive and racist stereotypical behaviour at the scene.
     He assumed that there had been a fight. He wholly failed to assess Duwayne
     Brooks as a primary victim. He failed thus to take advantage of the help
     which Mr Brooks could have given. His conduct in going to the Welcome
     Inn [the Inspector visited a public house at the scene for no apparent reason]
     and failing to direct proper searches was conditioned by his wrong and
     insensitive appreciation and conclusions.

ii   Family Liaison. Inspector Little's conduct at the hospital, and the whole
     history of later liaison was marred by the patronising and thoughtless
     approach of the officers involved ...

iii [This] sad failure was never appreciated and corrected by senior officers, in
     particular Mr Weeden, who in his turn tended to blame Mr & Mrs Lawrence
     and their solicitor for the failure of family liaison ...

iii Mr Brooks was by some officers side-lined and ignored, because of racist
     stereotyping particularly at the scene and the hospital. He was never
     properly treated as a victim.

iv   At least five officers ... simply refused to accept that this was purely a racist
     murder. This ... must have skewed their approach to their work.

v   DS Flook allowed untrue statements about Mr & Mrs Lawrence and Mr
     Khan to appear in his statement to Kent [the first inquiry into the police
     conduct of this case]. Such hostility resulted from unquestioning acceptance
     and repetition of negative views as to demands for information which Mr &
     Mrs Lawrence were fully entitled to make. DS Flook's attitude influenced
     the work which he did.

vi   The use of inappropriate and offensive language. Racism awareness training
     was almost non-existent at every level.

Most of these authors look to the future with considerable pessimism. Jenkins (see
above, '(3) Racism in Practice') pins many of his hopes on the formalisation of
recruitment procedures. This is an issue to which we will return when considering the
possible impact of equal opportunities policies.[17] Brown considers that voluntary
efforts will come to naught without a vigorous, active lead from government. This is
unlikely to be forthcoming, at least to the extent considered desirable. What is notable
is that neither considers that the law has the capacity to make a significant dent in the

---

17   See Chapter 18, especially p 594 et al.

social disadvantages experienced by minority ethnic groups. In contrast, Macpherson's analysis suggests that there are there are tangible solutions that rely heavily on the law. The Report's recommendations are set out below in Part 3 'Post-war Political and Legal Responses'.[18]

(5)   The Current Employment Position of Minority Ethnic Groups[19]

Annual Local Area Labour Force Survey 2001/02, Office for National Statistics:

Unemployment Rates by ethnic group and sex 2001/2002[20]

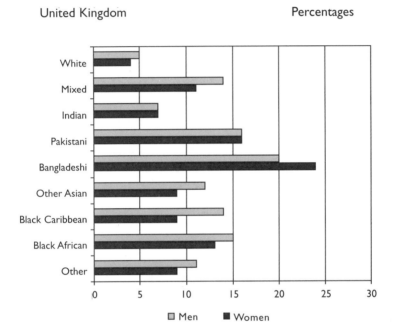

United Kingdom   Percentages

Economic Activity

There were marked differences between the economic activity rates of different ethnic groups, that is, the proportion of people who either have a job or are looking for a job.

Men and women from the White group are more likely to be economically active than their counterparts in minority ethnic groups.

18 Below, p 27.
19 See, also Modood, T et al (eds), *Ethnic Minorities in Britain: Diversity and Disadvantage*, 1997, London: Policy Studies Institute.
20 Published 12 December, 2002. Other Black and Chinese groups were omitted from the chart because sample sizes were too small for reliable estimates. This is an International Labour Organisation (ILO) recommended measure, used in household surveys such as the Labour Force Survey, which counts as unemployed those aged 16 and over who are without a job, are available to start work in the next two weeks, who have been seeking a job in the last four weeks or are waiting to start a job already obtained. The unemployment rate is based on the ILO definition as a percentage of all economically active.

In 2001/02 rates were 85 per cent for White men and 74 per cent for White women. Black Caribbean women had economic activity rates almost as high as White women at 72 per cent. Bangladeshis had the lowest economic activity rates among both men (69 per cent) and women (22 per cent). Pakistani women also had very low economic activity rates at 28 per cent.

Within all ethnic groups economic activity rates are higher for men than women.

Unemployment

In 2001/02 people from minority ethnic groups had higher unemployment rates than White people. This was the case for men and women.

Bangladeshi men had the highest unemployment rate at 20 per cent – four times that for White men. The unemployment rate among Indian men was only slightly higher than that for White men, 7 per cent compared with 5 per cent.

For all the other minority ethnic groups, unemployment rates were between two and three times higher than those for White men. This pattern was the same across different age groups.

For men from all ethnic groups unemployment was much higher among young people aged under 25 than for older people. Over 40 per cent of young Bangladeshi men were unemployed.

Young Black African men, Pakistanis, Black Caribbeans, and those belonging to the Mixed group also had very high unemployment rates – they ranged between 25 per cent and 31 per cent. The comparable unemployment rate for young White men was 12 per cent.

The picture for women was similar to that for men. Bangladeshi women had the highest unemployment rate at 24 per cent, six times greater than that of White women (4 per cent). Seven per cent of Indian women were unemployed.

Women in all other ethnic groups had rates between 9 per cent and 16 per cent. Rates for young women under the age of 25 years were considerably higher than for older women and this was true for all ethnic groups.

Self-employment

People from Pakistani and Chinese groups are far more likely to be self-employed than those in other groups. Around one-fifth of Pakistani (22 per cent) and Chinese (19 per cent) people in employment were self-employed in 2001/02 compared with only one in ten White people and less than one in ten Black people.

Certain ethnic groups were concentrated in particular industries. Self-employed Pakistani people were more likely than other people to work in the transport and communication industry, over half of them worked in this sector compared with 7 per cent of people overall.

Chinese people were more likely to work in the distribution, hotel and restaurant sector; 71 per cent did so compared with an overall figure of 18 per cent.

The growing diversity in economic performance between different ethnic groups, especially the relative success achieved by Indians, has implications for future policy and strategy. Modood argues that it is wrong to assume that 'being white or not is the single most crucial factor in determining the sociological profile of any non-white group in contemporary Britain, dwarfing class, employment, capital assets, skills, gender, ethnicity, religion, family, geography and so on'.[21] To some extent, the example of Indian success renders the simple divide between 'white' and 'black' increasingly outmoded. It is not denied that such problems may be true for many if not most ethnic groups; it is the assumption that economic underperformance is always directly traceable to racism which is questionable, as is any belief in the universality of purported solutions or policy interventions.

3   POST-WAR POLITICAL AND LEGAL RESPONSES

We start with the general political response to immigration in the 1950s and 1960s. In this first extract, Solomos explains successive governments' policy of linking integration to immigration control. In the second extract, Lester and Bindman observe that such a policy is fundamentally absurd.

Solomos, J, *Race and Racism in Britain*, 2nd edn, 1993, London: Macmillan, pp 82–84:

From the 1950s the question of what to do to counter racial discrimination emerged as a major dilemma in debates about immigration and race relations. Even in the early stages of black immigration there was an awareness that in the longer term the question of racial discrimination was likely to become a volatile political issue. In the early stages of post-war black immigration, political debates about race were centred upon the question of immigration controls. However, an underlying concern, even at that stage, was the future of race relations. The notion that the arrival of too many black immigrants would lead to problems in relation to housing, employment and social services was already widely articulated ...

Two problems were usually seen as in need of urgent attention. First, the negative response of the majority white population to the competition of black workers in the housing and labour markets ... Second, the frustration of black workers who felt themselves excluded from equal participation in British society by the development of a colour bar in the labour and housing markets, along with related processes of discrimination ...

The first attempts to deal with potential racial conflict and tackle racial discrimination can be traced back to the 1960s and took two basic forms. The first involved the setting up of welfare agencies to deal with the problems faced by black immigrants and to help the white communities understand the immigrants. The second stage of the policy response began with the passage of the 1965 and 1968 Race Relations Acts, and was premised on the notion that the State should attempt to ban discrimination on the basis of race, colour or ethnic origin through legal sanctions and public regulatory agencies charged with the task of promoting equality of opportunity ...

The notion that immigration was essentially an issue of race was consistent with the view that: (a) the growing number of black citizens resident in Britain was either actually or potentially the source of social problems and conflicts, and (b) that it was

21 Modood, T, 'The Indian economic success: a challenge to some race relations assumptions' (1991) Policy and Politics 177, p 178. He further argues that it is wrong to assume, first, that until 'racial prejudice and discrimination in all its forms is eliminated. Though some non-white individuals will be allowed to succeed, all non-white groups will share a below-average socio-economic profile; they will form a racial under-class' and, secondly, that the 'only way "black" people can improve their condition *as a group* is through political militancy and/or substantial State action'.

necessary for the State to introduce measures to promote the integration of immigrants into the wider society and its fundamental institutions.

The linking of immigration controls with integrative measures was a significant step since it signalled a move towards the management of domestic race relations as well as legitimising the institutionalisation of firm controls at the point of entry ... [S]ince the 1960s the two sides of State intervention have been seen as inextricably linked. According to Roy Hattersley's famous formula, 'integration without control is impossible, but control without integration is indefensible'.[22] The rationale of this argument was never articulated clearly, but it was at least partly based on the idea that the fewer immigrants there were, the easier it would be to integrate them into the English way of life and its social cultural values.

Lester, A and Bindman, G, *Race and Law*, 1972, Harmondsworth: Penguin, p 13:

The growth of racial feeling in Britain was both ignored and condemned during the first decade of immigration from the Commonwealth. In the next decade, the existence of a problem was reluctantly recognised; and, once more echoing earlier history, the initial governmental response was entirely defensive and negative. In 1962, after another ugly racist campaign, legislation was passed with the aim of limiting further coloured immigration. Since that date, public attitudes have become increasingly ambivalent. It is now conventional wisdom that Britain is too small and overcrowded to absorb fresh newcomers – unless they are white. At the same time, it is also widely accepted that racial discrimination is economically wasteful, socially divisive, harmful to international relations, or morally wrong (according to one's particular standpoint). The approach of successive governments has therefore been that Commonwealth citizens should therefore be excluded from this country because they are coloured, but that Commonwealth citizens who are already here should be treated equally, regardless of their colour. Understandably, few people have grasped the distinction. The more obvious conclusion that has generally been drawn is that if coloured immigration presents a threat to Britain's well-being, so does the coloured minority living in Britain.

The Race Relations Act 1965 was replaced with broader provisions by the 1968 Act. The next two extracts track their success.

Brown, C, 'Ethnic pluralism in Britain: the demographic and legal background', in Glazer, N and Young, K (eds), *Ethnic Pluralism and Public Policy*, 1986, Aldershot: Gower, p 51:

The 1965 Race Relations Act outlawed discrimination in specified places of public resort, such as hotels, restaurants ... and made it a criminal offence deliberately to stir up racial hatred by publishing or distributing written matter or by speaking in public. The Act set up the Race Relations Board ... which co-ordinated seven regional conciliation committees to deal with complaints of discrimination ... Although the number of complaints was small (690 in the year 1967–68), a large majority of them fell outside the scope of the Act, the most frequent of these being complaints about employment, the police and housing.

[As a result of reports confirming the continued existence of racial discrimination, the] Race Relations Act 1968 widened the coverage of the law to housing, employment, and the provision of goods and services. The Race Relations Board was given the power to investigate cases where there was reason to believe that discrimination had

---

22 *Hansard*, Vol 789 Cols 378–85.

taken place but no complaint had been received; the Board was also given the power to bring legal proceedings when attempts to conciliate failed ...

The more public indications of discriminatory practices, such as advertisements specifying 'no coloureds', and outright statements of racist job recruitment policies, all but disappeared ... But there were still high levels of discrimination, on a scale far greater than would have been judged from the still small number of complaints to the Race Relations Board. In addition, it had become apparent that direct discrimination was not always at the heart of racial disadvantage: regulations, policies and practices of organisations often discriminated indirectly against ethnic minorities, and the Act lacked any provision for dealing with these cases.

Davies, P and Freedland, M, *Labour Legislation and Public Policy,* **1993, Oxford: Clarendon, p 229:**

Perhaps the most significant aspect of the remedial provisions of the 1968 Act ... was its exclusion of the individual from direct access to the courts. Unlike the individual complaining of unfair dismissal or unequal pay, the complainant in a race relations case had to channel his or her complaint through the Board ... Even if these machineries failed to produce a settlement, the decision on taking proceedings in the courts lay exclusively in the hands of the Board, to whom indeed any award of damages was made, although the Board had to account to the individual for the money received. This procedure had two consequences. First, the resources of the Board were overwhelmingly deployed in the handling of individual complaints, so that it had very little opportunity to initiate independent investigations into situations which suggested that deep-seated patterns of discrimination had become established ... Second, from the point of view of the individual, the remedies against discrimination appeared rather ineffective. Especially in the employment field, where the voluntary machinery, if established, operated first, the procedures were cumbersome and slow, whilst the monopoly of the Board deprived the individual of control over the handling of the grievance. In fact, before 1975, only one employment case had reached the courts.

Pressure for more effective legislation came from a number of sources, concerned both with the apparent ineffectiveness of the legislation and the evidence of continued racial discrimination in practice. The 1967 Political and Economic Planning Report on Racial Discrimination demonstrated empirically what had until then been largely anecdotal evidence of the extent of discrimination. In addition, campaigning monographs by leading lawyers coherently and persuasively argued the case for more powerful legislation, which arrived in the shape of the 1976 Race Relations Act.[23]

Further pressure for more effective legislation came from evidence of what has come to be known as 'institutional discrimination',[24] factors which entrench patterns of social disadvantage within minority ethnic communities, although this was often attributed to the relatively recent arrival of the bulk of the black population. As the White Paper which preceded the 1976 Race Relations Act put it:

There is at work in this country ... the familiar cycle of cumulative disadvantage by which relatively low paid or low status jobs for the first generation of immigrants go

---

23 Eg, Lester, A and Bindman, G, *Race and Law*, 1972, Harmondsworth: Penguin; Hepple, B, *Race, Jobs and the Law in Britain*, 1968, Harmondsworth: Penguin. The fact that both were published by Penguin helped the debate to reach the public domain rather than being confined to the academic domain.

24 McCrudden, C, 'Institutional discrimination' (1982) 2 OJLS 303. See sections (4) and (5) above, pp 21 and 25 respectively.

hand in hand with poor and overcrowded living conditions, and a depressed environment. If, for example, job opportunities, educational facilities, housing and environmental conditions are all poor, the next generation will grow up less well equipped to deal with the difficulties facing them. The wheel then comes full circle as the second generation find themselves trapped in poor jobs and poor housing. If at each stage of the process an element of racial discrimination enters in, then an entire group of people are launched on a vicious downward spiral of deprivation. They may share each of the disadvantages with some other deprived group in society, but few groups in society display all their accumulated disadvantages.[25]

There is no doubt that racial disadvantage was and remains prevalent in our society. Whether such institutional disadvantage should properly be referred to as discrimination is less clear cut. The next three extracts suggest that the notion of institutional racism is too simplistic. Nonetheless, in 1999, the Macpherson Report delivered a widely accepted definition, which is repeated below, with its recommendations to combat it.

Miles, R, *Racism*, 1989, London: Routledge, pp 54–60:

[Institutional racism offers] a very different concept of racism from that used by [earlier] writers ... who defined it exclusively and specifically as an ideology. First, the concept has a generalised rather than a specific referent: it identifies as racism all those beliefs, actions and processes which lead to, or sustain, discrimination against and the subordination of 'black' people. Second, it denies that intentionality or motivation are measures of the presence or absence of racism. Whilst an explicit motive or intention to subordinate may be evident, it is not considered to be a necessary condition for the identification of racism. Third, by definition, racism is a prerogative of 'white' people. Fourth ... it asserts or assumes a theory of stratification in which the terms 'white' and 'black' have analytical status. The social formation under analysis is identified as constituted by the presence of two (homogeneous) groups, 'whites' and 'blacks', which have a hierarchical relationship with each other ...

[T]he concept is inseparable from a theory of stratification that is simplistic and erroneous because it states or assumes that the sole or primary division within a society is between 'white' people and 'black' people ... [T]his suppresses and denies the existence of class divisions and conflict, and the distribution of 'white' and 'black' people to different class positions ... Evidence of the extent of racist belief and sympathy for Fascist politics among sections of the 'white' unskilled working class ... is therefore more accurately understood as a response ... to powerlessness rather than the possession of power ...

Solomos, J and Back, L, *Racism and Society*, 1996, London: Macmillan, pp 77–79:

[T]he processes which help to structure racialised inequalities are by no means static. In the present economic and social climate racialised inequalities are being constantly transformed. A case in point is the relationship between the spatial restructuring of industries and jobs ... and its impact on employment opportunities for minorities ... [S]uch patterns of restructuring may end up having a major impact on those sections of racial and ethnic minorities who are most vulnerable and least likely to be able to benefit from equal opportunities policies.

[T]here has been a hardening of racial and ethnic cleavages among lower class groups. This is borne out by the evidence of racial disadvantage in the major urban conurbations and by what some have defined as the 'racialisation of poverty'. But at

---

25 *Racial Discrimination*, Cmnd 6234, 1975, London: HMSO, para 11.

the same time we have seen a noticeable growth of a black professional middle class and of ethnic minority small businesses with an impact at all levels of society ... This has led to much greater emphasis in recent studies on the role of economic and social processes which have helped to transform the class position of sections of minority communities.

Solomos, J, *Race and Racism in Britain*, 2nd edn, 1993, London: Macmillan, p 241:

[T]he basic problem confronting any account of the complex relations between race, class and the State is to be found in the very nature of racism in contemporary capitalist societies ... [T]here are at least two problems which have so far defied resolution. First, the question of the interplay between racial and ethnic categorisations and economic and class determinations. Second, the role of the State and political institutions of capitalist societies in the reproduction of racism, including the complex role of State intervention in many countries to control immigration, to manage race relations, and, more broadly, to integrate racial and ethnic groupings into the wider society ...

The Macpherson Report defined institutional racism as:

6.34 ... The collective failure of an organisation to provide an appropriate and professional service to people because of their colour, culture, or ethnic origin. It can be seen or detected in processes, attitudes and behaviour which amount to discrimination through unwitting prejudice, ignorance, thoughtlessness and racist stereotyping which disadvantage minority ethnic people.[26]

The Report then recommended: changes to Stop and Search procedures; amendments to the Race Relations and Freedom of Information Acts; changes in school practice; the creation of a police inspection system similar to OFSTED; and specific police training. They are summarised below.

46.31 The need to re-establish trust between minority ethnic communities and the police is paramount. Such distrust and loss of confidence is particularly evident in the widely held view that junior officers discriminate in practice at operational level, and that they support each other in such discrimination. We have referred (Para 45.8) to the primary problem of 'stop and search', including those stops which are unrecorded within the present statistics. The minority communities' views and perceptions are formed by their experience of all 'stops' by the police. They do not perceive any difference between a 'stop' under the Police and Criminal Evidence Act from one under the Road Traffic Act whilst driving a vehicle. It is essential to obtain a true picture of the interactions between the police and minority ethnic communities in this context. All 'stops' need to be recorded, and related self-defined 'ethnic data' compiled. We have considered whether such a requirement would create too great a bureaucracy for operational officers, and we are persuaded that this is not the case. The great weight of extra recording would undoubtedly relate to 'traffic stops' many of which are already recorded via the HORTI (production of driving documents) procedure. In this context we have also specifically considered whether police powers to 'stop and search' should be removed or further limited. We specifically reject this option. We fully accept the need for such powers to

---

26 *The Stephen Lawrence Inquiry, Report of an Inquiry by Sir William Macpherson, advised by Tom Cook, The Right Reverend Dr John Sentamu, Dr Richard Stone*, February 1999, presented to Parliament by the Home Secretary. Cm 4262-I, London: HMSO www.official-documents.co.uk/document/cm42/4262/4262.html, para 6.34; see above, '(2) Theories of Racism'.

continue, and their genuine usefulness in the prevention and detection of crime (Recommendations 60–63).

46.32 Seeking to achieve trust and confidence through the demonstration of fairness will not in itself be sufficient. It must be accompanied by a vigorous pursuit of openness and accountability across Police Services. Essentially we consider that the principle which should govern the Police Services, and indeed the criminal justice system, is that they should be accountable under all relevant legislative provisions unless a clear and specific case can be demonstrated that such accountability would be harmful to the public interest. In this context we see no justification for exemption of the Police Service from the full provisions of the Race Relations Act. Chief Officers should be vicariously liable for the actions of their officers. Similarly we consider it an important matter of principle that the Police Services should be open to the full provisions of a Freedom of Information Act. We see no logical grounds for a class exemption for the police in any area (Recommendations 9–11).

46.34 If racism is to be eliminated from our society there must be a co-ordinated effort to prevent its growth. This need goes well beyond the Police Services. The evidence we heard and read forces us to the conclusion that our education system must face up to the problems, real and potential, which exist. We therefore make a number of Recommendations aimed at encouraging schools to address the identified problems (Recommendations 67–69) ...

46.37 Systems of inspection and the existence of objective external appraisal are part and parcel of the process of accountability and reconciliation. They need to be strong and independent. In this context we are attracted by the 'standards based' approach adopted by OFSTED which in a transparent way shows the standards against which schools, colleges and other educational establishments will be judged. A similar approach in inspection of Police Services could have advantages and should be more broadly adopted. Furthermore in the future work may profitably be done by 'cross-cutting' inspection work across the criminal justice system as a whole, with appropriate and fair treatment as the aim. Perhaps a change of approach would help to produce a criminal justice service which is accessible and acceptable throughout to all those who experience it (Recommendation 5).

46.38 The public and the Police Services of the United Kingdom are justifiably proud of the tradition of an unarmed police service which polices with the consent of the public. The recent perceptive HMIC thematic report 'Winning the Race' reinforces our view that at present the confidence and trust of the minority ethnic communities is at a low ebb. Such lack of confidence threatens the ability of the Police Services to police by consent in all areas of their work, not simply in the policing of racist incidents and crimes.

46.42 We hope and expect that implementation of our Recommendations will ensure that the opportunity for radical thinking and root and branch action is seized. Nothing less will satisfy us and all those who so passionately spoke to us during our hearings in and out of London during the long months of the Stephen Lawrence Inquiry. We also hope that as Police Services reach out to local communities their approach will not be rejected. The gap between Police Services and local communities may seem to be great, but early steps welcomed and encouraged by both sides will surely lead to confidence and co-operation. This may then be the start of the beginning of change.

Following the Macpherson Report, the Race Relations Act 1976 was amended to make public authorities liable for discrimination, although decisions *not* to prosecute are exempt.[27] Further, the recommendation regarding the Freedom of Information Act 2000 was rejected: s 30(1) of that Act specifically exempts investigations that may lead to a decision to prosecute.

If evidence of serious social disadvantage is accepted, anti-discrimination legislation should be only one strand of a wider policy aimed at remedying social disadvantages, a policy which would require considerable expenditure of public money for it to have any chance of success. It is even possible to argue that passing legislation appears to take an activist stance while involving little or no expenditure of public funds, whereas real social change is more likely to result from appropriately targeted financial resources. We have seen why the 1968 Act was considered inadequate and why further legislation was considered necessary. In fact, the Race Relations Act 1976 was passed a year after the Sex Discrimination Act 1975, and is substantially identical to it.[28] The Macpherson Report stands out as identifying tangible problems with mainly *legal* solutions. Yet four years on, the shortcomings of its legal and cultural impact were exposed by Bowling's research, that found that blacks were 27 times more likely than whites to be stopped by the police. 'Under section 60 [of the Criminal Justice and Public Order Act 1994] police have the widest discretion, using their own beliefs about who is involved in crime, using their own stereotypes about who's worth stopping ...'[29]

---

27 See further, Chapter 13, p 370.

28 For the reasons for this identity, see McCrudden, C, 'Institutional discrimination' (1982) 2 OJLS 303, p 337.

29 *Per* Bowling, B (King's College, London), reported in *The Guardian*, 21 April 2003, and *Black Britain*, 23 April 2003.

CHAPTER 2

THE BACKGROUND TO SEX DISCRIMINATION LEGISLATION IN THE UK

The history of women's inequality is well-documented. Politically, legally, socially and economically, even partial freedom for women arrived only relatively recently.[1] Social disadvantages remain, if judged by the proportion of women in high political or judicial office, or senior professional or management positions, and by the stubbornly persistent gap in average pay levels between men and women. As with race issues, the causes of continuing inequality are complex and difficult to dislodge, throwing into doubt the capacity of any law to deal with them adequately.

However, the 20th century, and especially the years following the Second World War, have seen a social transformation in the economic and social position of women. Not all the changes are necessarily beneficial, and few would suggest that complete equality has been achieved, but it is undeniable that the changing expectations and opportunities for many women have been one of the major social changes experienced in the last 50 years by Western societies.

The task of this chapter is to trace the changes in the employment position of women through the 20th century and state the current position. It is then necessary to examine the causes of employment inequalities, both historically and presently. It is by examining such causes that we can begin to appreciate whether the law has contributed to any reduction in gender inequality and whether it has the capacity to bring about any further reduction in the future.

1 PARTICIPATION IN THE WORKPLACE – A RECENT HISTORY[2]

The distinction between paid work, performed outside the home, and unpaid work, usually at home, developed its modern clarity following the Industrial Revolution. Before that, the distinction was largely concealed by the prevalence of subsistence agriculture and craft work. It was the concentration of labour in factories necessitated by the Industrial Revolution which marked the shift towards the distinction which remains so significant today. It has been argued that it was a social choice that women should remain at home and that men should work in the factories – not a result which was in any sense inevitable. The proportion of married women in paid employment outside the home actually declined between 1851 and 1921 from 25% to 8.7%.[3] This ideology – for that is what it was – was also manifested in that women were excluded from certain jobs requiring physical strength and from night work. The assumption was that women could not and should not perform such jobs.[4] In addition, women were often required to leave paid employment on marriage.

---

1   See Fredman, S, *Women and the Law*, 1997, Oxford: Clarendon, Chapter 2, or Fredman, S, *Discrimination Law*, 2002, Oxford: Clarendon, Chapter 2, pp 27–36.

2   See 'Women in the labour market' (1998) 79 EOR 30.

3   Atkins, S and Hoggett, B, *Women and the Law*, 1984, Oxford: Robertson, pp 18–19.

4   See *op cit*, Fredman, fn 1, 1997, pp 67–74.

Walby, S, *Gender Transformations*, 1997, London: Routledge, pp 27–34:

There has been a massive growth in the number of women who are in formal waged employment since the Second World War ...

It suggests the possibility of rapid and substantial changes in the typical life experiences of women in this period. However, there is a series of caveats which place some qualifications on this picture ...

Much of the narrowing of the differences and inequalities between men and women in employment has taken place among full-time workers only. There are very significant inequalities and differences between full-time and part-time work. For instance, part-time work is on average paid significantly less than full-time work, and typically has fewer fringe benefits. ... [T]his acts as a serious qualification to any picture of the improvement in the position of women ...

The extent of part-time working among women means that the proportion of total working hours performed by women as compared with men has not risen as rapidly as the proportion of women holding jobs ... [But] part-time work should be ... recognised as a distinctive form of employment with its own significance for the position of women in society ...

While it has often been suggested that the absence of legal protection causes more jobs to be created, the fact that the growth in part-time employment occurred,[5] even though the majority of such employees were protected, casts doubt on this argument, and there is no indication of a reduction in part-time employment since the abolition of the hours threshold.[6]

Social Trends, 2002, No 32, London: HMSO, p 75, Table 4.10:[7]

One of the main themes already to emerge ... is the increased market participation of women over the last decades. However, the presence of a dependent child in the family still has a major effect on the economic activity of women. About 44 per cent of women of working age had dependent children in Spring 2001 [see Table below]. Only 18 per cent of women whose youngest child was under 5 worked full-time, but this proportion rose with the age of the youngest child so that for those whose youngest dependent child was aged 16–18 it reached 44 per cent, only five percentage points lower than for women with no dependent children. Among women with pre-school children, most were either working part-time (36 per cent) or were economically inactive and looking after family and home (38 per cent).

Between 1991 and 2001, the economic activity rate for women with pre-school children increased from 48 per cent to 57 per cent. Women on maternity leave are classified as in employment, so this rise reflects a greater number of women returning to the labour market sooner after the birth of their children than previously, and also an increase in the number who may leave the labour market at all while having their children. For women without dependent children the economic activity rate for 2001,

---

5   Since 1995. Until 1995, there was a 16-hours-per-week threshold for workers to obtain employment protection rights with two years' continuous employment. Below that, five years' continuous employment was required. This was abolished by SI 1995/31, following *Re Secretary of State for Employment v ex p EOC* [1995] 1 AC 1, HL, which held the threshold to be indirectly discriminatory.

6   See, eg, the arguments on the parallel issue of the (then) two-year qualifying period for unfair dismissal rights, put in *R v Secretary of State for Employment ex p Seymour-Smith* Case C-167/97, [1999] All ER (EC) 97 ECJ; [2000] 1 All ER 857, HL. For a casenote and commentary see [2000] 05/2 J Civ Lib.

7   *Social Trends*, 2002, No 32, London: HMSO, p 75, Table 4.10.

at 75 per cent, was the same as in 1991. Therefore the main driver behind the increase in female economic activity rates during the 1990s has been the increased economic activity of women with dependent children.

Economic activity status of women:[8] by age of youngest dependent child, 1991 and 2001

United Kingdom   Percentages

	Age of youngest dependent child				No dependent children	All
	Under 5	5–10	11–15	16–18		
1991						
Working full-time	14	21	31	38	50	38
Working part-time	28	44	42	37	20	27
Unemployed[9]	6	6	4	3	5	5
Looking after family/home	47	22	15	13	6	17
Students[10]	1	1	..	..	6	4
Other inactive	4	5	7	8	11	9
All (=100%)(millions)	3.1	2.1	1.4	0.5	9.7	16.8
2001						
Working full-time	18	26	37	44	49	39
Working part-time	36	44	38	37	23	30
Unemployed	3	3	4	2	3	3
Looking after family/home	38	18	12	7	4	13
Students	1	2	1	..	8	5
Other inactive	3	6	8	10	13	10
All (=100%)(millions)	3.0	2.4	1.6	0.6	9.9	17.4

It remains common, though less common than previously, for women who worked full-time before starting a family to return on a part-time basis either after maternity leave or some time later. This pattern is associated with downward occupational mobility – such women frequently return to a lower level job than they previously occupied. Furthermore, the longer the period out of the labour market, the greater the likelihood that return will be to a lower level job.[11] In Britain, there are very few high grade part-time jobs. This forces many women to choose between working full-time in a career or part-time in a low skilled job, and has the result of increasing the divergence in women's labour market experience, even in the case of women with similar qualifications. This is explored by Walby.

8   Aged 16–59. At Spring each year.
9   Based on the International Labour Organisation definition.
10 Those in full-time education.
11 Martin, J and Roberts, C, *Women and Employment: A Lifetime Perspective*, 1984, London: HMSO, p 137.

Walby, S, *Gender Transformations*, 1997, London: Routledge, pp 52–54:

The higher the woman's level of education and the higher her occupational level the more likely she is to be in paid employment while looking after young children. ... Possible reasons for this difference ... could include: that the cost of childcare is more within the reach of professionals ... [and] the relative balance of attractiveness of the activities of paid work and homework ... between these groups.

Women who are in full-time employment do less housework than those who are non-employed or work part-time ... However, ... studies suggest that married women who have full-time employment do more hours of work (housework plus paid work) than do women who do solely housework, with women who do part-time paid work and housework being in between.

People who were sick, elderly or disabled either inside or outside the household were reported to be looked after or given special help by 17% of women or 12% of men in the adult population in 1991 ... The women who provide this care are disproportionately aged between 45 and 64, while the most typical age of men carers is over 75.

(1)   Explaining the Change in Women's Participation Rates[12]

The reasons for the change are numerous and it is impossible to determine the precise degree to which each separate cause has contributed. The labour market factors which are relevant are the increased demand for female labour and the increased qualifications of women in the labour market. In the first extract below, Webb argues that the *demand* for labour is the relevant market factor, whilst in the second extract, Walby notes the *supply* side market factors.

Webb, M, 'Sex and gender in the labour market', in Reid, I and Stratta, E (eds), *Sex Differences in Britain*, 2nd edn, 1989, Aldershot: Gower, pp 136–37:

[T]he increase in the 'supply' of women workers was partly connected with changes in women's role and the decision of women to remain in gainful employment for longer before having a child. However, the changes in the pattern of childbearing may merely have resulted from, rather than caused, the increase in women's labour market participation. Childbearing patterns cannot be a complete explanation of the labour market changes, for the increase in paid work took place at all stages in the lifecycle including the period of childrearing ...

A better explanation of the increase in the proportion of women in work lies not on the 'supply' side but involves looking at economic 'demand'. During the 1950s and 1960s the economy was booming, whereas there was a recession after the mid 1970s and particularly after 1979. These periods match quite closely the periods of fastest and slowest rise in female employment. Therefore a key explanation of the rise in women's activity lies in the increased demand in the economy for people to undertake paid work; in recent years this has mainly been in the form of part-time work.

Walby, S, *Gender Transformations*, 1997, London: Routledge, pp 41–49:

One of the most important reasons for the changes in employment has been the increased educational qualifications gained by young women. Girls now achieve more educational qualifications than boys at school ... Women are much more likely to be in paid employment if they have received higher levels of education. ...

---

12 See *Women in the Labour Market: Results from the Spring 2001 Labour Force Survey*, Labour Market Trends, March 2002, pp 109–27.

Thus we have age-specific patterns of gender inequality. There can be no sweeping statement about women catching up with men ... The fact of very significant gender inequality in qualifications among people over 40 is not affected by the changes discussed for younger people ... We see a new form of inequality – that between women of different age cohorts ...

Other intervening variables include: structures of sex segregation; work commitment; discrimination. The correlation between educational qualifications and employment ... makes it clear that, whatever the remaining structures of disadvantage or differences in work commitment, educational changes are making a significant impact on gender relations in employment, at least for younger women.

The implications of this are highly significant. It is becoming less true to talk of patterns of disadvantage affecting women in general and more necessary to focus attention on particular groups of women. Secondly, and perhaps more controversially, the growth of families where both partners are in permanent well-paid jobs might be thought to be increasing *overall* inequality in society, as alongside this growth many households have no earner, or one part-time earner on a low wage.

However, examining the demand for female labour and the increased supply of qualified women workers is far from the whole answer. Availability for work is affected both by the greater control which women have over their own fertility, and by the greater availability of domestic labour-saving devices (and perhaps the greater need of money to pay for them). The fact that women can work more has resulted in a greater investment in human capital on the part of many women, but this hardly seems an adequate explanation of the huge increase in the number of women with young children who work.

Webb, M, 'Sex and gender in the labour market', in Reid, I and Stratta, E (eds), *Sex Differences in Britain*, 2nd edn, 1989, Aldershot: Gower, pp 168–69:

One survey found that 50% of the women questioned said that money was the overriding reason for working. The Women and Employment Survey [1984] found that 67% of working married mothers worked to earn money for basic essentials or extras.

Despite the importance of money, work may be performed out of a mixture of motivations, such as a desire to escape domestic drudgery ... and isolation ... and a desire for job satisfaction.

The expectation that most women work may itself be a factor in explaining why more women work. Isolation will be greater if one's peers work, and that will reinforce the belief that work is necessary, expected and desirable. Such reactions are, of course, dependent on the availability of such work, and so we are driven back to the position that the root cause of the increase in female employment, especially in the part-time sector, is the increased demand for such employees; indeed, many employers have chosen to organise their whole labour policy around part-time employment, in the confident expectation that the supply of such employees will be maintained.[13]

---

13   The measurement of female unemployment is notoriously problematic, because availability for work is partly dependent on knowing that there are available jobs. On whether women experience unemployment disproportionately to men, see, eg, Webb, M, 'Sex and gender in the labour market', in Reid, I and Stratta, E (eds), *Sex Differences in Britain*, 2nd edn, 1989, Aldershot: Gower, pp 157–61.

Furthermore, the dramatic rise in the participation rate of women with young children has occurred without any significant corresponding improvement in childcare provision.

2   THE CURRENT POSITION OF WOMEN AND WORK

(1)   Women's Pay Levels[14]

It is commonplace to point out and bemoan the fact that the gap between women's pay levels and those of men has not declined rapidly since the Equal Pay Act 1970 (which actually came into force in 1975). To ensure that like is compared with like, the usual comparison is of hourly pay rates. When that is done, it is seen that in the early 1970s, women full-time workers were paid, on average, between 63% and 67% as much as men. As a result of the Act, that figure increased to 72% in 1975. It had only reached 74% by 1986, but then followed a significant reduction in the gap.[15] The figures were 78% in 1991 and 80% in 1995.[16] However, the improvement has slowed since with the figure at 82% in 1999.[17]

Perhaps not surprisingly, there is no possible room for complacency when the pay levels of part-time women are concerned. The average hourly pay of part-time female employees, as a percentage of the hourly pay of full-time men, has varied from 54% in 1974 to 60% in 1977 and 1995.[18] The gap is far larger than between full-time men and full-time women, but there is no evidence that it is declining. In fact, the earnings of part-time women, as a percentage of the earnings of full-time women, has actually *declined* from 82% in 1974 to 75% in 1995.[19] The reason may not be the fact of part-time working as such, but that the occupations which are largely performed by part-time women employees tend to have significantly lower hourly rates of pay than those organised around full-time employees.[20] Nonetheless, in 1999, part-time women earned just 60% of the pay of part-time men.[21]

Thus, we have seen some increase in the relative pay of full-time workers. However, much of that increase has been achieved by women at the top end of the earnings curve. These gains are largely caused by a change in the distribution of employment towards higher paid non-manual work. Within the categories of non-manual and manual work, the increase in women's pay has been no more than

---

14 See also *Lower Earnings Limit in Practice: Part-Time Employment in Hotels and Catering – Research Findings*, 1999, London: EOC.

15 Walby, S, *Gender Transformations*, 1997, London: Routledge, pp 30–31.

16 The hourly figure tells only part of the story, as men are more likely than women to have overtime opportunities and to receive bonus payments. In 1987, 38.6% of men received overtime payments, compared with 18.2% of women. *Op cit*, Webb, fn 13, p 139.

17 *The Gender Pay Gap – A Research Review*, 2001, London: EOC

18 Walby, S, *Gender Transformations*, 1997, London: Routledge, p 32.

19 *Ibid*.

20 *Op cit*, Martin and Roberts, fn 11, p 58.

21 *The Gender Pay Gap – A Research Review*, 2001, London: EOC.

marginal. Furthermore, those at the bottom of the earnings distribution curve have seen no relative improvement in relation to male earnings.

There is a greater fragmentation and diversification in female labour-market experience, largely due to changes in the nature of the labour market itself. Factors contributing to this development include deregulation and the removal of labour standards, as industry-wide collective agreements became a thing of the past, the abolition of Wages Councils, which provided some measure of protection for lower paid workers, predominantly women,[22] and the use of subcontracting in the public sector.

'Minimum wage benefits women and ethnic minorities' (1997) 73 EOR 13, pp 15–18:

Though part-time workers make up a quarter of the labour force, they are disproportionately represented among the low paid ... 32% of all part-time employees earn less than £3.50 [per hour], compared with 8% of full-time employees. Over half of all part-timers earn less than £4.50, compared with a fifth of full-time employees.[23]

Around two-thirds of low paid employees are concentrated in four industries – wholesale, retail and motor trade; hotels and restaurants; manufacturing; and social work. Of the 3 million employees earning less than £3.50, around 30% are employed in the wholesale, retail and motor trade, 17% in hotels and restaurants, 15% in manufacturing, and 12% in health and social work.

Women workers are almost twice as likely to be low paid than male employees. Almost 10% of women earn less than £3.00 an hour, compared with just over 5% of men; 30% of women earn less than £4.00 and 40% less than £4.50 compared with 14% and 20% of male employees ... Overall, if a minimum wage was set at £4.00 an hour, over 3 million female employees and 1.6 million male employees would benefit.

The national minimum wage was set at £3.60 per hour upon introduction, which the government calculated would benefit 1.4 million women, 1.3 million part-time workers, 110,000 homeworkers, 175,000 working lone parents, and 130,000 workers.[24] Of course, these figures assume 100% compliance with the legislation. The minimum wage is now set at £4.50,[25] and due to rise to £4.85 on 1 October 2004.[26]

(2)   The Jobs Women Do

The issue here is the extent to which women perform, as a whole, different jobs from men, a phenomenon often referred to as occupational segregation, and the extent to which this segregation may be in decline. A comparison here must be made not only

---

22   Fredman, S, *Women and the Law*, 1997, Oxford: Clarendon, pp 264–67.

23   It has been observed that women's wage labour plays a crucial role in supporting the low-wage economy in the UK. 'Women are so poorly supported in their attempts to work through public provision of childcare, and wages are so low [that the majority cannot afford private childcare]. In addition, the low-wage economy in the UK has made use of women as a cheap labour force, as reflected in downward mobility after childbirth, even at the expense of under-utilising the skills and experience that women do have from their previous experience and training.' Fine, B, *Women's Employment and the Capitalist Family*, 1992, London: Routledge, p 161.

24   See Department of Trade and Industry Press Release P/98/489, 18 June 1998.

25   National Minimum Wage Regulations 1999 (Amendment) Regulations 2003, SI 2003/1923.

26   Government written statement to Parliament, 19 March 2003.

with the actual jobs performed by men and women, but with whether such jobs have the same or different socio-economic status.[27]

Walby, S, *Gender Transformations*, 1997, London: Routledge, pp 34–36:

There has been a decline in the extent to which top jobs in the upper socio-economic levels were monopolised by men ... Women have increasingly entered top positions, especially those managerial, administrative, and professional jobs for which university degrees are the effective entry qualifications ... Between 1975 and 1994, the percentage of economically active women who were in the upper [socio-economic groups] ... increased significantly, from 5% to 13%. This compares with a parallel male shift from 20% to 28% in the same period ...[28]

There has been a very significant change in the distribution of women across the occupational orders between 1981 and 1991 ... Whilst most occupations still show that they are staffed predominantly by one sex or the other, there has been a marked reduction in the extent of segregation. ...

It remains the case that women are crowded into a relatively narrow range of occupations. ... [I]t will be the norm rather than the exception for a female employee to have no male counterpart doing the same job for the same employer.[29]

3   THE CAUSES OF WOMEN'S INEQUALITY[30]

It is self-evident that explanations for differences and inequalities experienced by women in relation to work are connected with the division of labour in the household. After the Industrial Revolution led to a more general separation of work and home, women's primary responsibility for children had an impact on working opportunities. This operated both ideologically – what was perceived as appropriate for women to do – and practically – what in the real world could be done. The evidence suggests that these two factors or approaches continue to operate to the detriment of women. There are two major issues which need to be considered: first, the reasons why women

---

27   'A not wholly inaccurate caricature of women's occupations is provided by the list of the "10 deadly Cs": catering, cleaning, clerking, cashiering, counter-minding, clothes-making, clothes-washing, coiffure, childminding and care of the sick.' *Op cit*, Webb, fn 13, p 145.

28   '[T]he proportion of women working full time (44%) who are in the top two social classes is higher than that for men (41%). However, women still account for just over one-third of all those working full time in the top two social classes. And, although the number of women employed in many managerial and professional organisations has increased, they still only represent 32% of managers and administrators.'('Women in the labour market' (1998) 79 EOR 30, p 31.)

29   '[T]the pattern of career segregation over the lifetime ... is highly variable by sex and class. For men, career segregation is more accentuated at the top of the occupational hierarchies, both manual and non-manual, whereas for women it is more accentuated at the bottom of these hierarchies ... Many men in positions of power and influence ... will have had little experience of working with women in the same occupations, but women cannot reach such positions without working with men. The situation is reversed at the bottom of the occupational hierarchy where the men are more likely to have worked with men but the women are more likely to have worked only with other women.' MacEwan Scott, A and Burchell, B, 'Gender segregation and work histories', in MacEwan Scott, A (ed), *Gender Segregation and Social Change*, 1994, Oxford: OUP, pp 151–53.

30   For an excellent straightforward introduction to the subject specifically aimed at students, see Reskin, B and Padavic, I, *Women at Work*, 2nd edn, 2002, Sage, Thousand Oaks: Pine Forge.

perform the jobs that they do and, secondly, why on average women receive lower pay than men. However, many of the factors are so interrelated that it becomes extremely difficult to determine which is the primary or most important explanation, or even if there is one. It is important to appreciate that the social situation we are attempting to explain is in a permanent state of flux, so any explanations need both to be grounded in the history of women's employment and to be able to take account of changing conditions. The aim is to provide a foundation for consideration of the degree to which legal intervention is likely to make a significant impact on continuing gender inequality.[31]

(1)   Neo-Classical Economics

The first issue, however, is whether there is even a *problem* which needs to be explained. Those who believe in the primacy and the efficacy of the free market as the allocator of jobs and resources would argue that both the pay which women receive and the jobs which they perform are the result of market economics mediated by the free choices of the individuals concerned. On this view, the price of labour is determined in precisely the same way as the price of any other product, namely supply and demand. Wage levels are the lowest which the employer can pay while at the same time maintaining the ability to attract employees.

This approach implies that discrimination is irrational and that the discriminating employer would face higher labour costs than a non-discriminating counterpart.[32] In particular, the fact that women are apparently willing to work for lower wages than men would predict that employers would replace men with women. This would break down segregation and contribute to the reduction of the pay differential. The statistics considered earlier are only consistent with this happening to a very limited extent in the case of full-time workers. The problem is to account for the persistence of the pay gap and occupational segregation.

The first answer is to deny the analogy between product markets and labour markets: the supposedly 'simple' laws of supply and demand do not operate at all simply when dealing with labour. 'Opportunities for the marginal substitution of labour ... are severely constrained by the widespread acceptance by employers [and] workers of three key principles: the rate for the job, no money wage cuts and the right of all existing employees to retain their job in relation to all other potential recruits.'[33] The rate for the job means that it is normal practice, though becoming less so, to pay the same to everyone doing the same job irrespective of their productivity. Unlike the product market, oversupply of workers very rarely leads to wage cuts, which, if they occur, are more likely to result from lack of profitability. Equally, current employees are almost never displaced by a cheaper alternative – unless that alternative is mechanical rather than human. In the absence of redundancies, the social function of

---

31 The whole area continues to be a very fertile field of study for sociologists and others, many of whose answers vary diametrically from each other. It is not our task or within our capability to resolve these disputes; rather, the task is to outline the various different approaches.

32 See, for instance, Greenberger, 'A productivity approach to disparate impact and the Civil Rights Act of 1991' (1993) 72 Oregon Law Rev 253. Cf Epstein, R, *Forbidden Grounds*, Cambridge, Mass: Harvard UP, esp pp 226–29.

33 Craig, C, Garnsey, E and Rubery, J, *Payment Structures in Smaller Firms: Women's Employment in Segmented Labour Markets*, 1984, London: Department of Employment, p 5.

employment has led to the assumption that a competent employee will retain a job. In any event, the *external* job market has only a limited influence on pay levels. Large employers may lack effective competition and so set their own pay levels; many firms operate an *internal* market where there is progression through the hierarchy; and there is very considerable variation in pay between people doing the same job for different employers. The conclusion must be that social factors are more significant explanations of pay levels than the economic laws of supply and demand.

Furthermore, the *assumptions* of neo-classical economic theory are far removed from the way in which labour markets operate in practice.[34]

Browne, N, 'The fundamental tension between market wages for women and comparable worth' (1984) 2 Law and Inequality 473, pp 473, 476, 480–83:

It is argued that the market automatically and accurately determines the relative worth of individual male and female workers ... In part, the market defence achieves its intellectual appeal because of an unstated belief that a free and fair market is already dispensing incomes. Additionally, people who advocate the superiority of market mechanisms necessarily adopt certain assumptions describing the characteristics of the setting in which markets function.

Defenders continually describe markets as impersonal. Such a characterisation is highly convenient for those who have a disproportionate influence on the determination of relative wages. Market defenders cite 'the laws of supply and demand' as the determinants for what the proper gap between the income of a surgeon and a nurse both is and should be. These laws supposedly result from objective forces beyond individuals' control. Consequently, income differentials are calibrated not by a person who could conceivably be a misogynist, racist, homophobe or ignoramus, but by forces that would mysteriously and automatically make appropriate monetary distinctions ... Market proponents also argue that legislative or judicial intervention in resulting wage decisions is a clumsy and burdensome interference with impersonal processes.

A [further] belief held by those who defend market outcomes is that the *rational* employer and employee will each shape wage and employment decisions by calculating the net pecuniary benefit to herself. That economic actors might be motivated by altruism, community well being, or moral principles is dubbed 'remote' by market advocates. In neo-classical economic theory, human nature is not necessarily devoid of moral content; instead, moral actions are defined in terms of efficient and individualistic calculations. The moral employee or seller of labour acts to maximise her income; the moral employer or purchaser of labour acts to maximise her profit ... Supposedly, the employer always searches for the most productive employee, and the employee readily leaves a job when the wage lags behind the market value of her marginal output.

[Four assumptions underlie neo-classical theory.]

(1)   [T]hat product and factor markets are competitive ... If an employer pays employees less than their worth, higher wages elsewhere will lure the employees away. If the employer pays employees more than their worth, the employer will realise no profit. [In other words, no worker is forced to accept a

---

34   For an attack on the primacy of economic values in current social decision making, see Fredman, *op cit*, fn 1, pp 403–11.

wage lower than marginal productivity would dictate. Given the alternatives to paid employment, this assumption is totally unrealistic.]

(2)   Rational economic calculations depend on the existence of necessary information. Both the employer and the employee must have considerable information about a particular job to match precisely the employee's wages with the value of the employee's marginal output and simultaneously to provide the employer with the optimal bargain consistent with the profit maximisation objective. Many types of information, including the productivity of all pertinent potential employees, quality of alternative jobs in other geographic regions, and the market value of an employee must be considered prior to such wage setting. Without this data, market defenders' characterisation of a wage decision as objective and rational is absurd ...

(3)   Neo-classical labour market theory ascribes powerful efficiency effects to the market mechanism because it presumes that the market wage cannot exist below the value of an employee's output. Discrimination can exist temporarily, but soon some other profit-hungry employer will lure the justifiably dissatisfied employee to a workplace where her true value is appreciated. In reality, this may not be the case. Many employees will not abandon a job that pays less than the value of marginal output. Cultural or pecuniary reasons, as well as an employee's failure to perceive the discrimination, cause this immobility ... [Furthermore] in a period of high unemployment and persistent recession ... workers move from job to job less often than under more prosperous macroeconomic conditions. Macroeconomic conditions have a definite effect on the amount and degree of mobility that can realistically be expected from workers. Yet, no worker controls the macroeconomic conditions affecting her. Mobility, therefore, is not simply a matter of individual choice in society ...

(4)   For wages to serve as an accurate measure of the value of an employee's output, the individual must have a particular productivity that both the employer and the employee can measure and then compare to the productivity of other employees ... Measuring an individual's productivity would provide a meaningful yardstick of worker value only if discrete marginal output were attributable to each individual worker ...

Neo-classical economic theory attempts to treat the market as impersonal, separate from its participants. In reality, the market is no more than a sum of the attributes and behaviours of its participants, including what may be a propensity to discriminate. If we reject the purity of the market mechanism, we need to consider how discrimination continues to operate.

Becker asserted that some employers had a 'taste' for discrimination, though where these tastes originated, and in particular the extent to which society was responsible for their development, was never explained.[35] Whether a theory developed in the context of racial issues in the USA can satisfactorily translate to race or gender issues in the UK must be a matter of some doubt. In any event, the hiring of cheaper female or black labour should increase profits and thus rapidly lead to a change of heart, for commercial reasons, among those who are continuing to discriminate. The theory implies a personal contact between discriminator-employer and victim-employee which seems far removed from the impersonal reality of most

35   Becker, G, *The Economics of Discrimination*, 2nd edn, 1971, Chicago: Chicago UP.

employment situations. Finally, the theory cannot explain extremely stable patterns of job segregation in an era of very rapid social change.

(2)   Human Capital Theories

So the labour market devotees shifted to another approach: the human capital theory. Here, women's lower wages are said to result from a decision to invest less in education and skills training than men, coupled with the fact that skills and experience decline during the period when women are absent from the labour market for family reasons. Women may choose to make a lower investment than men because they anticipate significant periods of absence from the labour market. The conclusion from the theory is that women are, on average, less productive than men.

There is no doubt some validity in this approach: evidence has shown that the average pay of women declines for each year of absence from the labour market. Furthermore, it is clear that the reduction in the pay gap for full-time workers is due in substantial part to the fact that women are obtaining more and better qualifications, although whether the decline is in proper proportion to the level of women's improvement is open to serious doubt. But attempting to demonstrate a close correlation between women's pay levels and their qualifications and experience is fraught with problems. For example, pay rates are higher in jobs requiring scientific and technical qualifications, more often held by men. It is not clear from the theory why some investments should be valued more highly than others. Again, it may be questioned whether experience is as essential for jobs as is often made out; to reward those with long periods of continuous employment may be done for social more than managerial reasons. The evidence suggests that not all absences from work have the same consequences so far as pay and job position are concerned. It is the first return to work, usually after the birth of the first child, which is associated with declining earnings and status, and this is even more true if the return to work is on a part-time basis. So the reduction in earnings is not linear for each year of absence, as the theory predicts. The decline on first return suggests instead that institutional factors are at work, and that, if choice is involved, the choice is made by employers, not employees.[36]

The above criticism of the theory is the technical one, that it fails to explain the pay gap. The second and more fundamental defect with the human capital approach is that it implies that all decisions about how much to invest in human capital are freely and rationally made. Many decisions are made without full information as to the human capital consequences. More importantly, if women know or suspect that they are less likely to be hired for particular jobs, then they will not invest in the human capital training necessary for such jobs. The theory passes responsibility to the individual rather than blaming the discriminator. In addition, it simply assumes that women are more likely than men to take time out of the labour market for childrearing reasons. Why that should be is not considered, nor is the fact that the provision or lack of childcare may have significant influence on the working patterns of mothers. If employers act on the basis of stereotypes, it becomes rational from a human capital perspective to act as if the stereotype were true, for otherwise the

36 See England, P, 'The failure of human capital theory to explain occupational segregation' (1982) 17 Journal of Human Resources 356.

investment is in danger of being wasted. This perpetuates a vicious circle whereby employers assume that women will not be qualified or be able to perform a particular job, and thus women are not given the opportunity to do so.

The most persistent and damaging stereotypes concern the interaction for women between work and home. One is that women will leave work, at least temporarily, to have children. It is thus argued to be economically rational for employers not to hire women for jobs which require extensive on-the-job training. Another stereotype is that women employees with young children are more likely to prove unreliable than men with young children; indeed, for a man, having young children may be regarded as a plus factor, for such men are assumed to be reliable employees for domestic and financial reasons. A further stereotype is that women have higher turnover rates than men and thus overall training costs can be controlled by hiring only men. But turnover is a function of job status; the lower the status of a job, the higher the employee turnover tends to be. Thus, women's higher turnover rate may be because of the jobs they do, not because of supposed personal failings. Many of these approaches to hiring and training developed when a job for life was commonplace. Men may also be liable to move jobs, even though they may often do so for different reasons from women. The old-fashioned stereotypes may retain a hold in today's quite different labour market.

(3)   Segmented Labour Market Theories

The explanations so far considered have concentrated on the attributes women bring to the labour market and thus imply that the actions of employers are not responsible for any marketplace inequality; they might thus be regarded as 'blaming the victim'.[37] These fail to provide an adequate explanation of why men and women behave differently in the labour market. It is necessary to seek to explain why women are employed in particular jobs and why on average such jobs receive lower pay.

The first such approach argued that there are different labour markets operating in the economy.

Beechey, V, *Unequal Work*, 1987, London: Verso, pp 32–36:

Essential to the notion of the dual labour market is the assumption that the labour market is segmented into a number of structures ... Primary sector jobs have relatively high earnings, good fringe benefits, good working conditions, a high degree of job security and good opportunities for advancement, while secondary jobs have relatively low earnings levels, poor working conditions, negligible opportunities for advancement and a low degree of job security ... The difference between the opportunities for advancement offered by jobs in the primary sector and those in the secondary sector is usually related to the existence of structured internal labour markets to which primary jobs are attached. A highly structured internal labour

---

37   'In explaining the characteristic features of women's position in the labour force in terms of characteristics of women themselves, the common sense explanations are all individualistic forms of explanation ... They explain the position of women in the organisational structure in terms of assertions about women's nature, or capabilities or temperament, rather than social structures. Individualistic explanations very often implicitly or explicitly involve biologically determinist claims, that is, claims that women's capabilities are determined by their biological attributes.' Beechey, V, 'Women's employment in contemporary Britain', in Beechey, V and Whitegg, E (eds), *Women in Britain Today*, 1986, Milton Keynes: OU Press, p 103.

market contains a set of jobs organised hierarchically in terms of skill level and rewards, where recruitment to higher positions in the hierarchy is predominantly from lower positions in the same hierarchy and not from the external labour market. Only the lowest's positions in the firm's job hierarchy are not filled from within the organisation by promotion. Secondary jobs, on the other hand, are not part of a structured internal market; recruits to these jobs tend to come from outside the organisation ... Furthermore, because of the low skill requirement for most secondary jobs, training is non-existent or minimal, so that secondary workers rarely acquire skills which they can use to advance their status on the open market ...

[It has been argued] that there are five major attributes which make a group likely to be a source of secondary workers, and that women possess each of them. These are:

(1)   workers are easily dispensable, whether voluntarily or involuntarily;

(2)   they can be sharply differentiated from workers in the primary labour market by some conventional social difference; ,

(3)   they have a relatively low inclination to acquire valuable training and experience;

(4)   they are low on 'economism' – that is, they do not rate economic rewards highly;

(5)   they are relatively unlikely to develop solidarity with fellow workers ...

There is no doubt that the distinction between primary and secondary jobs provides some useful insights into the differences between work typically done by men and that typically done by women.[38] However, the neat distinction into two categories of jobs is impossible to substantiate empirically.[39]

Beechey, V, 'Women's employment in contemporary Britain', in Beechey, V and Whitegg, E (eds), *Women in Britain Today*, 1986, Milton Keynes: OU Press, p 111:

Dual labour market theory has little to say about horizontal occupational segregation – that is, the segregation of women into jobs like clerical work and selling, and men into jobs like security and protective services. It does, however, throw some light on the process of vertical occupational segregation, since it is centrally concerned with the question of hierarchy and privilege within the workforce, and with the strategies used by employers to privilege certain groups of workers in order to keep them within the firm ...

[M]any kinds of women's jobs do not fit easily into the category of secondary sector work. Some women's work in manufacturing industry is skilled work which is integral to the production process, for example, work in the textile industry. Although this may be low paid in comparison with men's work, it is not marginal or insecure as secondary sector work is. Much secretarial work throughout all sectors of the economy requires considerable training, and secretaries are an integral part of the workforce. Although secretarial work may not be well paid in comparison with men's work, and although it may not actually be defined as skilled, it is not marginal and insecure. Finally, a good number of women are employed in professional and technical jobs, especially in the public sector ... Dual labour market theory's

---

38   The distinction is between primary and secondary jobs, not primary and secondary employers. Many employers, of which the NHS is a good example, employ large numbers of workers in both categories.

39   '[S]ome areas of employment such as agriculture where men form the vast majority of workers and other areas of predominantly male employment such as construction where employment is highly insecure, show characteristics normally associated with the secondary sector.' Joseph, G, *Women at Work: The British Experience*, 1983, Deddington: Philip Allan, pp 223–24.

conception of women being a secondary sector workforce cannot adequately account for these kinds of women's work ... [Furthermore, the theory] does not explain why so many occupations have been constituted as 'women's work' – why, for instance, secretarial work is done almost exclusively by women, and why women predominate in sales work, domestic work, teaching and nursing.

Craig, C, Garnsey, E and Rubery, J, *Payment Structures and Smaller Firms: Women and Employment in Segmented Labour Markets,* **1984, London: Department of Employment, pp 92, 97:**

Contrary to the early labour market segmentation models, many 'secondary type' workers (that is, those drawn from relatively disadvantaged groups and in receipt of low wages) have considerable levels of skill and experience acquired through informal on-the-job training, and undertake work which makes heavy demands on the workers ...

Many of the apparently semi-skilled or unskilled jobs in the survey industries carried out by women require fairly long periods of on-the-job training and experience. Moreover, many of the jobs carried out by non-qualified men were often equally tedious, so that it was the difference in pay and grading of the jobs rather than differences in the content and nature of the jobs themselves that was the main cause of women's inferior employment status.

The dual labour market approach was the jumping-off point for more sophisticated theories arguing that the labour market was indeed divided into different segments, which at a practical level tended to operate to the disadvantage of women.

Craig, C, Garnsey, E and Rubery, J, *Payment Structures and Smaller Firms: Women and Employment in Segmented Labour Markets,* **1984, London: Department of Employment, p 6:**

[A] structured or differentiated labour supply is created through the interaction of the employment system and the system of social organisation ... [D]ifferentiation of the labour supply arises through four main but interrelated causes. In the first place, even if workers enter the labour market with similar characteristics and opportunities, they will acquire different work histories, experience and skills which subsequently limit their mobility and restrict them to particular firms and industries. Secondly, workers enter the labour market with unequal access to jobs due to differences in their social characteristics: these range from their different educational qualifications, which do not necessarily directly affect their productivity in the labour market but which are nevertheless used as screening devices by employers, to their different access to jobs because of their family connections.

Thirdly, workers are not usually independent individuals who rely entirely on their own wage or State-provided income but are members of social and family groups in which income is pooled or at least partly shared ... Firms make general assumptions about the relative income needs of specific demographic groups in structuring their pay and employment practices, and members of these groups may have to adjust to conventional assessments of their relative needs even if this does not correspond to their own specific family circumstances.

Fourthly, individuals accept different responsibilities for family or domestic commitments which restrict their availability in the labour market. These domestic commitments may in some cases make the employee less productive from the point of view of the employer, but they also provide a means by which firms can differentiate between different types of labour and take advantage of groups with limited access to the wage labour market by paying them wages which do not necessarily reflect their relative productivity.

The relatively disadvantaged position of women in the labour market can be seen to stem from the interaction of these four factors. Women are not only assumed to require less income, but they are also expected to take on the major share of family responsibilities, a division of responsibilities reinforced by unequal opportunities in the labour market. Expectations of limited commitment to wage labour and discrimination within the education system may result in women entering the labour market at a relative disadvantage even when young and single; this disadvantage can become reinforced through work experience as women are excluded from training or promotion through discrimination or as the result of an interrupted work history.

(4)   Ideology and Practice

The final extract epitomises a move from concentrating on the supposedly abstract qualities of labour markets to the importance of human agency and choice in the reproduction of women's employment disadvantage. It argues that jobs have been 'gendered' or 'sex-typed' – a process whereby it comes to be regarded as appropriate or natural for a job to be performed only or mainly by persons of one sex. The quest is to determine historically how this occurred and if, how and why it is reproduced in today's conditions.

There is no doubt that there is a link between women's position in the family and women's position at work. The way in which the link operates is, however, controversial. Some argue that it is the domestic division of labour which causes employment disadvantage; others argue that the causal factors largely operate the other way round. A further source of disagreement concerns the extent to which the primary cause of women's disadvantage has been capitalism or patriarchy. The former approach emphasises the inferior position of all workers, accepting that the manifestations of that inferiority may operate differently between men and women. The latter argues that society has been systematically structured by men in order to oppress and control women.[40] Resolution of these disputes is beyond the scope of this work; rather, the task is to identify, in relation to a number of different themes, the interlocking role of theory and practice in contributing to women's employment disadvantage.

(a)   The definition of skill

Historically, especially where pay has been determined by collective bargaining, there has been a distinction of great significance for levels of pay between work classified as 'skilled' and that classified as 'unskilled'. The extracts below suggest that the notion of skill has been manipulated in the interests of men.

Beechey, V, 'Women's employment in contemporary Britain', in Beechey, V and Whitegg, E (eds), *Women in Britain Today*, 1986, Milton Keynes: OU Press, p 121:

The first reason why women's jobs are often not classified as skilled is because they generally involve quite short periods of formal training ... A further important point is that many women's jobs use skills which women learn informally within the home ...

---

40   Walby, S, *Patriarchy at Work*, 1986, Cambridge: Polity.

This informal training, however, never counts as training in the more formal sense ... and is not generally considered a significant variable in the determination of women's pay.

A second reason why women's jobs are not defined as skilled is that women have frequently been unable to get their jobs defined as skilled through trade unions. Trade unions have fought to get jobs defined as skilled or to maintain their definition as skilled in the face of employers' endeavours to define jobs as unskilled or semi-skilled, and they have often tried to impose restrictions on entry into apprenticeships so that the number of skilled workers can be restricted.

[T]he concept of skill is socially constructed, and an adequate account of the exclusion of women from skilled jobs has to take account of this.

Beechey, V and Perkins, T, *A Matter of Hours: Women, Part-time Work and the Labour Market,* **1987, Cambridge: Polity, p 137:**

[T]he notions of skill and training are absolutely central to the ways in which the distinction between primary and secondary sector workers is drawn, and the theory assumes that what counts as skilled work can be treated positivistically – as an objective phenomenon which is unaffected by employers' conceptions or by the bargaining power or the social status of those who characteristically do it. It is quite clear, however ... that gender enters into the definition of skilled work and that it also plays a part in what counts and what does not count as training. That women's skills and training are systemically downgraded and undervalued is well documented.[41]

(b)   Gender-typing of jobs

This refers to processes, whether formal or informal, by which certain jobs come to be associated with women employees. The evidence suggests that this has happened by design rather than by accident.

Cockburn, C, *In the Way of Women: Men's Resistance to Sex Equality in Organisations,* **1991, Basingstoke: Macmillan, pp 38–41:**

People have a gender, and the gender rubs off on the jobs they do. The jobs in turn have a gender character which rubs off on the people who do them. Tools and machinery used in work are gendered too, in such a way that the sexes are expected to relate to different kinds of equipment in different ways ... In a training workshop where I have been doing fieldwork, it is impossible to get a teenage lad to wipe the floor with a mop, though he may be persuaded to sweep it with a broom. Any woman lifting a crowbar is likely to have some gender-conscious thought as she does so.

When a new invention arrives in the workplace it is already gendered by the activities and expectations of its manufacturers and owners. It may even be ergonomically sex-specific, scaled for the average height or anticipated strength of the sex that is to use it. Even if it arrives apparently gender-neutral it quickly acquires a gender by association with its user or its purpose. The computer was the brainchild of male engineers and was born into a male line of production technology. The fact that it has a keyboard rather like a (feminine) typewriter confuses no one for long. When a computer arrives in a school, for instance, boys and girls are quick to detect its latent masculinity ...

---

41   See also Phillips, A and Taylor, B, 'Sex and skill: notes towards a feminist economics' (1980) 6 Feminist Review 79.

The many technologists and technicians I have interviewed (almost all male) have expressed time and again their identification as men with technology and of technology itself with masculinity ...

There are good reasons for women's reluctance [to enter technical work]. It is not that women are set against the idea of non-traditional fields of work ... They are simply aware, however, of the high social costs that we all pay if we disobey gender rules. The gendering of jobs ... advertises loudly where women are not to enter. If we ignore the message we are made to feel silly, pushy, unnatural ... There is a relentless background noise of harassment. We become unlovable ...

The dichotomies, separations and power inequalities that occur at home and those that occur at work are related and mutually reinforcing.

Beechey, V, 'Women's employment in contemporary Britain', in Beechey, V and Whitegg, E (eds), *Women in Britain Today*, 1986, Milton Keynes: OU Press, pp 125–26:

Familial ideology asserts that men are primary breadwinners and that women are their dependants. It proclaims that a woman's primary role is that of housewife and mother. Familial ideology has in fact changed historically in Britain. In the 19th century it was thought to be unacceptable for married women to engage in paid employment outside the home at all, and single women's employment was only grudgingly accepted ... Today women's paid work is becoming more recognised and acceptable. Nevertheless, it is still assumed that a woman's work outside the home should not interfere with her domestic responsibilities in caring for her husband and particularly in caring for her children and other dependent relatives.

Despite the fact that fewer and fewer families correspond to the nuclear model with male breadwinner, non-working wife and dependent children, familial ideology remains pervasive. It is a crucial element of the dominant ideology. It plays an important role in structuring women's participation in the labour market and in restricting opportunities for paid work. It affects her participation in the labour market, deeming it unacceptable for her to work when she should be caring for others. It enters into the construction of certain jobs as 'women's jobs' and other jobs as 'men's jobs', with women's jobs frequently involving caring for and servicing others ... [I]t is embedded in the concept of the family wage – the notion that a man's major responsibility is as family breadwinner and that he should provide for a dependent wife and children – which is still prevalent in employers' and trade unions' ways of thinking about wages. When ideologies make differentiations among people on the basis of ascriptive characteristics such as age, sex or race they tend to be particularly pervasive because they represent social relations as though they were natural. Familial ideology, which assumes that women are primarily wives and mothers, plays an important role in the organisation of paid employment, while simultaneously portraying the sexual division of labour and women's position in the labour market in quasi-naturalistic terms.

Collinson, D, Knights, D and Collinson, M, *Managing to Discriminate*, 1990, London: Routledge, pp 131–35:

[There are] at least four common and recurrent rationalisations for sex discrimination ... First, managers were found to deny their responsibility for sex-discriminatory practices, while simultaneously exaggerating the choice and power of jobseekers. By emphasising supply side factors, recruiters tended to slip into 'blaming the victim' ... [W]hen managers required male breadwinners, it was often argued that women were 'their own worst enemy' because they were: too emotional; likely to leave for marriage or children; unreliable workers (particularly if they had children); lacked ambition, confidence, toughness and assertiveness; were not geographically mobile; were inflexible because they could not work nights or weekends and were not prepared to study in the evenings and sit professional examinations. Equally, when managers wished to appoint temporary or less ambitious staff they looked to appoint female homemakers since it was believed that these workers would accept highly routinised and controlled jobs which offered only poor pay and conditions.

Another way in which managers denied responsibility for their own practices and economic vested interests was by claiming to be the victim of 'tradition', 'history', 'culture', 'society', 'customers', 'other workers', 'clients/intermediaries', and other managers. Blaming other workers for the exclusion of one sex from a particular job was invariably interrelated with the concern of selectors to appoint candidates who are seen to 'fit in' with the organisation. Against the social conditioning and values of the wider society, recruiters claimed to be powerless to intervene ...

[A] recurrent explanation by personnel managers for the perpetuation of practices which have sex discriminatory effects was that change could be destabilising for production and control ...

It is precisely because of the 'common sense' plausibility that gender and managerial ideologies are routinely taken for granted and reproduced through the rationalisations and practices of personnel and line managers.

Cockburn, C, *In the Way of Women: Men's Resistance to Sex Equality in Organisations*, 1991, Basingstoke: Macmillan, pp 96, 100–02:

Many women experience the same conflicts. Ambitious women without children, some of whom are unmarried besides, know full well that having all these 'mother's privileges' serves to confirm men's beliefs that women as a sex are unreliable employees who have their mind half the time on domestic matters. Though part timing, jobsharing and career break schemes are now sometimes available to women to help them through the childrearing years, they know full well that this route is a succession of career impediments.

Women find the requirement of mobility hard to meet. This is because their husbands often require their own job to take precedence – he earns more, his career 'matters' more. Men, for their part, find mobility hard to sustain. Their wives and children often complain at being uprooted from their communities ... [M]en must discourage their wives from developing attachment to a job so as not to add to this family inertia.

There is a vicious circle ... Women's relatively low pay prevents men giving up their salary to care for the home, while women's domestic confinement limits their chance of earning a salary on which they could, wholly or partly, support man and child.

We are in a time of significant social change in which it might be argued that the above assumptions and ideologies are outdated – in the sense that they no longer influence behaviour. While there might be limited change, especially for women with high educational qualifications, evidence suggests that the impact of such changes should not be overestimated.[42]

---

42 Thus, eg, anecdotal evidence suggests that female solicitors may have greater difficulty than men in obtaining partnerships because male partners are concerned that a woman partner may leave in order to raise a family.

MacEwan Scott, A, 'Gender segregation and the SCELI research', in *Gender Segregation and Social Change,* **1994, Oxford: OUP, pp 34–35:**

Despite the economic changes of recent years, women's increased labour market participation, and changes in family structure, such as increases in divorce and single parenthood, there appears to be enormous stability in women's and men's domestic roles and the value system that underpins them ... [W]omen's role as primary childcarers causes severe disruption to their long term labour market position. This is mirrored in the fact that male breadwinners increase their career opportunities over their lifetime and enjoy a substantial earnings premium in the process ...

The primacy of the male breadwinner role continues to structure the labour market in a variety of ways, mainly through the material and ideological differentiation of labour supply. In many cases, this is translated into employment structures and payment systems, which further rigidifies segmentation (for example, part-time work). However, gender segregation is not based solely on primary or secondary earner status. There is much evidence that naturalistic beliefs about gender, embodied in notions of strength, dexterity, sensitivity and so on, play a fundamental role in the sex-typing of jobs. These beliefs seem to be much more enduring than economic and family structures. Finally, there is substantial inertia in the labour market; traditional employment practices persist despite pressure for change. Patterns of gender segregation are sustained by 'tradition' as much as by the rational strategies of individual employers and employees. All in all, despite marginal changes within specific occupations, there is much less evidence of desegregation than might have been expected given the extent of social and economic change during the 1980s.

Vogler, C, 'Segregation, sexism and the labour supply', in MacEwan Scott, A (ed), *Gender Segregation and Social Change,* **1994, Oxford: OUP, pp 59–63:**

Constraints resulting from an unequal division of labour within the home may force people into highly segregated or part-time work regardless of their attitudes ... It is therefore important to ask how far those working in segregated or part-time jobs were also living in households characterised by a traditional domestic division of labour and how attitudes mediated this linkage ...

[T]he data show that men living in households with a more traditional division of labour were more likely to be working in segregated jobs, whereas women's domestic tasks and responsibilities were related to gender segregation indirectly through their effects on part-time work ...

[A] partner's attitude and the presence of children were as important in explaining the pattern of women's labour market participation as their own attitudes, if not more so. These findings are consistent with the hypothesis that women's sexist attitudes are likely to be constrained by inequalities in the division of labour within the home. It cannot therefore be assumed, as human capital and cultural theorists have tended to do, that households are egalitarian consensual units in which both partners are free to realise their 'choices' on the labour market. Moreover, men's sexist attitudes had implications for women. By influencing the length of time women had spent out of employment, husbands were able to impose their sexism on women within the household as well as in the labour market, and this in turn affected the latter's chances of working in a segregated job.

Gender-typing of jobs occurs because of the attitude and behaviour of employers and because of the domestic circumstances of women. However, the role played by other employees must not be ignored. This operates in two main ways: the role historically played by trade unions in seeking to secure benefits for men, and the role played by notions of male sexuality having an impact on the different opportunities and experiences for men and women at work.

Beechey, V, 'Women's employment in contemporary Britain', in Beechey, V and Whitegg, E (eds), *Women in Britain Today*, 1986, Milton Keynes: OU Press, pp 117–18:

It has been argued that the *basis* of labour market segmentation lies in the fact that new supplies of wage labour have been introduced into the economy at different historical periods. Thus, in the UK, Commonwealth immigrants, blacks and married women have all entered the labour force more recently than men, and they have all been confined to the lowest strata of the labour market. They are often prepared to work at lower wage levels than white male workers, and this ... leads to hostility of white male workers towards these groups. If employers try to substitute any of these groups for white male workers ... this may well lead to a decline in relative wages within a given occupation, and reduce employment opportunities for men. This, in turn, may lead trade unions to try and confine them to a particular sector of the labour force by using a variety of mechanisms, ranging from union-organised apprenticeship schemes to promotion lines based upon strict seniority provisions ...

Hartmann argues that the development of capitalism threatened men's power over women. It threatened to bring all women and children into the labour force, and hence to destroy the family and the basis of men's power over women (which lay in control over men's labour power within the family). Men, she argues, therefore developed strategies to retain their power within the developing wage-labour system. One of these strategies was the development of techniques of hierarchical organisation and control within the labour market. Hartmann identifies a number of factors that partly account for the existence of job segregation by sex, and for women's lower wages: the exclusionary power of the male unions, the financial responsibility of men for their families, the willingness of women to work for less ... and women's lack of training. Most important of all, she argues, is the ability of men to organise in trade unions, which has played such an important role in maintaining job segregation and differentials and excluding women.

A further suggestion in which male control over women may operate is through the construction of women's sexuality in the workplace.

Beechey, V, 'Women's employment in contemporary Britain', in Beechey, V and Whitegg, E (eds), *Women in Britain Today*, 1986, Milton Keynes: OU Press, p 125:

Women are constructed within the ideology of femininity in relation to men throughout their lives ... Some white feminists have emphasised the importance of notions of glamour and sexuality in the construction of young women's jobs, especially jobs like secretarial work, telephone/receptionist work, hairdressing, and flight attendant, which represent women as being visibly attractive to men. Other have emphasised the servicing aspect of women's work which frequently underlie these glamorous representations ... Black women are frequently excluded from more glamorous jobs, it is suggested, precisely because it is white femininity which is required to be visible. The dominant representations which exist for black women are those of nurses, cooks, domestics and machinists, and their servicing role is often invisible 'below stairs'.

Adkins, L, *Gendered Work: Sexuality, Family and the Labour Market*, 1995, Buckingham: OU Press, pp 147–55:

At the two tourist workplaces [in her research], the labour market was shown to be gendered prior to occupations being differentiated. Specifically, women workers had to fulfil the condition of being sexualised workers regardless of their occupations. Men and women were constituted as different kinds of workers within these workplaces.

The gendering of production means that men and women within the two workplaces ... are different sorts of workers. They do different sorts of work even when working alongside each other, and have different relationships of and to production. Moreover, the gendering of production means that men occupy a structurally more powerful position in all these various areas of employment, a position from which they can control and appropriate some of the products of the work of women.

Women producing and maintaining a sexualised identity is both required and appropriated. Presenting a certain appearance and a sexualised way of being ... is part of their job ... Men, on the other hand, are not required to produce and maintain a particular sexual 'self' as part of their jobs.

[R]ather than being an intrusion into the workplace and unrelated to labour market practices, the sexual harassment and sexualisation of women is deeply embedded in such practices ... [S]exual harassment and the sexualisation of women is the outcome of the organisation of (gendered) relations of production.

(5)   Particular Groups of Workers[43]

It must not be assumed that all the various influences operate evenly throughout the labour market. There are three groups of workers who face particular problems: part-time workers, female minority group workers and homeworkers.

(a)   Part-time workers

The rapid growth in part-time employment in recent years has been almost entirely female.[44] It is more than a decade since writers began to analyse this sector of the labour market as possessing its own peculiar characteristics and as resulting in particular problems. We have seen that relatively low levels of pay are characteristic of part-time work.[45] Despite that, the growth in demand for part-time labour is partly due to the fact that, in the British labour market, part-time work suits many women with strong domestic commitments. Surveys consistently indicate a high level of job satisfaction among workers in this group.

> **Rubery, J, Horrell, S and Burchell, B, 'Part-time work and gender inequality', in MacEwan Scott, A (ed), *Gender Segregation and Social Change*, 1994, Oxford: OUP, pp 228–31:**
>
> Part-time jobs are differentiated from full-time jobs along a range of different dimensions. This differentiation cannot be explained solely in terms of gender as often the differences are more between full and part-time jobs than between female and male jobs, especially when male and female full-timers are compared. The main areas where there are strong differences ... are in job content and skills, in promotion prospects, access to benefits, and in types of working-time flexibility required. Thus

---

43 See, also, Dickens, L, *Whose Flexibility? Discrimination and Equality Issues in Atypical Work*, 1992, London: Institute of Employment Rights.

44 See *Social Trends*, 2002, No 32, London: HMSO, p 75, Table 4.10 (reproduced above, p 37).

45 See above, p 40.

part-time jobs appear to require less training, experience, and fewer qualifications, to involve relatively few responsibilities (especially those associated with supervisory duties), and to require relatively few attributes or talents for the job to be performed well. Part-timers are very unlikely to consider themselves to be in a job with promotion prospects and they have limited access to a wide range of employment benefits. Part-timers are also extensively used to provide unsocial and flexible working hours, involving weekend working, variable days, and evening and some nightwork ... All these characteristics taken together provide strong evidence for the view that part-timers constitute a distinct segment of the labour market ...

The evidence that part-time jobs are both low quality ... and are associated with long term career downgrading suggests the need to develop and promote new forms of part-time working which will enhance the quality of part-time jobs and integrate them better into career ladders and promotion chains. Without such a development it is likely that the female labour market will become increasingly polarised between those pursuing a continuous career in full-time jobs, and those who suffer permanent downgrading after leaving the labour market for childbirth and re-entering via part-time employment.

Beechey, V and Perkins, T, *A Matter of Hours: Women, Part-time Work and the Labour Market*, 1987, Cambridge: Polity, pp 8–9, 117–19, 145–49:

[E]mployers have gender-specific ways of organising their labour forces. Where the labour force is female ... employers use part-time workers as a means of attaining flexibility. On the other hand, where men are employed, other means of attaining flexibility are used. Thus ... many of the characteristics of part-time work do not stem from some generally defined economic process like de-skilling or the segmentation of the labour force into primary and secondary or core and peripheral workers, but from employment strategies which are related to gender ... [T]he division between full-time and part-time jobs is one crucial contemporary manifestation of gender within the sphere of production ... We take issue with theories which see part-time work as some kind of 'natural' outgrowth of relations within the family ... Cross-national comparisons show that part-time working is not always as closely correlated with married women's employment as it is in Britain ...

It is the need for flexibility which seems to be most central to people's conceptions of part-time workers. The part-timer is seen to be a woman with young children, who does not want full-time work but wants a job which gives her a bit of money, gets her out of the house, and which is compatible with her maternal/wifely role. The managers whom we interviewed talked about part-timers as if they were representative of *all* women. They spoke of women as having divided loyalties, requiring flexible hours ... And the employers often implied that they were doing women a favour by giving them part-time work.

The domestic responsibilities of women who were employed on a full-time basis were, by contrast, rarely mentioned ... The possibility that these women might like more flexible or shorter hours was never countenanced ...

[P]art time women workers are defined by their domestic responsibilities. Thus, when their labour is needed, employers seem prepared to recognise these and sometimes even prepared to accommodate them. In other circumstances, however, their domestic circumstances become a reason not to employ women on a part-time basis, and at times not to employ them at all ... [P]art timers are not generally seen as wishing to do interesting work, or as wanting training or promotion ... Promotion invariably entailed becoming full-time. And when they work full-time, the recognition of their domestic responsibilities, and their need for flexibility, seems to disappear ...

[I]t was simply not the case that employers used sex-blind criteria in their hiring practices, or in selecting people for training schemes, or in their definitions of what constitutes 'skill' or appropriate qualifications, but that they had very definite conceptions relating to gender. So did many trade unionists. Certain jobs ... had been constructed as part-time jobs because they were seen to be women's jobs. Various things followed from this. Part-time jobs were invariably low graded, they were rarely defined as skilled even when they involved a range of competencies and abilities, women doing them lacked opportunities for promotion and training ... Whether their work was central or marginal to particular production processes, part-time workers were regarded as marginal, their work was not defined as skilled, and they were badly paid ... [T]here is nothing *inherent* in the nature of particular jobs which makes them full-time or part-time. They have been constructed as such, and such constructions relate closely to gender ...

[T]he domestic division of labour is clearly an important part of the explanation of why women work part-time because it imposes real constraints upon women's participation in the labour market ... We do, however, wish to counter the view that this is the only way in which gender enters into the organisation of work relations ... In order to analyse why married women ... so often work part-time, it is necessary to analyse not only the domestic division of labour within the family, but also the ways in which this has been shaped through the operation of State policies ... [I]t is only in certain countries, of which Britain is a prime example, that high levels of women's activity rates are associated with high levels of part-time employment ... [I]t is the absence of adequate facilities for caring for children and for the elderly and the handicapped that is one of the crucial determinants of the fact that most married women with dependants work part-time ...

From the time of the industrial revolution, if not before, women have been constructed as marginal workers ... No matter what jobs they have done, however, their position has been defined as marginal because of a powerful form of gender ideology – the ideology of domesticity – which was deeply rooted in the emergence of bourgeois society and, indeed, became a defining characteristic of bourgeois class relations ...

It is certainly not the case that all women workers, nor even all part-time workers, are marginal to the production processes in which they work. Nor is it the case that all women have interrupted work histories in order to care for their families, or that all women have spells of part-time working. It is the case, however, that all women are defined as if there were a conflict between their paid work and their domestic responsibilities, and all women working part-time are defined as marginal workers, no matter what they actually do. Similarly, all men (with the possible exception of young men ...) are defined as if they have families to support, no matter what their actual situations may be.

(b)   Ethnic minority women in the labour market[46]

Ethnic minority women often have a double handicap in the labour market, being vulnerable to economic inequalities on the basis of their race as well as their gender. It seems clear that they form distinctive groups within the labour market, with patterns which differ both from white women and from ethnic minority men.

---

46 See Fredman, S and Szyszczak, E, 'The interaction of race and gender', in Hepple, B and Szyszczak, E (eds), *Discrimination: The Limits of Law*, 1992, London: Mansell.

Jones, T, *Britain's Ethnic Minorities: An Analysis of the Labour Force Survey*, 1996, London: Policy Studies Institute, p 63:[47]

[W]omen's economic activity rate varies according to whether or not they have dependent children in quite a different way for different ethnic groups. This suggests that a large part of the variation in economic activity rates ... is due to differences in culture concerning the role of women in home-making and childrearing. Afro-Caribbean women have relatively high rates of economic activity whether or not they are married or cohabiting or have dependent children. Pakistani and Bangladeshi women have much lower rates of economic activity than women of other groups, and this is true of both married and unmarried women.[48]

Webb, M, 'Sex and gender in the labour market', in Reid, I and Stratta, E (eds), *Sex Differences in Britain*, 2nd edn, 1989, Aldershot: Gower, p 179:

The differences in participation between the different ethnic minority groups are partly a reflection of their different age structures: all 'New Commonwealth' ethnic groups are relatively young, but the proportion of women in the childcare age ranges will vary. These ethnic minorities also have few persons over retirement age ... as a result it is likely that a smaller proportion of women's time is spent in the care of elderly relatives than is the case with the white population ...

The likelihood of women's participation in paid work may also be affected by the length of time individuals have spent in this country. Female immigrants may have followed their husbands to the UK after a considerable time lag, and so have had less opportunity to enter the employment networks, thus depressing their participation rate. The tendency for individuals to have a job may also increase as the ethnic group to which they belong becomes established. This is clearly relevant in the case of the West Indian community, and indeed the long standing recruitment of West Indian women by one employer (the NHS) may have contributed to their above average participation rate.

While ethnic minority women face specific labour market problems, it certainly should not be assumed that such problems are the same for each ethnic group and in every geographical location.

Cockburn, C, *In the Way of Women: Men's Resistance to Sex Equality in Organisations*, 1991, Basingstoke: Macmillan, pp 185–86:

The fact that white women share the racism of white men does not mean that there is no gender dimension to the race issue. There is a particularly intense relation of domination and resistance binding white men to black men. In fact, when black individuals were problematised in the discourse of either sex I found it was almost always a black *man* that was referred to. Black women were largely invisible ... It seemed that if a black woman was problematised it was more likely to be because she was a woman than because she was black. The reason race issues invoke in white men more anger and fear than do gender issues is because a male protagonist is involved. Black men are menacing in the eyes of white men in a way that women, white or black, can never be.

---

47   See, also, Bruegel, I, 'Sex and race in the labour market' (1989) 32 Feminist Review 49.

48   '[W]ork participation rates for black mothers with young children ranged in different towns from 13% to 33%, whereas the rate for white mothers was only from 20% to 23% ... The variations ... partly reflect the balance of ethnic groups ... of each town.' *Op cit*, Webb, fn 13, p 177.

The sexual contract ... gives white and black men some common ground. Black men in my study shared with white men a resistance to the women's movement and a distaste for positive action for sex equality.

(c)   Homeworkers

The term 'homeworker', taken literally, includes many relatively privileged workers such as authors and those utilising information technology to work at home. However, the bulk of homeworkers are those, almost exclusively female, engaged in jobs such as sewing, making Christmas crackers or filling envelopes. This group of workers is often considered to be among the most disadvantaged in the labour market.[49] Problems of definition, such as whether to include all homeworkers of whatever socio-economic status, and practical counting problems, mean that it is exceptionally difficult to determine the number of homeworkers.[50]

While it is clear that many women work at home because of the need to look after young children, that is only one factor among many. 'The existence of the homeworking labour force cannot be understood without reference to women's position in the labour market. For instance, differences in the relative amount and kinds of training received by women and men, the over-concentration of women's work opportunities within a very narrow range of low paid, often part-time, jobs and the differential impact of unemployment are also part of the explanation.'[51] Homeworking highlights in a very direct and physically immediate way the conflicts between home and work which are part of the lives of so many women. 'Husbands, children and elderly relatives are free to interrupt her paid work, and this may account for the preference by families that the woman work at home. Popular images of working at home – flexible working hours, more time to spend with one's children, a reduction of work pressure, a less stressful day – have nothing to do with the experience of homeworking ... [I]t is very far from being a boon to women, for instead of liberating them from or reducing the burden of the "double day", it intensifies the pressures of both waged work and unpaid domestic labour.'[52]

In addition, research has established a clear racial dimension to the pattern of homeworking.

Phizacklea, A and Wolkowitz, C, *Homeworking Women: Gender, Racism and Class at Work*, 1995, London: Sage, pp 45–46, 54–55:

[T]he sexual division of labour [is] the key factor producing a homeworking labour force ... [A] division in the female labour force between those women who put their families first, and those who develop lifetime careers, is now quite central to the organisation of production and reproduction in Western societies and simply cannot be seen as the result of women's own choices; the work of reproducing labour still has to be done and no one can point to an influx of men into this kind of work. Although it may be true that no one forces women to do this kind of work in the way that the concept of 'patriarchy' perhaps implies ... women will continue to do it for their families not only because they have internalised these responsibilities but because

---

49 See Allen, S and Wolkowitz, C, *Homeworking: Myths and Realities*, 1987, Basingstoke: Macmillan Education.

50 *Ibid*, pp 30–52.

51 *Ibid*, p 74.

52 *Ibid*, p 134.

there is no alternative given the persistence of segregated low paid work and the high price of childcare and domestic services.

[O]ur explanation of the role of homeworking in [Coventry] suggests that within the shared constraints that all women with children experience, there are racialised differences in levels of employment that force families into a situation where inadequate benefits have to be supplemented by low-wage, home-based work.

...

[H]ourly earnings in manual employment are extremely poor, and there is relatively little difference in average hourly earnings between white manual (£1.31) and Asian manual (£1.26) homeworkers. They compare badly with women's earnings in manual employment outside the home, which averaged £3.23 in the West Midlands in 1990; even among part-time women manual workers, only 11% earned less than £2.20 per hour ... Within this overall situation, however, the distribution of levels of earnings by ethnic group is distinctive, especially once clerical homework is included ... [H]ourly earnings for Asian homeworkers in the sample are concentrated in a narrow range; two-thirds earn between 75p and £1.50 per hour. In contrast, earnings for white homeworkers are more spread out across the wages span. The proportion of white homeworkers who earn very low wages (below 75p) is slightly higher, but nearly half earn £2 or more.

Discrimination law has little role to play in improving the lot of homeworkers. The national minimum wage applies, and is potentially by far the most significant legal protection for homeworkers.[53]

(6)   The Reproduction of Discrimination

Just as we saw in connection with race, discriminatory attitudes and stereotypes are reproduced at the level of individual decision making, often with no real awareness of the disadvantage and discrimination which women suffer in consequence.

Collinson, D, Knights, D and Collinson, M, *Managing to Discriminate,* **1990, London: Routledge, pp 60–61, 67:**

Curran[54] ... found that [selector]s tended to prioritise highly informal acceptability criteria that, in turn, required subjective evaluations which were very susceptible to both intentional and unintentional sex discrimination. The most common required attribute overall was that of 'personal qualities' which covered such intangibles as common sense, confidence and liveliness. Relevant experience and family and domestic circumstances were also revealed to be high priorities of selectors ... 70% of the gender preferences discovered by Curran were for women. These preferences were closely linked to job characteristics such as low pay, poor promotion prospects and female-dominated workforces and supervisory grades. They were also usually based on employers' 'common sense stereotypes' about male breadwinners and

---

53 Heyes, J and Gray, A, 'Homeworkers and the national minimum wage: evidence from the textiles and clothing industry' (2001) 15 Work, Employment and Society, p 863–73. This study investigated the initial impact of the National Minimum Wage on homeworkers in the textiles and clothing industry, using data from a survey of Asian homeworkers living in West Yorkshire. Most workers reported pay increases, although piece-workers fared less well than those paid an hourly rate.

54 Curran, M, *Stereotypes and Selection: Gender and Family in the Recruitment Process,* 1985, Manchester: EOC.

female homemakers. This was particularly the case where selectors attributed importance to the criteria of 'family commitments, married status and dependants' ...

[D]omestic responsibilities are viewed *positively* for men because they are believed to indicate stability and motivation, but *negatively* for women since they suggest divided loyalties between home and work. Resting on the assumption that domestic work is primarily women's responsibility, these gender stereotypes were seen to inform the criteria of recruitment acceptability. It is precisely because of such vague, impressionistic and non-job-related criteria of acceptability that conventional gender stereotypes continue to be so prevalent and influential ...

[I]nterviews may be self-reproducing in perpetuating class and sex inequality even where procedures are relatively systematic and standardised ... [W]here judgments are shaped by informal criteria and are heavily circumscribed by selectors' evaluation of the extent to which candidates either contrast, compare or identify with their own experience and perception of themselves, they almost inevitably reproduce the prevailing employment profile.

It is therefore appropriate to consider whether increased formalisation of the recruitment process can reduce the scope for such unacknowledged discrimination.[55]

Collinson, D, Knights, D and Collinson, M, *Managing to Discriminate*, 1990, London: Routledge, pp 72–75, 108, 209:

The danger of formalisation ... is that managers seeking to discriminate informally may be furnished with a formal alibi which is very difficult to penetrate.

[M]anagement cannot be treated as a homogeneous, monolithic and omniscient force ... [It] is characterised by heterogeneity, defensiveness and fragmentation, the politics of which can often militate against the achievement of equal opportunity. Attempts by corporate and local personnel to implement formal, accountable and lawful recruitment practices often failed because of these managerial divisions. In particular, line management resisted the intervention of personnel, resulting in the latter's marginalisation ... As the self-appointed organisational breadwinners, line managers typically dismissed formalisation as a bureaucratic encumbrance impeding their ability to recruit and manage production effectively. Formal procedures were seen as unnecessary, time consuming and costly.

[F]ormalisation can only ever be a *necessary* framework for the elimination of sex discrimination in recruitment. It is not, in itself, *sufficient*. Formalisation can facilitate recruitment by rendering practices more structured, visible and accountable. It cannot predetermine in a mechanical and uniform fashion the implementation of consistent recruitment practices at local level. The need to judge and evaluate candidates will always afford selectors a substantial element of discretion, regardless of the degree of bureaucracy and formality present in the selection process. The interactional nature of the interview, in particular, is not fully amenable to formalisation.

The issues considered in this chapter reveal only too clearly the difficulties faced by legal intervention. The deep structural causes of male and female working patterns and family life patterns inevitably limit the scope and ability of the law to transform the social and economic position of women. For more radical change, a radical shift in attitudes to work may be needed. 'What in the long run has to change is the pattern of men's lives. A 45 hour week, a 48 week year and a 50 year wage earning life cannot be

---

55   See below, Chapter 12, pp 317–21, Chapter 18, p 594 *et al*.

sustained by both sexes. It should be worked by neither.'[56] Even without such dramatic change '[p]rogress towards sex equality may in practice depend more on the spread of unionisation and collective bargaining to industries and jobs in which women are concentrated than on specific legislation designed to deal with inequality between men and women within firms'.[57]

4   PREGNANCY

(1)   Why have Pregnant Women been Discriminated Against?

Finley, L, 'Transcending equality theory: a way out of the maternity and the workplace debate' (1986) 86 Columbia L Rev 1118, pp 1118–19, 1126, 1129–35:

There is a persistent, deeply entrenched ideology in our society ... that men and women perform different roles and occupy different spheres. The male role is that of worker and breadwinner, the female role is that of childbearer and rearer. The male sphere is the public world of work, of politics and of culture – the sphere to which our legal and economic systems have been thought appropriately to be directed. The female sphere is the private world of family, home, and nurturing support for the separate public activities of men. Traditionally, in our culture, legal intervention in this private sphere has been viewed as inappropriate or even dangerous. The notion that the world of remunerative work and the world of home ... are separate has fostered the economic and social subordination of women in two interrelated ways. First, the values necessary for success in the home world, such as nurturing, responsiveness to others' needs, and mutual dependence, have been viewed as unnecessary, even incompatible with the work world. Since the work world is assigned economic importance, the traditionally 'female' tasks and qualities of the home world have come to be generally devalued in our society. Second, the separateness of the public and private worlds, and the consignment of women to the home world, is seen as natural, based on unquestioned assumptions stemming from the apparent immutability of roles derived from different reproductive capacity.

The fact that women bear children and men do not has been the major impediment to women becoming fully integrated into the public world of the workplace. The lack of integration of women into the public world has made the workplace unresponsive to values such as interconnectedness and concern for the needs of others. This unresponsiveness not only perpetuates barriers to the participation of women in the economically valued work world, it also denies men the opportunity to participate more meaningfully in the home world ...

Despite the changed composition of the workforce, the structures of the workplace remain built either around the needs of male management, or the assumption that the typical worker is a man with a wife at home to worry about the demands of the private sphere. Thus, when women return to work, they often find that workplace structures are utterly insensitive to the reality of a worker with both home and job responsibilities. Childcare arrangements are generally regarded as a woman's private problem, of no concern to the employer ... Flexible job scheduling ... is still far from

---

56 Cockburn, C, *In the Way of Women: Men's Resistance to Sex Equality in Organisations*, 1991, Basingstoke: Macmillan, p 104.
57 Craig, C, Garnsey, E and Rubery, J, *Payment Structures and Smaller Firms: Women and Employment in Segmented Labour Markets*, 1984, London: Department of Employment, p 99.

common. Most workplaces remain structured around an eight hour day, five days a week, even though such a schedule conflicts with employees' needs to do shopping and errands, to attend children's school functions or doctor's appointments, to be available to children when they are out of school, or to meet similar needs of other dependants. There is nothing inevitable or natural about this particular workplace structure ... Employers have too readily assumed that only the existing way of doing things can satisfy their needs.

Assumptions underlying pregnancy policies

(1)   The natural roles ideology

The ideology of separate spheres built upon natural roles has fostered both penalisation of and paternalism towards women. Underlying both the burdens and the protections has been an assumption that women's biological destiny incapacitates them as workers in the public sphere. This assumption of incapacity goes deeper than the view that mother and worker are inherently clashing roles, or that woman's primary responsibility is to the home world. It has caused women to be viewed as either especially vulnerable, in need of protection from the rigours and dangers of work for the good of the human race, or as unsafe and unreliable workers who must be excluded from certain jobs lest they endanger others ...

The premise that women's natural role makes them unsafe or unreliable as workers is reflected in policies that deny leaves or benefits on the assumption that women will not return full time or with full commitment to the workforce after having children. This assumption also underlies the tendency to call into question a woman's job commitment when she seeks some accommodation between her dual roles ...

(2)   Aesthetic and moral qualms

The twin problems of ignorance and failure to consider women's perspective are closely related to another set of values ... aesthetic and moral queasiness triggered by the sight of pregnant women. These qualms stem from our society's deeply ambivalent attitude towards female sexuality ... Because many of us, especially men, do not understand what it is like to be pregnant and are stirred by conflicting and complicated feelings of envy, fear and uncertainty about how the condition is actually affecting the woman, the sight of a pregnant woman can arouse either discomfiting protective impulses or disgust ... It is hard to treat [a pregnant woman] just like any other worker. Consequently, employers have sometimes feared that male workers would be distracted from their duties if they had to work alongside pregnant women ...

While proclaiming female sexual activity, pregnancy can simultaneously serve as a denial of sexual attractiveness or availability. The prevalent view in our culture is that to be sexually attractive a woman must be slim and should confine her curves to places other than her belly. A pregnant woman is often thought of as fat and sexually unattractive. It is no coincidence that the airlines, which fired or grounded women when they became pregnant, also had stringent attractiveness qualifications for flight attendants, including weight guidelines.

This important article was written nearly two decades ago. It sought to explain the exclusion of pregnant women from the workforce and their consignment to the domestic sphere; with the rapid increase in the number of women – including pregnant women and women with small children – in the workforce, attention has shifted to the practical problems involved in combining domestic and workplace responsibilities, and the way these tend to impinge more severely on women than on men.

Conaghan, J, 'Pregnancy and the workplace: a question of strategy?' (1993) 20 JLS 71, pp 71–72:

While most women exercise whatever rights are available, the reality is that the limited income replacement and right to return to work which British law provides, combined with the enormous gap between supply and demand in terms of the availability of decent and affordable childcare, leaves women with children in a significantly disadvantaged position in relation to the terms upon which they return to the workplace. The 'working mother' is still vulnerable to job loss during the period of her pregnancy and thereafter. She is still more likely to work part time, and part time work continues to be economically disadvantaged. She is also more likely to experience downward vertical mobility leading to lower pay and poorer working conditions. The constraints imposed by motherhood in an essentially unsympathetic working environment become another resource for employers to use in their increasing search for flexibility. A woman's lack of bargaining power, directly consequent upon the absence of significant legal protection of her economic position during pregnancy and thereafter, makes her economic vulnerability easy to exploit.

(2)   The Objectives of Legal Intervention

The law must deal with a number of issues: the treatment of pregnant women while they are pregnant and in the aftermath of the birth, and the broader issue of responsibility for childcare and the domestic division of labour. It is the former which has thrown into sharp focus the issue of what is meant in this context by equality and equality of treatment.

Conaghan, J, 'Pregnancy and the workplace: a question of strategy?' (1993) 20 JLS 71, pp 75–77:

In [the American] context pregnancy, as a biologically constituted difference between men and women, had historically been used to justify discrimination *against* women. Feminists, espousing an 'equal treatment' position, were understandably wary about calling attention to this difference in order to gain particular benefits, pointing to where arguments about women's 'difference' had got them in the past. They also argued that emphasising the special or unique nature of pregnancy risked reinforcing stereotypical notions of women's 'natural' role as mothers ...

Advocates of 'special' treatment, by contrast, insisted that pregnancy was neither a disability nor an illness and that it did not benefit women to characterise it as such, serving also to reinforce the damaging association of pregnancy with illness and vulnerability. Moreover, to subject pregnancy to the same conditions as disabilities generally was to fail to recognise that pregnancy *was* a unique and *enabling* condition requiring specially tailored policies. Furthermore, it failed to acknowledge the social *value* of pregnancy and childbearing. Finally, it was contended that differential treatment was not inconsistent with equality ... To require pregnant workers to conform to standards laid down without taking account of pregnancy was to require women to conform to a male norm, to assimilate to established male working patterns rather than to forge new ones.

MacKinnon argues for an approach to sexual equality which focuses primarily on power and dominance and only derivatively on questions of sameness and difference. More important than identifying difference or justifying differential treatment is the need to ask why it is *women* who are perceived to be different and who, on account of their difference, are accorded unequal treatment. Why is it that women who at one and the same time must assert their sameness to men (and thereby their entitlement to equal treatment) and their difference from men (and thus their need for special treatment), inevitably inviting the accusation that they want to have it both ways. Ultimately, this is a question of hierarchical ordering, a question of who gets to define the standard by which difference is measured.

Close analysis reveals that the concept of equality is perfectly consistent with either the equal/special treatment position, depending on how difference is defined. If equality requires that like cases be treated alike, the position of feminists who espouse equal treatment is to assert that men and women are, for all relevant purposes, alike and entitled to equal treatment. Hence the tendency to equate pregnancy with other 'similar' disabilities. Those arguing for special treatment, on the other hand, assert that pregnancy constitutes a significant difference between men and women. Equality does not require similar treatment because men and women are in fact differently situated.

Either position is supportable. If pregnancy is perceived in terms of its immediate financial and administrative consequences in the workplace, then it is arguably 'similar' to other disabilities. On the other hand, characterised as a normal, natural, often voluntary condition, pregnancy is distinguishable from disability resulting from disease or injury ... What is crucial is the power to decide what counts as difference, and how the difference counts. This suggests that the important issues in the equality debate are those of power, not philosophy ...

Fredman, S, 'A difference with distinction: pregnancy and parenthood re-assessed' (1994) 110 LQR 106, pp 110–11, 118–19:

In the pregnancy context, the equal treatment principle presents some intractable problems. Five central limitations will be dealt with here. First, the equal treatment principle requires an answer to the question 'Equal to whom?' The answer supplied by anti-discrimination legislation is, generally, 'equal to a man' ... In the pregnancy context, this central reliance on a male norm leads straight into the awkward question of who the relevant male comparator should be. Secondly, the reach of the equal treatment principles is necessarily restricted to those who are held to be similarly situated. It requires no explanation for the type of treatment meted out to those who are not equal in the relevant ways. Thus, no justification is required for detrimental treatment of women in cases in which there is no similarly situated male. In the pregnancy context, if no relevant comparator can be found, detrimental treatment is in effect legitimated. The third limitation of the equality principle is that it requires only consistency of treatment between men and women, not minimum standards. In the pregnancy context, this means that a woman's rights are entirely dependent on the extent to which comparable rights are afforded to comparable men [such as the rights afforded to sick men] ... Fourthly, the equal treatment principle leads to an inadequate consideration of the question of who should bear the social cost of pregnancy and childbearing. Because the principle translates into an obligation placed upon the individual employer, the courts are prompted to require justification for placing the cost of pregnancy on that employer. But this ignores the fact that sparing an 'innocent' employer leaves the whole cost with the woman and prevents any consideration of the potential cost-spreading role of the State. Finally, the equal treatment principle tends to operate symmetrically, striking down inequalities between men and women regardless of whether differential treatment favours women or men ... [Thus] maternity leave policies might be challenged on the grounds that they constitute a benefit which is not available to men.

The rights approach has at least four advantages over the equal treatment approach. First, there is no need for a male comparator. Secondly, minimum rights exist independently both of a finding of equality and a finding that a relevant man has the protection sought. Thirdly, the question of cost can be dealt with explicitly ... Arguments that greater maternity rights merely result in lower employment for women can be countered by allowing the employer to recoup the costs from the State ... The final and possibly most significant advantage of the specific rights approach is that it constitutes an explicit acknowledgment of the social value of pregnancy and parenthood. This percolates through to judicial attitudes ...

[T]he rights approach is controversial in at least three respects. The first is political. It may be difficult or impossible to persuade a legislature to enact pregnancy rights, whereas a general equal treatment right may already exist as a constitutional or statutory guarantee ... Secondly, legal enforcement may be problematic, frequently requiring each individual to find her way to a court or tribunal, and to prove her case on its own merits. Moreover, remedies may be too limited to make such effort worthwhile.

Thirdly, rights are only as good as their content. The decision to grant rights is only the first stage: there remains much difficult and controversial territory to cover in deciding the strength of the rights. One implication of this is that the impression given by the existence of specific rights may be quite misleading, particularly where other elements of the system operate to undermine those rights.

Conaghan, J, 'Pregnancy and the workplace: a question of strategy?' (1993) 20 JLS 71, pp 84–86:

[T]he consideration of *context* – political, legal and economic – is crucial to any strategic evaluation of the likely effects of a particular legal engagement. An approach which relies on 'workers' rights' may be of value in the British political climate of the 1970s but is less likely to produce results in the post-Thatcherist 1990s. Likewise, an approach which relies on liberal 'entitlements' such as the 'right' to equality, may be more in keeping with the legal tradition in the United States of America than the social welfarist approach implicit in British maternity law ...

[Furthermore], the equality approach should be regarded as valuable in so far as it produces results, *not* because it conforms to scholarly standards of logic and/or coherence. Equality is better viewed as a *means* than an end ... [E]quality has little fixed meaning except that which those with the power to define choose to allot it. This is not to say that equality is valueless in the struggle to achieve a just society (both for men and women) but rather to suggest that its value is tactical rather than inherent, pragmatic rather than principled ...

[P]ractical political concerns raise a host of broader questions about the regulation of the workplace ... Chief among these is who pays for such policies: parents, employers or the State? Who should assume the primary financial responsibility for childbearing – the individual or society?

Those who oppose the introduction of maternity and parental leave arrangements have very definite answers to these questions. Invoking the rhetoric of individual freedom and market efficiency [it is claimed that] maternity policies furnish employers with a disincentive to employ women.

This argument can to some extent be countered empirically. It is quite clear that more and more employers are introducing maternity polices which go beyond the minimum requirements established by law. The reasoning is economic: it is likely to cost more to hire and train a replacement for a well-qualified and experienced female employee who leaves a job because of what are perceived to be inadequate leave arrangements. It is also clear that the women left behind by these developments are those who have little or no market clout: it is they who have inadequate employment rights and are likely to remain confined to the low-pay, usually part-time, secondary sector of the economy. The assumption that it is the primary role of women to be responsible for family and childcare is largely responsible for that continued confinement.

5   SEXUAL HARASSMENT

(1)   The Causes of Harassment

Although the legal principles are applicable both to sexual and racial harassment, it is clear that the causes and motivations for sexual and racial harassment may well differ. While sexual harassment is normally viewed as an exercise of power over women, it may lack the overt hostility that tends to accompany much racial harassment, and the harassers may even delude themselves that such behaviour is appreciated. Perhaps not too much should be made of this point, as offensive language and banter form such a significant proportion of harassment complaints. Nevertheless, the attainment of sexual favours which may be the object of sexual harassment has no counterpart in racial harassment. Racial harassment perhaps follows more obviously from a belief in racial superiority or at least difference. When coupled with the still-expressed view that members of minority ethnic groups are an economic threat to indigenous white people, that may come to reflect a feeling that ill-treatment is acceptable as a means of preserving economic benefits. Nevertheless, it seems unlikely that much racial harassment is explicable, at least overtly, on economic grounds. In addition, the concept of harassment surely requires intention or at least knowledge that what is being done is offensive.

The following extracts summarise some of the main sociological theories on the causes of sexual harassment at work.

Stockdale, J, 'Sexual harassment at work', in Firth-Cozens, J and West, M (eds), *Women at Work: Psychological and Organisational Perspectives*, **1991, Milton Keynes: OU Press, pp 56–59:**

Gutek ... considers three classes of model which offer explanations of sexual harassment at work. The natural/biological explanation is used to argue that what has sometimes been called sexual harassment is really sexual attraction. According to this view such behaviour is neither sexist nor discriminatory and does not have harmful consequences. Most importantly, this approach admits the existence of the behaviour but denies the intent to harass ... This perspective is compatible with the individual deficit explanation ... which attributes sexual harassment to women's own deficiency in handling an approach or the deficiency of individual men in controlling their natural desires.

The organisational (or structural institutional) perspective assumes that sexual harassment is the result of opportunity structures created by organisational climate, hierarchy and specific authority relations. People in higher positions can use their power ... to coerce lower status individuals, who are usually women, into engaging in sexual interactions ... Socio-cultural or sex role models focus on the power differentials of men and women, the motivation of men to retain their dominance over women, and the socialisation of women to acquiesce in general or to specific female sex role ideals ...

Gutek proposes a model that incorporates elements of all three approaches, emphasising the effects of sex role expectations in an organisational context. This is known as sex role spillover ...

Sex role spillover refers to the carry-over onto the workplace of gender-based roles that are usually irrelevant or inappropriate to work ... Sex role expectations are carried over into the workplace for a variety of reasons. For example ... women may feel more comfortable with stereotypically female roles in some circumstances, especially if they feel men at work have difficulty accepting them in anything other than a traditional female role ... [Some research reports] women in non-traditional, male-dominated jobs ... reporting more sexual harassment than women in traditional female jobs ...

Occupational segregation and gendered working spheres are seen as playing an important role ... Gutek argues that sex segregation at work calls attention to gender ... and therefore facilitates sex role spillover, the assumption that people in particular jobs and the jobs themselves have the characteristics of only one gender ... According to Gutek's analysis, when the sex ratio of an occupation is significantly skewed, aspects of the sex role for the dominant gender spill over into the occupational work role, especially if the numerically dominant gender also occupies the high-status positions in the work group.

For example, the person in the minority – usually a woman – is seen as a role deviate, because of an incongruence between the sex role of the majority gender, which has spilled over onto the occupational sex role. The woman perceives the differential treatment she receives to be discriminatory, and to constitute harassment when the content is sexual. In contrast, a woman in an occupation which is female-dominated is expected to fulfil those aspects of the female sex role emphasised by the particular job, and there is substantial overlap between the work role and the female sex role. In this situation, although women may recognise that their job contains aspects of sexuality ... they are less likely to view and report sexual harassment as a problem at work, because it is 'part of the job'. Men in comparable situations do not encounter the same problems as women, because women do not focus on male sexuality in the same way that men choose to focus on female sexuality. Moreover, when men working in a female-dominated work group do encounter socio-sexual behaviour, they are less likely to perceive it as discriminatory or to label it as harassment because of the wider context of gender relations in society and the underlying issues of power and control.

Stanko ... argues that gendered working spheres provide the context but not the script for coercive sexuality at work. While concurring with Gutek that women's employment spheres, largely composed of care-giving and service jobs, contribute to the sexualisation of women in those positions, Stanko sees sexual harassment as another example of male domination in women's everyday lives. In her view, women's experiences of sexual harassment are not bound by traditional or non-traditional occupational spheres, but are bound by the wider spheres of male dominance, power and economic control ...

Sexual harassment serves to reinforce the status quo. The imposition of unwanted sexual attraction is a routine means of exercising the unequal power relations which exist between bosses – usually men – and workers – usually women. With its origins in polarised gender relations and inappropriate sex role expectations, sexual harassment makes it difficult for women to achieve equal working relationships and makes it unlikely that men will recognise the discrimination faced by women. The failure to initiate change and to eradicate sexual harassment reflects the pervasiveness of male power ... and men's understandable wish to retain this power by means of protectionist strategies, involving collusion and mutual support. Sexual harassment is a barrier to the full integration of women into the labour market, and its removal demands the degendering, both of work categories and of areas of responsibility and expertise in society as a whole ...

Adkins, L, *Gendered Work: Sexuality, Family and the Labour Market,* **1995, Milton Keynes: OU Press, pp 58–66:**

[W]omen entering 'non-traditional' areas of employment, especially previously all-male occupations, are more likely to report sexual harassment than women in 'traditional' areas of employment, because the former may assume that they are employed on a par with men and that harassment will not be part of their experience. In contrast, women in traditional areas of employment, such as those in service and care-giving jobs, have less 'right' to complain of sexual harassment and in consequence are less likely to report harassing behaviour.

MacKinnon argues that the sexual harassment of women is both productive and reproductive of gendered labour market divisions ... a reciprocal enforcement of two inequalities, one sexual and the other material.

It occurs not only because women occupy inferior job positions and job roles, but also because harassment works to keep women in such positions ... Rigid gender divisions in the labour market should therefore be understood as both created and reinforced by sexual harassment ...

The power relations of sexuality and capitalism interlock in the context of the labour market to specify women's position, keeping women sexually in thrall to men, at the bottom of the labour market. Women become jointly exploited in the workplace through both their sexuality and their work, when the work demands placed on women become sexual requirements of work ... Sexual harassment acts as a key mechanism in this more general process, sedimenting women's second-class status both sexually and economically ...

The sexual harassment of women within the labour market thus works to systematically disadvantage women in employment, for it is an abuse of economic power by men, but it operates in a structural situation in which women can be (and are) systematically subordinated to men sexually and in other ways ...

[Stanko] suggests that sexuality may serve as an organising principle in the labour market, that it may promote solidarity between men through which men may organise to exclude and segregate women workers from and within the labour market. What this part of her analysis implies is that sexuality may play a significant part in the production of gendered 'economic' divisions. With this suggestion, she moves away from assuming that sexuality only operates within the labour market in relation to the sexual harassment of women workers. Instead, she opens up the possibility of sexuality operating in a far broader sense – as a principle or organisation. As an outcome of this break, the significance to be attached to sexuality in the production of gender divisions changes dramatically. Instead of merely maintaining these divisions, it becomes – to some extent at least – productive of them ... [T]his suggests that forms of control of women's labour within the labour market may be produced through aspects of sexuality.

The strengths of these approaches are to link the causes of sexual harassment with gender relations outside the workplace, especially in the family. It shows how harassment is linked with attitudes to female sexuality and to power relations in the workplace. This emphasis on power echoes explanations of sexual violence against women. MacKinnon considers that the only adequate response 'is to eliminate the social inferiority of one sex to the other, to dismantle the social structure that maintains a series of practices that cumulatively ... disadvantage women'.[58] For that reason she is sceptical about the appropriateness or effectiveness of the discrimination model based on the comparative approach, as what is 'unjust about sex discrimination [is not irrationality but that] it supports a system of second-class status for half of humanity'.[59]

To say that power of men over women explains sexual harassment is only part of the answer. There are two further issues which require consideration: why does the prevalence of sexual harassment vary from workplace to workplace, and how does the theory deal with the fact that harassment is often committed by employees who, at least in the workplace context, do not have power over their victims?

Certain features of particular workplaces make sexual harassment more likely. There are clearly many jobs in which women are hired to be attractive either to fellow employees or to customers. Much of the entertainment, travel and leisure industry comes into this category. It is in such contexts that the line between a requirement to dress in a particular way and unlawful sexual harassment may be especially difficult to determine. This approach may be extended into those positions where a secretary, typically female, is required to bring to the job – and to her boss – characteristics which supposedly epitomise those of the submissive, domestic housewife, and where the job requirements easily slide into an obligation to meet more personal needs of the boss, which will not necessarily be sexual. Another context where sexual harassment may be especially prone to occur is where women are attempting to break into what has traditionally been an all-male working environment.[60] Here the harassment will typically be from fellow workers rather than superiors, although the reaction of management may be crucial to its future pattern. Many of the most extreme examples of harassment – at least in the sense that they have resulted in the highest levels of compensation or settlement – fall into this category, perhaps because they often feature a campaign of harassment by more than one individual. A further issue, which links closely with the previous point, concerns whether the extent of sexual harassment will be reduced if management has in place a well-publicised and comprehensive anti-harassment policy. Again, there is some evidence that this is the

---

58 MacKinnon, C, *Sexual Harassment of Working Women*, 1979, New Haven: Yale UP, p 103.

59 *Ibid*, p 105.

60 'It [has been suggested] that the subordination of women in the workplace is sometimes related to the sense of disempowerment that male workers feel ... [If a man] compensates for the low status he holds in the company through an exaggerated identification with his own maleness (and, explicitly, with the male social roles of worker and subordinator of women) then the presence of a female co-worker in his workplace, by challenging both of these traditional lines between male and female, will deprive him of an important sense of his self-identity. Her presence will not only make him feel emasculated, but will also threaten his very sense of self.'

'If it is true, then, that sexual harassment is partly a reaction to a socio-economic structure that disempowers and devalues workers at many levels, making them feel inadequate and unable to control their lives, its eradication will be no simple matter. Rather, to the extent that the male worker's acquiescence in the hierarchical and regimented structuring of the capitalist workplace is "bought" by allowing him to retain some sense of power by subordinating women, sexual harassment will be difficult to stop without changing the workplace structure itself.' Ehrenreich, N, 'Pluralist myths and powerless men: the ideology of reasonableness in sexual harassment law' (1990) 99 Yale LJ 1177, p 1228.

case, especially if employees genuinely come to believe that the penalty for harassment may include loss of a job.

It is also important to consider the particular contexts in which harassment operates or is allowed to operate.

Collinson, D and Collinson, M, 'Sexuality in the workplace. The domination of men's sexuality', in Hearn, J et al (eds), *The Sexuality of Organisation*, 1989, London: Sage, pp 107–09:

In the first case study, manual workers subscribed to a male sexual drive discourse which was designed to establish their sense of power, dignity and masculine identity in conditions of its erosion. The men's preoccupation with sexuality as an expression of personal power, significance and autonomy reflects their concern to resist management control and the organisational control system and to deny the reality of their subordination within the organisation. The second case study also illustrated how men may draw on sexuality as a means of maintaining power and control within organisations. In this example, attempts were made to discredit and undermine the commitment of the first female executive member of the trade union. The very presence of a woman in a relatively senior position was treated as problematic by colleagues, who, in turn, promulgated rumours about her sexual life that were entirely unfounded. The men's association and indeed conflation of 'woman' with 'sexuality' demonstrates how male-dominated labour organisations can be characterised by assumptions and practices which seek to discredit and exclude women ... [T]he final example highlights how a supervisor sought to manipulate his hierarchical position in order to sustain a sexual relationship. Moreover, even when the supervisor's abuse of his position was challenged and exposed, management adopted a protective approach towards him.

Together the three case studies provide detailed evidence of how men may seek to secure themselves and their identity by drawing upon conventional forms of masculine sexuality and organisational power. They illustrate how the domination of men's discourses and practices about sexuality can reflect and reproduce the male-dominated nature of contemporary organisations. Equally, they show how management may treat these expressions of men's sexuality as largely unproblematic ...

[But] women ... do recognise and resist some of the contradictions of men's conventional expressions of sexuality and power within organisations ...

The women's resistance was constructed in the face of extensive pressure from managers and male colleagues to discontinue their action. In each case the women were labelled as 'troublemakers' by those whom they were resisting. Whilst in both cases the original organisational 'problem' was initiated by men's preoccupation with sexuality, it was subsequently redefined as a reflection of women's inability to adjust to men's discourses and practices about sexuality. Yet, despite this pressure, the women were not only willing to pursue their grievance, but were also effective in challenging men's patriarchal assumptions.

Hearn, J and Parkin, W, *Sex at Work: The Power and Paradox of Organisation Sexuality*, 1987, Brighton: Wheatsheaf, pp 74, 82–85:

In most ... organisations formal induction ... may consist merely of suggesting that a certain style of dress, self-presentation or polite talk is appropriate 'here'. Initiation rites and rituals among co-members can be severe, sometimes including pronounced sexual and/or physical assaults. We have numerous examples of these sexual initiations from the armed forces, from junior cadets, the fire brigade, hospitals, coal mining, and engineering, chemical and textile factories. These may involve the use of glue to stick and smear on genitals, use of rope to tie, perhaps symbolising the intimacy of the bonds. Usually they are led by men, are common in men-only organisations and often part of male culture in mixed organisations ... Formerly, men-only homosexual overtones may become complicated by the mixed-sex and indeed sexually harassing nature of the ceremonies, as with the entry of a woman into the London Fire Service.

Organisations are not neat, uniform, asexual structures; they are more usually amalgamations of groups of women workers and groups of men workers, under the same control system of men. In mixed organisations where heterosexuality is dominant, this allocation in 'blocks' of women and men inevitably defines possible sex and love objects by means of job. Where one gender is in a minority, those few individuals are likely to receive greater attention in reality and/or in fantasy as scarce potential objects.

These divisions are powerful determinants of gender roles ... The social production of the gender role includes numerous aspects of the person that bear on sexuality: appearance, dress, emotionality, desire for others. Managerial control of dress through division of labour is particularly clear with aircraft cabin staff, nurses, shopworkers, amongst many others, especially women workers ...

Sexual harassment, despite the problems of definition, is a pervasive form of explicit sexual behaviour in many organisations. It is performed by management on workers and vice versa, by organisational members on clients and vice versa, and so on. However, to see harassment as a *process*, rather than just as specific actions, is important because it forms such a significant part of the *visible routine* of many organisations ... Policies and grievance procedures are often designed to deal with the more blatant forms of harassment, that are persistent and more easily verifiable, and that are between organisational members. As harassment becomes 'less blatant', 'more ordinary' and regular, yet less persistent with a single recipient or with non-organisational members in occasional contact, official policy becomes less easy to formulate and less effective.

[W]hat may be sexually implicit or ambiguous behaviour in the eyes of some participants may be sexual harassment for others ... A similar complex relationship of the implicit, the ambiguous and harassment is applicable to some speech and joking ... Implicit sexual behaviour often *underwrites* explicit sexual behaviour by providing the taken-for-granted routine of organisational life, which itself is more explicitly sexual at certain times in the form of harassment, display and so on.

(2)   The Effects of Harassment

'Sexual harassment pollutes the working environment and can have a devastating effect upon the health and safety of those affected by it. It imposes costs upon employers impeding efficiency and reducing profitability. It distorts the operation of the labour market by depriving women of the opportunities that are available to men without sexual conditions.'[61] Women who experience sexual harassment have an unenviable choice as to whether or not to complain. 'That women "go along" is partly a male perception and partly correct, a male-enforced reality. Women report being too

---

61 Rubenstein, M, *The Dignity of Women at Work. A Report on the Problem of Sexual Harassment in the Member States of the European Communities*, 1988, Luxembourg: Office for Official Publications of the European Communities, p 19.

intimidated to reject the advances unambivalently ...'[62] Women's most common
response is to attempt to ignore the whole incident, letting the man's ego off the hook
skilfully by appearing flattered in the hope he will be satisfied and stop.[63] 'These
responses may be interpreted as an encouragement or even as provocation.'[64] If
complaint is made, that in itself will lead to pressures at work, which may include
ridicule, disbelief, and so on.[65] Women who do not complain 'experience humiliation,
self-blame, anger, loss of self-confidence, and a drop in job performance as a result of
unwanted/imposed sexual attention ... There are very concrete effects and economic
consequences: some women resign, others are transferred or demoted and some lose
their jobs if they do not co-operate with sexual advances'.[66] Thus, sexual harassment
may contribute to absenteeism, high turnover, lower productivity rates and
motivation, job dissatisfaction and unemployment. It thus may help to reinforce the
stereotype that women are less effective as workers than men, and thus have effects
on the initial decision as to who should be hired.

---

62 'On the one hand there is the fear that resisting sexual advances may provoke violent assault
    and rape so it is safer to comply; at the same time there is a feeling of thankfulness that this
    particular approach was not as bad as it might have been – a feeling which stops women
    from making a complaint.' Hadjifotiou, N, *Women and Harassment at Work*, 1983, London:
    Pluto, p 17.
63 'By far the most usual response is to ignore it in the hope that it will eventually go away ... In
    75% of such cases, it eventually worsened.' *Ibid*, p 19.
64 MacKinnon, C, *Sexual Harassment of Working Women*, 1979, New Haven: Yale UP, p 48.
65 'The reasons respondents gave for doing nothing about sexual harassment reflect the
    widespread difficulties both individuals and organisations experience in dealing with such
    behaviour. Victims commonly thought that their complaints would not be taken seriously or
    they were too stunned and embarrassed to do anything. Other reasons for inaction included:
    harassment being the norm at work; the seniority of the harasser; individuals wanting to
    avoid retribution; and feeling that they needed to prove themselves in the company. The
    finding that in some cases no action was taken because there was no procedure or union
    representative available, and in others because of the identity of the person to whom they
    would have to report the incident ... highlights the importance of having clear company
    policies and a sympathetic reporting procedure.' Stockdale, J, 'Sexual harassment at work', in
    Firth-Cozens, J and West, M (eds), *Women at Work: Psychological and Organisational
    Perspectives*, 1991, Milton Keynes: OU Press, pp 59–60.
66 Adkins, L, *Gendered Work: Sexuality, Family and the Labour Market*, 1995, Milton Keynes: OU
    Press, p 57.

CHAPTER 3

BACKGROUND TO DISABILITY AND AGE LEGISLATION

1   DISABILITY

It is straightforward to discover the number of women in Britain, and reasonably straightforward to discover the numbers in each ethnic or national group. In the vast majority of cases, one's gender and racial status is clear and immutable. The concept of disability is far more fluid. It is problematic both to discover the number of disabled people in Britain and to define disability in a clear and comprehensive manner for the purposes of the legislation. The first two extracts make some observations before the Disability Discrimination Act (DDA) 1995 came into force. The table below reflects the position more recently.

> **Doyle, B, *New Directions Towards Disabled Workers' Rights*, 1994, London: Institute of Employment Rights, pp 3–6:**
>
> Using a broad definition, the [Office of Population Censuses and Surveys] found a disabled adult population in Britain of 6.2 million people, of whom 5.7 million were living in private households ... Some 42% of disabled adults living in private households were of working age (16–64 years old), compared with 74% of adults in the general population ... The [Social and Community Planning Research] study, using a narrower definition of disability (by reference to employability) estimated that 22% of adults of working age had a health problem or disability, and so measured the disabled adult population at 7.3 million persons ... [The researchers concluded] that disabled workers who are occupationally handicapped and economically active (in work or seeking work) represented nearly 4% of the population ...
>
> Seventy eight per cent of disabled adults are mobile without assistance and 92% with assistance if necessary, but [it was found] that disability placed some restrictions on mobility in terms of frequency and distance. Transport difficulties, lack of assistance, problems in affording mobility and obstacles to access were frequently cited to explain this picture ... Closely linked with mobility questions is the need of disabled persons for aid, equipment or adaptations. The OPCS researchers estimated that nearly 70% of disabled adults used some sort of equipment to assist or relieve their disability, while some 24% required domestic adaptations in order to sustain independent living ...
>
> Whereas 69% of the population under pension age are working, only 31% of disabled adults are similarly situated ...
>
> Disabled workers are nearly twice as likely as non-disabled workers to lack formal educational qualifications, while manual occupational status and low levels of qualifications tended to be associated with an increased incidence of disabled unemployment. When in employment, disabled employees are likely to be under-represented in the professional and managerial occupations or non-manual jobs, but disproportionately represented in manual, semi-skilled and unskilled employment ...
>
> The OPCS researchers found that the gross weekly earnings of disabled adults in full time employment [in 1988] averaged at £156.70 for men and £111.20 for women ... [T]his compared unfavourably with weekly earnings of £192.40 and £126.40 for men and women respectively in the general population ...

Weiss identified a number of problems faced by disabled workers in attempting to enter employment ... First, they must surmount physical and vocational obstacles during rehabilitation and training. Second, disabled persons must overcome the barriers confronted in architectural designs and transportation systems. Third, they will encounter resistance by employers to hiring persons with disabilities. Fourth, disabled jobseekers experience self-doubt as a product of previous prejudice. Fifth, they must master the tests created by inflexible medical examinations, which many employers use without questioning their value and utility.

Gooding, C, *Disabling Laws, Enabling Acts,* **1994, London: Pluto, p 6:**

[T]he majority of people with impairments become disabled during the course of their lives. For these people, disability frequently leads to the loss of a job. Only one-third of people who were in employment at the time they became disabled retained their jobs.

Economic activity status of disabled[1] people: by sex, *Social Trends,* **No 33, 2002[2]**

United Kingdom		Percentages	
	Males	Females	All
In employment			
Working full time	43	24	34
Working part time	6	21	13
All in employment	49	46	48
Unemployed			
Less than one year	3	3	3
One year or more	2	1	1
All unemployed	5	3	5
Unemployment rate	10	7	9
Economically inactive	45	51	48

Disability also has an impact on an individual's participation in the labour market. In spring 2002 one in five people of working age in the United Kingdom had a long-term disability, of whom just over half were economically active. This compares with an economic activity rate for the whole working age population of 79 per cent. Disabled men are more likely than disabled women to be in employment though the gap between the employment rates is smaller (just over 3 percentage points) than for the population as a whole (11 percentage points). Disabled men are also more likely to be unemployed than disabled women, at 5 per cent compared with 3 per cent

1   Males aged 16–64 and females aged 16–59 with current long-term disability.
2   Source: *Labour Force Survey,* Office for National Statistics. At spring. These estimates are not seasonally adjusted and have not been adjusted to take account of the Census 2001 results.

respectively. The unemployment rate among disabled people was much higher than those for the non-disabled (9 per cent compared with 5 per cent). Unemployed disabled people were also more likely to have been unemployed for at least a year, and to be economically inactive than non-disabled people.

(1)   The Causes of Discrimination and Disadvantage

There are two rather contradictory attitudes to the employment of disabled people. On the one hand there is evidence that employers who do employ disabled people testify to a high level of satisfaction with their work performance.

Doyle, B, *New Directions Towards Disabled Workers' Rights*, 1994, London: Institute of Employment Rights, p 7:

It was found that among employers employing disabled workers, one in 10 rated their level of performance as better than other employees, while seven in 10 thought such workers to be comparable with other employees. These employers reported that disabled employees' attendance records were about the same or better than their non-disabled workers, although nearly a quarter thought that their disabled personnel took more time off than their comparators.

On the other hand, a 1993 survey of a broad range of employers found that 42% of employers had no disabled employees.

Gooding, C, *Disabling Laws, Enabling Acts*, 1994, London: Pluto, pp 7–8:

One of the most frequently cited reasons for this was that there were no suitable jobs ... within the organisation ... [I]t is highly unlikely that the respondents truly had no posts which could be filled by anyone with any degree of disability ... The researcher comments: 'Many of the perceived difficulties are associated with somewhat stereotypical views of the range of difficulties likely to be encountered.' Thus, one of the commonest explanations for the unsuitability of the work was its 'physical nature'. And yet ... a higher proportion of disabled people work in manual jobs than do able bodied people ... [A]nother common reason given by employers ... was the lack of accessible premises. These employers equate disability with wheelchairs, and yet only 5% of disabled people use wheelchairs.

To an extent some of these 'reasons' are simply an excuse for discrimination. Some employers are blatant in their attitudes: 6% of employers ... said that they would not employ disabled workers under any circumstances. A survey of disabled solicitors found that 21% thought that their careers would be affected by prejudice. A further 8% said that they experienced 'appearance problems'. 'What clients would think' was the commonest reason for rejection given by potential employers ...

If the stereotyping and underestimation of disabled people's abilities is one half of the equation, the other half is a distorted sense of what abilities are required to carry out a job. A ... survey of employers' attitudes found that 65% thought that being able to climb stairs was 'vital for work in management' ... 75% thought that good eyesight was 'vital' for management work. Thirty one per cent stated that ability to walk fairly long distances was vital for a career as a business professional.

Doyle, B, *New Directions Towards Disabled Workers' Rights*, 1994, London: Institute of Employment Rights, p 6:

Discrimination against disabled persons often takes the form of prejudice. Prejudice is manifested in attitudes that distort social relationships by over-emphasis upon the characteristic of disability. Prejudice feeds the stereotypical, stigmatised view of disabled persons, exaggerates the negative connotations of impairment, and excludes or devalues other measures of social worth or attributes. The view of disabled persons as lesser individuals poisons their chances of full participation in employment opportunities. The assumption is that *disability* means *inability* and consequently many jobs are assumed to be beyond the capacity of disabled workers.

2   AGE

The possible extension of anti-discrimination legislation to cover age discrimination – ageism – depends on two things: the prevalence of discrimination on the basis of age, and the extent to which it is possible to analogise between racism and sexism on the one hand and ageism on the other.[3] While discrimination against older people may be more prevalent, younger people may also suffer discrimination on account of their age, perhaps due to a stereotype concerning unreliability. The setting of the national minimum wage for 18 to 20 year olds at £3.00 per hour (now £3.80)[4] will, of course, enshrine in law discrimination against younger workers.

'Age discrimination – no change!' (1993) 48 EOR 21, pp 21–24:

[W]e found that 30% of the job advertisements stated an age preference or requirement ... the vast majority in the private sector; less than 1% were in the public sector. Three-quarters of the advertisements specifying an age preference were placed on behalf of employers by recruitment agencies ... Overall, four out of five job advertisements giving an age preference required someone aged 45 or under ... Around half of the advertisements mentioning age gave a limit of 35 or under ...[5]

[M]any of the age-based assumptions are stereotypes having little basis in fact. Three main conclusions can be drawn from the growing body of research:

(a)   age-related declines in productivity, mental efficiency and reaction time are small and many of the losses can be, and are, compensated for by experience;

(b)   older workers are more satisfied with their jobs than are younger workers, are less likely to leave their jobs than are younger workers, are less likely to leave the organisation for another job and have lower rates of absenteeism and accidents; and

(c)   there is considerable variation in age-related losses. It is more meaningful to look at differences between individuals, which are far greater than differences between age groups.

---

3   See, generally, Bytheway, B, *Ageism*, 1995, Milton Keynes: OU Press. To illustrate the point, the author shows how ageist birthday cards are socially acceptable in a way that sexist and racist cards are not (pp 75–78).

4   National Minimum Wage Regulations 1999 (Amendment) Regulations 2003, SI 2003/1923.

5   The survey found that age is commonly used as a form of screening where there is a large number of applicants, and that older people may be denied the opportunity to go on training courses. There is some evidence of a decline in overtly ageist job advertising, although it may be replaced by wording such as 'Don't read this unless you want to join a young team'. See 'Drop in ageist job ads' (1997) 76 EOR 10.

The basis of the argument that ageism is analogous to racism and sexism is that the anti-discrimination principle rests on a human rights argument that one has a right to be considered on merit for a position for which one applies. On this view, the argument in favour of a law to deal with age discrimination could be said to be almost self-evident. If the anti-discrimination principle depends more on a history of stigmatised characteristics and economic disadvantage, the arguments for extension to cover age appear far more flimsy.

Buck, T, 'Ageism and legal control', in Hepple, B and Szyszczak, E (eds), *Discrimination: The Limits of Law*, **1992, London: Mansell, pp 246–54:**

[T]here are some immediately apparent similarities between [ageism] and sexism and racism. All three identify negative attitudes and stereotypes ascribed to a person by virtue of nothing more than belonging to one of these categories ... [T]hese pejorative attitudes have been, to a greater or lesser extent, institutionalised, although one has to say that the empirical evidence in relation to ageism in the UK is still at a formative stage. The problem in relation to ageism, certainly in the UK, is that it has not fully emerged in the public consciousness.

There are perhaps four qualifications to be made to the latter proposition. First, 'youth culture' has on occasion been a significant social and political entity ... Second, on the personal and psychological plane, individuals persist in being acutely aware of their age ... indeed many individuals could be described as being obsessed with their chronological age. Third, in public affairs, sporadic outbursts from politicians and the press may be occasioned by firms refusing to employ anyone over 35 or 40. Finally, there would appear to be an increasing interest among feminists in the particular position of older women ...

The balance of evidence relating to the use of age limits in job advertising ... would suggest that age is frequently a marginal factor in the decision. Furthermore, employers frequently breach their own age limits in recruitment. Of course, the difficult question here is whether ageism is more covert precisely because age consciousness is generally low or whether it is the nature of the phenomenon that it operates in a less potent fashion than either sexism or racism?

[It has been argued] that men are 'allowed' to age without the same penalties as women. Men's ageing crisis is often linked to pressures on them to be 'successful', while women's ageing crisis relates to their sexual attractiveness and loss of reproductive function ...

The relationship between racism and ageism is also problematic. Each ethnic group imposes its own distinctive social meaning on the individual's experience of ageing. Some commentators have argued that black Americans do not suffer the same discontinuities in their lives as their white peers. Other argue that the 'triple jeopardy' of being old, poor and belonging to a racial minority has an additive discriminatory effect ...

The obvious difference about being old compared with being female or a member of a racial minority is that it is an attribute achieved over a long period of time and ... it is achieved by most members of society. The experience of ageing can, therefore, claim to have a more universal application. If equality legislation can be made wide enough to accommodate some rational model of equality between age cohorts, it is arguable that all members of such a society will have a direct interest in supporting the equality principle ...

It may ... be the case that one of the strongest arguments in support of age discrimination legislation ... is that it is (potentially) a protection for all workers.

Arguably, a clear, simple measure is required, perhaps predominantly as a public relations exercise. A law making age-discriminatory advertising unlawful has much to recommend it in this respect. There is ample evidence to show that age limits in employment advertising are fairly widespread ... Such a law would 'bite' in a clearly defined area and cause many employers, for the first time perhaps, to pause and reconsider their opportunities policies in the age context.

CHAPTER 4

THE AIMS OF ANTI-DISCRIMINATION LEGISLATION

1   INTRODUCTION

We are concerned in this chapter with ideas about what the aims of anti-discrimination both are and should be. There is a distinction between equality of opportunity, which seeks to enable all people to compete equally, in particular in the employment market, and equality of outcome or results, a notion which pays at least some regard to the distribution of outcomes between the various different groups. A further question is whether the law can and should take account of group rights, as opposed to the more traditional approach which focuses on individual rights. Consideration of these issues also requires analysis of rather broader questions concerning the nature of discrimination and why it is unlawful – at least in certain contexts; why racial groups and women have been isolated as groups most worthy of the benefits of anti-discrimination legislation; and whether the ideas lying behind such legislation are appropriate for extension to other groups. Finally, it is necessary to consider whether the law is a suitable weapon or forum for remedying the disadvantages caused by discrimination, or whether it should be abandoned in favour of a more overtly political stance.[1]

It is first essential to distinguish clearly between what might be perceived as the actual aims of the current legislation – though it is naive to believe that it is possible to isolate one sole aim – and ideas as to the aims which an ideal or model legislative regime might seek.

Wasserstrom, R, 'Racism, sexism and preferential treatment: an approach to the topics' (1977) 24 UCLA L Rev 581, pp 583–84:

There are three different perspectives within which the topics of racism, sexism and affirmative action can most usefully be examined. The first of these perspectives concentrates on what in fact is true of the culture, on what can be called the social realities. Here the fundamental question concerns the way the culture is: what are its institutions, attitudes and ideologies in respect to matters of race and sex?

---

1   I have consciously avoided too lengthy an excursion into jurisprudential theory, partly because of a desire to include material relevant to both race and gender.

In relation to race, see: Crenshaw, K, 'Race, reform and retrenchment: transformation and legitimation in anti-discrimination law' (1988) 101 Harv L Rev 1331; Delgado, R, 'The ethereal scholar: does critical legal studies have what minorities want?' (1987) 22 Harv CR CL LR 301; Freeman, A, 'Legitimating race discrimination through anti-discrimination law' (1982) 62 Minn LR 96; Freeman, A, 'Racism, rights and the quest for equality of opportunity: a critical legal essay' (1988) 23 Harv CR CL LR 295; Bell, D, 'Racial realism' (1992) 24 Conn LR 363; Caldwell, V, 'Review of *Critical Race Theory: The Key Writings that Formed the Movement*' (1996) 96 Columbia L Rev 1363; Lustgarten, L, *Legal Control of Racial Discrimination*, 1980, London: Macmillan.

In relation to gender, see: Barnett, H, *Sourcebook on Feminist Jurisprudence*, 1997, London: Cavendish Publishing; Rhode, D, *Justice and Gender*, 1989, Cambridge, Mass: Harvard UP; MacKinnon, C, *Feminism Unmodified*, 1987, Cambridge, Mass: Harvard UP; MacKinnon, C, *Towards a Feminist Theory of the State*, 1989, Cambridge, Mass: Harvard UP; Olsen, F, 'The family and the market: a study of the ideology of legal reform' (1983) 96 Harv L Rev 1497; Littleton, C, 'In search of a feminist jurisprudence' (1987) 10 Harvard Women's LJ 1; Lacey, N, 'Feminist legal theory beyond neutrality' [1995] CLP 1; Bartlett, K, 'Feminist legal methods' (1990) 103 Harv L Rev 829.

The second perspective is concerned with the way things ought to be ... Here the fundamental question concerns ideals: What would the good society ... look like in respect to matters involving race and sex?

The third perspective looks forward to the means by which the ideal may be achieved. Its focus is on the question: what is the best or most appropriate way to move from the existing social realities ... to a closer approximation of the ideal society? ...

[W]hat might be an impermissible way to take race or sex into account in the ideal society, may also be a desirable and appropriate way to take race or sex into account, given the social realities.

Sunstein, C, 'Three civil rights fallacies' (1991) 79 California L Rev 751, p 751:

From the early 1950s until the present day, three propositions have permeated the arguments of lawyers and others interested in advancing the cause of civil rights.

The first proposition is that the target of the civil rights movement is discrimination, which is always or usually a product of irrational hatred, fear, or prejudice. In this view, the purpose of civil rights law is to eliminate these forms of irrationality from the public and private realms.

The second proposition is that the principal function of civil rights law is compensatory. Just as an injured person in a tort action has a right to be made whole, so victims of a history of discrimination (including slavery) are entitled to be put into the place they would have occupied if discrimination had never occurred ...

The third proposition is that the judiciary is the appropriate institution for the making and enforcement of civil rights law. Reliance on the courts, principally though interpretation of the Constitution, has been a distinctive feature of the civil rights movement ...

The issues of discrimination and group inequality can never be understood in isolation from the particular society in which it is alleged to be occurring. Historically, in America, black people – a minority – were excluded from economic and political power. In other countries, notably South Africa, minorities have oppressed majorities. The same legal and/or political solutions may not be appropriate for different societies. While Wasserstrom's questions are of universal relevance, it does not follow that the answers will be the same in all countries. For example, it is clear that slavery necessarily leads to a different understanding of the American black experience from that of black people in Britain. At the same time, Sunstein's arguments concerning the role of and faith in the law, while powerful and relevant, are probably too strongly stated to be directly transferable to Britain, especially as the absence of a written constitution and a tradition of judicial activism in support of individual rights means that few would have the faith in the British judiciary's capacity for the creative law making that might on occasion emanate from the United States Supreme Court.

2   WHAT IS MEANT BY DISCRIMINATION

We need to examine the concept of discrimination and its relationship with the concept of equality. This involves consideration of the sense, if at all, in which patterns or practices which give rise to group economic disadvantage ought properly to be included within the term 'discrimination' and whether race- or gender-conscious remedies are equally within its boundaries. It will be argued that the concept derives its strength from moral arguments, but that these are necessarily contingent and variable.[2]

(1)   From Hostility to Unconscious Discrimination

While the first and most obvious meaning of discrimination emphasises hostility or prejudice, it is necessary to use a wider definition adopted because, first, the evidence shows that adverse treatment, or adverse effect, frequently occurs in the absence of prejudice or hostility and, secondly, it is difficult to define or prove prejudice or hostility. In the first extract, Sunstein discusses prejudice, whilst in the second, Rutherglen argues that 'discrimination' has several meanings.

Sunstein, C, 'Three civil rights fallacies' (1991) 79 California L Rev 751, pp 752–53:

For present purposes, perhaps we can understand 'prejudice' to encompass three sorts of mistakes. The first consists of a belief that members of a group have certain characteristics when in fact they do not. Here the relevant belief has no basis in reality and its irrationality is especially conspicuous. The second consists of a belief that many or most members of a group have certain characteristics when in fact only a few of them do. Here the error is an extremely over-broad generalisation. The third mistake consists in reliance on fairly accurate group-based generalisations when more accurate (and not especially costly) classifying devices are available. Here the members of a group actually have an undesirable characteristic in fairly large numbers ... but it is possible and more rational to use other, more direct devices to filter out that characteristic. The failure to use those more direct devices reflects a kind of prejudice ...

The theory of civil rights law has often identified 'discrimination' with prejudice, and defined an act as discriminatory when it is caused by prejudice ... For present purposes, I will understand discrimination to include a decision to treat a black person or a woman differently from a white person or a man, regardless of the motivation.

Rutherglen, G, 'Discrimination and its discontents' (1995) 81 Virginia L Rev 117, pp 127–28:

'Discrimination', as it is ordinarily used, refers to a process of noticing or marking a difference, often for evaluative purposes. The two most common synonyms for the verb 'discriminate' are 'distinguish' and 'differentiate', which in turn denote recognising, discerning, appreciating or identifying a difference ... The phrase 'intentional discrimination' is a redundancy according to the ordinary sense of 'discrimination'. All discrimination is intentional in the sense that anyone who discriminates acts on the ground for the discrimination. It is conceptually impossible to discriminate on the ground of race without taking race into account. Conversely, most forms of affirmative action explicitly require consideration of race or sex. They plainly involve discrimination in the ordinary sense: they require race or sex to be taken into account in awarding benefits or advantages. From the perspective of

---

2   There is a strong argument for not making all discrimination unlawful, even where it is immoral. 'For example, a person who, in choosing a spouse ... excludes members of a particular race solely because of a bias, may be acting within her moral rights even if she is acting immorally.' Alexander, L, 'What makes wrongful discrimination wrong? Biases, preferences, stereotypes and proxies' (1992) 141 Penns UL Rev 149, p 201.

common usage, the typical liberal position is therefore doubly paradoxical: it insists that non-discriminatory actions with 'discriminatory effects' are nevertheless discriminatory just as it maintains that affirmative action plans that plainly take account of race or sex are not ...

[This] is not a conceptual point about what 'discrimination' must mean, for a term can have a technical legal sense in addition to its ordinary sense, but it is a point about how the term is understood by ordinary citizens. And it is the understanding of ordinary citizens that is crucial in a democracy ...

[T]he technical legal usage invites the question whether it is similar enough to ordinary usage to support a different sense of the same term. And it is in these controversial cases, when understanding of the issues is most needed in a democracy, that misunderstanding is most likely. Lawyers are likely to use the term in its technical sense while ordinary citizens understand it in its usual sense. Yet it is the ordinary citizens whose support is necessary for the enactment and enforcement of civil rights law.

Rutherglen argues that the liberal position on affirmative action and unintentional discrimination is 'paradoxical'. But is this not taking the definition out of the context of the place where it is meant to operate? For instance, an employer, with a disproportionately male workforce, may adopt (conscious) affirmative action to redress the result of years of (unconscious) discrimination.

We saw from consideration of the statistics and the causes[3] that in many situations the focus is not so much on discrimination as is commonly understood but on processes that lead to social and economic disadvantage – that is, to inequality. The introduction into British and American anti-discrimination law of the concept of indirect discrimination – which is clearly intended in some more or less limited sense to reduce inequality – might be thought to confuse the issue: whether indirect discrimination ought to be called discrimination is one question; whether it is appropriate for the law to seek to provide a remedy for disadvantage is quite another. It seems that the unlawfulness is easier to accept if it is called 'discrimination', for that builds upon the stigma implied by that term,[4] but arguably at a cost of introducing some intellectual sleight-of-hand.

The basis of this strand of the argument is, therefore, that discrimination is wrong because it leads to inequality. But most economic and social inequality is not the result of discrimination in the narrow sense. Why should discrimination leading to racial or gender inequality be a focus of attention? What precisely is wrong – in the moral sense – with discriminating against women and black people? In particular, is it wrong to discriminate against people because in so doing we are harming them, or is it because we are treating them unfairly – not according to their own individual merit or worth? In broad terms, the latter approach utilises a human rights perspective, the former

---

3   See Chapters 1–3.

4   In *Khan v Chief Constable of West Yorkshire* [2000] All ER (D) 237, CA, at para 14, the then Master of the Rolls, Lord Woolf said: 'To regard a person as acting unlawfully when he had not been motivated either consciously or unconsciously by any discriminatory motive is hardly likely to assist the objective of promoting harmonious racial relations.' In *Nagarajan v London Regional Transport* [1999] 4 All ER 65, HL, at 70, Lord Browne-Wilkinson (dissenting) said: 'To introduce something akin to strict liability into the Acts which will lead to individuals being stamped as racially discriminatory ... where these matters were not consciously in their minds when they acted is unlikely to recommend the legislation to the public as being fair and proper protection for the minorities that they are seeking to protect.'

more of a group economic rights perspective. The perspective which is adopted makes a difference, for reliance on the harm principle would imply that only members of historically disadvantaged groups would be able to utilise the law, while the unfairness principle would allow claims by white males and, potentially, by *anyone* who has been unfairly or inappropriately rejected for employment.[5]

Gardner, J, 'Liberals and unlawful discrimination' (1989) 9 OJLS 1, pp 2–8:

For those who subscribe to ... liberalism, it immediately matters whether we classify some social event, circumstance or practice as an injustice or as a harm ... The harm principle operates ... to implicate individual members of society. Citizens may be held personally responsible for those harms which take place under their control, and may be subject to enforced treatment of some kind in the light of their personal blameworthiness. By contrast, the injustice of a distribution is attributed to no one but the society as a whole.

Given the similarities between direct discrimination and more conventional crimes and torts, it is hardly surprising that theorists frequently opt for the ready assumptions that direct discrimination is unlawful because it is harmful ... [T]he fact that otherwise indirectly discriminatory processes may be 'justified' indicates that what is at stake is not a harm, but a redistributive goal which must be balanced against some other interests which citizens are at liberty to pursue ... Unlike the direct discriminator, it appears that the indirect discriminator is not marked off as a wrongdoer, but is implicated in our collective responsibility for social injustices ...

It is not the large *amount* of stigmatisation and denied opportunity which brings discrimination within the harm principle, but the *quality* of the stigmatisation and rejection. We respond, in our classification of harms, to the cultural context of our subject matter. Taking this line, there seem to be two broad ways in which cultural context might allow intentional acts of discrimination to count as harms.

The first of these points to a strong relationship between stigma and denied opportunity on the one side, and their historical significance as instruments of wholesale disenfranchisement and disadvantage on the other. We might say that, in the classification of ethnic groups as unworthy, or women as inferior, a set of momentous and enduring collective disadvantages has been inflicted ... and that our willingness to treat continuing disparate treatment as a harm is a product of its close historical significance with distributional injustice ...

The other way of isolating a harm involves pointing out a rather weaker relationship between stigma, denial of opportunities and the historical facts of disadvantage. In this weaker connection, we have developed an historically informed view that race- and gender-dependent decisions are *unfair*, and this claimed *unfairness* is sufficient to turn stigmatisation and denial of opportunities into harms of the required sort ...

If we trace a strong link between the history of disadvantage and our present view that intentional discrimination is harmful, we can really only include discrimination which compounds that disadvantage among the activities which we count as harmful. If we make the strong connection, then the only sort of discrimination which falls within the harm principle is discrimination against certain sorts of people – primarily blacks and women. It would then be difficult to see the exclusion of a white male from

---

5   The unfair dismissal provisions already provide such a remedy for those who have been *dismissed from* employment, at least after one year's continuous employment. A universal right not to be unfairly rejected for a job would involve very substantial control over what have traditionally been regarded as private decisions.

some sort of opportunity as a relevant 'harm' ... If, on the other hand, we trace the rather weaker link between disadvantage and harm, through the mediating principle of 'unfairness', then we perceive the whole business of taking race and gender into account as a harm ...

Once the 'unfairness' takes over from the harm in this way, we risk identifying the wrongness of sexual subjugation or slavery with the failure of those invidious and enduring historical traditions to be perfectly meritocratic, and we start, illiberally, to treat all non-meritocratic preferences as being on all fours with slavery. So in the liberal tradition, the harmful unfairness must ... be narrowly tied to the degradation of those whose race or gender have been devalued, and the cultural meanings which race and gender have, on that account, assumed for us ...

Gardner has tried to show why a law with origins in the harm principle is linked to a liberal world view based on individual human rights, or fairness. Indeed, as discrimination law already covers all races (including the 'white male'), disability, and is due to cover age, religion and sexuality, the 'fairness' aspect of the law seems to be in the ascendancy. For those of a more radical persuasion, who are sceptical of the rights-based approach to law, the harm analysis takes on a more overtly political tinge. The next three extracts try to separate particular cases of social inequality and a theoretical sense of justice for all.

Lacey, N, 'From individual to group', in Hepple, B and Szyszczak, E (eds), *Discrimination: The Limits of Law*, 1992, London: Mansell, p 104:

[A]nti-discrimination legislation ... picks out certain features or categories only in order to prohibit their operating as reasons for certain kinds of decisions. This represents the liberal notion that all have *the same right* not to be discriminated against. It opens up the possibility of white male legal actions which exploit the vulnerability of any legal recognition of race or gender difference ... It can do so precisely because the legislation is framed in terms of difference rather than disadvantage: it constructs the problem to be tackled as race and sex discrimination, rather than as discrimination against and disadvantage of women and certain ethnic groups. Quite apart from the fact that this seriously misrepresents the social problems to which the legislation purports to respond, it means that any kind of protective measure addressing disadvantage is suspect. In particular, it rules out affirmative action, even of a moderate kind, as objectionable in principle ...

Wasserstrom, R, 'Racism, sexism and preferential treatment: an approach to the topics' (1977) 24 UCLA L Rev 581, pp 591–93:

[R]acism and sexism consist in taking race and sex into account in a certain way, in the context of a specific set of institutional arrangements and a specific ideology which together create and maintain a *system* of unjust institutions and unwarranted beliefs and attitudes ...

The primary evil of the various schemes of racial segregation against blacks that the courts were ... called upon to assess was not that such schemes were a capricious and irrational way of allocating public benefits and burdens ... The primary evil of such schemes was instead that they designedly and effectively marked off all black persons as degraded, dirty, less than fully developed persons who were unfit for full membership in the political, social and moral community ...

Sunstein, C, 'Three civil rights fallacies' (1991) 79 California L Rev 751, pp 770–71:

[O]ne who claims discrimination does not seek the prevention of certain irrational acts ... but asks instead for the elimination, in places large and small, of something like a caste system. Instead, a large mistake of civil rights policy has been to treat the issue as one of discrimination at all, since the term tends to connote irrational differentiation – an unacceptable practice to be sure, but not an appropriate description of the problem at hand, which is second-class citizenship ... A systemic disadvantage is one that operates along standard and predictable lines, in multiple important spheres of life, and that applies in realms like education, freedom from private and public violence, wealth, political representation, and political influence, all of which go to basic participation as a citizen in a democratic society ... In the areas of race and sex discrimination, and of disability as well, the problem is precisely this sort of systemic disadvantage ...

In the following extract, Wasserstrom resolves the conflict between anti-discrimination law and ('pro-discrimination') quotas on moral grounds.

Wasserstrom, R, 'Racism, sexism and preferential treatment: an approach to the topics' (1977) 24 UCLA L Rev 581, pp 617–18:

The racial quotas and practices of racial exclusion that were an integral part of the fabric of our culture ... were pernicious. They were a grievous wrong and it was and is important that all morally concerned individuals work for their eradication from our social universe. The racial quotas which are a part of contemporary affirmative action programmes are, I think, commendable and right. [But even if they are wrong] they are wrong for reasons very different from those which made quotas against blacks wrong ... [They] were wrong both because of the direct consequences of these programmes on the individuals most affected and because the system of racial and sexual superiority of which they were part was an immoral one in that it severely and without any adequate justification restricted the capacities, autonomy and happiness of those who were members of the less favoured categories.[6]

Whatever may be wrong with today's affirmative action programmes and quota systems, it should be clear that the evil, if any, is not the same. Racial and sexual minorities do not constitute the dominant social group. Nor is the conception of who is a fully developed member of the moral and social community one of an individual who is either female or black. Quotas which prefer women or blacks do not add to the already relatively overabundant supply of resources and opportunities at the disposal of white males. If racial quotas are to be condemned or if affirmative action programmes are to be abandoned, it should be because they will not work well to achieve the desired result. It is not because they seek either to perpetuate an unjust society or to realise a corrupt ideal ...

Many of these writers are concerned to demonstrate that affirmative action – however defined – designed to benefit women and black people should not be judged by the same standards as direct discrimination *against* women and black people. The point is perhaps clearest when the issue of disability is considered. It is common sense that many disabled people will not be able to perform a job until some specific accommodation is made to their needs. The Disability Discrimination Act 1995 recognised this reality both by mandating employers to make such reasonable accommodation and by preventing a non-disabled person from claiming discrimination in respect of such accommodation.[7] There is no logical reason why such an approach could not have been taken in respect of race and gender. It is, however, true that the approach taken in respect of disability marries more easily to an

6   See, also, *op cit*, Alexander, fn 2, pp 162–63.
7   See below, Chapter 16.

individual rights focus, because of the great variety of disabilities of which the law must take account, whereas accommodation for black people and women would of necessity focus more on the needs of the group as a whole.

(2)   Principles of Harm and Fairness

The next question is whether the focus on harm can also be used to explain why indirect discrimination is wrong. The task is harder here: for one thing, an employer may be liable for indirect discrimination without knowledge of the fact that such discrimination is occurring; for another, the inequality on which a claim of indirect discrimination is based may be the result of factors over which the individual employer or employers in general have no immediate control.

Gardner, J, 'Liberals and unlawful discrimination' (1989) 9 OJLS 1, pp 10–11, 18–20:

Waldron [has argued that] '[I]n the case of indirect discrimination, the wrongness of the employers' actions is nothing more than that they are not doing their bit to promote racial or sexual equality' ... [T]he duty not to discriminate indirectly seems to be imposed on citizens in a way that is partly arbitrary from the point of view of relative advantage. Employers, in other words, seem to be required by the State to do more than that which is entailed by their ordinary share of collective responsibility for disadvantage ...

At least two factors about the employment relationship give it a special institutional role in our culture. First, whether or not I am employed, and in what capacity, plays in our culture an absolutely decisive role in the relative advantages which I may enjoy throughout my life; secondly, the formation and preservation of the employment relationship involves a peculiarly large amount of control for one of the parties ... The employer finds himself in a special privileged position in the distributive mechanics of society, which makes him, for every individual employee or applicant, every bit as strong and as peremptory a distributive agency as the State itself ... When the employer's social significance is realised, requiring him not to discriminate indirectly is merely a proper response to current patterns of advantage and disadvantage, coupled with an understanding of the distribution of effective social power ...

Raz suggests that the harm principle does indeed set the boundaries of the use of State power, but that the harm principle is a wide harm principle: it allows governments 'to use coercion both in order to stop people from actions which would diminish people's autonomy and in order to take actions which are required to improve people's options and opportunities' ... So understood, distributive justice is not a principle which competes with the harm principle, but is rather a concomitant of it. 'Sometimes failing to improve the situation of another is harming him' ... [A]n employer who fails to provide opportunities to a woman, because his criterion of selection disadvantages women, harms her in the sense required by the wide harm principle – he fails to enhance her opportunities in the way that respect for her autonomous agency requires. We are all involved in a participative enterprise of protecting autonomy, an enterprise which carries with it obligations of mutual life-enhancement ...

For Raz, we are pursuing a culture in which the value of personal autonomy is understood to be the core value. Since the value of personal autonomy requires a culture of toleration and competitive pluralism, one of the reasons for precluding certain institutional structures in our society is that they fail to contribute to the ideals of toleration and competitive pluralism.

This argument is both complex and controversial.[8] It argues that even indirect discrimination is wrong, primarily because it is harmful rather than because it is unfair or anti-meritocratic – such employment practices might lead to inefficiencies, but that hardly represents the gist of their undesirable social effects. It treats employment as more than a relationship between private parties, and employment law as having a deeper function than merely holding the fort between such parties. Employment becomes a semi-public state, the absence of which in a real sense produces harm, especially if the effects on the group are such that the harmful consequences are reproduced extensively or from generation to generation. Thus, the harm is still linked with membership of and identity in a particular group. The harm, however, is contingent on the particular circumstances of the group against which the bias is manifest. It is impossible to understand discrimination without some grasp of the history of the group's experience under the particular regime at issue.

This raises a number of subsidiary questions. First, what is characteristic about the experiences of women and black people which have resulted in their being selected for specially favourable legislation? Secondly, are their experiences sufficiently similar as to warrant a fundamentally identical legislative approach? Thirdly, how does this approach respond to the fact that inequalities *between* women and between and within minority ethnic groups are increasing; is it still plausible to treat women as one single group and so entitled to benefit from anti-discrimination legislation? Fourthly, after reading the next extract, you might consider whether this socio-historical approach can apply equally to other groups who claim the right to have anti-discrimination legislation extended to them, or whether only a notion of 'fairness' or individual rights can explain this.

Lacey, N, 'From individual to group', in Hepple, B and Szyszczak, E (eds), *Discrimination: The Limits of Law*, 1992, London: Mansell, pp 109–12:

[I]t is implicit in the feminist project that some features of ... subordination are common to all women in a particular society, at least at some level – although the forms and nature of women's oppression are recognised to be historically and culturally specific ... [But] not all women's oppression, even in one society, is just the same. Since the subordination experienced by Afro-Caribbean women, Asian women, working class women, lesbian women, women who are single mothers and so on is qualitatively different, the feminist claim must be that gender is always *one factor*, and a fundamentally important one, in constituting the social position and experience of

---

8   It is not my purpose to explore all the details of the controversy. See Morris, A, 'On the normative foundations of indirect discrimination law: understanding the competing models of discrimination law as Aristotelian forms of justice' (1995) 15 OJLS 199, and the reply by Gardner, J, 'Discrimination as injustice' (1996) 16 OJLS 353.

all women and men, but it is overlaid by many other factors, most notably in our society by race and class ...[9]

As social institutions, sexism and racism clearly exhibit certain important differences. The centrality of naturalistic and biologistic arguments in constituting and maintaining racism and sexism, at least in the UK, is arguably different; membership of particular racial groups is significantly correlated with social class and poverty, as conventionally understood, in a way which is not so obviously true of gender; the experience of racial oppression is arguably more diverse than that of sexism given the variety of stereotypes about different racial groups ...

There are also similarities between racism and sexism. Both are strongly associated with a variety of forms of political and social disadvantage ... and both rely to a significant extent on stereotyped views about what is normal to, appropriate for or to be expected of members of that group simply by virtue of that membership. Perhaps most importantly, both have been recognised as social institutions – parts of the structure and patterning of social relations – rather than as merely cumulations of individual prejudices, actions and decisions ...

3   THE OBJECTIVES OF LEGAL INTERVENTION

Assuming that discrimination is either 'harmful' or 'unfair', or both, the next question is what should be the overall aim of such intervention.[10] Here, Wasserstrom provides some challenging ideas.

---

9   Posner's response to this kind of reasoning claims that because of the 'heterogeneity of women as an economic class and their interdependence with men, laws aimed at combating sex discrimination are more likely to benefit particular groups of women at the expense of other groups rather than women as a whole. And to the extent that the overall effect of the law is to reduce aggregate social welfare because of the allocative and administrative costs of the law, women as a group are hurt along with men. Sex discrimination has long been on the decline, for reasons unrelated to law, and this makes it all the more likely that the principal effect of public intervention may have been to make women as a group worse off by reducing the efficiency of the economy ...'. Posner, R, 'An economic analysis of sex discrimination laws' (1989) 56 Chicago UL Rev 1311, pp 1334–35. His argument is that sex discrimination laws are economically inefficient and are unnecessary as the operation of the free market is itself causing discrimination to decline. Even if he is correct on the economics, which is highly controversial, he fails, rather typically of the law and economics school, to give weight to other objectives of law such as justice and the vindication of rights. The only non-economic gain which is mentioned in the article is a gain in self-esteem which law might induce, thus propelling more women into the marketplace. Posner's underlying position seems to be that the sum total of human happiness will not be advanced if more women work. It is curious that as economic beings we are entitled and indeed virtually required by the theory to act in accordance with individual self-interest, but when it comes to the social consequences of legal intervention, no account is apparently taken of individual rights and liberties. See, further, Epstein, R, *Forbidden Grounds: The Case Against Employment Discrimination Laws*, 1992, Cambridge, Mass: Harvard UP.

10   Hugh Collins identified three 'deviations' from a simple equal treatment principle. First, different *treatment* is required in some cases, eg, pregnancy and disability. Secondly, equal treatment is not permitted where it causes unjustifiable indirect discrimination. Thirdly, affirmative action is required. See Collins, H 'Discrimination, equality and social inclusion' (2003) 66 MLR 16, at pp 16–17.

Wasserstrom, R, 'Racism, sexism and preferential treatment: an approach to the topics' (1977) 24 UCLA L Rev 581, pp 585–89, 603–14:

It is even clearer in the case of sex than in the case of race that one's sexual identity is a centrally important, crucially relevant category within our culture. I think, in fact, that it is more important and more fundamental than one's race ...

But to be female, as opposed to being black, is not to be conceived of as simply a creature of less worth. That is one important thing that differentiates sexism from racism: the ideology of sex, as opposed to the ideology of race, is a good deal more complex and confusing. Women are both put on a pedestal and deemed not fully developed persons ... Because the sexual ideology is complex, confusing and variable, it does not unambiguously proclaim the lesser value attached to being female ... nor does it unambiguously correspond to the existing social realities. For these, among other reasons, sexism could plausibly be regarded as a deeper phenomenon than racism. It is more deeply embedded in the culture and thus less visible. Being harder to detect, it is harder to eradicate. Moreover, it is less unequivocally regarded as unjust and unjustifiable ...

What would the good or just society make of race or sex, and to what degree, if at all, would racist and sexist distinctions even be taken into account? Indeed, it could plausibly be argued that we could not have an adequate idea of whether a society was racist or sexist unless we had some idea of what a thoroughly non-racist or non-sexist society would look like ...

[O]ne picture of a non-racist society is that which is captured by what I call the assimilationist model. A non-racist society would be one in which the race of an individual would be the functional equivalent of the eye colour of individuals in our society today ... The assimilationist ideal is not, however, the only possible, plausible ideal. There are two others that are closely related, but distinguishable. One is the ideal of diversity; the other, the ideal of tolerance. Both can be understood by considering how religion, rather than eye colour, tends to be thought about in our culture. According to the ideal of diversity, heterodoxy in respect to religious belief and practice is regarded as a positive good. In this view there would be a loss – it would be a worse society – were everyone to be a member of the same religion. According to the other view, the ideal of tolerance, heterodoxy with respect to religious belief and practice would be seen more as a necessary, lesser evil. In this view there is nothing intrinsically better about diversity in respect to religion, but the evils of achieving anything like homogeneity far outweigh the possible benefits ...

My view is that the assimilationist ideal may be just as good and just as important an ideal in respect to sex as it is in respect to race. But many persons think there are good reasons why an assimilationist society in respect to sex would not be desirable ... [T]o make the assimilationist ideal a reality in respect to sex would involve more profound and fundamental revisions of our institutions and our attitudes than would be the case in respect to race ... [I]n that event, for example, marriage, all sex-role differentiation, and any kind of sexually exclusive preference would be treated either as anomalous or as statistically fortuitous.

It may be that in respect to sex (and, conceivably, even in respect to race) something more like the ideals in respect to religion – pluralistic ideals founded on diversity or tolerance – is the right one. But the problem then ... is to specify with a good deal of precision and care what that ideal really comes to. Which legal, institutions and personal differentiations are permissible and which are not? Which attitudes and beliefs concerning sexual identification and difference are properly introduced and maintained and which are not? Part, but by no means all, of the attraction of the assimilationist ideal is its clarity and simplicity ...

Race as a naturally occurring characteristic is also a socially irrelevant category. There do not in fact appear to be any characteristics that are part of this natural concept of race and that are in any plausible way even relevant to the appropriate distribution of any political, institutional or interpersonal concerns in the good society. Because in this sense race is like eye colour, there is no plausible case to be made on this ground against the assimilationist ideal ... [But] it may be ... that one could argue that a form of the pluralist ideal ought to be preserved in respect of race, in the socially created sense, for reasons similar to those that might be offered in support of the desirability of some version of the pluralist ideal in respect to religion ...

It is sex-role differentiation, not gender *per se*, that makes men and women as different as they are from each other, and it is sex-role differences which are invoked to justify most sexual differentiation ... Even though there are biological differences between men and women in nature, this fact does not determine the question of what the good society can and should make of these differences ... [T]here appear to be very few, if any, respects in which the ineradicable, naturally occurring differences between males and females *must* be taken into account ... [T]he only fact that seems required to be taken into account is the fact that reproduction of the human species requires that the foetus develop *in utero* for a period of months ...

I think it important to see ... that the case against the assimilationist ideal ... must rest on arguments concerned to show why some other ideal would be preferable; it cannot plausibly rest on the claim that it is either necessary or inevitable ... If it is true, as I think it is, that the sex-role differentiated societies we have had so far have tended to concentrate power in the hands of males, have developed institutions and ideologies which have perpetuated that concentration and have restricted and prevented women from living the kinds of lives that persons ought to be able to live for themselves, then this says far more about what may be wrong with any non-assimilationist ideal than does the conservative premise say about what may be right about my non-assimilationist ideal ...

(1)   Equality of Opportunity Versus Equality of Outcomes[11]

(a)   The theories explained

The concepts of discrimination and disadvantage are intimately linked with concepts of equality.

Lustgarten, L, *Legal Control of Racial Discrimination*, 1980, London: Macmillan, pp 6–7:

One may begin with a broad distinction between two distinct, and ultimately conflicting, ideas of racial equality. Drawing upon Leon Mayhew, these will be called the 'equal opportunity' and 'fair-share' approaches[12]... In its purest or most extreme form the first accepts that discrimination has been abolished when all formal and deliberate barriers against blacks have been dismantled. Its concern stops with

---

11 For a discussion of EC discrimination law as a substantive rights, or anti-discrimination, model, see Barbera, M, 'Not the same? The judicial role in the new community anti-discrimination law context' [2002] 31 ILJ 82.

12 Mayhew, L, *Law and Equal Opportunity*, 1968, Cambridge, Mass: Harvard UP, pp 59–74.

determining whether the factor of race has caused an individual to suffer adverse treatment. At the furthest point at the other end of the spectrum the unalloyed fair-share approach is concerned only with equality of result, measured in terms of proportionality. Its inherent logic leads to the adoption of quotas as a remedy once a finding of discrimination is made.

The two approaches derive from different, also ultimately conflicting, philosophical foundations. Equality of treatment is inherent in the feeling of a fundamental human connectedness. In the striking phrase of Patrick Fitzgerald, 'Why would it be offensive, at the end of King Lear, for only Lear and Cordelia to take bows, and not the minor characters? It would be like equating the minor characters with tables and chairs. It is not just a question of equality, but of humanity.[13] Grounded in sentiments so deep, it is consequently a minimalist view, requiring only that each individual be judged by the same standards – whatever these may be in any particular instance – and not favoured or disfavoured by the application of socially ascribed status characteristics ...

The fair-share approach, by contrast, is more complex and controversial. It is also of much more recent origin, having arisen in response to a history of ill treatment of socially distinct groups – which history, it is argued, makes the defining group characteristic relevant to the distribution of social goods. Justice is therefore seen as collective, at least in the negative sense that it is considered wrong for the ill-treated group to have proportionately less of whatever is valued. The fair-share idea also embodies what Robert Nozick calls 'a patterned distribution' – a norm based upon abstract philosophical principles by which a given distribution is to be judged.[14] This norm, whilst not necessarily socialist or egalitarian, does entail a judgment about the relative deserts of different groups; as such it is incompatible with the liberal individualism of the nineteenth century, which not only accepted the results of the market but could not conceive of enquiring into the handicaps some competitors brought with them when they entered its competitions. However – as one might have suspected from its American antecedents fair-share approach is in no way compatible with great inequalities of income, wealth and social resources: it merely requires that blacks fit into the existing patterns of inequality in the same proportions as whites.

Equality of opportunity implies that all people should be treated as individuals in the sense of having the opportunity to compete on equal terms for the goods which society has to offer. The problem, though, is that reliance on equal opportunity alone provides no guarantee that, in practice, those goods will be spread proportionally between the protected groups and the rest. Equality of outcome implies an equitable division of the economic cake between different groups in society. Lacey argues that, for women, the law does not go far enough.

Lacey, N, 'Legislation against sex discrimination: questions from a feminist perspective' (1986) 14 JLS 411, pp 413–17:

[T]he limitations of formal equality as a feminist goal are now widely recognised: it has little bite in view of the disadvantages which women suffer in private areas such as family life, untouched by the sex discrimination legislation. No concept of discrimination which is based exclusively on formal equality can take proper account of aspects of women's different position resulting from prior discrimination and disadvantage in spheres which fall outside the relatively limited ambit of the

---

13 This occurred in private conversation with Professor Fitzgerald, formerly of the Law Faculty of the University of Kent.

14 Nozick, R, *Anarchy, State and Utopia*, 1974, Cambridge, Mass: Harvard UP, pp 155–64.

legislation ... Given the history and structure of sex discrimination, merely ruling out sex as a reason for action in certain areas promises little progress in terms of dismantling women's disadvantage. It may even be counterproductive in ruling out sex as remedially relevant reason in the context, for example, of affirmative action programmes ...

[T]he discourse of equality of opportunity presupposes a world inhabited by autonomous individuals making choices. These choices may differ along gender lines, resulting in a very different distribution of jobs or other goods as between women and men ... An equal opportunity principle is inadequate to criticise and transform a world in which the distribution of goods is structured along gender lines ... Differential treatment and unequal impact, even within the ambit of *prima facie* discrimination, may be legitimated subconsciously by Industrial Tribunal[15] members who believe that women and men just do typically make different choices. Different finishing points are not seen as problematic. In this way, the very stereotypes which the legislation is presumably meant to undermine inevitably and invisibly affect the tribunal's reading of legal issues ... [By] conceptualising the problem as sex discrimination rather than *discrimination against women*, the legislation renders invisible the real social problem and deflects away a social ideal or goal which would identify and address it ...

[T]he comparative approach ... presupposes (yet suppresses) the idea of a norm with which the scrutinised behaviour is compared. In the case of claims brought by women, that norm is the treatment usually accorded to men: thus, in so far as the sex discrimination legislation prescribes equality, it is *equality in terms of a norm set by and for men* – the logic of discrimination allows no challenge to general practices in any area. By definition, sex discrimination cases do not provide a jumping off point for criticism of general social practices or real debate about what kind of equality is worth having, and with whom. At best, the legislation promises some dismantling of practices restrictive of access to goods and resources which present (that is, male-dominated) culture has determined as valuable. It may go some way towards reducing the overt significance of sex in the allocation of certain goods, but it has no cutting edge against the significance of gender in setting them up as goods in the first place.

Ward, T, 'Beyond sex equality: the limits of sex equality in the new Europe', in Hervey, T and O'Keeffe, D (eds), *Sex Equality Law in the European Union*, 1996, Chichester: John Wiley, pp 370, 375:

The pervasive argument in sex equality, until recent years at least, has been that of sameness and difference ... [This approach] gives women just two choices; they can either aspire to be the same as men, and to enjoy the same rights, or they can campaign to have their difference from men recognised in law.[16] Either way, women are compared with a male norm, and by presenting women with these two choices, and these two choices only, the debate immediately establish parameters.

Any ... rights-based approach tends to be founded on a 'claim to similarity'. A collateral argument here is that the formal enactment of rights for women ... will not

---

15 Under the Employment Rights (Dispute Resolution) Act 1998, s 1(1), Industrial Tribunals were re-named Employment Tribunals.

16 'The negative, narrow and exclusive features of the concept of discrimination, no doubt, made it an effective weapon against segregation. They have made it much less effective, if not entirely ineffective, in breaking down barriers to equality which are now both less obvious and more pervasive.' Rutherglen, G, 'Discrimination and its discontents' (1995) 81 Virginia L Rev 117, p 130.

in reality address the myriad of substantive inequalities that women face. In other words, a liberal rights-based approach ... actually serves to entrench the real inequalities that women encounter, and does more harm in practice, than good. Thus, as MacKinnon concludes, the phrase 'sex equality law' contains three particular preconceptions. First, it assumes a particular determination of sex as denoting difference. Second, it then presumes that any 'inequalities' must be the result of 'mistakes' in addressing difference. Third, 'law' explicitly assumes that the problem is something that can somehow be resolved by law ...

Next, Lacey argues that the existing law, giving individual rights, can only benefit those in the best position historically to enforce their rights, ie, men.

Lacey, N, 'From individual to group', in Hepple, B and Szyszczak, E (eds), *Discrimination: The Limits of Law*, 1992, London: Mansell, pp 103–04, 106–07:

[T]he standard or treatment of the outcome which represents the point of comparison and hence the Acts' conception of what is normal or legitimate is necessarily a norm set by (and generally by) men. This poses particular problems in areas such as pregnancy ... [T]he legislation ... cannot provide any platform for litigants to criticise the formulation of the 'normal' standard: they must content themselves with arguing for assimilation to it. Complaints about formal difference rather than substantive critique is the name of the game ...

Feminists have criticised this ahistorical, pre-social view of human nature which underlies liberal rights theory and legal individualism, and have pointed out the ways in which the need to frame legal arguments in terms of individual claims systematically obstructs the project of revealing and dismantling structures and institutions which disadvantage women. These arguments have developed into a more general critique of the discourse of rights, which are seen as not only inherently individualistic, but also competitive and hence anti-socialistic. They are also seen as tied in with the notion of formal equality – hence the need to ascribe equal rights to all and the inevitable obscuring of real social problems and disadvantages. In a world in which white, male and middle class people both have more effective access to legal forums and meet a more sympathetic response when they get there, the ascription of formally equal rights will in effect entrench the competitively asserted rights of these privileged people. Far from dismantling the disadvantage of women, people from ethnic minorities and socio-economically underprivileged groups, it may even have the opposite effect ...

(b)   Arguments for and against

Thus, equality of opportunity is primarily concerned with formal equality under the law rather than with substantive or material equality. It may have no regard to the fact that women or black people may have difficulty in obtaining the relevant qualifications or experience. The equality of opportunity approach is based upon the notion of individual merit as supposedly the chief criterion for success in the labour market and in society as a whole. The next three extracts attack the notion of equality of opportunity. Wasserstrom suggests that that in a sea of inequalities, it seems pointless, philosophically and practically, to redress just one. Townshend-Smith fears that the law could simply reinforce equally male-based values. O'Donovan explains that equality of opportunity is only credible if there is an equal starting point. In the fourth extract, Lacey takes a pragmatic view.

Wasserstrom, R, 'Racism, sexism and preferential treatment: an approach to the topics' (1977) 24 UCLA L Rev 581, pp 619–20:

Affirmative action programmes almost always make sex or race a relevant condition, not a conclusive one. As such, they function the way all other classificatory schemes do. The defect, if there is one, is generic, and not peculiar to programmes such as these. Part of what is wrong with even talking about qualifications and merit is that the argument derives some of its force from the erroneous notion that we would have a meritocracy were it not for affirmative action ...

To be at all persuasive, the argument must be that those who are the most qualified deserve to receive the benefits ... because they are the most qualified ... But why do the most qualified deserve anything? ... Most of what are regarded as the decisive qualifications for higher education have a great deal to do with things over which the individual has neither control nor responsibility: such things as home environment, socio-economic class of parents, and of course the quality of the primary and secondary schools attended. Since individuals do not deserve having had any of these things vis à vis other individuals, they do not, for the most part, deserve their qualifications. And since they do not deserve their abilities they do not in any strong sense deserve to be admitted because of their abilities ...

Townshend-Smith, R, *Sex Discrimination in Employment: Law, Practice and Policy*, 1989, London: Sweet & Maxwell, pp 25–26:

The extent to which one is personally responsible for job performance is ... problematic. Many required abilities are innate; others are learned in a culture where there is no guarantee of equal opportunities to engage in such learning.

Success at work may be measured by factors to which men and women have unequal access. Ability to work long hours is a clear example, so is the ability to remain for a very long period with the same employer. Most difficult is the manifestation of characteristics such as aggression or dynamism which may be considered, rightly or wrongly, to be associated with being male. If women are conditioned to be submissive and to consider other people, how can they later be said to deserve less at work for failure to possess [other] characteristics?

[I]t is important to see how deep-rooted is the notion of merit in our society, and that merit has historically been determined in [white] male terms. The danger is that the law will accept male definitions of what is meritorious in employment, and that this will not correspond with the desires or best interests of many or most women.

O'Donovan, K and Szyszczak, E, *Equality and Sex Discrimination Law*, 1988, Oxford: Blackwell, pp 4–5:

Other writers contrast equality of opportunity with equality of outcome. For example, socialist feminists argue that equal opportunity is procedural and formal whereas equality of outcome is substantive. Equal opportunity as a concept is criticised for being concerned merely to ensure that the rules of entry into competition are the same for all. Equality of outcome as a concept looks to the results of competition and then raises questions about the rules of entry ...

[I]n discussions of anti-discrimination legislation it is often assumed that once barriers to competition are removed, women, who have historically been discriminated against, will show their prowess and compete equally. But this conception of equality is limited, for it abstracts persons from their unequal situations and puts them in a competition in which their prior inequality and its effects are ignored ... Williams explains [that] equal opportunity 'requires not merely that there should be no exclusion from access on grounds other than those appropriate or rational for the good in question, but that the grounds considered appropriate for the good should themselves be such that people from all sections of society have an equal chance of satisfying them'.

Equality of opportunity in its full sense requires a fair, rational and appropriate competition for goods and benefits. This means that competitors must have an equal starting point, where possible. It goes further than lowering barriers to education, services and the labour market. For women to compete equally with men, both sexes must start equally.

Lacey, N, 'Legislation against sex discrimination: questions from a feminist perspective' (1986) 14 JLS 411, p 414:

Equality of opportunity represents only one among many of the more programmatic conceptions of equality described and defended in modern political theory. Equality of welfare, results, resources and consideration of interests, to name but a few, have been energetically and ably defended. Any of these conceptions *might* be easier to extend beyond a liberal world-view or more susceptible of being given a distinctively feminist content than is equality of opportunity ... [T]he idea [of equality of opportunity] provided a crucially important campaigning slogan for the legislation, but ... by the same token, it was not discussed or analysed in any open or rigorous way. Had it been, it seems likely that both its ambiguity and its potentially radical implications would have come to the surface and it would have lost its capacity to unite diverse political groups. How many liberal supporters of the current legislation, for example, would have been content to reflect on the implications of a thorough-going commitment to equality of opportunity in terms of socialisation of childrearing or even genetic engineering? Thus, we should not expect to find that the legislation conforms to a unitary or coherent ideal of equality. We should rather recognise equality of opportunity as a crucial piece of political rhetoric which also provides guiding and limiting principles ...

(c)   The problem with the compensation remedy

Much of the criticism of the approach based on equality of opportunity focuses on the nature of the rights which are protected – or the rights which are excluded – under a doctrine of equality of opportunity. But even a more thorough and realistic approach designed to foster *genuine* equality of opportunity may founder on the problem of remedies. For the *legal* model of equality of opportunity is closely bound up with the view that the law's function is to compensate the victims of wrongdoing. This may have a number of unfortunate consequences. First, the political association of anti-discrimination law with wrongdoing is so strong that defendants resist all efforts to have them classified in this way, and this may hinder the promotion of out-of-court settlements with the potential to improve the position of disadvantaged groups. Secondly, the levels of compensation awarded are unlikely in most cases to be sufficient to act as a deterrent against repetition of such behaviour.[17] Thirdly, in a

---

17 The absence of creative remedies may not flow as a logically necessary consequence of an equality of opportunity frame of reference, although it certainly seems to have done so in the British context. In the American context, however, where, again, equality of opportunity has been the dominant rhetoric, class actions and patterns and practice suits have led in some instances to very substantial awards of compensation. See below, Chapter 17, p 566.

variation of the previous point, the assumption is that there is no entitlement to a remedy *unless* the claimant can prove that measurable financial loss has been suffered.

Sunstein, C, 'Three civil rights fallacies' (1991) 79 California L Rev 751, pp 762–64:

In important respects ... the model of compensatory justice inadequately captures the nature of the problem and is therefore a recipe for confusion ... For example, the requirement of 'discriminatory intent' might well be understood as an effort to adhere to compensatory principles ... The question, thus conceived, is whether an identifiable actor has harmed an identifiable person in an identifiable way. To abandon the touchstone of intent would lead courts far from the compensatory model. It would lead courts to require redress of social wrongs committed by third parties in the distant past, which would involve conspicuous social re-ordering and harms to innocent persons, rather than a restoration of some well defined *status quo ante* ... In this more expansive view, the redress of harms other than those created by the particular practice in question would be the goal of the equality principle. The notion of compensation would remain, but it would require public and private employers to ensure that the distribution of benefits and burdens between blacks and whites would be roughly what it would have been without the legacy of discrimination.

The general problem is that the compensatory model, in any form, is based on notions of causation, injury and restoration to the *status quo ante* that are well adapted to the tort or contract setting, but singularly ill-suited to the problem of discrimination ...

Many people have concluded that equality of opportunity is inadequate as a fundamental philosophy for anti-discrimination legislation, but there are also problems with the more radical approach based on equality of outcome.[18]

O'Donovan, K and Szyszczak, E, *Equality and Sex Discrimination Law*, 1988, Oxford: Blackwell, p 6:

Another answer to perceived limitations of equal opportunity is to propose equality of outcome or results ... It is evident that the creation of outcome equality would require a major social revolution ... Whilst liberal political theory advocates equality of opportunity in an unspecified way, equality of outcome is characteristic of radical and socialist society. Liberals object that 'equality of outcomes could be maintained only at a substantial cost to liberty'. The argument is that maintenance of strict equality would require coercive interference to maintain an egalitarian distribution pattern ...

Lustgarten, L, *Legal Control of Racial Discrimination*, 1980, London: Macmillan, p 7:

At both the philosophical and legal levels the latent conflict erupts when the fair-share approach requires denial of something desirable to a white person in order to achieve justice defined in terms of collective advancement. The daunting task confronting policymakers and theorists is to minimise the extent of the conflict, to transcend the

18   It is sometimes argued that the philosophy of direct discrimination is equality of opportunity, while the philosophy of indirect discrimination is equality of results. For many reasons, this is too radical a view of the way indirect discrimination law operates. First, the way the group comparison must be made focuses only on the particular employer rather than the wider society. Secondly, the defence of justification means that equality of result may sometimes be trumped by other values, including the defendant employer's own economic well-being. Thirdly, the remedial framework for indirect discrimination remains firmly wedded to an individualistic equality of opportunity model. These points will be developed further in Chapter 10; the aim of this chapter is to consider not whether current legislation does aim at equality of results, but whether ideal legislation should do so.

limited effectiveness of the first approach while avoiding the injustices of the second. No more important question exists in relation to racial discrimination than how to eliminate the inferior conditions of blacks without trampling upon important social values.

(2)   The Recognition of Differences

To move to an approach based fairly and squarely on equality of results is theoretically and practically problematic, as taken literally it would appear to require equality of distribution between black and white, male and female, over a whole range of economic goods. Given that redistribution of wealth is conceptually intertwined with the relief of poverty, it is entirely unclear why certain victims of poverty and not others should be entitled to relief under the doctrine. Far more appropriate is an approach based on pluralistic political philosophies, which argues that equality can only be attained if appropriate recognition is given to the factors which render formal equality inadequate or ineffective.

O'Donovan, K and Szyszczak, E, *Equality and Sex Discrimination Law*, 1988, Oxford: Blackwell, pp 7–9:

The question of whether equality is viewed as a competition between men and women starting from the same point, or as a pluralistic recognition of different qualities and needs, is fundamental to theories of sex equality ... If the model for whom the competition ... is designed is male then women may find it difficult to fit ... Economic and social institutions, willing to admit women under a policy of equality, will not necessarily adapt to accommodate them.

If treatment as an equal implies respect for others, avoidance of stereotypes and viewing the world from another's point of view, then pluralism goes further than equal treatment. For it allows for differences in persons, their situations, their needs ... In this guise equality does not mean giving or receiving the same treatment, but rather giving or receiving equal concern ... Pluralism goes further than equal treatment because it allows the dissimilarities between the sexes to enter in. A focus on inequality puts differential treatment to the forefront. This is a deeper perspective which enables the standpoint or perspective of those, unequal in social reality, to emerge. But instead of women's difference from men being a signal for unequal treatment to follow, as it has done in the past, it would be a sign for suspicion of the existing inequality ...

The argument, therefore, is that, in the name of equality, the law must take account of the differences between groups which affect their capacity for equal competition in the marketplace. The argument has been in the forefront of feminist thinking concerning the way in which the law should seek to reconcile tension between work life and family life. Such an approach should inform the way the law deals with pregnancy, which is a biological difference between men and women. The same approach may be applied to social differences, and thus the law may allow for the fact that women continue to have prime responsibility for care of children and other dependants. It may do this by protecting part-time workers, giving rights to time off and by encouraging or permitting a more flexible pattern of work. It is far less clear what the recognition of differences approach has to say about racial discrimination in the labour market,[19] though it has plenty to say about the recognition of differences, primarily cultural, outside the labour market.[20]

The issue of ensuring the appropriate legal response to pregnancy has, as we will see in Chapter 8, caused serious problems for British – and American – anti-discrimination law. The reason is that the non-discrimination principle depends on a comparison, a comparison which in the case of pregnancy is either impossible or inappropriate. English law – with more than a little help from the EC – has now largely resolved the debate by the direct provision of employment rights which do not depend on the concept of discrimination.

Rutherglen, G, 'Discrimination and its discontents' (1995) 81 Virginia L Rev 117, p 141:

On the one hand, discrimination on the basis of pregnancy is formally equivalent to discrimination on the basis of sex ... On the other hand, this way of looking at the issue systematically underestimates the barriers to employment of women created by the traditional division of labour within families ... The question whether an employer should be required to take account of these burdens led to the more general debate among feminists whether women have the right to be treated the same as men or the right to be treated differently. However this debate over sameness and difference should be resolved, the concept of discrimination leaves no room for it to arise in the first place. It pre-empts the debate in favour of sameness.

The issue of childcare, which many regard as essential for any move towards genuine workplace equality, has, in Britain at least, largely escaped regulation by law. This may reflect the ideological position that the family, the domestic, are private matters and thus the concern of the parties rather than the State.

Townshend-Smith, R, *Sex Discrimination in Employment: Law, Practice and Policy*, 1989, London: Sweet & Maxwell, p 28:

Neither the State nor employers have provided childcare adequate to enable most women to exercise a real choice as to whether they wish to continue working ... Even where childcare is available, school holidays and illness may cause problems, and a woman employee who is absent during such periods has no legal or collectively negotiated protection. Her absences may be treated as personal failings.

In this social context equality of opportunity is insufficient ... The purpose even of indirect discrimination law is to improve women's integration into the labour market ... If women's family commitments prevent such integration then the law will provide no help, though if limited accommodation can be made at no serious cost to efficiency then individual employers may be required to alter their practices. It may, for example, sometimes be discriminatory not to allow a jobshare.[21]

Indirect discrimination law cannot overcome the inherent labour market disadvantages facing many women. Equality theory has been useful in gaining some limited access to male preserves, but is problematic in other areas where there are real

---

19 Cultural pluralism might require, eg, employers to permit employees to take time off for celebration of religious festivals.

20 See Poulter, S, 'The limits of legal, cultural and religious pluralism' and Montgomery, J, 'Legislating for a multi-faith society: some problems of special treatment', in Hepple, B and Szyszczak, E (eds), *Discrimination: The Limits of Law*, 1992, London: Mansell, Chapters 10 and 11 respectively.

21 See below, Chapter 10, pp 283–88.

biological or social differences between men and women. True equality can only occur both when employers are obliged to take such differences into account and when the social differences are of less significance.

4   THE ROLE OF LAW

Some would argue that it is misconceived to rely on the law to bring about improvements in the social position of women and minority groups. Passing legislation may create the false impression that the problem of discrimination and disadvantage has been tackled and perhaps even solved, as ordinary people often assume that laws necessarily achieve their purpose. This criticism fails to take adequate account of the symbolic function of the law; in particular, the message that would accompany any decision, for whatever reason, to repeal anti-discrimination legislation is hardly likely to be welcomed by the prior beneficiaries of such legislation. The strength of the argument, however, lies in its clear recognition that law can only ever be one strand in what is effectively a political campaign concerning the allocation of resources, in which legal victories may themselves have symbolic importance at the political level – as may legal defeats!

O'Donovan, K and Szyszczak, E, *Equality and Sex Discrimination Law*, **1988, Oxford: Blackwell, p 12:**

The State, through anti-discrimination legislation, affirms its interest in the quality of citizens. It recognises individuals as members of the polity and the wider social interest in social solidarity. It makes a legal statement prohibiting discrimination as wrong. That the statement may be limited, that the means may be ineffective, should not cause us to overlook the importance of such a statement in official discourse.

Lacey, N, 'Legislation against sex discrimination: questions from a feminist perspective' (1986) 14 JLS 411, pp 418–20:

[D]oubts must arise as to whether the legal forum really represents a useful place in which to attempt to advance arguments for women's liberation, or to seek concrete improvements in the position of women in our society The more specific features relevant to these doubts would include the male domination of the legal forum in terms of its personnel; the male domination of the legal system in terms of the composition of the legislature and powerful interest groups; and the construction of disputes in individual terms and their resolution through a closed system of reasoning. It is hardly surprising that many feminists see the 'equality' legislation as a sop intended to promote false consciousness; it enables women to think that things are getting better or enables men to resist women's further claims, while actually making no real contribution to the dismantling of sexism in our society.

[W]e should acknowledge the limitation of legislation designed to give individual remedies ... [P]rimacy should rather be given to action at the policy level such as contract compliance; changes in the practice of education; adequate provision of childcare facilities and parental leave [and] revaluation of women's work.

We must continue to struggle for a proper emphasis on changes to material conditions which both reflect and consolidate sexism and women's disadvantage ... And we must campaign for policies which reach a much broader range of women – particularly those such as black women, working class women, and single mothers – who suffer specific disadvantages and discriminations ...

[I]f we are to exploit the ideal of equality, our focus must be equality not in terms of opportunity within the liberal model, but in terms of welfare, power resources and goods ...

[W]e could argue for the abandonment of formal equality legislation and the adoption of a specific Act of Parliament prohibiting discrimination against women ... This would not, of course, be to imply that discrimination against men on grounds of sex is morally unproblematic, although it certainly does imply that non-discrimination on grounds of sex conceived in formal equality terms is not a moral absolute. But the main thrust of such a strategy would be to acknowledge that sex discrimination against men is not a social phenomenon of the same order, does not involve comparably damaging and oppressive effects as does sex discrimination against women, and that this clear social difference justifies, and indeed calls for, a totally different legal response ...

[I]f we are to minimise both the dangers attaching to the legislation and its limitations, I would argue that we must abandon equality of opportunity as an important underlying principle. The images it conjures up in both political and legal discourse are closely associated with a minimal and atomistic libertarian vision which fails to address the factors implicated in women's oppression. The opportunity ideal's presupposition of a world of autonomous individuals starting a race or making free choices has no cutting edge against the argument that men and women are simply running different races. And it poses the real danger of actually serving to legitimate existing differences: inequality of impact or results can just be defined as to do with different 'free' choice – or natural sex difference! ... [W]e would be better advised to aim for a determinate measure of equality of results (as through affirmative action programmes) than to run the risks presented by the manipulable notion of equality of opportunity ...

We should neither abandon anti-discrimination legislation just because of its inherent limitations nor regard it as the *only* appropriate *legal* response to women's oppression ... The reform of anti-discrimination law *can* form part of a genuinely feminist political strategy, but it cannot be more than a minor part.

Sunstein, C, 'Three civil rights fallacies' (1991) 79 California L Rev 751, pp 765–68:

The courts' insulation – from an electoral process that is often said to have produced civil rights violations in the first place – is considered a comparative virtue, allowing the judges to implement anti-discrimination principles without being affected by political biases. There can be no question that because of their insulation, judges have often been in an unusually good position to elaborate and implement principles of anti-discrimination. But for several reasons, reliance on the judiciary may have been a mistake. It may have diverted attention from more productive alternatives and at the same time disserved the very causes at issue. In any case, such reliance seems a poor strategy for the future. Three considerations are relevant here.

(a)   Efficacy

       Judicial decisions are of limited efficacy in bringing about social change. Study after study has confirmed this basic conclusion ... [T]he evidence suggests that judges are less effective than the elected branches of the government in attempting to reform systems of discrimination.

(b)   Democracy, citizenship, compromise and legitimacy

       For achieving sensible and effective reform, political channels are often far better than the courts. The resort to politics can produce a kind of citizen mobilisation that is a public and private good, and can inculcate political commitments, broader understanding, feelings of citizenship and dedication to the community

... [R]eliance on the courts has large and hidden disadvantages. It may divert energy and resources from political processes, and the substitution effect imposes large costs on these processes. And if questions of morality tend to become questions of constitutional law, their resolution before nine judges can harm the practice of citizenship.

(c)   The narrowing focus of adjudication

[L]egal thinking and legal procedures are most suited to ideas growing out of the tradition of compensatory justice, which is poorly adapted to the achievement of serious social reform. Adjudication is ill-suited to undertaking the necessary changes. Many of the important problems in current civil rights policy are systemic and complex. The lack of adequate schools, job training, or jobs creates a cycle of poverty, vulnerability to drugs and to crime, teenage pregnancy and single-parent households. Courts simply lack the tools to respond to these problems.

Lacey, N, 'From individual to group', in Hepple, B and Szyszczak, E (eds), _Discrimination: The Limits of Law_, 1992, London: Mansell, pp 106–08, 114–20:

The liberal legal world is one in which legal rules are applied and enforced in a politically neutral and formally equal way; the legal sphere is seen as relatively autonomous from the political sphere; all are equally subject to the law and formally equal before it. There are stringent limits on the proper ambit of State intervention by means of law, which is seen as positively protecting individual rights and interests against political encroachment, and negatively as protecting a sphere of private life in which public regulation is inappropriate and indeed oppressive ...

One possible strategy ... is for feminists and anti-racists to attempt to intervene in the legal forum, reworking legal concepts and definitions so as to reflect Afro-Caribbean, Asian, female and other perspectives. A notable example of such a strategy is law defining and making actionable sexual harassment – a concept which reconstructs, from a feminist perspective, behaviour conventionally regarded as acceptable and even favourable to women as unacceptable, oppressive and illegal. This kind of social and legal reconstruction is one of the most important potential contributions of critical social theory, and in the anti-discrimination area it raises a number of possibilities for reform. One example might be the recognition of groups' rather than individuals' claims, combating the notion of the legal subject as an abstract individual and putting the position and experience of an oppressed group explicitly on the legal agenda ...

Could a move to the recognition of group rights and/or collective remedies help to overcome the problems of legal individualism or to deconstruct the notion of the abstract legal subject in acknowledging as subjects entities recognised precisely because of their substantive political position? ...

I want to assess the potential of a ... conception of group rights which I shall call 'remedial' rights. These rights would apply to groups which were suffering disadvantage as a result either of present oppression or the present effects of past oppression. The essence of the right would be that positive and effective steps be taken to combat and overcome that disadvantage within a reasonable period of time ...

The assertion of group rights would be met with remedies not only of the traditional legal kind ... but also with a wide range of radically different remedies ... This feature would be crucial in breaking the conceptual link between loss and remedy which characterises the individual legal form. Hence contract compliance, quota systems and affirmative action programmes, urban development programmes, educational reforms and money to set up community projects of various kinds would be possible responses to the legal assertion of the violation of a group right ...

A more serious problem for the notion of group rights seems to be the fact of fragmentation and diversity of individual and group identity. People in any social world are members of a number of different communities and groups, and suffer or enjoy a number of overlapping and interacting identities, advantages and disadvantages as a result ... [W]e certainly cannot assume any kind of identity of interest among members of a group just because of one shared oppression, nor can we assume that, for example, racial oppression will have had the same kind of impact on the experience, consciousness and life chances of all members of that group. A recognition of this kind of diversity, and a commitment to recognition of a plurality of oppression, experiences and interests, seems to bring with it a nightmarish vision of a potential explosion of overlapping groups defined along different lines all competing with other (and implicitly with parts of themselves) for the resources or changes necessary to dismantle their specific disadvantages ... [T]he practical and conceptual difficulties raised by the diversity of social oppression and the consequent fragmentation of group identity cannot be underestimated.

On the present construction of the boundary between law and politics, remedial decisions with the kinds of significant resource implications likely to be effective in tackling racial and sexual disadvantage could only come from government institutions. As things stand at the moment ... I suspect that effective recognition of group-based remedial rights would have to be at a political rather than a legal level ...

Concepts such as equality of opportunity and equality of results are only a means to an end. That is why their usefulness is as much symbolic as purely philosophical. The law and the legal system are also a means to an end, rather than a closed system with a life and a rationale of their own. From this standpoint, it is perfectly consistent to be at the same time cynical and sceptical about the usefulness of the law and yet to seek to have it strengthened and to make use of it to its full capacity. What is essential for anyone concerned with the economic and social position of disadvantaged groups is that the law is never seen as the only way forward for tackling the problems.

PART 2

DISCRIMINATION LAW

CHAPTER 5

THE SOURCES OF ANTI-DISCRIMINATION LAW

1   INTRODUCTION

There is vast range of legislation covering discrimination, coming from various sources with the inherent problem of differing styles and competing status.[1] Legislation specifically covers race, religion or belief, sex, gender reassignment, sexual orientation and disability, and will in due course cover age. The principal domestic legislation is the Race Relations Act (RRA) 1976, the Sex Discrimination Act (SDA) 1975 and Equal Pay Act (EqPA) 1970. In addition (deriving from European Community law) there are statutory instruments covering religion or belief (in force since 2 December 2003) and sexual orientation (in force since 1 December 2003). European legislation specifically covers equal pay between sexes (Art 141 of the EC Treaty), sex (Equal Treatment Directive 76/207), race (Race Directive 2000/43), nationality (Art 39 of the EC Treaty) and religion and belief, disability, age and sexual orientation (Equal Treatment in Employment Directive 2000/78). This EC-derived legislation[2] is confined to employment matters, except for the Race Directive, which, like the RRA 1976 and SDA 1975, extends to other fields such as the provision of services, housing and education.

In addition, the Human Rights Act 1998, which incorporated the European Convention on Human Rights, came into force on 2 October 2000.[3] It covers discrimination 'on any ground such as sex, race, colour, language, religion, political or other opinion, national or social origin, association with a national minority, property, birth or other status'. Note that this list is non-exhaustive. However, the Convention only covers discrimination in connection with any of the free-standing rights, such as freedom of association or the right to respect for private and family life, although freedom of religion is specifically protected by Art 9.[4]

---

1   The problems arising from this is explored in Part 4 of this chapter, 'A single Equality Act'.
2   For a commentary on the recent Directives and the Human Rights Act 1998, see Fredman, S, 'Equality: a new generation?' [2001] ILJ 145.
3   Human Rights Act 1998 (Commencement No 2) Order 2000, SI 2000/1851.
4   The 12th Protocol provides a free-standing right against discrimination. It has been adopted, but has yet to be ratified and the UK Government are not likely to ratify it in the foreseeable future. For a discussion of the protocol, see Moon, G (2000) 1 EHRLR 49; Schokkenbroek, J, 'Towards a stronger European protection against discrimination: the preparation of a new additional protocol to the ECHR' and Cooper, J, 'Applying equality and non-discrimination rights through the Human Rights Act 1998', both in *Race Discrimination*, 2000, Oxford: Hart; and Khaliq, V, 'Protocol 12 to the ECHR: a step forward or a step too far?' [2001] PL 457.

2   THE RELATIONSHIP OF DOMESTIC, EC AND HUMAN RIGHTS LEGISLATION

(1)   Supremacy of EC Law

The basic legal foundation of the European Community is the Treaty of Rome, although its subsequent amendment means that it is now more accurate to refer to it as the European Community Treaty (or EC Treaty). European Community law has supremacy over domestic law.

> *Costa v ENEL* **Case 6/64 [1964] ECR 585; [1964] CMLR 425:**
>
> *Judgment (p 586):*
>
> By contrast with ordinary international treaties, the EEC Treaty has created its own legal system which, on the entry into force of the Treaty, became an integral part of the legal systems of the Member States and which their courts are bound to apply ... [T]he Member States have limited their sovereign rights, albeit within limited fields, and have thus created a body of law which binds both their nationals and themselves ...
>
> The transfer by the States from their domestic legal system to the Community legal system of the rights and obligations arising under the Treaty carries with it a permanent limitation of their sovereign rights, against which a subsequent unilateral act incompatible with the concept of the Community cannot prevail.[5]

Community law gives rights to, and creates obligations on, individuals as well as Member States, unlike treaties governed by conventional international law doctrine, which tend only to bind the State parties.

> *Amministrazione delle Finanze v Simmenthal* **Case 106/77 [1978] ECR 629:[6]**
>
> *Judgment (pp 643–44):*
>
> [The Treaty provisions are] a direct source of rights and duties for all those affected thereby, whether Member States or individuals, who are parties to legal relationships under Community law ...
>
> Furthermore, in accordance with the precedence of Community law, the relationship between provisions of the Treaty and directly applicable measures of the institutions on the one hand and the national law of the Member States on the other is such that those provisions and measures not only by their entry into force render automatically inapplicable any conflicting provision of current national law but ... also preclude the valid adoption of new national legislative measures to the extent to which they would be incompatible with Community provisions ...
>
> It follows ... that every national court must ... apply Community law in its entirety and protect rights which the latter confers on individuals and must accordingly set aside any provision of national law which may conflict with it, whether prior or subsequent to the Community rule.[7]

---

5   This principle forms part of UK domestic law as a result of the European Communities Act 1972, ss 2 and 3.

6   See also [1978] 3 CMLR 263.

7   See also *Van Gend en Loos v Niederlandse Administratie der Belastingen* Case 26/62 [1963] ECR 1; [1963] CMLR 105.

(2)   Direct Effect of EC Treaty Articles

The doctrine of the supremacy of Community law makes it necessary to determine the precise mechanism by which provisions of the Treaty take effect within the domestic law of the Member States. One essential question is whether a Treaty Article may have only *vertical* direct effect (creating an obligation on the State to the individual) or whether it has also *horizontal* direct effect (creating obligations between individuals). In the context of EC discrimination law, that amounts to a question of whether or not private employers – as well as State employers – can be sued by a worker.

Defrenne v SABENA Case 43/75 [1976] ECR 455[8]

Sabena, a Belgium airline, paid their male air stewards more than their hostesses, although their jobs were identical. Ms Defrenne brought an equal pay claim under Art 119 (now Art 141). Sabena argued that that as Art 119 was primarily concerned with relationships between private employers and their workers, it was not suitable to be given direct effect.

Judgment (para 39):

> ... the prohibition on discrimination between men and women applies not only to the action of public authorities, but also extends to all agreements which are intended to regulate paid labour collectively, as well as to contracts between individuals.

Thus, Art 119 (now Art 141) is directly effective, vertically and horizontally, requiring no implementation by Member States. It can therefore be utilised by individuals against employers in both the public and the private sector. The rights thereby conferred may be enforced by individuals despite there being no equivalent right under domestic legislation. In such a case, the applicant will be relying on the precise wording of the Treaty, which itself becomes part of domestic law. It follows that in the event of a conflict between domestic law and Art 119, the latter must prevail. Thus, the direct effectiveness of Art 119 necessarily implies that in some cases the provisions of domestic law are overridden and cannot be applied, because of the overriding principle that EC law is supreme.[9]

(3)   Direct Effect of Directives

Directives are addressed to governments of Member States rather than to individuals, requiring each government, within a specified time period, to amend domestic law so as to ensure that the requirements of the directive are complied with. The precise way in which that is done is a matter for each Member State. The question here is what is the legal effect of the directive should the Member State not implement it properly, or at all. The answer was given in *Marshall*.

---

8   See also [1976] 2 CMLR 98; [1976] ICR 547.

9   See, eg, *Macarthys Ltd v Smith* Case 129/79 [1980] ECR 1275; [1981] QB 180; [1981] 1 All ER 11; [1980] IRLR 210, in which the claim was brought against an individual. In *R v Secretary of State for Employment ex p Equal Opportunities Commission* [1995] 1 AC 1; [1994] ICR 317; [1994] 1 All ER 910; [1994] IRLR 176, the EOC obtained a declaration that British unfair dismissal legislation was contrary to Art 119 and the Equal Treatment Directive because in affording part-time workers (predominately female) less rights, it indirectly discriminated against women. The decision thus disapplies domestic legislation.

Marshall v Southampton and South West Hampshire AHA Case 152/84 [1986] IRLR 140:[10]

Judgment (p 149):

[W]herever the provisions of a directive appear, so far as their subject matter is concerned, to be unconditional and sufficiently precise, those provisions may be relied on by an individual against the State where that State fails to implement the directive in national law by the end of the period prescribed or where it fails to implement the directive correctly ...

[T]he binding nature of a directive, which constitutes the basis for the possibility of relying on the directive before a national court, exists only in relation to each Member State to which it is addressed. It follows that a directive may not of itself impose obligations on an individual and that a provision of a directive may not be relied on as such against such a person.

[W]here a person ... is able to rely on a directive as against the State he may do so regardless of the capacity in which the latter is acting, whether employer or public authority. In either case it is necessary to prevent the State from taking advantage of its own failure to comply with Community law.

So a directive has direct *vertical* effect, but not horizontal effect. Of course, the disadvantage of this approach is that whether there is a remedy depends entirely on whether the defendant is a State or an individual employer. The anomaly is defendable because it would be unjust to permit State organs to rely on the State's own failure to implement the directive in question. Note that a directive cannot be directly effective before its time limit for implementation has expired.[11]

Another consequence of the European Court of Justice (ECJ)'s limiting of the direct effectiveness of directives to vertical direct effect against the Member State is a natural tendency to construe the notion of 'the State' widely. In *Foster v British Gas*,[12] the ECJ said this included 'a body, whatever its legal form, which has been made responsible, pursuant to a measure adopted by the State, for providing a public service under the control of the State and has for that purpose special powers beyond those which result from the normal rules applicable to relations between individuals is included in any event among the bodies against which the provisions of a directive capable of having direct effect may be relied upon'.[13] This included the nationalised British Gas Corporation.[14]

There are three subsequent English domestic cases on the point. In *Doughty v Rolls-Royce Ltd*,[15] the Court of Appeal held that Rolls-Royce, even when in public ownership, was not part of the State as, even though it was under State control, it was neither a public service nor dependent on special powers granted by the State in the same sense as British Gas had been. In *Griffin v South West Water Services Ltd*,[16] the High Court held that a privatised water company was an emanation of the State, as it provided a particular service under the control of the State which derived from special

---

10 See also [1986] ECR 723; [1986] 1 QB 401; [1986] ICR 335.
11 *Pubblico Ministero v Ratti* Case 148/78 [1979] ECR 1629.
12 Case C-188/89 [1990] 3 All ER 897; [1990] IRLR 353; [1990] ECR I-3133.
13 *Ibid*, at para 20.
14 *Foster v British Gas* [1991] 2 AC 306, HL.
15 [1992] IRLR 126, CA.
16 [1995] IRLR 15; High Court, ChD.

statutory powers granted to it. Finally, in *National Union of Teachers v Governing Body of St Mary's Church of England (Aided) Junior School*,[17] the Court of Appeal considered that the concept of an emanation of the State was very broad, embracing all organs of administration; there was no one exclusive formula to resolve the issue and the approach of the ECJ in *Foster* had not suggested otherwise. Furthermore, the estoppel rationale of *Marshall* itself supports a wide view. Voluntary aided schools rely significantly on the State, which has considerable control and influence over them, and thus they are sufficiently closely tied to the State education system to be regarded as an emanation of it.[18]

(a)   Indirect effect – construing domestic law to conform with Community law[19]

Where a directive does not have direct effect, a claimant may still have a remedy if the domestic legislation can be interpreted conform to the directive. This is *indirect* effect. It was declared by the ECJ in *Van Colson*, but unenthusiastically applied by the House of Lords in *Duke v GEC*. The ECJ responded in *Marleasing* by removing the obstacles expressed by the House of Lords.

Von Colson and Kamann v Land Nordrhein-Westfalen Case 14/83 [1984] ECR 1891:[20]

Judgment (p 1909):

[T]he Member States' obligation arising from a directive to achieve the result envisaged by the directive and their duty under Art 5 [now Art 10] of the Treaty to take all appropriate measures ... to ensure the fulfilment of that obligation, is binding on all the authorities of Member States ... including the courts. It follows that, in applying the national law and in particular the provisions of a national law specifically introduced in order to implement [a directive], national courts are required to interpret their national law in the light of the wording and the purpose of the directive in order to achieve the [required] result ...[21]

Duke v GEC Reliance [1988] IRLR 118, HL[22]

The issue here was whether the exclusion concerning provisions relating to retirement which was contained in the SDA 1975 could or should be interpreted so as to conform to the requirements of the Equal Treatment Directive. It was argued for the applicant that, in the light of *Marshall*, the exception should be interpreted narrowly so as to refer only to the consequences of retirement, but not to the age of retirement.

---

17 [1997] ICR 334; [1997] IRLR 242, CA.

18 For comment, see Eady, J, 'Emanation of the State. *National Union of Teachers and Others v Governing Body of St Mary's Church of England (Aided) Junior School and Others*' (1997) 26 ILJ 248.

19 See Craig, P, 'Directives: direct effect, indirect effect and the construction of national legislation' (1997) 22 EL Rev 519.

20 See also [1986] 2 CMLR 430.

21 For leading examples of the way in which domestic courts have reacted to the *Von Colson* imperative, see *Litster v Forth Dry Dock and Engineering Co* [1990] 1 AC 546; [1989] ICR 341; [1989] IRLR 161 (a case on the Transfer of Undertakings Regulations 1981); *Pickstone v Freemans plc* [1989] AC 66; [1988] ICR 697; [1988] IRLR 357 (an equal pay case), and *Webb v EMO Air Cargo (UK) Ltd* Case C-32/93; [1994] ECR I–3537; [1994] QB 718; [1994] ICR 770; [1994] IRLR 482; and [1995] ICR 1021; [1995] IRLR 645, HL (a pregnancy case – see below, pp 199–202).

22 See also [1988] AC 618; [1988] ICR 639.

Lord Templeman (pp 122–23):

Of course a British court will always be willing and anxious to conclude that United Kingdom law is consistent with Community law. Where an Act is passed for the purpose of giving effect to an obligation imposed by a directive or other instrument, a British court will seldom encounter difficulty in concluding that the language of the Act is effective for the intended purpose. But the construction of a British Act of Parliament is a matter of judgment to be determined by British courts and to be derived from the language of the legislation considered in the light of the circumstance prevailing at the date of enactment ... [The Equal Pay Act (EPA) 1970 and the Sex Discrimination Act (SDA) 1975] were not passed to give effect to the Equal Treatment Directive and were intended to preserve discriminatory retirement ages ... [T]he words of s 6(4) [of the unamended SDA 1975] are not reasonably capable of being limited to the meaning ascribed to them by the appellant. Section 2(4) of the European Communities Act 1972 does not ... enable or constrain a British court to distort the meaning of a British statute in order to enforce against an individual a Community directive which has no direct effect between individuals.

This case lays down the principle that domestic legislation, especially that passed before the directive in question, should only be construed so as to conform with the directive if capable of being interpreted in that way. The following case casts doubt on that limiting principle, holding that there is an obligation on national courts to construe national legislation so far as possible so as to ensure conformity with a directive.[23]

Marleasing SA v La Comercial Internacional de Alimentacion SA Case C-106/89 [1990] ECR I-4135:[24]

Judgment (p 4159):

[T]he Member States' obligation arising from a directive to achieve the result envisaged by the directive and their duty under Art 5 of the Treaty to take all appropriate measures ... to ensure the fulfilment of their obligation, is binding on all the authorities of Member States including ... the courts. It follows that, in applying national law, whether the provisions in question were adopted before or after the directive, the national court called upon to interpret it is required to do so, as far as possible, in the light of the wording and the purpose of the directive in order to achieve the result pursued by the latter ...

Clearly, there is tension between the ECJ and domestic courts here. As we shall see in the forthcoming chapters, British courts have not always been as reluctant as the House of Lords in *Duke v GEC*, but the record is a mixed one.

---

23   See Docksey, C and Fitzpatrick, B, 'The duty of national courts to interpret provisions of national law in accordance with Community law' [1991] 20 ILJ 113.

24   See also [1992] 1 CMLR 305.

(4)   Actions against the State – the *Francovich* Principle

An individual may suffer financial loss as a result of a State's failure to implement a directive or implement it correctly. In such a case, there may be a remedy against the State.[25] This principle was established in *Francovich*.

Francovich and Others v Italian State Cases C-6/90 and C-9/90 [1992] IRLR 84:[26]

Judgment (p 88):

The full effectiveness of Community rules would be impaired and the protection of the rights which they grant would be weakened if individuals were unable to obtain redress when their rights are infringed by a breach of Community law for which a Member State can be held responsible.

It follows that the principle whereby a State must be liable for loss and damage caused to individuals as a result of breaches of Community law for which the State can be held responsible is inherent in the system of the Treaty.

[T]he full effectiveness of that rule of Community law requires that there should be a right to reparation provided that three conditions are fulfilled.

The first of those conditions is that the result prescribed by the directive should entail the grant of rights to individuals. The second condition is that it should be possible to identify the content of those rights on the basis of the provisions of the directive. Finally, the third condition is the existence of a causal link between the breach of the State's obligation and damage suffered by the injured parties.

(5)   Enforcement and Interpretation of EC Law

Many key sex discrimination cases have arisen where a national court has referred a case to the ECJ under Art 234 (formerly Art 177) of the EC Treaty for clarification of EC law.[27] Such cases, from whichever Member State they originate, become law which an English court is bound to apply.[28]

A further way in which EC law develops is through the procedure under Art 226 (formerly Art 169), which enables the European Commission to bring a Member State before the European Court alleging failure to comply with a Treaty obligation.[29] There are numerous cases where the UK has been found wanting under this provision. From the sex equality perspective, the most important is *Commission of the European*

---

25 In *Secretary of State for Employment v Mann* [1997] ICR 200, CA, it was held that such claims had to be instituted in the High Court and could not be made before an Industrial Tribunal, as the latter's jurisdiction was entirely governed by statute. This decision was not contested in the House of Lords: [1999] ICR 898.

26 See also [1991] ECR I-5357; [1995] ICR 722.

27 See Ellis, E and Tridimas, T, *Public Law of the European Community: Text, Materials and Commentary*, 1995, London: Sweet & Maxwell, pp 466–92.

28 Eg, in *Bilka-Kaufhaus v Weber von Hartz* Case 170/84 [1986] ECR 1607; [1986] 2 CMLR 701; [1987] ICR 110; [1986] IRLR 317, it was held to be unlawful to exclude part-time workers from occupational pension schemes unless the employer could demonstrate that such exclusion was justified.

29 *Op cit*, Ellis and Tridimas, fn 27, pp 340–60.

Communities v United Kingdom[30] which held that the then existing British equal pay law failed to comply with Art 119 (now Art 141) and the Equal Pay Directive in that it had no provision for a woman to allege that her work was of equal value to that of a man (rather than 'same work').[31] A finding of breach under this procedure does not automatically change domestic law, but both the political pressures and the likelihood of claims based on *Francovich* are likely to bring about such change. In this instance, the EqPA 1970 was amended by the Equal Pay (Amendment) Regulations 1983.[32]

(6)   The Human Rights Act 1998[33]

Many cases of discrimination will fall outside of the legislative scheme. For instance, discrimination on the grounds of sexual orientation or religion or gender reassignment, in the fields of the provision of services or housing are not covered by specific legislation. However, such cases *may* be covered by the European Convention on Human Rights (ECHR), which has been incorporated into domestic law by the Human Rights Act 1998. The European Convention, and the Court of Human Rights (ECtHR), are separate from the European Union, although, as we shall see, there are important similarities and connections between the two.

The Convention gives no free-standing right against discrimination,[34] but Art 14 does provide that the rights in the convention must be 'secured' without discrimination 'on any ground such as sex, race, colour, language, religion, political or other opinion, national or social origin, association with a national minority, property, birth or other status'. Not only are the specific examples far wider than current domestic or European anti-discrimination legislation, it is clear that the use of the words 'such as' mean that other unstated grounds for discrimination might contravene the Article. 'The Strasbourg authorities have characterised a large number of "other statuses", including sexual orientation, marital status, illegitimacy, status as a trade union, military status, conscientious objection, professional status and imprisonment as falling within this residual category.'[35] Further, the Court of Appeal

---

30 Case 61/81 [1982] ECR 2601; [1982] ICR 578; [1982] IRLR 333. See, also, *Commission of the European Communities v United Kingdom* Case 165/82 [1983] ECR 3431; [1984] 1 All ER 353; [1984] ICR 192; [1984] IRLR 29, which concerned three allegations of failure to comply with the Equal Treatment Directive and was one of the progenitors of the Sex Discrimination Act 1986.

31 The Treaty of Amsterdam amended Art 119, now Art 141, so that it now specifically refers to work of equal value.

32 SI 1983/1794.

33 See Foster, N, 'The European Court of Justice and the European Convention for the Protection of Human Rights' (1987) 8 Human Rights LJ 245; Aras, Y, 'The ECHR and non-discrimination' (1998) 7 *Amicus Curiae*, the Journal of the Society for Advanced Legal Studies 6. See generally, Clarke, B (Editor), *Challenging Racism*, 2003, London: Lawrence & Wishart, in association with the Discrimination Law Association, ILPA, Cre and 1990 Trust. See also Chapter 16, pp 515–16.

34 The 12th Protocol provides a free-standing right against discrimination. It has been adopted, but not yet ratified and the UK Government are not likely to ratify it in the foreseeable future. For a discussion of the Protocol, see Moon, G (2000) 1 EHRLR 49; Schokkenbroek, J, 'Towards a stronger European protection against discrimination: the preparation of a new additional protocol to the ECHR' and Cooper, J, 'Applying equality and non-discrimination rights through the Human Rights Act 1998', both in *Race Discrimination*, 2000, Oxford: Hart; and Khaliq, V, 'Protocol 12 to the ECHR: a step forward or a step too far?' [2001] PL 457.

35 Harris, D, O'Boyle, M and Warbrick, C, *Law of the European Convention on Human Rights*, 1995, London: Butterworths, Chapter 9, fn 43, p 470.

observed in *Mendoza v Ghaidan*:[36] 'As it is put in Grosz, Beatson & Duffy, *Human Rights* (2000), § C14-10: "It would appear, however, that even the most tenuous link with another provision in the Convention will suffice for Article 14 to enter into play ..."'

The free-standing rights given by the Convention are to life (Art 2), against torture (Art 3) and slavery (Art 4), to liberty (Art 5) and a fair trial (Art 6), against punishment without law (Art 7), to respect for family and private life (Art 8), to freedom of thought, conscience and religion (Art 9), to freedom of expression (Art 10), assembly and association (Art 11) and to marry (Art 12).

The way in which the ECtHR has interpreted the concept of discrimination shows similarities to EC jurisprudence, but is less fully developed. In order to establish discrimination, the applicant has to show less favourable treatment than of another person in an analogous situation. The State defendant then has the opportunity to justify the discriminatory measure. In other words, direct discrimination is potentially justifiable.[37] In the *Belgian Linguistic*[38] case, the Court held that the non-discrimination principle was only violated if the measure had 'no reasonable and objective justification. The existence of such a justification must be assessed in relation to the aim and effects of the measure under consideration'. The objective of the measure must be legitimate, and the means chosen must be both appropriate and proportionate to that objective. While the criteria appear relatively stringent, the manner of their interpretation has been less so. It is normally not difficult for States to show that the policy under challenge has a rational aim. As regards the means chosen, the Court is relatively deferential to what is termed the 'margin of appreciation', that is, the State's discretion as to the appropriate manner in which to achieve its policy objectives. This resembles the ECJ's approach to indirect discrimination, that a measure must be 'appropriate and necessary' to achieve the aim, but allowing a State a 'margin of appreciation' in the pursuance of social and employment policies.[39]

Section 6 of the Human Rights Act (HRA) 1998 states that it is 'unlawful' for a public authority, which includes the courts and tribunals, to act in a way incompatible with the Convention. Section 2 provides that a court or tribunal, when determining a Convention right, must take into account the jurisprudence of the ECtHR. Accordingly, the judiciary at every level will be exposed to new forms of reasoning.

In the USA, there is a twin-track system of anti-discrimination law, the private law model based on the 1964 Civil Rights Act, and the public law model based on the 14th amendment to the Constitution, which guarantees to everyone the equal protection of the law. This area has been especially significant in the law on affirmative action. For example, cases on the admissions policies of universities[40] and on the policy of a city

---

36   [2002] 4 All ER 1162; [2002] EWCA Civ 1533, at para 9. See also Livingstone, S, 'Article 14 and the prevention of discrimination in the ECHR' (1997) 1 EHRR 25.

37   For a discussion on whether direct discrimination generally should be justifiable see Bowers, J and Moran, E, 'Justification in direct discrimination law: breaking the taboo' [2002] 31 ILJ 307. For a response see Gill, T and Monaghan, K, 'Justification in direct sex discrimination law: taboo upheld' [2003] 32 ILJ 115.

38   Belgian Police and Swedish Engine Drivers Union cases, respectively (1975) 1 EHRR 578; (1975) 1 EHRR 617.

39   See, eg, *R v Secretary of State for Employment ex p Seymour-Smith* Case C-167/97 [1999] All ER (EC) 97 ECJ, at paras 74–75, considered in Chapter 10.

40   *Regents of the University of California v Bakke* 435 US 265 (1978).

to allocate at least 30% of its contracting work to minority businesses[41] have been argued under the Equal Protection clause rather than the specific provisions of the Civil Rights Act 1964. In the UK, the private law model has been, with rare exceptions, the only game in town. It is a matter for speculation whether, in 10 or 20 years time, incorporation of the ECHR will have increased the scope for public law rights and remedies to be at least one of the jurisprudential models around which discrimination cases are resolved.

Two further, more general points may be made. First, the ECHR is concerned with individual and not with group rights. The Convention is not primarily concerned to protect minority rights, though this may be a side effect of its jurisprudence. It follows that there can be no *redistributive* thrust to Art 14. Secondly, a holding that a State has violated ECHR imposes an obligation on that State to ensure non-repetition, often via a change in domestic law. It does not, in itself, provide a remedy for the individual whose rights have been violated. This is especially the case under the HRA 1998, where the only 'remedy' may be a 'declaration of incompatibility' between a Convention right and domestic law.[42] This will frequently act as a disincentive to the bringing of individual claims. It may be more promising to argue that the specific discrimination legislation should be interpreted in the light of ECHR, rather than simply alleging a breach of the Convention.

One also has to consider the part of European Community law in all of this. The Convention has not been incorporated into Community law. However, the ECJ will follow the Convention's principles.[43] Accordingly, claims under Community discrimination law may rely on the Convention, and the decisions under it by the ECtHR. This becomes particularly significant if the claim pre-dates the incorporation of the Convention into UK law (by the HRA 1998 on 2 October 2000). Where a domestic court must apply Community law, it must apply Convention principles, even in cases where the HRA is not applicable. The point was illustrated in *A v Chief Constable of West Yorkshire*.

A v Chief Constable of West Yorkshire (2002) *The Times*; 14 November; [2002] EWCA 1584; [2002] All ER (D) 50, CA:

The claimant was a male-to-female transsexual and was refused a job as a police constable. She made a claim of sex discrimination. The Chief Constable defended by stating that police searches had to be carried out by a person of the same sex as the person searched (s 54(9) of the Police and Criminal Evidence Act 1984) and as the claimant, who now considered herself a woman, was *legally* a man, this was not possible. He therefore relied on the 'Genuine Occupational Qualification' given in s 7 of the SDA 1975. After the decisions of the Employment Tribunal and the EAT, the ECtHR, in *Goodwin v UK*,[44] held that a reassigned transsexual was entitled to a birth certificate to reflect her present sex. A's case now came to the Court of Appeal, which held that in light of *Goodwin*, the claimant could now be treated *legally* as a woman.[45]

---

41 *City of Richmond v JA Croson* 488 US 469 (1989).

42 HRA 1998, s 4.

43 See, eg, *R v Kirk* Case 63/83 [1984] 2 ECR 2689; 3 CMLR 522; [1985] 1 All ER 453; *Johnston v Chief Constable of the Royal Ulster Constabulary* Case 222/84 [1986] ECR 1651; [1986] 3 CMLR 240; [1987] QB 129; [1986] 3 WLR 1038; [1987] ICR 83; [1986] 3 All ER 135.

44 [2002] EHRR 447; [2002] 2 FCR 577. See Chapter 6, p 158.

45 At the time of writing an appeal was due in the House of Lords.

Buxton LJ:

33   ... I consider that this case must be determined according to the law as set out in *Goodwin*. I was not persuaded by [the] ... argument that the state of the law as perceived in *Goodwin* should be held to apply only from the date of that ruling by the Strasbourg court, and that therefore the Chief Constable's decision, which predated the ruling in *Goodwin*, should be adjudicated upon according to the pre-*Goodwin* law. That the law at the time at which he made his decision was uncertain is of course another factor that goes towards acquitting the Chief Constable of any actual fault ... However, as a matter of human rights law the court has to apply the law as it is now developed by the Convention organs. And I am fortified in that view by the consideration that, as set out below, the Convention jurisprudence enters domestic law in this case because of its status in Community law. It has always been assumed in Community jurisprudence that decisions on the meaning of the treaties apply *ex tunc*, that is, from the date of the treaty and not from the date of the decision; the much controverted decision to the contrary in Case 43/75 *Defrenne v Sabena* [1976] ECR 455 [69]–[75] being the exception that proves that rule ...

41   ... it is important to be clear that *Goodwin* decides that it will be a breach of article 8 [Respect for Private Life] in cases 'where there are no significant factors of public interest to weigh against the interest of this individual applicant in obtaining legal recognition of her gender re-assignment', to refuse to recognise that re-assigned gender [*Goodwin*, §93]. Accordingly, in any case to which the Human Rights Act 1998 [the HRA] applies, it will in future be necessary to consider whether a failure or refusal to treat a post-operative transsexual as being of the reassigned gender involves a breach of Article 8. Since the application of article 8 is case-specific, and does not confer absolute rights, the court will have to consider in every case whether the subject's interest in achieving respect and recognition for her gender re-assignment is outweighed by countervailing considerations of the public interest.

42   In the present case we have to add the fact that, because of the date at which the acts complained of took place, the Convention jurisprudence is introduced into domestic law not by the medium of the HRA, but by the medium of the Equal Treatment Directive [ETD]. That means that not only is any case subject to the considerations of balance already referred to, but also that the ETD, and thus the potential breach of article 8, does not, as it would under the HRA, potentially arise in connexion with every issue arising in domestic law, but rather only applies in relation to the employment field to which the ETD is limited.

3   THE JUDICIARY

(1)   The Common Law

The common law has never developed general principles of equality or non-discrimination. This may be the result of the common law being reactive in nature and its tradition of freedom of contract.[46] The general position is explained by Jowell.

---

46   Robilliard, St John A, 'Should Parliament enact a Religious Discrimination Act?' [1978] PL 379, p 380.

Jowell, J, 'Is equality a constitutional principle? (1994) 47 CLP (Part 2, Collected Papers) 1, pp 4–91:

In elaborating the rule of law Dicey said that 'With us every official, from the Prime Minister down to a constable or collector of taxes, is under the same responsibility for every act done without legal justification as any other citizen.' Dicey is here espousing a concept of what has been called formal equality, by which he meant that no person was exempt from the enforcement of the law. Rich and poor, revenue official and individual taxpayer are all within equal reach of the arm of the law.

... Its reach however is limited because its primary concern is not with the content of the law but with its *enforcement* and *application* alone. The Rule of Law is satisfied so long as laws are applied and enforced equally, that is evenhandedly, free of bias and without irrational distinction. The Rule of Law requires formal equality which prohibits laws from being enforced unequally, but it does not require substantive equality. It does not therefore prohibit unequal laws. It constrains, say, racially bias enforcement of laws, but does not inhibit apartheid-style laws from being enacted.

... we find some ancient duties placed [by the common law] upon the likes of innkeepers, common carriers and some monopoly enterprises such as ports and harbours, to accept all travellers and others who are 'in a fit and reasonable condition to be received'.

A rare (if not only) example of one of these 'ancient duties' coinciding with racial discrimination arose in *Constantine v Imperial Hotels*,[47] where the black West Indian cricketer (and later a member of the Race Relations Board) was refused accommodation for fear of upsetting white American soldiers. The King's Bench Division awarded Constantine nominal damages for the breach of the innkeepers' duty to receive all travellers. The general attitude of the common law towards specific cases of equality and discrimination was epitomised by the House of Lords in *Roberts v Hopwood*.

Roberts v Hopwood [1925] AC 578, HL

By s 62 of the Metropolis Management Act 1855, Metropolitan Borough Councils were empowered to allow wages to workers as the Council 'may think fit'. Poplar Borough Council paid to its lowest grade of workers, whether men or women, a minimum wage of £4 per week. The council considered that as a model employer, this was the minimum wage that should be paid. The district auditor found that these payments were not wages but gratuities to the employees, and were unlawful. The House of Lords agreed.

Lord Atkinson (at pp 594 and 599):

[A]s wages are remuneration for services, the words 'think fit' must, I think, be construed to mean 'as the employer shall think fitting and proper' for the services rendered. It cannot, in my view, mean that the employer, especially an employer dealing with moneys not entirely his own, may pay to his employee wages of any amount he pleases. Still less does it mean that he can pay gratuities or gifts to his employees disguised under the name of wages. The only rational way by which harmony of administration can be introduced into the various departments of Local Government covered by s 62 of the Act of 1855, and by the several more recent statutes aforesaid, is by holding that in each and every case the payment of all salaries and wages must be 'reasonable.' I see no difficulty in so construing the words of s 62.

---

47   [1944] 1 KB 693, KBD.

(2)   Judicial Statutory Interpretation[48]

Although the common law has failed to develop substantive principles of equality and non-discrimination, the judiciary plays a major part in the development of discrimination law in their role as interpreters of the legislation. There are many theories of statutory interpretation, from 'framer's intent' to 'living tree',[49] from 'literal' to 'purposive'. Most cases fall into the literal/purposive dichotomy.

For English judges, the literal rule of interpretation has its roots in the constitutional settlement of 1688. Article 9 of the Bill of Rights proclaimed that '... the freedom of speech and debates or proceedings in Parlyament ought not to be impeached or questioned in any court or place out of Parlyament'. By the Victorian era, the deference afforded to statutory words by the judiciary amounted to a rule of interpretation that would do no more than give the words their literal meaning.[50] The consequence is that a judge cannot go behind the face of the statute to discover its meaning and purpose, even if the result is absurd. In *Fisher v Bell*,[51] the defendant displayed flick-knives in his shop window with price tags attached. He was charged under the Restriction of Offensive Weapons Act 1959, which made it an offence to 'offer for sale' offensive weapons. The defendant was acquitted because, under contract law, goods on display were not capable of being an offer in the sense that such an offer could be accepted to form a contract. Quite clearly, the purpose of the statute was defeated by this decision, which relied on no more than the literal meaning of the word 'offer'. For the court, the problem was one to be resolved by Parliament, which subsequently amended the statute with the phrase 'offer or display for sale'. A consequence of the literal rule was ever more complex Acts of Parliament with torturous formulas to cover every imagined scenario within the statutes' purpose.[52] In more recent years, some movement from this position could be detected. Some judges began to reject the literal approach and gave words their 'natural' and 'ordinary' meaning,[53] but this was not universal. Another development came in *Pepper v Hart*,[54] where the House of Lords ruled that in cases of ambiguity, a court could look to parliamentary debates to resolve the meaning of a statute. But this practice is the exception, rather than the rule. The third development undermining the literal rule is the increasing need for judges to interpret the legislation of the EC. This law is entrenched in the 'Purposive' school of interpretation. European legislation spells out general principles for the judiciary to develop and apply. That has always been the practice of the ECJ. Britain's obligations under EU membership require the

---

48   See Barbera, M, 'Not the same? The judicial role in the new Community anti-discrimination law context' [2002] 31 ILJ 82.

49   *Per* Lord Sankey, *Edwards v AG of Canada* [1930] AC 124 PC, at 136. For an exploration into the Framer's Intent/Living Tree dichotomy, see Wilson, B, 'The making of a constitution' [1988] PLJ 370.

50   See Lord Bramwell, *Hill v E & W India Dock Co* (1884) 9 AC 448, HL, at 464–65 and later Lord Loreburn LC, *London & India Docks v Thames Steam & Lighterage* [1909] AC 15, HL, at 19, and Lord Atkinson, *Vacher & Sons v London Society of Compositors* [1913] AC 107, HL, at 121–22.

51   [1961] 1 QB 394.

52   Lord Diplock once remarked – in *Fothergill v Monarch Airlines* [1980] 3 WLR 209, at 222 – that 'the current style of legislative draftsmanship' was an 'unhappy legacy of this judicial attitude'.

53   See, eg, *Fothergill v Monarch Airlines* [1980] 3 WLR 209, HL and *Brutus v Cozens* [1973] AC 854, HL.

54   [1983] 1 All ER 42, HL.

judges to give its legislation a purposive interpretation. In *Litster v Forth Dry Dock & Engineering Co*,[55] the Regulations implementing the Acquired Rights Directive[56] provide that those employed immediately before a business is transferred shall be employed by the new business, or transferee. In this case, a new company, Forth Estuary Engineering, was set up to take over FDD, who were in receivership. The two companies colluded and the whole workforce was sacked one hour before the transfer in an attempt to evade the Regulations. The House of Lords held that, in order to serve the purpose of the Directive, the Regulations applied to this case, even though, literally, the workforce was not employed immediately before the transfer. Again, this approach is not universal practice. On occasion, the courts still use the literal rule when applying European law[57] and elsewhere English judges still employ the literal rule as their basic tool of statutory interpretation.

A fourth development that may change the judges' approach to statutory interpretation, at least so far as human rights are concerned, was the passing of the Human Rights Act 1998, which came into force in October 2000. This Act introduces the European Convention on Human Rights into domestic law.

The question is whether the Human Rights Act will usher in a universal purposive approach to all human rights legislation. A further question is whether any new approach will be applied to discrimination legislation, which at present is not specified *per se* by the Convention. The body of case law on the rights under the Act belongs to the Strasbourg European Court of Human Rights, which takes a purposive, rather than literal, approach. Domestic courts are obliged by s 2 of the HRA 1998 to take into account ECtHR jurisprudence and so ought to adopt a purposive approach when interpreting the Act.[58] The Judicial Studies Board was established to give judges training in applying the Act, but their specific training exercises remain confidential. There is some evidence upon which the British judicial approach to human rights legislation may be predicted. In the Privy Council, senior British judges preside over cases from the Commonwealth, some of which concern the interpretation a country's particular human rights legislation. In *AG for Gambia v Momodou Jobe*,[59] Lord Diplock said: 'A constitution ... which protects fundamental human rights ... is to be given a generous and purposive interpretation.'[60] However, in *Robinson v The Queen*,[61] the defendant's trial for murder – a hanging offence – was adjourned 19 times. On the 20th, his lawyer resigned because, apparently, his fees were unpaid. The trial judge was keen not to lose a key witness and so persisted with the trial, even though the defendant had no representation. He was convicted and appealed to the Privy Council under the Jamaican Bill of Rights, which provided that every person on trial for a capital offence shall be *permitted* to be represented by a lawyer. Lord Roskill examined

---

55   [1989] ICR 341, HL.

56   The Transfer of Undertakings (Protection of Employment) Regulations 1981 implementing Council Directive 77/187/EEC.

57   See, eg, *Secretary of State v Spence* [1986] ICR 651, CA, actually approved (albeit distinguished) by Lord Oliver in *Litster*.

58   In *Barclays Bank v Ellis* (unreported, 9 August 2000, CA), Schiemann LJ stated: '... if Counsel wish to rely on provisions of the Human Rights Act then it is their duty to have available ... decisions of the European Court of Human Rights upon which they wish to rely or which will help the court in its adjudication.'

59   [1984] 3 WLR 174.

60   *Ibid* at p 183b.

61   [1985] 2 All ER 594.

the statutory word *permitted* and concluded that it did not give an *absolute right* to a defence lawyer. He held that the trial accorded with the Bill of Rights and sent Mr Robinson to his death following a trial without legal representation.[62] Lords Keith and Templeman concurred. Lords Scarman and Edmund-Davies dissented, preferring a purposive construction of the Bill of Rights.[63]

An alternative to this literal/purposive dichotomy is provided by Lord Browne-Wilkinson who argues that English judges, when interpreting statutes, merely 'seek to ensure that the meritorious triumph and the dirty dogs lick their wounds'.[64] The point is that the decision is made on moral grounds, but articulated on legal reasoning. That may explain why no one approach is universal. In recent years, judges may have simply identified the 'dirty dog' and then chosen the reasoning, be it literal, 'ordinary', 'natural' or purposive as a matter of convenience to justify the decision. The HRA 1998 will change this in two ways, according to Lord Browne-Wilkinson. Judgments on the Act will be made *and* articulated on moral grounds, but this will no longer be the moral standpoint of the individual judge, but the code of morals developed, *inter alia*, by the Strasbourg Court of Human Rights and the social and political realities of the day. This approach resembles the 'living tree' school of interpretation articulated by Lord Sankey in *Edwards v AG of Canada*,[65] which holds that legislation of constitutional nature should be read according to the values of the present day, as opposed to the time it was enacted. Meanwhile, Lord Woolf has stated that 'judges should be robust in resisting inappropriate' arguments based on the Human Rights Act.[66] The judgments in *Ahmad v ILEA* illustrate the living tree/framer's intent dichotomy.

Ahmad v Inner London Education Authority [1978] QB 36; [1978] 1 All ER 574, CA

The applicant teacher was a devout Muslim who felt it was his religious duty to attend a Mosque each Friday afternoon. The authority terminated his full-time contract and offered him a contract for four-and-a-half days each week, excluding Friday afternoon. He refused to accept the offer, resigned and lost his claim for constructive unfair dismissal. The Court of Appeal, with Lord Scarman dissenting, dismissed his appeal. Lord Scarman's dissent represents the 'living tree' approach whilst the majority's reasoning represented the 'framer's intent'.

Lord Denning (at p 39):

On the appeal, Mr Ahmad relied much on section 30 of the Education Act 1944. It was a section inserted so as to safeguard the position of teachers. It said:

> ... no teacher ... shall be required to give religious instruction or receive any less emolument or be deprived of, or disqualified for, any promotion or other advantage by reason of the fact that he does or does not give religious instruction or by reason of his religious opinions or of his attending or omitting to attend religious worship: ...

---

62 Robinson was eventually reprieved following the intervention of the United Nations.
63 See also *Pratt v AG for Jamaica* [1993] 3 WLR 995, PC; *Riley v AG for Jamaica* [1985] 1 AC 719, PC.
64 In Markesinis (ed), *The Impact of the Human Rights Act on English Law*, 1998, Oxford: OUP, p 22.
65 [1930] AC 124, PC, at 136. See Wilson, B, 'The making of a constitution' [1988] PLJ 370.
66 *Daniels v Walker* (2000) *The Times*, 17 May.

If the words were read literally without qualification, they would entitle Mr Ahmad to take time off every Friday afternoon for his prayers without loss of pay. I cannot think this was ever intended ...

During the argument Scarman, LJ drew attention to article 9 [Freedom of Religion] of the European Convention on Human Rights ...

The convention is not part of our English law, but, as I have often said, we will always have regard to it. We will do our best to see that our decisions are in conformity with it. But it is drawn in such vague terms that it can be used for all sorts of unreasonable claims and provoke all sorts of litigation. As so often happens with high-sounding principles, they have to be brought down to earth. They have to be applied in a work-a-day world. I venture to suggest that it would do the Muslim community no good – or any other minority group no good – if they were to be given preferential treatment over the great majority of the people. If it should happen that, in the name of religious freedom, they were given special privileges or advantages, it would provoke discontent, and even resentment among those with whom they work. As, indeed, it has done in this very case. And so the cause of racial integration would suffer. So, whilst upholding religious freedom to the full, I would suggest that it should be applied with caution ... I see nothing in the European Convention to give Mr Ahmad any right to manifest his religion on Friday afternoons in derogation of his contract of employment: and certainly not on full pay.

Orr LJ (at p 44):

... I am unable to accept ... [Mr Ahmad's interpretation of s 30]. In the first place it is to be noted that the words 'shall ... receive any less emolument' do not appear in the earlier part of the section which applies both to teachers and to persons otherwise employed in a school and in my judgment it would be very surprising if a teacher were, but a domestic or clerical employee of a school were not, allowed to be absent during school hours without loss of pay for the purpose of attending religious worship. In the second place I do not think that the prohibition against receiving any less emolument can only have been directed to such a case as this. It is more likely, in my judgment, to have been inserted because there was thought to be a danger that a teacher might be offered a lower rate of remuneration either because he did or because he did not give religious instruction. Finally, if the provision was intended to permit a teacher to break his contract by absenting himself from school during school hours I would have expected much clearer and more specific language to be used.

Lord Scarman, dissenting (at p 46):

... there were until recently no substantial religious groupings in our country which fell outside the broad categories of Christian and Jew. So long as there was no discrimination between them, no problem was likely to arise. The five-day school week, of course, takes care of the Sabbath and of Sunday as days of special religious observance. But with the advent of new religious groups in our society section 30 assumes a new importance.

... society has changed since 1944: so also has the legal background. Religions, such as Islam and Buddhism, have substantial followings among our people. Room has to be found for teachers and pupils of the new religions in the educational system, if discrimination is to be avoided. This calls not for a policy of the blind eye but for one of understanding. The system must be made sufficiently flexible to accommodate their beliefs and their observances: otherwise, they will suffer discrimination – a consequence contrary to the spirit of section 30, whatever the letter of that law. The change in legal background is no less momentous. Since 1944 the United Kingdom has accepted international obligations designed to protect human rights and freedoms, and has enacted a series of statutes designed for the same purpose in certain critical areas of our society. These major statutes include the Trade Union and Labour Relations Act 1974, the Employment Protection Act 1975, the Sex Discrimination Act 1975, and the race relations legislation.

They were enacted after the United Kingdom had ratified the European Convention on Human Rights (signed November 1950: in force since September 3, 1953) and in the light of our obligations under the Charter of the United Nations. Today, therefore, we have to construe and apply section 30 not against the background of the law and society of 1944 but in a multi-racial society which has accepted international obligations and enacted statutes designed to eliminate discrimination on grounds of race, religion, colour or sex ...

With these general considerations in mind, I conclude that the present case, properly considered, begins but does not end with the law of contract. It ends with a very difficult problem – the application to the particular circumstances of this appellant of the new law associated with the protection of the individual's human rights and fundamental freedoms ...

The question is what the contract, which admittedly incorporates section 30, means. Is the section to be given a broad or a narrow construction? ...

A narrow construction of the section would mean that a Muslim, who took his religious duty seriously, could never accept employment as a full-time teacher, but must be content with the lesser emoluments of part-time service. In modern British society, with its elaborate statutory protection of the individual from discrimination arising from race, colour, religion or sex, and against the background of the European Convention, this is unacceptable, inconsistent with the policy of modern statute law, and almost certainly a breach of our international obligations. Unless, therefore, the language of section 30 forces one to adopt the narrow construction, I would think it wrong to do so. But it does not: the section, linguistically speaking, can be construed broadly or narrowly. No doubt, Parliament in 1944 never addressed its mind to the problem of this case. But, if the section lends itself, as successful human rights or constitutional legislation must lend itself, to judicial interpretation in accordance with the spirit of the age, there is nothing in this point, save for the comment that Parliament by refusing to be too specific was wiser than some of us have subsequently realised. The choice of construction, while it must be exercised judicially, is ours: for the reasons which I have attempted to formulate, the decision must be in favour of the broad construction.

It is easy to assume that some of Lord Denning's reluctance to advance the law for fear that the resulting 'preferential treatment' would do no good to race relations contains populist sentiment from a bygone era, where judges were afraid to stand up for the rights of unpopular minorities. However, some recent judicial statements have echoed that sentiment. Lord Woolf MR (as he then was) commented in 2000: 'To regard a person as acting unlawfully when he had not been motivated either consciously or unconsciously by any discriminatory motive is hardly likely to assist the objective of promoting harmonious racial relations.'[67] In 1999, Lord Browne-Wilkinson opined:

---

67 *Khan v Chief Constable of West Yorkshire* [2000] All ER (D) 237, CA, at para 14, a case on victimisation, where in spite of this opinion, Lord Woolf felt bound by precedent. However, his decision was reversed by the House of Lords, which underpinned his opinion: [2001] 1 WLR 1947; see Chapter 11, p 306.

To introduce something akin to strict liability into the [discrimination] Acts which will lead to individuals being stamped as racially discriminatory or victimisers where these matters were not consciously in their minds when they acted is unlikely to recommend the legislation to the public as being fair and proper protection for the minorities that they are seeking to protect.'[68]

Two recent and contrasting cases on discrimination under the HRA suggest that, in its early stages of dealing with the Act, the judiciary remain unpredictable.

Mendoza v Ghaidan [2002] 4 All ER 1162; [2002] EWCA Civ 1533, CA[69]

Paragraph 2 of Sched 1 to the Rent Act 1977 provided:

2(1) The surviving spouse (if any) of the original tenant, if residing in the dwelling-house immediately before the death of the original tenant, shall after the death be the statutory tenant if and so long as he or she occupies the dwelling-house as his or her residence.

(2) For the purposes of this paragraph, a person who was living with the original tenant as his or her wife or husband shall be treated as the spouse of the original tenant.

Mendoza and Mr Walwyn-Jones lived together in a same-sex relationship in Mr Walwyn-Jones' rented flat. When Mr Walwyn-Jones died, Mendoza claimed a right to succeed the tenancy under Sched 2 to the Rent Act 1977, relying in particular on para 2(2). The problem was that only recently the House of Lords, in *Fitzpatrick v Sterling HA*,[70] held that para 2(2) extended the right of succession only to unmarried heterosexual cohabitees. However, since *Fitzpatrick*, the HRA 1998 had come into force. Mendoza claimed that his right to respect for home and private life under Art 8 should be secured without discrimination in accordance with Art 14. To achieve that, he argued, para 2(2) had to be interpreted to cover same-sex relationships.

The Court of Appeal found in his favour. Buxton LJ found first that the claim fell within the ambit of Art 8 (at para 9). He then rejected the arguments that the discriminatory interpretation of Sched 1 (made in *Fitzpatrick*) could be justified and considered (at para 32) that 'sexual orientation' came within Art 14. Finally, he offered a new interpretation of Sched 1.

Buxton LJ (para 9):

Article 14 reads:

The enjoyment of the rights and freedoms set forth in this Convention shall be secured without discrimination on any ground such as sex, race, colour, language, religion, political or other opinion, national or social origin, association with a national minority, property, birth or other status.

An uninformed reading of the bare words of that provision might suggest that a complainant had to establish an actual breach of another article of the Convention before he could rely on article 14. Jurisprudence has however established that that is not so. As it is put in Grosz, Beatson & Duffy, *Human Rights* (2000), § C14-10: 'It would

---

68   Dissenting in *Nagarajan v LRT* [1999] 4 All ER 65, at p 70; see Chapter 11, p 304.

69   At the time of writing due for appeal in the House Lords. See also *Bellinger v Bellinger* [2003] UKHL 21; [2003] All ER (D) 178 (Apr), HL, and *AG for Ontario v M and H* [1999] DLR (4th) 577, discussed in Hitchings, E, '*M v H* and same-sex spousal benefits' (2000) 63 MLR 595.

70   [1999] 4 All ER 705; [1999] 3 WLR 1113; [2000] 1 FCR 21; [2000] Fam Law 14.

appear, however, that even the most tenuous link with another provision in the Convention will suffice for Article 14 to enter into play' ...

The state's margin of judgement

16   ... Mr Small [Counsel for the defendant] said that in the present case there were at least four competing interests that had to be taken into account, and that it fell well within the legitimate function of Parliament to decide where the balance between them should be struck. Those interests were the rights of the landlord; the desire of the survivor of the tenant to remain in place; the need to maintain fluidity in the housing market; and the policy of the Rent Act, or at least of the Schedule, to protect the family ...

17   There are at least three reasons why any principle of deference to the will of Parliament cannot assist in this case.

18   First, we are concerned with the fourth question in *Michalak*.[71] That makes it quite clear that once, as in this case, discrimination is demonstrated, it is for the discriminator to establish an objective and reasonable justification for that discrimination. That is not simply a literalistic argument about burden of proof. Rather, the form of the questions in *Michalak* reflects the seriousness with which Convention jurisprudence views discrimination, and the limited extent to which such discrimination can be tolerated. In seeking to discharge that burden, it is simply not enough to claim that what has been done falls within the permissible ambit of Parliament's discretion: because all that that shows is that the decisions taken are not to be regarded as necessarily unjustified. A much more positive argument is required if the burden imposed by *Michalak* is to be discharged.

19   Second, guidance has been given on the limits of the principle of deference by Lord Hope of Craighead in *R v DPP ex p Kebilene* [2002] 2 AC 326 at p 380:

> It will be easier for [a 'discretionary area of judgment'] to be recognised where the issues involve questions of social or economic policy, much less so where the rights are of high constitutional importance or are of a kind where the courts are especially well placed to assess the need for protection.

The general organisation of housing policy, and in particular of public housing ... clearly involves complex questions of social or economic policy that the courts should only enter with trepidation. But I have no hesitation in saying that issues of discrimination, which it is conceded we are concerned with in this case, do have high constitutional importance, and are issues that the courts should not shrink from. In such cases deference has only a minor role to play.

20   Third, once it is accepted that we are not simply bound by whatever Parliament has decided ... then we need to see whether the steps taken in implementation of the supposed policy are, not merely reasonable and proportionate, but also logically explicable as forwarding that policy. If it is accepted for the moment that Parliament seeks by the Schedule to promote the interests of landlords; flexibility in the housing market; and the protection of the family; how is any of that significantly forwarded by depriving the survivors of same-sex partnerships of statutory but not of assured tenancies? Since this part of the argument rested simply on assertion, no actual facts or evidence were available to assist us; so the court has to fall back on common sense.

21   The fundamental weakness of this whole argument is two-fold. First, as to the interests of landlords and flexibility in the housing market, Parliament has, by paragraph 2(2) of the Schedule, already extended full Rent Act protection to

survivors of heterosexual unmarried partnerships, a class that one would instinctively think to be much more numerous, and thus whose recognition was much more threatening to flexibility, than would be the category of same-sex partnerships. And so far as protection of the family is concerned, it is quite unclear how heterosexual family life (which includes unmarried partnerships) is promoted by handicapping persons who are constitutionally unable, or strongly unwilling, to enter into family relationships so defined. Second, if deterrence is really the objective, the means used to that end are singularly unimpressive. The more that we were told that a person holding an assured tenancy was very little if at all worse off than a statutory tenant, the less that it seemed that any effective social policy could be achieved through the award of an assured rather than a statutory tenancy.

22   I am therefore quite un-persuaded that the requirements of question (iv) in *Michalak* are made out in this case ...

32   This court bears the burden of having to construe the Convention as a living instrument. It has to ask itself ... whether discrimination on grounds of sexual orientation is excluded from the protection of Article 14. Looking at that question in 2002 it seems to me that there can only be one answer. Sexual orientation is now clearly recognised as an impermissible ground of discrimination, on the same level as the examples, which is all that they are, specifically set out in the text of Article 14. To include sexual orientation within this list does not depend on taking the step that was thought impossible in *Grant*,[72] of analysing discrimination on grounds of sexual orientation as a case of discrimination on grounds of sex. Rather, it applies to sexual orientation the more general principles inherent in Article 14.

33   In *Salgueiro v Portugal* (2001) 31 EHRR 47 the Strasbourg Court said, at §§ 28 and 36:

> ... the Court can only conclude that there was a difference in treatment between the applicant and [the comparator], which was based on the applicant's sexual orientation, a concept which is undoubtedly covered by Article 14 of the Convention. The Court notes in this regard that the list set out in this provision is of an indicative nature and is not definitive, as is evidenced by the adverb *notamment* (in English: 'any ground such as') the [national] Appeal Court used a distinction dictated by considerations relating to the applicant's sexual orientation, a distinction which cannot be tolerated under the Convention.

I respectfully agree. No other rational reason having been advanced for the exclusion of same-sex relationships from paragraph 2 of the Schedule, the conclusion is inescapable that paragraph 2, as construed by the House of Lords in *Fitzpatrick*, infringes article 14.

Remedy

34   In order to remedy this breach of the Convention the court must, if it can, read the Schedule so that its provisions are rendered compatible with the Convention rights of the survivors of same-sex partnerships. The width of this duty, imposed by section 3 of the HRA, has been emphasised by Lord Steyn, *R v A* [2001] 2 WLR 1546 at 1563, in terms too well-known and respected to require repetition.

---

72 *Grant v South West Trains* Case C-249/96 [1998] IRLR 206, ECJ.

35   That duty can be properly discharged by reading the words 'as his or her wife or husband' to mean 'as if they were his or her wife or husband'.[73] That wording achieves what is required in the present case, and does not open the door to lesser relationships (such as, for instance, sisters sharing a house, or long-term lodgers) because those relationships do not enjoy the marriage-like characteristics that for instance Lord Nicholls discerned in *Fitzpatrick*, and which the judge found to have characterised the relationship between Mr Walwyn-Jones and Mr Mendoza. It is quite true, as Mr Small pointed out, that the words 'husband' and 'wife' are in their natural meaning gender-specific. They are also, however, in their natural meaning limited to persons who are party to a lawful marriage. Parliament, by paragraph 2(2), removed that last requirement. And Parliament having swallowed the camel of including unmarried partners within the protection given to married couples, it is not for this court to strain at the gnat of including such partners who are of the same sex as each other.

This judgment carries some progressive and significant declarations. Buxton LJ said that discrimination was of 'high constitutional importance', that deference to parliament should be 'minor' and that the ECHR was a 'living instrument'. This last observation, of course, alludes to the 'living tree' school of interpretation. This was an encouraging judgment for those concerned with the gaps in Britain's legislative scheme. Less encouraging was the judgment of a differently constituted Court of Appeal in *A v Secretary of State for the Home Department*.

A and Others v Secretary of State for the Home Department [2002] EWCA Civ 1502, CA

As a consequence of the attacks which took place in the USA on 11 September 2001, legislation was passed that empowered the Home Secretary to detain non-nationals who resided in the UK if he suspected that they were terrorists; however, he could not deport them as being a threat to national security because, for example, they would suffer death or torture if returned to their home country. Article 5 of the Convention provides a right to liberty, but the legislation allowed the Home Secretary to derogate under Art 15, which is permissible 'in times of war or other public emergency threatening the life of the nation'. The Home Secretary detained 11 persons under this power. However, the Special Immigration Appeals Commission (SIAC) allowed their appeal against detention on the ground, *inter alia*, that the legislation (coming within the ambit of Art 5) was incompatible with the HRA 1998 because it discriminated on the grounds of nationality; only suspected terrorists who were non-nationals could be detained when there were equally dangerous British nationals who could not be detained. The Court of Appeal allowed the Home Secretary's appeal.

Lord Woolf CJ:

45   ... Was the UK government entitled to single out non-nationals who could not be deported in the foreseeable future as the subject of the Order and the 2001 Act? Here I differ from SIAC, largely because of the tension between Article 15 and Article 14. Article 15 restricts the extent of the derogation to what is strictly necessary. That is what the Secretary of State has done on his evidence. Of course, he did so for national security reasons. No doubt, by taking action against nationals as well as non-nationals the action from a security point of

73   See *Bellinger v Bellinger* [2003] UKHL 21; [2003] All ER (D) 178 (Apr), HL, where the House of Lords could not reinterpret the phrase 'respectively male and female' (in s 11(c) of the Matrimonial Causes Act 1973) to recognise a marriage between a male-to-female transsexual and a male. See further Chapter 6, p 161.

view would have been more effective. Equally, if the non-nationals were detained notwithstanding the fact that they wanted to leave this country, the action would be more effective. However, on his assessment of the situation, the Secretary of State was debarred from taking more effective action because it was not strictly necessary.

46   SIAC came to the conclusion at paragraph 94 that if an 'alien cannot be deported he must be allowed to remain'. That is correct, but as already stated that does not create a right to remain, only a right not to be removed. For example, if later the alien can be deported, he can be removed and pending removal detained. Because of this difference alone, aliens can be objectively distinguished from non-aliens.

47   SIAC go on to say that the threat is not confined to aliens (and that is agreed), but SIAC then wrongly conclude that this means there must be discrimination on the grounds of nationality as aliens are not nationals. This is an over-simplification. It was eloquently urged on behalf of the respondents, and particularly by Mr Pannick. It is an over-simplification because the position here is that the Secretary of State has come to the conclusion that he can achieve what is necessary by either detaining or deporting only the terrorists who are aliens. If the Secretary of State has come to that conclusion, then the critical question is, are there objective, justifiable and relevant grounds for selecting only the alien terrorists, or is the discrimination on the grounds of nationality? As to this critical question, I have come to the conclusion that there are objectively justifiable and relevant grounds which do not involve impermissible discrimination. The grounds are the fact that the aliens who cannot be deported have, unlike nationals, no more right to remain, only a right not to be removed, which means legally that they come into a different class from those who have a right of abode.

48   The class of aliens is in a different situation because when they can be deported to a country that will not torture them this can happen. It is only the need to protect them from torture that means that for the time being they cannot be removed.

49   In these circumstances it would be surprising indeed if Article 14, or any international requirement not to discriminate, prevented the Secretary of State taking the restricted action which he thought was necessary. As the respondents accept, the consequences of their approach is that because of the requirement not to discriminate, the Secretary of State would, presumably, have to decide on more extensive action, which applied both to nationals and non-nationals, than he would otherwise have thought necessary. Such a result would not promote human rights, it would achieve the opposite result. There would be an additional intrusion into the rights of the nationals so that their position would be the same as non-nationals.

50   The ECHR is essentially a pragmatic document. In its application it is intended to achieve practical benefits for those who are entitled to its protection ...

52   However, contrary to the view of SIAC, I consider the approach adopted by the Secretary of State, which involves detaining the respondents for no longer than is necessary before they can be deported, or until the emergency resolves, or they cease to be a threat to the safety of this country, is one which can be objectively justified. The individuals subject to the policy are an identifiable class. There is a rational connection between their detention and the purpose which the Secretary of State wishes to achieve. It is a purpose which cannot be applied to nationals, namely detention pending deportation, irrespective of when that deportation will take place.

53   The fact that deportation cannot take place immediately does not mean that it ceases to be part of the objective. This is confirmed by the fact that two of the respondents were able to leave this country. It is suggested that the action is not proportionate. However, I disagree. By limiting the number of those who are subject to the special measures, the Secretary of State is ensuring that his actions are proportionate to what is necessary. There is no alternative which the respondents can point to which is remotely practical ...

54   In *Michalak v London Borough of Wandsworth* [2002] EWCA Civ 271 at [20] Lord Justice Brooke helpfully summarised the questions that may be asked where discrimination arises, while stressing that he was only providing a framework and indicating that there is a potential overlap between the considerations. He also warned against treating the questions as a series of hurdles. However, the questions were:

      1) Do the facts fall within the ambit of one or more of the substantive Convention provisions?

      2) If so, was there different treatment as respects that right between the complainant on the one hand and other persons put forward for comparison ('the chosen comparators') on the other?

      3) Were the chosen comparators in an analogous situation to the complainant's situation?

      4) If so, did the difference in treatment have an objective and reasonable justification: in other words, did it pursue a legitimate aim and did the differential treatment bear a reasonable relationship or proportionality to the aims sought to be achieved?

55   Lord Justice Brooke added that the third test addresses the question whether the chosen comparators were in a sufficiently analogous situation to the complainant's situation for the different treatment to be relevant to the question whether the complainant's enjoyment of his Convention right has been free from Article 14 discrimination.

56   I will shortly answer each of those questions. As to the first question, the answer is yes. As to the second question, the answer is also yes, the chosen comparators, here being aliens and nationals who are suspected terrorists. As to the third question, I say those comparators were not in an analogous situation because the nationals have a right of abode in this jurisdiction but the aliens only have a right not to be removed. Finally, as to the fourth question, as I set out above, I consider the distinction between the position as to removal of nationals and non-nationals, together with the fact that the non-nationals but for the problem of torture could be removed, means that the difference in treatment does have an objective and reasonable justification.

Lord Woolf suggested (at para 45) that detaining nationals alongside non-nationals 'would have been more effective', but the Home Secretary could do no more than was 'strictly necessary'. This reasoning appears contradictory. If it was not strictly necessary to detain equally dangerous British suspects, then why was it so for the non-nationals? It seems that the detention could be justified if the numbers were kept down to an 'acceptable minimum'. In this case that was achieved by picking a sub-class, of non-nationals. The Home Secretary may as well have chosen those who wear sandals as the criterion. Accordingly, the conclusion flowing from this reasoning – that it would not promote human rights if more persons were detained (at para 49) – reduces the justification argument to one of pure numbers, irrespective of any substantial reasons to detain persons. Of more general importance in this context is the flavour of the judgment in contrast to that in *Mendoza*, in particular, the deference shown to Parliament and powers it gave to the Home Secretary.

In contrast to the British uncertainties of how to interpret this type of law, the American approach is clear. In the USA, the judiciary – with over two centuries' experience under a written constitution – has developed a purposive interpretation for constitutional or fundamental legislation. Holmes J's observation in 1919 that a word 'is the skin of a living thought'[74] illuminates the issue to this day. Some time later Learned Hand J said: '[I]t is one of the surest indexes of a mature and developed jurisprudence not to make a fortress out of a dictionary; but to remember that statutes always have some purpose or object to accomplish, whose sympathetic and imaginative discovery is the surest guide to their meaning.'[75] Roberts J said that: '... remedial ... legislation should ... be given a liberal interpretation ... [and] exceptions from its sweep should be narrow and limited to effect the remedy intended.'[76] In the context of discrimination law, the Supreme Court has said that 'Congress intended to prohibit *all* practices in *whatever form* which create inequality in employment opportunity due to discrimination on the basis of race, religion, sex or national origin'.[77]

4   A SINGLE EQUALITY ACT[78]

The complex situation with UK discrimination legislation was outlined at the beginning of this chapter and will be a theme throughout the book. Here the report by Hepple *et al* explains the position in more detail and proposes a single equality Act.[79]

Hepple, B, QC, Coussey, M and Choudhury, T, *Equality: A New Framework Report of the Independent Review of the Enforcement of UK Anti-Discrimination Legislation,* **2000, Hart:**

(1)   Outdated legislation

1.1   ... In our consultations and case studies the current legislation was widely criticised for being outdated, fragmented, inconsistent, inadequate, and at times incomprehensible.

1.2   The Sex Discrimination Act (SDA) came into force, with the Equal Pay Act (EqPA), at the end of 1975, and the Race Relations Act (RRA), replacing an Act of 1968, was passed in 1976. Each of these Acts has been amended on several occasions. Their essential feature remains a negative prohibition on discrimination, rather than a positive duty to promote equality. There are separate commissions – the EOC and CRE – with responsibility for enforcing each Act. These Acts formed the model for the Disability Discrimination Act

---

74   *Towne v Eisner* 245 US 418 (1919), at p 425.

75   *Cabell v Markham* 148 F 2d 737 (2nd Cir 1945), at p 739 (aff'd 326 US 404 (1945)).

76   *Piedmont & Northern R Co v Interstate Commerce Commission* 286 US 299 (1932), at pp 311–12. See also *Spokane & Inland Empire R Co v United States* 241 US 344, at p 350 (1916).

77   Emphasis added. *Franks v Bowman Transportation Co* 424 US 747 (1976), at p 763. See also *Alexander v Gardiner-Denver Co* 415 US 36 (1974), at p 44.

78   See, especially, for comparisons with South Africa, Fredman, S, *The Future of Equality in Britain,* EOC Working Paper 5 (2002) available at www.eoc.org.uk.

79   See Harrington, J, 'Making sense of equality law: a review of the Hepple Report' (2001) 64 MLR 757 and McKay, S, 'Proposing a new framework to combat discrimination' [2001] 30 ILJ 133.

(DDA) in 1995, but with the significant additions of a general defence of justification of direct discrimination and a positive duty to make reasonable adjustments for disabled persons, and the absence of the concept of indirect discrimination. In April 2000, another separate commission – the DRC – came into being to enforce this legislation.[80] There are numerous differences between each of the Acts, and between the powers of the various commissions.

1.3 Meanwhile, in Northern Ireland, the Fair Employment Act 1976 (FEA) applied the British model to the problem of discrimination between the Protestant and Roman Catholic communities. This was unsuccessful in removing entrenched practices. A significant change came with a new FEA in 1989. This shifted the emphasis from the elimination of unlawful discrimination on grounds of religion or political opinion to the reduction of structural inequality in the labour market, whether caused by discrimination or not. Positive duties on employers were introduced to monitor and review the composition of the workforce and to take affirmative action, under the supervision of an enforcement agency, the FEC. The evidence ... indicates that in its first ten years this legislation had a significant impact in reducing inequalities in the workplace. Another innovation in Northern Ireland, resulting from the Good Friday Agreement of 1998, was the enactment of a positive duty on public authorities to promote equality of opportunity not only between the Protestant and Roman Catholic communities, but also between persons of different racial group, age, marital status or sexual orientation; between men and women generally, between persons with a disability and without, and between persons with dependants and without.[81] The three separate commissions dealing with religion, race and sex respectively were merged, from October 1999, into a single equality commission (ECNI) which also took on responsibilities for disability discrimination, and monitoring the positive duty on public authorities. However, the new commission continues work under four separate regimes – for religious, race, sex and disability discrimination. The ECNI functions alongside the new Northern Ireland Human Rights Commission whose remit is wide enough to cover general equality issues.

1.4 These developments in Northern Ireland were bound to raise questions about the continuing emphasis in Britain on negative duties not to discriminate and the fragmentation of legislation and institutions. Indeed, following the Stephen Lawrence[82] inquiry, which highlighted institutional racism in the Metropolitan Police the Government has introduced a positive duty on public authorities in the current Race Relations (Amendment) Bill, and has committed itself do the same in respect of gender and disability when legislative time permits.[83]

1.5 The inspiration for British and Northern Irish legislation in the 1960s and 1970s was found in the USA and Canada. The Street Report of 1967 made a study of the workings of anti-discrimination in North America and contained detailed proposals for a 'second generation' Race Relations Act to replace the limited first Act of 1965.[84] This Report had some influence on the shape of the Race Relations Act 1968, but it was not until the 'third generation' legislation the SDA and RRA – that its most important advice was heeded, particularly by strengthening the

80 Set up under the Disability Rights Commission Act 1999.
81 Northern Ireland Act 1998, s 75.
82 For extracts, see Chapter 1, pp 11, 12 and 31.
83 Equality Statement, Cabinet Office, 30 November 1999.
84 *Anti-Discrimination Legislation: The Street Report*, London: PEP (Political and Economic Planning), 1967. The other members of the committee under Professor Harry Street's chairmanship were Geoffrey (later Lord) Howe and Geoffrey Bindman. See generally on the earlier legislation, Hepple, R, *Race, Jobs and the Law in Britain*, 1970, Penguin; Lester, A and Bindman, G, *Race and Law*, 1972, Penguin.

commissions and the enforcement provisions.[85] The White Papers which preceded the 1975 and 1976 Acts, drafted by Anthony (later Lord) Lester, marked a major turning point. The resulting legislation provided a right for individuals to bring proceedings for compensation for unlawful sex and race discrimination in industrial (later employment) tribunals, or for damages in designated county and sheriff courts in non-employment cases, while at the same time entrusting strategic enforcement in the public interest to the EOC and CRE. The Acts also imported the novel American concept of adverse impact or indirect discrimination.

1.6   The third-generation legislation did not copy the American concept of affirmative action plans (introduced by President Kennedy in 1961 in respect of government contractors) to increase the representation of minorities and of women in the workforce. The exception, as we have seen was Northern Ireland, in response to the deteriorating political situation there and to the campaign in the US to persuade corporations, state legislatures and municipal governments with investments in Northern Ireland to adopt the 'MacBride Principles' which encouraged employers to adopt affirmative action.[86] No similar political imperative existed in Britain. Pressures are now growing, however, for the UK as a whole to move towards a fourth generation of legislation prescribing positive duties on public authorities, employment and pay equity plans, and contract compliance regimes. Several models now exist, apart from fair employment legislation in Northern Ireland, such as employment and pay equity legislation in Canada, affirmative action for women in Australia, and recent employment equity legislation in South Africa. Although the political and social situations in those countries differ from those in the UK, the processes which lead to status discrimination and structural inequality are comparable.

(2)   The law of the European Union

1.7   The third generation legislation has developed under the strong influence of EU law. Article 119 of the EC Treaty, contained a directly applicable right for women and men to equal pay for equal work. (Following the Treaty of Amsterdam this is now embodied in revised form in Article 141 of the EC Treaty.) It was complemented by a series of directives, the most important of which is the Equal Treatment Directive 76/207/EC, implementing the principle of equal treatment in relation to access to employment, vocational training, promotion, working conditions and termination of employment. Many of the extensions of the rights of women resulted from the test case strategy adopted by the EOC, and from infringement proceedings brought by the European Commission. A dynamic relationship has grown up between EC law and domestic UK sex discrimination law, with the former exposing gaps in the coverage of UK law, and concepts from the UK, such as unintentional indirect discrimination, helping to shape EC law. EC directives and recommendations on sex discrimination have widened the gap between the law on this and other forms of discrimination which were not within the scope of the EC Treaty.

1.8   The Treaty of Amsterdam has now inserted a new Article 13 into the EC Treaty, empowering the Council to 'take appropriate action to combat discrimination based on sex, racial or ethnic origin, religion or belief, disability, age or sexual orientation.' Two ... directives[87] ... [o]ne – the so-called 'vertical' directive –

---

85 *Equality for Women*, Cmnd 5724, 1974, London: HMSO; *Racial Discrimination*, Cmnd 6234, 1975, London: HMSO.

86 McCrudden, C, 'Mainstreaming equality in the governance of Northern Ireland' (1999) 22 Fordham International Law Journal 1676–1775, at 1706.

87 Council Directives 2000/78/EC and 2000/43/EC respectively.

covers only employment and occupation but deals with direct and indirect discrimination on all the grounds mentioned in Article 13, except sex, which is already covered in other directives. The second – 'horizontal' – directive covers not only employment but also education, social security, the provision of goods and services and cultural activities, but is limited to discrimination on grounds of race and ethnic origin. The two overlapping directives are not entirely consistent, and will, if enacted, result in different standards in respect of the 'new' grounds of discrimination compared to those applying to equal treatment between men and women. The EC proposals are modelled on the negative duties and the individualistic, adversarial approach of third-generation British legislation, rather than the fourth-generation positive duties and affirmative action legislation. Whatever future legislation emerges from the EU, UK legislation will have to be brought into line with it.

1.9   Constitutional changes in the UK are already beginning to have a significant effect on equality issues. One of these changes is devolution, which may increase fragmentation of policy and executive decisions within the UK, since Scotland, Wales, and Northern Ireland now have some scope to develop their own equal opportunities policies. All the devolved bodies are subject to the basic ground rule that they cannot act in a way which is incompatible with the ECHR ...

1.13   Another major constitutional change affecting equality is the HRA ... The Act provides for the enforcement in UK courts and tribunals of rights secured by the ECHR. Article 14 of the ECHR requires Convention rights to be secured 'without discrimination on any ground such as sex, race, colour, language, religion, political or other opinion, national or social origin, association with a national minority, property, birth or other status.' (The italicised grounds are not covered by current UK legislation, except for religion and political opinion in Northern Ireland.)

Summary

1.17   There are thus numerous challenges to the present framework – dissatisfaction with the fragmentation and inconsistencies between four separate anti-discrimination regimes in the UK, and three separate commissions in Britain; demands for the legislation to be made more comprehensible and user-friendly; international, European and domestic pressures to extend the grounds of unlawful discrimination; the commitment of government to impose positive duties on public authorities; the relative success of fair employment legislation in Northern Ireland in reducing structural inequality; the continuing need to keep in line with EU law; the pressure from devolved legislatures and executives in the UK: and the building of a new legal and political culture of equality based on the ECHR and international human rights treaties. These legal and political challenges cannot be met without an understanding of the wider social changes which have occurred since the l970s ...

A Single Statute?

(1)   Defects of the present framework

2.1   The first and most obvious defect of the present framework is that there is too much law. At present, there are no less than 30 relevant Acts, 38 statutory instruments, 11 codes of practice, and 12 EC directives and recommendations directly relevant to discrimination (Appendix 2). Nearly every year there are amendments or fresh rules.[88] To this is added the weight of an ever-expanding case law, with many thousands of decided cases being available through law reports, the internet and commercial digests. The statutes are written in a language and style that renders them largely inaccessible to those whose actions they are intended to influence. Human resource managers, trade union officials, officers of public authorities, and those who represent victims of discrimination find difficulty in picking their way through it all ...

2.3   The complexity and inaccessibility of all this anti-discrimination legislation and case law were identified by our respondents as being among its greatest weaknesses.

2.4   The second main defect is that the law is inconsistent and inherently unsatisfactory ... We may limit ourselves here to a few examples—

- the DDA, unlike the SDA and RRA does not include the concept of indirect discrimination
- the SDA and RRA, unlike the DDA, do not include the concept of 'reasonable adjustment'
- the British legislation, unlike the FETO in Northern Ireland, does not include a positive
  duty to secure 'fair participation' in employment
- the SDA and RRA make it unlawful to discriminate only in respect of 'access' to existing
  opportunities or benefits (eg to a job share), while the DDA is not limited in this way
- the RRA places a duty on local authorities to promote racial equality (currently being
  extended to all public authorities), but there is no similar duty in respect of sex or disability
- the RRA and FETO cover only partnerships of six or more partners, while the SDA covers
  all partnerships
- the SDA allows recovery of compensation for unintentional indirect discrimination, while
  the RRA does not
- there are inconsistencies between the powers of the EOC, GRE and DRC, and the ECNI ...

2.5   There are gaps and anomalies between the EqPA Act and the SDA ... A number of inconsistencies have been resolved only by judicial interpretation, such as the application of the concept of indirect discrimination to equal pay claims, and differences between the test of objective justification under the SDA and 'material factor' in the EqPA. But important differences remain, for example—

- the SDA permits a comparison with a hypothetical male, the EqPA does not
- claims for payment of money or for a matter regulated by the 'equality clause' in a contract of employment can be brought only under the EqPA, while non-contractual claims can be brought only under the SDA
- the SDA includes discrimination against married person, the EqPA does not
- the SDA and EqPA have different time limits for bringing claims.

---

88 Of course, since the publication of this report the Government has introduced four sets of Regulations covering race, sexual orientation, religion and equal pay. Regulations on age discrimination are forthcoming. See above, p 107.

2.6 Although important changes have been made in the SDA so as to bring it into closer conformity with EC law, there remain a number of significant respects in which the SDA and EqPA appear to fall short of the standards demanded by EC law. In Working Paper No 1 for this project, Professor Evelyn Ellis ... has identified no less than 15 differences where, subject to two possible exceptions, judicial adaptation[89] appears to be impossible and the statute requires to be amended.

2.8 The Government is already committed to harmonising the provisions of the SDA, RRA and DDA.[90] We canvassed a number of options for achieving this. The most radical would be a single Equality Act. This is the model which can be found in several countries, such as Australia, Canada, Ireland,[91] New Zealand and the United States. An alternative would be to follow the EOC's proposal that the SDA, EqPA and other relevant laws, including EC law, should be replaced by a single Sex Equality Act, but to retain a similarly structured law on racial discrimination, and another on disability discrimination. Presumably, if new grounds of unlawful discrimination were added these would each be the subject of a new Act or they would be included with an analogous Act (eg religion with race, sexual orientation with sex etc) ...

2.10 There were, however, some reservations. The CRE argued that:

A separate Race Relations Act is useful for campaigning and education purposes as well as law enforcement. To move to a single equality statute would blur the focus on specific types of discrimination. For so long as institutional racism persists it must be tackled directly, and general concepts of equality and diversity will not have the same sharp impact.

In our view, this reservation confuses a 'general' concept with a unified one. The same concept of equality can be applied to each ground of discrimination without undermining specific action against particular grounds of discrimination. RADAR, which works on behalf of disabled people, expressed concern about merging all areas of discrimination under a single equality statute, 'because disability discrimination is still not an equal partner in comparison with other legislation'. This is really aimed at the way in which an equality statute is enforced rather than the substance of the law, namely whether the focus on particular forms of discrimination should be entrusted to different agencies ...

Recommendation 1

- There should be a single Equality Act in Britain
- This Act should be supplemented by regulations and by regularly up-dated codes of practice on specific subjects
- The Act and other documents should be written in plain language so as to facilitate comprehension, and should be available in forms which take into account the needs of disabled people ...

Recommendation 2

The framework should be based on the following five principles—

---

89 Ie, indirect effect; see above, p 111.
90 Cabinet Office, Equality Statement (30 November 1999): but contrast the Northern Ireland Office (1998). The White Paper (1998) stated that it was not proposed to bring together the separate statutes as they apply in that province. The Better Regulation Task Force (1999), para 3.1, was not persuaded of the need for a major legislative overhaul.
91 See Buckley, L, 'Employment Equality Act 1998 (Ireland)' [2000] 29 ILJ 273.

- the goal of legislation and other measures is to eliminate unlawful discrimination and to promote equality regardless of sex, race, colour, ethnic or national origin, religion or belief, disability, age, sexual orientation, or other status
- there must be clear consistent and easily intelligible standards
- the regulatory framework must be effective, efficient and equitable, aimed at encouraging personal responsibility and self-generating efforts to promote equality
- there must be opportunities for those directly affected to participate, through information, consultation and engagement in the process of change
- individuals should be free to seek redress for the harm they have suffered as a result of unlawful discrimination, through procedures which are fair, inexpensive and expeditious, and the remedies should be effective.

CHAPTER 6

THE PROHIBITED GROUNDS OF DISCRIMINATION

Legislation specifically covers race, religion or belief, sex, gender reassignment, sexual orientation, disability and will cover, in due course, age. The definition of 'disability' is discussed in Chapter 16. The principal domestic legislation is the Race Relations Act (RRA) 1976 and the Sex Discrimination Act (SDA) 1975. In addition (deriving from European Directives), there are statutory instruments covering religion or belief (in force since 2 December 2003) and sexual orientation (in force since 1 December 2003). European legislation specifically covers sex,[1] racial and ethnic origin,[2] nationality,[3] and religion and belief, disability, age and sexual orientation.[4] However, this European legislation is limited in that most of it extends only to employment matters.[5] The exception is the Race Directive, which, like the RRA 1976 and SDA 1975, extends to other fields such as the provision of services, housing and education.

In addition, the Human Rights Act (HRA) 1998, which incorporated the European Convention on Human Rights, covers discrimination on all of the above grounds plus many others, but only in connection with any of the free-standing rights, such as freedom of association or the right to respect for private and family life, although freedom of religion is specifically protected by Art 9.

1   THE MEANING OF RACE

Race Relations Act 1976:

Section 3

(1)   In this Act ...

'racial grounds' means any of the following grounds, namely colour, race, nationality or ethnic or national origins;

'racial group' means a group of persons defined by reference to colour, race, nationality or ethnic or national origins.

(2)   The fact that a racial group consists of two or more distinct racial groups does not prevent it from constituting a particular racial group for the purposes of this Act.

---

1   Equal Treatment Directive 76/207 and Article 141 (Equal Pay) EC Treaty.
2   Race Directive 2000/43/EC.
3   Article 39 of the EC Treaty.
4   Equal Treatment in Employment Directive 2000/78/EC.
5   Employment and vocational training.

Council Directive 2000/43/EC of 29 June 2000 implementing the principle of equal treatment between persons irrespective of racial or ethnic origin

Article 1

The purpose of this Directive is to lay down a framework for combating discrimination on the grounds of racial or ethnic origin ...

Article 3

2   This Directive does not cover difference of treatment based on nationality ...

As a result of the Directive, the RRA 1976 has been heavily amended by statutory instrument[6] under powers given to the Government by the European Communities Act 1972. The problem with amending the 1976 Act in this way (ie, not by Act of Parliament) is that only those parts of the Act affected by the Directive could be revised. For the purposes of this chapter, it means that there is a slightly narrower definition of race for the areas subject to amendment.[7] The Directive covers only 'racial or ethnic origin', although there is little doubt that the European Court of Justice (ECJ) would interpret this broadly. Accordingly, the draftsmen have included 'national origins' in the amendment to reflect the true meaning of the Directive. However, 'colour' and 'nationality' are excluded from the amendments. Again, there is little doubt that the ECJ would interpret 'race' to include most cases of discrimination on the grounds of colour. However, there are a few instances where this may be difficult, for example, where a dark-skinned black person discriminates against a light-skinned black person.[8] However, the ECJ will not interpret the Directive to cover claims under 'nationality', as Art 3 of the Directive expressly reserves such matters for Art 39 (formerly Art 48) of the EC Treaty, which is principally concerned with the free movement of workers.[9]

That said, the RRA 1976 has not been narrowed in any way.[10] Consequently, where a 'nationality' claim fails under, say, the new definition of indirect discrimination in s 1A of the RRA 1976, the claimant may fall back on the old (s 3) definition (which includes nationality) combined with the narrower definition of indirect discrimination within in s 1(1)(b). There is no overlap between s 3 and the new provisions, which use the word 'race'. Section 3 only defines 'racial grounds' and 'racial group', but not 'race'. Thus, it is not possible to argue, for instance, that the new definition of indirect discrimination includes 'nationality' via the definition in s 3.

(1)   Race

As we saw in Chapter 1,[11] writers have concluded that there is no scientific definition of 'race' which could serve any purpose under discrimination legislation. In Britain

---

6   Race Relations Act 1976 (Amendment) Regulations 2003, SI 2003/1626.
7   This becomes especially complicated in fields other than employment: see Chapter 13.
8   *See Walker v Secretary of the Treasury* 713 F Supp 403, explained below, '(2) Colour.'
9   Discussed below, '(3) Nationality', p 141.
10   Article 6 of the Directive prevents this.
11   Chapter 1, Part 2(2) 'Theories of Racism'.

there is an absence of case law on the issue.[12] However, there has been much litigation over the definition of race in the USA.

Saint Francis College v Al-Khazraji **481 US 604 (1987) Supreme Court**[13]

The Civil Rights Act 1866 encoded s 1981:

(a)   All persons within the jurisdiction of the United States shall have the same right ... to the full and equal benefit of all laws ... as is enjoyed by white citizens ...

Al-Khazraji, a US citizen, born in Iraq, brought a s 1981 action[14] against his former employer, St Francis College. The College argued that modern scientific theory placed humans into three major racial groups: Caucasoid, Mongoloid, and Negroid.

During his Opinion, White J noted:[15]

There is a common popular understanding that there are three major human races – Caucasoid, Mongoloid, and Negroid. Many modern biologists and anthropologists, however, criticize racial classifications as arbitrary and of little use in understanding the variability of human beings. It is said that genetically homogeneous populations do not exist and traits are not discontinuous between populations; therefore, a population can only be described in terms of relative frequencies of various traits. Clear-cut categories do not exist. The particular traits which have generally been chosen to characterize races have been criticized as having little biological significance. It has been found that differences between individuals of the same race are often greater than the differences between the 'average' individuals of different races. These observations and others have led some, but not all, scientists to conclude that racial classifications are for the most part sociopolitical, rather than biological, in nature.

White J then reviewed a number of reference book definitions and the legislative history of the Civil Rights Act 1866 (at 612–13):

These dictionary and encyclopedic sources are somewhat diverse, but it is clear that they do not support the claim that for the purposes of § 1981, Arabs, Englishmen, Germans, and certain other ethnic groups are to be considered a single race. We would expect the legislative history of § 1981 ... to reflect this common understanding, which it surely does. The debates are replete with references to the Scandinavian races, Cong. Globe, 39th Cong, 1st Sess, 499 (1866) ... as well as the Chinese, *id*, at 523 ..., Latin, *id*, at 238 ... Spanish, *id*, at 251 ... and Anglo-Saxon races, *id*, at 542 ... Jews, *ibid*, Mexicans, see *ibid*, blacks, *passim* [there and throughout], and Mongolians, *id*, at 498, were similarly categorized. Gypsies were referred to as a race ... Likewise, the Germans ...

---

12   The Court of Appeal in *Mandla v Dowell Lee* [1983] QB 1 discussed the meaning of race incidentally whilst ruling on whether Sikh's fell into the category of 'ethnic origins'. See *per* Lord Denning MR, at p 10F, Oliver LJ, at p 15H and Kerr LJ, at p 22D. The court's conclusion was reversed by the House of Lords.

13   For a full review of this and other cases on the issue, see the Californian Court of Appeal in *Sandhu v Lockheed Missiles* 26 Cal App 4th 846 (1994).

14   Section 1981 does not expressly protect 'national origins' or 'religion', but it can provide better remedies than the modern Title VII. See *Johnson v Railway Express Agency* 421 US 454 (1975), at p 460 and *Sandhu v Lockheed Missiles* 26 Cal App 4th 846 (1994). So Al-Khazraji compressed his claim under the head of 'race', which is accepted as a protected group under s 1981.

15   481 US 604, at p 610, fn 4.

Based on the history of § 1981, we have little trouble in concluding that Congress intended to protect from discrimination identifiable classes of persons who are subjected to intentional discrimination solely because of their ancestry or ethnic characteristics. Such discrimination is racial discrimination that Congress intended § 1981 to forbid, whether or not it would be classified as racial in terms of modern scientific theory ... It is clear from our holding ... that a distinctive physiognomy is not essential to qualify for § 1981 protection. If respondent ... can prove that he was subjected to intentional discrimination based on the fact that he was born an Arab, rather than solely on the place or nation of his origin, or his religion, he will have made out a case under § 1981.

The argument that there were only three racial groups for the purposes of the legislation was rejected for another reason by a lower court (the Third Circuit) in this case. It found that the strict 'three race' approach would lead to anomalies: 'while a white would be able to claim anti-white discrimination under the statute ... a Mexican-American or an Indian would be unable to make out a claim, unless they contended they were unfairly treated by virtue of being Caucasians.'[16] This shows that the US courts are prepared to give the word 'race' a liberal and purposive interpretation, free of any scientific dimension. It remains to be seen if the British courts follow this approach, although Lord Fraser, in *Mandla v Dowell Lee* (below)[17] suggested that the definition of a racial group should not depend upon scientific proof.

(2)   Colour

There has been no litigation over the meaning of the word 'colour' in s 3 of the RRA 1976. The matter has arisen occasionally in the USA. It was noted in *Felix v Marquez*[18] that a claim based solely on 'colour' will be rare. This is because 'color may be mixed or subordinated to claims of race discrimination'. However, such a rare case arose in *Walker v Secretary of the Treasury*.[19]

Ms Walker was a light-skinned black woman who worked in an office of predominantly dark-skinned black persons. She claimed that she was dismissed because of her lighter skin colour and brought an action under Title VII. Ms Walker, as a black person, could not claim that she was discriminated on grounds of 'race'; this claim was peculiar to 'colour'. The defendants argued that legislative history and case law all pointed towards the statutory word 'colour' meaning the same thing as 'race'. Thus, it was not possible to bring an action on colour without some proof of a 'racial' element.

An Atlantean District Court[20] discussed the issue at length and dismissed the defendants' argument for two reasons. First, to give two words (that is 'colour' and 'race') in the same phrase a single meaning would make one of those words redundant. The second reason was drawn from the Supreme Court's definition of 'race' in *Saint Francis College v Al-Khazraji*.[21] In that case, White J adopted the view that

---

16   784 F 2d 505, 520.
17   [1983] AC 548 HL. See below, p 144, '(5) Ethnic Origins'.
18   24 Empl Prac Dec (CCH) para 31,279 (DDC 1980), discussed briefly in *Walker v Secretary of the Treasury* 713 F Supp 403 (1989), at 406–07.
19   713 F Supp 403 (1989) and 742 F Supp 670 (1990).
20   For the Northern District of Georgia, Atlanta Division.
21   481 US 604 (1987). See above: '(1) Race'.

a distinctive physiognomy was not necessary to bring a claim of discrimination based on 'race'. The court in *Walker* extended this logic to cover 'colour'. Thus, it was unnecessary for Ms Walker to prove a distinctive physiognomy: a claim based solely on colour could succeed. It was noted in *Felix*[22] that colour may be the 'most practical' claim where the victim has mixed heritage.

(3) Nationality

This category was introduced into the 1976 Act as a result of the House of Lords' decision in *Ealing LBC v CRE*,[23] a case on the 1968 Race Relations Act, which prohibited discrimination on grounds of 'national origin', but not 'nationality'. The House of Lords held that a Polish national, whom the Council had refused to put on their housing list, had no claim under the 1968 Act. Lord Cross stated: 'It is not difficult to see why the legislature in enacting the ... Act used this new phrase "national origins" and not the word "nationality" which had a well-established meaning in law. It was because "nationality" in the strict sense was quite irrelevant to the problem with which they were faced. Most of the people against whom discrimination was being practised or hatred stirred up were in fact British subjects.' Section 78 of the 1976 Act provides that, unless the context otherwise requires, '"nationality" includes citizenship'. Consequently Polish, or any other, nationals, or citizens, are protected under the 1976 Act.[24]

There is an overlap with EC law here. The EC Treaty recognises that there shall be freedom of movement within the Community for Member State nationals. Consequently, discrimination on grounds of nationality is outlawed in several areas. For instance, Art 39 (previously Art 48) outlaws discrimination against workers on grounds of nationality.

EC Treaty

Article 39 (formerly Art 48)

1   Freedom of movement of workers shall be secured within the Community.

2   Such freedom of movement shall entail the abolition of any discrimination based on nationality between workers of the Member States as regards employment, remuneration and other conditions of work and employment.

The wording of Art 39 reflects its principal purpose, which is to secure free movement, rather than to outlaw irrational discrimination.[25] Consequently, Art 39 does not cover

---

22   24 Empl Prac Dec (CCH) para 31,279 (DDC 1980), discussed briefly in *Walker v Secretary of the Treasury* 713 F Supp 403 (1989), at pp 406–07.

23   [1972] AC 342; see also below, '(4) National origins'.

24   There is one area where the US courts have been uncharacteristically conservative when recognising racial groups for protection. A fine distinction between 'national origin' and 'citizenship' is made to exclude aliens from Title VII. In *Espinoza v Farah Manufacturing* Co 414 US 86 (1973), the defendant company hired only American citizens. Mrs Espinoza was a Mexican citizen and a first generation American immigrant who was married to an American citizen. She was refused a job and the Supreme Court held (Douglas J dissenting) that the defendant was not discriminating on grounds of 'national origin'. (In fact 98% of the company's employees were of Mexican origin.) This was discrimination solely based on citizenship and consequently she was not protected under USA discrimination law.

25   See de Búrca, G 'The role of equality in European Community law', in Dashwood, A and O'Leary, S, *The Principle of Equal Treatment in European Community Law*, 1997, London: Sweet & Maxwell.

discrimination in a Member State against a national of that State,[26] and should not cover, for example, discrimination in England against a Welsh person.[27]

(4)   National Origins

There are a number of situations where a claim under 'national origins' may succeed where a claim under 'nationality' would not, for instance, where a nation no longer exists, or least no longer exists as a nation State (eg, Wales). The following judgments confirm that discrimination within the Great Britain against Scots, Welsh or English may fall into this category.[28]

Ealing LBC v Race Relations Board [1972] AC 342, HL[29]

Ealing Council refused to put Mr Zesko, a Polish national, on their housing list. He brought an action for discrimination under the 1968 Race Relations Act, which included the term 'national origins', but not 'nationality'. His claim failed because Mr Zesko could not be defined by national origin. During his judgment, Lord Simon discussed the meaning of 'national origins':

Lord Simon (pp 363–64):

I have already indicated that these words ['national origins'] are part of a passage of vague terminology in which the words seem to be used in a popular sense. 'Origin', in its ordinary sense, signifies a source, someone or something from which someone or something else has descended. 'Nation' and 'national', in their popular in contrast to their legal sense, are also vague terms. They do not necessarily imply statehood. For example, there were many submerged nations in the former Hapsburg empire.[30] Scotland is not a nation in the eye of international law; but Scotsmen constitute a nation by reason of those most powerful elements in the creation of national spirit – tradition, folk memory, a sentiment of community. The Scots are a nation because of Bannockburn and Flodden, Culloden and the pipes at Lucknow, because of Jenny Geddes and Flora Macdonald, because of frugal living and respect for learning, because of Robert Burns and Walter Scott. So, too, the English are a nation – because Norman, Angevin and Tudor monarchs forged them together, because their land is mostly sea-girt, because of the common law and of gifts for poetry and parliamentary government, because (despite the Wars of the Roses and Old Trafford and Headingly) Yorkshireman and Lancastrian feel more in common than in difference and are even prepared at a pinch to extend their sense of community to southern folk. By the Act of Union English and Scots lost their separate nationalities, but they retained their separate nationhoods; and their descendants have thereby retained their separate national origins. So, again, the Welsh are a nation – in the popular, though not in the legal, sense – by reason of Offa's Dyke, by recollection of battles long ago and pride in the present valour of their regiments, because of musical gifts and religious dissent, because of fortitude in the face of economic adversity, because of the satisfaction of all

---

26 *Morsen* and *Jhanjan* Joined Cases 35 and 36/82 [1982] ECR 3723 ECJ. See also *R v Saunders* Case 175/78 [1979] ECR 1129, para 10, ECJ.

27 See McLeod, W, 'Autochthonous language communities and the Race Relations Act', Web Journal of Current Legal Issues [1998] 1 Web JCCI-htm.

28 On the specific issue of 'national' minorities within the UK, see MacEwen, M, 'Racial grounds: a definition of identity' (1998) 3 IJDL 51.

29 See also [1972] 1 All ER 105; [1972] 2 WLR 71; 70 LGR 219; 136 JP 112; 222 EG 31; [1972] EGD 223.

30 Or 'Habsburg'.

Wales that Lloyd George became an architect of the welfare state and prime minister of victory. To discriminate against Englishmen, Scots or Welsh, as such, would, in my opinion, be to discriminate against them on the ground of their 'national origins'. To have discriminated against Mr Zesko on the ground of his Polish descent would have been to have discriminated against him on the ground of his national origin.

Northern Joint Police Board v Power [1997] IRLR 610, EAT

The applicant claimed that he was rejected for a Chief Constable position in Scotland because he was English. The Employment Appeal Tribunal (EAT) upheld the decision of the industrial tribunal[31] that it had jurisdiction to hear the complaint.

Lord Johnston (p 613):

Nationality, we consider, has a juridical basis pointing to citizenship, which, in turn, points to the existence of a recognised State at the material time. Within the context of England, Scotland, Northern Ireland and Wales the proper approach to nationality is to categorise all of them as falling under the umbrella of British ... Against that background, therefore, what context should be given to the phrase 'national origins'? It seems to us ... what has to be ascertained are identifiable elements, both historically and geographically, which at least at some point in time reveals the existence of a nation ... [W]hat cannot be in doubt is that both England and Scotland were once separate nations. That in our opinion, is effectively sufficient to dispose of the matter, since thereafter we agree with the proposition that it is for each individual to show that his origins are embedded in such a nation.[32]

The conclusion that the English,[33] Scots, Irish and Welsh[34] have separate national origins seems clearly correct in terms of the policy of the law. On this basis, Walloons (Belgiums of French origin), Catalans, Basques, Sicilians, Bretons and Cornish should have a claim under 'national origins'. It is clear they would succeed in the US courts. For instance, in *Pejic v Hughes Helicopters*,[35] it was held that Serbians were a protected class under by national origin, although Serbia (at the time, in 1988) was no longer an independent State. The Court of Appeals stated 'Unless historical reality is ignored, the term "national origin" must include countries no longer in existence'.[36] In *Roach v Dresser*,[37] a District Court went further and held that a Cajun whose ancestry derived from Acadia (now Nova Scotia) fell within the meaning of 'national origin' even though Acadia as a nation never existed.[38] The reasoning given was that: 'Distinctions between citizens solely because of their ancestors are odious to a free people whose institutions are founded upon the doctrine of equality ...'[39] The American courts may

---

31 By the Employment Rights (Dispute Resolution) Act 1998, s 1(1), Industrial Tribunals are renamed Employment Tribunals.

32 Having held that the applicant could bring a case based on discrimination on the basis of national origins, the EAT went on to hold that a claim could not be maintained on the basis of different ethnic origins.

33 *BBC Scotland v Souster* [2001] IRLR 150, CS.

34 *Griffiths v Reading University Students Union* (1996) unreported, Case 16476/96, see 31 DCLD 3.

35 840 F 2d 667.

36 *Ibid* at 673.

37 *Roach v Dresser Industrial Valve & Instrument Div* 494 F Supp 215 (1980) District Court, Western District Louisiana, Alexandria Division.

38 It was a colony.

39 494 F Supp 215 (1980), at 218.

have been more generous here because the legislation – unlike the EC and British versions – does not include 'ethnic origins'.

(5)   Ethnic Origins

Under this head it has been argued (successfully) that Sikhs, Jews, 'Gypsies' and (unsuccessfully) Rastafarians fall within the definition of 'ethnic origins'. The leading case on the definition of 'ethnic origins' in the RRA 1976 is *Mandla v Dowell Lee*.

Mandla v Dowell Lee [1983] AC 548, HL

According to the rules of a private school, boys had to wear the school uniform (including a cap), and keep their hair cut 'so as not to touch the collar'. The school refused Gurinder Singh admission as a pupil because he would not comply with those rules. As an orthodox Sikh, he was obliged not to cut his hair and to restrain it by wearing a turban, so he could not wear the school cap. The main issue was whether or not Sikhs were a 'racial group' for the purposes of the RRA 1976. At first instance, and in the Court of Appeal, it was held that they were not. The Court of Appeal held that 'ethnic' meant 'race'[40] and as Sikhs could show no common biological characteristic, they did not form a racial group. The House of Lords reversed that decision.

Lord Fraser (at pp 560–63):

It is not suggested that Sikhs are a group defined by reference to colour, race, nationality or national origins. In none of these respects are they distinguishable from many other groups, especially those living, like most Sikhs, in the Punjab. The argument turns entirely on whether they are a group defined by ethnic origins ...

I recognise that 'ethnic' conveys a flavour of race but it cannot, in my opinion, have been used in the 1976 Act in a strict racial or biological sense. For one thing it would be absurd to suppose that Parliament can have intended that membership of a particular racial group should depend on scientific proof that a person possessed the relevant distinctive biological characteristics (assuming that such characteristics exist). The practical difficulties of such proof would be prohibitive, and in the clear that Parliament must have used the word in some more popular sense. For another thing ... within the human race, there are very few, if any, distinctions which are scientifically regarded as racial ...

For a group to constitute an ethnic group ... it must, in my opinion, regard itself, and be regarded by others, as a distinct community by virtue of certain characteristics. Some of these characteristics are essential; others are not essential but one or more of them will commonly be found and will help to distinguish the group from the surrounding community. The conditions which appear to me to be essential are these:

(1)   a long shared history, of which the group is conscious as distinguishing it from other groups, and the memory of which it keeps alive;

(2)   a cultural tradition of its own, including family and social customs and manners, often but not necessarily associated with religious observance.

In addition to those two essential characteristics, the following characteristics are, in my opinion, relevant;

(3)   either a common geographical origin, or descent from a small number of common ancestors;

---

40   [1983] QB 1, *per* Lord Denning MR, at p 10F, Oliver LJ, at p 15H and Kerr LJ, at p 22D.

(4)   a common language, not necessarily peculiar to the group;

(5)   a common literature peculiar to the group;

(6)   a common religion differing from that of neighbouring groups or from the general community surrounding it;

(7)   being a minority, or being an oppressed or a dominant group within a larger community ...

A group defined by reference to enough of these characteristics would be capable of including converts, for example, people who marry into the group, and of excluding apostates. Provided a person who joins the group feels himself or herself to be a member of it, and is accepted by other members, then he is, for the purposes of the 1976 Act, a member ...

The conclusion at which I have arrived ... is greatly strengthened by ... the decision of the Court of Appeal in New Zealand ... in *King-Ansell v Police* [1979] 2 NZLR 531 ... that Jews in New Zealand did form a group with common ethnic origins ...[41]

The respondent admitted, rightly in my opinion, that, if the proper construction of the word 'ethnic' in section 3 of the 1976 Act is a wide one, on lines such as I have suggested, the Sikhs would qualify as a group defined by ethnic origins for the purposes of the Act. It is, therefore, unnecessary to consider in any detail the relevant characteristics of the Sikhs. They were originally a religious community founded about the end of the fifteenth century in the Punjab by Guru Nanak, who was born in 1469. But the community is no longer purely religious in character. Their present position is summarised sufficiently for present purposes in the opinion of the county court judge in the following passage:

> The evidence in my judgment shows that Sikhs are a distinctive and self-conscious community. They have a history going back to the fifteenth century. They have a written language which a small proportion of Sikhs can read but which can be read by a much higher proportion of Sikhs than of Hindus. They were at one time politically supreme in the Punjab.

The result is, in my opinion, that Sikhs are a group defined by a reference to ethnic origins for the purpose of the 1976 Act, although they are not biologically distinguishable from the other peoples living in the Punjab. That is true whether one is considering the position before the partition of 1947, when the Sikhs lived mainly in that part of the Punjab which is now Pakistan, or after 1947, since when most of them have moved into India.

Lord Templeman (p 569E).

In my opinion, for the purposes of the 1976 Act a group of persons defined by reference to ethnic origins must possess some of the characteristics of a race, namely group descent, a group of geographical origin and a group history. The evidence shows that Sikhs satisfy these tests. They are more than a religious sect, they are almost a race and almost a nation. As a race, the Sikhs share a common colour, and a common physique based on common ancestors ... They fail to qualify as a separate race, because in racial origin prior to the inception of Sikhism they cannot be distinguished from other inhabitants of the Punjab ... [T]hey fail to qualify as a separate nationality because their kingdom never achieved a sufficient degree of recognition or permanence. The Sikhs qualify as a group defined by ethnic origins

---

41   It was the Government's intention that persons of the Jewish faith be protected under the Race Relations Act 1965. In a debate on that Act, the Home Secretary stated that the word 'ethnic' would 'undoubtedly' include Jews (HC Deb Vol 711 Cols 932–33, 3 May 1965).

because they constitute a separate and distinct community derived from the racial characteristics I have mentioned.

It appears that a unanimous House of Lords clarified the meaning of 'ethnic origin', but an examination of the speeches reveals some confusion.[42] Lords Brandon and Roskill concurred with the speeches of both Lord Fraser and Lord Templeman, whilst Lord Edmund-Davies restricted himself to concurring with just the decision. Yet the criteria set out in each speech actually differ. Lord Templeman spoke of (a) group descent, (b) geographical origin and (c) group history, yet only 'group history' was stated by Lord Fraser to be an 'essential' characteristic. 'Group descent' and 'geographical origin', said Lord Fraser, were merely 'relevant' characteristics. In *Crown Suppliers v Dawkins*, the Court of Appeal stated[43] that there were no inconsistencies of substance between the speeches in *Mandla*. However, there is clearly some difference between Lord Fraser's and Lord Templeman's definitions. In practice, Lord Fraser's test has become fashionable and it is the one usually applied by the lower courts and tribunals.

In *Crown Suppliers v Dawkins*,[44] Dawkins was refused a job as a van driver because he was unwilling to cut his hair. This was because his Rastafarian faith obliged him to keep it in dreadlocks. Dawkins claimed that Rastafarians were a racial group defined by 'ethnic origins' within the meaning of s 3 of the RRA 1976. The Court of Appeal applied Lord Fraser's 'test', and held that as Rastafarians did not have a long shared or 'group' history they did not form a racial group for the purposes of the RRA 1976. Of course, since 2 December 2003, religious discrimination in employment matters is covered by the Employment Equality (Religion or Belief) Regulations.[45] In the next case, the Court of Appeal applied Lord Fraser's 'test' to travellers.

CRE v Dutton [1989] QB 783; [1989] 1 All ER 306; [1989] IRLR 8, CA

The defendant, a publican, displayed 'no travellers' signs outside his public house and refused to serve persons from caravans parked nearby. The Commission alleged that that indirectly discriminated against gypsies, or travellers. The county court judge applied *Mandla* (above) and stated that those few travellers who satisfied Lord Fraser's two 'essential characteristics' had been absorbed by a larger group of travellers, some of whom had abandoned the nomadic way of life and/or were indistinguishable from the general public. This larger group could not satisfy the two essential conditions and could 'barely satisfy' Lord Fraser's five 'non-essential' conditions. Thus, the judge held that gypsies did not form a racial group for the purposes of the Act. The Court of Appeal reversed that decision.

Nicholls LJ (at 795–801):

[I]n my view the word 'gipsy' has ... more than one meaning. The classic 'dictionary' meaning can be found as the primary meaning given in the Oxford English Dictionary (1933): 'A member of a wandering race (by themselves called Romany), of Hindu

---

42 For criticisms of *Mandla*, see Pagone, GT, 'The lawyer's hunt for snarks, religion and races' [1984] CLJ 218 and Benyon, H and Love, N, '*Mandla* and the meaning of "racial group"' (1984) LQR 120.

43 [1993] ICR 517, at p 526H.

44 [1993] ICR 517.

45 SI 2003/1660, discussed below, p 150.

origin, which first appeared in England about the beginning of the 16th century and was then believed to have come from Egypt' ... Alongside this meaning, the word ... also has a more colloquial, looser, meaning ... [i]n short, a nomad ...

I can anticipate here by noting that if the word 'gipsy' is used in this second, colloquial sense it is not definitive of a racial group within the Act. To discriminate against such a group would not be on racial grounds, namely, on the ground of ethnic origins. As the judge observed, there are many people who travel around the country in caravans, vans, converted buses, trailers, lorries and motor vehicles, leading a peripatetic or nomadic way of life. They include didicois, mumpers, peace people, new age travellers, hippies, tinkers, hawkers, self-styled 'anarchists', and others, as well as (Romany) gipsies. They may all be loosely referred to as 'gipsies', but as a group they do not have the characteristics requisite of a racial group within the Act ...

On the evidence it is clear that such gipsies are a minority, with a long shared history and a common geographical origin. They are a people who originated in Northern India. They migrated thence to Europe through Persia in mediaeval times. They have certain, albeit limited, customs of their own, regarding cooking and the manner of washing. They have a distinctive, traditional style of dressing with heavy jewellery worn by the women, although this dress is not worn all the time. They also furnish their caravans in a distinctive manner. They have a language or dialect, known as 'pogadi chib' spoken by English gipsies (Romany chals) and Welsh gipsies (Kale) which consists of up to one-fifth of Romany words in place of English words. They do not have a common religion, nor a peculiar, common literature of their own, but they have a repertoire of folk tales and music passed on from one generation to the next. No doubt after all the centuries which have passed since the first gipsies left the Punjab, gipsies are no longer derived from what, in biological terms, is a common racial stock, but that of itself does not prevent them from being a racial group as widely defined in the Act ...

... with respect to the judge, I do not think that there was any evidence justifying his conclusion that gipsies have been absorbed into a larger group, if by that he meant that substantially all gipsies have been so absorbed. The fact that some have been so absorbed and are indistinguishable from any ordinary member of the public, is not sufficient in itself to establish loss [of a historically determined social identity]. In my view, the evidence was sufficient to establish that, despite their long presence in England, gipsies have not merged wholly in the population, as have the Saxons and the Danes, and altogether lost their separate identity. They, or many of them, have retained a separateness, a self-awareness, of still being gipsies.[46]

This judgment makes clear that the only travellers protected by the Act are 'gipsies'. In contrast, the Race Relations (Northern Ireland) Order 1997[47] expressly includes the Irish Traveller community as a racial group. This should include both nomadic and settled members of the community.

The different ethnic origins of at least some of the various constituent parts of the UK are clear: at one time, for example, Celts, Saxons and Danes would probably have satisfied the modern definition. But assimilation, if not total, has proceeded so far that claims to separate ethnic identity, while in some contexts still having an emotional

---

46 The Court of Appeal remitted the case to the county court to decide whether the signs were justified (under the RRA 1976, s 1(1)(b)(ii)).

47 Art 5(2): 'In this Order "racial grounds" – (a) includes the grounds of belonging to the Irish Traveller community, that is to say the community of people commonly so called who are identified (both by themselves and by others) as people with a shared history, culture and traditions including, historically, a nomadic way of life on the island of Ireland ...'

appeal, are far too flimsy to be accepted in law. The court implied in *Dutton* that there may come a time when gipsies are no longer sufficiently separate to be entitled to protection under the Act.

(a)   Language requirements and ethnic origins

A particular issue explored by McLeod (below) is whether a racial group can be defined by language. The matter was discussed by the EAT in *Jones*.

Gwynedd County Council v Jones [1986] ICR 833, EAT

The council required applicants to speak Welsh. Two Welsh complainants – who spoke English only – brought a claim of discrimination on grounds of their ethnic origins. An industrial tribunal[48] found in their favour. However, the EAT reversed this holding that it was 'wrong in law' to define a racial group by a language factor alone and that even if it was a question of fact, the tribunals finding was 'wholly unreasonable'.

Sir Ralph Kilner Brown (p 834):

We cannot believe that, for example, a Mrs Jones from Holyhead who speaks Welsh as well as English is to be regarded as belonging to a different racial group from her dear friend, a Mrs Thomas from Colwyn Bay who speaks only English. The concept seems to us to be as artificial as the proposition that 5,000 or so spectators at Cardiff Arms Park who are fluent in Welsh are a different racial group from the 45,000 or so whose command of the Welsh language is limited to the rendering of the Welsh national anthem, or 'Sospan fach'. An Englishman who dared to suggest this would be in danger of his life!

The *ratio decidendi* of *Jones* is that direct discrimination against English-only-speaking Welsh persons is not unlawful under the RRA 1976. However, the decision, and the statement that language alone could not be used to define a racial group, implied that Welsh speakers did not form a racial group. McLeod considers the position of Welsh and (Scottish) Gaelic speakers.

McLeod, W, 'Autochthonous language communities and the Race Relations Act', Web of Current Legal Issues [1998] 1 Web JCCI-html:[49]

The term 'autochthonous language' ... may ... seem unfamiliar and unwieldy, but is becoming an important term of art. At a European level, autochthonous minority languages have been distinguished from immigrant minority languages and granted special protections, most notably through the Council of Europe's European Charter for Regional or Minority Languages and certain European Community funding programmes set in place for the autochthonous languages of member states (European Commission Budget Line No. B3-1006).

[There is a] ... 500,000 strong Welsh-speaking community and [a] 65,000-strong Scottish Gaelic community, whose potential claim to recognition as a distinct 'ethnic group' – and thus a protected 'racial group' within the meaning of the Act – is arguably the strongest of the autochthonous language communities ...

48 By the Employment Rights (Dispute Resolution) Act 1998, s 1(1), Industrial Tribunals are renamed Employment Tribunals.
49 See also for the United States, Locke-Steven, I, 'Language discrimination and English-only rules in the workplace: the case for legislative amendment of Title VII' (1996) 27 Texas Tech Law Review, pp 33–72.

Turning first to the question of the Welsh language community, the *Jones* decision is of central importance. In concluding that English-monoglot Welsh people did not constitute a protected racial group, the EAT adopted a view of the Welsh as an undifferentiated unit and thus implicitly determined that Welsh speakers were also not a protected group ...

The analysis in *Jones* was superficial, indeed cryptic, and a range of important sociological and legal questions were ignored ...

Although its decision may ultimately have been correct in light of the overall position of the Welsh language in Wales and the nature of the Welsh-speaking community, the EAT in *Jones* clearly failed to consider the question with any serious analysis. Language cannot properly be considered as something that stands alone; in particular, it very often tends to create among its speakers 'a cultural tradition of [their] own' (*Mandla* [1983] 2 AC 548, at 562), and it is certainly arguable that such a distinct tradition can be discerned among Welsh speakers. It is unfortunate that the status of the Welsh language community was determined in this essentially negative context; a much more vigorous and culturally sensitive case could have been mounted within the *Mandla* framework if the question affirmatively presented had been the status of the Welsh-speaking minority community, rather than the English-monoglot majority.

The analysis in *Jones* was also distorted to some extent by the unhelpful terminology of the RRA, with its reliance on the term 'racial group' as the unit of analytic currency. Although *Mandla* took the proper analytic approach and spoke of 'ethnic groups' – the pertinent subset of the 'racial group' under the statute – the EAT's reasoning in *Jones* seems to have been confused by the 'racial group' terminology. The EAT's evident difficulty in seeing Welsh-speakers and English-monoglots as separate 'racial groups' in the ordinary lay sense led it to explain its decision with peculiar images ... [ie, Mrs Jones and Mrs Thomas].

Part of the difficulty [of recognising Gaels under the RRA] arises from the fact that the Gaels are, in many respects, a group in transition, part way – far along the way? – toward assimilation into a greater Britain and the global village. A sensitive evaluation of the Gaels' position, however, requires attention to the larger historical trajectory, and not some artificial snapshot of the present situation ...

Although the principal factor differentiating the Gaels from other Scots is the use of the Gaelic language itself, it can well be argued that the language is actually the medium of a distinct and separate culture, manifested in a variety of ways including deep-rooted traditions of poetry, song and music, and unique forms of religious worship. To some extent at least, this distinctiveness extends to material existence as well, the present-day crofting communities remaining substantially different in their way of life from the highly urbanised Scottish mainstream.

The claim of Gaelic speakers to recognition as an ethnic group is also strengthened by the fact that a very high proportion of Gaelic speakers, relative to the UK's other autochthonous language communities, are native speakers born and brought up in Gaelic-speaking communities in the Hebrides and West Highlands. It would be safe to say that at least 90% of Gaelic speakers come from such backgrounds, whereas the Welsh language community contains significant proportions of learners and non-traditional speakers. In the case of Gaelic, then, there is a very significant link between the ability to speak the language and a distinct culture and way of life, and the language is the badge of a community that has long been outside the societal mainstream.

Significantly from a legal standpoint, this 'combination of shared customs, beliefs, traditions and characteristics' is largely 'derived from a common ... past', distinct from the social institutions and practices of Lowland Britain (*King-Ansell* [1979] 2 NZLR 531, at 543) ...

On balance, it appears very difficult to articulate a viable basis for protection of Welsh speakers, given the constraint of Jones. The position of Gaelic speakers is considerably stronger, but by no means certain. A simplistic analysis, emphasising the 'racial' dimension without deep probing, would tend to work against recognition of the Gaels as an ethnic group, while a more complex, culturally informed inquiry could well produce a different result ...

McLeod puts a strong case for (Scottish) Gaels – and a borderline case for Welsh speakers – to fall within the definition of 'ethnic origins'. Although he is critical of the reasoning in *Jones*, he does not attack the *decision*. Of course there remains an anomaly. An English woman resident in Wales, who could not comply with a Welsh language requirement, could bring a claim of *indirect* discrimination based on her national origin.[50] A considerably smaller proportion of English than Welsh could comply with the requirement. To build on the imagery of Sir Ralf Kilner Brown (in *Jones*, above), of two non-Welsh speaking neighbours, only Mrs Smith enjoys the protection of the Act. Mrs Jones can be discriminated against because she is Welsh.

2   RELIGION OR BELIEF[51]

The Employment Equality (Religion or Belief) Regulations 2003[52]

2(1)   In these Regulations, 'religion or belief' means any religion, religious belief, or similar philosophical belief.

The Regulations came into force on 2 December 2003. They cover only employment matters.[53] Until these Regulations, there was no express protection for religious discrimination in Great Britain. There has been, since 1976 legislation against discrimination on grounds of 'religious or political opinion' in Northern Ireland.[54] Otherwise, the position for religious groups was capricious. They could claim under the RRA 1976 if the religion coincided with Lord Fraser's *Mandla* criteria,[55] and so Sikhs succeeded, but Rastafarians failed,[56] for want of a long shared history. According to the Court of Appeal, 60 years' history was not enough, although the court did not venture to suggest how many years amounted to 'long'.[57] According to Lord Fraser in *Mandla*, Jews would fall into his definition of 'ethnic origins'. Another possibility was where a religion and national origin coincided. This is explained by Poulter, who articulates the position for Muslims in the extract below.

---

50   See above, '(4) National Origins', p 142. Of course, such a requirement would be lawful if it were justified. For the ease of justifying language requirements, see *Groener v Minister of Education* Case 397/87 [1989] 2 ECR 3967, ECJ.

51   See Cumper, P, 'The protection of religious rights under section 13 of the Human Rights Act 1998' [2002] PL 254.

52   SI 2003/1660, implementing the Equal Treatment at Work Directive 2000/78/EC. See Vickers, L, 'The *Draft* Employment Equality (Religion or Belief) Regulations' (2003) 32 ILJ 23.

53   See Chapter 12.

54   Fair Employment (Northern Ireland) Act 1976.

55   See above '(5) Ethnic Origins', p 144.

56   *Crown Suppliers v Dawkins* [1993] ICR 517, CA. See above, '(5) Ethnic Origins', p 144.

57   *Ibid*, at p 526.

Poulter, S, 'Muslim headscarves in school: contrasting approaches in England and France' [1997] OJLS 43, p 64:

So far, in four cases decided by industrial tribunals and the Employment Appeal Tribunal, it has been held that Muslims are not an ethnic group but a religious one. As the South London Industrial Tribunal explained in *Nyazi v Rymans Ltd*:[58]

> Muslims include people of many nations and colours, who speak many languages and whose only common denominator is religion and religious culture.

More importantly perhaps, Muslims worldwide do possess a 'shared history' and many perceive themselves not as members of an ethnic group but as part of an essentially religious community or *'ummah'*. To some extent, this definitional hurdle can be circumvented through a plaintiff's reliance on membership of a group which does fall clearly within the terms of the Act. A Muslim pupil whose parents came to Britain from Pakistan could plead, for example, that any discrimination against her was based on her Pakistani nationality, her Pakistani 'national origin' (if she was a British citizen) or her Asian 'race'. On the other hand, the daughter of a growing number of white or black (Afro-Caribbean) British converts to Islam could not take advantage of this approach.

The inclusion of the word 'belief' in the recent Regulations widens the scope beyond conventional religions. Indeed, the Regulations state that this includes any 'religious' or 'philosophical' belief. At the least, this should avert detailed in-depth debates over whether, say, Catholicism is a religion or a denomination of Christianity.[59] However, the inclusion of *philosophical* beliefs allows the courts to go beyond recognised religions. This has been the approach taken by the USA courts, which have been interpreting the statutory word 'religion' for decades.

Organised religions recognised by American courts include Sikhs,[60] Tantric Buddhists,[61] Jews[62] and Rastafarians.[63] Further, in *Frazee v Illinois Department of Employment Security*,[64] the Supreme Court held that a man who expressed a Christian belief but belonged to no religious church or sect was protected. Atheists also have been held to come within the definition of 'religion'.[65]

The American courts have protected political beliefs that were rooted in a religion. In *Wilson v United States West Communications*,[66] a Roman Catholic employee made a religious vow to wear an anti-abortion button displaying a colour photograph of a foetus and two anti-abortion slogans. It was held that this practice came within the

---

58 EAT/6/88 (unreported).

59 Contrast the exception in reg 7(3), which is limited to 'religious ethos.' See below, Chapter 12, p 344.

60 See *Bhatia v Chevron* 734 F 2d 1382 (1984).

61 See *State v Rocheleau* 64 451 A 2d 1144 (1982).

62 *Lapine v Edward Marshall Boehm Inc* 1990 US Dist LEXIS 3459.

63 Formally known as *The Twelve Tribes of Israel*. See *Whyte v United States* 471 A 2d 1018 (1984) District of Columbia Court of Appeals, under the Free Exercise Clause of the First Amendment.

64 489 US 829 (1989).

65 *EEOC v Townley Engineering* 859 F 2d 610 (1988). See also *Young v Southwestern Saving and Loan Association* 509 F 2d 140, at p 144.

66 58 F 3d 1337 (1994).

meaning of 'religion'.[67] In *Dorr v First Kentucky*,[68] a member of a religious group[69] committed to equal rights for homosexual men and women fell within the definition of 'religion'. In *American Postal Workers Union v Postmaster General*,[70] two window clerks refused to handle draft (conscription) papers on the grounds that their religion prohibited them from doing anything to facilitate war. Their employer's refusal to accommodate this was held to be religious discrimination under Title VII. The limit of this liberal approach was, perhaps, expressed by the Supreme Court when noting that an asserted belief might be: 'so bizarre, so clearly non-religious in motivation, as not to be entitled to protection ...'[71]

3   SEX, GENDER REASSIGNMENT AND SEXUAL ORIENTATION

These three categories are drawn together under one general heading because they each have a relationship to the definition of 'sex' in the Sex Discrimination Act 1975. The position today is as follows. The relevant legislation is the SDA 1975, the Equal Treatment Directive,[72] Art 141 (formerly Art 119) of the EC Treaty (equal pay), the Equal Treatment at Work Directive,[73] the subsequent Employment Equality (Sexual Orientation) Regulations 2003,[74] and the Human Rights Act (HRA) 1998. The SDA 1975 covers discrimination against men as well as women,[75] and discrimination on the grounds of pregnancy.[76]

The coverage becomes more complex in relation to gender reassignment and sexual orientation. Here, the SDA 1975 covers *direct* discrimination only, on the grounds of gender reassignment, and only in the field of employment or vocational training.[77] Claims of indirect discrimination should be possible under the Equal Treatment Directive and, in other fields, a claim may be possible under the general equality article of the HRA 1998.[78] As we shall see, it may be possible, with some ingenuity, to extend the SDA 1975 to cover indirect discrimination in *all* fields.

Sexual orientation discrimination will be covered by the Employment Equality (Sexual Orientation) Regulations 2003.[79] The Regulations extend only to employment matters. In other fields, the SDA 1975 may be used where, for instance, the defendant

---

67   58 F 3d 1337 at p 1340. Although the evidence showed that the wearing of the badge was within the vow, the *displaying* of it was not, and so was outside of the meaning of 'religion'.
68   *Dorr v First Kentucky National Corporation; First National Bank of Louisville* 796 F 2d 179 (1986).
69   A group called *Integrity*, affiliated to the Episcopal Church.
70   781 F 2d 772 (1986) Court of Appeals for the Ninth Circuit.
71   *Thomas v Review Board of Indiana Employment Security Div* 450 US 707 (1981), at p 715; a case under the Free Exercise Clause.
72   Council Directive 76/207/EEC.
73   Council Directive 2000/78/EC.
74   SI 2003/1661.
75   SDA 1975, s 2.
76   *Webb v EMO Air Cargo (No 2)* [1994] QB 718; [1995] IRLR 645, HL.
77   SDA 1975, s 2A.
78   *A v Chief Constable of W Yorkshire* (2002) *The Times*, 14 November; [2002] EWCA 1584; [2002] All ER (D) 50, CA. See Chapter 5, p 116.
79   SI 2003/1661. In force since 1 December 2003.

treated a gay man less favourably than he would have treated a lesbian.[80] As with gender reassignment, a claim may also be possible under the general equality article of the HRA 1998.[81]

Finally, the SDA 1975 and the Equal Treatment Directive make it unlawful to discriminate on grounds of a person's marital status, but both pieces of legislation are confined to employment matters.[82]

(1)   Gender Reassignment

(a)   *P v S and Cornwall CC*

In this landmark case, the ECJ held that discrimination against transsexuals was discrimination on the grounds of sex.

P v S and Cornwall CC Case C-13/94 [1996] ECR I-2143, ECJ[83]

When the applicant was hired as a general manager, he was male. A year later, his employer learned that he intended to undergo gender reassignment. He was dismissed. An industrial tribunal held that this case fell outside the scope of the SDA 1975, but referred the case to the ECJ for consideration of whether the Equal Treatment Directive applied.

Advocate General (para 24):

I am well aware that I am asking the Court to make a 'courageous' decision. I am asking it to do so, however, in the profound conviction that what is at stake is a universal fundamental value, indelibly etched in modern legal traditions and in the constitutions of the more advanced countries: *the irrelevance of a person's sex with regard to the rules regarding relations in society.* Whosoever believes in that value cannot accept the idea that a law should permit a person to be dismissed because she is a woman, or because he is a man, or because he or she changes from one of the two sexes ... by means of an operation which – according to current medical knowledge – is the only remedy capable of bringing mind and body into harmony. Any other solution would sound like a moral condemnation – a condemnation, moreover, out of step with the times – of transsexuality, precisely when scientific advances and social change in this area are opening a perspective on this problem which certainly transcends the moral one.

I am quite clear ... that in Community law there is no precise provision *specifically* and literally intended to regulate the problem; but such a provision can readily and clearly be inferred from the principles and objectives of Community social law, the statement of reasons for the Directive underlining 'the harmonisation of living and working conditions while maintaining their improvement', and also the case law of the Court itself, which is ever alert and to the fore in ensuring that disadvantaged persons are protected.

---

80   See *Smith v Gardener Merchant* [1998] IRLR 510, CA.
81   See *Mendoza v Ghaidan* [2002] 4 All ER 1162; [2002] EWCA 1533, CA, set out in Chapter 5, p 124.
82   SDA 1975, s 3.
83   See also [1996] ICR 795; [1996] IRLR 347.

Judgment (paras 19–22):

[T]he right not to be discriminated against on grounds of sex is one of the fundamental human rights whose observance the Court has a duty to ensure ...

Accordingly, the scope of the [Equal Treatment] Directive cannot be confined simply to discrimination based on the fact that a person is of one or other sex. In view of its purpose and the nature of the rights which it seeks to safeguard, the scope of the Directive is also such as to apply to discrimination arising ... from the gender reassignment of the person concerned.

Such discrimination is based, essentially if not exclusively, on the sex of the person concerned. Where a person is dismissed on the ground that he or she intends to undergo, or has undergone, gender reassignment, he or she is treated unfavourably by comparison with persons of the sex to which he or she was deemed to belong before undergoing gender reassignment.

To tolerate such discrimination would be tantamount, as regards such a person, to a failure to respect the dignity and freedom to which he or she is entitled, and which this Court has a duty to safeguard.

Flynn, L, 'Case note: *P v S and Cornwall CC'* (1997) 34 CML Rev 367, pp 375–84:

Whether [the decision] is to be regarded as the principled stand of a body entrusted with a constitutional task requiring it to ensure the protection of human rights, or as the activism of individuals who are creating rights which the legitimate legislator has for its own reasons chosen not to grant, must rest on the commentator's vision of the Community legal order ...

[T]he Court ... states that a person dismissed for undergoing or proposing to undergo gender reassignment is treated unfavourably 'by comparison with persons of the sex to which he or she was deemed to belong [beforehand]'. As P was male under English law at all times and the Court does not seem to suggest that she was legally female as a matter of Community law, it appears that the 'comparison' is between persons of the same sex ... The comparison between P and other male employees is not a comparison based on biological sex but between persons, all of the same sex, of whom one has a feminine gender identity while the others have stable masculine gender identities ...

[A] far more liberal approach is taken by the Court [than in the past] to discover if a human rights' matter falls within its jurisdiction. The operative part of the Court's reasoning starts with the declaration that fundamental human rights include the principle of equality and that this non-discrimination principle extends to transsexuals. On this basis the Court concludes that the scope of the Directive must be read in the light of this principle. The traditional approach would have been to have first looked at the scope of the Directive and then to find that the principle of equality applied within its scope. The reasoning of the Court quite literally overturns its earlier perspective on this point ...

The difficulty for transsexuals being recognised under the heading of 'sex' discrimination has been in the comparison. The ECJ appeared to sidestep this obstacle by declaring that 'the Directive cannot be confined simply to discrimination based on the fact that a person is of one or another sex', but then the Court provided a formula for a comparison (with the claimant's past sex).[84] Flynn argues that this comparison is really one between persons of the same sex.

---

84 Or, in cases before planned reassignment, presumably, with the sex that the claimant plans to become.

(b)   Section 2A of the SDA 1975

P v S and Cornwall CC led to s 2A of the SDA 1975 coming into force on 1 May 1999. However, s 2A (being passed under the European Communities Act 1972) is confined to cases of direct discrimination in the field of employment matters only. As we shall see, it is possible to extend the protection beyond that given by s 2A.

Sex Discrimination Act 1975

2A Discrimination on the grounds of gender reassignment[85]

(1)   A person ('A') discriminates against another person ('B') ...

if he treats B less favourably than he treats or would treat other persons, and does so on the ground that B intends to undergo, is undergoing or has undergone gender reassignment.

...

(5)   For the purposes of subsection (1), a provision mentioned in that subsection framed with reference to discrimination against women shall be treated as applying equally to the treatment of men with such modifications as are requisite.

By expressly identifying gender reassignment as a ground of discrimination, s 2A removes the problem of comparing a male with a female. This did not help the claimant in the next case, who was pre-operative transsexual. The facts are given by Lindsay J.

Croft v Consignia (ex Post Office) [2002] IRLR 851, EAT; affd [2003] IRLR 592, CA

Lindsay J:

1.   Sarah Croft. ... is a pre-operative transsexual. Under our current domestic law she is male; she was male at birth and remains so biologically and genitally. She is, though, an instance of gender dysphoria and has embarked on the 'real life test' of dressing and generally 'presenting' as a woman. In accordance with that wish, she wanted to use the female toilet facilities which the employer provided. Other female employees objected. The employer ... refused her permission to do so ...

5.   The other matter we mention at the outset is the remarkable rarity of the problem which faced employer and employee. Whilst we would not wish this statistic to be taken to be reliable generally, the Post Office, a nationwide employer with some 160,000 employees at the time, prior to Ms Croft's case knew of only four other cases of transsexualism amongst its employees, a rate of 0.0025%. Moreover, whilst it is not unknown for transsexuals, embarking on the 'real life test' and wishing to escape the prurient interest which the press, particularly the tabloid press, has in such matters, to undertake the test in surroundings where, for example, she had not been known as male, Ms Croft remained at the same workplace where she had been known for over 10 years as a man. Whilst such considerations do not necessarily affect whether or not there had been discrimination or any breach of contract, they need to be borne in mind when one is to consider whether an employer, moving in such exceptional circumstances, has moved as adroitly as law may require ...

---

85   Inserted by SI 1999/1102, reg 2(1). It came into force 1 May 1999: see reg 1(2).

54. [W]e need to mention the Workplace Directive (89/654/EEC) of 30 November 1989. ... Annex I para 18.1.3 requires provision of separate changing rooms or separate use of changing rooms for men and women ... Para 18.3 provides:

'Provision must be made for separate lavatories or separate use of lavatories for men and women' ...

55. The terms 'men' and 'women' were not defined in either the Directive or the Regulations but, as it seems to us, in 1989 and 1992 the references would be to those at law or believed by the employer to be male and female respectively. Moreover, it seems to us inherently improbable that the terms 'men' and 'women' should then be referring to the gender a person might choose for himself or herself as that interpretation would require contemplation of the shower rooms, similarly provided to be separate, nonetheless possibly having amongst their users, in the women's facilities, persons still wholly anatomically male and, in the men's, persons surgically adapted as far as possible to resemble females. Further, if the Directive was contemplating 'men' or 'women' as including persons asserting a gender other than congruent with their sex at law or that sex believed by the employer to be the appropriate sex at law, one could reasonably have expected provision to be made to exclude, for example, temporary masquerades, by referring to the steps taken to adopt the discongruent gender and as to its intended duration.

56. If that is right, then a woman finding a person at law male using the facilities separately assigned for use by women might not be asserting only a right to a conventional form of privacy or propriety but also a breach of Directive or Regulation. In the light of these workplace provisions, ordinary good practice requires, as it seems to us, that an employer is to be expected to require those who are, or who are believed by him to be, at law males to use only the men's facilities and those who are at law or who are believed by him to be females to use only the women's ...

63. ... [Section 2A] by its reference to the treatment of others, invites a comparative process. We see the force, in general, of Miss Rose's [counsel for Ms Croft] submission that the comparison is to be with the treatment of those, of either sex, who are not transsexuals. It might, still dealing in general, be necessary to qualify that by reference to the treatment of other employees who are not known to the employer to be transsexual in the sense of intending to undergo, undergoing as or having undergone gender reassignment. But we do not see the general case as applicable in the particular circumstances of the use of toilet facilities and the effect, as we have understood it, of the Workplace Directive and Regulations ... The bar put on Ms Croft's use of toilet facilities dedicated to a sex other than the legal sex to which the Post Office knew her to belong was not a treatment, in respect of toilet facilities, other than would have been afforded to anyone else where there was a known discongruity between the way a person was presenting and his or her legal or putative sex. It was not less favourable treatment within s 2A and, if it were to be so regarded, s 2A would, in our view, need, in the particular circumstances of the applicability of the Workplace Directive, to be disapplied.

Lindsay J added[86] that his decision was consistent with *Goodwin* (see below), which concerned a post-operative transsexual. It is arguable that this decision is consistent with *P v S and Cornwall CC* (above) where the ECJ envisaged a comparison between a male and a female. However, under s 2A, the comparison must be between the

---

86 [2002] IRLR 851, at para 72.

claimant (in this case intending to undergo gender reassignment) and another. Lindsay J compared the treatment of Ms Croft with that 'afforded to anyone else where there was a known discongruity between the way a person was presenting and his or her legal or putative sex'. In other words, he compared her to someone intending, or at least, contemplating, gender reassignment. His alternative, to disapply s 2A in favour of the Directive, is more convincing. However, Lindsay J left an impression of being influenced by the practical problems facing the employer, noting the 'rarity' of claimants (suggesting a disproportionate adjustment for very few workers) and the complaints of fellow workers. Neither factor should contribute to a case of direct discrimination.

(c)   Protection beyond s 2A of the SDA 1975

As mentioned above, in reflecting actual decision in *P v S*, s 2A only covered *direct* discrimination in the field of employment and occupation. However, subsequent cases have broadened the protection beyond the strict wording of s 2A. The decision in *Chessington World of Adventures v Reed* suggests that the SDA 1975 *as a whole* may apply to transsexuals. The European Court of Human Rights in *Goodwin v UK*[87] held that the Government violated the Convention by refusing a new birth certificate to a male-to-female transsexual. In turn, *Goodwin* will become part of ECJ jurisprudence, so EC sex discrimination law must be interpreted accordingly. This may expose shortfalls of the SDA 1975 in employment matters.[88]

Chessington World of Adventures Ltd v Reed [1997] IRLR 556, EAT

In 1991, the applicant announced a change of identity from male to female. For the next three years she was subjected to a campaign of harassment by some of her male colleagues. Eventually, she took sick leave and five months later was dismissed on the ground of lack of capability.

The EAT upheld the decision of the industrial tribunal that the SDA 1975 could, in the light of *P v S*, be construed so as to cover unfavourable treatment following a person's statement of intention to undergo gender reassignment.

Judge Peter Clark (pp 518–19):

[W]here, as in this case, the reason for the unfavourable treatment is sex based, that is, a declared intention to undergo gender reassignment, there is no requirement for a male/female comparison to be made. In these circumstances we interpret the 1975 Act consistently with the ruling of the European Court in *P v S*.

Reed could have only achieved the remedy upon this interpretation. At the time, that is, before the amendment to SDA 1975, Reed had no claim under the Equal Treatment Directive, as the employer was from the private sector. Of course, the new s 2A remedied that, but the decision that the word 'sex' in s 1 of the SDA 1975 can apply to transsexuals arguably means that the Act applies beyond the restrictions of s 2A to

87 (2002) EHRR 447; [2002] 2 FCR 577.
88 In *A v Chief Constable of West Yorkshire* (2002) *The Times*, 14 November; [2002] EWCA 1584; [2002] All ER (D) 50 (Nov), the Court of Appeal suggested that, in light of the ECtHR decision in *Goodwin* recognising the right to a new birth certificate in the new sex (see below), the claimant was entitled to be treated as his post-assignment sex, for all purposes, including intimate body searches, the right flowing through the Equal Treatment Directive. At the time of writing an appeal was due in the House of Lords. See further Chapter 5, p 116.

cover indirect discrimination and fields beyond employment, such as the provision of services and housing.

The obstacle to applying s 1 in this way is that s 2A then becomes redundant. The counter argument is that s 2A serves a purpose of 'amplifying' s 1(1)(a). To assess the strength of the arguments, the cases need to be divided into those within employment, and those in other fields. The 'amplifying' argument may appear artificial, but, for cases in the employment field, it allows a domestic tribunal to apply the Act in accordance with the Equal Treatment Directive. Although the ECJ's decision in *P v S* extended only to direct discrimination, it is inconceivable that the ECJ would restrict the Directive to cover only direct discrimination where the case concerned gender reassignment. As domestic courts and tribunals are obliged to interpret domestic legislation in accordance with EU law, so far as it is possible to do so,[89] this 'artificial' argument should be all that is needed to achieve that.

Of course, in the second class of cases – those in a field other than employment – such reasoning cannot be used. What can be said to support the 'artificial' argument is that it gives the statutory word 'sex' its ordinary meaning, in accordance with *Reed* and the ECJ in *P v S*. This avoids the anomaly of the word 'sex' in s 1 of the SDA 1975 having one meaning for employment cases (assuming the above argument would succeed) and another meaning other fields. It also avoids another anomaly of the Act outlawing discrimination in employment, but not elsewhere, although of course that anomaly exists in racial,[90] religious and the forthcoming age discrimination law. However, another path to recognition may be through the Human Rights Act 1998.

Goodwin v UK (2002) EHRR 447; [2002] 2 FCR 577, ECtHR

Christine Goodwin had undergone male-to-female gender reassignment. At the heart of her case, was her inability to obtain a new birth certificate recognising that she was a woman. The Court highlighted some of the consequences of being denied a birth certificate and found the UK in breach of Arts 8 and 12, but not Art 14.

Judgment of the Court

I. ALLEGED VIOLATION OF ARTICLE 8 OF THE CONVENTION

59.   The applicant claims a violation of Article 8 of the Convention, the relevant part of which provides as follows:

'1.   Everyone has the right to respect for his private ... life ...

2.   There shall be no interference by a public authority with the exercise of this right except such as is in accordance with the law and is necessary in a democratic society in the interests of national security, public safety or the economic well-being of the country, for the prevention of disorder or crime, for the protection of health or morals, or for the protection of the rights and freedoms of others.'

60.   The applicant submitted that ... [t]he lack of legal recognition of her changed gender had been the cause of numerous discriminatory and humiliating experiences in her everyday life. In the past, in particular from 1990 to 1992, she

---

89   The doctrine of indirect effect. Domestic courts should interpret domestic legislation as far as possible to accord with a Directive whether the domestic law in question was enacted *before or after* the Directive: *Marleasing SA v La Comercial Internacional de Alimentacion* Case C 106/89 [1990] 1 CMLR 305, at para 13. See further Chapter 5, p 112.

90   Largely cured by the Race Directive 2000/43/EC and the consequent Race Relations Act 1976 (Amendment) Regulations 2003, SI 2003/1626, in force since 19 July 2003.

was abused at work and did not receive proper protection against discrimination. She claimed that all the special procedures through which she had to go in respect of her NI contributions and State retirement pension constituted in themselves an unjustified difference in treatment, as they would have been unnecessary had she been recognised as a woman for legal purposes. In particular, the very fact that the DSS operated a policy of marking the records of transsexuals as sensitive was a difference in treatment. As a result, for example, the applicant cannot attend the DSS without having to make a special appointment.

61.   The applicant further submitted that the danger of her employer learning about her past identity was real. It was possible for the employer to trace back her employment history on the basis of her NI number and this had in fact happened. She claimed that her recent failure to obtain a promotion was the result of the employer realising her status.

62.   As regarded pensionable age, the applicant submitted that she had worked for 44 years and that the refusal of her entitlement to a State retirement pension at the age of 60 on the basis of the pure biological test for determining sex was contrary to Article 8 of the Convention. She was similarly unable to apply for a free London bus pass at the age of 60 as other women were but had to wait until the age of 65. She was also required to declare her birth sex or disclose her birth certificate when applying for life insurance, mortgages, private pensions or car insurance, which led her not to pursue these possibilities to her advantage. ...

64.   Referring to the Court's case-law, the Government maintained that there was no generally accepted approach among the Contracting States in respect of transsexuality and that, in view of the margin of appreciation left to States under the Convention, the lack of recognition in the United Kingdom of the applicant's new gender identity for legal purposes did not entail a violation of Article 8 of the Convention. They disputed the applicant's assertion that scientific research and 'massive societal changes' had led to wide acceptance, or consensus on issues, of transsexualism.

...

The Court's assessment

71.   This case raises the issue whether or not the respondent State has failed to comply with a positive obligation to ensure the right of the applicant, a post-operative male to female transsexual, to respect for her private life, in particular through the lack of legal recognition given to her gender re-assignment.

72.   The Court recalls that the notion of 'respect' as understood in Article 8 is not clear cut, especially as far as the positive obligations inherent in that concept are concerned ... In determining whether or not a positive obligation exists, regard must also be had to the fair balance that has to be struck between the general interest of the community and the interests of the individual, the search for which balance is inherent in the whole of the Convention (*Cossey v the United Kingdom* judgment of 27 September 1990, Series A no 184, p 15, § 37) ...

The state of any European and international consensus

84.   Already at the time of the *Sheffield and Horsham* case,[91] there was an emerging consensus within Contracting States in the Council of Europe on providing legal recognition following gender re-assignment (see § 35 of that judgment). The latest survey submitted by Liberty in the present case shows a continuing

---

91   *Sheffield and Horsham v UK* (1998) 27 EHRR 163.

international trend towards legal recognition ... In Australia and New Zealand, it appears that the courts are moving away from the biological birth view of sex (as set out in the United Kingdom case of *Corbett v Corbett*)[92] and taking the view that sex, in the context of a transsexual wishing to marry, should depend on a multitude of factors to be assessed at the time of the marriage ...

87. It may be noted however that exceptions are already made to the historic basis of the birth register system, namely, in the case of legitimisation or adoptions, where there is a possibility of issuing updated certificates to reflect a change in status after birth. To make a further exception in the case of transsexuals (a category estimated as including some 2,000–5,000 persons in the United Kingdom according to the Interdepartmental Working Group Report, p 26) would not, in the Court's view, pose the threat of overturning the entire system ...

88. Furthermore, the Court notes that the Government have recently issued proposals for reform which would allow ongoing amendment to civil status data ...

Striking a balance in the present case

90. ... the very essence of the Convention is respect for human dignity and human freedom. Under Article 8 of the Convention in particular, where the notion of personal autonomy is an important principle underlying the interpretation of its guarantees, protection is given to the personal sphere of each individual, including the right to establish details of their identity as individual human beings (see, *inter alia, Pretty v UK*[93] ... § 62, and *Mikulic v Croatia*[94] ... § 53 ... In the twenty first century the right of transsexuals to personal development and to physical and moral security in the full sense enjoyed by others in society cannot be regarded as a matter of controversy requiring the lapse of time to cast clearer light on the issues involved. In short, the unsatisfactory situation in which post-operative transsexuals live in an intermediate zone as not quite one gender or the other is no longer sustainable. Domestic recognition of this evaluation may be found in the report of the Interdepartmental Working Group and the Court of Appeal's judgment of *Bellinger v Bellinger* ...[95]

93. Having regard to the above considerations, the Court finds that the respondent Government can no longer claim that the matter falls within their margin of appreciation, save as regards the appropriate means of achieving recognition of the right protected under the Convention. Since there are no significant factors of public interest to weigh against the interest of this individual applicant in obtaining legal recognition of her gender re-assignment, it reaches the conclusion that the fair balance that is inherent in the Convention now tilts decisively in favour of the applicant. There has, accordingly, been a failure to respect her right to private life in breach of Article 8 of the Convention.

II.   ALLEGED VIOLATION OF ARTICLE 12 OF THE CONVENTION

94. The applicant also claimed a violation of Article 12 of the Convention, which provides as follows:

---

92 [1971] Probate Reports 83.
93 (2002) 35 EHRR 1.
94 [2002] 1 FCR 720.
95 [2001] EWCA Civ 1140, [2002] 1 All ER 311; [2002] 2 WLR 411; [2001] 3 FCR 1; [2001] 2 FLR 1048; [2001] Fam Law 807; 64 BMLR 1. Affirmed [2003] UKHL 21; [2003] All ER (D) 178 (Apr), HL.

'Men and women of marriageable age have the right to marry and to found a family, according to the national laws governing the exercise of this right.' ...

102. ... The Government have argued that in this sensitive area eligibility for marriage under national law should be left to the domestic courts within the State's margin of appreciation, adverting to the potential impact on already existing marriages in which a transsexual is a partner. It appears however from the opinions of the majority of the Court of Appeal judgment in *Bellinger v. Bellinger* that the domestic courts tend to the view that the matter is best handled by the legislature, while the Government have no present intention to introduce legislation ...

104. The Court concludes that there has been a breach of Article 12 of the Convention in the present case.

III. ALLEGED VIOLATION OF ARTICLE 14 OF THE CONVENTION

108. The Court considers that the lack of legal recognition of the change of gender of a post-operative transsexual lies at the heart of the applicant's complaints under Article 14 of the Convention. These issues have been examined under Article 8 and resulted in the finding of a violation of that provision. In the circumstances, the Court considers that no separate issue arises under Article 14 of the Convention and makes no separate finding.

Although this was, ultimately, not a case of discrimination, but of human rights, this decision was a major development in discrimination law regarding transsexuals. The inability to obtain a new birth certificate was the cause of the 'numerous discriminatory and humiliating experiences' suffered by Christine Goodwin. It should also resolve the problems associated with unrecognised marriages, such as in *Bavin v NHS Trust Pensions Agency*.[96] Ms Bavin was legally disabled from marrying her partner, who had undergone female-to-male reassignment, but, in the eyes of the law, remained a woman. She challenged the rule that restricted survivors' pensions to widows and widowers. The EAT rejected her claim since, it observed, the benefit was withheld because Bavin's partner was unmarried, *not* because he was a transsexual. Since *Goodwin*, a person in Bavin's position *should* be able seek a remedy under the HRA 1998, at the least. If the claim falls within the employment field, the claim may be made under EC law. This is because the ECJ takes into account ECtHR jurisprudence.[97] Of course, this would apply even to cases pre-dating the HRA 1998, (which came into force in October 2000).[98] However, the House of Lords in *Bellinger v Bellinger*[99] refused to recognise a marriage between a male-to-female transsexual and a male, preferring to leave the full implementation of *Goodwin* to Parliament.[100] The

---

96 *Bavin v NHS Trust Pensions Agency and Secretary of State for Health* [1999] ICR 1192.

97 See, eg, *R v Kirk* Case 63/83 [1984] 2 ECR 2689; 3 CMLR 522; [1985] 1 All ER 453; *Johnston v Chief Constable of the Royal Ulster Constabulary* Case 222/84 [1986] ECR 1651; [1986] 3 CMLR 240; [1987] QB 129; [1986] 3 WLR 1038; [1987] ICR 83; [1986] 3 All ER 135.

98 *A v Chief Constable of West Yorkshire* (2002) *The Times*, 14 November; [2002] EWCA 1584; [2002] All ER (D) 50 (Nov), CA. At the time of writing an appeal was due in the House of Lords. See further Chapter 5, p 116.

99 [2003] UKHL 21; [2003] All ER (D) 178 (Apr), HL.

100 The House held that, in light of *Goodwin*, s 11(c) of the Matrimonial Causes Act 1973, which stated that a marriage was void unless the parties were 'respectively male and female', was incompatible with the HRA 1998.

Government announced on 13 December 2002[101] that it proposed to implement *Goodwin* fully with legislation.

Finally, note that the judgment in *Goodwin* renders Flynn's criticism of *P v S* (above) immaterial. If a person's new sex is recognised *legally*, it is no longer possible to argue that the ECJ (in comparing the treatment given before and after gender reassignment) compared persons of the same sex.

(2)   Sexual Orientation

Sexual orientation discrimination is covered by the Employment Equality (Sexual Orientation) Regulations 2003, in force since 1 December 2003. They were implemented in response to the Equal Treatment at Work Directive.[102] Accordingly, the Regulations extend only to employment and vocational training.

Employment Equality (Sexual Orientation) Regulations 2003

2.(1) In these Regulations 'sexual orientation' means an orientation towards
   (a) persons of the same sex,
   (b) persons of the opposite sex, or
   (c) persons of the same sex and of the opposite sex.

Regulation 2 covers homosexual, heterosexual and bisexual persons. 'Sexual orientation' was inserted into Equal Treatment at Work Directive following the ECJ's decision in *Grant v South West Trains Ltd*[103] that the existing EU sex discrimination legislation did not extend to discrimination on the grounds of sexual orientation. Domestic courts have taken the same line.[104] The result is that outside the field of employment, there is no specific protection against such discrimination. However, there are some cases outside of employment that may fall under the SDA 1975 or the HRA 1998.

(a)   Sex Discrimination Act 1975

The key to success here is making the correct comparison and showing that, for instance, a gay man was treated less favourably than a gay woman.

Smith v Gardner Merchant Ltd [1998] 3 All ER 852; [1999] ICR 134; [1998] IRLR 510, CA

The claimant, a homosexual man, alleged that a work colleague had subjected him to harassment by constantly asking personal questions regarding his sexuality and making offensive remarks about him being gay (for example, saying that he probably had all sorts of diseases and that gay people who spread AIDS should be put on an island). He claimed that this amounted to a breach of the SDA 1975 by his employer.

---

101 A draft Gender Recognition Bill was published in July 2003. See www.lcd.gov.uk (due to be replaced by www.dca.gov.uk) and click on 'People's Rights'.
102 2000/78/EC.
103 Case C-249/96 [1998] IRLR 206. See Bamforth, N, 'Sexual orientation discrimination after *Grant v South-West Trains*' (2000) 63 MLR 694.
104 In *Macdonald v Secretary of State for Defence* [2003] UKHL 34; [2003] All ER (D) 259 (Jun), the House of Lords upheld the majority decision of the CS ([2001] IRLR 431; [2002] ICR 174) that 'sex' in the SDA did not include sexual orientation, reversing the decision of the EAT, which held that 'sex' should be given broad interpretation because of the Human Rights Act. On the CS decision, see Hannett, S 'Sexual orientation and the SDA 1975' (2001) 30 ILJ 324.

The industrial tribunal and EAT dismissed his claim on the basis that the SDA 1975 did not extend to discrimination on the grounds of sexual orientation. The Court of Appeal allowed his appeal.[105]

Ward LJ (paras 2 and 4)

To identify whether or not there has been direct sex discrimination it is necessary to compare the treatment meted out to the employee and the treatment which was or would have been meted out to a member of the opposite sex and to ask whether the employee has received less favourable treatment ...

The industrial tribunal and the Appeal Tribunal were, therefore, correct to conclude that there is a difference between discrimination on the ground of sex and discrimination on the ground of sexual orientation and that a person's sexual orientation is not an aspect of his or her sex ...

The error lies in the conclusion, which was virtually a conclusion of *cadit quaestio*[106] when, as I now see it, the right question had not been addressed. The right question framed in terms of s 1(1)(a) is whether the applicant, a man, had been less favourably treated than his employers treated or would have treated a woman. By focusing on the applicant's homosexuality, the drift of the argument pushes one almost ineluctably – as I myself was carried along – to ask the wrong question: was he discriminated against because he was a man (sex) or because he was a homosexual (sexual orientation)? In concentrating on that, one falls into the error that one does not make the comparison which the statute requires, namely between his position as a man, and the comparative position of a woman. The fault in the argument is that it precludes consideration of a vital question, namely whether or not discrimination against him based upon his homosexuality may not also be discrimination against him as a man. I am grateful to Ms Cox [counsel for the claimant] for withstanding a fairly hostile judicial barrage and for opening my eyes to errors made by the tribunal.

It is upon that further reflection that I have come to the conclusion that the task imposed on the tribunal by s 1(1)(a) read with s 5(3) is to ascertain: (a) what, as a matter of fact, was the treatment received by the employee; (b) was he treated less favourably than the woman with whom he falls to be compared; and (c) would he have been so treated but for his sex? ...

To compare like with like, a male homosexual must be compared with a female homosexual.

(b)   Human Rights Act 1998

The HRA 1998 brought the European Convention on Human Rights into domestic law. The Convention has no free-standing right regarding discrimination.[107] But rights in the Convention must be 'secured' without discrimination (Art 14). And so the State (including the courts) may not apply Convention rights (such as freedom of expression, or right to respect for home and private life) in a discriminatory way,

---

105 Contrast *Pearce v Governing Body of Mayfield Secondary School* [2003] UKHL 34, extracted below, Chapter 9, p 221.

106 The matter admits of no further argument. Literally, *the question falls.*

107 The 12th Protocol, which gives a free-standing right against discrimination has been adopted, but not yet ratified. It covers the same grounds as Art 14, ie, sex, race, colour, language, religion, political or other opinion, national or social origin, association with a national minority, property, birth or other status.

unless it can show it is justified in doing so. In *Mendoza v Ghaidan*,[108] the Court of Appeal held that a cohabitee in a same-sex relationship had the same right of succession to a lease as a cohabitee in a heterosexual relationship. The judgment in *Mendoza* is set out in Chapter 5.[109]

(3)   Marital Status

Sex Discrimination Act 1975

2   Direct and indirect discrimination against married persons in employment field

(1)   ... a person discriminates against a married person of either sex if

    (a) on the grounds of his or her marital status he treats that person less favourably than he treats or would treat an unmarried person of the same sex ...

Section 3(1)(b) of the SDA 1975 outlaws indirect discrimination against married people. There are two key points in the SDA 1975 definition. First, while s 3(1)(a) refers to marital status, which could be thought to include the status of being single, it is clear from the wording (eg, 'against a married person') that only discrimination against a married person is covered; discrimination against a single person is lawful under the SDA 1975. Secondly, the comparison is with an unmarried person of *the same sex* as the complainant, so that the provision applies even where the workforce is wholly female. It follows that it is irrelevant that male married people are treated in the same way as female married people if a female married person is treated less favourably than a female single person.

The drafting appears to require that the complainant be married at the time of the action of which complaint is made. This excludes those intending to be married, those about to be married, those living together who are not formally married, and those who have once been married. Article 2(1) of the Equal Treatment Directive is more extensive, covering discrimination 'in relation to marital or family status'. While the ECJ has not ruled on the extent of this provision, the context would appear to support a wide interpretation. This may be important if, for example, someone is dismissed having announced their intention of marrying or divorcing, although the rights would only be against organs of the State.

4   AGE

Age discrimination was included in the Equality at Work Directive, although the Government have negotiated an extension to 2006 for implementation.[110] Unlike the US model (see below), the Directive is not expressly aimed at older persons. The obvious candidate for a challenge here is the minimum wage legislation, which provides for lower pay for 18 to 20 year olds. However, Article 6, which offers some specific examples of justifiable discrimination, includes 'the setting of special conditions ... including remuneration ... for young people'.

---

108 [2002] 4 All ER 1162; [2002] EWCA Civ 1533. At the time of writing an appeal was due in the House of Lords.
109 At p 124.
110 On the British position, see Desmond, H [2000] 29 ILJ 403.

To gain some notion of how it work in the UK, we can look at the American experience. The Age Discrimination in Employment Act (ADEA) was passed in 1977. The basic legal model adopted reflected existing law on race and sex discrimination, known as Title VII.[111] The impact of the law has been less in terms of granting significant legal or political rights to a disadvantaged group, and more in terms of granting certain legal rights to individuals which were not previously available.

Rutherglen, G, 'From race to age: the expanding scope of employment discrimination law' (1995) 24 Journal of Legal Studies 491, pp 495–501, 509, 520:

With several exceptions, the [Age Discrimination in Employment Act] covers all employees at or above the age of 40, regardless of race or sex.[112] Although Title VII nominally has equally broad coverage, it was intended to protect mainly racial minorities, women and other traditional victims of discrimination ... What the reported cases reveal, and what the empirical evidence confirms, is that white males have been the principal beneficiaries of the ADEA. Whatever be the justification for protecting white males aged 40 or over, it cannot be that they have been excluded from political and economic power. The justification for the ADEA must therefore be based on entirely different grounds. These turn out to have a surprising resemblance to the justification for recognising claims for wrongful discharge [or unfair dismissal in British terms] ...

ADEA cases usually concern a discharge from employment, or less frequently, denial of promotion or refusal to hire. These cases are decided under the same structure of proof as claims of racial or sexual discrimination ...

In constitutional law, there is no need to protect the old from the rest of the population, most of whom will live to the same age. So too, in employment, there is no evidence that older workers on the whole are worse off than younger workers, although the earnings of unskilled workers do tend to decrease before retirement.

Nor can discrimination against older workers be condemned as an inefficient form of statistical discrimination ... A statistical theory of age discrimination would have to establish that the balance of efficiency lies with prohibiting generalisations on the basis of age. This conclusion is implausible for several reasons: first, everyone's physical and mental abilities decline at some point with age, more steeply for some individuals than others and more steeply in some jobs than others; second, the countervailing benefits of age, such as experience and judgment, do not invariably outweigh the loss of these abilities; third, the period over which older workers can gain and utilise new skills necessarily is shorter than for younger workers; and fourth, more accurate methods of evaluation, such as individualised testing, may cost enough to outweigh the gain in accuracy that they achieve ...

[Claims have been] mainly concerned with protecting the investment that long term employees have made in developing skills specific to their jobs ...

[T]he average recovery for each ADEA action ... was two-and-one-half times the average recovery in each Title VII case ...

By every measure, plaintiffs in ADEA cases are better off than plaintiffs in other employment discrimination cases ... [T]hey are much more likely to be managerial and professional employees ... They are, of course, likely to be older than other

---

111 Procedurally, there were originally significant differences, especially as regards the ability of age discrimination plaintiffs to obtain trial by jury. Since the Civil Rights Act 1991, trial by jury is now more frequently available in race and gender cases.

112 It follows that affirmative action *in favour* of those over 40 is permissible.

> plaintiffs and to have a longer tenure on the job ... It is therefore not surprising to find that the average salary of ADEA plaintiffs is almost twice the average salary of other plaintiffs ...

> Claims under the ADEA bear a far stronger resemblance to wrongful discharge claims than other claims of employment discrimination precisely because they are not claims on behalf of a discrete and insular group in our society. Like wrongful discharge claims, they are usually brought by white males, and they can usually be avoided by employers who establish general safeguards against unjust dismissal. The institutional reform stimulated by the ADEA, apart from changes in retirement and benefits policies, is indistinguishable from the reform caused by the law of wrongful discharge.

The logic of this argument is that age discrimination law is unlikely to be used frequently by those who are denied job opportunities. Even if it were, it is arguable that compensation levels would be lower than in race and gender cases; if ageism is less stigmatising than racism or sexism, the degree of injury to feelings and thus compensation will consequently be lower. The law would be used in some promotions cases, although problems of proof and the difficulty of establishing the level of loss of earnings may depress awards and so reduce claims.

Proof of discrimination on the basis of age would often be difficult. It was pointed out in *Laugesen v Anaconda Co*[113] that, even without discrimination, a dismissed older worker will normally be replaced by someone younger. 'This factor of progression and replacement is not necessarily involved in cases involving the immutable characteristics of race, sex and national origins. Thus, while the principle thrust of the Age Act is to protect the older worker from victimisation by arbitrary classification on account of age, we do not believe that Congress intended automatic presumptions to apply whenever a worker is replaced by another of a different age.' On the other hand, even though the American legislation only protects those over 40, it is perfectly possible that the Act could be violated where, for example, a 55 year old was replaced by a 45 year old.

(a)   Age and indirect sex discrimination

Until the age discrimination legislation comes into force, it may be possible that an age related requirement or practice amounts to indirect discrimination on a protected ground, such as sex. It has been held that a preference for young workers (aged between 17 and a half and 28) adversely affected women[114] and discrimination against older workers – post-retirement-age – adversely affected men (see *Rutherford*, below). Of course, in such cases, the practice may be justifiable.[115] However, proving an adverse impact can be complex and difficult, as *Rutherford* illustrates.

Harvest Town Circle Ltd v Rutherford **[2001] IRLR 599; [2002] ICR 123, EAT**[116]

Mr Rutherford, aged 67, was made redundant. Sections 109 and 156 of the Employment Rights Act 1996 respectively excluded persons aged 65 or over from a

---

113 510 F 2d 307 (6th Cir 1975), at 312.
114 *Price v Civil Service Commission* [1977] IRLR 291; [1977] 1 WLR 1417; [1978] 1 All ER 1228, EAT. See further Chapter 10, p 254.
115 Discussed generally below, Chapter 10 p 273 *et al*.
116 See, also, for justification, Chapter 10, p 291.

claim for unfair dismissal or a redundancy payment. Mr Rutherford claimed that these exclusions indirectly discriminated against men, and as such were contrary to Art 141 of the EC Treaty. An industrial tribunal upheld his claim, but the EAT allowed the appeal, holding that the tribunal based its finding of adverse impact upon flawed statistics.

Lindsay J:

20. There are, as it seems to us, serious flaws in ... [the tribunal's] approach. To illustrate by reference only to the figures for 1998, the tribunal's figures can be tabulated as follows:

	1998 '000	
	Females	Males
All in employment (a)	168	266
Economically active (b)	172	275
Economic activity Rate (b/b + c)	3.0%	8.0%
Economically inactive (c)	4,834	3,345
Total	5,006	3,620

These figures are, firstly mistaken; the true computation of the 'Economic activity rate' is 3.4% (not 3%) for the female 'economic activity rate' and 7.6% (not 8.0%) for the male. The comparison – 3.0% to 8.0% – on which the tribunal relied was thus not a correct one to make. The 5% gap (8%–3%) was truly one of 4.18% (7.60%–3.44%). With only small figures being in issue, that difference (itself of a reduction of 16.4%) is not to be overlooked.

21. Secondly although this point was not taken below and is not relied upon before us, we find it hard to see how it can be correct, when assessing the possible disparate effect of unfair dismissal and redundancy provisions on the over-65s, to have in mind all over-65s describable as economically active, a figure which (on the definitions used) will include, for example, numbers of self-employed, numbers of those – directors and partners perhaps – in practical control of their own employment and numbers of persons on fixed term contracts to whom contractual relief would exceed anything statutorily available. It could not be assumed that such classes, unlikely to be affected by unfair dismissal or redundancy legislation, would fall equally or in any other as yet ascertained ratio between men and women.

22. Thirdly, reference to the totals, 5,006,000 women and 3,620,000 men, will surely include literally millions to whom unfair dismissal or redundancy is utterly meaningless; to include, for example, 80 and 90 year olds who have no wish or who have no longer the physical and mental ability to work, amongst the comparison serves only to distort the picture, especially since, as women in general live longer than men, the figure for women over 65 either unable or unwilling to work at any one time is likely to be larger than the corresponding figure for men.

23. Fourthly, these figures throw no real light on the impact of ss 109 and 156 as they look only at those who have survived to 65 and have remained in or have taken up employment. All men and women unfairly dismissed or made redundant upon their attaining 65 will not appear in these figures. Those who

retired because they knew that they might otherwise be dismissed, will not appear in the figures. One is thus attempting to judge the impact of the legislation by looking only at those upon whom it has not, at the time of the statistics, had an impact but upon whom it might later have an effect. One is leaving out those upon whom its effect has, by the same date, perhaps already been crucial.

24.   These factors, taken together, illustrate, in our view, the inutility of the figures laid before the tribunal: they cannot serve the purpose for which it was intended they should be used ...

30.   It may be thought cowardly on our part if having described the statistics laid before the employment tribunal as inadequate for the task, we fail to say what statistics would have been adequate. At first blush it seems to us that those put at a disadvantage by the primary legislation in issue would consist of or would need to include all those who, on arriving at age 65, would have wished, and would have been physically and mentally able, to continue in employment properly so called but who either were then dismissed or made redundant by reason of the relative freedom which the legislation conferred upon their employer or who were so fearful of that freedom being exercised against them that they accepted retirement. We would not wish to include in any statistics reference to persons who were neither physically nor mentally able, nor wished, to be employed. However, we have no means of knowing whether statistics of such kinds could be made available or whether adequate inferences sufficient for the task could be drawn from other statistics. Moreover, as the argument before us has largely been, on the one hand, that the statistics presented below were sufficient and, on the other, that what was drawn from them was inappropriate, what range of alternative statistics might have been possible to have been laid before the tribunal below has not been explored. We thus shrink from telling the employment tribunal what statistics it is to require upon the remission if adequate consideration is to be given to the questions before it; that will be a primary subject which upon hearing argument on the point, and upon having the range of possible alternative statistics explained, it will need to grapple with.

The case was remitted to another tribunal, which found, upon this guidance, that there was an adverse impact and it was not justified.[117]

---

117 *Rutherford v Towncircle Ltd (t/a Harvest) (in Liquidation) and Secretary of State for Trade and Industry (No 2); Bentley v Secretary of State for Trade and Industry* [2002] IRLR 768.

CHAPTER 7

DIRECT DISCRIMINATION

1   INTRODUCTION TO THE LEGISLATION

Two forms of discrimination on the prohibited grounds (race, sex, religion, etc) are identified in the legislation: direct and indirect. Direct discrimination arises where, for instance, an advertisement reads: 'Librarians wanted, no women need apply.' This directly discriminates against women. The advert may be amended to read: 'Librarians wanted, applicants must be over six foot tall.' This is not direct discrimination, but it has broadly the same effect as the first, and as such, may *indirectly* discriminate against women (and possibly some racial groups), unless it can be justified. Unlike indirect discrimination, there is no general defence[1] to direct discrimination, only specific exceptions provided by the legislation, such as genuine occupational qualifications.[2] The definitions of direct discrimination across the legislation are broadly the same, although there are some relatively minor differences, which will be highlighted in this chapter when appropriate.

Race Directive 2000/43/EC[3]

Article 2

Concept of Discrimination

2 ... (a) direct discrimination shall be taken to occur where one person is treated less favourably than another is, has been or would be treated in a comparable situation, on grounds of racial or ethnic origin ...

Race Relations Act 1976

1(1)   A person discriminates against another ... if:
   (a) on racial grounds[4] he treats that other less favourably than he treats or would treat other persons ...

Sex Discrimination Act 1975

Section 1

(1)   ... a person discriminates against a woman if:
   (a) on the ground of her sex he treats her less favourably than he treats or would treat a man ...[5]

---

1   For a discussion on whether direct discrimination generally should be justifiable, see Bowers, J and Moran, E, 'Justification in direct discrimination law: breaking the taboo' [2002] 31 ILJ 307. For a response see Gill, T and Monaghan, K, 'Justification in direct sex discrimination law: taboo upheld' [2003] 32 ILJ 115.

2   These are considered in Chapters 12 and 13.

3   Equal Treatment at Work Directive 2000/78/EC, Art 2, is materially the same.

4   'Racial grounds' is defined by s 3(1) to mean 'colour, race, nationality or ethnic or national origins'. See above, Chapter 6, pp 137–50.

5   SDA 1975, s 3, prohibits discrimination on the ground of being married, this prohibition being restricted to the field of employment. Here the comparison is with how an unmarried person of the same gender as the applicant was or would have been treated. See above, Chapter 6, p 164.

The Employment Equality (Sexual Orientation) Regulations 2003[6]

3(1) For the purposes of these Regulations, a person ('A') discriminates against
another person ('B') if –

(a) on grounds of sexual orientation, A treats B less favourably than he treats or
would treat other persons ...

The Employment Equality (Religion or Belief) Regulations 2003[7]

3(1) For the purposes of these Regulations, a person ('A') discriminates against
another person ('B') if –

(a) on grounds of religion or belief, A treats B less favourably than he treats or
would treat other persons ...

What these definitions have in common are two broad elements: (a) 'less favourable
treatment' and (b) 'on the grounds of ...'

2   LESS FAVOURABLE TREATMENT

(1)   'Treatment'

In *De Souza v Automobile Association*,[8] Maria De Souza overheard her office manager
refer to her as 'the wog', whilst she was standing outside his office. The remark was
not directed towards her and was not intended to have been overheard by her. It was
held that the office manager had not discriminated against Ms De Souza. May LJ
explained that although she had been 'considered' less favourably, she had not been
'treated' less favourably.[9] Note that *De Souza* is not an authority that racial insults
cannot amount to less favourable treatment.[10]

(2)   'Less Favourable'

(a)   *What is 'less' favourable?*

R v Birmingham CC ex p EOC [1989] AC 1155, CA and HL[11]

The council defended their policy of favouring boys in the admission to grammar
schools with an argument that there was no evidence that grammar schools were
better than the other schools, and hence there had been no less favourable treatment.
The Court of Appeal and the House of Lords rejected the argument.

---

6   SI 2003/1661. In force since 1 December 2003.
7   SI 2003/1660. In force since 2 December 2003.
8   [1986] ICR 514, CA.
9   *Ibid* at p 524E.
10 See further, Chapter 9. For cases on racial insults, see below, p 171.
11 See also [1989] 1 All ER 769; [1989] IRLR 173, HL.

Dillon LJ (p 1176):

The loss, because of sex, of the chance of getting something which is reasonably thought to be of value is enough to constitute sex discrimination. It is not necessary for the Commission, in order to establish less favourable treatment, to prove ... that selective schools are, either generally, or in the case of particular pupils, objectively better or more suitable than comprehensive schools.

Lord Goff of Chieveley (p 1193):

It is enough that, by denying the girls the same opportunity as the boys, the council is depriving them of a choice which (as the facts show) is valued by them, or at least by their parents, and which ... is a choice obviously valued, on reasonable grounds, by many others ...

It would seem that it is enough that the victim considered – reasonably – that they had been treated less favourably, even in the face of objective evidence. The key is that there must be some reasonable grounds for that perception. It is not enough that the claimant simply considered that she was treated less favourably.[12]

In a different context, the Court of Appeal was less liberal with the definition of 'less favourable'. In *Simon v Brimham Associates*,[13] Mr Simon, a Jew, attended an interview with a firm of job consultants. When asked, he refused to disclose his religion. The interviewer then explained that the job was with an Arab company and those of the Jewish faith might not be selected. Mr Simon ended the interview there and then and made a claim for direct discrimination. It was held that as all applicants were asked about their religion, the interviewer had treated Mr Simon no less favourably than he would treat any other applicant. This narrow interpretation defeats the broad aim of the legislation of promoting equality. If, as the decision suggests, the practice was neutral, it would have been appropriate to argue, in the alternative, that this was a case of *indirect* discrimination.

(b) Stereotyping and insults

Treatment based upon stereotyping can amount to 'less favourable treatment'. The courts have recognised this in several situations. In *Alexander v Home Office*,[14] a prisoner complained that he was refused (more desirable) work in the prison kitchen. This was because he displayed 'the usual traits associated with people of his ethnic background being arrogant, suspicious of staff, anti-authority, devious and possessing a very large chip on his shoulder ... [which seemed] ... common in most coloured inmates'.[15] The Court of Appeal found that this was discrimination.

There are a number of higher profile cases involving stereotyping of the sexes. In *Ministry of Defence v Jeremiah*,[16] the reason that women doing overtime were not required to work in the dirty part of the factory related to the greater discomfort to a

---

12 *Burrett v West Birmingham HA* [1994] IRLR 7, EAT.
13 [1987] ICR 596; [1987] IRLR 307, CA. See also below, p 187.
14 [1988] 2 All ER 118, CA. See also *RRB v Mecca Ltd*, RRB Report 1974 p 39, Westminster county court; *Effa v Alexandra Healthcare NHS Trust* (1997) unreported, Case No 45390/95, 33 DCLD 9; *Hussain v Canklow Community Centre* CRE Report 1980, p 85, Leeds county court; *RRB v Botley Motor Vehicle Repairs*, CRE Report 1977, p 118, Westminster county court.
15 *Ibid*, at p120h.
16 [1980] QB 87; [1979] 3 All ER 833; [1979] IRLR 436, CA.

woman in having her hair and clothes dirtied. This example of gender stereotyping was held to be unlawful. Employers frequently utilise stereotypes, partly to reduce the costs of hiring and partly based on perceptions as to the average cost or productivity of particular groups of employee. The evidence is clear that such stereotyping remains commonplace, yet it is clearly unlawful. Basing a decision in an *individual* case on stereotypes or averages about women or a particular racial group will amount to unlawful discrimination. An obvious example concerns the exclusion of women from jobs requiring physical strength on the ground that women, on average, are less strong than men. This is clearly unlawful.[17] Other such stereotypes relate to the social reality of the lives of many women, such as being a single parent or having a partner who works or seeks to work in another part of the country.

Hurley v Mustoe [1981] IRLR 208, EAT[18]

The applicant was rejected for a waitressing job because she had four young children; it was the employer's policy not to employ women with young children because in his experience they were unreliable.

Browne-Wilkinson J (p 210):

> Even if ... one concedes that some women with small children are less reliable than those without, it does not follow that it is necessary in order to achieve reliability to exclude all women with children ... In general, a condition excluding *all* members of a class from employment cannot be justified on the ground that *some* members of that class are undesirable employees ... Parliament has legislated that women with children are not to be treated as a class but as individuals. No employer is bound to employ unreliable employees, whether men or women. But he must investigate each case and not simply apply a rule of convenience, or a prejudice, to exclude a whole class of women or married persons because some members of that class are not suitable ...

Three comments are needed on this important case:

(a) The claim of direct discrimination succeeded, as there was no evidence that the employer would have applied the same criterion to *fathers* with young children. Had he done so, the policy could still have been attacked as being unjustifiable indirect discrimination. A claim may be brought under either theory of discrimination: the applicant does not have to opt for one or the other and indeed it may not become apparent until relatively late in the proceedings, which is the more appropriate theory.

(b) The claim succeeded even though economists might argue that the policy was efficient and rational in a profit-maximising sense. For this reason, the law's attempt to change behaviour, while not by any means doomed to failure, clearly faces formidable obstacles.[19]

---

17 *FM Thorn v Meggit Engineering Ltd* [1976] IRLR 241, IT. What the employer must do is to decide what level of strength is required for the job and how it is to be measured. On the assumption that fewer women can meet the requirement than men, there will be a *prima facie* case of indirect discrimination, but the employer may very well be able to justify the requirement. See also *Dothard v Rawlinson* 433 US 321 (1977).

18 See also [1981] ICR 490.

19 See, eg, Epstein, R, *Forbidden Grounds*, 1992, Cambridge, Mass: Harvard UP, esp pp 226–229. For contrary view in the context of indirect discrimination see Greenberger, 'A productivity approach to disparate impact and the Civil Rights Act of 1991' (1993) 72 Oregon Law Review 253, at pp 292–97.

(c) It is still a case of unlawful sex discrimination even though the employer did not discriminate against all women, but only against a subset of women,[20] in this case women with young children. In such a case the appropriate comparison is with how a man possessed of the same characteristic would have been treated, and of course the employer would have almost certainly shown no interest in whether such an applicant had children.

Horsey v Dyfed CC [1982] IRLR 395, EAT[21]

The applicant began employment as a trainee social worker in 1979. The job involved starting in work but she was required to start a social work course within one year. She was also required to undertake that after completing the course she would return to work for the council for at least two years. She wanted to attend a course in Kent as her husband lived in London. The council refused to allow her to attend that particular course as they considered that she would probably not return afterwards. She won her claim for discrimination.

Browne-Wilkinson J (pp 397–98):

The Act covers generalised assumptions in relation to particular characteristics. Most discrimination flows from generalised assumptions of this kind and not from a simple prejudice dependent solely on the sex or colour of the complainant. The purpose of the legislation is to secure equal opportunity for individuals regardless of their sex, married status or race. This result would not be achieved if it were sufficient to escape liability to show that the reason for the discriminatory treatment was simply an assumption that women or coloured persons possessed or lacked particular characteristics and not that they were just women or coloured persons ...

Mr Evans assumed that Mr Horsey would not give up his job to join his wife, but that Mrs Horsey would give up her job to join her husband, ie, he had made a general assumption on the basis of her sex ... [even though] on two occasions previously Mr Horsey had followed his wife.

(c)   Segregation

Section 1(2) of the RRA 1976 provides that 'segregating a person from other persons on grounds of race is treating him less favourably than they are treated'. There are no parallel provisions for religion or sexual orientation. In the White Paper *Racial Discrimination*,[22] the Government adopted the observation of the Race Relations Board that '... for a time segregation may represent a form of accommodation acceptable to all, but if it hardens into patterns, tensions and conflicts will occur when pressures to change that pattern arise'.

In *Pel Ltd v Modgill*,[23] a paint shop in a factory was staffed solely by Asians. Originally, there had been white workers there as well. However, over the years as vacancies arose they were filled by friends or relatives of the Asians through word of mouth. The personnel department did no recruiting. The paint spray work was the

---

20 In the USA, this is known as 'sex-plus' discrimination, as the treatment is based on gender *plus* the particular characteristic. See *Phillipps v Martin Marietta Corp* 400 US 542 (1971).
21 See also [1982] ICR 255.
22 Cmnd 6234, para 62.
23 [1980] IRLR 142, EAT.

dirtiest in the factory and the Asians were unhappy at this. They complained, alleging segregation. The EAT held that the claim failed.

Slynn J (at para 40):

> ... had there been evidence of a policy to segregate, and of the fact of segregation arising as a result of the company's acts, that might have well constituted a breach of the legislation ... We do not consider that the failure of the company to intervene and to assist on white or non-Asian workers going into to the shop, contrary to the wishes of the men to introduce their friends, itself constituted an act of segregating ...

Slynn J is saying, in effect, that there must be a *positive* act of segregation by the defendant, to fall within the definition given by s 1(2) of the Race Relations Act (RRA) 1976. In this case, the employer merely *acquiesced* in the segregation. This decision is, at the least, contrary to the sentiment expressed in the White Paper (above). There are also technical problems with the Employment Appeal Tribunal's interpretation of the Act. On the face of it, the word employed by the Act 'segregating' is a verb, suggesting that there must be some positive act by the discriminator. However, s 78 provides that, for the purposes of the RRA 1976, an act includes a deliberate omission, and clearly, in this case, segregation arose *as a result of* the company's 'deliberate omissions'. Further, by allowing the practice to continue, the employer might have been in breach of s 33 of the RRA 1976, which proscribes aiding unlawful acts. The simple 'non-intervention' of the personnel office is a powerful weapon in the workplace. It is possible to read a further error into Slynn J's judgment. He alluded to an absence of a company 'policy' on several occasions. It appears that by policy he meant an 'intention to segregate'. Yet intention should be irrelevant to liability (*R v Birmingham CC ex p EOC* and *James v Eastleigh BC*)[24] and if that absence is the reason that the claim failed, the decision was wrong.[25]

Finally, all parties in this case referred to the job of working in the paint shop as 'the dirtiest in the factory'. That should not matter when s 1(2) provides that segregation *in itself* amounts to less favourable treatment.

Where gender is concerned, it is not the case that segregation *necessarily* entails less favourable treatment. This clearly reflects the cultural reality that men and women should sometimes be separate, especially, but not only, as respects washing and bathroom facilities. The other area where segregation occurs is in the field of education, where there is some evidence to suggest that girls do better – or at least achieve better exam results – where they are educated in an all-female environment. The provision of single-sex schools is specifically permitted by s 26 of the Sex Discrimination Act (SDA) 1975, but the way in which such provision was forthcoming led to problems in *R v Birmingham CC ex p EOC*.[26]

The specific legislative protection for single-sex education is required because not all providers of education operate both boys' schools and girls' schools. The *Birmingham* case, however, demonstrates that where separate facilities are provided, they must be equal as between males and females. Thus, the provision of as many places for girls as boys in single-sex grammar schools would not have been unlawful.

---

24 [1989] AC 1155 and [1990] AC 751 respectively; see below, p 182.
25 For the difficulties of analysing cases of large scale 'passive' segregation, see *Wards Cove v Antonio* 490 US 642 (1989), discussed in Chapter 10, pp 252–53.
26 [1989] AC 1155. See below, p 182.

As segregation on the ground of sex is not automatically unlawful, it may be permissible to provide separate facilities or teaching for boys and girls even within the confines of a mixed school – as long, of course, as the facilities so provided are equal. It is not equal to offer boys metalwork classes and girls needlework classes, but it would be permissible for boys' metalwork classes and girls' metalwork classes to take place at different times. Nor is the argument limited to schools: separate leisure centre gymnastic or trampolining classes for boys and girls are not unlawful because there is no element of less favourable treatment.[27] It is clear and of fundamental importance that the same arguments should be totally impermissible as regards race.

(d)   The comparison between the victim and another

> **Race Relations Act 1976**
>
> **Section 3**
>
> (4)   A comparison of the case of a person of a particular racial group with that of a person not of that group under section 1(1) must be such that the relevant circumstances in the one case are the same, or not materially different, from the other.[28]

By employing the phrase 'or would treat', the statutory definition of direct discrimination (set out at the beginning of this chapter) makes it clear that the comparator may be a hypothetical person. The domestic legislation makes it clear that the relevant circumstances of comparator must be materially the same as the claimant. In other words, the comparison must be 'like-with-like', the only difference between the two being the challenged ground, for example, sex. The first point to make (*Matins v Marks & Spencer*) is that a comparison *must* be made. Next, there are three potential errors to avoid. Finally, social norms may become 'relevant circumstances' for the comparison between men and women in challenges to dress, or appearance, codes.

(i)   The compulsory comparison

Martins v Marks & Spencer plc [1998] IRLR 326; [1998] ICR 1005, CA

Ms Martins, who was Afro-Caribbean by origin, applied a post as a trainee manager. Her performance at the interview was graded poorly and she was rejected. Ms Martins brought a complaint of race discrimination. An industrial tribunal found that 'nothing but bias' could explain the low marks she had received from the recruitment panel. On the basis of her evidence before them, the tribunal found it inconceivable that Ms Martins could properly be described as 'inarticulate'. The Court of Appeal found for Marks & Spencer.

Mummery LJ (331–32):

... was Ms Martins treated by Marks & Spencer less favourably than they treated or would treat another person of a different racial group in the same or relevantly similar circumstances? The answer to this question requires a comparison to be made between the treatment of Ms Martins and the treatment of a 27-year-old applicant of a

---

27 See below, Chapter 13, pp 372–73, for discussion of the provision of facilities, especially sport, known to be more likely to be attractive to men than women.

28 The relevant provisions for discrimination on the grounds of sex, sexual orientation and religion are materially the same.

different racial group with similar experience and qualifications applying for the same job. The tribunal did not attempt to make the compulsory comparison. Instead, it simply asked itself whether there was 'bias' on the part of [the interview panel] ... against Ms Martins and concluded that there was. This approach is defective. In a complaint under the 1976 Act, the focus is not on whether the conduct of the employer or putative employer towards the complainant is biased or unreasonable or unfair: as Lord Browne-Wilkinson said in *Zafar v Glasgow CC*,[29] ... the fact that an employer has acted unreasonably ... casts no light whatsoever on the question whether he has treated the employee 'less favourably' for the purposes of the 1976 Act ... The tribunal wholly failed to address itself to the issue, which Ms Martins had to establish in order to make out a claim for racial discrimination, whether she had been treated less favourably than the interviewers would have treated another applicant in the same circumstances. The finding that Marks & Spencer interviewers were guilty of 'bias' against Ms Martins is not a relevant or meaningful finding for the purpose of the 1976 Act.

(ii)   Three further problems

Three further potential errors can be identified from the cases. First, inappropriate comparators; secondly, different circumstances attributed to the comparator; and thirdly, where the discrimination is on the grounds of somebody else's race, using a comparator with a different attitude to race.

The first error was illustrated in *Re EOC for Northern Ireland's Application*[30] (a case brought on the Sex Discrimination (Northern Ireland) Order 1976, which is set out in similar terms to the SDA 1975 and RRA 1976). In Northern Ireland, the Department of Education allocated non-fee paying grammar school places equally to boys and to girls; each group received 27% of the places. However, that discriminated against the girls because they performed better in the entrance exam. Consequently 422 boys were awarded places, even though they had achieved lower marks than a group of 555 girls, who were not awarded places. In an earlier action, that was held to be discrimination. However, the Department decided not to withdraw the boys' offers out of 'fairness': unlike the girls, the boys had not had their hopes raised. The Equal Opportunities Commission (EOC) challenged that decision as being discriminatory. The Department argued that the difference was based, not upon sex, but on 'fairness'. Hutton LCJ held that it was incorrect to compare the two groups as they were, because the relevant circumstances (that is that the boys had already been offered places) were created by sex discrimination in the first place. Thus, the 555 girls should be awarded places instead of the boys.

The second possible error arose in *Grieg v Community Industry*.[31] Ms Grieg was refused a job with an all-male decorating team because otherwise it would have 'created an imbalance to the composition of the team'. In defending an action of sex discrimination, the Community Industry argued that Ms Grieg had not been treated less favourably because, equally, a man would have been refused a job with an all-woman team. It was held by the EAT that the comparison must be between Ms Grieg and a man applying for the same job. The 'relevant circumstances' (see s 3(4) above) would not be the same if the job was changed.

29   [1998] IRLR 36, HL; see further, below, p 191.
30   [1989] IRLR 64, NI High Court.
31   [1979] ICR 356, EAT.

Thirdly, in *Showboat Entertainment Centre Ltd v Owens*,[32] Mr Owens, who is white, was sacked for refusing to obey an order to exclude black youths from an amusement arcade. Counsel for Showboat argued, *inter alia*, one should compare how Mr Owens was treated with the treatment that would have been meted out to another manager who also refused to obey the order. However, Browne-Wilkinson J (in the EAT) felt that to be misconceived. He stated:[33]

> Although one has to compare like with like, in judging whether there has been discrimination you have to compare treatment actually meted out with the treatment which would have been afforded to a man having all the same characteristics as the complainant except his race *or attitude to race* [emphasis added].

So the correct approach is to endow the comparator with all the features of the complainant *except* his attitude to race. Note that this will not apply to cases of sex discrimination because s 1 of the SDA 1975 only covers less favourable treatment on the grounds of the *claimant's* sex, rather than 'on the grounds of sex'.

(iii)   Dress codes

This issue is connected to stereotyping. The question is the extent to which the anti-discrimination legislation constrains the ability of an employer to regulate the appearance or clothing of employees. In principle, the SDA 1975 comes into play if the employer's rules involve unequal treatment between men and women. The difficulty is that, for most people, social convention dictates that men and women do present themselves differently. It could be argued that it is discriminatory to require them so to do; it could also be argued to be discriminatory to require men and women to look the same when conventionally they appear different. It is dangerous to refer in this context to the view taken by society. Grooming and appearance codes are enormously moulded by one's racial, religious and cultural background, and may alter rather rapidly with the passage of time. The law has to tread a fine line between accepting what has traditionally been the norm – such traditions are likely to be relatively recent and, in any event, the anti-discrimination legislation aims to challenge tradition and stereotyping – while on the other hand avoiding outcomes which might be thought by many people to bring the law into disrepute.

Schmidt v Austicks Bookshops Ltd [1977] IRLR 360, EAT[34]

The applicant's employers required her to wear a skirt (and not trousers) to work, and while serving the public to wear overalls. The only restriction on men was not to wear tee-shirts. Her claim of sex discrimination failed. Phillips J dismissed the overalls complaint as too trivial to amount to a 'detriment' within s 6.[35] He then dealt with the compulsory skirt issue.

Phillips J (p 361):

> [T]he rules were plainly designed to assist in creating what to the employers was a satisfactory image and to assist in relations with the public ... [T]he restriction applied only when she was working with and in sight of the public ...

---

32   [1984] 1 All ER 836; see also below, p 187.
33   *Ibid*, at p 842c–g.
34   See also [1978] ICR 85.
35   See Chapter 12, p 325.

[T]he evidence showed that although there was less scope for positive rules in the case of the men, in that the choice of wearing apparel was more limited, there were restrictions in their case, too. For example, they were not allowed to wear tee-shirts; and it is quite certain, on a reasonable examination of the evidence, that they would not have been allowed to wear, had they sought to do so, any out-of-the-way clothing ... [T]here were in force rules restricting wearing apparel and governing appearance which applied to men and also applied to women, although obviously, women and men being different, the rules in the two cases were not the same. We should be prepared to accept ... an alternative contention ...'that in any event, in so far as a comparison is possible, the employers treated both female and male staff alike in that both sexes were restricted in the choice of clothing for wear whilst at work and were both informed that a certain garment should not be worn during working hours' ...

It seems to us ... that an approach of that sort is a better approach and more likely to lead to a sensible result, than an approach which examines the situation point by point and garment by garment ...

[A]n employer is entitled to a large measure of discretion in controlling the image of his establishment, including the appearance of staff, and especially so when, as a result of their duties, they come into contact with the public.

In *Schmidt*, women were more constrained by the code than men – women were presumably not allowed to wear tee-shirts either – and thus the rules could not be said to have operated even-handedly. No objective reason for the no-trousers rule was put forward; the EAT was content to hold that such a rule lies within the scope of the employer's discretion to regulate his business. The next two extracts offer less legalistic commentaries.

Flynn, L, 'Gender equality laws and employers' dress codes' [1995] 24 ILJ 255, pp 257, 260:

The reasoning of the EAT [in *Schmidt*] rests on a questionable assumption, namely that it is not open to men to wear certain items of apparel which are open to women. This premise removes the possibility of strict comparability between the sexes in matters of dress and necessitates the use of a modified, equivalence analysis. Neither of these elements in the EAT's reasoning ... stands up to scrutiny ... The boundaries of acceptable male and female dress can, and have, shifted significantly over the centuries and have altered with dramatic speed in the last few decades. Efforts to fix the process through an ascription of natural limits to 'female' and 'male' apparel cannot be reconciled with the basic philosophy of anti-discrimination legislation.

McColgan, A, *Discrimination Law*, 2000, Oxford: Hart, p 399:

Schmidt permits employers to reinforce, through dress codes, the very stereotypes of 'male' (serious, responsible, mature) and 'female'(decorative handmaidens) which disadvantage women at work. Because they are in line with stereotyped notions of what is appropriate to men and women respectively, these dress codes are not seen 'objectively' to 'demean' women even where they serve to mark them out [alluding to the overalls giving a presumably subordinate image in comparison with the men] as 'second class.'

McConomy v Croft Inns Ltd [1992] IRLR 561, High Ct of NI

Men with earrings were not allowed admission to a particular pub in Belfast. The complainant was asked to leave when it was noticed that he was wearing two small stud earrings in one ear. No objection was raised to women with earrings.

The claim of unlawful sex discrimination was brought under the Northern Ireland equivalent of s 29 of the SDA 1975, concerning the discriminatory provision of services to a section of the public.

The lower court said what is required is equal rather than identical treatment, applied *Schmidt* and rejected the claim. The applicant's appeal was allowed.

Murray LJ (pp 563–64):

> [W]hile I can see that in comparing like with like one would have to take account of certain basic rules of human conduct – such as the ordinary rules of decency ... which might permit or require different dress regulations as between men and women, I find it difficult to see how in today's conditions it is possible to say that the circumstances are different as between men and women as regards the wearing of personal jewellery or other items of personal adornment ...

> [The judge was clearly unhappy with the decision he felt bound to reach, as he commented that] there are people about who would take a robust view of this, would regard it with some scorn as effeminacy, and could, under the influence of drink, be moved to violence towards the wearers of such things. [If this be the employer's position] their motive in wishing to avoid disorder in their premises is entirely laudable.

This is not an employment case, and it may be that courts are instinctively prepared to give employers greater discretion in regulating the appearance of employees than bar owners the appearance of customers. However, if regard is had, as surely it must be, to changing social convention, it is very hard to defend *Schmidt* 20 years after it was decided. Nevertheless, two recent cases have reinstated and approved the *Schmidt* approach, with no recognition that times have changed and are continuing to change. The first, *Burrett v West Birmingham Health Authority*,[36] concerned a requirement to wear a cap that some departments imposed on female but not on male nursing staff. The applicant was disciplined and transferred for refusing to wear a cap on the ground that she found it demeaning and undignified and that it stereotyped nurses, an action she claimed breached the SDA 1975. While a majority of the female staff appeared to favour the practice, it was clear that it could not be justified for any operational reason such as hygiene. The EAT rejected her claim on the basis that *Schmidt* was the appropriate authority; the fact that men and women were each required to wear uniforms, albeit not identical, was sufficient to show that less favourable treatment had not occurred.

The following case is the first case on the issue to reach the Court of Appeal; it is notable for the clear difference of approach and philosophy between the EAT and the Court of Appeal.

Smith v Safeway plc [1995] IRLR 132, EAT[37]

A delicatessen assistant was dismissed because his pony-tail became too long to be contained under his hat. The applicable rule for male employees insisted on: 'Tidy hair not below shirt collar length. No unconventional hair styles or colouring.' For women, the equivalent provision stated: 'Shoulder-length hair must be clipped back. No

---

36   [1994] IRLR 7, EAT.
37   See also [1995] ICR 472.

unconventional hair styles or colouring.' There was no suggestion that the rule was based on considerations of hygiene.

The industrial tribunal[38] said it that was lawful to have different lengths of hair for men and women. They applied *Schmidt*, reasoning that the law permits different standards to be applied to men and women provided they enforce a common standard of smartness if read as a whole.

By a majority, the EAT allowed the appeal.

Pill J (pp 134–35):

[The applicant argued that hair length] could not be equated with dress. Dress can be changed on leaving work whereas hair is worn into public life. Hair length is not a function of any physiological difference between men and women. Differences are a question only of custom or fashion. Unlike differences in dress, there is no counterbalancing feature; the rule discriminates against men ...

The lay members of this tribunal have no difficulty in holding that the treatment was less favourable and self-evidently so. The requirements ... with respect to hairstyle are capable of being applied to both men and women in such a way as to take account of convention (and therefore be compatible with *Schmidt*) without placing the restriction they do on hair length for men only ...

[According to the chair] *Schmidt* [is] concerned with appearance. Employers are entitled to lay down reasonable requirements as to the way employees present themselves at work, if, for example, they come into contact with the public. Employers can have regard to current conventions and decline to accept what is 'out-of-the-way' ... What is conventional and what is out-of-the-way for men will often be different [than] ... for women.

If the employer is entitled to require an appearance which is not out-of-the-way, it is difficult to distinguish between dress and other aspects of personal appearance including hairstyle. Provided requirements for men and women can reasonably be related to current perceptions of what is a conventional appearance for men and for women, the requirements do not treat one sex less favourably than the other. The sexes are treated differently but equally by the standards of what is conventional.

[1996] IRLR 456, CA[39]

The Court of Appeal reversed the decision of the EAT and restored the decision of the industrial tribunal.

Phillips LJ (pp 458–59):

[It was submitted] that the principle to be derived from *Schmidt* ... has become unsound in law as a result in changes in society [and that it does not apply to these facts] ...

In my judgment, a package approach to the effects of an appearance code necessarily follows once one accepts that the code is not required to make provisions which apply identically to men and women ... [O]ne has to consider the effect of any [one] item in the overall context of the code as a whole ...

---

38 By the Employment Rights (Dispute Resolution) Act 1998, s 1(1), industrial tribunals are re-named employment tribunals.
39 See also [1996] ICR 868.

Appearance depends in part on ephemera: clothes, rings and jewellery worn; but it also depends on more permanent characteristics: tattoos, hairstyle, hair colouring and hair length. The approach adopted in *Schmidt* can in my judgment properly be applied to both types of characteristic ...

I can accept that one of the objects of the prohibition of sex discrimination was to relieve the sexes of unequal treatment resulting from conventional attitudes, but I do not believe that this renders discriminatory an appearance code which applies what is conventional. On the contrary, I am inclined to think that such a code is likely to operate unfavourably with regard to one or other of the sexes unless it applies such a standard ... A code which applies conventional standards is one which, so far as the criterion of appearance is concerned, applies an even-handed approach between men and women, and not one which is discriminatory ...

[We do not] lay down a rule of law that it can never be discriminatory to require men to wear their hair short, but is simply to say that in this case it was not perverse for the Industrial Tribunal to hold that a code containing the requirement that men's hair should be collar length was not discriminatory on the facts of the case.

Wintemute, R, 'Recognising new kinds of direct sex discrimination: transsexualism, sexual orientation and dress codes' (1997) 60 MLR 334, pp 354–55:

The 'package approach' adopted in Safeway is clearly inconsistent with the House of Lords' decision in *James v Eastleigh Borough Council*. 'But for' his sex, Mr Smith would not have been dismissed. The Court of Appeal reasoned that the dress code 'as a whole' treated men and women equally by applying different, but somehow equivalent and compensating, restrictions to their freedom to choose their clothing, make up, jewellery and hairstyles. But there was clearly 'less favourable treatment' if individual items of the code are examined. In particular, men could not have hair below shirt-collar length, whereas women could have shoulder length hair so long as it was clipped back. The Court of Appeal attempted to escape a finding of 'less favourable treatment' by using direct sex discrimination against women in individual items of the code to justify the direct sex discrimination against men in individual items of the code. It is unlikely that the House of Lords in *James* would have found no 'less favourable treatment' and therefore no direct sex discrimination, if the Council's admission prices 'as a whole' had treated men and women aged 60–64 equally: for example, swimming (75p for men, free for women); badminton (free for men, 75p for women). Sex distinctions applying to different choices cannot be lumped together and their net effect examined. Courts must look instead at their net effect on the ability of individuals to make each specific choice. For the woman who wants badminton at the same price as a man, free swimming is no consolation. For the man who wants to wear a pony-tail or a skirt, it is no consolation that women are prevented from wearing short hair or trousers.

Even if courts come to accept the view of the EAT in *Safeway*, the limits of that approach should be noted. A full blown anti-discrimination standard was applied only to those aspects of appearance which necessarily spill over from the workplace into other aspects of the applicant's life, and thus can be viewed as relating to freedom of expression and personal autonomy. This approach would continue to permit, for example, differential rules concerning clothing, jewellery and make-up, all of which may be altered on leaving work. But these are all aspects of appearance where there have in recent history been conventional differences between men and women, differences which in some small ways are being reduced. Even the approach of the EAT in *Safeway*, let alone that of the Court of Appeal, permits the employer to insist on maintaining such differences amongst his employees. The main reason given for such a view is the need to allow employers discretion in controlling staff appearances. This is an assertion, not an argument, and comes close to permitting discrimination because that policy would be favoured by customers or fellow employees, arguments normally rejected. The argument that, were the law otherwise, any man would be able to insist on wearing a skirt, is simply wrong. The courts have adopted a view of convention as allowing for only one convention, rather than many different conventions among different groups. People should have a right to whatever appearance they choose as long as their choice is that made by a reasonably sized group from within their gender; sex discrimination law does not and should not protect the discriminatory whims of individuals.

3   'ON GROUNDS OF'

(1)   Intention, Motive and the 'But For' Test

R v Birmingham CC ex p EOC [1989] 1 AC 1156, HL

The council allocated more grammar school places to boys than to girls. Consequently, a higher entrance exam pass mark was required of girls. The council argued that, for liability, there had to be an *intention* or *motive* to discriminate. The House of Lords rejected that view.

Lord Goff (p 1194):

> There is discrimination under the statute if there is less favourable treatment on the ground of sex, in other words if the relevant girl or girls would have received the same treatment as the boys but for their sex. The intention or motive of the defendant to discriminate, though it may be relevant so far as remedies are concerned ... is not a necessary condition of liability; it is perfectly possible to envisage cases where the defendant had no such motive, and yet did discriminate on the ground of sex. Indeed, as Mr Lester pointed out in the course of his argument, if the council's submission were correct it would be a good defence for an employer to show that he discriminated against women not because he intended to do so but (for example) because of customer preference, or to save money, or even avoid controversy. In the present case whatever may have been the intention or motive of the council, nevertheless it is because of their sex that the girls in question receive less favourable treatment than the boys, and so are subject to discrimination under the Act of 1975.

James v Eastleigh BC [1990] 2 AC 751, HL

The municipal swimming baths admitted persons 'of pensionable age' free of charge. In the UK, men reach pensionable at 65 and women at 60. So when Mr and Mrs James, both aged 61, visited the baths, Mrs James as admitted free whilst Mr James was required to pay. Mr James complained that he was receiving less favourable treatment on the grounds of sex. The Court of Appeal found against him. That decision was reversed by a bare majority of the House of Lords.

Lord Goff (p 774B-C):

> ... cases of direct discrimination under section 1(1)(a) can be considered by asking the simple question: would the complainant have received the same treatment from the

defendant but for his or her sex? This simple test possesses the ... virtue that ... it avoids, in most cases at least, complicated questions relating to concepts such as intention, motive, reason or purpose, and the danger of confusion arising from the misuse of those elusive terms. I have to stress, however, that the 'but for' test is not appropriate for cases of indirect discrimination under s 1(1)(b), because there may be indirect discrimination against persons of one sex under that subsection, although a (proportionately smaller) group of persons of the opposite sex is adversely affected in the same way.

Lord Lowry (dissenting, p 775):

On reading s 1(1)(a), it can be seen that the discriminator does something to the victim, that is, he treats him in a certain fashion, to wit, less favourably than he treats or would treat a woman. And he treats him in that fashion on a certain ground, namely, on the ground of his sex. These words, it is scarcely necessary for me to point out, constitute an adverbial phrase modifying the transitive verb 'treats' in a clause of which the discriminator is the subject and the victim is the object. While anxious not to weary your Lordships with grammatical excursus, the point I wish to make is that the ground on which the alleged discriminator treats the victim less favourably is inescapably linked to the subject and the verb; it is the reason which has caused him to act. The meaning of the vital words, in s 1(1)(a), where they occur, cannot be expressed by saying that the victim receives treatment which on the ground of (his) sex is less favourable to him than to a person of the opposite sex. The structure of the sentence makes the words 'on the ground of his sex' easily capable of meaning 'due to his sex' if the context so requires or permits.

Lord Lowry then alluded to Mr Lester's 'fears' raised by Lord Goff in *Ex p EOC* (above):

It would have had to be admitted that the [Birmingham City] council, however regretfully, knew it was treating the girls less favourably ... and ... had deliberately decided so to treat them because they were girls. The defence, based on absence of intention and motive, was rightly rejected ... If a man's hairdresser dismisses the only woman on his staff because the customers prefer to have their hair cut by a man, he may regret losing her but he treats her less favourably because she is a woman, that is, on the ground of her sex.

(Lords Acker and Bridge agreed with Lord Goff. Lord Griffiths dissented with Lord Lowry.)

Lord Goff's simple 'but for' test was designed avoid defences of 'benign motive'. A good example of the problem arose in *R v Commission for Racial Equality ex p Westminster CC*.[40] Vacancies for council refuse workers had previously been filled through friends or family of current employees, as a result of which no black people were hired. The employer introduced a new system, but the workforce insisted on the resumption of the former procedure, and even backed up the demand with the threat of industrial action. In response, the management dismissed the black worker hired under the new system. It was clear that this discrimination was unlawful, even though the management claimed to have been motivated, not by race, but by the desire to avoid industrial unrest. However, the 'but for' test carries problems of its own and may not be necessary.

---

40   [1985] ICR 827; [1985] IRLR 426, CA.

Connolly, M, 'Race, gender and *mens rea'* [2001] J Civ Lib 151

Technical shortcomings of the 'but for' test were articulated in Lord Lowry's dissenting speech in *James* ... This skilful judgement does two things. First, it shows that the 'but for' test does not accurately reflect the statutory formula. Instead of asking: 'Was the less favourable treatment on the ground of sex?' the 'but for' test asks: 'Did the treatment disfavour her because she was female?' There is a significant difference between the two questions. This difference can be realised by considering the legislation beyond s 1(1)(a). The SDA and RRA define *two* types of discrimination: direct and indirect ... However, *indirect* discrimination was added to catch cases where an apparently neutral practice, which cannot be justified, causes an adverse effect to a racial or gender group.[41] For example a long-standing requirement that pupils wear the school-uniform cap would adversely affect Sikh boys.[42] The victim was disfavoured by the school-cap requirement because he was an orthodox Sikh. But (for liability at least) we do not need to establish that the school imposed the uniform requirement on grounds of race. Now take a contrasting case. A school simply says: 'No Sikhs'. That is direct discrimination. Here, we have to establish that the school treated the Sikh applicant less favourably on grounds of race. In *either* case we could say that *but for* his race the school would have admitted him. However, we need more than that for the latter ('No Sikhs') case, otherwise we cannot distinguish it from the school-cap case of *indirect* discrimination. The problem with the 'but for' test is it cannot distinguish direct from *indirect* discrimination.

Lord Goff qualified the 'but for' test by emphasizing that it was only suitable for cases of direct discrimination and not suitable for cases of indirect discrimination. But this qualification merely exposes the error. If a test designed to identify direct discrimination should only be used in cases of direct discrimination, it is fundamentally flawed. It is asking a tribunal to identify the case before using the test of identification.

The second feature of Lord Lowry's judgement was that he illustrated that a strict interpretation of the legislation would not seriously reduce its scope. He did not say that motivation must be a factor, only that the 'ground' for the treatment must be sex or race. Consequently there would still be liability for direct discrimination in all of the 'fear' cases (ie Grammar school allocation, customer preference, saving money, avoiding controversy) despite the absence of a discriminatory motive.

In fact, the only case to fall outside of Lord Lowry's interpretation is *James* itself. And there is good reason for that: James was in fact an example of *(prima facie) indirect* discrimination. It is true that Lord Bridge stated that the requirement 'pensionable age' was 'convenient shorthand'[43] for direct sex discrimination. But shorthand needs translating, and so the relationship between the challenged practice and gender is necessarily *indirect*. Many requirements are 'convenient shorthand' for discrimination. Job specifications have included 'an excellent command of English',[44] 'be clean shaven',[45] 'be under 30 years of age',[46] 'must have lived in the area all your life'.[47] All these could be examples of *indirect* discrimination, and – to a lesser or greater degree –

---

41 Indirect discrimination is defined in the RRA 1976, s 1(1)(b) and the SDA 1975.
42 See *Mandla v Dowell Lee* [1983] ICR 385, HL.
43 [1990] 2 AC 751, at p 764.
44 See *Perera v Civil Service Commission (No 2)* [1983] ICR 428.
45 *Panesar v Nestle Co Ltd* [1980] ICR 144 and *Gilbert v United Parcel Service* (1996) unreported, 26 April, CA.
46 See *Price v Civil Service Commission (No 2)* [1978] IRLR 3.
47 See *Meer v LB of Tower Hamlets* [1988] IRLR 399.

are 'shorthand' for discrimination. But they are not examples of *direct* discrimination. Indeed, the Labour Government, when introducing the SDA, envisaged a body offering reduced prices for pensioners as an example of *prima facie* indirect discrimination. Further, they suggested it was one that could be justified ...[48]

Lord Lowry's strict interpretation includes the statutory word 'ground' but not any element of motive or discriminatory intent. Consequently this would not seriously reduce the scope of s 1(1)(*a*). Cases – such as *James* – that do fall outside of Lord Lowry's interpretation may be considered under the definition of *indirect* discrimination, where the defendant will have the opportunity to 'justify' the challenged practice.

... If the facts reveal more than one ground of the treatment, (*eg*, she was black *and* handled customers badly), then the case remains one of direct discrimination. This is because race or sex need only be one of the grounds for liability for direct discrimination.[49]

A different view was expressed by Ross, in her commentary on the Court of Appeal's decision[50] *in favour* of Eastleigh Council.

Ross, J, 'Reason, ground, intention, motive and purpose' (1990) 53 MLR 391[51]

It is arguable that that there was 'overt' discrimination in *James* with the 'covert' or underlying motive not being discriminatory. The rule of the Council, that people over state pension age are admitted free, was described ... as not being overtly discriminatory in that ground of the discrimination on the face of it did not relate to sex. ... While the ground for refusing Mr James admission involved other factors than his sex, nevertheless his sex was certainly a crucial ground for the decision to charge him 75p. When Browne-Wilkinson VC observed that '[h]e [the discriminator] had not acted on the ground of the plaintiff's sex, since that was not his reason for having adopted the policy ...' the reason referred to is of a different nature to a 'ground' for acting ... While the sign at the public baths did not say 'women over 60 and men over 65 admitted free' and did not therefore qualify for the Vice-Chancellor's definition of an overt act of discrimination, nonetheless the reference to persons of a pensionable age was a short hand way of saying exactly that.

What the statute demands is that the unfavourable treatment to be shown to have been because of the sex (or race) of the aggrieved person. There may have been additional underlying intentions, motives, purposes or even reasons but these do not detract from the fact that the ground for acting was sex. It appears that the Court of Appeal was wrong in rejecting the causative approach, ie, the 'but for' or 'because of' approach, which was surely more consonant with the meaning of ground approved in *R v Birmingham City Council*.

---

48 HL Deb Vol 362, Cols 10116–17 (14 July 1975). That is the reason the Government preferred 'justified' to 'necessary', which they thought would bar a defence in such cases. (See now *Matthews v UK* (Application No 40302/98) (2002) *The Times*, 30 July, a case which was settled in light of the Travel Concessions (Eligibility) Act 2002.)

49 See *Owen and Briggs v James* [1982] ICR 618, CA.

50 [1989] IRLR 318, CA.

51 This article was cited with approval by the majority in *Nagarajan v London Regional Transport* [1999] 4 All ER 65; [2001] 1 AC 502, HL, but subsequently the House of Lords, in *Khan v Chief Constable of West Yorkshire* [2001] 1 WLR 1947, appeared to have backtracked somewhat. Both cases concerned parallel provisions on victimisation; see Chapter 11, pp 304–11.

(2)   Race Need Not Be the Only Ground of the Less Favourable Treatment

In *Owen and Briggs v James*,[52] a firm of solicitors refused to employ a black applicant, Ms James. The industrial tribunal found that an important factor in that decision was race. A partner in the firm had stated to the successful candidate: 'I cannot understand why an English employer would want to take on a coloured girl when English girls are available.' However, race was not the only factor in the decision to reject the applicant. The industrial tribunal found for Ms James and the firm appealed to the Court of Appeal *inter alia* on the ground that the decision not to employ Ms James was not solely motivated by race. It was held that to make out a case of discrimination, it was sufficient that race was an important factor in the decision not to employ Ms James. On the other hand, in *Seide v Gillette Industries Ltd*,[53] the EAT said that it was insufficient that race was merely part of the background which led to the treatment in question. Here, anti-Semitic remarks made to the complainant led to his transfer (about which no complaint was made). He subsequently sought to involve another employee in the dispute, which led to a further transfer in order to minimise disruption, this transfer entailing loss of wages. The question was whether this second transfer was on racial grounds. While it was clear that the train of events would not have occurred had he not been Jewish, the EAT said that was insufficient. 'It does not seem to us to be enough merely to consider whether the fact that the person is of a particular racial group ... is any part of the background ... [T]he question which has to be asked is whether the activating cause of what happens is that the employer has treated a person less favourably than others on racial grounds.'[54] The finding that the second transfer was not on racial grounds was undoubtedly made easier by the acceptance that the second employee involved had no anti-Semitic views.[55] This approach should be contrasted with *Din v Carrington Viyella Ltd*,[56] in which the EAT correctly observed that it will normally be unlawful to remove the victim from the source of the discrimination, whether or not any loss of pay or status is involved, and even if the motive is simply the avoidance of future unrest.[57]

---

52 [1982] ICR 618, CA.

53 [1980] IRLR 427, EAT.

54 *Ibid*, p 431.

55 See also *Simon v Brimham Associates* [1987] IRLR 307, CA, where a claim of racial discrimination was rejected in circumstances where an applicant, who, unknown to the defendants, was Jewish, withdrew his application for a position which involved working with Arab employers. He refused to answer a direct question about his religion and was then informed that being Jewish might prejudice his application. In a narrow interpretation of the law, it was held that there was no less favourable treatment, as the employers were simply explaining why they felt a need to inquire about the religion of applicants.

56 [1982] ICR 256; [1982] IRLR 281, EAT.

57 See also *Kingston v British Railways Board* [1984] ICR 781; [1984] IRLR 146, CA.

(3)   Discrimination on the Ground of Another's Race

Under the SDA 1975, the less favourable treatment must be on the ground of the sex of the complainant.[58] Under the RRA 1976, on the other hand, the less favourable treatment may be on the ground of the race of a third party. This latter approach has been adopted in the Religion and Sexual Orientation Regulations.[59]

In *Showboat Entertainment Centre Ltd v Owens*,[60] Mr Owens, who was white, was a manager of an amusement centre. He was instructed by his employer to refuse admission to black youths. He declined to obey this order and was dismissed. The question for the EAT was whether the instruction (plainly amounting to racial discrimination against any excluded black youths) constituted racial discrimination against the (white) applicant. Browne-Wilkinson J held that although s 1(1)(a) was capable of a broad or a narrow interpretation, the broad interpretation was in accordance with the intention of Parliament (*that is*, to address racially discriminatory instructions). Thus, it was held that Showboat had discriminated against Mr Owens. Browne-Wilkinson, J relied, in part, on an *obiter dictum* of Lord Simon in *Race Relations Board v Applin*[61] (a case on the predecessor to the RRA 1976, the Race Relations Act 1968), which provided a similar definition of direct discrimination. In the House of Lords, Lord Simon had stated:

> It is inadmissible to read s 1(1) as if it read 'on the ground of his colour'. Not only would this involve reading into the subsection that is not there; it would also mean that some conduct which is plainly within the 'mischief' would escape – for example, discriminating against a white woman on the ground that she married a coloured man.[62]

(4)   Discrimination Without Knowledge of the Person's Race

In *Simon v Brimham Associates*,[63] Mr Simon, a Jew, attended an interview with a firm of job consultants. When asked, he refused to disclose his religion. The interviewer then explained that the job was with an Arab company and those of the Jewish faith would not be selected. Mr Simon ended the interview there and then and claimed that he had been discriminated against. The industrial tribunal held that for there to be discrimination, it must be shown that the discriminator was aware of the claimant's race. The Court of Appeal disagreed in part, stating that it was a question of fact in

---

58   But action taken against someone on the basis of the sex of a third party may be actionable under s 4, the victimisation provision. In addition, where an employee discloses unlawful discriminatory behaviour to the employer or other person, there may in some circumstances be protection under the Public Interest Disclosure Act 1998, the Act designed to protect whistleblowers.

59   The definitions are set out at the beginning of this chapter.

60   [1984] 1 All ER 836, EAT. See also above, p 177. Approved by the Court of Appeal in *Weathersfield (t/a Van & Truck Rentals) v Sargent* [1999] IRLR 94.

61   [1975] AC 259, HL.

62   *Ibid*, at p 289. In *Wilson v TB Steelwork* (1978) COIT 706/44 (see IDS Employment Law Handbook 48 (1990) p 9), IT, a white woman was refused employment because her husband was black.

63   [1987] ICR 596, CA. See also above, p 171.

each case and that such knowledge could be a factor. It agreed with the industrial tribunal that there had not been discrimination in this case.[64]

4   PROOF OF DIRECT DISCRIMINATION

Direct discrimination can be covert, resulting from a state of mind which, by its very nature, is not likely to be susceptible to direct proof.[65] A claim may develop from a feeling, whether based on instinct or a certain amount of knowledge, that the best person has not been appointed. Defendants will almost always put forward an alternative explanation for their behaviour, in some cases because they have every incentive to do so, and also as it is possible to be unaware that one is engaging in discriminatory behaviour. Discrimination often results from stereotypes, assumptions and the like which may lead an employer to behave in a particular manner. Furthermore, the law must counter the fact that almost all the information as to what did occur is within the employer's control. It is important that tribunals are prepared to draw *inferences* of discrimination in cases where direct evidence is not and cannot be forthcoming.

As discrimination is a civil matter, the burden of proof is satisfied if the applicant proves the case on a balance of probabilities.[66] Traditionally, the burden lies on the party making the allegation. However, all cases falling under EC law are subject to a specific rule of a shifting burden. This covers discrimination on the grounds of sex, religion or belief, sexual orientation and racial or ethnic origin. The first three categories are confined to employment matters. The specific rule will shift the burden to the defendant once the claimant has proved a *prime facie* case and will be considered presently. Whatever the formal burden of proof, defendants, who normally have at their disposal greater information about what happened than applicants, are almost invariably required to provide their version of events.[67]

It may be that the more formalistic approach to the ordering of proof, which is characteristic of American law, would ease the task of tribunals in knowing when to draw adverse inferences and, perhaps not incidentally, make it more likely that complainants will win their cases. According to the United States Supreme Court in *McDonnell Douglas Corp v Green*,[68] the applicant has to show:

(a)   that he belongs to a racial minority;

(b)   that he applied and was [minimally] qualified for a job for which the employer was seeking applicants;

---

64   The EAT in *O'Neill v Symm & Co* [1998] IRLR 233 relied on *Simon* in a case under the Disability Discrimination Act 1996, when it held that for liability, the defendant had to have been aware of the claimant's disability. This is to misunderstand *Simon*, which states only that such knowledge is relevant to liability.

65   See *Anya v University of Oxford* [2001] IRLR 377, CA, below p 193.

66   It is sometimes suggested that tribunals see an allegation of discrimination as very serious, almost quasi-criminal in nature, and as a result may, consciously or subconsciously, demand a rather higher standard than the normal balance of probabilities test. See Bourn, C and Whitmore, J, *Anti-Discrimination Law in Britain*, 3rd edn, 1996, London: Sweet & Maxwell, p 116.

67   See *Oxford v DHSS* [1977] ICR 884; [1977] IRLR 225, EAT.

68   411 US 792 (1973).

(c)   that ... he was rejected; and

(d)   that after such rejection the position remained open.

The burden then shifts to the employer to articulate some legitimate non-discriminatory reason for the employer's rejection.

The applicant also has the opportunity to establish that the employer's stated reason for rejection was a pretext for the real reason.[69] The British position before the Burden of Proof Directive took effect was explained in *King* and *Zafar*.

King v Great Britain-China Centre [1991] IRLR 513, CA[70]

The applicant was Chinese but had been educated in Britain. She applied for the post of deputy director of the centre, a government-sponsored organisation which aims to foster closer ties with China. She met the requirements of fluent spoken Chinese and personal knowledge of China. All eight shortlisted candidates were white and the appointee was an English graduate in Chinese.

The tribunal upheld her complaint on the ground that the employers had failed to demonstrate that she had not been treated unfavourably because of her race. The employers had admitted that none of the five ethnically Chinese applicants had been shortlisted and that no ethnically Chinese person had ever been employed in the centre. The majority concluded that it was entitled to draw the conclusion that she was discriminated against because she did not come from the 'same, essentially British, academic background' as the existing staff.

The EAT allowed the appeal on the ground that the tribunal had approached the case on the basis that there was a burden on the employers to disprove discrimination.

The Court of Appeal restored the decision of the industrial tribunal.

Neill LJ (p 518):

From [the] several authorities it is possible ... to extract the following principles and guidance:[71]

(1)   It is for the applicant who complains of racial discrimination to make out his or her case. Thus if the applicant does not prove the case on the balance of probabilities he or she will fail.

(2)   It is important to bear in mind that it is unusual to find direct evidence of racial discrimination. Few employers will be prepared to admit such discrimination even to themselves. In some cases the discrimination will not be ill-intentioned but merely based on an assumption that 'he or she would not have fitted in'.

(3)   The outcome of the case will therefore usually depend on what inferences it is proper to draw from the primary facts found by the tribunal. These inferences can include, in appropriate cases, any inferences that it is just and equitable to draw in accordance with s 65(2)(b) of the 1976 Act from an evasive or equivocal reply to a questionnaire.

(4)   Though there will be some cases where, for example, the non-selection of the applicant for a post or for promotion is clearly not on racial grounds, a finding of discrimination and a finding of a difference in race will often point to the

---

69   Clearly, the same logical principles can be applied to gender cases and to other cases of discrimination not involving a failure to hire.

70   See also [1992] ICR 516.

71   These guidelines were approved by the House of Lords in *Glasgow CC v Zafar*, below, p 191.

possibility of racial discrimination. In such circumstances, the tribunal will look
to the employer for an explanation. If no explanation is then put forward or if
the tribunal considers the explanation to be inadequate or unsatisfactory it will
be legitimate for the tribunal to infer that the discrimination was on racial
grounds. This is not a matter of law, but, as May LJ put it in *Noone*,[72] 'almost
common sense'.

(5)   It is unnecessary and unhelpful to introduce the concept of a shifting evidential
       burden of proof. At the conclusion of all the evidence the tribunal should make
       findings as to the primary facts and draw such inferences as they consider
       proper from those facts. They should then reach a conclusion on the balance of
       probabilities, bearing in mind both the difficulties which face a person who
       complains of unlawful discrimination and the fact that it is for the complainant
       to prove his case.

The process of reasoning [in the Industrial Tribunal] did not involve a reversal of the
burden of proof but merely a proper balancing of the factors which could be placed in
the scales for and against a finding of unlawful discrimination.

The danger of a relatively informal approach to the ordering of proof is that it may
lead tribunals to assess the facts in too broad and insufficiently rigorous a fashion.
There is evidence that this used to be true of far too many tribunals.[73] In particular, too
much weight was placed on evidence that employers were not motivated by hostility
towards the applicant. However, it may be that greater experience has lead tribunals
to appreciate that hostile motivation is not required, that direct discrimination may
originate in unconscious stereotyping, and thus that a claim may succeed without
proof that the employer was overtly racist or sexist.

In cases where the applicant appears to be better or at least as well qualified as the
successful candidate and the employer articulates a reason as to why the latter was
chosen, there are a number of ways of showing that the employer's stated reason
was a pretext: that the employer's reason had never been utilised before, that the
applicant was treated unfairly, and by the use of statistics. It has been held in Northern
Ireland, however, that no inference of any kind is raised by the mere fact that the
members of the appointing panel were all of a different religion from a candidate.[74]
This is correct as a general rule, as otherwise an obligation would arise to ensure that
the panel had a member of the same race and gender as each applicant. There is no
recommendation in the Codes of Practice[75] that attempts need be made to ensure that
the panel is as representative as possible, but the membership must be relevant
evidence, especially if normal procedures were not followed or there is evidence that
the panel's composition was in some way manipulated.

Examples of proving pretext by relying on a reason which is not applied to
everyone include pregnancy dismissals where the period of absence had never led to
dismissal of a sick man, or applying different criteria of misconduct or satisfactory
work performance. The evidence of unfair or prejudiced questioning at interview may
be sufficiently powerful to prove the applicant's case. However, the more equal the
candidates are on merit, the more difficult it will be to prove a case simply on the basis

---

72   *Noone v North West Trains RHA* [1988] IRLR 195, CA.
73   Leonard, A, *Judging Inequality: The Effectiveness of the Industrial Tribunal System in Sex
     Discrimination and Equal Pay Cases*, 1987, London: The Cobden Trust, pp 38–51, 78–85.
74   *Armagh DC v Fair Employment Agency* [1994] IRLR 234, NICA.
75   Issued by the EOC or CRE. See Chapter 12, p 317.

of such unfairness,[76] but unfairness in the sense of incompetence will not necessarily lead to a finding of unlawful discrimination. In *Qureshi v LB of Newham*,[77] it was held that failure to follow the employer's own equal opportunities policy was insufficient to establish discrimination. 'Incompetence does not, without more, become discrimination merely because the person affected by it is from an ethnic minority.' It was assumed, rather than for the employer to prove, that similar incompetence would also have affected any white applicant. As in most cases this would be hard to prove, in effect this case turns on the allocation of the burden of proof.

Glasgow CC v Zafar [1998] IRLR 36, HL

The applicant was dismissed after being found guilty of serious sexual harassment. The industrial tribunal found that procedure for dealing with the allegations had been so seriously defective as to constitute unreasonable treatment, and that such unreasonable treatment amounted to less favourable treatment which gave rise to a presumption that it had been on grounds of race. The tribunal further held that, as the presumption had not been rebutted, there was no choice but to conclude that discrimination was proved.

The EAT dismissed the appeal, but the Court of Session allowed the employer's further appeal, a decision upheld by the House of Lords.

Lord Browne-Wilkinson (p 38):

[T]he conduct of a hypothetical reasonable employer is irrelevant. The alleged discriminator may or may not be a reasonable employer. If he is not a reasonable employer he might well have treated another employee in just the same unsatisfactory way ... in which case he would not have treated the complainant 'less favourably' for the purposes of the Act of 1976. The fact that, for the purposes of the law of unfair dismissal, an employer might have acted unreasonably casts no light whatsoever on the question whether he has treated the employee 'less favourably' for the purposes of the Act of 1976.

I cannot improve on the reasoning of Lord Morison ... who stated that it 'cannot be inferred, let alone presumed, only from the fact that an employer has acted unreasonably towards one employee, that he would have acted reasonably if he had been dealing with another in the same circumstances'.

Connolly, M, 'The Burden of Proof Regulations: change and no change' [2001] 30 ILJ 375:

The Sex Discrimination (Indirect Discrimination and Burden of Proof) Regulations 2001[78] ... implement the 'Burden of Proof' Directive (97/80) ... The Directive relates to sex discrimination in employment and consequently the Regulations are limited so in scope.

---

76 See, eg, *Saunders v Richmond upon Thames LBC* [1978] ICR 75; [1977] IRLR 362, EAT.
77 [1991] IRLR 264, CA.
78 See also regs 29 and 32 of either the Employment Equality (Religion or Belief) Regulations 2003 (SI 2003/1660) or the Employment Equality (Sexual Orientation) Regulations 2003 (SI 2003/1661); ss 54A and 57ZA of the RRA 1976 (inserted by SI 2003/1626).

The Regulations implement this by amending the SDA with a new s 63A: ...

> (2)   Where, on the hearing of the complaint, the complainant proves facts from
>   which the tribunal could, apart from this section, conclude in the absence of
>   an adequate explanation that the respondent
>
> (a)   has committed an act of discrimination against the complainant ...
>
> the tribunal shall uphold the complaint unless the respondent proves that he did
> not commit, or, as the case may be, is not to be treated as having committed, that
> act.[79]

This amendment appears to disturb the existing law on proving a case of direct
discrimination. The established guidelines were handed down by the Court of Appeal
in *King v Great Britain-China Centre* [1991] IRLR 513 and approved by the House of
Lords in *Zafar v Glasgow City Council* [1998] IRLR 36 ...

[Guideline (4) in *King* (above)] ... becomes clearer if the first 'discrimination' in the
sentence is replaced with 'less favourable treatment'. Its significance can be illustrated
by looking at the facts of *King* and *Zafar* ...

What these cases have in common is that there was less favourable treatment and
each victim belonged to a protected group. Lord Browne-Wilkinson is saying that that
alone is not enough for a finding of racial (or sex) discrimination. In *Zafar* there was
no more evidence than that. The same could be said for *King* except that the same
evidence (the racial make-up of the Centre's staff, of those short-listed for interview
and of the claimant) pointed to the less favourable treatment being on the grounds of
race. The Centre's failure to explain the less favourable treatment on grounds other
than race confirmed this. Combined with the less favourable treatment and racial
origin of the claimant, this was enough to draw an inference of racial discrimination.
The facts of *King* illustrate Neill LJ's guideline ... [(4)]: where there is no direct
evidence of racial (or sex) discrimination, inferences of such discrimination from
circumstantial evidence may be made, if the defendant cannot refute those inferences
with contrary evidence. *Zafar* tells us that less favourable treatment to a claimant
belonging to a protected group is not enough in itself to establish racial or sex
discrimination. This is a point of law (incidentally, first argued by Lord Browne-
Wilkinson in *James v Eastleigh BC* [1989] IRLR 318, at 321, reversed by a bare majority
of the House of Lords [1990] IRLR 288), not evidence. And so the Regulations on the
burden of proof should not disturb *Zafar* at all. What they will do is formalize the
Neill LJ's guideline cited above for *all* cases of direct discrimination, thus upsetting
his view that a concept of a shifting burden is unnecessary.

The rhetoric in *King* and *Zafar* envisage three classes of direct discrimination cases
before tribunals. First, where there is direct evidence of racial or gender
discrimination (eg, an employer states: 'I cannot understand why an English
employer would want to take on a coloured girl when English girls are available.' See
Owen and Briggs v James [1982] ICR 618, CA). Second, where there is only
circumstantial evidence of such discrimination (as in *King*). Third where there is only
evidence of less favourable treatment of a claimant from a protected group. These
cases will fail with or without the Regulations because as a matter of law (according
to *Zafar*) this does not amount to racial or gender discrimination.

A recent Court of Appeal judgment put this law into context.

---

79   There is a new s 66A that repeats the formula above for county or sheriff court claims
     regarding barristers, advocates and vocational training.

Anya v University of Oxford **[2001] IRLR 377; [2001] ICR 847, CA**[80]

Sedley LJ (p 381):

The present case is a textbook example of a race discrimination claim. It makes it possible to see with some clarity how the principles established by authority ought to work out in practice. Here we have a shortlist of two candidates, one black, one white, both by definition qualified by training and experience for a specialised post. Whichever is to be chosen, good administration requires that he be chosen fairly; and to this the law has now added for a quarter of a century that the choice must not be affected in any way by his race. If it is, the unsuccessful candidate will have been treated less favourably on racial grounds and the university will be liable for direct discrimination ... Very little direct discrimination is today overt or even deliberate. What *King* and *Qureshi* tell tribunals and courts to look for, in order to give effect to the legislation, are indicators from a time before or after the particular decision which may demonstrate that an ostensibly fair-minded decision was, or equally was not, affected by racial bias.

---

80 See also *Deman v AUT* [2003] All ER (D) 211 (Mar), where the Court of Appeal reversed the employment tribunal's and EAT's (EAT/746/99, [2002] All ER (D) 162 (Apr)) decisions because the employment tribunal failed to look for subconscious discrimination.

CHAPTER 8

ANTI-DISCRIMINATION LAW, PREGNANCY AND CHILDBIRTH[1]

1   INTRODUCTION

The fact that women get pregnant and give birth, while men do not, raises issues of great theoretical and practical importance for those concerned with equality issues. This is because, first, pregnancy has historically been the cause and the occasion for the exclusion of many women from the workplace and, secondly, because of the practical difficulties which many women face in juggling the demands of work and family responsibilities.

There are two areas pertaining to anti-discrimination legislation which are specifically concerned with the fact that women and not men get pregnant, the offspring develops inside the female uterus, and the woman then gives birth, the birth itself giving rise to after-effects which vary enormously in their duration and intensity. The first area of concern is the employment rights of pregnant women and women who have recently given birth. The second area concerns issues of health and safety, both of the mother and the unborn or new-born baby. This may manifest itself, first, in purported attempts to 'protect' all women or pregnant women from certain jobs or work at certain times – in particular, at night – where it is considered to be inappropriate or dangerous for women to work and, secondly, where it is suggested that continuing to work may, usually because of some product or discharge associated with the work process, risk damaging the health of the unborn child.

The first two of these issues arise because of the fact of women's physical difference from men. This raises conceptual problems for anti-discrimination legislation; such legislation may be predicated on the assumption that those in similar positions should be treated equally, with the inference being that those in different situations may be treated unequally. If a woman cannot compare herself with a similarly situated man, how can adverse treatment of a pregnant woman amount to discrimination?[2] Indeed, pregnancy is perhaps the starkest example of the perceived inadequacies of the comparative approach. The answers to the problem have varied: some purported solutions have emphasised an approach whereby failing to take account of the disadvantages in which pregnancy may result itself amounts to discrimination; other approaches have abandoned a discrimination model in favour of an approach which gives direct rights to women. Some such rights may be specifically job-related; others place greater emphasis on the health and safety issues surrounding pregnancy.

---

1   See Fredman, S, *Women in Labour: Parenting Rights at Work*, 1995, London: Institute of Employment Rights; Palmer, C, *Maternity Rights*, 1996, London: Legal Action Group.

2   In the US Supreme Court, a majority held that a distinction between pregnant and non-pregnant persons was not one based on sex, as there were non-pregnant women (*General Electric v Gilbert* 429 US 125 (1976), pp 134–35). The position was remedied by the Pregnant Discrimination Act, which amended s 701, Title VII by adding a new sub-s (k). For an analysis of the USA position, see Magid, JM, 'Pregnant with possibility: re-examining the Pregnancy Discrimination Act' (2001) 38(4), American Business Law Journal 819 and for a comparative study of Australia and the USA, see Casas, N, 'Sex discrimination on the basis of pregnancy' (2001) 11 Transnation Law & Contemporary Problems 141.

British law has, in the last few years, been transformed by European developments, both legislative and case law. In addition, the premises and objectives of the law are not free from controversy. The law on pregnancy rights may be seen as a stepping stone for those who wish to see the law foster, first, a more equitable division of domestic responsibilities between men and women and, secondly, greater possibilities to take temporary absences from the workplace without experiencing significant employment disadvantages in consequence.

2   THE LAW

European Community law has, like the UK, adopted a twin track approach. The first track asks whether disadvantageous treatment of pregnant women is sex discrimination in contravention of the Equal Treatment Directive (76/207/EEC).[3] The second track, manifested especially in the Pregnant Workers Directive,[4] grants direct rights to such workers irrespective of discrimination. That Directive was incorporated into English law by the Trade Union Reform and Employment Rights Act 1993 and re-enacted in the Employment Rights Act 1996, which has been amended and supplemented several times since. The relationship between the two different tracks may become problematic: in particular, may an employee choose whichever track is likely to give her a more favourable outcome, or is the track based on the Directive and subsequent legislation to take precedence over the case law established under the anti-discrimination principle?

In addition, the approach based on health and safety sits uneasily alongside the other two approaches. Both in domestic and European law, women sometimes receive *additional* health and safety protection because of pregnancy, and have sometimes received additional protections on the grounds that they are new mothers or simply on the grounds that they are women. What is permissible under this heading is still somewhat unclear.

There are three different areas of law which need to be considered: dismissal because of pregnancy, pay and other benefits consequential on being pregnant and, finally, health and safety issues connected with pregnancy.

(1)   Dismissal

Given that a man cannot get pregnant, remorseless logic unaffected by consideration of the purpose of the law would suggest that the dismissal of a woman because she is pregnant cannot therefore amount to sex discrimination. It was precisely this reasoning which prevailed in *Turley v Allders Department Stores Ltd*,[5] the first such case to reach an appellate court. This 'no comparison possible' approach fell on exceptionally stony critical evaluation and proved very short-lived. The next approach, the 'sick man' standard, provided the first mechanism by which protection was granted, and it may still today be relevant in contexts other than dismissal.

---

3   Council Directive 76/207/EEC; OJ L39/40, 1976.
4   Council Directive 92/85/EEC; OJ L348/1, 1992.
5   [1980] ICR 66; [1980] IRLR 4, EAT.

Hayes v Malleable Working Men's Club and Institute [1985] IRLR 367, EAT[6]

The applicant was dismissed after telling her employers that she was pregnant; she lacked sufficient service to be able to claim unfair dismissal, so any claim had to be under the Sex Discrimination Act (SDA) 1975. Her appeal to the Employment Appeal Tribunal (EAT) was successful and the case remitted for a rehearing.

Waite J (pp 368, 370):

[T]he Industrial Tribunal[7] applied *Turley v Allders* to hold that dismissal because of pregnancy was incapable, as a matter of law, of amounting in any circumstances to discrimination between the sexes. The logic appears flawless ... If you dismiss a woman on the ground of her pregnancy, no one can say that you have treated her less favourably than you would treat a man, because nature has ensured that no man could ever be dismissed upon the same ground ...

To say of someone that she has been dismissed 'on the ground of pregnancy' can never be more than at best a half-told tale, because it begs too many questions. It must in practice be extremely rare these days for anyone to be dismissed simply because they were going to have a baby, and for no other reason ... It will usually be the consequences of pregnancy rather than the condition itself, which provides the grounds for dismissal: the general effect, that is to say, upon the employee's performance at work of the need to take time off for confinement and for periods of rest both before and afterwards. Those consequences will vary greatly in importance and significance from case to case ...

[W]e have not found any difficulty in visualising cases – for example, that of a sick male employee and that of a pregnant woman employee, where the circumstances, although they could never in strictness be called the same, could nevertheless properly be regarded as lacking any material difference.

Thus, the comparison mandated was with how the employer would have treated a similarly situated sick man; there appeared no necessity to postulate that the illness had to relate to a man's reproductive system unless there was evidence that such illnesses were treated differently from other male illnesses. This approach is open to criticism on four grounds. First, pregnancy is not an illness but a normal, natural and necessary event which should be celebrated. While the approach may give practical protection, its theoretical foundation is thus demeaning to women. Secondly, in any event, the amount of time off which results even from a normal pregnancy is far in excess of typical examples of sick leave and allows for the possibility that men requiring long absences would not receive generous provision. Thirdly, the approach means that pregnant women must not be treated worse than sick men. If a sick man with less than one year's service would be instantly dismissed, or if the employer made no provision for sick pay, the employer would be free to treat pregnant women in the same way. Fourthly, given that so many women have no male colleagues doing the same job, or that the organisation may lack formalised personnel policies, it may be impossible to rebut an employer's assertion that a hypothetical sick man would have been treated just as unfavourably as the applicant was treated.

---

6   See also [1985] ICR 703.
7   As a result of the Employment Rights (Dispute Resolution) Act 1998, s 1(1), industrial tribunals are re-named employment tribunals.

This approach was, in the absence of anything better from the English courts, accepted as law for a number of years. The transformation wrought by the European Court began with the next case.

Dekker v Stichting Vormingscentrum voor Jonge Volwassen (VJV-Centrum) Plus **Case C-177/88 [1991] IRLR 27**[8]

The complainant applied, when pregnant, for employment as a training instructor. She was told that she could not be employed; their insurer would not reimburse the sickness benefits which she would have to be paid because the fact she was pregnant at the time of her application meant that such absences would be regarded as a foreseeable incapacity. The claim was that this decision was in contravention of the Equal Treatment Directive.

Judgment (pp 29–30):

> As employment can only be refused because of pregnancy to women, such a refusal is direct discrimination on grounds of sex. A refusal to employ because of the financial consequences of absence connected with pregnancy must be deemed to be based principally on the fact of pregnancy. Such discrimination cannot be justified by the financial detriment in the case of recruitment of a pregnant woman suffered by the employer during her maternity leave ...

> [A]n employer is acting in direct contravention of the principle of equal treatment ... if he refuses to enter into a contract of employment with a female applicant found suitable by him for the post in question, where such refusal is on the ground of the possible adverse consequences for him arising from employing a woman who is pregnant at the time of the application, because of a government regulation concerning incapacity to work which treats inability to work because of pregnancy and confinement in the same way as inability to work because of illness ...

> [T]he answer to the question of whether the refusal to recruit a woman constitutes direct or indirect discrimination depends on the motive for such a refusal. If this motive resides in the fact that the person concerned is pregnant, this decision is directly related to the applicant's sex ... [I]t is of no importance ... that there were no male applicants ...

> [T]he Directive does not make the liability of the discriminator in any way dependent upon the evidence of fault or the absence of any grounds of legal justification ... [A] contravention of the prohibition of discrimination in itself should be sufficient in order for full liability of the discriminator to arise. No grounds for justification existing in national law can be accepted.

The European Court unequivocally stated that refusal of employment on the ground of pregnancy is direct discrimination on the ground of sex.[9] The reasoning is that pregnancy is a condition unique to women; in consequence, an adverse decision made on the ground of pregnancy is, *by definition*, a decision made on the ground of sex. That the employer had no male employees cannot affect the conclusion that the non-

---

8   See also [1990] ECR-I 3941; [1992] ICR 325.

9   It has been argued that pregnancy discrimination is better viewed as a species of indirect sex discrimination. See Wintemute, R, 'When is pregnancy discrimination indirect sex discrimination?' [1998] 27 ILJ 23. In response, it was argued that it is *neither* direct or indirect sex discrimination, and that there should be a separate Pregnancy Discrimination Act, as well as legislation providing pregnant women positive benefits: Honeyball, S [2000] 29 ILJ 43.

discrimination principle has been violated. The reason or motive that impelled the employer not to hire on ground of pregnancy, be it financial, social or whatever, cannot provide a defence.

It cannot be argued that it is necessarily sex discrimination to dismiss a pregnant woman: for example, she might be made redundant or be guilty of gross misconduct. It must therefore be established that there is a causal link between the dismissal and the fact of her pregnancy. However, this allows for the possibility of a defence that the pregnancy was the occasion, not the cause, of the dismissal, and courts who have seemed unable or unwilling to accept the breadth of the *Dekker* principle have sometimes grasped at this line of reasoning so as to deny the applicant's claim.

Webb v EMO Air Cargo (UK) Ltd [1993] IRLR 27, HL[10]

The firm had an import department of four people, including an import operations clerk. When the holder of that job became pregnant, Ms Webb was hired, as it was considered that she would need six months' training in order to be able to act on her own as a temporary replacement. It was nevertheless anticipated that Ms Webb would probably remain employed when Ms Stewart returned. Several weeks after starting work, Ms Webb discovered she was pregnant, whereupon the employers dismissed her.

The Court of Appeal said that dismissal of a pregnant woman can be, but is not necessarily, direct discrimination. The question is whether a man with a condition as nearly comparable as possible which had the same practical effect upon his ability to do the job would, or would not, have been dismissed. *Dekker* was distinguished on the ground that that case was not concerned with whether a woman was incapable of doing her job. The House of Lords referred the case to the European Court of Justice (ECJ), but made certain observations in the process.

Lord Keith of Kinkel (pp 29–30):

There can be no doubt that in general to dismiss a woman because she is pregnant or to refuse to employ a woman of childbearing age because she may become pregnant is unlawful direct discrimination. Childbearing and the capacity for childbearing are characteristics of the female sex. So to apply these characteristics as the criterion for dismissal ... is to apply a gender-based criterion ... In the present case, there was not any application of a gender-based criterion. If the appellant's expected date of confinement had not been so very close to that of Ms S she would not have been dismissed. It was her expected non-availability during the period when she was needed to cover ... which was the critical factor.

If [this] is not legitimate, then cases can be envisaged when somewhat surprising results would follow. For example, an employer might require to engage extra staff for an event due to take place over a particular period, such as the Wimbledon fortnight or the Olympic Games. [Is there direct discrimination if the employer refuses to hire a woman whose confinement is expected to be on the first day of the event?] ...

The circumstances in the case of a woman due to have a hysterectomy are different from the circumstances in the case of a man due to have a prostate operation. The question is whether they are materially different, and the answer must be that they are not, because both sets of circumstances have the result that the person concerned is not going to be available at the critical time. Then it has to be considered whether there is something special about pregnancy which ought to lead to the conclusion that the case of a woman due to be unavailable for that reason is materially different from the case of a man due to be unavailable because of an expected prostate operation. In logic, there would not appear to be any valid reason for that conclusion ... [T]he correct comparison is not with any man but with a hypothetical man who would also be unavailable at the critical time ... The precise reason for the unavailability is not a relevant circumstance.

[It is hardly surprising that this opinion brought forth a torrent of criticism, since it appears to fly in the face of *Dekker* and to resurrect the supposedly discredited 'sick man' comparison. Moreover, it does so by quoting examples which are far removed from the typical experience of working women – a very small tail being made to wag a very large dog.]

Case C-32/93 [1994] IRLR 482, ECJ[11]

Advocate General (p 491):

[I]t is ... difficult to separate and distinguish pregnancy from inability to work for a specific length of time which coincides, moreover, with the duration of maternity leave. In such cases, absence from work is determined by the pregnancy ... a condition which affects only women. While it may be true that the woman in question was engaged for the purpose of replacing for a short time another employee during the latter's maternity leave, the fact remains that she was engaged on the basis of a contract for an indefinite period and therefore her inability to carry out the task for which she was engaged affects only a limited period in relation to the total length of the contract ...

[T]he absence from work is the result ... of the employer's concern to avoid possible financial or in any event organisational burdens arising from the need to engage an employee to perform – on a temporary basis – the tasks which the female employee who was subsequently dismissed had been recruited to carry out ...

[I]t is of no significance whatever ... that the employer would not have recruited [her] if he had been aware of her pregnancy ... [T]he dismissal cannot in any case be considered lawful when the appellant herself ... was not aware of her condition.

Judgment (p 494):

[T]here can be no question of comparing the situation of a woman who finds herself incapable, by reason of pregnancy discovered very shortly after the conclusion of the employment contract, of performing the task for which she was recruited with that of a man similarly incapable for other reasons ...

[T]he protection afforded by Community law to a woman during pregnancy and after childbirth cannot be dependent on whether her presence at work during maternity is essential to the proper functioning of the undertaking in which she is employed. Any contrary interpretation would render ineffective the provisions of the Directive.

In [these] circumstances ... termination of a contract for an indefinite period on grounds of the woman's pregnancy cannot be justified by the fact that she is prevented, on a purely temporary basis, from performing the work for which she has been engaged.

The case was returned to the House of Lords for final resolution.

---

11   See also [1994] ECR I-3567; [1994] ICR 770; [1994] 4 All ER 115.

Webb v EMO Air Cargo (UK) Ltd (No 2) **[1995] IRLR 645**[12]

Lord Keith of Kinkel (pp 647–48):

The emphasis placed by the court upon the indefinite nature of the appellant's contract of employment suggests the possibility of a distinction between such a case and the case where the woman's absence due to pregnancy would have the consequence of her being unavailable for the whole of the work for which she had been engaged. [If the latter situation] does not fail to be distinguished, so that an employer who fails to engage a woman who, due to pregnancy, will not be available for any part of the period of the proposed engagement, is to be made liable for wrongful discrimination, the result would be likely to be perceived as unfair to employers and as tending to bring the law on sex discrimination into disrepute ...

The ruling of the European Court proceeds upon an interpretation of the broad principles dealt with in Arts 2(1) and 5(1) of Directive 76/207. Sections 1(1)(a) and 5(3) of the 1975 Act set out a more precise test ... and the problem is how to fit the terms of that test into the ruling. It seems to me that the only way of doing so is to hold that, in a case where a woman is engaged for an indefinite period, the fact that the reason why she will be temporarily unavailable for work at a time when to her knowledge her services will be particularly required is pregnancy is a circumstance relevant to her case, being a circumstance which could not be present in the case of the hypothetical man. It does not necessarily follow that pregnancy would be a relevant circumstance in the situation where the woman is denied employment for a fixed period in the future during the whole of which her pregnancy would make her unavailable for work, nor in the situation where after engagement for such a period the discovery of her pregnancy leads to the cancellation of the engagement.

It follows that, as a general principle, having regard to pregnancy in reaching a decision to dismiss constitutes the application of a sex-based criterion and, according to the European Court, the application of a sex-based criterion necessarily amounts to sex discrimination. It does not follow that the dismissal of a pregnant woman is automatically unlawful. It still has to be shown that the treatment she has received was on the *ground* of her pregnancy. The question which must be asked in order to satisfy the comparative approach is whether the woman would have received the same treatment had she not been pregnant. The employer thus remains free to argue that the pregnancy was irrelevant or no more than a background cause of the dismissal, and that the real cause is different.[13] The approach of the courts to these difficult cases of causation – as problematic here as in other branches of the law – will

---

12 See also [1995] ICR 1021; [1995] 4 All ER 577.

13 A harbinger of the appropriate approach had been seen in *Stockton-on-Tees BC v Brown* [1989] AC 20; [1988] 2 All ER 129; [1988] IRLR 263, where the applicant was selected for redundancy because she was pregnant. Here, the reason for the dismissal was not pregnancy but redundancy, so the general unfair dismissal provisions applied rather than the SDA 1975. It was held, though, that the same principles apply; if the pregnancy was a significant factor leading to the dismissal, that would be sufficient to make it unlawful. The 'but for' test applies; she would not have been chosen for redundancy had she not been pregnant.

largely determine the width and the effectiveness of the protections proclaimed by the European Court in *Dekker* and *Webb*.[14]

(a)   Pregnancy or immorality[15]

O'Neill v Governors of St Thomas More RCVA School and Bedfordshire CC [1996] IRLR 372, EAT[16]

The applicant was a teacher of religious education expected to teach Catholic principles. She became pregnant as the result of a relationship with a Roman Catholic priest in the locality. Effectively she was forced to leave her post. It was accepted that the dismissal was unfair but the issue was whether it was also a case of sex discrimination. The tribunal said it was a mixed motives case and that pregnancy *per se* was not the dominant motive for the dismissal. The EAT allowed the appeal.

Mummery J (pp 376–78):

The consequence of [*Webb (No 2)*] is that the applicant's pregnancy is a circumstance relevant to her case, though it is not a circumstance which would be present in the case of a hypothetical man. The appellant's claim ... is not, therefore, to be determined by a comparison of her treatment with the treatment of a hypothetical male comparator proposed by the governors as a male teacher of RE ... who had fathered a child by a Roman Catholic nun and where there had been press publicity about that relationship. Such a comparison is not legally appropriate under the interpretation of the 1975 Act in the light of the ruling of the ECJ. Pregnant women in employment occupy a special position which attracts special protection ...

The basic question is: what, out of the whole complex of facts before the tribunal, is the 'effective and predominant' cause or the 'real and efficient' cause of the act complained of? ... [T]he event or factor alleged to be causative of the matter complained of need not be the only or even the main cause of the result complained of (though it must provide more than just the occasion for the result complained of) ...

In our view, the distinction made by the tribunal between pregnancy *per se* and pregnancy in the circumstances of this case is legally erroneous ... The concept of 'pregnancy *per se*' is misleading, because it suggests pregnancy as the sole ground of dismissal. Pregnancy always has surrounding circumstances, some arising prior to the state of pregnancy, some accompanying it, some consequential on it. The critical question is whether, on an objective consideration of all the surrounding circumstances, the dismissal or other treatment complained of ... is on ground of pregnancy. It need not be only on that ground. It need not even be mainly on that ground. Thus, the fact that the employer's ground for dismissal is that the pregnant

---

14 In the two consolidated cases of *Dixon v Rees; Hopkins v Shepherd and Partners* [1994] ICR 39; [1993] IRLR 468, decided before the decision of the ECJ in *Webb*, the EAT held in *Dixon* that the dismissal of a pregnant employee was acceptable as they had found an adequate replacement and did not wish to lose the opportunity to employ her; and in *Hopkins* that the dismissal of a veterinary nurse was acceptable because the employers took the view that it was unsafe to continue her employment because of health risks to the baby. It was stated that the employers would have treated a similarly situated man in the same way and thus the dismissals were not on ground of pregnancy. In the light of the first House of Lords' decision in *Webb*, the cases are probably wrong; after the decision of the European Court they are certainly wrong.

15 For a case on pregnancy or misconduct, see *Shomer v B and R Residential Lettings Ltd* [1992] IRLR 317, CA.

16 See also [1997] ICR 33.

woman will become unavailable for work because of her pregnancy does not make it any the less a dismissal on the ground of pregnancy ... [I]n the present case the other factors in the circumstances surrounding the pregnancy ... are all causally related to the fact that the applicant was pregnant – the paternity of the child, the publicity of that fact and the consequent untenability of the applicant's position ... Her pregnancy precipitated and permeated the decision to dismiss her ...[17]

(b)   Pregnancy or illness

Pregnancy may itself disable an employee from continuing to work, and the effects of the pregnancy or the birth may lead to further periods of absence through sickness. These periods of illness may fall within the permitted maternity leave or may extend beyond it. In each situation, the question arises whether the dismissal is on the ground of pregnancy, in which case the protected status will mean that the Equal Treatment Directive is contravened, or on the ground of sickness, in which case comparison with a man's treatment becomes appropriate. It is clear that a woman absent through illness arising because of and during her pregnancy – not extending afterwards – may not be dismissed even if a man absent for an equivalent length of time would have been dismissed. The pregnancy, at least while it lasts, confers a protected status. The position is less clear as regards illnesses which originate in pregnancy but continue after childbirth.

> *Handels- og Kontorfunktionaerernes Forbund i Danmark (acting for Hertz) v Dansk Arbejdsgiverforening (acting for Aldi Marked K/S)* **Case C-179/88 [1991] IRLR 31**[18]

The applicant experienced a complicated pregnancy involving considerable periods of absence. When the child was between one and two she was off work for 100 days as a result of an illness arising from the pregnancy and childbirth. She was dismissed as a result of these absences and claimed that such dismissal was in breach of the Equal Treatment Directive. The ECJ rejected her claim.

> *Judgment (pp 32–33):*
>
> It is submitted on the one hand that the dismissal of a woman because of her pregnancy, confinement, or reported absence due to an illness which has its origin in a pregnancy or confinement, at whatever moment this illness may occur, is contrary to the principle of equal treatment in so far as such problems cannot affect a male worker and he could not, therefore, be dismissed for the same reason.
>
> On the other hand, it is submitted that an employer cannot be forbidden to dismiss a female worker because of a large amount of sick leave simply for the reason that the illness has its origin in pregnancy or confinement ...
>
> [T]he Directive does not deal with the case of an illness which has its origin in pregnancy or confinement. It does, however, allow for national provisions which ensure specific rights for women in respect of pregnancy and maternity, such as

---

17   This decision casts serious doubt upon the previous EAT decision in *Berrisford v Woodard Schools (Midland Division)* [1991] ICR 564; [1991] IRLR 247, where a matron at a Church of England school was dismissed after telling the head she was pregnant but had no immediate plans to marry. It was held that she was dismissed not because she was pregnant but because the pregnancy manifested extra-marital sex. It was concluded that a man acting in a similar way would also have been dismissed.

18   See also [1990] ECR I-3979; [1992] ICR 332.

maternity leave. It follows that during the maternity leave from which she benefits under national law, a woman is protected from dismissal because of her absence.

In regard to an illness which appears after maternity leave, there is no reason to distinguish an illness which has its origin in pregnancy or confinement from any other illness. Such a pathological condition therefore falls under the general scheme applicable to an illness.

Female and male workers are in fact equally exposed to illness. Although it is true that certain problems are specifically linked to one sex or another, the only question is whether a woman is dismissed for absence due to illness on the same conditions as a man: if that is the case, there is no direct discrimination on grounds of sex.

Advocate General (p 37):

[On the applicant's argument] if the complications caused by a confinement are very serious, the female worker may be unable to work for long periods of time without her employer being allowed to dismiss her ... [T]he efficient operation of the company may be compromised by the difficulty of employing a replacement for that post immediately. But the most serious difficulties arise where the employer, prevented from dismissing his employee, is legally bound to contribute, even partially, directly or indirectly to the payment of social security payments which are due to the employee ...

It seems to me equally that the financial difficulties which confront an employer obliged to retain on his payroll a female employee who is incapable of work ... may lead numerous employers to refuse to employ pregnant women (very probably under false pretext) or even women of childbearing age ... It must be considered how a solution which would protect those women who have serious post-natal difficulties – [a small proportion] – carries dangers for all women wishing to enter the labour market.

[There should be no protection for] medical conditions which do not arise from the normal risks of pregnancy and which should therefore receive the same treatment as illness under the normal law.[19]

The judgment appeared clear that dismissal for illness within the national period of statutory maternity leave was unlawful. The following case attempted to distinguish *Hertz* on the basis that there, the illness did not come to light until after the statutory

---

19 '[Hertz] gives us a non-medical, male view of what represents normal pregnancy, childbirth and post-confinement recovery. For a woman who does not fit this normal model (she and/or her baby may have post-confinement problems), the protection of the law is partially removed. If we are beginning to recognise the special nature of pregnancy and motherhood, what justification is there for protecting a mother only before childbirth and not afterwards, when she and her new-born baby are equally as vulnerable? ... [T]he rationale for distinguishing between the two [periods] can only be on policy, that is, economic grounds – precisely those grounds rejected in *Dekker.*' Szyszczak, E, 'Community law on pregnancy and maternity', in Hervey, T and O'Keeffe, D (eds), *Sex Equality Law in the European Union*, 1996, Chichester: John Wiley, p 54. In the same volume (pp 85–86), Kilpatrick responds that 'although the *Hertz* decision is heavily criticised, it is less clear what the Court should have done. Does it mean that the length of the "protected period" should have been extended by the Court to cover Ms Hertz or that open-ended protection should be provided for pregnant employees? ... [M]any feel that the anchoring of maternity rights in discrimination law weds it to the sameness/difference debate in a way that involves the use of artificial comparisons and makes pregnancy rights a derogation from equality, a special right or preferential treatment ... [T]he critiques of *Hertz* are directed against not protecting the pregnant woman *enough* by not recognising the realities of pregnancy complications, which can continue long after the birth of the child and by providing a cut-off point for protection after which she is thrown back into the comparative approach'.

maternity leave period had ended. Here, her illness began during the pregnancy and continued after the expiry of her maternity leave.

> *Handels- og Kontorfunktionaererernes Forbund i Danmark (acting on behalf of Larsson) v Dansk Handel and Service (acting on behalf of Fotex Supermarket)* **Case C-400/95 [1997] IRLR 643**[20]

During her pregnancy, she was on sick leave in August 1991 and from November 1991 to March 1992 when her maternity leave commenced. That finished in September 1992 after which she took four weeks' annual leave. She again went on sick leave, after which her contract of employment was terminated on the ground of 'your lengthy period of absence and the fact that it is scarcely likely that you will at any time in the future be in a position to carry out your work in a satisfactory manner'. The European Court held that there was no breach of the Equal Treatment Directive.

> *Judgment (p 650):*
>
> Outside the periods of maternity leave ... a woman is not protected against dismissal on grounds of periods of absence due to an illness originating in pregnancy ... [A]s male and female workers are equally exposed to illness, the Directive does not concern illnesses attributable to pregnancy or confinement.
>
> [A]bsence during the protected period, other than for reasons unconnected with the employee's condition, can no longer be taken into account as grounds for subsequent dismissal.

After this decision, the only clearly discriminatory dismissal is one which occurs during the period of maternity leave. Dismissals arising after that period has ended should logically be compared with how a similarly situated sick man would have been treated. In making that calculation, policy demands that the whole of the period of illness during maternity leave be ignored – the illness clock will only begin to tick the day after the end of maternity leave; otherwise, dismissal might be permissible even if the illness only lasted a very short time after maternity leave had ended.

The problem that remained concerned the effect of illness in pregnancy *before* maternity leave commenced. *Fotex* (above) had implied that pre-maternity leave absences could be added to post-maternity leave absences to determine whether a woman was treated less favourably than a comparable man. The European Court has now rejected that approach and held that *all* absences due to pregnancy must be disregarded.

> *Brown v Rentokil Ltd* **Case C-399/96; [1998] IRLR 455, ECJ**

The applicant became unable to work some two months into her pregnancy because of various pregnancy-related disorders. She was dismissed after 26 weeks of absence in accordance with the company rule that sickness absence for 26 consecutive weeks would lead to dismissal. The Court of Session[21] purported to distinguish between pregnancy and illness arising from pregnancy and held that no breach of the Equal Treatment Directive had occurred.

---

20   See also [1997] ECR I-2757.
21   [1995] IRLR 211.

Judgment:

[D]ismissal of a woman during pregnancy cannot be based on her inability, as a result of her condition, to perform the duties which she is contractually bound to carry out. If such an interpretation were adopted, the protection afforded by Community law to a woman during pregnancy would be available only to pregnant women who were able to comply with the conditions of their employment contracts, with the result that the provisions of Directive 76/207 would be rendered ineffective ...

[P]regnancy is a period during which disorders and complications may arise compelling a woman to undergo strict medical supervision and, in some cases, to rest absolutely for all or part of her pregnancy. Those disorders and complications, which may cause incapacity for work, form part of the risks inherent in the condition of pregnancy and are thus a specific feature of that condition.

[T]he principle of non-discrimination ... requires ... protection throughout the period of pregnancy ... However, where pathological conditions caused by pregnancy or childbirth arise after the end of maternity leave, they are covered by the general rules applicable in the case of illness ... In such circumstances the sole question is whether a female worker's absences, following maternity leave, caused by her incapacity for work ... are treated in the same way as a male worker's absences of the same duration ...

Where a woman is absent owing to illness resulting from pregnancy or childbirth, and that illness arose during pregnancy and persisted during and after maternity leave, her absence not only during maternity leave but also during the period extending from the start of her pregnancy to the start of her maternity leave cannot be taken into account for computation of the period justifying her dismissal under national law ...

The effect of this decision is that the principle of non-discrimination protects a woman from the time she informs her employer she is pregnant until the time she returns from maternity leave.[22] She is, however, not protected from all sickness dismissals in the period before the birth, only those connected with the pregnancy. Employers will therefore need to ensure that they are informed of the precise cause of each sickness absence during pregnancy.

(c)   Pregnancy or unavailability

Caruana v Manchester Airport plc [1996] IRLR 379, EAT

The applicant worked as an independent contractor as a researcher under a series of fixed term contracts, the final one being for a period of 12 months. When she became pregnant, she was told that her contract would not be renewed for a further period because she would not be available for work at its commencement. As she was self-employed, she could not claim unfair dismissal (nor did she have any right to maternity pay). The EAT upheld her claim under the SDA 1975.

Buxton J (pp 380–81):

There is no doubt that although the employers decided not to offer Mrs Caruana a new contract because of her future unavailability, that unavailability was because of ...

---

22   In *Caledonia Bureau v Caffrey* [1998] IRLR 110; [1998] ICR 603, the Scottish EAT held that post-natal depression that arose during maternity leave, but persisted beyond that, was an illness related to pregnancy, so that the dismissal amounted to sex discrimination on the ground of pregnancy.

her pregnancy ... Since pregnancy was a circumstance relevant to her case ... and that circumstance could not be present in the case of a man, she ... was the object of unlawful discrimination.

The contention [that the principle does not apply to fixed term contracts] is not consistent with Lord Keith's limitation of a possible special rule for fixed term contracts to cases where the employee would be available for no part of the term. [All that Lord Keith is saying is that] it does not necessarily follow from the ECJ's ruling that pregnancy would be a relevant circumstance where the woman will be absent for the whole duration of the contract ... That approach gives little ground for confidence that there are other, entirely unstated, exceptions ...

To disqualify Mrs Caruana from the protection of the ECJ's ruling would be a positive encouragement to offer or to impose, not a continuous and stable employment relationship, but a series of short-term contracts, with the object or collateral advantage of avoiding the impact of the discrimination laws. We are confident that neither the ECJ nor the House of Lords did or would support such an approach.

Thus, there *may* be an exception for one-off fixed term contracts, as opposed to renewed or renewable contracts as in *Caruana*. Lord Keith in *Webb* took pains to exclude from the scope of the protection an employee whose pregnancy caused her to be unavailable for the whole duration of the contract. Such a contract would perforce be relatively short. However, this exception does not appear in the Equal Treatment Directive, did not find favour with the Advocate General in *Webb*, runs contrary to the general policy of seeking to improve the legal position of atypical workers, and may indeed provide an incentive for employers to hire women on short-term temporary contracts.[23]

Availability for work is premised on the assumption that the woman will, after the birth, return to the same job she was performing beforehand.

British Telecommunications plc v Roberts and Longstaffe [1996] IRLR 601, EAT

The two applicants decided they wanted to work on a jobsharer basis when they both returned from maternity leave. Their plan was rejected on the basis that the operational needs of the job required Saturday working, which was only available if they worked part-time. The industrial tribunal upheld their complaint of sex discrimination, purporting to follow *Dekker* and *Webb*.

The EAT allowed the employer's appeal in respect of direct discrimination, but remitted the case for an industrial tribunal to consider whether there had been indirect discrimination.

Tucker J (pp 602–03):

[T]he finding of direct discrimination arose solely from the tribunal's view that, since the requests and refusals followed directly from the pregnancy and maternity, there was automatically direct discrimination on the grounds of sex ...

In our opinion ... the situation did not arise because the respondents sought to exercise their statutory rights, but because they did not seek to do so, but rather sought to alter the terms of their employment ...

Once a woman returns to work after her [maternity] leave, the statutory protection finishes, and her work thereafter is to be considered in the same circumstances as if

---

23   See *op cit*, Szyszczak, fn 19, pp 54–57.

she was a man ... [W]hat happened to these two respondents had nothing to do with them being pregnant, but with them having children to look after ... They were not permanently entitled to rely on having had babies as a protecting feature.

There is thus no *automatic* right to return to work on a part-time basis, or to be granted the benefit of other modifications to the contract of employment in order to reconcile work and parenthood. Refusal of such changes is likely to amount neither to direct discrimination nor to breach of the Employment Rights Act 1996. Such a refusal may, however, amount to indirect discrimination, as it is likely that such employer policies will disproportionately affect women as compared with men. In such situations, employers may argue that they were justified in refusing to permit such changes to be made.[24]

(d)   Section 99 of the Employment Rights Act 1996

Employment Rights Act 1996

99   Leave for family reasons

(1)   An employee who is dismissed shall be regarded ... as unfairly dismissed if—

    (a)   the reason or principal reason for the dismissal is of a prescribed kind, or

    (b)   the dismissal takes place in prescribed circumstances.

(2)   In this section 'prescribed' means prescribed by regulations made by the Secretary of State.

(3)   A reason or set of circumstances prescribed under this section must relate to:[25]

    (a)   pregnancy, childbirth or maternity,

    (b)   ordinary, compulsory or additional maternity leave,

    (ba) ordinary or additional adoption leave,

    (c)   parental leave, or

    (ca) paternity leave, or

    (d)   time off under section 57A [time off for dependants]; and it may also relate to redundancy or other factors.

Section 99, which came into force in October 1999,[26] means that it is automatically unfair dismissal if the principal reason for dismissal is related to pregnancy. There is no time threshold for it to be effective,[27] although there may be one to qualify for 'prescribed circumstances', such as additional maternity leave.

However, three comments are needed. Although pregnancy (or the related matters prescribed) must be the reason for the dismissal, and so the worker should inform the employer of her pregnancy,[28] it is not necessary that the worker discloses the pregnancy at the time of recruitment.[29] However, pregnant employees who are absent or likely to be absent for extended periods need to ensure the employer is aware of the

---

24 See Cox, S, 'Flexible working after maternity leave: the legal framework' (1998) 78 EOR 10; see also *Home Office v Holmes*, below, Chapter 10, pp 284–86.

25 Confirmed by Secretary of State by Maternity and Parental Leave etc Regulations 1999, SI 1999/3312.

26 Substituted by the Employment Relations Act 1999, s 9, Sched 4, Pt III, paras 5, 16: see SI 1999/2830, art 2(2), Sched 1, Pt II.

27 Section 108(3)(b). The upper age limit does not apply either: s 109(2)(b).

28 Pregnant Workers Directive, 92/85/EC, Art 2(a).

29 *Tele Danmark v HK (Acting for Brandt-Nielson)* Case C-109/00 [2001] IRLR 853, ECJ.

reason. In addition, a causal connection between the pregnancy and the dismissal must be shown and causal tests are notoriously difficult to pin down. For example, if an employer, within his contractual rights, orders a pregnant employee to move to a different office – for organisational reasons, not simply because she is pregnant – and she refuses because she is pregnant and does not want the additional hassle, it is unclear whether the dismissal would be connected with her pregnancy. The same problem might arise, where misconduct is in some sense triggered by the pregnancy.[30]

The second problem is where pregnancy-related illness is long-lasting. Literally, if the illness was a complication of the pregnancy or childbirth it is surely covered, but the economic argument that this may potentially cause unfair economic hardship for employers may lead to the words being given a more restricted meaning. But, in *Caledonian Bureau Investment and Property v Caffrey*,[31] the Scottish EAT held that a dismissal for post-natal depression was automatically unfair under this provision, even though its effects continued after the protected period of maternity leave and even though, on a very narrow reading of the legislation, it could be argued that the condition was connected with childbirth rather than pregnancy. Whether this approach will stand the test of time remains to be seen.

Finally, and most importantly, the different compensation rules in the UK mean that there may still be a strong incentive to allege breach of the SDA 1975. The new rights take effect as part of the general law on unfair dismissal, for which there is a maximum limit on compensation. At the time of writing, the maximum compensatory award for unfair dismissal was £52,600.[32] Until the decision in *Marshall (No 2)*,[33] the same limit applied to the SDA 1975, but the decision of the European Court and resulting legislation means that there is now no limit in such cases.[34] Some sex discrimination cases may involve greater loss than may be awarded for an unfair dismissal; in such cases a claim under the SDA 1975 should also be brought.[35]

(2)   Pregnancy, Pay and Benefits

The Pregnant Workers Directive provides that Member States must establish a right to maternity pay for which a qualifying period of no more than one year is permissible.[36] The amount of such pay must be at an adequate level, which is defined as at a level at

---

30 [1992] IRLR 317, CA. See *Shomer v B and R Residential Lettings Ltd* [1992] IRLR 317, CA.

31 [1998] IRLR 110.

32 Employment Rights Act 1996, s 124. In 1998, the Government proposed to abolish this limit: *Fairness at Work*, Cm 3968, 1998, London: HMSO, para 3.5.

33 *Marshall v Southampton and South West Hampshire AHA (No 2)* Case C-271/91 [1993] ECR I-4367; [1994] AC 530; [1994] QB 126; [1993] IRLR 445.

34 See below, Chapter 17, pp 535–36.

35 The abolition of the limit on compensation proved crucial in the cases where the armed forces admitted a long-standing policy of dismissing those who became pregnant. As the claim was against an organ of the State, damages could be awarded for losses arising in respect of any period after the UK's failure to implement the Equal Treatment Directive. The Government was forced to concede the unlawfulness of its policy, so the litigation concerned the proper approach to compensation in such cases. See, eg, *Ministry of Defence v Cannock* [1994] ICR 918; [1995] 2 All ER 449; [1994] IRLR 509, EAT; Arnull, A, 'EC law and the dismissal of pregnant servicewomen' [1995] 24 ILJ 215; and the Sex Discrimination Act 1975 (Application to Armed Forces, etc) Regulations 1994 SI 1994/3276. See below, Chapter 12, p 356.

36 Directive (92/85/EEC), Art 11(3) and (4). See *Banks v Tesco & Secretary of State for Employment* [1999] ICR 1141, EAT.

least equal to the value of the minimum State sick pay in the Member State concerned, which is of course in many cases lower than employer-provided occupational sick pay. This maternity pay is 'pay' for the purposes of Art 141 (equal pay). However, if the pay is less than the contractual sick pay, there is no breach of the principle of equal pay. Here the Pregnant Workers Directive prevails. This was explored in the following cases.

Gillespie v Northern Health and Social Services Board Case C-342/93 [1996] IRLR 214; [1996] ICR 498, ECJ

Gillespie's maternity pay was less than her normal pay. She argued that she should have continued to receive her normal pay throughout her maternity leave as otherwise she was being discriminated against on the ground of her pregnancy.

Judgment (p 224):

[Women on maternity leave] are in a special position which requires them to be afforded special protection, but which is not comparable either with that of a man or with that of a woman actually at work ...

Directive [92/85] does not apply *ratione temporis* to the facts of the present case. It was therefore for the national legislature to set the amount of the benefit to be paid during maternity leave ...

[A]t the material time neither Art 119 [now 141] ... nor Art 1 of Directive 75/117 [the Equal Pay Directive] required that women should continue to receive full pay during maternity leave. Nor did those provisions lay down any specific criteria for determining the amount of benefit to be paid to them during that period. The amount payable, however, could not be so low as to undermine the purpose of maternity leave, namely the protection of women before and after giving birth ...

The reasoning in the case is thin, the outcome inevitable. The Pregnant Workers Directive, which set no more than minimum levels of maternity pay which employers should be obliged to pay, was the outcome of a compromise among the Member States; for the ECJ to hold that, after all, *full* pay was payable *throughout* the pregnancy would have been politically unthinkable.

When the case was returned to the Northern Ireland Court of Appeal,[37] it was held, inevitably, that there was no case for concluding that contractual maternity pay, which was at a higher level than statutory sick pay, was inadequate. In *Todd v Eastern Health and Social Services Board*, heard together with *Gillespie*, it was contended that it was unlawful for contractual maternity pay to be less generous than the contractual sick pay, as sick pay covered all forms of disability which could be encountered by a man, but not all the forms which could be met by a woman, such as pregnancy. The argument was accepted by the industrial tribunal, but rejected by the Northern Ireland Court of Appeal on the basis that the contractual maternity and sickness provisions could not be rolled up together into one term providing for disability; a healthy pregnancy fell outside the contractual provisions relating to sickness and disability as pregnancy cannot be compared with sickness. This reasoning is flawed. If a pregnant woman requires time off because of illness, it seems clear that she should be treated the same as an employee off sick for any other reason. The argument is that the employer should have treated all disabling conditions in the same way, as

---

37   [1997] IRLR 410.

otherwise the woman is being treated worse than a similarly situated man. The fact that pregnancy is not an illness is irrelevant to a comparison of benefits for different periods of absence; even worse is to deny the claim on the basis that the courts had previously decided that to treat pregnancy as an illness was inappropriate and demeaning.[38]

However, in *Boyle v EOC*,[39] the ECJ took the same approach and held that an employment contract could make maternity pay in excess of the statutory minimum dependent upon a return to work, even though there was no corresponding term in relation to contractual sick pay. Accordingly, the employer could claw back the payments made in excess of the statutory minimum, should the woman not return to work.

Wynn, M 'Pregnancy discrimination: equality, protection or reconciliation?' (1999) 62 MLR 435, p 441:

The result of *Boyle and Gillespie* is that women on maternity leave are left without effective recourse where employers exploit the modicum of protection provided by Directive 92/85/EC. Financial detriments will continue to be incurred by women who chose to combine work and childbearing and employers will not be penalised for minimising their costs as long as the threshold of adequacy of income is not undermined. These cases indicate that the limits of maternity protection are determined by the European Court's perception of national autonomy in matters of social welfare. The result of balancing competing interests on the social plane is that the cost of applying the principle of equal treatment militates against the equal treatment of individual rights. As Advocate General Iglesias noted in *Gillespie*, to give full protection to pregnant mothers 'would threaten to upset the balance of the entire social welfare system'.

The ECJ in *Gillespie* made clear that none of this means that a woman on maternity leave cannot be deprived of normal pay rises and benefits because of her maternity leave. In *GUS Home Shopping*[40] the EAT held that depriving a woman of a loyalty bonus because she was absent through pregnancy was unlawful sex discrimination.

The definition of maternity pay is narrower than that of pay in Art 141 (formerly Art 119), under which certain non-monetary payments constitute pay.[41] So these decisions should not affect other benefits. Accordingly, where there an employer deprives a worker of other benefits because of pregnancy, a claim of discrimination or equal pay should be possible. Legislation provides that a woman taking maternity leave is entitled to all other benefits arising from the employment.

---

38 For discussion of the complicated interaction between pregnancy rights and sickness benefits, see Cox, S, 'Maternity and sex discrimination law: where are we now?' (1997) 75 EOR 23, pp 26–28.

39 Case C-411/96 1998 ECR I-6401; [1998] IRLR 717, ECJ, and see Casenote, Caracciolo di Torella, E, 'Recent developments in pregnancy and maternity rights' [1999] 28 ILJ 276.

40 [2001] IRLR 75, EAT.

41 *Garland v British Rail Engineering* [1982] ECR 359, ECJ. See Chapter 14, p 381.

Maternity and Parental Leave etc Regulations 1999, SI 1999/3312

Application of terms and conditions during ordinary maternity leave[42]

9(1) An employee who takes ordinary maternity leave:

    (a) is entitled, during the period of leave, to the benefit of all of the terms and conditions of employment which would have applied if she had not been absent, and

    (b) is bound, during that period, by any obligations arising under those terms and conditions ...

(2) In paragraph (1)(a), 'terms and conditions' has the meaning given by section 71(5) of the 1996 [Employment Rights] Act, and accordingly does not include terms and conditions about remuneration.

(3) For the purposes of section 71 of the 1996 [Employment Rights] Act, only sums payable to an employee by way of wages or salary are to be treated as remuneration.

Section 71 of the Employment Rights Act 1996 provides that the terms of employment 'includes matters connected with the employee's employment whether or not they arise under her contract of employment'. In *CNAVTS v Thibault*,[43] the ECJ held that to deprive a woman on maternity leave of her annual assessment, and the resulting possibility of promotion, was discrimination under the Equal Treatment Directive.

(3) Protective Legislation

Equal Treatment Directive 76/207

Article 2

(3) This Directive shall be without prejudice to provision concerning the protection of women, particularly as regards pregnancy and maternity.[44]

Historically, a great deal of legislation was passed to 'protect' women, and thereby had the effect of restricting their hours of work, their opportunities to engage in night work and the type of work they were legally permitted to undertake.[45] The effect of such provisions is to deny employment opportunities for women, so is of practical economic benefit to men as restricting the supply of labour in particular areas of the labour market. In addition, such legislation reflected and confirmed patriarchal assumptions that the appropriate place for women was in the home rather than in the male world of work.

The SDA 1975 threw down little or no challenge to this traditional view, which collapsed for two ideologically separate, though converging, reasons. First, the restrictions on female labour market participation were seen as an unnecessary and outdated fetter on the operation of the free market economy. Secondly, European law saw such restrictions as breaching the fundamental principle of equality between men and women, which was manifested in the Equal Treatment Directive. That Directive is

---

42 Inserted by the Maternity and Parental Leave (Amendment) Regulations 2002, SI 2002/2789, applicable where the expected week of birth was on or after 6 April 2003 (reg 2(1)).

43 *Caisse nationale d'assurance vieillesse des travailleurs salaries (CNAVTS) v Evelyne Thibault* Case C-136/95 [1998] ECR I-2011; [1998] IRLR 399.

44 See the SDA 1975, ss 51 and 51A, inserted by the Employment Act 1989, s 3.

45 Fredman, S, *Women and the Law*, 1997, Oxford: Clarendon, pp 67–74.

subject to two relevant exceptions: first, by virtue of Art 2(2), in relation to occupational activities where 'the sex of the worker constitutes a determining factor' and, secondly, by virtue of Art 2(3) (above). The scope of these exceptions was considered in the following cases.

Silke-Karin Mahlburg v Land Mecklenburg-Vorpommern Case C-207/98 [2000] ECR I-549, ECJ

Ms Mahlburg was employed as a nurse on fixed-term contracts. She applied for a permanent post working in the operating theatre. At the time she was pregnant. The hospital rejected her application because, under the *Mutterschutzgesetz* (German Law on the Protection of Working Mothers), it was unlawful to employ a pregnant woman where there was a risk to the woman or her foetus. There was such a risk working in the operating theatre. Her challenge to the ECJ under the Equal Treatment Directive was successful, despite the defence arguments under Art 2(3) of that Directive.

Judgment

21   It must, however, be pointed out that, in contrast to the *Dekker* case ... the unequal treatment in a case such as the present is not based directly on the woman's pregnancy but on a statutory prohibition on employment attaching to that condition.

22   That prohibition, imposed by the Mutterschutzgesetz, is based on Article 2(3) of the Directive, according to which that directive is to be without prejudice to provisions concerning the protection of women, particularly as regards pregnancy and maternity.

23   The question to be considered, therefore, is whether the Directive allows an employer not to conclude an employment contract for an indefinite period on account of the fact that compliance with the prohibition on pregnant women's employment would prevent the woman carrying out, from the outset, the work in the post to be filled.

24   It must be pointed out, first of all, that the Court has held that dismissal of a pregnant woman recruited for an indefinite period cannot be justified on grounds relating to her inability to fulfil a fundamental condition of her employment contract. The availability of an employee is necessarily, for the employer, a precondition for the proper performance of the employment contract. However, the protection afforded by Community law to a woman during pregnancy and after childbirth cannot be dependent on whether her presence at work during maternity is essential to the proper functioning of the undertaking in which she is employed. Any contrary interpretation would render ineffective the provisions of the Directive (Case C-32/93 *Webb* [1994] ECR I-3567, paragraph 26).

25   Secondly, a statutory prohibition on night-time work by pregnant women, which is in principle compatible with Article 2(3) of the Directive, cannot, however, serve as a basis for terminating a contract for an indefinite period (see to that effect Case C-421/92 *Habermann-Beltermann* [1994] ECR I-1657, paragraphs 18 and 25) Such a prohibition takes effect only for a limited period in relation to the total length of the contract (Habermann-Beltermann ...).

26   Lastly, the Court has held, in Case C-136/95 *Thibault* [1998] ECR I-2011, paragraph 26, that the exercise of the rights conferred on women under Article 2(3) of the Directive cannot be the subject of unfavourable treatment regarding their access to employment or their working conditions and that, in that light, the result pursued by the Directive is substantive, not formal, equality.

27   It follows from that case-law that the application of provisions concerning the protection of pregnant women cannot result in unfavourable treatment regarding their access to employment, so that it is not permissible for an employer to refuse to take on a pregnant woman on the ground that a prohibition on employment arising on account of the pregnancy would prevent her being employed from the outset and for the duration of the pregnancy in the post of unlimited duration to be filled ...

29   The Court has already held, in that regard, that a refusal to employ a woman on account of her pregnancy cannot be justified on grounds relating to the financial loss which an employer who appointed a pregnant woman would suffer for the duration of her maternity leave (*Dekker* ...). The same conclusion must be drawn as regards the financial loss caused by the fact that the woman appointed cannot be employed in the post concerned for the duration of her pregnancy.

30   The answer must therefore be given that Article 2(1) and (3) of the Directive precludes a refusal to appoint a pregnant woman to a post for an indefinite period on the ground that a statutory prohibition on employment attaching to the condition of pregnancy prevents her from being employed in that post from the outset and for the duration of the pregnancy.

Johnston v The Chief Constable of the Royal Ulster Constabulary **Case 222/84 [1986] IRLR 263, ECJ**[46]

The applicant was a reservist with the Royal Ulster Constabulary on a full-time, fixed term contract. Until 1980, she performed regular police duties, although she was not armed when doing them. It was the policy of the RUC that women officers should not carry firearms or receive training in their use; it was considered that it would increase the risk that they would become targets for assassination, that armed women officers would be less effective in areas for which women are 'better suited' such as welfare work, and the public would regard women carrying firearms as a much greater departure from the ideal of an unarmed force.

In 1980, her contract was not renewed on the basis that a substantial part of the duties would involve the use of firearms. She claimed sex discrimination. The Secretary of State for Northern Ireland issued a certificate stating that the reason for the refusal was for the purpose of safeguarding national security and protecting public safety or public order, which was a conclusive defence to the claim.

It followed that she could not succeed under domestic legislation. However, as she contended that the Equal Treatment Directive applied, the industrial tribunal referred the case to the ECJ, before which the claim succeeded.

Judgment (pp 277–78):

The reasons which the Chief Constable gave for his policy relate to the special circumstances in which the police must work in the situation existing in Northern Ireland ...

[I]t must be recognised that the context in which the occupational activity of members of an armed police force is carried out is determined by the environment in which that activity is carried out. In this regard, the possibility cannot be excluded that in a situation characterised by serious internal disturbances the carrying of firearms by policewomen might create additional risks of their being assassinated and might therefore be contrary to the requirements of public safety.

---

46   See also [1986] ECR 1651; [1987] QB 129; [1986] 3 All ER 135.

In such circumstances, the context of certain policing activities may be such that the sex of police officers constitutes a determining factor for carrying them out ...

[The] principle [of proportionality] requires that derogations remain within the limits of what is appropriate and necessary for achieving the end in view and require the principle of equal treatment to be reconciled as far as possible with the requirements of public safety, which constitute the decisive factor as regards the context of the activity in question ...

It is clear from the express reference to pregnancy and maternity that the Directive is intended to protect a woman's biological condition and the special relationship which exists between a woman and her child. That provision of the Directive does not therefore allow women to be excluded from a certain type of employment on the ground that public opinion demands that women be given greater protection than men against risks which affect women and men in the same way and which are distinct from women's specific needs of protection ...

A total exclusion of women from ... an occupational activity which, owing to a general risk not specific to women, is imposed for reasons of public safety is not one of the differences in treatment that Art 2(3) of the Directive allows out of a concern to protect women.

Thus, the national security defence was permitted to succeed on the very specific facts of the case, although the Court held that the ministerial certificate to that effect could not be conclusive, as that would deprive the applicant of the right under Art 6 to a judicial hearing of a complaint. This aspect of the decision is clearly vulnerable to the criticism that it allows social attitudes as to what role is appropriate for women to justify their exclusion, thereby adopting a much less rigorous approach to equality than under Art 2(3). *Johnston* is the only example where the European Court has upheld a so called 'special protection' which does not relate to pregnancy or maternity issues; the decision is explicable only in relation to the situation in Northern Ireland at the time. Outside the context of national security, the Court decided that the *only* protective legislation which was permissible was that which related specifically to pregnancy and maternity. Generalised assumptions that women were unsuited to particular areas of work were outdated and unlawful.

The upshot was the 1989 Employment Act. The equality rationale relied on by the Court in *Johnston* dovetailed with the then Conservative Government's intention to sweep away unnecessary legislation restricting the operation of a free labour market, but by both routes the end result would be the same. Most of the restrictions on the employment of women were swept away, such as the restriction on the employment of women working underground in mines and the restrictions on women cleaning machinery in factories. It is, however, still possible to justify a requirement – most obviously a height or strength requirement – if it can be shown to be necessary to comply with health and safety duties.[47]

The objectives of health and safety policies reflect theoretical and practical problems. If the goal is equality, it would be satisfied by a dangerous playing field but one which was level as between men and women: permitting women to work at night on the same terms as men is vulnerable to this criticism. If the goal is improving standards for all working people, the aim should be to extend to men those protections which had previously only been available to women.

---

47 See below, Chapter 10, pp 289–90.

CHAPTER 9

HARASSMENT

1   INTRODUCTION

When the Sex Discrimination Act (SDA) 1975 was passed, the *concept* of sexual harassment, though not of course the experience of it, was almost unknown. Racial harassment was seen as an issue, perhaps without using that exact phrase, but here the focus was – and to a large extent remains – on violence and intimidation away from the workplace. Yet within 20 years, sexual harassment has become one of the most discussed and significant aspects of the anti-discrimination legislation,[1] one where the removal of the statutory limit on compensation had an immediate impact in some cases.[2] The change in awareness is startling,[3] although of course it should certainly not be inferred that the problem of sexual harassment has somehow been solved.

The legal definition of sexual or racial harassment was developed entirely by case law, as a form of direct discrimination.[4] The case law has been predominantly concerned with sexual harassment. However, now, or in the near future, the various grounds of discrimination have, or will have, a free-standing statutory definition of harassment. This is a result of a number of recent EC Directives providing a more-or-less uniform definition of harassment. The relevant EC legislation consists of Equal Treatment Amendment Directive,[5] the Race Directive[6] and the Equal Treatment in Employment Directive.[7] The first of these Directives amended the Equal Treatment Directive[8] (which prohibits sex discrimination in employment matters) to read:

Article 2

2.   For the purposes of this Directive, the following definitions shall apply ...

— harassment: where an unwanted conduct related to the sex of a person occurs with the purpose or effect of violating the dignity of a person, and of creating an intimidating, hostile, degrading, humiliating or offensive environment,

— sexual harassment: where any form of unwanted verbal, non-verbal or physical conduct of a sexual nature occurs, with the purpose or effect of

---

1   The publication in 1979 of MacKinnon, C, *Sexual Harassment of Working Women*, 1979, New Haven: Yale UP, is generally considered to have been a key development in this growth of consciousness.

2   Issues of compensation and other remedies for sexual and racial harassment will be considered below, in Chapter 14. See also Kelly, J and Watt, B, 'Damages in sex harassment cases: a comparative study of American, Canadian and British law' (1996) 16 New York Law School Journal of International and Comparative Law 79.

3   A survey of 112 organisations, covering 742,000 employees, found that almost the entire sample had a policy for dealing with complaints of sexual harassment. Six in 10 respondents had introduced or revised policies within the past three years: (2002) 102 EOR 8.

4   For an argument that discrimination law is the wrong legal home for sexual harassment, see Dine, J and Watt, B, 'Sexual harassment: moving away from discrimination' (1995) 58 MLR 343.

5   Council Directive 2002/73/EC (due for implementation by 5 October 2005).

6   2000/43/EC.

7   2000/78/EC.

8   76/207/EEC.

violating the dignity of a person, in particular when creating an intimidating, hostile, degrading, humiliating or offensive environment.

3.   Harassment and sexual harassment within the meaning of this Directive shall be deemed to be discrimination on the grounds of sex and therefore prohibited.

A person's rejection of, or submission to, such conduct may not be used as a basis for a decision affecting that person.

The other Directives offer a less extensive definition. For instance, the Equal Treatment in Employment Directive provides:[9]

Article 2

Harassment shall be deemed to be a form of discrimination ... when unwanted conduct related to any of the grounds [ie, religion or belief, disability, age, or sexual orientation] takes place with the purpose or effect of violating the dignity of a person and of creating an intimidating, hostile, degrading, humiliating or offensive environment.

The consequential changes to the Race Relations Act (RRA) 1976 came into force on 19 July 2003. They came into force for sexual orientation on 1 December 2003, for religion or belief on 2 December 2003, and are due to come into force for disability on 1 October 2004, for sex by 5 October 2005 and for age sometime in 2006. Apart from sex[10] and disability,[11] the definitions are uniform. For instance, s 3A of the RRA 1976 provides:

(1)   A person subjects another to harassment ... where, on grounds of ethnic or national origins, he engages in unwanted conduct which has the purpose or effect of –

(a) violating that other's dignity, or

(b) creating an intimidating, hostile, degrading, humiliating or offensive environment for him.

(2)   Conduct shall be regarded as having the effect specified ... only if, having regard to all the circumstances, including in particular the perception of that other person, it should reasonably be considered as having that effect.

The major significance of the free-standing definition is that it will no longer be necessary to prove that the treatment was 'less favourable' than the treatment afforded to a comparator (real or hypothetical). The significance of this will be explored below. Also note that the harassment need not relate to the *claimant's* race, sexual orientation, religion or belief or sex, as the case may be. So, for instance, harassing a colleague because of his son's homosexuality, or because his daughter is a Muslim convert, or because of a belief that he is a Muslim, will be unlawful. This feature follows the definition of direct discrimination in the RRA, but extends the more limited one in the SDA.[12]

There will be a residual class of cases that are not bound by the Directives. Most obviously, these will include those arising before the law on the particular ground comes into force. Save for the Race Directive, the Directives only cover the field of

---

9   Race Directive, Art 2, para 3, provides an identical formula, on the grounds of racial or ethnic origin.

10   At the time of writing, no amendment had been published by the Government, but it is likely to be more expansive to reflect the Directive.

11   The harassment must relate to the *claimant's* disability.

12   Discussed in Chapter 7, p 187.

employment matters. So, for instance, a case of sexual harassment arising in the provision of housing will fall outside of the Directive. In addition, the Race Directive, unlike the Race Relations Act (RRA) 1976, does not extend to discrimination on the grounds of colour or nationality. So, for instance, a case of harassment purely on colour, would not be governed by the statutory definition.[13] Strictly speaking, these residual cases should be governed by the pre-existing case law. Just how much judges will be influenced by the new definition remains to be seen. What follows is a review of the elements of harassment developed under case law, prior to the statutory definition.

2 THE ELEMENTS OF HARASSMENT

(1) The Comparison

Here lies the major difference between the pre-existing case law and the statutory definition. The new statutory definition merely requires that the conduct is 'related to' sex, sexual orientation, race, religion or belief, or disability, as the case may be. No comparison with how someone else not belonging to the protected group in question would be treated is necessary. However, the case law developed the concept of sexual harassment as a form of direct discrimination under s 1(1)(a) of the SDA 1975. So it appears, until the new definition comes into force, that tribunals are bound to include *less* favourable treatment as an element and with it, they must use a comparator, as specified in s 5 of the SDA 1975. This seems illogical because harassment is, in its nature, gender- (or race-, etc) specific. *Some* judges have followed this reasoning and ignored the comparison. This has not been the norm and so there is some confusion over which is the correct approach. The majority of the Court of Appeal, in *Smith v Gardner Merchant*, disapproved of the 'gender-specific' approach taken by the Employment Appeal Tribunal (EAT) in *British Telecom v Williams*. However, a differently constituted Court of Appeal in *Sidhu* less than two years later, *obiter*, endorsed the 'gender-specific' approach, without reference to *Smith*. Recently, the House of Lords in *Pearce* endorsed *Smith*, without reference to *Sidhu*.

> **Smith v Gardner Merchant Ltd [1998] IRLR 510; [1998] 3 All ER 852; [1999] ICR 134, CA**

The facts are set out on p 162, above.

> *Ward LJ (p 516):*
>
> A different argument for avoiding the necessity to look for a comparator of the opposite sex may arise in connection with allegations of sexual harassment. The argument is taken from the judgment of Morison, J in the EAT in *British Telecom v Williams* [1997] IRLR 668 at 669 ...:
>
>> To affect a person's dignity on the grounds of sex will, as with other forms of sexual harassment, cause a detriment to that person. Thus, proof of sexual harassment, of whatever form, will satisfy the criterion. *Because* the conduct which constitutes sexual harassment is itself gender-specific, there is no

---

13 For a rare case of colour discrimination, see *Walker v Secretary of the Treasury* 713 F Supp 403 (1989); see Chapter 6, p 140.

necessity to look for a male comparator. Indeed, it would be no defence to a complaint of sexual harassment that a person of the other sex would have been similarly so treated: see *Porcelli v Strathclyde Regional Council* ([1986] ICR 564).' (My emphasis.)

The judgments of the President of the EAT always command respect but I regret I do not fully agree with what fell from him on this occasion. I agree that the kind of conduct which constitutes sexual harassment can be, indeed usually is, gender-specific. It was in *Porcelli's*[14] case. The abuse to which she was subjected was being shown a screw nail and asked if she wanted a screw and being shown a penis-shaped glass rod holder and asked if she had use for it. It was this sort of behaviour which ineluctably compelled the conclusion that:

> In my opinion this particular part of the campaign was plainly adopted against the applicant because she was a woman. It was a particular kind of weapon, *based upon the sex of the victim*, which, as the industrial tribunal recognised would not have been used against an equally disliked man [see [1986] ICR 564 at 569 per the Lord President; my emphasis] ...

These are conclusions of fact. Why I disagree with the observations of Morison J is that he seems to elevate a conclusion of fact – usually, in the context of the case, an absolutely inevitable conclusion of fact – into a principle of law. Picking up the emphasis I added to his judgment, it is not the case that because the abusive conduct is gender-specific that there is no necessity to look for a male comparator; but it is rather the case that if it is gender-specific, if it is sex-based, then, in the nature of the harassment, it is almost certainly bound as a matter of fact to be less favourable treatment as between the sexes. The male employee would never have been subjected to the indignity of being asked if he wanted a screw or had use of the phallic rod holder. Thus, in those circumstances, there is no need for a comparator simply because *res ipsa loquitur* [the thing speaks for itself].

Sir Christopher Slade agreed with Ward LJ on this point. However, Beldam LJ endorsed Morison's J approach.

Beldam LJ (dissenting on this point, at p 520):

I agree with Morison J that in general in cases of sexual harassment there is no necessity to look for comparison with a particular person of the opposite sex. In the case of a man who sexually harasses a woman at work, it will usually be the case that the man would not have sexually harassed another man and it is in this sense that Morison J used the phrase 'sex specific' but ... the question is whether the sexual harassment took place because of the sex of the victim, not whether it would have amounted to sexual harassment of a person of the opposite sex ...

Sidhu v Aerospace Composite Technology [2000] IRLR 602; [2001] ICR 167, CA

Peter Gibson LJ (p 606)

[After citing the RRA 1976, ss 1(1)(a) and 3(4)] It is clear therefore that what the statute requires in order to find direct racial discrimination under s 1(1)(a) is that the complainant must show that he has been treated less favourably by the discriminator than the discriminator treats or would treat other persons in the same circumstances.

But in certain cases the comparison need not be demonstrated by evidence as to how a comparator was or would be treated, because the very action complained of is in itself less favourable treatment on sexual or racial grounds. Thus in a sex

---

14 See also below, p 228.

discrimination case if it can be shown that the less favourable treatment meted out to a woman was only because she was a woman, it follows that the woman was treated less favourably than a man (*Porcelli v Strathclyde Regional Council*).[15] In the jargon of employment lawyers, that conduct is gender-specific. So also if a person is harassed or abused because of his race, that conduct is race-specific and it is not necessary to show that a person of another race would be treated more favourably (*Burton v De Vere Hotels*).[16]

Brooke and Robert Walker LJJ agreed with Peter Gibson LJ.

Pearce v Governing Body of Mayfield Secondary School [2003] UKHL 34; [2003] All ER (D) 259 (Jun), HL

Shirley Pearce is a lesbian and she regularly experienced homophobic taunts and abuse by pupils at the school at which she taught. This mainly took the form of oral abuse, including words such as 'lesbian', 'dyke', 'lesbian shit', 'lemon', 'lezzie' or 'lez'. At a meeting with her head teacher, he told her to 'grit your teeth'. The abuse continued and her new head of department suggested that she either looked for another job or joined the supply list. Ms Pearce went off sick for a second time and took early retirement on health grounds a year later. She brought a complaint of unlawful sex discrimination, but the House of Lords dismissed her appeal.

Lord Nicholls:

8 ... The disgraceful way she was treated by some of the pupils was because of her sexual orientation, not her sex. Ms Pearce accepted that the children would have pursued a comparable campaign of harassment against a homosexual man.

16 In some cases there are suggestions of a different approach. It has been suggested that if the form of the harassment is sexual, that of itself constitutes less favourable treatment of the ground of sex. ... Degrading treatment of this nature differs materially from unpleasant treatment inflicted on an equally disliked male colleague, regardless of equality of overall unpleasantless: ... *Porcelli* [1986] ICR 564, 568–70. Because the form of the harassment is gender specific, there is no need to look for a male comparator. It would be no defence to a complaint of sexual harassment that a person of the opposite sex would have been similarly treated: see ... *BT v Williams* [1997] IRLR 668, 669.

17 ... I respectfully think some of these observations go too far. They cannot be reconciled with the language of scheme of the statute. The fact that the harassment is gender specific in form cannot be regarded as of itself establishing conclusively that the reason for the harassment is gender based: 'on the ground of her sex.' It will certainly point in that direction. But this does not dispense with the need ... that the reason why the victim was being harassed was her sex. The gender specific form of the harassment will be evidence, whose weight will depend on the circumstances, that the reason for the harassment was gender based. A male employee who subjects a female colleague to persistent, unwelcome sexual overtures may readily be inferred to be doing so on the ground of her sex.

---

15 [1986] IRLR 134, EAT. The essential facts are set out in Ward's LJ judgment in *Smith v Gardner Merchant*, above. See also below, p 228.

16 [1996] IRLR 596, EAT. See below, p 232.

Smith and *Pearce* concerned homophobic harassment, which would of course be decided in the claimants' favour[17] under the Employment Equality (Sexual Orientation) Regulations 2003, should they have been force at the time. Nevertheless, it is clear that the dominant view is that there must be a comparison and this is still relevant for some other areas. The need for a comparison proved fatal to the claim in the next case.

Stewart v Cleveland Guest (Engineering) Ltd [1994] IRLR 440; [1996] ICR 535, EAT

A female inspector had to go through the manufacturing area where calendars and pin-ups of nude and partially nude women were on display. She complained to the works manager that she was embarrassed and degraded by the pictures. His view and that of the managing director was basically that the pictures were acceptable as they did not show the genital area. They treated her complaint as so trivial as not to be worthy of a reply. After she complained to the union, an order was issued to take the pictures down, whereupon a deputation of women employees said they had no objection to the pictures. When she realised that everyone knew it was she who complained, she resigned, saying she had no confidence in the employers being prepared to protect her from embarrassment and distress caused by the other employees' attitude. She claimed sex discrimination and constructive dismissal.

The industrial tribunal upheld the complaint of constructive dismissal on the ground that the employers had broken the implied term of mutual confidence. There was no appeal from that decision. The Employment Appeal Tribunal (EAT) upheld the decision of the industrial tribunal and rejected the claim of sex discrimination.

Mummery J (p 443):

It was argued that the Tribunal erred in law in finding that the treatment of Miss Stewart was not less favourable to her on the ground of her sex. Reference was made to the EC Commission Code of Practice on sexual harassment which includes, in the range of behaviour which constitutes sexual harassment, 'conduct which creates an intimidating, hostile or humiliating working environment' (para 2). It was argued that it was perverse of the Tribunal to conclude that the display of pictures was not aimed at women and was sexually neutral. The display was of women in a sexually explicit fashion in a workplace where most of the workers were men and where there was a prevalent attitude of the men epitomised by remarks and conduct which treated women as sex objects. The display was 'gender-specific', operating in a 'gender-specific environment' where women, not men, were exposed to the treatment complained of by Miss Stewart.

It was also perverse [it was argued] of the Tribunal to conclude that a man might well find this sort of display as offensive as Miss Stewart did. A man's objection to such a display would be based on other grounds (eg, moral grounds), not on the ground of his sex. As the pictures depicted women, and not men, a man, even one who objected to the pictures, would not have found the pictures offensive in the same way as Miss Stewart did. The display was not in an environment where men were in the minority, nor in an environment where men, as against women, were subjected to suggestive remarks. The true position was that, in the words of Lord Brand in *Porcelli v Strathclyde Council*,[18] this form of treatment was unfavourable to a women because she was more vulnerable to it than a man was. ...

---

17   In the event Smith won his case under the SDA 1975; see below, p 224, and Chapter 6, p 162.
18   [1986] IRLR 134 CS, at p 138, para 18.

We have reached the conclusion, after careful consideration of Ms Gill's arguments, that no error of law on the part of the Industrial Tribunal has been demonstrated ... The decision to dismiss this appeal does not mean that it is never an act of sex discrimination for a company to allow its male employees to display pictures of that kind in the workplace. A decision to allow this appeal would not mean that such an employer would in every such case be liable for sex discrimination ...

A feature of this case was that Miss Stewart was not singled out as a target. But should that make a difference? It is possible to harass a person by creating an unpleasant environment. The new statutory definition endorses this by outlawing conduct of a sexual nature with the effect of violating the dignity of a person, 'in particular when creating an intimidating, hostile, degrading, humiliating or offensive environment'.

A comparison need not be fatal to a claim of harassment, as the next two cases demonstrate.

Insitu Cleaning Co Ltd v Heads [1995] IRLR 4, EAT

The victim was area supervisor for a contract cleaning firm. The harasser, who was the son of two directors, and a manager, entered a room and said 'Hiya, big tits'. She said that she found the remark very embarrassing and distressing, especially as she was nearly twice his age. She received no internal support in making a complaint and eventually resigned and successfully claimed sex discrimination.

Morison J (p 5):

[T]he defence argued the following points:

(1)   The remark was not sex-related and therefore could not amount to direct discrimination on the ground of sex. It is said that a similar remark could have been made to a man, for example in relation to a balding head or beard. ...

The first ground seemed to us to be absurd. A remark by a man about a woman's breasts cannot sensibly be equated with a remark by a woman about a bald head or a beard. One is sexual and the other is not.

Driskel v Peninsula Business Services [2000] IRLR 151, EAT

Mrs Driskel was employed by Peninsula and alleged that her Head of Department, Mr Huss, subjected her to sexual banter and comments in February and April 1996. In July 1996, she had an interview scheduled with Mr Huss for a promotion. On the day before the interview, she claimed that he had remarked that she should wear a short skirt and see-through blouse showing plenty of cleavage if she wanted to be successful. Following the interview itself, she brought a formal complaint of sexual harassment. Her complaint was rejected after investigation by the director of consultancy. When Mrs Driskel refused to return to her job unless Mr Huss was moved elsewhere, she was dismissed. An employment tribunal dismissed her claims of sex discrimination. The EAT allowed her appeal.

Holland J (at para 13):

In making its judgment a tribunal should not lose sight of the significance in this context of the sex of not just the complainant but also that of the alleged discriminator. Sexual badinage of a heterosexual male by another such cannot be completely equated with like badinage by him of a woman. *Prima facie* the treatment is not equal: in the latter circumstance it is the sex of the alleged discriminator that potentially adds a material element absent as between two heterosexual men. ...

[W]hat is relevant is that by this remark ... [Mr Huss] was undermining her dignity as a woman when, as a heterosexual, he would never similarly have treated a man. Again, the tribunal seriously misdirected itself in putting any weight on Mr Huss's sexual vulgarity towards male employees for the reasons already set out in this judgment, that is, that being heterosexual that which he said to men was vulgar without being intimidatory.

These last two cases reveal that a comparison need not prove fatal to a claim of harassment. The polarised debate between the 'gender-specific' and comparison arguments should be immaterial. What matters is the nature of the comparison. For instance, in *Smith*, the Court of Appeal went on to compare the claimant (a gay man who had been subjected to homophobic abuse regarding AIDS) with a woman, who of course, would not have been subjected to such abuse. Similar comparisons were made in *Insitu* and *Driskel*. In *Stewart*, the industrial tribunal found that the display in a factory of pictures of nude women might be as offensive to a man, which surely was a perverse finding of fact, despite the EAT's refusal to interfere. However, in *Pearce*, the House of Lords compared the complainant to a homosexual male and then latched on to the admission that the comparator would have suffered a 'comparable campaign', albeit using different language. The result was inevitable. The House was clearly wary of finding homophobic harassment actionable under the SDA, which had been held not to cover discrimination on the grounds of sexual orientation.[19] However, as the Court of Appeal in *Smith* showed, this is a misplaced fear which leads to comparisons based on sexual orientation, rather than upon sex.

Curiously, the courts have not found this dilemma when dealing with racial harassment. For instance, in *Commission for Racial Equality v United Packing Industry Ltd*,[20] the insult to a Pakistani worker was 'We used to buy you when you were slaves'. In *De Souza v Automobile Association*,[21] a worker overheard her office manager refer to her as 'the wog'. In these cases, no attempt was made to substitute an equivalent insult to a white person. However, although these cases were not cited, this approach was disapproved by Lord Nicholls in *Pearce v Governing Body of Mayfield Secondary School*.[22]

(2)   Treatment

In *De Souza v Automobile Association*,[23] Maria De Souza overheard her office manager refer to her as 'the wog' whilst she was standing outside his office. The remark was not directed towards her and not intended to have been overheard by her. It was held that the office manager had not discriminated against Ms De Souza. May LJ explained that although she had been 'considered' less favourably, she had not been 'treated' less favourably.[24] Of course, this is not an authority that a racial insult cannot amount to less favourable treatment.

---

19   Case C-249/96, *Grant v South West Trains* [1998] IRLR 206, ECJ.
20   Commission for Racial Equality Report, 1980, p 20, IT.
21   [1986] ICR 514, CA.
22   [2003] UKHL 34; [2003] All ER (D) 259 (Jun), HL, at para 30. See above, p 221.
23   [1986] ICR 514, CA; see further below, p 230.
24   *Ibid*, at 524E.

(3)   Assessing Whether There Has Been Harassment

(a)   Relevance of the perception of the victim

In conventional cases of direct discrimination, the House of Lords, in *R v Birmingham CC ex p EOC*,[25] has held that it is enough that the victim considered – reasonably – that they had been treated less favourably, even in the face of objective evidence. There must be some reasonable grounds for that perception; it is not enough that the claimant simply considered that she was treated less favourably.[26] A similar approach was taken by Holland J in *Driskel* (above):[27]

> The ultimate judgment ... reflects an objective assessment by the tribunal of all the facts. That said, amongst the factors to be considered are the applicant's subjective perception of that which is the subject of complaint and the understanding, motive and intention of the alleged discriminator. Thus, the act complained of may be so obviously detrimental, that is, disadvantageous (see *Insitu*)[28] to the applicant as a woman by intimidating her or undermining her dignity at work, that the lack of any contemporaneous complaint by her is of little or no significance. By contrast she may complain of one or more matters which if taken individually may not objectively signify much, if anything, in terms of detriment ... By contrast the facts may simply disclose hypersensitivity on the part of the applicant to conduct which was reasonably not perceived by the alleged discriminator as being to her detriment – no finding of discrimination can then follow.

The Government expressly endorsed this approach in the *pre-consultation* Explanatory Notes to the new Regulations on Sexual Orientation and Religion or Belief, and the amendment regulations to the Disability Discrimination Act, hence this part of *Driskel* is codified in the Government's transposition of the Race and Equality in Employment Directives. For example, reg 5 of the Religion or Belief Regulations 2003 provides:

> ... conduct shall be regarded as having the effect [of violating a person's dignity or creating an intimidating, hostile, degrading, humiliating or offensive environment for a person] ... only if, having regard to all the circumstances, including, in particular, the perception of B [the victim], it should reasonably be considered as having that effect.[29]

This approach, in mixing the subjective and objective, does not reflect the recommendation of the Lawrence Inquiry to define a racist incident (criminal and

---

25   [1989] AC 1155; [1989] 1 All ER 769; [1989] IRLR 173, HL.
26   *Burrett v West Birmingham HA* [1994] IRLR 7, EAT.
27   *Driskel v Peninsula Business Services* [2000] IRLR 151, at 155, EAT.
28   [1995] IRLR 4, EAT; see above, p 223.
29   The same formula is used by the RRA 1976, s 3A and the Sexual Orientation Regulations 2003, reg 5. A curiosity here is the different emphasis placed on the formula in the respective *pre-consultation* Explanatory Notes. For disability: 'The intention is ... Tribunals should be required to take into account all relevant circumstances, in particular, the perception of the person alleging harassment.' In contrast, for religion or belief, and sexual orientation: 'Therefore, an over-sensitive complainant who takes offence unreasonably at a perfectly innocent comment would probably not be considered as having been harassed.' The difference of emphasis should add up to nothing, as they are different ways of explaining the same principle.

non-criminal) as: 'any incident which is perceived to be racist by the victim or any other person.'[30]

(b)　One-off and serial incidents and the victim's response

It is common for victims not to complain at the time of the harassment. This can be the case also where there is a series of unwelcome conduct. The cases make clear that a one-off incident may amount to harassment and a series of incidents should be assessed as a whole, not in isolation. Holland J in *Driskel* (below) suggested that a failure to make a contemporaneous indication that the conduct was unwelcome may be 'material'. This position will be modified by the Equal Treatment Amendment Directive.[31] Once in force, Art 2, para 3 of the Equal Treatment Directive will provide:

> A person's rejection of, or submission to, such conduct may not be used as a basis for a decision affecting that person.

The anomaly here is that the same rider is not included in the Race or Equal Treatment in Employment Directives and nor, of course, in the ensuing regulations and amendments. Consequently, Holland's J statement in *Driskel* may be good law in all grounds save sex, which is not due for the new definition until October 2005.

Below, *Insitu* involved a one-off incident, whilst the EAT in *Driskel* and *Reed* explained how to assess a series of 'minor' incidents coupled with the victim's response.

Insitu Cleaning Co Ltd v Heads [1995] IRLR 4, EAT

The facts are set out above, p 223.

Morison J (p 5):

> For the bosses' son to make a sexual remark to a female employee nearly twice his age was calculated to, and did, cause distress which no doubt was a mixture of rage, humiliation and genuine embarrassment. This is a form of bullying and is not acceptable in the workplace in any circumstances. The wrong done was compounded by B's status, the aggressive way he responded to the complaint, and his arrogant and dismissive manner at the Industrial Tribunal ... [S]uch conduct is likely to create an intimidating, hostile and humiliating work environment for the victim.

> Whether a single verbal act of sexual harassment is sufficient to found a complaint is also a question of fact and degree[32] ... No one, other than a person used to indulging in loutish behaviour, could think that the remark used in this case was other than obviously unwanted.

30　*The Stephen Lawrence Inquiry, Report of an Inquiry by Sir William Macpherson, advised by Tom Cook, The Right Reverend Dr John Sentamu, Dr Richard Stone*, February 1999, presented to Parliament by the Home Secretary, Cm 4262-I, London: HMSO, (available at www.official-documents.co.uk/document/cm42/4262/4262.htm). Chapter 47 paras 12–13. See also Chapter 1.

31　Council Directive 2002/73/EC. Due for implementation by 5 October 2005.

32　See also *Bracebridge Engineering Ltd v Darby* [1990] IRLR 3, EAT.

Driskel v Peninsula Business Services **[2000] IRLR 151, EAT**

The facts are set out above, p 223.

Holland J (p 155):

Thus, the act complained of may be so obviously detrimental, that is, disadvantageous (see *Insitu* ...) to the applicant as a woman by intimidating her or undermining her dignity at work, that the lack of any contemporaneous complaint by her is of little or no significance. By contrast she may complain of one or more matters which if taken individually may not objectively signify much, if anything, in terms of detriment. Then a contemporaneous indication of sensitivity on her part becomes obviously material as does the evidence of the alleged discriminator as to his perception. That which in isolation may not amount to discriminatory detriment may become such if persisted in notwithstanding objection, vocal or apparent. The passage cited from the judgment of the US Federal Appeal Court is germane[33] ...

The fact that Mr Huss had been so consistently and wrongly 'in denial' about the incidents complained of was a factor obscured to the tribunal by its approach to the case but which was highly germane to the weight of his professed perception that Mrs Driskel contemporaneously regarded all that she later complained of as acceptable sexual banter ...

We turn to the crucial incident of [the pre-interview remark] ... In our judgment, had the tribunal correctly directed itself as to the law, it would first, have sought to put the incident in context, that is, as the latest in a line of incidents with 'its predecessors'. Second, it would readily have found that that which was complained of amounted *prima facie* to discrimination of a high order. She was in the unenviable position of having to seek promotion by way of a one-to-one interview with a man for whom she had an antipathy. In such circumstances she was in receipt of remarks that in an appalling fashion sought to exploit the situation by reference to the sex of respectively, interviewee and interviewer, as in *Insitu* ... that which was complained of was objectively *prima facie* discriminatory and it would need some exceptional findings to negate that inference by reference to the respective perceptions of Mrs Driskel and Mr Huss. As it was, the tribunal was heavily influenced by Mrs Driskel's failure to make an immediate complaint without reminding itself that any instinct to complain must perforce be inhibited by the fact that she wanted the promotion that would come from the approval of Mr Huss – and that she did in fact complain on the day following when she perceived that she had no chance of promotion. Further and in any event, given the nature of the remarks, how significant was any failure to complain? ...

We allow much of the appeal as related to the dismissal of Mrs Driskel's complaint of sexual discrimination ...

Reed and Another v Stedman **[1999] IRLR 299, EAT**

Morison J (p 302):

As to whether the conduct is unwelcome, there may well be difficult factual issues to resolve. In general terms, some conduct, if not expressly invited, could properly be described as unwelcome. A woman does not, for example, have to make it clear in advance that she does not want to be touched in a sexual manner. At the lower end of the scale, a woman may appear, objectively, to be unduly sensitive to what might

---

33 'The trier of fact must keep in mind that each successive episode has its predecessors, that the impact of the separate incidents may accumulate, and that the work environment created may exceed the sum of the individual episodes.' *Burns v McGregor Elec Indus* 955 F 2d 559, at 564 (8th Cir 1992).

otherwise be regarded as unexceptional behaviour. But because it is for each person to define their own levels of acceptance, the question would then be whether by words or conduct she had made it clear that she found such conduct unwelcome. It is not necessary for a woman to make a public fuss to indicate her disapproval; walking out of the room might be sufficient. Tribunals will be sensitive to the problems that victims may face in dealing with a man, perhaps in a senior position to herself, who will be likely to deny that he was doing anything untoward and whose defence may often be that the victim was being over-sensitive. Provided that any reasonable person would understand her to be rejecting the conduct of which she was complaining, continuation of the conduct would, generally, be regarded as harassment. But at all times, the tribunal should not lose sight of the question at issue: was the applicant subjected to a detriment on the grounds of her sex? The answer to that question does not depend upon the number of incidents. A one-off act may be sufficient to damage her working environment and constitute a barrier to sexual equality in the workplace, which would constitute a detriment.

(c)   Discriminatory intent

Being a form of direct discrimination, there is no need to prove an intention, or motive, to cause harassment.[34] This is confirmed in the next three extracts.

Strathclyde Regional Council v Porcelli [1986] IRLR 134; [1986] ICR 564, CS

The plaintiff was harassed as part of a campaign to try to get her to leave the school where she worked as a laboratory technician. The campaign included suggestive remarks and deliberate brushing against her, but no sexual favour was sought. Eventually she applied for a transfer and complained that the employers had discriminated against her in that they were vicariously liable for the acts of sexual harassment committed against her. The main argument for the defence, which was accepted by the industrial tribunal, was that much of the behaviour was of a non-sexual nature and that they would have harassed a man they wished to get rid of in largely the same way, even though some specific instances would have differed.

The EAT, in a decision upheld by the Court of Session, allowed the applicant's appeal.

Lord Emslie, the Lord President (p 137):

Section 1(1)(a) [of the SDA 1975] is concerned with 'treatment' and not with the motive or objective of the person responsible for it. Although in some cases it will be obvious that there is a sex-related purpose in the mind of a person who indulges in unwanted and objectionable sexual overtures to a woman or exposes her to offensive sexual jokes or observations, that is not this case. But it does not follow that because the campaign ... as a whole had no sex-related motive or objective, the treatment ... which was of the nature of 'sexual harassment' is not to be regarded as having been 'on the ground of her sex' ... In my opinion this particular part of the campaign was plainly adopted ... because she was a woman. It was a particular kind of weapon, based on the sex of the victim ... which would not have been used against an equally disliked man.

---

34   *R v Birmingham CC ex p EOC* [1989] AC 1155; [1989] 1 All ER 769; [1989] IRLR 173, HL. See Chapter 7, p 182. For a consideration of alternative actions in tort (under *Wilkinson v Downton* [1897] 2 QB 57) or criminal law (Public Order Act 1986, s 5), see Mullender, R, 'Racial harassment, sexual harassment and the expressive function of law' (1998) 61 MLR 236.

***Driskel v Peninsula Business Services* [2000] IRLR 151, EAT**

The facts are set out above, p 223.

Holland J (p 155, para 14):

> Turning to Mr Huss, the tribunal's finding ... that the remark was flippant and was
> not meant to be taken seriously effectively misses the point. It is irrelevant that he
> never expected her to turn up for the interview in sexually provocative dress – what is
> relevant is that by this remark (flippant or not) he was undermining her dignity as a
> woman ...

(4)   Detriment

So far, we have established that outside of the new statutory definition, harassment is
a form of discrimination. Consequently, a claimant must show that the discrimination
occurred in one of the fields covered by the relevant legislation. Nearly all claims will
be in the field of employment. Section 6 of the SDA 1975 provides that it is unlawful
for an employer to discriminate against a woman in recruitment, access to promotion
etc, dismissal *or by subjecting her to some other detriment*. Unless the harassment causes
dismissal,[35] or some other specified disadvantage in s 6, a claimant has the further
burden of showing that the harassment caused a 'detriment'. In *Porcelli,* the EAT held
that the detriment should be work-related.

***Strathclyde Regional Council v Porcelli* [1984] IRLR 467; [1985] ICR 177, EAT**

Lord McDonald MC (at p 469):

> An employer who dismisses a female employee because she has resisted or ceased to
> be interested in his advances would, in our view, be in breach of s 6(2)(b) and s 1(1) of
> the 1975 Act for reasons arising from sexual harassment. Similarly if, for the same
> reason, he takes other disciplinary action against her short of dismissal, he would also
> be in breach. This action could be suspension, warning, enforced transfer, etc all of
> which would be to the detriment of the female employee although open to an
> employer under her contract of service in a genuine case not associated with sexual
> harassment.

The EAT held that the claimant, in seeking a transfer because of the harassment, had
suffered a detriment. The Court of Session upheld the decision, where the issue of
detriment was not contended. However, Lord Emslie gave the word a less strict
interpretation.

***Strathclyde Regional Council v Porcelli* [1986] ICR 564; [1986] IRLR 134, CS**

Lord Emslie (at pp 568–69):

> Although it is necessary for a woman seeking to found a claim upon s 6(2)(b) of the
> Act to establish that her employer had discriminated against her by dismissing her or
> subjecting her to some other detriment it is accepted by the appellants for the
> purposes of this appeal, that if Mrs Porcelli who was not dismissed, was
> discriminated against within the meaning of s 1(1)(a) she was subjected to a detriment
> within the meaning of s 6(2)(b). The appellants, in my opinion, were well advised to
> make that concession on the facts of this case for, as was pointed out by Brightman LJ

---

35 Which of course is most likely to be constructive dismissal.

(as he then was) in *Ministry of Defence v Jeremiah* [1979] IRLR 436, 'detriment' simply means 'disadvantage' in its statutory context.

Lord McDonald's view was also rejected by the Court of Appeal in *De Souza*.

De Souza v Automobile Association [1986] IRLR 103; [1986] ICR 514, CA

May LJ (p 107):

Racially to insult a coloured employee is not enough in itself, even if that insult cause him or her distress; before the employee can be said to have been subjected to some 'other detriment' the court or tribunal must find that by reason of the act or acts complained of a reasonable worker would or might take the view that he had been disadvantaged in the circumstances in which he had thereafter to work.

If in the passage from his judgment Lord McDonald [above] must be read as holding that an employee could only be said to have been subjected to a detriment within ... s 6 [SDA] ... if the result of the ... discrimination ... was either dismissal or other disciplinary action by the employer, or some action by the employee such as leaving the employment on the basis of constructive dismissal, or seeking transfer to another plant, then with respect I think that this was too limited an approach.

Thus if in another case the discrimination was such that the putative reasonable employee could justifiably complain about his or her working conditions or environment, then whether or not these were so bad as to be able to amount to constructive dismissal, or even if the employee was prepared to work on and put up with the harassment, I think this too could contravene the subsections.

May, LJ stated that a worker who continued in her job could still bring an action for harassment.[36] However, his definition appears narrower than Lord Emslie's (and *Jeremiah's*) for two reasons. First, he asks whether the *reasonable* worker (as opposed to the claimant) was disadvantaged. Secondly, such disadvantage has to be work-related. In *Thomas v Robinson*,[37] the EAT said of May's LJ interpretation: 'That *dictum* must now be treated with some reserve because it is clear that some levels of distress will now be regarded as detriment, and in any event, working in an environment where racist remarks are tolerated may itself be a detriment.'[38]

However, the EAT in *Thomas* also affirmed that detriment is an essential element for liability.[39]

Thomas and Comsoft Ltd v Robinson [2003] IRLR 7, EAT

Ms Robinson, of black Afro-Caribbean origin, born and bred in England, was told by a colleague that Caribbeans 'come over here and scrounge off the system and then go back'. Ms Robinson's parents had recently returned to the Caribbean and, during her claim for harassment in an industrial tribunal, she testified that she was 'shocked and deeply offended' by the remark. The tribunal did not allow cross-examination of Ms Robinson, stating that the racist remark alone amounted to a detriment. This was despite evidence that after the remark, Ms Thomas and Ms Robinson socialised and appeared to get on well. The EAT reversed that decision.

---

36   The facts are set out above, p 224. De Souza lost her claim on the issue of 'treatment'.
37   [2003] IRLR 7, EAT.
38   *Ibid*, at para 24.
39   This is confirmed by s 78 of the RRA: '"detriment" does not include conduct of a nature such as to constitute harassment under section 3A' (inserted by SI 2003/1626).

Judge JR Reid QC (para 25):

[A] Tribunal which is considering whether an employee has been
against by the use of racist language should consider both whether the ₁ₐ.₋ᵤ
been used and whether the employee has suffered detriment as a result. If botn
elements are established, then as a matter of shorthand it can be said that the
employee has been racially harassed. In very many cases the second element will be
extremely easy for the employee to establish, but this is does not entitle the Tribunal
to assume the second element, nor (as the Tribunal seems to have done here) to decide
that the proof of the language created an irrebuttable presumption of detriment. There
are some work environments in which (undesirable though it may be) racial abuse is
given and taken in good part by members of different ethnic groups. In such cases the
mere making of a racist remark could not be regarded as a detriment.

There is, of course, a residual class of cases[40] unaffected by the European derived free-
standing definition of harassment. This will include the provision of goods, facilities
and certain services under the SDA 1975. Section 29 of that Act provides that it is
unlawful to discriminate: 'by refusing or deliberately omitting to provide ... goods,
facilities or services of the like quality, in the like manner and on the like terms as are
normal in his case in relation to male members of the public ...' This section does not
employ the phrase 'any other detriment'. Sexual harassment in the provision of
services is most likely fall foul of s 29 because the service was not provided 'in the like
manner' as is 'normal'.

3   EMPLOYER RESPONSIBILITIES

There are three issues which must be distinguished: the way in which complaints are
investigated by the employer; the subsequent treatment of the complainant in relation
to the harasser; and the responsibility of the employer to protect employees from
harassment at the hands of fellow employees; in addition, the issue may arise of the
employer's legal responsibility for the actions of the harasser.

Failure to deal adequately with a claim of sexual harassment is not in itself an act
of sexual harassment or sex discrimination, but should be regarded in the same way
as failure to deal with any other employment complaint, assuming, of course, that the
way the complaint was dealt with fell short of being an act of victimisation. As a
matter of law, this conclusion is probably correct, but it leaves the victim with the
general problem of how to enforce this implied term in the contract of employment.
Suing for damages is unlikely to be practical or beneficial; resigning and claiming
constructive unfair dismissal is the ultimate step and, while it is a price victims may
well feel they must pay, not all would wish to do so. In addition, unlike claims under
the SDA 1975, constructive unfair dismissal claims are only open to employees who
have acquired one year of continuous employment. Thirdly, many cases reveal tension
between the actions of the alleged harasser and those of the employer. Arguably, the
claims in *Insitu, Stewart* and *Balgobin*[40a] were only brought because of the employer's
failure to respond adequately to the original complaint, thereby revealing the
importance, from the employer's perspective, of having proper procedural
mechanisms in place. Such procedural failure may be a breach of contract, even if the

40   See above, pp 218–19.
40a See, respectively, pp 223, 222 and 232.

,riginal action is insufficiently serious or detrimental on its own to amount to unlawful harassment.

In *Balgobin and Francis v London Borough of Tower Hamlets*,[41] two female employees complained of sexual harassment by a cook. The cook was suspended during an investigation, but the complaints could not be substantiated. The women were then required to continue working alongside their alleged harasser, and they argued that to have to continue working in that way itself constituted sex discrimination. The argument was rejected, Popplewell J observing that there:

> ... is no doubt that the intolerable situation to which these ladies were exposed had a sexual context but the reason they were exposed to that intolerable situation which affected them because they were women was not on account of their being women; the consequence of working with Mr C was no doubt a detriment to them as women; but they were not required to work with Mr C because they were women ... We have to say that the employers did not require these applicants to work with Mr C because of their sex.[42]

Just as with complaints of failure to investigate, such behaviour might constitute a breach of contract, but it is not sex discrimination.

Balgobin was not a case where the employer knew or had reason to anticipate that the actions might be repeated. However, even where the employer *knows* or *should know* that harassment may occur, the outcome may still be the same.

Pearce v Governing Body of Mayfield Secondary School [2003] UKHL 34; [2003] All ER (D) 259 (Jun), HL

For the facts, see above, p 221. A third (and, in the event, unnecessary) issue in *Pearce* was whether her employer could be liable for discriminatory acts by the school pupils. The House of Lords held, *obiter*, that it was not so liable and, in doing so, disapproved of the EAT decision in *Burton and Rhule v De Vere Hotels Ltd*.[43]

Lord Nicholls:

28   ... In *Burton* ... two black waitresses, clearing tables in the banqueting hall of a hotel, were the butt of racist and sexist jibes made by a guest speaker entertaining the assembled all-male company at a private dinner party. The Employment Appeal Tribunal held that the employer of the waitresses had racially discriminated against the waitresses. Had the assistant managers in charge for the evening been properly instructed, the two young women would not have suffered embarrassment. They could, and should, have been withdrawn from the room.

29   This is not a satisfactory decision. ... Viewed in the broadest terms, the *Burton* decision has much to commend it. There is, surely, everything to be said in favour of a conclusion which requires employers to take reasonable steps to protect employees from racial or sexual abuse by third parties. But is a failure to do so 'discrimination' by the employer? Where the *Burton* decision is, indeed, vulnerable is that it treats an employer's inadvertent failure to take such steps as discrimination even though the failure had nothing to do with the sex or race of the employees. In this crucially important respect, the decision gives insufficient

---

41   [1987] IRLR 401; [1987] ICR 829, EAT.
42   *Ibid*, at p 404.
43   [1996] IRLR 596; [1997] ICR 1 EAT. For comment, see Mullender, R, 'Racial harassment, sexual harassment and the expressive function of law' (1998) 61 MLR 236.

heed to the statutory discrimination provisions. An essential element of 'direct' sex discrimination by an employer is that, on the grounds of sex, the employer treats the employee less favourably than he treats or would treat an employee of the opposite sex. Similarly with 'direct' racial discrimination ... Unless the employer's conduct satisfies this 'less favourable treatment' test, the employer is not guilty of direct sex or racial discrimination. In making this comparison acts of persons for whose conduct an employer is vicariously responsible are to be attributed to the employer. It is otherwise in respect of acts of third parties for whose conduct the employer is not vicariously liable ...

31   ... [T]he harassment in *Burton* was committed by third parties for whose conduct the employer was not vicariously responsible. Despite this, the tribunal seems to have proceeded on the basis that the racial harassment of the waitresses by the speaker and some of the guests constituted discrimination on the part of the employer, and that the only issue left outstanding on the appeal, if the discrimination claim were to succeed, was whether the employers had by active or passive conduct subjected the waitresses to racial harassment by the speaker and the offending guests. This cannot be right. In order to succeed the two Caribbean waitresses had to prove discrimination by their employer.

32   On the sole outstanding issue before the tribunal Smith J said, at [1997] ICR 1, 10, para 38:

'The [employment] tribunal should ask themselves whether the event in question was something which was sufficiently under the control of the employer that he could, *by the application of good employment practice*, have prevented the harassment or reduced the extent of it. If such is their finding, then the employer has subjected the employee to the harassment.' (Emphasis added) ...

35   ... The hotel's failure to plan ahead properly may have fallen short of the standards required by good employment practice, but it was not racial discrimination. I consider the case was wrongly decided by the Employment Appeal Tribunal ...

36   Had the factual position been otherwise, and had the employer permitted exposure of the black waitresses to racist remarks by a third party when it would not have treated white employees similarly in a corresponding situation, this would have been a case of racial discrimination. This conclusion would follow from the difference in treatment afforded to black waitresses on the one hand and the treatment which would have been afforded to white waitresses on the other hand. In such circumstances the employer would be liable without it being necessary, or appropriate, to have recourse to 'good employment practice'
        ...

37   Some will regard this as a deficiency in the structure and scope of the discrimination legislation. I have already noted the desirability of employers taking reasonable steps to protect employees from sexual and racial harassment by third parties. But the discrimination legislation is targeted in precise terms. A fundamental feature of this aspect of the legislation is that attention is focused on the conduct of the particular employer, not the conduct of a reasonable employer. Further, the circumstances where an employer is liable for the acts of others are stated expressly in the legislation. It is not for the courts to extend the ambit of the discrimination legislation, however desirable this may seem, under the guise of interpretation of provisions which are unambiguously clear. As the legislation stands, the employer cannot be in a worse position regarding sexual or racial harassment of an employee by a third party for whose behaviour he is not vicariously liable than he is regarding sexual or racial harassment

committed by himself. If his conduct in the latter case must meet the statutory definition of discrimination before it will become unlawful, so also must his conduct, whether by way of act or omission, in the former case.

Section 32(1) of the RRA 1976[44] provides that anything 'done by a person in the course of his employment shall be treated for the purposes of this Act as done by his employer as well as by him, whether or not it was done with the employer's knowledge or approval'.[45] The meaning of that provision was at issue in the following case.

Jones v Tower Boot Co [1997] IRLR 168; [1997] ICR 254; [1997] 2 All ER 406, CA

The applicant was seriously racially harassed while working for the employers. Among other incidents, his arm was burnt with a hot screwdriver, metal bolts were thrown at his head and he was repeatedly called racially abusive names. The EAT held that the employers were not liable for these acts of harassment. They applied the traditional and well-known tort test of vicarious liability and concluded, not surprisingly, that the employers were not liable, as the acts of harassment were committed outside the course of employment.

The Court of Appeal allowed the appeal.

Waite LJ (pp 171–72):

A purposive construction ... requires s 32 of the Race Relations Act (and the corresponding s 41 of the Sex Discrimination Act) to be given a broad interpretation. It would be inconsistent with that requirement to allow the notion of the 'course of employment' to be construed in any sense more limited than the natural meaning of those everyday words would allow ... [T]here is no sufficient similarity between the two contexts to justify, on a linguistic construction, the reading of the phrase 'course of employment' as subject to the gloss imposed on it in the common law context of vicarious liability ... [If such a construction were adopted], the more heinous the act of discrimination, the less likely it will be that the employer will be liable.

The policy ... is to deter racial and sexual harassment in the workplace through a widening of the net of responsibility beyond the guilty employees themselves, by making all employers additionally liable for such harassment, and then supplying them with the reasonable steps defence ... which will exonerate the conscientious employer who has used his best endeavours to prevent such harassment, and will encourage all employers who have not yet undertaken such endeavours to take the steps necessary to make the same defence available in their workplace.

It would be particularly wrong to allow racial harassment on the scale that was suffered by the complainant in this case ... to slip through the net of employer responsibility by applying to it a common law principle evolved in another area of the law to deal with vicarious responsibility for wrongdoing of a wholly different kind. To do so would seriously undermine the statutory scheme of the Discrimination Acts and flout the purposes which they were passed to achieve.[46]

---

44 See also SDA 1975, s 41(1).

45 It was held in *UP and GS v N and RJ*, unreported, IT, Case 10781/95, see 35 DCLD 11, that this potential exclusion of employer liability was contrary to European law, as neither the Equal Treatment Directive nor the European Commission Code of Practice make any mention of such possibility.

46 *Irving and Irving v The Post Office* [1987] IRLR 289, EAT, was distinguished on the basis that there it was *assumed* rather than argued and decided that the common law test of vicarious liability was appropriate for use in the discrimination context.

The tribunals are free, and indeed bound, to interpret the ordinary and understandable words 'in the course of employment' in the sense in which layman would understand them ... The application of the phrase will be a question of fact for each Industrial Tribunal to resolve, in the light of the circumstances presented to it, with a mind unclouded by any parallels sought to be drawn from the law of vicarious liability in tort.

[The Court of Appeal restored the order of the IT, which had held the employers to be vicariously liable without making reference to that doctrine as it is applied in the tort context.]

The harasser can only be liable personally under the anti-discrimination legislation for aiding unlawful acts, which in turn depends on the employer being liable. The legislation does not permit action against the harasser to the exclusion of the employer. The law of harassment has been included within anti-discrimination law partly because that is what occurred in the USA and partly for want of a better alternative under English law. The issue, of which this case is a paradigm example, of whether the employer or the actual harasser is the more appropriate defendant, has been ignored by both judiciary and legislature. There are conceptual difficulties in applying a law based on comparative treatment on grounds of race or gender to a situation based on bullying, abuse or misuse of sexuality:

Furthermore, harassment may occur on grounds other than race or gender and in situations other than at the workplace. As the conceptual base of the law on sexual and racial harassment is so fragile, it is unsurprising that there are difficulties in attributing appropriate blame to either employer or employee. The law on vicarious liability [was] not responsible for [the decision of the EAT in] *Jones*; that should be laid at the feet of the failure by the judiciary and the legislature to deal adequately with harassment at a more conceptual level.[47]

The approach taken by the Court of Appeal, that the claim here is of an entirely different nature from one in tort, is not at all convincing. The applicant suffered personal injuries and might well have brought a tort claim. It is unclear in policy terms why an employer should be liable for racial discrimination but not liable in tort. It is apparently now the case that the employer will be liable for any actions of harassment committed by employees against fellow employees while at work, as long as the harassment is on ground of race, gender or disability. Logic suggests that the same principle applies if the victim is a customer or client. The employer may therefore be liable, and labelled as a discriminator, whether or not there was knowledge or means of knowledge of what was occurring, unless proper efforts had been made to prevent harassment from occurring.

Section 41(3) of the SDA 1975 states that in: 'proceedings brought ... against any person in respect of an act alleged to have been done by an employee of his it shall be a defence for that person to prove that he took such steps as were reasonably practicable to prevent the employee from doing that act ...'[48] This provision is particularly relevant to harassment cases, where employers may seek to argue that an equal opportunities policy or other management strategy had been precisely designed

47 Townshend-Smith, R, 'Case note' (1996) 2 IJDL 137, pp 139–40. For development of the argument, see Townshend-Smith, R, 'Harassment as a tort in English law: the boundaries of *Wilkinson v Downton*' (1995) 24 Anglo-Am LR 299; Dine, J and Watt, B, 'Sexual harassment: moving away from discrimination' (1995) 58 MLR 343, fn 3.
48 See also RRA 1976, s 32(3).

to prevent harassment from occurring. The question is what steps must employers take to avail themselves of this defence. In *Balgobin and Francis v London Borough of Tower Hamlets*,[49] it was conceded that the employers were vicariously liable for the acts of sexual harassment, but the employers argued that they had a defence under s 41(3). The industrial tribunal found that no one in authority knew what was going on, there was proper and adequate supervision, they had made known their policy of equal opportunities, and that in this light there were no other practicable steps they could have taken to stop the harassment from occurring. The EAT said that this was a finding which, on the evidence, the tribunal was entitled to reach, even though no evidence was given that any employees were given instruction or guidance on the operation of the equal opportunities policy, or that any particular efforts were made to combat sexual harassment. It took little to persuade the EAT that there was nothing more the employers could reasonably have done. This approach is dubious in law and on the facts. The section expressly places on the employer the burden of showing that all reasonable steps were taken, a burden which should require employers to show both that the policy was effectively implemented and communicated to the employees, and that under it, sexual harassment was a specific disciplinary offence. It cannot be enough merely to tell employees not to discriminate.[50]

If the employer is *not* responsible for the alleged harassment, for example, because it occurred outside working hours, there will be no protection under the victimisation provisions for the employee who makes a complaint.[51] This extremely narrow and technical reading of the legislation fails to provide the protection which is needed to employees who, at the time they are considering making a complaint, may be unaware or have no means of knowing whether the employer will be held liable for the acts of the actual harasser.

---

49 [1987] IRLR 401, EAT.
50 See European Commission Code of Practice, ss 5–7.
51 *Waters v Commissioner of Police of the Metropolis* [1997] ICR 1073; [1997] IRLR 589, CA. See below, Chapter 11, pp 301–03.

CHAPTER 10

INDIRECT DISCRIMINATION

1 THEORETICAL BASIS OF INDIRECT DISCRIMINATION LAW[1]

Different concepts of discrimination reflect different social goals and philosophies and thus are generally the products of legal positivists, although it cannot be denied that there is a general sense of justice underlying all concepts of discrimination. On the one extreme, some believe that only overt intentional discrimination should come under legal scrutiny. Lord Woolf CJ has stated: 'To regard a person as acting unlawfully when he had not been motivated either consciously or unconsciously by any discriminatory motive is hardly likely to assist the objective of promoting harmonious racial relations.'[2] At the other end of the scale, there are demands for quotas. The profile of a businesses' staff should reflect the profile of the community in which it exists. This has been labelled a 'fair share' theory or 'unalloyed' discrimination law.[3] Somewhere between these extremes there is a goal that all unnecessary discriminatory barriers should be eliminated.

There is a sense in which the law of direct discrimination parallels criminal law and the law of tort in its focus on individual responsibility and blameworthiness. The law is less certain in its justification for imposing liability for indirect discrimination: one approach focuses on the knowledge or conduct of the defendant employer, restricting liability to situations where the employer has a degree of responsibility for the particular instance of adverse impact; another approach imposes liability if the defendant fails to take adequate steps to remove barriers which have historically existed, even though the employer may in no way have been responsible for the existence of such barriers. There is a close parallel between the justification for imposing liability for indirect discrimination and the justification for requiring employers to engage in some form of positive action.

> **Rutherglen, G, 'Disparate impact under Title VII: an objective theory of discrimination' (1987) 73 Virginia L Rev 1297, pp 1310–11:**
>
> The prevailing economic theories of discrimination confirm the need for objective evidence of discrimination, because objective economic incentives, as much as an employer's state of mind, motivate employers to engage in discrimination. According to Gary Becker, employers engage in discrimination in order to satisfy tastes for discrimination: their own desire or the desires of their employees, customers, or suppliers not to associate with members of a disfavoured group. If employers cannot

---

1   See also, above, Chapter 4.

2   *Khan v Chief Constable of West Yorkshire* [2000] All ER (D) 237, CA, at para 14. See also comments of Lord Browne-Wilkinson in *Nagarajan v London Regional Transport* [1999] 4 All ER 65, HL, at 70. But note that discriminatory intent is not necessary for liability. See, eg, RRA 1976, s 56, and in the USA, *Griggs v Duke Power Co* 40 US 424 (1971), at p 434; below, p 240.

3   Mayhew labels this a 'fair share approach': *Law and Equal Opportunity*, 1968, Cambridge, Mass: Harvard UP, pp 59–74. Lustgarten, calls it an 'unalloyed' approach: Lustgarten, *Legal Control of Racial Discrimination*, 1980, London: Macmillan, p 54; see Chapter 4, p 92. Carvin names it a 'pure' standard: 'Disparate impact claims under the new Title VII' 68 Notre Dame Law Rev 1153, at p 1154.

engage in explicit discrimination because it is obviously illegal, they will use other means to minimise contact between the group with discriminatory tastes and the disfavoured group: for example, neutral selection procedures that disproportionately screen out members of the disfavoured group. Moreover, employers could adopt these procedures without any taste for discrimination themselves or any intent to discriminate on their part. They might seek to obtain the benefits of satisfying others' tastes for discrimination, and they might even be unaware that these benefits derive from tastes for discrimination.

Likewise, according to the theory of statistical discrimination, employers screen out members of a disfavoured group because of the difficulty of accurately assessing their productivity. Employers can minimise the cost of assessing productivity and making mistakes in so doing by minimising the number of employees that they hire from the disfavoured group. They can do so by adopting neutral employment practices with adverse impact on the disfavoured group. For example, by setting artificially high minimum standards with an adverse impact on the disfavoured group, the employer can be assured of hiring only those members of the group most likely to be productive. It can screen out other members of the group whose productivity is more uncertain. Again, the employer may take these steps without any explicit intent to discriminate but simply to improve the predicted productivity of its work force as evaluated according to neutral standards.

This is a useful if somewhat conservative approach. Its strength is that it provides a justification for the imposition of liability for criteria over the existence of which the employer has no direct control and even, it seems, no knowledge of their adverse impact. Its weakness is that it proceeds from a purely meritocratic and individualistic approach to the allocation of employment benefits and opportunities. Indirect discrimination law does have the potential to recognise the ethical demand that society should make some attempt to secure some degree of redistribution of wealth and opportunities from privileged groups to those who have been historically less privileged.

Indirect discrimination is concerned with group disadvantage – situations where the attainments of a particular group are, on average, lower than those of another group – usually white males. The concern is with group rights, but this fails to resolve the issue of precisely what status such rights are to have. The two most extreme positions are as follows. First, indirect discrimination applies where we suspect that the employer is guilty of direct discrimination but the evidence is inconclusive. For example, in *Griggs v Duke Power Co*,[4] the direct discrimination claim failed – perhaps marginally – but the inequality in educational achievement was so well known that the employer could hardly deny knowledge that his demand for High School diplomas would adversely affect blacks. Secondly, the objective of indirect discrimination may be seen as equality of outcome, whereby the employer is not permitted to utilise any employment practice which significantly differentiates between different relevant groups. This would require employment benefits to be allocated regardless of merit and in proportion to group membership in the relevant population – in other words, quotas. The main argument of principle against quotas is that they depart from the accepted mechanism of distributing goods and benefits in society based on individual merit. However, as a practical defence mechanism, quotas may be inevitable unless employers are permitted to justify or provide an explanation for an observed difference between groups.

Willborn, S, 'The disparate impact model of discrimination: theory and limits' (1985) 34 American UL Rev 799, pp 801–03:

A pure disparate impact model would find discrimination whenever there is a disparate impact. A pure model would apply to all protected groups, would apply to all types of employer action, and would recognise no defences. A pure model, therefore, proposes that disparate impact equals discrimination. That proposition has not been accepted. There is a generally shared intuition that employment decisions need not always affect various groups equally. There are both ideological and practical reasons for this intuition. Ideologically, a pure disparate impact model seeking group justice conflicts with fairness and meritocracy [in] a society accustomed to individual justice concepts. Practically, a proportional distribution of employment benefits on the basis of group characteristics seems, at best, uneconomical and, at worst, impossible ...

The disparate impact model, therefore, recognises a limitation – business necessity. An employer practice is illegal only if it creates a disparate impact and is not justified by business necessity. The inquiry into business necessity examines the relationship between the employment criterion that has a disparate impact and the skills that are required to perform the job. If the criterion, despite its disparate impact, distinguishes between persons who are capable of performing the job and persons who are not capable of performing the job, the criterion is not illegal under current disparate impact theory.

Is Willborn correct in his definition of a 'pure' model of indirect discrimination? If an employer, with an unbalanced racial make-up of staff, can justify his recruitment procedure on the basis of, say, qualifications essential for the job, he has not *discriminated* in relation to race. It is arguable that a strict test of justification completes a 'pure' theory, by identifying if, or how much, discrimination exists.[5]

Rutherglen, G, 'Discrimination and its discontents' (1995) 81 Virginia L Rev 117, pp 136–39:

The theory of disparate impact has had its principal effects ... in causing employers to abandon facially neutral employment practices, such as general aptitude tests, that have been successfully attacked using the theory and in encouraging employers to adopt affirmative action plans to eliminate the most obvious forms of disparate impact ... The theory was not originally devised as an inducement to engage in affirmative action, or at least it was not justified in those terms. It derived instead from the need to prevent evasion of Title VII through pretextual forms of discrimination. Judicial development of the theory, however, soon went beyond this limited goal ...

In its weakest form, the theory imposes only a light burden of justification upon the employer; it only extends the central prohibitions against discrimination and segregation to root out hidden discrimination. In its strongest form, the theory moves beyond the concept of discrimination to force employees to justify non-discriminatory practices that deny equal opportunity ... Faced with ambiguous statutory language codifying previous ambiguous case law, employers have apparently continued to do what proved successful in the past: abandon practices which have been condemned

---

5   See Connolly, M, 'Discrimination law: justification, alternative measures and defences based on sex' [2001] ILJ 311, extracted below, p 280.

under the theory of disparate impact and engage in more or less voluntary (sometimes much less than voluntary) affirmative action ...[6]

In both American and English law, an employer is permitted to argue that a *prima facie* indirectly discriminatory practice is nevertheless justifiable if it can be shown to be essential in the interests of the business, especially if it enables the employer to select employees who are the best on merit. Thus, a requirement that a job applicant have a degree in engineering will no doubt have an adverse impact on women, but normally this type of requirement will be justified, as it is presumably essential for the job and leads to a higher quality of applicant. However, to assume that it is easy to determine whether one applicant would be better for a business than another is unrealistic. To assume that merit both is and ought to be the basis for all hiring and promotion decisions is problematic both practically and ethically.[7]

2   HISTORY OF INDIRECT DISCRIMINATION LEGISLATION

The British indirect discrimination legislation has its origins in the USA's Civil Rights Act of 1964 and the Supreme Court's landmark decision in *Griggs v Duke Power Co*.[8] The Civil Rights Act 1964 contained many Titles outlawing discrimination in such areas as voting rights, public accommodation, facilities and education, and federally assisted programmes. Title VII covered employment. Section 703(a)[9] provided that it was unlawful for an employer to discriminate 'because of' a worker's race, colour, religion, sex or national origin. The Act contained no specific definition of *indirect* discrimination. The Supreme Court recognised indirect discrimination and developed the 'disparate impact' theory to outlaw it.[10]

Griggs v Duke Power Co **401 US 424 (1971), US Supreme Court**

The defendant utility company, which had a history of segregation in employment, instituted a practice whereby all employees except those hired to the lowest paying jobs were required to have successfully completed high school, and to have achieved satisfactory scores on two professionally prepared aptitude tests. It was accepted that 'there was no showing of a racial purpose or an invidious intent ... and that these standards had been applied fairly to whites and [black people] alike'. Nevertheless, the statistics showed that while 34% of white males had completed high school, only 12% of black males had done so, and that the use by a different employer of these aptitude tests had in one instance resulted in a pass rate of 58% for whites and 6% for

---

6   If the objective of indirect discrimination law is to promote voluntary action, there is no doubt that the British law has utterly failed in this regard.

7   See above, Chapter 4, especially pp 92–97.

8   401 US 424 (1971).

9   Codified as 42 USCS s 2000e-2 (c).

10 In the years that followed, the Supreme Court developed the disparate impact theory in accordance with the basic tenets of *Griggs*. However, in the late 1980s, this was checked by judicial and political divisions. The Supreme Court upset many well-established principles of the theory. Most notable was the bare majority decision in *Wards Cove Packing Co v Atonio* 490 US 642 (1989) which followed the plurality decision in *Watson v Fort Worth Bank & Trust* 487 US 977 (1988). In response, Congress passed the Civil Rights Act 1991. Although this statute re-established some of the earlier principles, it also codified some parts of the *Wards Cove* decision. See further below, pp 252–53.

blacks. Burger CJ illuminated his opinion with the fable of the milk, the fox and the stork.

Chief Justice Burger (pp 429–32):

The objective of Congress ... was to achieve equality of employment opportunities and remove barriers that have operated in the past to favour an identifiable group of white employees over other employees. Under the Act, practices, procedures or tests, neutral on their face, and even neutral in terms of intent, cannot be maintained if they operate to 'freeze' the status quo of prior discriminatory employment practices ...

Congress has now provided that tests or criteria for employment or promotion may not provide equality of opportunity merely in the sense of the fabled offer of milk to the stork and the fox. On the contrary, Congress has now required that the posture and condition of the job-seeker be taken into account. It has – to resort again to the fable – provided that the vessel in which the milk is proffered be one all seekers can use.

The Act proscribes not only overt discrimination but also practices that are fair in form but discriminatory in operation. The touchstone is business necessity. If an employment practice which operates to exclude [black people] cannot be shown to be related to job performance, the practice is prohibited ...

[N]either the high school completion requirement nor the general intelligence test is shown to bear a demonstrable relationship to successful performance of the jobs for which it was used. Both were adopted ... without meaningful study of their relationship to job performance ability.

Congress directed the thrust of the Act to the *consequences* of employment practices, not simply the motivation. More than that, Congress has placed on the employer the burden of showing that any given requirement must have a manifest relationship to the employment in question.

It is clear from this case that the theory of indirect discrimination (or 'disparate impact' or 'adverse effect') is based upon two broad limbs. First, the claimant must show that a practice has led to an adverse impact on a protected group. For example, where a high school diploma is a condition of employment and a larger proportion of whites than blacks complete high school. Second, the burden shifts to the defendant to prove that the practice was *necessary* to achieve the (non-discriminatory) aim. For instance, was a high school diploma necessary to perform the job? Note where the burden lies for each element. This is important when assessing the practicality of bringing or defending a claim of indirect discrimination.

The inclusion of indirect discrimination in Britain's legislation is a direct result of the then (Labour) Home Secretary's (the late Roy Jenkins) discovery of *Griggs* whilst on a trip to the USA. Mr Jenkins, upon his return, introduced s 1(1)(b) (defining and outlawing *indirect* discrimination) in a late amendment to the 1975 Sex Discrimination Bill. That explains why the White Paper[11] that preceded the Bill contained no indication of the Government's understanding of, and policy towards, indirect discrimination. In fact, the average politician of the day had no understanding of the concept of indirect discrimination. The Conservative Opposition objected to the inclusion of indirect discrimination in the Bill because:

---

11 *Equality for Women*, Cmnd 5724, 1974, London: HMSO.

... we do not know what it means. Secondly we do not think the Government knows what it means; and, thirdly, if we did know what it meant, we do not think that we would like it, but we cannot be sure.[12]

Nonetheless, the Government added a formula defining indirect discrimination to the Bill and that became law. A year later, Parliament used the same formula in the Race Relations Act (RRA) 1976. This time the respective White Paper on race relations[13] included *some* indication of the Government's aims in introducing indirect discrimination laws. However, the imprecise use of language reflected the Government's less than full appreciation of the concept of indirect discrimination.[14] From its inception in Britain, the legislators have offered very little guidance about their aims and ambitions for their legislation on indirect discrimination. Consequently, the judges had only the statutory words as guidance.

When the American two-limbed theory (see *Griggs*, above) of indirect discrimination was translated into British legislation (ie, the Sex Discrimination Act (SDA) 1975 and the RRA 1976), more detail was added. There were seven elements contained in the British statutory scheme (six belonging to the first limb). The prospect is that the more detailed British legislation will prove more rigid. In time, tension developed between the narrow British and the broad ECJ definitions. This began with the Equal Pay Act[15] and then the Sex Discrimination Act.[16] Eventually, a series of Directives forced the broader definition into domestic law, but only in areas of EC competence. The new definition amended the SDA 1975 in 2000,[17] but only for employment matters. The RRA 1976 was amended in July 2003 in all fields, but not for discrimination on the grounds of colour or nationality. The Sexual Orientation and Religion or Belief Regulations contained the new definition from the their outset.[18] Essentially, the new version substitutes the phrase 'requirement or condition' with 'provision, criterion or practice' and provides a more detailed definition of justification. What follows is the original (narrow) definition, the new one, and the Directive upon which it is based.

Race Relations Act 1976[19]

Section 1

1(1)   'A person discriminates against another ... if—

...

---

12 *Per* Ian Gilmour, Standing Committee B (22 April 1975), col 36.
13 *Racial Discrimination*, Cmnd 6234, 1975, London: HMSO.
14 See especially p 244, below.
15 See *Enderby v Frenchay HA* [1991] ICR 382, EAT and [1994] ICR 112, CA and ECJ, below pp 247, 251 and 276.
16 See *Falkirk Council v Whyte* [1997] IRLR 560; below, p 247.
17 This was achieved by the Burden of Proof Directive 97/80/EC. This definition is due for a slight amendment by 5 October 2005 by Equal Treatment Amendment Directive, Art 2.
18 Which came into force 1 on December 2003 and 2 December 2003, respectively.
19 This repeated the formula used in SDA 1975, s 1: '(1) A person discriminates against a woman ... if— ... (b) he applies to her a requirement or condition which he applies or would apply equally to a man but— (i) which is such that the proportion of women who can comply with it is considerably smaller than the proportion of men who can comply with it, and (ii) which he cannot show to be justifiable irrespective of sex, and (iii) is to the detriment of that other because she cannot comply with it.'

> (b) he applies to that other a requirement or condition which he applies or would apply equally to persons not of the same racial group as that other but—
>
>> (i) which is such that the proportion of persons of that same racial group who can comply with it is considerably smaller than the proportion of persons not of that racial group who can comply with it; and
>>
>> (ii) which he cannot show to be justifiable irrespective of the colour, race, nationality or ethnic or national origins of the person to whom it is applied; and
>>
>> (iii) is to the detriment of that other because he cannot comply with it.

The new definition is given in s 1(1A):

> A person ... discriminates against another if ... he applies to that other a provision, criterion or practice which he applies or would apply equally to persons not of the same race or ethnic or national origins as that other, but—

> (a) which puts or would put persons of the same race or ethnic or national origins as that other at a particular disadvantage when compared with other persons,

> (b) which puts that other at a disadvantage, and

> (c) which he cannot show to be a proportionate means of achieving a legitimate aim.

Race Directive 2000/43/EC

Article 2

> 2.   ... (b) indirect discrimination shall be taken to occur where an apparently neutral provision, criterion or practice would put persons of a racial or ethnic origin at a disadvantage compared to other persons, unless that provision, criterion or practice, is objectively justified by a legitimate aim and the means of achieving that aim are appropriate and necessary.

The elements raised by these definitions are: protected group (discussed in Chapter 6); applying a provision, criterion or practice (or 'requirement or condition'); causation (or 'cannot comply'); a comparison between groups; a disparate impact (considerably smaller/larger); detriment, or disadvantage, to the claimant;[20] and justification. Five of these merit discussion here.

3   THE ELEMENTS OF INDIRECTION DISCRIMINATION

(1)   Requirement or Condition/Provision, Criterion or Practice

(a)   Requirement or condition

For the residual[21] class of sex and race cases, the legislation demands that for *prima facie* discrimination to be proved, the discriminator must have applied a *requirement or*

---

20 This element is included merely to ensure a claimant has *locus standi*: See, eg, 893 HC 1491-2 18 June 1975. There is no need to discuss it.

21 See above, p 242. For this purpose these will include race cases arising before 19 July 2003 or brought on the grounds of colour, and possibly nationality, and for cases under the SDA 1975, those outside the fields of employment and vocational training.

condition to the victim that adversely affects the victim's group. Often, that will not be a problem. For example, a job advertisement might read: 'Librarians wanted. Applicants must be over six feet tall.' That would adversely affect many groups. However, what if the advertisement were amended to read: 'Librarians wanted. Applicants who are at least 6 feet tall will be *preferred'*? Does the exchange of the word *preferred* for *must* take this job advertisement out of the scope of the British legislation? Particular racial groups remain disadvantaged by the modified criterion, yet it is arguable that, strictly speaking, it falls outside of the statutory words *requirement or condition*. Thus, the judges have a choice of giving the words a strict literal interpretation or – to serve the purpose of the legislation – a liberal one. Confusion in the White Paper on Racial Discrimination has not helped them in this task.[22] For example, it stated that *direct* discrimination laws alone could not address the 'practices and procedures which have a discriminatory effect' and 'practices which are fair in a formal sense but discriminatory in their operation and effect'.[23] Further on[24] the Government outlined the intended legislation. In the place of the words 'practice and procedure', one finds 'requirement and condition'.

If the judges prefer the narrow interpretation, they create a loophole in this law. Employers could evade the legislation simply by relegating any discriminatory requirements to 'mere preferences'. Consequently, with this element in particular, the role of the judges is critical. The cases show that in the early days tribunals wavered between narrow and broad interpretations. However, since 1983, the judges, with some minor exceptions, have firmly supported the narrow one. First, a line of Employment Appeal Tribunal (EAT) cases indicated a willingness to give the Act a broad and purposive interpretation.[25] For instance, in *Watches of Switzerland v Savell*,[26] the EAT found that the '... vague, subjective, unadvertised promotion procedure which does not provide ... any adequate mechanisms to prevent subconscious bias unrelated to the merits of the candidates ... for the post ...' amounted to a *requirement or condition* within the meaning of the Act.[27]

The Court of Appeal came to the matter for the first time in *Perera v Civil Service Commission (No 2)*.[28] Here, an advertisement for a legal assistant stated that candidates with a good command of the English language, experience in the UK and with British nationality would be at an advantage. It was held that these 'mere preferences' did not amount to a *requirement or condition* within the meaning of the s 1(1)(b). To come within the Act, the court stated, an employer should elevate the preference to a requirement or 'absolute bar' which has to be complied with in order to qualify for the job. Stephenson LJ justified the decision thus:

---

22 *Racial Discrimination*, Cmnd 6234, 1975, London: HMSO.
23 *Ibid*, para 35. Note that even within one paragraph there is inconsistent use of terms, *practices and procedures* followed by *practices* alone, a sentiment clearly derived from *Griggs* (above).
24 *Ibid*, para 55.
25 Eg, *Clarke v Eley (IMI) Kynoch* [1983] ICR 165, at p 171; *Home Office v Holmes* [1985] 1 WLR 71.
26 [1983] IRLR 141.
27 Ms Savell's claim only failed because that procedure did not adversely affect women. See further below, p 249.
28 [1983] ICR 428.

... a brilliant man whose personal qualities made him suitable as a legal assistant might well have been sent forward ... in spite of being, perhaps, below standard on his knowledge of English ...[29]

That comment reveals the problem. If a candidate has to be 'brilliant' to compensate for a racially based 'weakness', then he is at a disadvantage because of his race. A 'brilliant' black person will obtain a post otherwise suitable for an 'average' white person. The Court of Appeal also rejected Mr Perera's strongest argument, that several 'preferences' which could not be complied with added up to an absolute bar. If a candidate lacked a good command of the English language, experience in the UK and British nationality, he stood no chance of being selected. Nonetheless, the Court of Appeal followed *Perera* in *Meer*.

Meer v London Borough of Tower Hamlets [1988] IRLR 399, CA

The employer attached twelve 'selection criteria' to an advertised post. One of these was experience in the Tower Hamlets district. That put persons of Indian origin at a disadvantage because a higher than average proportion of them were new to the area. The Court of Appeal rejected Meer's claim of indirect discrimination, holding that the criterion (or 'mere preference') of Tower Hamlets experience did not amount to a *requirement or condition*.

Staughton LJ (at p 403):

If I had not held that we ought to follow [*Perera*], I am by no means sure that I would have reached a different conclusion ... That is because s 1(1)(b), of the Race Relations Act 1976 would have such an extraordinarily wide and capricious effect ... Once an employer takes into account any factor whatsoever, which is not justifiable in terms of s 1(1)(b)(ii), he may be exposed to a charge of racial discrimination. That is so whether or not he had the slightest intention to discriminate on racial grounds ... I say that because it must almost always be possible to find a racial group with a smaller proportion of persons able to pray in aid [of] that factor than the proportion of persons not in that group who can pray it in aid, and there will be a risk that someone in that racial group may have applied for a job and not been awarded it.

To illustrate the point I take an extreme example. Suppose an employer takes into account, amongst other things, whether an applicant's surname begins with the letter 'A'. If it does, that is a factor to be taken into account in his favour. Suppose also, and this is not difficult, that the letter 'A' has no relevance to the job on offer and the requirement or factor is not justified – it is just adopted at the whim of the employer. I do not doubt that a racial group could be found somewhere in which the proportion of persons whose surnames begin with the letter 'A' is considerably smaller than the proportion of persons not in that group whose surnames begin with the letter 'A'. There will be a risk that a person from that racial group whose surname does not begin with the letter 'A' will have applied for the job and not been awarded it. The applicant will be able to say that he suffered a detriment in the shape of an inability to take advantage of a factor which would have told in his favour. That is an extreme example in order to make the point clear.

---

29 [1983] ICR 428, at pp 437H–438A.

A number of comments are necessary. First, liability is not dependent on discriminatory intent.[30] Staughton LJ is suggesting that interpretation of s 1(1)(b) should be restricted to exclude cases of unintentional discrimination. Plainly, that is incorrect. Next, this employer's 'whim' could conceivably amount to discrimination if a higher than average proportion of a protected group were affected by it. For instance, excluding those whose name begins with the letter 'P' would exclude all Patels, who make up a significant part of the Indian population. Staughton LJ failed to appreciate the *effect* of the 'whim', one which almost certainly could not be justified as related to job performance.

It is clear from the facts of these two cases that mere preferences can amount *de facto* to race or sex discrimination. Yet the decisions hold that anti-discrimination law is not applicable to mere preferences. This reveals the loophole. A bigot could simply reclassify his job conditions as 'preferences', so that his job advertisement might read:

> Librarians wanted. Candidates would be at an advantage if they: had an excellent command of English,[31] were clean shaven,[32] were over six feet tall, had a Home Counties accent, were under 30 years old,[33] and had lived in the area all their lives.[34] Free lunch (roast pork) will be provided to those interviewed.

If the reasoning of the Court of Appeal in *Perera* and *Meer* were extended to this advertisement, those criteria would not infringe British discrimination legislation, even though they would disadvantage and in many cases effectively bar most ethnic minorities and women.

In summary, the Court of Appeal maintains that the words *requirement or condition* in s 1(1)(b) should be given a narrow interpretation because: (a) employers may not intend to discriminate when using mere preferences;[35] (b) '... a brilliant man ...' may overcome a disadvantageous preference;[36] and (c) otherwise the section would have '... such an extraordinary wide and capricious effect.'[37] All of this is in the face of the White Paper that states that *direct* discrimination laws alone could not address the 'practices and procedures which have a discriminatory effect' and 'practices which are fair in a formal sense but discriminatory in their operation and effect'.[38]

So far, the debate has been on policy grounds. There are also technical reasons to question the *Perera* decision. The Court of Appeal felt that the statutory words could only be read to mean an 'absolute bar to the job'. However, there is no reason why they could not cover an absolute bar to gaining an advantage in the job selection procedure. This interpretation in no way distorts the statutory words and accords

---

30 This is implied by RRA 1976, s 57(3), which provided that no damages shall be payable in cases of unintentional indirect discrimination (discussed Chapter 17, p 543). See, for example, *Orphanos v Queen Mary College* [1985] AC 761. Cf *Barry v Midland Bank*, where the House of Lords relied on the 'object' of a severance scheme to hold that there was no adverse impact (see also p 287).

31 See *Perera v Civil Service Commission (No 2)* [1983] ICR 428.

32 *Panesar v Nestle Co Ltd* [1980] ICR 144 and *Gilbert v United Parcel Service* (1996) unreported, 26 April, CA.

33 See *Price v Civil Service Commission (No 2)* [1978] IRLR 3. See below, p 254.

34 See *Meer v LB of Tower Hamlets* [1988] IRLR 399.

35 *Per* Staughton LJ, *Meer v Tower Hamlets* [1988] IRLR 399, at p 403, para 20.

36 *Per* Stevenson LJ, *Perera v Civil Service Commission (No 2)* [1983] ICR 428, at pp 437H–438A.

37 *Per* Staughton LJ, *Meer v Tower Hamlets* [1988] IRLR 399, at p 403, para 20.

38 *Racial Discrimination*, Cmnd 6234, 1975, London: HMSO.

with the purpose of the legislation. There is support for this view in Australia, where under similarly worded legislation, the Federal Court of Western Australia refused to follow *Perera*, holding that 'mere preferences' that disadvantaged women, were within the phrase 'requirement or condition'.[39]

A further weakness of *Perera* is that it was always going to be under threat from EC discrimination law. Community legislation provided an open-ended definition of discrimination, leaving the detail to the European Court of Justice (ECJ). For instance, the Equal Treatment Directive[40] simply alluded to the 'principle of equal treatment', expressing this in context as meaning 'that there will be no discrimination whatsoever on the grounds of sex'. The ECJ had no doubts when interpreting Community legislation to cover discriminatory 'preferences', and so, in time, conflicts were due. In *Enderby v Frenchay Health Authority*,[41] the ECJ held that under Art 119 (now Art 141) EC Treaty (and thus the Equal Pay Act 1970) there was no need for to show that there had been a 'requirement or condition' in a claim of equal pay based upon indirect discrimination. Domestic courts could live with this as the Equal Pay Act contained no definition of indirect discrimination. Thus, British judges could isolate equal pay claims from *Perera* without too much embarrassment.[42] The first court to face fully the issue and disregard *Perera* in favour of conflicting Community law was the Scottish EAT in *Falkirk Council v Whyte*.[43] Here the employer advertised a post of first-level line manager. One of the selection criteria stated that 'management training and supervisory experience' was *'desirable'* (not absolutely necessary). The three female complainants each made unsuccessful applications for the post. They alleged that the criterion above amounted to unlawful sex discrimination because a considerably lesser proportion of women than men had such experience. (The applicants themselves had no such experience.) The EAT held that *Perera* was not binding as it was a case under the RRA 1976. Instead, Lord Johnston interpreted the SDA 1975 according to Community law and more general principles:

> In many ways this was a classic situation of indirect sex discrimination, with mostly women in basic grade posts, and mostly men in promoted management posts – a vivid example of what the Act and its forerunners in the United States set out to eliminate, ie those practices which had a disproportionate impact on women and were not justifiable for other reasons ...[44]

The next development was the publication of the Burden of Proof Directive,[45] which (as well as dealing with proof) introduced the new liberalised definition of indirect discrimination into sex discrimination law. It was implemented and came into force on 12 October 2001.[46] The following Directives on Race and Equal Treatment in

---

39 *Secretary of Department of Foreign Affairs and Trade v Styles* (1989) 88 ALR 621; see also *Waters v Public Transport Corporation* (1991) 173 CLR 349, High Court of Australia.

40 Council Directive 76/207/EC.

41 [1991] ICR 382, EAT and [1994] ICR 112, CA and ECJ. See further, pp 247, 251 and 276.

42 See *British Coal v Smith* [1994] ICR 810, CA, at p856E; *Ratcliffe v North Yorkshire CC* [1995] 3 All ER 597, HL, at 603b; *Bhudi v IMI Refiners* [1994] ICR 307, EAT, at p 315.

43 [1997] IRLR 560. For a commentary, see Connolly, M, 'Discrimination law: requirements and preferences' [1998] 27 ILJ 133.

44 [1997] IRLR 560, at p 562.

45 Council Directive 97/80/EC.

46 See SI 2001/2660, reg 3.

Employment carried a similar definition, so *Perera* should only now be an issue in the residual class of cases not covered by EC law, which will be rare.[47]

Apart from the policy consideration stated by Lord Johnston (above), much of the reasoning in *Whyte*, depending as it did on Community law, will be of little help to a claimant in these residual cases. Short of an appeal to the House of Lords, the possibilities of avoiding *Perera* are as follows. First, a court may find, *as a question of fact*, that the practice amounted to a requirement, or bar. In *Jones v University of Manchester*,[48] a job advertisement stated that the successful candidate would be 'a graduate, preferably aged 27–35 years'.[49] An industrial tribunal found that although the advertisement expressed age as a *preference*, in practice the employer had applied the age limit as a *requirement*. The Court of Appeal had doubts over the tribunal's interpretation of the evidence,[50] but refused to interfere with their finding of fact, that the employer had applied a 'requirement' for the purposes of s 1(1)(b) of the SDA 1975.

Secondly, in residual cases of sex discrimination, it may be argued that *Perera* is confined to the RRA 1976. This technical argument succeeded in *Whyte*. Thirdly, discrimination on the grounds of nationality was expressly excluded from the Race Directive and, accordingly, from the new definition of indirect discrimination in the RRA 1976. Nationality was excluded from the Directive because Community law, by Art 39 (formerly Art 48) already prohibits discrimination against nationals of Member States. Thus, in a 'residual' case that fell under Art 39,[51] a court should not be bound by *Perera*. In cases under Art 39, the ECJ has recognised 'mere preferences' as amounting to discrimination.[52] Outside of the scope of Community law, a claimant would have to fall back on the *Jones* argument.

(b)   Provision, criterion or practice

As well as abolishing the *Perera* doctrine, the new definition (using 'provision, criterion or practice') has the potential to include two particular situations. The first is subjective hiring practices. The second is 'result-only' cases, which, some fear, might lead to quotas.

---

47 See above, p 242. These will include race cases arising before 19 July 2003 or brought on the grounds of colour, and possibly nationality, and for cases under the SDA 1975, those outside the fields of employment and vocational training.

48 [1993] ICR 474.

49 See also *Price v Civil Service Commission (No 2)* [1978] IRLR 3, where an upper age limit of 28 years was held to adversely affect women, who took time out from work in their twenties to have children.

50 See, for instance, Ralf Gibson LJ [1993] ICR 476, at pp 490G–491E.

51 Ie, discrimination on the grounds of nationality against a national of a Member State in the field of employment contrary to the principle of the free movement of workers. This is unlikely to cover discrimination, say, against an English person in Wales. See *Morsen* and *Jhanjan* Joined Cases 35 and 36/82 [1982] ECR 3723, ECJ; *R v Saunders* Case 175/78 [1979] ECR 1129, para 10, ECJ; McLeod, W, 'Autochthonous language communities and the Race Relations Act', Web Journal of Current Legal Issues [1998] 1 Web JCCI-htm; and the discussions above, Chapter 6, pp 142 and 148.

52 See, for instance, *Ingetraut Scholz v Opera Universitaria di Cagliari* Case C-419/92 [1994] ECR 1-507; (1994) *The Times*, 23 February.

(i)   Subjective hiring practices

A major impact of the new definition is that it will cover claims against subjective hiring practices. This seemed possible before *Perera,* as *Savell* illustrates. This decision was influenced by the American case law. A more recent and the most prominent example from the USA is *Watson.*

Watches of Switzerland v Savell [1983] IRLR 141, EAT

The claim was of a failure to be promoted to branch manager. The applicant argued that there were serious defects in their procedure which meant that women were less likely to be considered for promotion. The industrial tribunal held that there was no direct discrimination, but that a claim of indirect discrimination was made out.

The EAT allowed the employer's appeal on indirect discrimination on the decidedly dubious ground that the procedure in question did not operate to her detriment, but the significance of the case lies in the holding that the employer had applied a requirement or condition.

Waterhouse J (pp 145–46):

[T]he relevant criticisms of the promotions procedure ... were as follows:

(1)   Impending appointments were not advertised to staff and women were less likely than men to ask to be considered for promotion.

(2)   Persons under consideration for promotion were not interviewed.

(3)   There were no clear guidelines to branch managers about the criteria to be applied in the regular assessments and appraisals; and some appraisals, including those of Mrs Savell, were out of date.

(4)   The criteria for promotion were not written; they were subjective and not made known to persons in line for promotion.

(5)   The employers made a point of promoting their own staff and paid particular attention to training when searching for potential managers, but Mrs Savell was unaware of the importance attached to training for which she could have volunteered ...

[On appeal] the requirement or condition was phrased as follows:

'... that to be promoted to the post of manager ... one must satisfy the criteria of a vague, subjective, unadvertised promotion procedure which does not provide any or any adequate mechanisms to prevent subconscious bias unrelated to the merits of candidates ...'

[A] requirement or condition of the kind formulated on behalf of Mrs Savell is capable of being a requirement or condition to which the Act applies ...

In America, both academic argument and judicial authority supports the use of indirect discrimination law in this type of case.

Bartholet, E, 'Application of Title VII to jobs in high places' (1982) 95 Harv L Rev 947, pp 955–58, 978–80:

For candidates who satisfy minimum objective qualifications, the final decision making tends to be largely subjective, based on evaluations of the candidates' previous work and potential for future performance.

Selection systems of this sort are likely to have an adverse racial impact. Blacks as a group are far less likely than whites to have had the education and experience that have traditionally been the prerequisites for these jobs. Use of such credentials – either as minimum objective requirements or as part of a subjective evaluation process – seriously limits black access to upper level positions. Subjective systems ... allow for the expression both of conscious bias and of the unconscious bias that is likely to result in the exclusion of persons who are visibly different from those doing the selecting ...

[Disparate impact litigation in the United States] has helped destroy the notion that the meritocratic principle is the norm governing job allocation. The systems exposed have not been outlawed because employers could not meet an impossibly strict standard of validation; they have been outlawed because they were revealed to be inconsistent with merit selection ... The *Griggs*[53] doctrine, with its demand for proof of business necessity, can and should serve a similar function with respect to upper level employment systems ...

Enforcement of *Griggs* at the upper level would generate pressure for racially proportionate hiring from among the pool of those with conceded minimum qualifications ... [This] is as it should be. Validation and other proof of business necessity are particularly difficult on the upper level, largely because we are unsure what we mean by effective performance in our most important jobs. Our notions of effective performance are necessarily value laden, reflecting what are often essentially political choices. These considerations militate in favour of opening such jobs to groups traditionally excluded from them ...

[A] differential standard is elitist. The courts distinguish between selection systems primarily on the basis of the social and economic status of the job involved. They have intervened freely in low-status jobs, even when poor performance in those jobs might have threatened significant economic and safety interests. But with high-status jobs, a hands-off attitude has prevailed.

Judges defer to the employers with whom they identify, and they uphold the kinds of selection systems from which they have benefited. When they deal with prestigious jobs, the courts show an appreciation of the apparent rationality of the employment procedures at issue and a respect for the decision makers involved that can only be explained by the fact that these confront the courts with their own world. Judges have a personal investment in traditional selection procedures on the upper level ...

Judges must develop ... analytic distance in looking at upper level selection systems. The *Griggs* doctrine encourages such detachment. By rejecting apparent common sense as a sufficient defence, it forces courts to analyse their own assumptions. By insisting that employers produce evidentiary justifications for their systems, the doctrine educates courts about the actual strengths and weaknesses of these justifications.

Watson v Fort Worth Bank and Trust 487 US 977 (1988), US Supreme Court

The black applicant was rejected for promotion to supervisory positions in the bank. The employers had no formal criteria for the position, but relied on the subjective judgment of white supervisors. The US disparate impact theory was developed from Title VII of the Civil Rights Act 1964,[54] which simply made a discriminatory 'employment practice' unlawful. The Supreme Court held that this included subjective procedures.

---

53   See above, p 240.
54   Section 703, codified as 42 USCS s 2000e-2.

Justice O'Connor (pp 989–91, 999):

We are persuaded that our decisions in *Griggs*[55] and succeeding cases could largely be nullified if disparate impact analysis were applied only to standardised selection practices. However, one might distinguish 'subjective' from 'objective' criteria, it is apparent that selection systems that combine both types would generally have to be considered subjective in nature ... So long as an employer refrained from making standardised criteria absolutely determinative, it would remain free to give such tests almost as much weight as it chose without risking a disparate impact challenge. If we announced a rule that allowed employers so easily to insulate themselves from liability under *Griggs*, disparate impact analysis might effectively be abolished.

We are also persuaded that disparate impact analysis is in principle no less applicable to subjective employment criteria than to objective or standardised tests. In either case, a facially neutral practice, adopted without discriminatory intent, may have effects that are indistinguishable from intentionally discriminatory practices ... [E]ven if one assumed that any ... discrimination can be adequately policed through disparate treatment analysis, the problem of subconscious stereotypes and prejudices would remain ... If an employer's undisciplined system of subjective decision making has precisely the same effects as a system pervaded by impermissible intentional discrimination, it is difficult to see why Title VII's proscription against discriminatory action should not apply ...

In the context of subjective or discretionary employment decisions, the employer will often find it easier than in the case of standardised tests to produce evidence of 'a manifest relationship to the employment in question'. It is self-evident that many jobs, for example, those involving managerial responsibilities, require personal qualities that have never been considered amenable to standardised testing.

(ii) 'Result-only' cases and quotas

The following commentary on the new definition explores the possibility of 'result only' cases and quotas.

Connolly, M, 'The Burden of Proof Regulations: change and no change' (2001) 30 ILJ 375:

A perhaps unintended consequence of the relaxation of the 'requirement or condition' rule ... was raised by Watt ((1998) 27 ILJ 121, at 129).[56] He argued that if *Perera* is abolished the simple demonstration of numerical inequality in the result would be enough for a *prima facie* case. (We can call these 'result only' cases.) And thus 'the caseload and complexity of the cases would simply cause the courts to grind to a halt'. His fear is based on the Equal Pay case *Enderby* where the ECJ held that where there is a difference in pay between man and women doing work of equal value, the burden shifts to the employer to 'objectively justify' the difference irrespective of sex under the *Bilka-Kaufhaus v Weber von Hartz* [1987] ICR 110 (ECJ) formula.

One could object to this argument on the basis that the new definition of indirect discrimination demands that there be a 'provision, criterion or practice.' A case brought purely on statistics would fail for lack of evidence of a practice, or succeed where the statistical evidence was such that an inference of a practice could be made.

---

55 See above, p 240.
56 This issue was also raised by Fenwick, H and Hervey, T, 'Sex equality in the single market: new directions for the ECJ' (1995) CMLR 443, p 461 and Campbell, A and Voyatzi, M, 'Sex discrimination and the burden of proof' (1994) 13 SLT 127, at p 129.

Seeing as inferences can be made under direct discrimination (and indeed in virtually all areas of law) there is no reason why that should not happen here or lead to the courts 'grinding to a halt'. Furthermore, when two groups (or more) are doing work of equal value (in *Enderby* it was speech therapists, 98% female, and pharmacists, 63% female) but one group is being paid more than the other a clear inference can be made that there is a facially neutral 'practice' of paying one group more than the other. The connection between this and the end result of women being adversely affected is so obvious it hardly deserves a word. The ECJ held that Ms Enderby did not have to prove that there was a 'requirement' *with which she could not comply*. Of course the only 'requirement' to receive higher pay was to become a pharmacist and Ms Enderby *could* comply with that. But she did prove a practice causing an adverse impact on women. The Directive, which applies to Equal Pay claims, is in accordance with this. Thus neither *Enderby* nor the Directive should lead to 'result only' cases.[57]

The issue of 'result-only' cases and quotas was the subject of a fierce debate in the USA. It surfaced in the Supreme Court in *Wards Cove Packing Co v Antonio*.[58] Wards Cove ran salmon canneries in Alaska where skilled (mainly white) and unskilled (mainly Filipino or native Alaskan) workers were divided by separate accommodation, dining halls and pay. A class of non-white unskilled workers brought a case – heavily based on statistical evidence – of indirect discrimination. A bare majority of the Supreme Court rejected the claim, holding that there had to be a specific, identifiable employment practice which caused the disparate impact. White J stated that an alternative result would mean that any employer with a racially imbalanced workforce could be 'haled into court' to justify to the situation.[59] The alternative was to adopt quotas. Congress acted to clarify the law and passed s 105 of the Civil Rights Act 1991, which provided that:

> ... the complaining party shall demonstrate that each particular challenged employment practice causes a disparate impact ...

This follows the *Wards Cove* line. However, the reform came with the exception:

> ... if the complaining party can demonstrate to the court that the elements of a respondent's decisionmaking [*sic*] process are not capable of separation for analysis, the decisionmaking process may be analyzed as one employment practice.

An example of this exception was given in the statute. In *Dothard v Rawlinson*,[60] height and weight requirements designed to measure strength were used in the recruitment of prison officers, but discriminated against women. According to the exception, these requirements could not be separated for analysis and so could be taken as a whole when linking them to the adverse impact. The American experience shows that the new definition 'provision, criterion or practice' can be applied to subjective hiring practices, such as those in *Savell*,[61] not but to 'result-only' cases. This is not to say this

---

57   This view was confirmed by the ECJ in *Specialarbejderforbundet i Danmark v Dansk Industri* (the *Royal Copenhagen* case) C-400/93 and *Angestelltenbetriebsrat der Wiener Gebietskrankenkasse v Wiener Gebietskrankenkasse* C-309/97. For a casenote, see Abanulo, A, 'Equal pay for work of equal value: the "results-oriented" approach that never was' [1999] 28(4) ILJ 365.

58   490 US 642 (1989).

59   *Ibid*, at p 652.

60   433 US 321 (1977).

61   Above, p 249.

is the correct: it is arguable that this interpretation does not reflect the 'discriminatory barriers'[62] theory of indirect discrimination.

There are two classes of 'result-only' cases that merit further consideration under the indirect discrimination theory. The first is where there is simply employer acquiescence in a disorganised recruitment or promotion process. In *Butler v Home Depot*,[63] a case post-1991 Civil Rights Act, statistics showed that over a four-year period, women made up just 6.4% of the new recruits, whereas women made up some 36–39% of the labour market qualified for the jobs. This alone raised a reasonable suspicion of the defendant's employment 'practice', which was no more than a delegation to managers who used irregular subjective criteria when recruiting. It was held to be a 'practice' for Title VII.

The second class of 'result-only' cases arises where statistics reveal large disparities, in the workforce and/or recruitment success. Without an identifiable provision, criterion or practice, there is no 'barrier' to challenge.[64] A conspicuous case here is *Wards Cove Packing Co v Antonio*[65] and its underlying fear of quotas. There are two reasons why the recognition of these cases should not lead to quotas.

First, if an employer, in the face of say, a racially imbalanced workforce, panics and adopts quotas, he will face discrimination claims from those disadvantaged under the quotas. An employer could hardly justify, say, a disparate impact on white workers, on the grounds that it favours another race.[66] Secondly, any significant imbalance should alert the employer that something is wrong. An investigation will identify a cause, which should be eradicated, refined or justified. If the employers in *Butler v Home Depot*[67] had taken that action, there would have been no expensive litigation. In fact, disparate impact theory ought to lead to the desired result, to remove unlawful discrimination from the workplace. Further, the discipline imposed which refines or removes discriminatory practices (including omissions) could create business efficiencies.[68] If business practices are tainted by race, gender or any irrelevancies, the employer can hardly tell the shareholders that the business is 100% efficient. The problem with this approach, or course, is that it is difficult to square it with the legislation, which requires a provision, practice or criterion. The solution would seem to be that where the disparities are so significant, an inference that a practice exists, *and* that that practice causes the disparity, may be made.

---

62 See above, pp 237–40 and generally, Chapter 4.
63 No C-94-4335 SI, C-95-2182 SI, 1997 US Dist LEXIS 16296 (District Court for the Northern District of California).
64 There are, of course, cases where large statistical disparities are accepted as evidence of causation: see, eg, *Dothard v Rawlinson* 433 US 321 (1977) where statistics showed that height and weight requirements would exclude 40% of women and under 1% of men.
65 490 US 642 (1989).
66 See Chapter 18, below, especially pp 579–81.
67 No C-94-4335 SI, C-95-2182 SI, 1997 US Dist LEXIS 16296 (District Court for the Northern District of California).
68 For an extensive study of business efficiency and Title VII, see Greenberger, S, 'A productivity approach to disparate impact and the Civil Rights Act of 1991' (1993) 72 Oregon Law Rev 253. Cf Epstein, R, *Forbidden Grounds: The Case Against Employment Discrimination Laws*, 1992, Cambridge, Mass: Harvard UP, especially pp 226–29.

(2)   Causation and 'Can Comply'

This is a causative element, demanding a connection between the challenged practice and the claimant's sex, race, religion or belief, or sexual orientation, as the case may be. The old definition, still relevant for the residual cases,[69] demands that: 'the proportion of women[70] who *can comply* [with a requirement] is considerably smaller than the proportion of men[71] who *can comply* with it ...' The current definition in the SDA 1975 for employment matters requires that the provision, practice or criterion *'would be to the detriment* of a considerably larger proportion ...' of the claimant's group. The new definitions in the domestic legislation require that the claimant's group is 'put at' a 'particular disadvantage'. The Directive, upon which the new definition is based, uses the verb 'disadvantages'. These differences should be of little significance in this context,[72] especially after the liberal and purposive interpretation given to the phrase 'can comply' in the old definition.

(a)   The old definition – can comply

Price v Civil Service Commission [1977] IRLR 291; [1977] 1 WLR 1417; [1978] 1 All ER 1228, EAT

At the time the Civil Service had a requirement that to be appointed as an Executive Officer, one had to be aged between 17-and-a-half and 28, a requirement which the applicant claimed was indirectly discriminatory against women on the basis that many women between those ages are unavailable for work for family reasons. The tribunal rejected the claim on the basis that 'can comply' meant physically able to comply, an argument overturned by the EAT.

Phillips J (p 293):

In one sense it can be said that any female applicant can comply with the condition. She is not obliged to marry, or to have children, or to mind children ... Such a construction appears to us to be wholly out of sympathy with the spirit and intent of the Act ... It should not be said that a person 'can' do something merely because it is theoretically possible for him to do so: it is necessary to see whether he can do so in practice ... [I]t is relevant to take into account the current usual behaviour of women in this respect, putting on one side behaviour and responses which are unusual or extreme ...

---

69 See above, p 242. These include race cases arising before 19 July 2003 or brought on the grounds of colour, and possibly nationality, and for cases under the SDA 1975, those outside the fields of employment and vocational training.

70 Or persons of the claimant's racial group.

71 Or persons not of the claimant's racial group.

72 For the significance of using 'positive' or 'negative' statistics, see below, p 273.

> Knowledge and experience suggest that a considerable number of women between the mid twenties and the mid thirties are engaged in bearing children and minding children, and that while many find it possible to take up employment, many others, while desiring to do so, find it impossible.[73]

Mandla v Dowell Lee [1983] 1 QB 1, CA; [1983] 2 AC 548; [1983] 1 All ER 1062; [1983] IRLR 209, HL

A Sikh boy could not wear the school cap because of his turban.[74] The Court of Appeal held he could *physically* comply by simply cutting his hair, removing the turban and fitting the school cap.[75] Kerr LJ suggested that as he had decided that the definition of a racial group is based upon unalterable characteristics, 'cannot comply' must be equated with impossibility: 'It was not intended to be measured against criteria of free will, choice, or conscience.'[76] The House of Lords reversed that decision.

Lord Fraser (at p 565):

> [A] literal meaning of the word 'can' would deprive Sikhs ... of much of the protection which Parliament evidently intended the Act to afford to them. They 'can' comply with almost any requirement or condition if they are willing to give up their distinctive customs and cultural rules ... The word 'can'... must ... have been intended by Parliament to be read not as meaning 'can physically', so as to indicate a theoretical possibility, but as meaning 'can in practice' or can consistently with the customs and cultural conditions of the racial group.

The question whether the applicant can or cannot comply with the requirement depends only on whether they can comply with it at the time when the requirement or condition is applied. In *Clarke v Eley (IMI) Kynoch Ltd*,[77] Browne-Wilkinson J stated that the relevant point in time at which the ability of a part-time worker to comply with the requirement of being full-time was at the date the detriment was imposed – the date she was made redundant. It was irrelevant that she could previously have become a full-time worker, in which event she might have been able to comply. Similarly, in *Commission for Racial Equality v Dutton*,[78] a landlord, who displayed 'no travellers' signs at the entrances of his public house argued that gypsies *could* comply with that requirement and remain gypsies by giving up the nomadic way of life after seeing the sign, and returning as 'non-travellers'. The Court of Appeal held that the

---

73 When the case was remitted, the industrial tribunal ([1978] IRLR 3) held that the requirement was not justified; it had been introduced for reasons of convenience, not necessity, and there were other ways of achieving the same objective. The exclusion of younger workers will often be indirectly discriminatory against women and will be very difficult to justify. (But see *Leavers v Civil Service Commission* (1986), IT, unreported – see 8 EOR 38 – where it was held that a relatively low age limit for entry into the Diplomatic Service was justifiable as, without it, entrants would be unlikely to achieve before retirement age sufficient years of experience to be appointed as an ambassador.) Until the age discrimination legislation comes into force (due 2006), discrimination against older workers may be challenged as indirect sex discrimination against men: *Harvest Town Circle Ltd v Rutherford* [2001] IRLR 599; [2002] ICR 123, where the EAT explained the proper comparison for such cases and [2002] IRLR 768 where it was applied by an employment tribunal. See further Chapter 6, p 167. On the issue of justification, see below, p 291.
74 The facts are set out above, Chapter 6, p 144.
75 [1983] 1 QB 1, at p 16.
76 *Ibid*, at pp 24D–E. See also Oliver LJ; *ibid*, at p 16f.
77 [1983] ICR 165; [1982] IRLR 482, EAT.
78 [1989] QB 783. The details are set out in Chapter 6, p 146.

time of compliance with the requirement was when it was invoked, ie, when a person stood outside the public house wishing to enter. The result was satisfactory but the reasoning is not. This was a technical, rather than purposive interpretation. What the court failed to appreciate is that this was exactly the same argument rejected by the House of Lords in *Mandla*. The emphasis on the *time* of compliance is misleading. Mandla also was told to go away, change his particular custom, and then return. In fact, Dutton was being asked to forgo a custom associated with his racial group, just as Mandla was. The court's reasoning, based around the 'time issue', side-stepped the real argument.

(b)   The new definition and causation

As seen above,[79] the new definition opens the way to challenges to subjective employment practices and perhaps even some 'result-only' cases, brought largely, or purely, on statistical evidence. Causation will often be a major issue in these cases. Once again, the American experience can give some guidance on how the law may develop here.

A connection between a practice and the victim's race (or religion) has became an express element of the American scheme following the *Wards Cove* decision, where an apparent 'result-only' case was rejected mainly for fear of encouraging quotas. Congress codified this theory by legislating that a plaintiff must identify practices which *cause* the disparate impact. Ordinarily, proving causation is not a problem: it is so obvious that it does not require explanation. For instance, in *Dothard v Rawlinson*,[80] minimum height and weight requirements combined with statistics showing the likely impact of such a measure on women was enough, without more, to prove a causal link between the two. This was largely because the disparity was so great that it would offend common sense to come to any other conclusion, or to demand further evidence.[81] The main issue was whether the employer could justify the requirements.

There is, however, is a series of cases where causation is not so obvious. Typically, there may be an identified suspect practice (eg, nepotism in recruitment) and evidence of some racial disparity (eg, amongst successful applicants). Yet there is no tangible link between the two. The question is in what circumstances, if at all, can proof of the practice and disparity *per se* be used to prove a causal link between the two? The American position was summarised in *Waisome*.

Waisome v Port Authority of New York & New Jersey, 948 F 2d 1370 (1991), US Court of Appeals for the 2nd Circuit

Cardamon, Circuit Judge (at p 1375):

To prove disparate impact, a plaintiff must first identify the specific employment practice he is challenging, see *Wards Cove v Atonio*;[82] *Watson v Fort Worth Bank*,[83] and then show that the practice excluded him or her, as a member of a protected group,

---

79 See above, pp 248–53.
80 433 US 321 (1977).
81 National statistics showed that the requirements would exclude over 40% of the female population but less than 1% of the male population.
82 490 US 642, at pp 656–57.
83 487 US 977, at p 994.

from a job or promotion opportunity. See *Watson*.[84] Statistical evidence may be probative where it reveals a disparity so great that it cannot be accounted for by chance, see *Bridgeport Guardians* [*v City of Bridgeport*],[85] or, to state it in other words, the 'statistical disparities must be sufficiently substantial that they raise ... an inference of causation.' *Watson*.[86]

The loose term ('sufficiently substantial') employed in the last sentence alludes to the courts' practice of not adhering to a particular formula when deciding whether there has been a disparate impact. There is nothing more precise than that.

It would seem from *Bushey v New York State Civil Service Commission*[87] and *Bridgeport Guardians*[88] that where the 'four-fifths' or 'probability of chance' rules are used, an inference of causation will be made from a simple finding of disparate impact. There are other cases where causation was proved without the formulas of 'four-fifths' and 'probability of chance'. For instance, in *Butler v Home Depot*,[89] the plaintiffs presented statistics that showed a 20% disparity between the women in the qualified labour market and those within the workforce. The court held simply that the statistical evidence was 'of a *kind* and *degree* from which causation may reasonably be inferred'.[90] This decision was made without reference to the 'four-fifths' rule. From this, it would seem that even if the disparity falls below 20%, it is at least *conceivable* that a court may find that there is causation, should it find that disparity to be 'sufficiently substantial'.

The guiding principle for proving an adverse impact in the ECJ and the British courts has been a 'considerable difference', which is being replaced with 'a particular disadvantage'.[91] In the absence of other evidence, this is unlikely to be suitable, by itself, for proving causation, but there is no reason why statistical evidence of a disadvantage could not coincidentally raise an inference of causation, where appropriate.

(3)   The Basis of the Comparison

Race Relations Act 1976[92]

Section 3

(4)   A comparison of the case of a person of a particular racial group with that of a person not of that group under section 1(1) [or (1A)] must be such that the relevant circumstances in the one case are the same, or not materially different, from the other.

---

84   *Ibid*, at p 994.
85   933 F 2d 1140, at p 1146. See below, p 265.
86   487 US at 977, at p 995.
87   733 F 2d 220 (1984) Court of Appeals for the Second Circuit, cert denied, 469 US 1117 (1985). See further below, p 264.
88   933 F 2d 1140, at p 1146. See below, p 265.
89   1997 US Dist LEXIS 16296. See above, p 253.
90   *Ibid*, at p 49 (emphasis supplied).
91   See below, p 269.
92   All domestic discrimination (save disability) legislation carries this rubric, adapted for the ground in question.

This element applies to cases under the old and new definitions of indirect discrimination with only minor differences. It concerns who should be compared with whom – or, in more technical language, what is the appropriate pool for comparison? It is vital to grasp that we are dealing with proportions rather than numbers. To illustrate, suppose that a test is taken by 500 women and 200 men. Suppose further that the test is passed by 100 women and 100 men. It is clear that a *prima facie* case of indirect discrimination will have been made out. It is irrelevant that the same *numbers* of men and women pass the test; what matters is that only 20% of women pass while 50% of the men do so. It is also clear that on these figures any tribunal will find that there has been a significant disparity in outcome – a considerably smaller proportion of women than men passed the test.

Stage one involves identifying the provision, practice or criterion (or requirement or condition), whilst stage two involves selecting the appropriate pool for comparison. Stage three is a comparison between the protected group (say, women) and the others in the pool (say, men) of the proportions who are adversely affected. Stage four is to ask whether the proportion of the protected group is considerably larger than the proportion of the other group. Under the old definition, the principle is the same except that the question is inverted. The comparison is between the proportions who *can* comply with the requirement, and the proportion of the protected group must be considerably *smaller* than the other group. For the moment, we will concentrate on choosing the pool and making the comparison. What amounts to 'considerably larger' (or smaller) will be explored afterwards. The following cases demonstrate how this process operates.

McAusland v Dungannon DC [1993] IRLR 583, NICA

This claim, under the Fair Employment (Northern Ireland) Act 1989 (outlawing discrimination on grounds of religious belief or political opinion), alleged that a job requirement indirectly discriminated against Catholics. The post of chief works manager was open only to local government staff in Northern Ireland. The other requirement was a 'standard occupational classification' (SOC) of 1, 2 or 3. The pool chosen was the whole Northern Ireland workforce with the SOC 1, 2 or 3. The comparison was between the proportion of Catholics, and the proportion of Protestants who could comply with the requirement to be in local government.

McDermott LJ (p 585):

(1) The relevant class of employee to be considered was comprised of those in the grades referred to as standard occupational classifications (SOC) 1, 2 and 3.

(2) The number of district council employees ... in SOC 1, 2 and 3 were Protestant: 1,039; Roman Catholic: 423 ... [Thus] 71% ... was Protestant and 29% Roman Catholic.

(3) In the total Northern Ireland workforce there were, in SOC grades 1, 2 and 3, Protestant: 50,170; Roman Catholic: 28,159 ... 64% Protestant and 36% Roman Catholic.

(4) [There must be] a comparison between the group fulfilling the condition or requirement (LGS – SOC 1, 2 and 3) and the appropriate comparable group, those in SOC grades 1, 2 and 3 in the general workforce in Northern Ireland; a formula had to be applied. That favoured by the tribunal and accepted by both parties before us was PY/PT compared to CY/CT. In it, P refers to Protestant, C refers to Roman Catholic, Y refers to those who can comply with the requirement, T refers to the total in the comparable class.

(5) Using that formula, the result was PY/PT = 0.0207 (say 0.021) and CY/CT = 0.015.

(6) Grossing up those figures, 1.5 (Roman Catholics) can be expressed as 71% of 2.1 (Protestants). Thus, it can be said that the success chance for Roman Catholics ... is 29% less ... than for Protestants ...

In order to determine who should be compared, it is essential to ensure that the comparison made is with those who are otherwise qualified for the job apart from the requirement being challenged.

Jones v University of Manchester [1993] IRLR 218, CA[93]

The employers wanted a graduate careers adviser aged 27–35; the desire was for a younger person, to have someone closer in age and outlook to the students. The applicant was 46 and claimed that the requirement was indirectly discriminatory against women who were mature students – she did not get her degree until she was 41. The essence of the claim was that female mature students are, on average, rather older than male mature students. Her claim failed.

Evans LJ (pp 228–29):

If the numbers of women and of men, respectively, remaining after the requirement is applied are to be compared as 'proportions' of something other than the total number of those who can comply, then the question arises, as proportions of what? One possibility is, as proportions of 'all men' and 'all women', even of 'all humanity' ... The other possibility is what Mustill LJ called 'the relevant population', meaning all persons who satisfy the relevant criteria apart from the requirement or condition which is under consideration ... In my judgment, [this approach] is much to be preferred ... It is, in effect, the total number of all those persons, men and women, who answer the description contained in the advertisement, apart from the age requirement. Here, that means all graduates with the relevant experience.

[D]iscrimination ... cannot be established; the statistics only support the applicant's case if comparison is limited to mature graduates aged between 25 and 29 ... years of age ...

I have wondered throughout this appeal whether Parliament can have envisaged the kind of detail which has been produced in this case. Even these figures involve a considerable amount of approximation; for example, the numbers and ages of those attending university are taken apparently as the numbers and ages of those who obtain degrees, and there are no precise figures for those who graduate and are able to acquire the relevant experience, before or after graduating, before the age of 35.

Ms Jones' statistics were too narrow, focusing on female mature students rather than female students in general. While female mature students may tend to be older than men, and thus less likely to meet the requirement in question, the requirement only required a graduate, aged between 27 and 35, and so mature graduates would have

---

93 Criticised by Hervey, T, 'Structural discrimination unrecognised' (1994) 57 MLR 307.

been considered. There was no evidence to suppose that women graduates as a whole were disadvantaged by that requirement.[94]

The selection of the appropriate pool may be a highly technical exercise fraught with difficulty both for litigants and tribunals. The EAT has attempted to deflect the problem by emphasising that the question of the appropriate pool is one of fact for the tribunal. In *Kidd v DRG (UK) Ltd*,[95] Waite J said that the 'choice of an appropriate section of the population is in our judgment an issue of fact ... entrusted by Parliament to the good sense of the tribunals ... [There was no] error in deciding that the proper section of the community for the purposes of making the statutory comparison ... was the section of the population living in households needing to provide home care for children to an extent that would normally be incompatible with the acceptance of full-time employment ...' In *Greater Manchester Police Authority v Lea*,[96] it was the policy of the police authority not to employ persons receiving an occupational pension. This was to take account of the needs of the unemployed. Accordingly, they refused to employ Mr Lea, because he was receiving an occupational pension following retirement, which resulted from a road traffic accident. Lea claimed that the policy amounted to (indirect) sex discrimination because a larger proportion of men than women were receiving occupational pensions. The industrial tribunal chose a pool of all economically active men and women in the UK. It was argued before the EAT that using the economically active population as the pool was far too wide because it included those who could not, for intellectual and other reasons, realistically apply for the post and also people who would have been over-qualified and would not have been interested in applying for such a job. The EAT said that the 'underlying consideration [is] that this is an issue of fact and judgment and that this is a matter in which it has to be shown that the tribunal has adopted a course which is outside the range of selection for any reasonable tribunal ...'.[97] Furthermore, while it was accepted that the applicant's statistics were not perfect, the employers had put in no statistics of their own and thus were in effect estopped from denying the applicability of the only statistics which were available.

There are three further problems with selection of the appropriate pool. The first two demonstrate how much easier it may be to utilise indirect discrimination law as regards internal employment practices (such as promotion and redundancy) rather than recruitment. The first problem is that to compare the success rate of black and white applicants to a firm may be misleading, as it leaves out of account any reasons which may dissuade people from applying in the first place. There may be many factors, some discriminatory and others not, which may prevent the applicant pool

---

94 A similar need to ask the right question is apparent from *Kirshammer-Hack v Sidal* Case C-189/91 [1993] ECR I-6185; [1994] IRLR 185. Under German law, firms employing fewer than five workers are exempt from unfair dismissal law and, in making that calculation those who work less than 10 hours per week are disregarded. The applicant, a woman who worked more than 10 hours per week, claimed that the law contravened the Equal Treatment Directive as being indirectly discriminatory. The appropriate issue was not whether disproportionately more women work part-time, but whether disproportionately more women worked for employers employing less than five employees.

95 [1985] ICR 405; [1985] IRLR 190, EAT.

96 [1990] IRLR 372, EAT.

97 *Ibid*, at p 374, para 11.

being in any sense a representative sample. In *Orphanos v QMC*,[98] Lord Fraser stated: '[I]f [the pool] is limited to persons who actually apply ... it would omit all those who may have been deterred from applying because they knew they could not comply with the [requirement].'[99]

The second problem concerns choosing the appropriate labour market. The concern here is to identify the proportion of qualified minorities in the labour market from whom the employer might reasonably be expected to hire. This is not usually a problem in sex discrimination cases as, without more detailed evidence, it can safely be assumed that women and men with any given qualifications are evenly distributed throughout the community. Similarly, the court in *McAusland* regarded Northern Ireland as sufficiently small that it could be treated as one labour market. The issue is especially acute with race: the different races are extremely unevenly distributed and are likely to have very different proportions with appropriate qualifications. One possible explanation of why this issue has not troubled the courts is simply the unavailability of detailed local labour market statistics pertaining to race. In *Hazlewood School District v United States*,[100] the allegation was that the employers had engaged in a pattern and practice of direct discrimination. The case was largely built on the statistical evidence that few black teachers were employed compared with their number in the surrounding geographical area. The question, to which there is no logical answer, is what is the appropriate labour market for the purpose of comparison? It will often be the case that the smaller the market utilised, the higher will be the black population within it, and thus the easier the task to demonstrate significant statistical disparity.

The third problem with identifying the appropriate pool arises when a job is created for a particular person.

Coker v Lord Chancellor [2002] ICR 321, CA[101]

The Lord Chancellor wanted to appoint Garry Hart as his Special Adviser. By letter, he sought the Prime Minister's approval. His letter stated: 'A number of people have approached me with a view to becoming my Adviser, but I have so far declined: they have not struck me as of sufficiently high quality. I now believe that I may be able to attract a first class Adviser, Garry Hart ...' Approval was given and Mr Hart was appointed. The post was never advertised, and the Lord Chancellor had not looked outside his circle of acquaintances when making the appointment.

An employment tribunal[102] upheld Ms Coker's claim of indirect discrimination, finding that the Lord Chancellor had applied a requirement that the successful candidate must be personally known to him. As this class of persons were predominantly white males, it indirectly discriminated on the grounds of sex and race. However, the EAT and the Court of Appeal found for the Lord Chancellor

---

98 [1985] AC 761. See also Garaud, M, 'Legal standards and statistical proof in Title VII litigation: in search of a coherent disparate impact model' (1990) 139 Penns UL Rev 455, p 474.

99 [1985] AC 761, at 771.

100 433 US 299 (1977).

101 See also [2001] EWCA Civ 1756; [2002] IRLR 80.

102 [1999] IRLR 396.

Lord Phillips MR:

7.   These proceedings are supported by both the Equal Opportunities Commission
       and the Commission for Racial Equality. They deny any political motivation.
       Nor are they supporting the proceedings simply to attack the manner of
       appointing Special Advisers, objectionable though they say that is. The object of
       these proceedings is to challenge the practice of closed, or internal, recruitment.
       ...

22.   Sometimes an employer will create a post in order to employ a specific
       individual. The most common example is the husband who employs his wife as
       a part-time secretary. In such circumstances no 'vacancy' ever exists, no selection
       for a post ever occurs and there is no question of any requirement or condition
       being applied to anyone else. We were inclined to wonder whether this was not
       the position in the present case. May it not have been that the Lord Chancellor
       decided to appoint a Special Adviser only because he thought that Mr Hart
       would be of value to him in that role? ...

32.   The legal representatives on both sides ... had some difficulty in identifying the
       appropriate pool. The applicants advanced a number of alternatives: all adults;
       all Labour Party voters; political advisers who had been appointed to local
       authorities; senior officers in local authorities; and the whole of local
       government. Counsel for the LCD suggested that it was all who were eligible for
       the post. The tribunal held that the pool was 'those people who were eligible for
       the position given the criteria set out in the letter [see headnote, above] ...' Thus
       the tribunal restricted the pool to persons with the following qualities:
       —   first class common sense, judgment and ability to assess situations;
       —   a profound knowledge of how a broad area of government works in
            practice;
       —   a commitment to New Labour;
       —   a comprehensive knowledge of the whole politics of the law;
       —   all the qualities and experience of the law necessary to offer sound
            political advice across the whole range of the work of the Lord
            Chancellor's Department ...

[The employment tribunal held]:

36.   '... the situation in this case is artificial, and indeed wholly unusual. We consider
       that the legal principles afford us a degree of latitude to meet the circumstances
       of this case in a straightforward and commonsense way. Given the requirement
       which we have set out, we have to ask ourselves whether that requirement had
       a disproportionate impact as between men and women. Given the answer by
       the Lord Chancellor to the question posed by the tribunal, the answer is clearly
       that it did.'

37.   This passage is Delphic. We believe, however, that we can identify the reasoning
       of the tribunal. The answer of the Lord Chancellor to the question posed by the
       tribunal included the statement that had he considered (which he did not) the
       pool of his acquaintances for the appointment 'he would have considered more
       white men than women and those of African, Caribbean or Afro-Caribbean
       ethnic origin would have been in a very small minority'. We believe that the
       tribunal must have concluded from this that the requirement that candidates
       should be personally known to the Lord Chancellor would have screened out a
       considerably larger proportion of women and of the racial minorities than of
       white men.

38.   If this was the reasoning of the tribunal, it was fundamentally flawed. The test
       of indirect discrimination focuses on the effect that the requirement objected to

has on the pool of potential candidates. It can only have a discriminatory effect within the two statutes if a significant proportion of the pool are able to satisfy the requirement. Only in that situation will it be possible for the requirement to have a disproportionate effect on the men and the women, or the racial groups, which form the pool. Where the requirement excludes almost the entirety of the pool it cannot constitute indirect discrimination within the statutes.

39.   For this reason, making an appointment from within a circle of family, friends and personal acquaintances is seldom likely to constitute indirect discrimination. Those known to the employer are likely to represent a minute proportion of those who would otherwise be qualified to fill the post. The requirement of personal knowledge will exclude the vast proportion of the pool, be they men, women, white or another racial group.

40.   If the above proposition will be true in most cases of appointments made on the basis of personal acquaintanceship, it was certainly true of the appointment of Mr Hart by the Lord Chancellor. This was because those members of the elite pool who were personally known to the Lord Chancellor were, on the unchallenged evidence, reduced to a single man. However many other persons there may have been who were potential candidates, whatever the proportions of men and women or racial groups in the pool, the requirement excluded the lot of them, except Mr Hart. Plainly it can have had no disproportionate effect on the different groupings within the pool ...

53.   For the reasons that we have given, the attack advanced in these proceedings on the practice of making appointments from a circle of family, friends and acquaintances has failed .... It does not follow, however, that this practice is unobjectionable. It will often be open to objection for a number of reasons. It may not produce the best candidate for the post. It may be likely to result in the appointee being of a particular gender or racial group. It may infringe the principle of equal opportunities.

54.   In conclusion, we would emphasise that this judgment is not concerned with the practice of recruiting by word of mouth. The Code of Practice issued by the Equal Opportunities Commission in 1985 under s 56A(1) of the 1975 Act, which contains valuable practical guidance for the elimination of discrimination in the field of employment and for the promotion of equality of opportunity between men and women, has this to say about that practice:

> ... recruitment solely or primarily by word of mouth may unnecessarily restrict the choice of applicants available. The method should be avoided in a workforce predominantly of one sex, if in practice it precludes members of the opposite sex from applying.

55.   A Code of Practice was also issued by the Commission of Racial Equality in 1983 under s 47(1) of the 1976 Act, and nothing in this judgment detracts from the desirability of complying with the Codes of Practice.

In his commentaries to *Coker* in the Industrial Relations Law Reports, Michael Rubenstein noted, 'The prohibition of discrimination in selection arrangements – a concept which lies at the heart of discrimination law – can be circumvented by the simple expedient of not having any selection arrangements.'[103] He also noted:

[T]he Court of Appeal seems to be answering the wrong question of whether it was indirectly discriminatory to appoint Mr Hart rather than whether the tribunal was right to find the arrangements for selection were indirectly discriminatory. The

---

103 Comment to EAT decision, [2001] IRLR 115, at p 116.

applicants were not challenging the appointment of Mr Hart as such – the reduction of the 'elite pool ... to a single man'. They were challenging the selection arrangements whereby the potential candidates were confined to an 'elite pool'. The statutes rightly treat these as separate and distinct causes of action.[104]

It is arguable that Ms Coker would succeed under the Equal Treatment Directive which provides 'that there shall be no discrimination *whatsoever* on the grounds of sex ...'.[105]

(4)   Proving Adverse Impact

Once the pool has been established, the next step is to ascertain whether the protected group has suffered an adverse impact. This step raises a number of issues: first, if appropriate, choosing a suitable statistical model; secondly, the relationship between the rules of evidence (or admissibility) and the significance of statistics. Thirdly, the problems associated with the 'considerable difference' rubric adopted by the courts and some of the legislation. Finally, the consequence of using comparable success rates ('positive' figures) instead of failure rates ('negative' figures).

(a)   Choosing a statistical model

Different statistical models can be used, but ultimately, it is a question of fact in each case. The American experience is instructive here. In the USA, courts have adopted several common methods in appropriate circumstances. There is, for instance, the 'four-fifths' or '80%' rule. Alternatively, a court may assess the probability of the statistics occurring by chance. Then there are a number of cases where apparently good claims have been rejected because the statistics have not told the 'whole truth'.

Guidelines issued by the US Equal Employment Opportunity Commission (EEOC) state that an inference of adverse impact should not be made unless the rate of recruitment of the victim's group is less than four-fifths (or 80%) of the rate at which the group with the highest rate is selected.[106] In *Bushey v New York State Civil Service Commission*[107] a written examination was used for the post of Captain in the State prisons. The results were as follows:

	Number taking test	Number passing	Per cent passing
White	243	119	49%
Non-white	32	8	25%

104 Comment to CA decision, [2002] IRLR 1, at p 3.
105 Article 2, 76/207/EC (emphasis supplied).
106 29 CFR 1607.4(D) (1978) revised 1 July 2000. See http://frwebgate.access.gpo.gov/cgi-bin/get-cfr.cgi?TITLE=29&PART=1607&SECTION=4&YEAR=2000&TYPE=TEXT or www.eeoc.gov.
107 733 F 2d 220 (1984) Court of Appeals for the Second Circuit, cert denied, 469 US 1117 (1985).

As the passing rate for non-whites was approximately 50% that of whites, a *prima facie* case was made out. Similarly, in *Firefighters Institute v St Louis*,[108] 16.7% of whites passed a test in comparison to 7.1% of blacks. The black pass rate was 42.5% of whites. As this fell well short of the '80%' rule, the test was held to be discriminatory.

An alternative model is based upon the probability of chance, ie, the statistical significance concerning the likelihood that a particular result arose by chance. If 10 people passed a test, seven men out of 10 (male) applicants and three women out of 10 (female) applicants, the male pass rate is 70% and the female pass rate 30%. While there appears to be a significant disparity, both common sense and statisticians would accept that the result might have arisen for other reasons. However, if 100 had passed the test, 70 men and 30 women, the proportions and percentages would be identical, but we should now be suspicious, and if there were 1,000 successes, 700 men and 300 women, we should be almost certain that a gender-related factor was involved to give rise to a *prima facie* case of discrimination.[109]

In *Bridgeport Guardians v City of Bridgeport*,[110] tests used in the promotion of police officers to the rank of sergeant were challenged. One hundred and seventy persons applied for 19 posts. The results were as follows:[111]

Race of candidate	Number taking exam	Number passing	Percent passing	Highest rank
White	115	78	68%	1–19
Black	27	8	30%	20
Hispanic	28	13	46%	22

Two things can be seen from these results: first, a substantially lower proportion of non-whites passed the test; secondly, that each of the 19 best performers was white, and so the 19 vacancies were filled by whites. Statistical analysis was presented which showed that the disparity between the whites' and blacks' results would occur by chance once in 10,000 times and the disparity between the whites and Hispanics would occur twice in 10,000. Relying on the 'rule of thumb' that anything less than one in 20 could not be put down to chance, the Court of Appeals held that the statistics raised an inference of causation, which helped establish a *prima facie* case.

American courts are not bound by these models and are at liberty to reject a statistical model. In *Bushey* (see above), the category of non-whites included four Hispanics, two of whom passed the test. Thus, their pass rate (50%) was comparable to the whites'. The Court of Appeals held that in the case of the Hispanics, no *prima*

---

108 616 F 2d 350 (1980), cert denied *sub nom St Louis v United States* 452 US 938 (1981).
109 If there were 10,000 applicants, even a 1% difference might be regarded as statistically significant, but it is questionable whether it should carry any legal weight. '[T]he fact that a disparity is not statistically significant does not necessarily mean that it is not "practically significant" in the sense that it may be of a size which is considered important and indicative of possible discrimination. Conversely, a small disparity which is of little or no practical significance may nevertheless be shown to be "statistically significant" if based upon a sufficiently large sample of cases.' Sugrue, T and Fairley, W, 'A case of unexamined assumptions: the use and misuse of the statistical analysis of *Castenada/Hazlewood* in discrimination legislation' (1983) 24 Boston College L Rev 925, p 933, n 39.
110 933 F 2d 1140 (1991), Court of Appeals for the Second Circuit.
111 933 F 2d 1140, at p 1143.

facie case could be made out. In *Fudge v Providence Fire Department*[112] statistics were ruled to be too small and incomplete. In *Hazelwood School District v United States*,[113] statistics based upon an applicant pool including some lacking minimal qualifications for the job were rejected. In *Carroll v Sears, Roebuck & Co*,[114] statistics based solely upon test results were rejected because the test was only part of the decision making process, and in *Harper v Trans World Airlines*,[115] the statistics consisted of only five persons, whilst some 65 blacks had taken the written examination at issue. What these cases have in common is that circumstances peculiar to each case undermined the credibility of the statistical evidence.

(b)   Evidence and statistical significance distinguished

The issues of legal proof and statistical significance must be kept distinct. Statisticians may not accept that a given result is significant at less than the 95% significance – a less than 5% chance that the observed result occurred by chance. But such a high level of proof is unnecessary and inappropriate in a court of law.[116] The plaintiff's burden is to establish a *prima facie* case merely on a balance of probabilities; the defendant has the opportunity to justify the practice which leads to adverse impact, and the weight of the burden of establishing justification should vary according to the degree of adverse impact which is established. The relationship between the rules of evidence (or admissibility), and the quality of statistics was explored in some detail in the next extract, from a case on age discrimination.

Kadas v MCI Systemhouse Corporation 255 F 3d 359, US Court Of Appeals for the Seventh Circuit[117]

Posner, Circuit Judge (at pp 362–63):

Some cases suggest that statistical evidence is not admissible to show discrimination unless it is significant at the conventional 5 percent significance level (that is, the coefficient of the relevant correlation is at least two standard deviations away from zero) ... – in other words, unless there is no more than a 5 percent probability that we would observe a statistical correlation between the dependent variable (such as whether terminated) and the independent variable having legal significance (such as age) even if the variables were uncorrelated in the population from which the sample was drawn. Other cases – including our own – reject the suggestion ... The 5 percent test is arbitrary; it is influenced by the fact that scholarly publishers have limited space and don't want to clog up their journals and books with statistical findings that have a substantial probability of being a product of chance rather than of some interesting underlying relation between the variables of concern. Litigation generally is not fussy about evidence; much eyewitness and other nonquantitative evidence is subject to significant possibility of error, yet no effort is made to exclude it if it doesn't satisfy some counterpart to the 5 percent significance test. A lower significance level

---

112 766 F 2d 650, at pp 656–59 (1985).
113 433 US 299 (1977), at p 308.
114 708 F 2d 183 (1983), at p 189.
115 525 F 2d 409 (1975).
116 Garaud, M, 'Legal standards and statistical proof in Title VII litigation: in search of a coherent disparate impact model' (1990) 139 Penns UL Rev 455, pp 468–69.
117 2001 US App LEXIS 13583; 85 Fair Empl Prac Cas (BNA) 1720; 80 Empl Prac Dec (CCH) P40, 597.

may show that the correlation is spurious, but may also be a result of 'noise' in the data or collinearity (correlation between independent variables, such as sex and weight), and such evidence, when corroborated by other evidence, need not be deemed worthless. Conversely, a high significance level may be a misleading artifact of the study's design; and there is always the risk that the party's statistical witness ran 20 regressions, one and only one of which supported the party's position and that was the only one presented, though, in the circumstances, it was a chance result with no actual evidentiary significance. (Careful pretrial discovery by the other party should unmask this trick.)

But the question whether a study is responsible and therefore admissible ... is different from the weight to be accorded to the significance of a particular correlation found by the study. It is for the judge to say, on the basis of the evidence of a trained statistician, whether a particular significance level, in the context of a particular study in a particular case, is too low to make the study worth the consideration of judge or jury.

And so, in both America and Britain, the ultimate analysis remains a question of fact, as the following British cases illustrate.

Staffordshire CC v Black [1995] IRLR 234, EAT

The case concerned benefits available to part-time teachers made redundant compared with those available to full-time teachers. The tribunal said there was a requirement or condition that in order to qualify for the maximum additional service credit, an employee had to be employed full-time at the date of dismissal. While the proportion of women teachers over 50 who were full-time (89.5%) was held not to be considerably smaller than the same proportion of male teachers (97.0%), the industrial tribunal upheld the complaint under Art 119 (now Art 141) of the EC Treaty on the basis that the condition affected a far greater number of women than men.

The EAT allowed the employer's appeal.

Morison J (pp 237–38):

What is or is not a 'considerably smaller proportion' is a matter for the Industrial Tribunal. The figures speak for themselves. Overall there are more full-time women teachers than men. No doubt for historical reasons there are proportionately slightly less women than men in the over-50 age range, although, again, in absolute terms there are more women than men doing full-time work in that bracket. A difference of 7.5 percentage points, in the context, is very small ... It is not unhelpful to keep in mind that the European Court refers to 'a much lower proportion' or a 'considerably lower percentage'...

McAusland v Dungannon DC [1993] IRLR 583, NICA

The facts and statistics are set out above, p 258. The applicant argued that the 'four-fifths' rule should be adopted.

McDermott LJ (pp 585–86):

[The words 'considerably smaller'] are words in daily usage and do not require definition. They were not defined by Parliament and we think no useful purpose would be served by any judicial definition or interpretation ... In our judgment, Parliament has chosen to leave these words undefined, relying on the good sense and experience of [the tribunal] to produce a fair and relevant conclusion ...

The introduction of [the four-fifths] rule, if considered wise or helpful, should be by Parliament and not by judicial decision. We think it would be unwise to introduce such a test without a real knowledge of American law, a true understanding of the application of the rule in practice and the benefit of in-depth research on the impact of such a rule on industrial relations in the UK ...

[I]t could be said that the success chance for Roman Catholics ... was 29% less than for Protestants and, having regard to this, the tribunal was entitled to reverse its decision on the 'considerably smaller' question.

London Underground Ltd v Edwards (No 2) [1997] IRLR 157, EAT

A single mother with a young child was employed as a train operator. Her rostering arrangements allowed her to be at home in the mornings and evenings. She normally worked from 8 am to 4 pm or 8.30 am to 4.30 pm, with Saturday as a rest day, and as a result she did not receive shift bonuses for working between 6 pm and 7 am.

In 1991, a new flexible shift pattern was announced – duties were to begin at 4.45 am and were to include Sundays. Although it was possible to change shifts so as to avoid early and late work, the trade-off was a longer shift for the same money. She was not prepared to work the new system and when negotiations between management and unions about special arrangements for single parents were unable to reach agreement, she resigned and claimed indirect sex discrimination.

The second industrial tribunal[118] found that 100% of the 2,023 male train operators could comply with the requirement. Mrs Edwards was the only one of the 21 female train operators who positively complained that she could not comply, so that the proportion of women who could comply was 95.2%. However, the tribunal had regard to the small number of female train operators, stated that it was common knowledge that females are more likely to be single parents with sole responsibility for a child than males, and held that this meant that a considerably smaller proportion of females could comply with the requirement.

This approach was upheld by the EAT.

Morison J (p 160):

[A]s a matter of principle it seems to us that, when weighing the extent of the disproportionate effect that a condition has upon men and women in the relevant pool, the tribunal can properly have regard to the number of female train operators as against the number of male train operators. The industrial tribunal is entitled to have regard to the possibility that, where the number of women as against the number of men is, in percentage terms, very slight, some kind of generalised assumption may exist at the workplace that the particular type of work is concerned is 'men's' and not 'women's' work. Further, the tribunal is also entitled to consider whether the number of women drivers is so small as to be statistically unreliable ... The impact is ... to be assessed at the date of the complaint. But in assessing the extent of the disproportionate impact, the tribunal is entitled to take account of a wider perspective. It is for this reason that statistics showing the percentage of women in employment who have primary care responsibility for a child, in contrast to the percentage of men in that position, are relevant. The disproportionate impact of the condition may be assessed by looking both at the picture as it was at the time, and as it may be, had the small pool of women been larger and statistically significant ... With such a small pool, the tribunal were right to recognise that the percentage proportion would be substantially larger if just one more woman were unable to

118 [1995] ICR 574; [1995] IRLR 355, EAT.

comply with the requirement due to temporary or permanent childcare responsibilities.[119]

The EAT is saying that the whole ethos of the organisation may itself have contributed to the small number of women doing the job in question – and, no doubt, many other jobs. Thus, the female workforce was self-selecting and, as a result, arguably more likely to be able to comply with the changed working arrangements than a more representative group of women might have been. Thus, there was a finding of disparate impact despite the absence of statistical significance, although if there is statistical significance, that will normally establish the *prima facie* case. This sophisticated and commendable approach still leaves two unanswered questions. First, there was still a 5% disparity in ability to comply. Would the tribunal have been so bold if she had been one woman among 50 who objected to the new arrangements? Secondly, and more importantly, the EAT emphasised that the tribunal was *entitled* to have regard to the wider perspective. It did not hold that the tribunal was *bound* to have done so. The issue remains one of fact for the employment tribunal. It is unlikely that the EAT would have held it to be an error of law if a different employment tribunal had failed to take such an enlightened approach.

(c)   The meaning of 'considerable difference'

We come now to the rubric used in British and EC law: 'considerable difference.' Before examining its meaning, however, some complications arising from the new definitions of indirect discrimination need to be explained. The original position is that none of the EC legislation contained a definition of indirect discrimination. The ECJ have always maintained that to establish a *prima facie* case, the claimant had to show that the difference was considerable.[120] The Burden of Proof Directive, which came into force in 2001, introduced a definition of indirect discrimination, which provided that the difference had to be substantial.[121] This was transposed into the Sex Discrimination Act (for employment matters only) as 'considerably larger'.[122] This is due to be revised by the Equal Treatment Amendment Directive, by 5 October 2005,[123] with a less stringent demand that the claimant's group are 'put at a particular disadvantage'.[124] The other Directives on Race[125] and Equal Treatment at Work[126] use this ('particular disadvantage') formula as well, which has been transposed into

---

119 The Court of Appeal [1998] IRLR 364 dismissed the appeal on this point, adopting largely the same approach as the EAT, and emphasised both that the issue is one of fact for industrial tribunals, and that it would be unwise to lay down a figure which would be of general application in determining the 'considerably smaller' question.

120 Eg, *Jenkins v Kingsgate* ('considerably smaller') [1981] IRLR 228, at p 234; *Teuling* ('considerably smaller') [1988] 3 CMLR 789, at p 805; *Rinner-Kuhn FWW* ('considerably less') [1989] ECR 2743, at p 2760 and *Bilka-Kaufhaus v Weber Von Hartz* ('much lower proportion') [1987] ICR 110, at p 125.

121 Article 2, 97/80/EC. See generally Chapter 5.

122 SDA 1975, s 1(2)(b)(i).

123 Article 2, para 1, 2002/73/EC.

124 Article 1, para 2, 2002/73/EC.

125 2000/43/EC.

126 2000/78/EC, covering religion or belief, disability, age and sexual orientation.

domestic law.[127] The original domestic legislation (the SDA 1975 and the RRA 1976) used the rubric 'considerably smaller', which means the position now is that the phrase 'put at a particular disadvantage' applies to all cases of race discrimination falling under EC competence,[128] and all cases of discrimination on the grounds of sexual orientation and religion or belief. But the sex discrimination legislation carries the modifier 'considerable' or 'substantial' until, probably, 2005. It is arguable, that as the ECJ has always insisted upon a 'considerable difference', the anomaly should make no difference. However, the next case exposed the limitations of looking for a *considerable* difference.

R v Secretary of State for Employment ex p Seymour-Smith, ECJ and HL[129]

The Unfair Dismissal (Variation of Qualifying Period) Order 1985 (the Order) extended the qualification period for unfair dismissal rights to two years.[130] Ms Seymour-Smith challenged this as being contrary to Art 119 (now Art 141) of the EC Treaty because it discriminated against women, who are more transient in the workforce than men.

Both sides accepted the Annual Labour Force Surveys as evidence of the impact of the two-year requirement. These are surveys of the UK's total workforce. They reveal that in 1985, for example, the total workforce in the UK was 18.73 million. If the two-year requirement were neutral in its effect, some 8.48 million men and 5.44 million women would have qualified under the two-year rule. However, the survey revealed that, in fact, only 5.07 million women qualified, so some 370,000 women were adversely affected. That was the situation expressed as *numbers*. Here are the *proportions* of male and female qualifiers for the years 1985 (when the Order was introduced) to 1991 (when Ms Seymour-Smith was dismissed). The calculations of disparity are to the right:

Year	% of Males with more than 2 years	% of Females with more than 2 years	Disparity	% of women to men in advantaged group
1985	77.4	68.9	8.5	89
1986	77.2	68.4	8.8	88.6
1987	75.3	67.1	8.2	89.1
1988	73.4	65.6	7.8	89.4
1989	72.0	63.8	8.2	88.6
1990	72.5	64.1	8.4	88.4
1991	74.5	67.4	7.1	90

127 Respectively, RRA 1976, s 1(1A); Employment Equality (Sexual Orientation) Regulations 2003, reg 3(1)(b)(i); Employment Equality (Religion or Belief) Regulations 2003, reg 3(1)(b)(i), which came into force on 19 July 2003, 1 December 2003 and 2 December 2003, respectively.

128 Covering employment matters and the provision goods, facilities and services, but *not* discrimination on the grounds of colour or nationality.

129 Case C-167/97 [1999] All ER (EC) 97; [1999] 3 WLR 460; [1999] ICR 447; [1999] IRLR 253; [1999] 2 CMLR 273, ECJ; [2000] 1 All ER 857; [2000] 1 WLR 435; [2000] ICR 244; [2000] IRLR 263, HL.

130 Now reduced to one year where the effective date of termination is after 1 June 1999: Unfair Dismissal and Statement of Reasons for Dismissal (Variation of Qualifying Period) Order 1999, SI 1999/1436.

For 1985, the disparity was 8.5 percentage points. That means that, roughly, for every 10 men who qualified for unfair dismissal rights, only nine women did so (expressed in the far right column as 89%). That figure remained roughly constant until 1991. In a nutshell, the problem was whether a 'small' difference could be 'considerable' when it was established and constant over a number of years.

The Divisional Court found that the disparity was not considerable. The Court of Appeal reversed that decision. The House of Lords referred the case to the ECJ for a ruling and subsequently held by a bare majority that there was a considerable difference.[131]

ECJ:

49.   With regard ... to statistics, it may be appropriate to take into account not only the statistics available at the point in time at which ... [the Order] was adopted, but also statistics compiled subsequently which are likely to provide an indication of its impact on men and on women ...

60.   As the Court has stated on several occasions, it must be ascertained whether the statistics available indicate that a considerably smaller percentage of woman than men is able to satisfy the condition of two years' employment required by the disputed rule. That situation would be evidence of apparent sex discrimination unless the disputed rule were justified ...

61.   That could also be the case if the statistical evidence revealed a lesser but persistent and relatively constant disparity over a long period ...

House of Lords [2000] 1 All ER 857

Lord Nicholls (for the majority at pp 870–71):

... the Court of Justice has adopted an approach similar to that provided in s 1(1)(b) of the Sex Discrimination Act 1975. A considerable disparity can be more readily established if the statistical evidence covers a long period and the figures show a persistent and relatively constant disparity. In such a case a lesser statistical disparity may suffice to show that the disparity is considerable than if the statistics cover only a short period or if they present an uneven picture ...

I find myself driven to the conclusion that a persistent and constant disparity ... in respect of the entire male and female labour forces of this country over a period of seven years cannot be brushed aside and dismissed as insignificant or inconsiderable ... I think that these figures are adequate to demonstrate that the extension of the qualifying period had a considerably greater adverse impact on women than men.

Lord Slynn (for the minority, at 866):

[I]t cannot be said that [the Order] actually affects a considerably higher percentage of women than men ... It would in any event ... be odd if there was no discrimination in 1985, but in 1991 on a slightly higher percentage on women qualifying (and one as part of a rising trend) there was discrimination.[132]

---

131 However, it was held that the Order was justified; see below, p 295.

132 By 1993, the Survey showed that the percentage of women to men in the advantaged group had risen to 95%.

Connolly, M, 'Commentary, *R v Secretary of State for Employment, ex parte Seymour-Smith*' [2000] 5(2) J Civ Lib 212, pp 217–19:

... the ECJ formula is not entirely clear. ... On the one hand the disparity must be 'considerable'. On the other, it can be 'less than considerable'. Lord Nicholls attempted to reconcile this by stating – in effect - that a *less than* considerable disparity over a long period can amount to a *considerable* disparity. This has the convenience of being consistent with the domestic legislation, which demands a 'considerable difference'. But ... [w]hat happens when another novel case arises, where even the new 'flexible formula' is inappropriate? For instance, a case with a large sample, a marginal impact, but only one set of data: a large company making hundreds redundant, selects part-timers first, with the result being that a marginally higher proportion of women are made redundant. Statisticians may testify that the disparity is significant. They could not have used the 'long, persistent and constant' formula to conclude this, but their method would have been credible. A tribunal would have the choice between verbally distorting this appropriate and credible method to accord with the modifier 'considerable', or denying that there was discrimination. The better view is that the ECJ added an alternative to the 'considerable' test. And *where appropriate*, the lower courts should be able to add other credible tests or calculations. There should no longer be a need, in every case, for a *considerable* disparity.

More fundamentally, this case highlights an apparent difference, between the European legislation and the case law, over the degree of disparity required to establish a *prime facie* case of discrimination. The legislation is absolute. For instance, Article 141 (ex 119) provides for ensuring 'full' equality.[133]

However, the ECJ has always held[134] that there should be a *considerable* disparity in cases of indirect discrimination. It appears that the ECJ has diluted the legislation to outlaw only discrimination which is *considerable*. This seems more peculiar when, in cases of *direct* discrimination, the courts do not demand a *considerable* difference in treatment.[135]

The only way to explain this difference is to treat the legislation as a rule of law, and the ECJ guidance as a rule of *proof*. One of the purposes of proof in cases of indirect discrimination is to prevent *prime facie* cases being brought, where the disparity is the result of chance. The 'considerable difference' rule can do this in many cases, but not all. That rule should not be used to disqualify *genuine* cases of discrimination ...

The ECJ may have recognised this, but the House of Lords did not. During his judgment Lord Nicholls said: 'The obligation is to avoid ... requirements having a considerable disparity of impact.' The majority found that there had been considerable *discrimination*, not that there was considerable *evidence* of discrimination. The minority proceeded on the same basis. Lord Slynn found the figures to be reliable

---

133 It is obviously desirable that this legislation uses a single definition of indirect discrimination. It would be perverse otherwise: eg, in this case, if Ms Seymour-Smith was seeking reinstatement instead of compensation, her claim would have fallen under the Equal Treatment Directive. See Case C-167/97, paras 30 and 41 [1999] All ER 97, at pp 131 and 132. The Equal Treatment in Employment Directive (2000/78/EC) uses the adjective 'whatsoever', but the Race Directive (2000/43/EC) does not. The point is slightly undermined by the temporary use of the modifier 'substantial' in the Burden of Proof Directive.

134 Eg, *Jenkins v Kingsgate* ('considerably smaller') [1981] IRLR 228, at p 234; *Teuling* ('considerably smaller') [1988] 3 CMLR 789, at p 805; *Rinner-Kuhn FWW* ('considerably less') [1989] ECR 2743, at p 2760; and *Bilka-kaufhaus v Weber Von Hartz* ('much lower proportion') [1987] ICR 110, at p 125.

135 See, eg, *Gill v El Vino* [1983] 1 QB 425, [1983] 1 All ER 398; [1983] IRLR 206, CH.

(or not 'fortuitous').[136] The figures showed that women were disadvantaged. Yet he held there was no discrimination. That can only be explained if he was looking for proof of considerable *discrimination*, rather than considerable *proof* of discrimination.

> What comes out of this case is not an answer to the ... question: 'what degree of disparity was necessary to establish a *prime facie* case?' Rather, it is a realisation that the rubric 'considerable difference' can be no more than one of several methods of evaluating a *prime facie* case. A specific answer to the question ... would shackle the courts with one narrow rigid definition ... that would deny some legitimate claims and defeat the goal of 'no discrimination whatsoever.'

(d) *Positive or negative figures?*

Another feature of *Seymour-Smith* has new significance upon the publication of the new definition of indirect discrimination. Council for Ms Seymour-Smith advanced an alternative comparison. He compared the *disadvantaged* groups in this case. In 1985, for example, 22.6% of women could not meet the two-year requirement. The figure for men was 31%. Thus, for every 10 women disadvantaged, there were only seven men. That is clearly a considerable difference. However, all the courts in this case based their decisions on the 'positive' figures: the proportions of those who *could* comply with the Order. The 'negative' argument is attractive for no other reason than the legislation is designed to protect those disadvantaged by a measure. The old formula in the domestic legislation, which required the comparison between those who *can* comply, is a barrier to using 'negative' figures. The current formula for sex discrimination uses 'substantially disadvantages'[137] women or 'would be to the detriment of a considerably larger proportion'[138] of women. The new formula requires that the provision, criterion or practice 'puts' the protected group 'at a particular disadvantage'. All but the old formula is open-ended enough to allow the use of positive or negative figures.

(5) The Justification Defence

This topic will be taken in two stages. First, there is an attempt to establish the precise meaning of the defence and, secondly, a review of the defence being used in a variety of circumstances.

(a) *The meaning of the justification*

There are two issues to explore here. First, the differences (if any) between the EC and British definitions and, secondly, where the defence itself is based upon discrimination. Before exploring the issues associated with the justification defence, it may be helpful to unravel (so far as possible) the complications arising from the new definitions of indirect discrimination. The Burden of Proof Directive,[139] which came into force in 2001, stated that a challenged measure must be 'appropriate and

---

136 [2000] 1 All ER 857, at p 864.
137 The Burden of Proof Directive 97/80/EC.
138 SDA 1975, s 1(2). This applies to employment matters only.
139 87/80/EC.

necessary and can be justified by objective factors unrelated to sex'. This was transposed to the SDA 1975 as 'justifiable irrespective of ... sex'.[140] The new definition in the Equal Treatment Amendment Directive,[141] due in force by 5 October 2005, states that a measure 'is objectively justified by a legitimate aim, and the means of achieving that aim are appropriate and necessary'. The Race and Equal Treatment in Employment Directives[142] carry the same formula. These have been transposed into domestic legislation as a proportionate means of achieving a legitimate aim.' We can observe three elements from the definitions. First, there must be a legitimate aim, that is, one not related to sex or race, etc. Secondly, the means of achieving that aim must be appropriate. Thirdly, the means of achieving that aim must be necessary. The SDA 1975, (old and new definitions) and the old definition in the RRA 1976 simply state that the justification must be 'irrespective of sex/race'. The other domestic legislation carries all three elements, assuming that 'proportionate' encapsulates 'appropriate and necessary'.[143]

Some of these anomalies can be explained with a review of the case law. In the early years of the British legislation, tribunals (influenced by US case law, upon which our legislation was based), working with the statutory phrase 'justifiable irrespective of ... sex' spoke of 'necessity'. For example, in *Steel v Union of Post Office Workers*,[144] Phillips J, President of the EAT, said that the practice must be *inter alia* 'genuine and necessary'.[145] In 1982, however, the Court of Appeal in *Ojutiku v Manpower Services Commission*[146] contrasted the word 'necessary' with the statutory word 'justifiable'; Kerr LJ stated that 'justifiable ... clearly applies a lower standard than ... necessary'.[147] Eveleigh LJ considered it to mean 'something ... acceptable to right-thinking people as sound and tolerable'.[148] Balcombe LJ in *Hampson v Department of Education*[149] drew back from this loose interpretation and stated that the courts should balance the discriminatory effect of the requirement against the defendant's reasonable need for it.[150] This has become widely known as the '*Hampson* balancing test'. It was approved by House of Lords in *Webb v EMO Air Cargo*.[151]

Meanwhile, the ECJ was developing its jurisprudence on indirect discrimination, upon which the EC legislative definitions were based. *Bilka* set the standard.

---

140 SDA 1975, s 1(2)(b)(ii).
141 Council Directive 2002/73/EC.
142 Respectively, 2000/43/EC and 2000/78/EC, covering religion or belief, disability, age and sexual orientation.
143 The EC definition has its root in the general principle of proportionality, developed by the ECJ in the *Cassis de Dijon* case, C-120/78 (*Rewe-Zentral AG v Bundesmonopolverwaltung für Branntwein*) [1979] ECR 649.
144 [1978] ICR 181 EAT, at p 187.
145 In Parliament, the Government resisted amendments to the Sex Discrimination Bill that would have replaced 'justifiable' with 'necessary'. Lord Harris stated that where a body offered reduced fares for pensioners, the policy might be justifiable, but not necessary (HL Deb Vol 362 Cols 10116–17, 14 July 1975).
146 [1982] ICR 661, CA.
147 *Ibid*, at p 670.
148 *Ibid*, at p 668.
149 [1989] ICR 179.
150 *Ibid*, at p 196F.
151 [1992] 4 All ER 929, at p 936d.

Bilka-Kaufhaus v Weber von Hartz **Case 170/84 [1986] IRLR 317, ECJ**[152]

Full-time employees automatically qualified for a non-contributory pension on retirement, while part-time employees only qualified if they had been employed full-time for at least 15 years.

Judgment (pp 319–21):

> Bilka ... argued that it was not guilty of any breach of the principle of equal pay since there were objectively justified economic grounds ... [I]t emphasised ... that in comparison with the employment of part-time workers the employment of full-time workers involves lower ancillary costs and permits the use of staff throughout opening hours ...
>
> Bilka argues that the exclusion of part-time employees ... aims solely to discourage part-time work, since in general part-time workers refuse to work in the late afternoon and on Saturdays. In order to ensure the presence of an adequate workforce during those periods it was therefore necessary to make full-time work more attractive than part-time work ...
>
> It is for the national court, which has sole jurisdiction to make findings of fact, to determine whether, and to what extent, the grounds put forward by an employer to explain the adoption of a pay practice which applies independently of the employee's sex, but which in fact affects more women than men, can be regarded to be objectively justified for economic reasons. If the national court finds that the means chosen by Bilka correspond to a real need on the part of the undertaking, are appropriate with a view to attaining the objectives pursued and are necessary to that end, the fact that the measures in question affect a far greater number of women than men is not sufficient to show that they constitute an infringement of Art 119 ...

The three-stage test in the last paragraph is the nub of the judgment and is the basis of the new definitions provided by the EC legislation.

(i)   British and EC definitions contrasted

There is clearly a difference, of language at least, between the *Hampson* balancing test and the *Bilka* test. Most obviously, *Bilka's* third element, 'necessity', is absent from the balancing test. However, for many years now, British courts have insisted that *Hampson* and *Bilka* amounted to the same thing. This was restated recently in the next case.

Allonby v Accrington & Rossendale College **[2001] IRLR 364; [2001] EWCA Civ 529; [2001] ICR 1189, CA**

For the facts, see pp 279–80, below.

Sedley LJ (para 23):

> The House of Lords in *Barry v Midland Bank plc*[153] endorsed the decision in this court, where Peter Gibson LJ had said:
>
>> [After citing the *Bilka* test] In our judgment it would be wrong to extrapolate from those words written in that context that an employer can never justify indirect discrimination in a redundancy payment scheme unless the form of the

---

152 [1986] ECR 1607; [1986] 2 CMLR 701; [1987] ICR 110.
153 [1999] IRLR 581. See below, p 288.

scheme is shown to be necessary as the only possible scheme. One must first consider whether the objective of the scheme is legitimate. If so, then one goes on to consider whether the means used are appropriate to achieve that objective and are reasonably necessary for that end.

That approach, as Peter Gibson LJ went on to point out, has the support of the House of Lords in *Rainey v Greater Glasgow Health Board* [1987] IRLR 26 and in *Webb v EMO Air Cargo (UK) Ltd* [1993] IRLR 27, 30, where the judgment of Balcombe LJ in *Hampson v Department of Education and Science* [1989] IRLR 69, 75, was expressly approved. Balcombe LJ said:

> In my judgment, 'justifiable' requires an objective balance between the discriminatory effect of the condition and the reasonable needs of the party who applies the condition.

This is not convincing. The closest that any of this comes to represent *Bilka* is where Peter Gibson LJ qualified 'necessary' with *reasonably*. The effect that is explored in the following commentary on Sedley LJ's judgment.

Connolly, M, 'Discrimination law: justification, alternative measures and defences based on sex' [2001] 30 ILJ 311:

This is the neatest integration yet of the *Bilka* and *Hampson* 'tests'. Hitherto, British courts have done no more than treat the tests as expressing the same thing in different language ...

However, Sedley's LJ assimilation of *Bilka* – or more precisely *proportionality* – and *Hampson* is not perfect. The obvious difference is in the language. The word 'necessary' appears nowhere in the *Hampson* test. But there is a difference in substance as well. Asking if a practice is suitable and necessary is different from asking whether it is outweighed by its discriminatory effect. This becomes clear where ... there exists an alternative. Under *Hampson* the existence of a less-discriminatory alternative practice achieving the same goal is merely an ingredient in the 'balance' test; under *Bilka* it will always defeat a justification defence. The case of *Enderby v Frenchay Health Authority* [1994] 1 All ER 495 illustrates the point.

In *Enderby* the Health Authority was trying to justify a difference in pay between speech therapists (98 per cent female) and pharmacists (63 per cent female). The pharmacists were paid about 40 per cent more than the speech therapists. As women were over-represented in the lower paid group the Health Authority were obliged to justify the difference. It argued that market forces caused the difference. But the evidence was that only an extra ten per cent pay was needed to recruit a sufficient number of pharmacists. Thus there existed a less-discriminatory alternative of paying the pharmacists a ten per cent premium. The ECJ held (at para 27): 'If ... the National Court has been able to determine precisely what proportion of the increase in pay is attributable to market forces, it must necessarily accept that that the pay differential is objectively justified to the extent of that proportion.' In other words, proportionality means *no more than* necessary.

If we applied the *Hampson* 'objective balance' test to the facts of *Enderby* the result may be different. On the one hand there is the 40 per cent difference in pay, on the other, the need for sufficient pharmacists. Given that stark choice, a tribunal could easily hold that the difference in pay was justified. Indeed that was the result in the EAT in *Enderby* [1991] ICR 382 ...

A similar uncertainty has dogged American case law. In the seminal US Supreme Court case *Griggs v Duke Power* (1971) 401 US 424, Burger CJ stated (at 431): 'The touchstone is business necessity. If an employment practice which operates to exclude

Negroes cannot be shown to be related to job performance, the practice is prohibited.' However, later he said (at 432): 'Congress has placed on the employer the burden of showing that any given requirement must have a manifest relationship to the employment in question.' Here we have two standards ('business necessity' and 'manifest relationship') in the same speech. Subsequent Supreme Court pronouncements have vacillated between the two, giving for instance, 'significant correlation' and 'necessary'. (From respectively *Albermarle Paper v Moody* 1975 422 US 405, at 431 and *Dothard v Rawlinson* 1977 433 US 321, at 331.) This uncertainty was codified by the Civil Rights Act 1991, which stated that a practice must be 'job related for the position in question and consistent with business necessity.' (42 USCS s 2000e-2, (k)(1)(A)(i)).

However, different standards of justification in the United States matter little where alternatives exist because the Supreme Court has developed a separate 'alternative practice' doctrine. ...[154]

None of this is to say that British courts will refuse to *consider* alternatives in the justification debate ... Indeed the Court of Appeal remitted *Allonby's* case for reconsideration because, among other things, the tribunal had not considered the 'obvious' alternatives open to the College. Of course asking a tribunal to 'consider' an alternative in the 'balance' test is different from ruling that the mere existence of an alternative will defeat the justification defence. Sedley LJ's judgement further departs from *Bilka* ... [He] diluted *Bilka* by qualifying 'necessary' with '*reasonably* necessary' ... He spoke only of *obvious* alternatives. This is the language of compromise. One can only conclude that he intended a broad-brush approach. Tribunals should only consider 'fairly obvious' alternatives. This deepens the impression (eg, given in *Ojutiku* and *Hampson*) that the English courts will apply *Bilka* in form only, whilst actually subjecting employers to the lower *Hampson* standard of justification ...

[T]his does not mean that the difference between *Hampson* and *Bilka* is merely a matter of degree. It is a fundamental difference. The compromise in the *Hampson* test upsets the theory of indirect discrimination. Where a practice having a disparate impact is shown to be absolutely necessary to achieve a genuine non-discriminatory goal, then the cause of the disparate impact lies elsewhere. No action lies against the employer. The cause(s) of any disparate impact can only be identified if the courts impose a strict test of necessity. A lesser standard gives employers leeway to discriminate and blurs the causes of a disparate impact. As *Enderby's* case illustrates, 'excess' disparate impact amounts to discrimination.

Logically, this difference should disappear with the new domestic statutory definitions, which expressly include 'proportionate'. Yet if the courts persist with the view that 'necessary' (or proportionate) means *reasonably* necessary, and is satisfied with the *Hampson* balancing test, the difference will remain. However, the following extract suggests that the complexities of assessing an employer's justification may well blur any differences between the two definitions.

Townshend-Smith, R, 'Justifying indirect discrimination in English and American law: how stringent should the test be?' (1995) 1 IJDL 103, pp 106–10:

The task of the law is to reconcile the competing interests of the employer in efficiency and profits with those of members of the group seeking economic advancement. The assumption is that the employer must be allowed to hire, promote and pay more to those who are truly better employees, while at the same time artificial and irrational

---

154 See below, p 281.

barriers to the economic advancement of protected groups can be challenged. As it will already have been shown that the challenged condition has a disparate impact, it logically follows that the burden of proof is on the employer to show that it is justified. As the rationale for permitting justification is that the employer's economic and other business objectives must be respected, it further follows that the employer's argument is only worthy of respect if it can be shown that the employer's policy will indeed have the result claimed for it.

This point is the heart of the requirement for objective justification. But even if the employer is successful in proving this causal connection, he may still fail on the basis of what has come to be known as the principle of proportionality. First, the plaintiff may win if it can be established that there was a means of achieving the same objective which had less of a disparate impact. Secondly, the employer may also lose if the court considers that the gain to the employer from being allowed to continue with the practice is outweighed by the discriminatory consequences to the protected group ... [T]he decision on this issue is at bottom an issue of competing social policy values, is a matter for the court and of course depends enormously on judicial sensitivity to the social objectives of the legislation.

[O]n the question of objective proof that there is a causal link between the challenged policy and the employer's objectives, the two competing policy objectives are ... clear. On the one hand, employers must not be permitted to utilise practices with an adverse impact which cannot be proved to achieve business objectives. On the other hand, the standard at which that proof is set must not be so stringent as to be virtually unattainable, for that would logically lead to the use of surreptitious quotas, contrary to legislative policy ...

The task of the law is to produce a standard of justification which is sensitive to both of these policy objectives ... While it is important to examine what courts have said on the matter, it is contended that too often judicial *dicta* have been uttered with no awareness of the practical problems of application, or of how employers are supposed to discharge the burden laid upon them ...

There are three interconnected reasons why a standard less than full objective justification must necessarily be applied by courts and tribunals. The first reason concerns the appropriate role for statistics in an indirect discrimination claim. The second reason is to ensure that subjective employment practices are potentially challengeable via indirect discrimination law. The third concerns the very notion of the concept of 'necessity'.

A standard of literal objective justification requires that the employer prove on a balance of probabilities that the challenged practice will have the effect claimed for it. Almost by definition, this entails statistical proof that the workers concerned manifest higher productivity or efficiency. To require proper statistical proof would demand of tribunals and, more importantly, applicants, a familiarity with statistical techniques which is inappropriate. I am not arguing that statistics are always irrelevant, either to the original establishment of adverse impact or to prove of justification; I am simply arguing that these matters should in appropriate cases be provable without elaborate statistical techniques ...

The second reason why statistical proof should not be essential follows on from the above ... It is appropriate that a *prima facie* case of indirect discrimination should be raised merely by a statistically significant numerical disparity ... If such procedures cannot be validated, courts and tribunals will not allow the *prima facie* case to be established. The process of justification must permit reliance on best practice even if such practice cannot be proved to be effective. As jobs increase in their complexity and as people are increasingly hired for what they are rather than what they can do, it is essential that indirect discrimination is not relegated to traditional low-level jobs. In many situations it is impossible to define good job performance in such a way as to permit its scientific measurement ... If such practices were immune from legal challenge based on indirect discrimination, that would be some incentive for employers to utilise subjective and therefore unchallengeable practices in preferences to more objective procedures ...

The third reason why a statistical numerical approach cannot by itself be adequate concerns the very concept of 'necessity'. Necessity is not an abstract concept; whether something is necessary requires consideration for what and to whom the requirement is said to be necessary. This means that necessity has to be decided in the light of the employer's objective ... The law rightly requires the employer to identify which objective is sought to be achieved via the challenged requirement, but has fought shy of evaluating the merits of the objective itself. There is a great deal of difference between saying that a requirement is necessary to achieve an objective, and saying that the objective is itself necessary. While the former is admittedly extremely difficult, the second is highly interventionist and judgmental ...

It is therefore appropriate that courts are relatively deferential to the objectives of the employer. They should be far less deferential to the means chosen. Even if it can be shown that the means chosen will achieve the objective, the employer's case is not proven. It is necessary ... to consider the degree of adverse impact and thus the amount of social harm in need of remedy, and whether there are any alternatives which might achieve nearly the same result in a less discriminatory way ... There is no escape from the need to make a value judgment evaluating the degree of the adverse impact ... the social benefit of the employer's objective, whether the objective is likely to be achieved by the requirement, and whether or not the objective can be achieved by an alternative method.

(ii)   Defences based upon discrimination

It is implicit in the *Bilka* test that the justification must not be related to the ground of discrimination in question. The ECJ has expressed this consistently. For example, in *Jenkins v Kingsgate*,[155] it stated the factors used as a defence should be objectively justified and 'in no way related to any discrimination based on sex'. This was expressed in the SDA 1975 and the RRA 1976 (eg, 'justifiable irrespective of sex/race'), but was not restated in the new domestic definitions. However, it should come under the general expressed principle of proportionality, and it is inconceivable that the new definitions, based upon EC law, differ in substance on this matter. The issue is likely to arise where employers respond to a law giving rights to a protected group by manoeuvring that group into a position where those rights are not applicable. This appeared to be the case in *Allonby*.

> *Allonby v Accrington & Rossendale College* [2001] EWCA Civ 529; [2001] IRLR 364; [2001] ICR 1189, CA

Accrington & Rossendale College employed 341 part-time lecturers on successive one-year contracts. In 1996, legislation came into force obliging the College to afford to

---

155 [1981] IRLR 228, para 13. See below, p 286. See also *Bilka* [1986] IRLR 317, para 19.

their part-time lecturers equal benefits to those given to their full-time lecturers.[156] Faced with the extra expense, the College responded by terminating the contracts with all its part-time lecturers and re-employing them as sub-contractors, through an agency. Consequently, the part-timers were paid less and lost a series of benefits (eg, sick pay). Ms Allonby, a part-time lecturer, brought several actions against the College. One was for indirect sex discrimination.

In the employment tribunal, Ms Allonby proved her *prima facie* case that the new arrangement had caused a disparate impact on women, who made up some two-thirds of the part-time lecturers, but only about half of the full-timers. In effect, the dismissals fell disproportionately upon women. However, the tribunal found that the new arrangement was *justified* for two reasons: first, to save money, estimated at about £13,000 per year; secondly, to impose control over the hiring of part-time staff, which had in the past been left to individual team leaders. Ms Allonby appealed to the Court of Appeal, arguing that the College had failed to justify the measures because (a) less-discriminatory alternative measures existed to achieve the College's goals, and (b) the measures were themselves based on discrimination. The Court of Appeal allowed her appeal chiefly because the tribunal failed to consider any 'fairly obvious' alternatives or apply an 'objective balance' (*Hampson*) test. On this failure, Sedley LJ said that: 'In particular there is no recognition [by the tribunal] that if the aim of the dismissal was itself discriminatory ... it could never afford justification.'[157] Surprisingly, the judge said no more than that on the issue. This point was explored in the following commentary on the case.

Connolly, M, 'Discrimination law: justification, alternative measures and defences based on sex' [2001] 30 ILJ 311, pp 316–17:

Ms Allonby cited *R v Sec of State, ex p EOC* [1994] 1 All ER 910 and *R v Sec of State, ex p Seymour-Smith*.[158] In *Ex p EOC* (the case that led to the Regulations) Lord Keith held (at 922) that the existing Regulations that afforded lesser benefits to part-time workers constituted a 'gross breach of the principle of equal pay and could not be possibly regarded as a suitable means of achieving an increase in part-time employment.' In *ex p Seymour-Smith* the ECJ, when giving a ruling on justification, stated (at para 75) that a Government measure 'cannot have the effect of frustrating the implementation of a fundamental principle of Community law such as that of equal pay ...'

Those cases concerned Government measures made in pursuance of a social policy. In such cases the ECJ allows a Government a 'broad margin of discretion' (see eg *ex p Seymour-Smith* at para 74), which is less onerous than the *Bilka* test. In *Allonby* the 'measure' (ie dismissals) was taken by a College employer and should be judged by the stricter *Bilka* standard. The express aim of the measure was to give (predominantly female) part-time lecturers less benefits and pay. That too was a gross breach of the fundamental principle of equal pay and accordingly should never be justified. On this point alone Ms Allonby should prevail.

---

156 Although not specified by the EAT or the Court of Appeal this was presumably the Employment Protection (Part-time Employees) Regulations 1995, passed in response to *R v Secretary of State for Employment ex p EOC* [1994] 1 All ER 910, where the House of Lords held that existing legislation prescribing inferior rights to part-time workers was incompatible with Community sex discrimination law.

157 At para 29.

158 See p 109 (fn 9) and p 295 respectively.

There lies a related line of argument here. Section 1(1)(b), SDA provides that the measure must be justified 'irrespective' of sex ... The dismissals were made in response to the Regulations of 1995 passed to afford equal benefits to part-time workers because they are predominantly female. The reports are vague as to the relationship between the stated goals – to save money and control the hiring of part-time lecturers – and the introduction of the Regulations. In the EAT (EAT/1081/98, Transcript) Lindsay's J sole observation was (at para 6): 'The College took the view that the costs attendant upon recent changes in the law as to part-time workers were too high for it'. In the Court of Appeal, Sedley LJ noted only (at para. 3) that things had become 'financially more onerous because of legislative changes which required part-time lecturers to be afforded equal ... benefits to full-time lecturers.'

It can be said, at the least, the new Regulations were the background of the dismissals. The question is, were the dismissals unrelated to sex? The immediate goal was to save money and gain control over hiring part-time staff. In *Orphanos v Queen Mary College* [1985] 2 All ER 233 the plaintiff challenged a requirement to be three-years ordinarily resident within the European Community, so to be exempt from full overseas student fees. The immediate goal for the requirement was to curtail public expenditure on education. The House of Lords held (at 239–230) that the requirement was 'so closely related' to nationality that it could not be justified and amounted to indirect racial discrimination. In *Allonby* the dismissals of a predominantly female group were inspired by Regulations aimed to afford equal benefits to women. It is at least arguable that the requirement is 'so closely related' to sex that it should not be justifiable ...

[I]t was surprising that the Court of Appeal made no comment on the law cited to support Ms Allonby's ... argument ... Could this be an early sign of another long-running difference between UK and EU discrimination law?

(iii)   The US alternative practice doctrine

In the USA, the Supreme Court developed the alternative practice doctrine. Should a *prima facie* case be met with a proper business necessity defence, the plaintiff may still win by proposing an alternative business practice which has a lesser discriminatory effect. This has since been recognised in the 1991 Civil Rights Act.[159] The rubric generally used, was set in *Albermarle Paper Co v Moody*[160] where it was stated that the alternative should 'also serve the employer's legitimate interest in "efficient and trustworthy workmanship"'.[161]

An example of a successful demonstration of an alternative practice can be seen in *Bridgeport Guardians v City of Bridgeport*,[162] where tests used in the promotion of police officers to the rank of sergeant were challenged. One hundred and seventy persons applied for 19 posts and the results showed[163] that the tests had a disparate impact on blacks and Hispanics, with only 30% and 46% respectively passing in comparison with 68% of whites. Hiwever, the real impact was worse than that because the 19 best performers were selected, leaving no minorities with promotion. The employer

---

159 Section 105, codified as 42 USCS s 2000e-2(k)(1), which also provides that the alternative practice doctrine should be applied according to pre-*Wards Cove* principles (see above, p 252).
160 422 US 405 (1975).
161 422 US 405, at p 425, citing *McDonnell Douglas Corp v Green* 411 US 792, at 802 (1973).
162 933 F 2d 1140 (1991) (CA 2nd Cir). See also above, p 265.
163 933 F 2d 1140 (1991), at p 1143. The results table is set out above, p 265.

successfully justified the tests as a reliable and accurate predictor of job performance. However, what the chart above does not reveal is that, of all those passing, the marks were extremely close. The plaintiffs put forward evidence that the difference between a few marks was insignificant. Accordingly, the plaintiffs suggested that the marks should be banded: that is, marks within, say, 8% of each other placed in a single band. The successful candidates could then be selected from those bands, using other (non-discriminatory) factors to decide. In this way the best performers were selected without a disparate impact. The court found that the use of banding would alleviate the disparate racial effect of the examination without imposing any significant burden on the defendants, whilst serving their legitimate interests.[164]

The doctrine has not been adopted by the EC or British schemes. However, a strict test of proportionality should achieve the same result. If a claimant can identify a less discriminatory alternative means of achieving the same aim, the justification should fail for being disproportionate. A rare British example arose in *Bohon-Mitchell v Common Professional Examination Board*.[165] It was the defendants' policy that persons with a degree in a subject other than law were required to take a course in academic law to qualify to take the Bar finals. This was normally a 12 month course. However, those with a non-British or non-Irish degree were required to complete a 21 month course. In 1978, Ms Bohon-Mitchell applied to take her Bar finals. She had been living in England (except for one year) since 1972 and was married to an Englishman. When she was informed that, as an American graduate, she would have to sit the 21 month course, she complained of discrimination under the RRA 1976 on grounds of nationality or national origin. The defendants tried to justify that requirement on the grounds that barristers needed a wide knowledge of the English way of life, and the simplest way of identifying those without such experience was by their degrees. The industrial tribunal held[166] that the requirement to sit a 21 month course was not justified because it was not *necessary* to achieve the aim. Instead, each candidate's familiarity with the English way of life could be assessed on a case by case basis. If the tribunal had taken the 'objective balance' *Hampson* approach, it may well have concluded that the means was justified. The evidence was that just eight out of 191 applicants with a non-law degree had 'overseas' degrees. Probably fewer than that eight had been resident in Britain and were therefore 'familiar with the English way of life'. In any case the discriminatory effect was relatively minor. If this discriminatory effect were weighed against the administrative costs of changing the system, a court may well find that defendant's administrative needs justified the practice. In other words, discrimination could be allowed to continue because that would be more convenient for the defendant.[167]

---

164 *Ibid*, at pp 1145 and 1148.
165 [1978] IRLR 525. Also contrast the respective approaches of the EAT and ECJ in *Enderby v Frenchay HA*; see pp 276 and 420.
166 *Ibid*, at 530, para 29.
167 See also Connolly, M, 'Discrimination law: justification, alternative measures and defences based on sex' [2001] 30 ILJ 311, extracted above, p 276.

(b)   Examples of the defence

(i)   Seniority

Seniority may be relevant to employment benefits in a number of different ways. For example, incremental pay systems mean that greater seniority may be associated with higher pay; total accumulated seniority profoundly affects pension entitlement; priority for promotion or other benefits may be dependent on seniority as may access to fringe benefits; and reverse seniority – last-in, first-out – remains an extremely common method of selecting employees for redundancy. In the USA, where employment benefits are even more dependent on seniority than in the UK, many indirect discrimination cases have arisen where a prior pattern of direct discrimination prevented black people from acquiring the seniority which at a later date might be crucial for the allocation of benefits, even though s 703(h) of the Civil Rights Act 1964 provides a specific defence for 'bona fide seniority systems'.[168]

(ii)   Part-time workers and family issues

It is now a truism to say that any distinction between part-time and full-time workers is *prima facie* indirect discrimination against women, so much so, that discrimination against part-time workers is now provided for in legislation.

Part-time Workers (Prevention of Less Favourable Treatment) Regulations 2000[169]

5 Less favourable treatment of part-time workers

(1)   A part-time worker has the right not to be treated by his employer less favourably than the employer treats a comparable full-time worker—

(a) as regards the terms of his contract; or

(b) by being subjected to any other detriment by any act, or deliberate failure to act, of his employer.

(2)   The right conferred by paragraph (1) applies only if—

(a) the treatment is on the ground that the worker is a part-time worker, and

(b) the treatment is not justified on objective grounds.

(3)   In determining whether a part-time worker has been treated less favourably than a comparable full-time worker the *pro rata* principle shall be applied unless it is inappropriate.

(4)   A part-time worker paid at a lower rate for overtime worked by him in a period than a comparable full-time worker is or would be paid for overtime worked by him in the same period shall not, for that reason, be regarded as treated less favourably than the comparable full-time worker where, or to the extent that, the total number of hours worked by the part-time worker in the period, including overtime, does not exceed the number of hours the comparable full-

---

168 See *International Brotherhood of Teamsters v United States* 431 US 324 (1977); *California Brewers Association v Bryant* 444 US 598 (1980).

169 SI 2000/1551, which came into force on 1 July 2000, implementing Directive 97/81/EC. For a commentary concluding that the protections given by the regulations are too few and too narrow, see McColgan, A, 'Missing the point? The Part-time Workers (Prevention of Less Favourable Treatment) Regulations 2000 (SI 2000, No 1551)' [2000] 29 ILJ 260. See also Schmidt, M 'The right to part-time work under German law: progress in or a boomerang for equal employment opportunities?' [2001] 30 ILJ 335.

time worker is required to work in the period, disregarding absences from work and overtime.

Accordingly, most cases of discrimination against part-time workers will turn on the justification.

Many employees would value the opportunity to work part-time; the question has arisen whether it may be indirectly discriminatory to deny women the opportunity to jobshare or work only part of a week.[170]

Home Office v Holmes [1984] IRLR 299; [1985] 1 WLR 71; [1984] 3 All ER 549, EAT

After the birth of her baby, a woman applied to return to her previous full-time post on a part-time basis. The request was refused. An industrial tribunal found this to be unlawful indirect discrimination and that the condition or requirement of full-time work was not justified.

The EAT dismissed the appeal.

Waite J (pp 301–02):

The scheme of the anti-discrimination legislation involves casting a wide net throwing upon employers the onus of justifying the relevant requirement or condition ... One must be careful, however, not to fall into the error of assuming that because the net is wide, the catch will inevitably be large. [Counsel for the employers] eloquently invited us to consider the shock to British industry and to our national and local government administration which, he submitted, would be bound to be suffered if ... they had to face a shoal of claims by women full-time workers alleging that it would be discriminatory to refuse them part-time status ... [W]e emphasise ... that this one case of the employee and her particular difficulties within her particular grade in her particular department stands very much upon its own ... There will be cases where the requirement for full-time staff can be shown to be sufficiently flexible as arguably not to amount to a requirement or condition at all. There will be cases where a policy favouring full-time staff exclusively within a particular grade or department is found to be justified. There will be cases where no actual or no sufficient detriment can be proved by the employee. All such cases will turn upon their own particular facts.

Greater Glasgow Health Board v Carey [1987] IRLR 484, EAT

A health visitor wanted to return to work following maternity leave on the basis that she would work full days for two-and-a-half or three days a week. The employers were only prepared to let her work every day of the week, either mornings or afternoons. The employer's view was that this arrangement was necessary to avoid the need for patient-sharing. The tribunal were not convinced that it was necessary for a health visitor to be available on each day of the week.

The EAT upheld the employer's appeal.

Lord Mayfield (p 489):

[W]e do not think that [the tribunal] had the efficiency of the service at the forefront of their mind ... The reasons stated [for the policy] were that health visiting work was mainly on a personal contact basis with the patient and not task-oriented; that therefore the family would discuss their personal problems with the health visitor, which were not always suitable to be recorded on the records; personal observations

---

170 See Cox, S, 'Flexible working after maternity leave: the legal framework' (1998) 78 EOR 10, esp pp 13–15.

of the home surroundings and relationships with other members of the family not always be put in detail on the record ... with the increasing emphasis on health visiting in cases of child abuse and granny abuse, if the same health visitor was not available on each day of the week that led to poor communication with general practitioners, social workers and other agencies. That was one of the problems which had been highlighted in cases of child abuse which had proceeded to court.

While it must be a question of fact whether part-time work or jobsharing will impair the efficiency of the organisation, the failure of the EAT in *Holmes* to give *any* guidance as to the appropriate criteria is dismal, especially as the facts were so typical. *Carey* shows, correctly, that the factors relevant to efficiency are not necessarily economic; there was not, and could not, be proof that the arrangements the employers favoured were strictly *necessary*; the concept of necessity seems inappropriate where the aim is for healthcare to be as effective as possible. It is also important to consider the degree of adverse impact: if the challenged policy is one with the potential to affect all female employees, it will be harder to justify than a policy, as in *Carey*, where the adverse impact is in part due to her individual situation and where the employer was prepared to countenance some degree of accommodation.

The European Court in *Bilka* held that Art 119 (now Art 141) 'does not have the effect of requiring an employer to organise its occupational pension schemes in such a manner as to take into account the particular difficulties faced by persons with family responsibilities in meeting the conditions for entitlement to such a pension'. There is thus no obligation on employers to assist with childcare and no obligation to count periods out of the workforce towards seniority or pension entitlements. However, the following case shows that there may be an obligation to take account of the fact that women have primary responsibility for childcare.

London Underground v Edwards (No 2) [1997] IRLR 157, EAT[171]

Having concluded that the new rostering arrangement had an adverse impact on women (see above, p 268), the EAT also concluded that its imposition was not justified.

Morison J (p 161):

There was evidence to justify the conclusion that London Underground could – and, we would add, should – have accommodated [her] personal requirements. She had been working for them for nearly 10 years. Her family demands were of a temporary nature. There were no complaints about her work ... London Underground were, we think, probably fully justified in rejecting the idea of a creche which would be unsuitable as a solution for a parent working unsocial hours. But ... there was good evidence that London Underground could have made arrangements which would not have been damaging to their business plans but which would have accommodated the reasonable demands of their employees ...

Although there is no direct correlation between the two, we would anticipate that ... the less justification London Underground had for the way they treated [her], the less likely it is that a tribunal will conclude that she has failed to show that the disproportionate effect of the condition was considerable.

---

171 The decision was upheld by the Court of Appeal [1998] IRLR 364, but there was no appeal on the justification issue.

This case is significant in two respects. First, the court demonstrated a real sympathy for the problems working mothers may have in juggling home and work responsibilities. The employer must at least consider whether assistance or accommodation is possible. While this is a potentially major advance, much will depend on the willingness of tribunals and the EAT to follow through this relatively interventionist perspective. Secondly, the link made between the issues of adverse impact and justification marks a rejection of a mechanistic point-by-point analysis of indirect discrimination law and a willingness to focus on the overall merits of the case. The caveat must be that the merits here may be have been too one-sided for the case to be of great use as a precedent: there was evidence that the employers were originally willing to accede to her demands but changed their mind following pressure from the predominantly male workforce.

It is normally unjustifiable to pay part-time workers at a lower rate than full-time workers.

Jenkins v Kingsgate **Case 96/80 [1981] IRLR 228; [1981] ECR 911; [1981] ICR 592; [1981] 1 WLR 972, ECJ**

The employers paid full-time workers 10% more than part-time workers, who were mostly women. The EAT referred the matter to the ECJ, asking whether Art 119 (now Art 141) and Directive 75/117 required parity of pay even where different hours were worked.

The ECJ held (para 13) that the difference in rates did not contravene Art 119 where: 'the difference in pay ... is attributable to factors which are objectively justified and are in no way related to any discrimination based on sex. Such may be the case, in particular, when ... the employer is endeavouring, on economic grounds which may be objectively justified, to encourage full-time work irrespective of the sex of the worker.'[172]

Rinner-Kuhn v FWW Spezial-Gebäudereinigung GmbH and Co KG **Case 171/88 [1989] IRLR 493; [1989] ECR 2743, ECJ**

German law required employers to pay sick pay for six weeks, but excluded from the entitlement those who worked less than 10 hours per week or 45 per month. Employers received an 80% rebate from the State on all payments made.

The European Court concluded that the payments constituted 'pay' under Art 119 (now Art 141); there was clearly *prima facie* indirect discrimination; the further question was whether the exclusion of some part-time workers could be justified.

---

172 The parts of the judgment quoted appear to reflect the standard approach to indirect discrimination. Elsewhere in the judgment, though, the Court appears to suggest that such a pay policy would only be unlawful if it was 'in reality discrimination based on the sex of the worker'. When the case returned to the EAT ([1981] IRLR 388; [1981] 1 WLR 1485), Browne-Wilkinson J identified the contradiction at the heart of the judgment of the ECJ, but held that, whatever European law provided, English law required the employer to show that the difference in pay was 'reasonably necessary in order to obtain some result (other than cheap female labour) which the employer desires for economic or other reasons'. Subsequent European Court decisions show that the proper interpretation of *Jenkins* is the same as that given to English law by the EAT.

Judgment (p 496):

[The employers' defence was] that workers who work less than 10 hours a week or 45 hours a month are not integrated in and connected with the undertaking in a way comparable to that of other workers.

However, these considerations only represent generalised statements concerning certain categories of workers and do not therefore admit the conclusion of objective criteria unrelated to any discrimination on grounds of sex. If, on the other hand, the Member State is in a position to establish that the means selected correspond to an objective necessary for its social policy and are appropriate and necessary for the attainment of that objective, the mere fact that the legislative provision affects a considerably greater number of female than of male workers cannot be regarded as an infringement of Art 119.

Kowalska v Freie und Hansestadt Hamburg Case C-33/89 [1990] IRLR 447; [1990] ECR I-2591; [1992] ICR 29, ECJ

The applicant was a part-time law clerk whose employment relationship was governed by a public sector collective agreement. That agreement provided for a severance payment where the employment was terminated for reasons not attributable to the person concerned, such as reaching retiring age. Entitlement to such payments was limited to those who worked at least 38 hours per week.

The European Court again held that the payment constituted pay and that there was *prima facie* indirect discrimination.

The Court held that the outcome of collective agreements was just as subject to Art 119 (now Art 141) as other means of determining pay levels. To establish justification, the *Bilka* test would need to be satisfied.

These cases establish a number of basic principles. First, it makes no difference what is the source for the pay discrimination – or any other form of discrimination – against part-time workers. Whether it be employer fiat, collective bargaining or statutory regulation, the same principles of justification apply. The employer's argument must be tightly focused on the precise objective and whether the policy will achieve the objective. Generalised assumptions or traditions will not suffice. Given that it is the employers' choice to organise a workplace with part-time employees, presumably because some benefit is perceived from such a system, it is hard to imagine that *any* employer-generated differentiation between part-time and full-time workers will be justifiable. A possible exception is a rule which excludes membership of pension schemes – and perhaps other fringe benefits – to employees who work very few hours per week; arguably the inevitably high turnover amongst such employees provides an adequate administrative justification for differentiating between full-time and part-time workers. However, the principles may be applied rather less rigorously where a social policy argument is advanced by the government for a statutory distinction whose primary focus is not to differentiate between full-time and part-time employees as regards terms and conditions of employment.[173]

However, if the differentiation does not impact upon all part-time workers, the employer's task may be easier.

173 See below, pp 290–98.

Barry v Midland Bank plc [1999] 1 WLR 1465; [1999] ICR 859; [1999] 3 All ER 974, HL

The case concerned the way in which severance payments were calculated. Ms Barry argued that to base the calculation upon the fact that, when she left the bank's employ, she worked part-time, took insufficient account of the fact that 11 of her 13 years' service had been full-time. She was arguing for a *pro rata* method of calculation rather than one based on final salary. The House of Lords held that the scheme did not, in any case, adversely affect women. Lord Nicholls went on to hold that, even if the scheme did adversely affect women, it could be justified.[174]

> Lord Nicholls (p 1477):
>
> Further, under a restructured [*pro rata*] scheme there would be losers as well as winners. Some employees, such as Mrs Barry, would benefit, but others would be worse off. By the same token that it is reasonable to infer that the disadvantaged group is predominantly comprised of women, so it is reasonable to infer that the presently advantaged group (those whose average hours are less than their hours at termination) is mostly comprised of women. There is no evidence showing how these groups compare in size ... In 1992 the majority of changes in hours by female employees were increases, not decreases, but this is not a satisfactory basis for drawing any clear conclusions about the size or extent of the two groups. However, even in the absence of evidence it is reasonable to infer that under the restructured scheme there would be a significant number of losers, and that these would be mostly women. They would be mostly women because, as already noted, fluctuating hours of work is a characteristic principally confined to women.
>
> In these circumstances ... the bank's scheme is lawful. Its objects are of sufficient importance to override the weight to be given to the fact that under a different scheme with a different object a group of employees, mostly women, would be better off. To decide otherwise would be to compel the bank to abandon its scheme and substitute a scheme where severance pay is treated and calculated, not as compensation for loss of a job, but as additional pay for past work. That could not be right. I am reassured in my conclusion by noting that the same point was decided in the same way by the German Federal Labour Court (*Bundesarbeitsgericht*) in case no 10 AZR 129/92 (28 October 1992), *Entscheidungssammlung zum Arbeitsrecht* 247/65.

(iii)   Testing and educational qualifications[175]

Tests are potentially beneficial from an equal opportunities standpoint. It is an inappropriate and dangerous strategy to insist on such high and expensive standards of validation that testing will be abandoned. In America, such abandonment sometimes led to the use of quotas. Whatever is felt about this development, it would not happen in the UK; more subjective and thus potentially discriminatory practices would be substituted. It is, however, perfectly consistent both to defend testing and to demand that tests follow best professional practice, with a potential indirect

---

174 Lords Steyn, Hoffmann and Clyde concurred. Lord Slynn confined his decision to the issue of adverse effect.

175 See also the discussion on causation above, p 254.

discrimination claim if they fail.[176] This imposes an appropriate standard which is capable of being met.

Wood, R, 'Psychometrics should make assessment fairer' (1996) 67 EOR 27, pp 32–33:

It is undeniable that certain kinds of ability tests, specifically those of the verbal reasoning variety, will tend to disadvantage people from ethnic minorities, the reason being – and this will vary within and between minorities ... – that their understanding of written English is less secure than that of the people from the majority group they are competing against ... [O]utlawing tests is not the answer ... You would only end up using something less valid and reliable, like an interview, and make worse hiring decisions ... In the *Brent Council* case ... the council allowed the test results to be overridden by interview results, which only worsened the position of many ethnic minority applicants ...

In these circumstances it is necessary to proceed carefully. When using test scores to exclude applicants, set the lowest pass score which is sensible given the numbers involved. This will tend to minimise the numbers of those who score poorly on the tests, but could do the job if hired ... As a result of employing [such] a conservative strategy, most of the people you have rejected will be people who are appropriately rejected. It is likely that there will still be a disproportionate number of people from ethnic minorities among this number but there is nothing you can do about this given that, as well as being historically rooted, the causes lie elsewhere.

What you can do is to make sure that minority people have access to practice materials and the opportunity to familiarise themselves with the tests, and with testing generally. [British Rail did this] for people already employed – doing it for people you are not yet employing is another matter altogether.

As for personality questionnaires, there is no body of evidence which would substantiate bias against people from ethnic minorities, but ... it could happen. There may also be bias against women in some circumstances. But ... we do not know very much about what happens when these questionnaires are used in a 'hard' way. Just because they seem harmless is not a good reason for rushing around using them.

(iv)   Physical and health and safety justifications

While the decline in the proportion of jobs which require physical strength is a factor in the increasing proportion of women in the labour market, it remains the case that strength or other physical attributes continue to be job requirements in some areas of employment. No requirement of physical strength or stamina may be a genuine occupational qualification.[177] It is unlawful direct discrimination to exclude *all* women from a job on the basis that few will be able to meet the relevant strength requirement. Employers are required to impose a standard common to both male and female applicants and, on the assumption that fewer women than men meet the standard,

---

176 In *Guardians Association v Civil Service Commission* 630 F 2d 79 (2d Cir 1980), it was said that the requirements for an acceptable test were: a suitable job analysis, reasonable competence in the actual construction of the test, test content must relate to and be representative of job content, and the system of scoring must appropriately select those better at performing the job. On testing generally, see Pearn, M, Kandola, R and Mottram, R, *Selection Tests and Sex Bias: The Impact of Selection Testing on the Employment Opportunities of Men and Women*, 1987, Manchester: EOC; *Towards Fair Selection: A Survey of Test Practice and Thirteen Case Studies*, 1993, London: Commission for Racial Equality.

177 SDA 1975, s 7(2)(a).

that is potentially justifiable. How this is to be done will vary according to the circumstances. Employers may not, for example, be able to test ability to lift weights, because failure leading to injury might conceivably lead to a tort claim and a health and safety prosecution. It may thus be permissible to use a height or weight requirement as a proxy for strength, or to require experience in the kind of work, a requirement which would clearly tend to exclude women.[178] Moreover, machinery designed for the average man may make the job impractical for most women; a height requirement would be imposed not because the job intrinsically needs it but because of the machine used to do the job. A requirement to make adjustments to previously accepted ways of working might be appropriate, but tribunals might understandably be reluctant to impose such obligation on employers with few employees. Safety rules with an adverse impact will arguably be easier to justify than many other rules with an adverse impact. Many cases where a justification is alleged raise issues of competing social values; it is arguable that the avoidance of physical injury is a more fundamental value than the avoidance of discrimination.

In relation to gender, the focus of attention so far as health and safety is concerned has been on issues relating to pregnancy and reproductive risks, discussed earlier.[179] Here, the discrimination is likely to be direct rather than indirect. In relation to race, the issue has surfaced where a cultural norm in relation to clothing or appearance might carry a health and safety risk. Thus, in *Singh v British Rail Engineering Ltd*,[180] it was held to be justifiable to insist that all employees, including Sikhs, wear protective headgear, and in *Singh v Rowntree Mackintosh Ltd*[181] and *Panesar v The Nestle Co Ltd*,[182] it was held to be justifiable to prohibit the wearing of beards in confectionery factories in order to reduce the risk of contamination by facial hair. It was held that the defence of justification was not defeated by the fact that the employers did not adopt the 'no beards' policy in each of their factories. Such argument might often be conclusive against the employers, but in the health and safety context it might to be permissible to introduce new criteria, even if only as an experiment to determine whether safety might indeed be improved. However, this experiment must still be shown to be a suitable means of achieving a real need.

(v)   Social policy justifications

It may happen that justifications are put forward which seek to advance a broader social policy than merely the efficient and profitable operation of the enterprise. For example, in *Greater Manchester Police Authority v Lea*,[183] the plaintiff was not appointed to a police job because he was in receipt of an occupational pension following his compulsory medical retirement. The policy was to exclude those in receipt of such pensions and to consider only those who were unemployed. However high-minded the policy might have been, it was not justifiable because the reason for the policy was not related to a particular need of the employer for workers who met the requirement.

---

178 For a detailed American case on this issue, see *Dothard v Rawlinson* 433 US 321 (1977), above, p 252.
179 See above, p 212 *et al*.
180 [1986] ICR 22, EAT.
181 [1979] ICR 554; [1979] IRLR 199, EAT.
182 [1980] IRLR 60, EAT; upheld by CA [1980] ICR 44 (note); [1980] IRLR 64.
183 [1990] IRLR 372, EAT.

In *Board of Governors of St Matthias Church of England School v Crizzle*,[184] it was held that a requirement that the head teacher of a church school should be a 'committed communicant Christian' was justifiable despite its adverse impact on Asians. The EAT concluded that the school's objectives could legitimately be regarded as wider than the mere provision of an efficient education, and that the challenged requirement was appropriate, bearing in mind the ethos of the school. This is a social policy justification, prioritising the right of religious groups to employ those whose beliefs accord with the employers. The EAT had no difficulty in finding for the employers, failing to grasp the competing policy issues at stake.

However, in some instances, the effective cause of the adverse impact is not a policy or practice of the employer, but a legislative or other State-employed requirement. Two issues arise here. One is procedural, the other is the standard of justification required in such cases.

The procedural problem is that unless the case proceeds by judicial review, the employer may be in the position of defending the government's social policy. Where the case progresses to the ECJ, a Member State may make representations.[185] For domestic courts, the issue arose in *Rutherford*.

Harvest Town Circle Ltd v Rutherford [2001] IRLR 599; [2002] ICR 123, EAT

Sections 109 and 156 of the Employment Rights Act exclude persons over 65 years of age from unfair dismissal rights and redundancy payments, respectively. Mr Rutherford was dismissed, aged 67, and argued that ss 109 and 156 were contrary to EC discrimination law as they indirectly discriminated against men. The employment tribunal found that the exclusions adversely affected men,[186] and as Harvest Ltd produced no evidence to justify the exclusions, the tribunal concluded that the exclusions were not justified. The EAT held this to be an error of law. It should have, if necessary, summoned the Secretary of State.

Lindsay J (President, pp 604–05):

> The employment tribunal was obliged to conduct the hearing in such manner as it considered most appropriate for the clarification of the issues before it – employment tribunal rule 9(1). It would be quite unreasonable to expect a small company such as Harvest Town Circle Ltd itself to be familiar with the objective justifications arguably available to support important primary legislation such as ss 109 and 156. Where the validity of primary legislation affecting literally hundreds of thousands of people is in issue, it seems to us essential, if the parties have not themselves made adequate arrangements for evidence being given on the subject of objective justification, that the tribunal itself should take pains to see that it is sufficiently informed on the

---

184 [1993] IRLR 112; [1993] ICR 401, EAT. The Employment (Religion or Belief) Regulations 2003, reg 7, provide exceptions where there is a genuine and determining occupational requirement related to a religion or belief, or where the employer has an ethos based on religion or belief and a religion or belief is a genuine occupational requirement. The Human Rights Act 1998, s 13, requires courts to have 'particular regard to the importance of' the right to freedom of religion in Art 9. It was introduced following concern by churches that the Act may curtail their freedom to exclude persons as employees or church members and to choose who can be married in church.

185 See, eg, *Jenkins v Kingsgate*, C-96/80; [1981] ECR 911; *Barber v Guardian Royal Exchange* C-262/88 [1990] ECR I-1889.

186 The EAT found that the employment tribunal used the wrong comparison and remitted the case for a rehearing, where, using a different comparison, an employment tribunal found, again, that men were adversely affected by the exclusions. See [2002] IRLR 768. Discussed in Chapter 6, p 167.

subject. The matter cannot properly be left simply on the basis that there is an onus on one party or another and that the onus has been left undischarged. The obvious course, in a case such as the one at hand, was for the employment tribunal to have requested an invitation to be sent to the Secretary of State in order that he might consider what arguments there were by way of objective justification. Given that State and other pensions are commonly paid from age 65 or even earlier and that in a sense it may be that every employee over 65 who remains in work might thereby exclude some younger (unpensioned) person from the same job, the existence of possible objective justifications irrespective of sex seems to us so obvious, and informed argument on the point to be so essential to a just decision, that for the employment tribunal to fail invite the Secretary of State to be joined represents, in our view, an error of law.[187] Of course, he could decline to be joined or, even if joined, could decline to take any active part. If necessary, witness summonses could be used and the Secretary of State may, if necessary, be joined as a party against his will ... Where literally hundreds of similar cases could arise, it would plainly be unjust for some cases, indistinguishable from one another, to be decided in his absence to one effect and then others to be decided otherwise because of his presence, nor would it be helpful if he was bound by the result in one (having been joined as a party) but not in others (because he was not so joined).

For the second issue – the standard of justification in these cases – special considerations apply. The *Bilka* test is modified, first because it is the objective of the *policy*, not the employer, which must be considered and, secondly, because it is arguable that a somewhat more lenient approach should be taken. This is not at all to say that justifications in such cases will ever be straightforward. They will still require proper evidence. In *Rinner-Kuhn*,[188] the statutory policy of excluding some part-time workers from sick pay was subject to *Bilka*, and in *R v Secretary of State for Employment ex p EOC*,[189] the evidence provided by the Government as to why it was necessary to exclude part-time workers from statutory protections was so inadequate as clearly to fail the test. These cases, however, concern part-time workers, where the degree of adverse impact is so great that the operation of the proportionality test is likely to mean that any purported justification will fail.

Where the facts are less clear-cut, there are now numerous examples of a less rigorous standard being applied.

Kirshammer-Hack v Sidal Case C-189/91 [1994] IRLR 185; [1993] ECR I-6185

The German law on protection from unfair dismissal does not apply to small businesses – businesses with five or less than five employees. In determining this number, no account is taken of those who work less than 10 hours per week or 45 per month.

The applicant's complaint of unfair dismissal was inadmissible, not because of her lack of hours but because of those of some of the others who worked in her dental surgery.

---

187 In the rehearing, the Secretary of State offered a rather lamer defence than this, which the ET rejected. See [2002] IRLR 768.

188 See above, p 286.

189 See above, p 109 (fn 9).

Judgment (p 188):

[L]egislation like that in question forms part of a group of measures intended to alleviate the constraints on small businesses, which play an essential role in economic development and job creation within the Community ... [I]t should be stressed that by providing that directives adopted relating to the health and safety of employees shall avoid imposing administrative financial and legal constraints in a way which hold back the creation and development of small and medium-sized undertakings, Art 118A ... indicates that these undertakings can be the object of special economic measures.

This decision is out of line with the more rigorous approach adopted in other cases, and with British law as epitomised by the *EOC* case. However, the finding on justification followed a holding that no adverse impact was established. Again, the two issues run together to reach what is overall considered to be a fair result. Such arguments as were here successful are, in any event, inapplicable to a case against an individual employer.

There is some evidence that the European Court will be at its most lenient in relation to matters of social security; here, the policy decisions may most suitably be resolved by national courts and a finding of indirect justification in relation to one benefit would be very likely to have serious knock-on effects elsewhere.

Nolte v Landesversicherungsanstalt Hannover **Case C-317/93**

Megner v Innungskrankenkasse Vorderpfalz **Case C-444/93**

[1996] IRLR 225; [1996] All ER (EC) 212

The first case concerned a challenge to German social security rules which classed employment for less than 15 hours per week as 'minor employment', on which contributions were not payable. In consequence, when she became ill, she received no benefits. In the second case, the complainants sought a ruling that deductions should be made from wages for similar employment.

There is no doubt that such provisions were indirectly discriminatory. The Court, in effectively identical judgments in the two cases, concluded that the German Government had provided adequate justification.

Judgment (p 235):

[T]he German Government argues, in particular, that the exclusion of persons in minor employment from compulsory insurance corresponds to a structural principle of the German social security scheme.

The German Government further explains that there is a social demand for minor employment, that it considers that it should respond to that demand in the context of its social policy by fostering the existence and supply of such employment and that the only means of doing this within the structural framework of the German social security scheme is to exclude minor employment from compulsory insurance.

In addition, the German Government contends that the jobs lost would not be replaced by full or part-time jobs subject to compulsory insurance. On the contrary, there would be an increase in unlawful employment (black work) and a rise in circumventing devices (for instance, false self-employment) in view of the social demand for minor employment.

[I]n the current state of Community law, social policy is a matter for the Member States ... Consequently, it is for the Member States to choose the measures capable of achieving the aim of their social and employment policy. In exercising that competence, the Member States have a broad margin of discretion.

It should be noted that the social and employment policy aim relied on by the German Government is objectively unrelated to any discrimination on grounds of sex and that, in exercising its competence, the national legislature was reasonably entitled to consider that the legislation in question was necessary to achieve that aim.[190]

However, the more lenient approach is not restricted to matters of social security.

Kuratorium für Dialyse und Nierentransplantation Ev v Lewark Case C-457/93 [1996] IRLR 637

German legislation which gives members of staff committees a right to time off without loss of pay in order to attend relevant training courses provides that both full-time and part-time workers attending a course are compensated up to the limit of their normal working hours. In *Botel*,[191] it was held that such a provision is indirectly discriminatory and requires objective justification.

The complainant in this case worked four days a week and attended a course in respect of a day when she would not otherwise have been working. She was not compensated for that day.

Judgment (p 646):

The German Government considers that ... it is justified by the principle that staff council members are not paid, which is intended to ensure their independence ... from both internal and external pressures.

Such a social policy aim appears in itself to be unrelated to any discrimination on grounds of sex [and in itself is a worthy aim].

[T]he legislation is likely to discourage part-time workers from performing staff council functions or acquiring the knowledge necessary for performing them, thus making it more difficult for that category of worker to be represented by qualified staff council members.

Advocate General (pp 642–43):

A distinction can ... be drawn between economic grounds and social policy grounds. Where it is alleged that a difference in treatment between men and women is justified on economic grounds, it is usually necessary to evaluate the specific circumstances of the case, taking into account, *inter alia*, the requirements of the market and of the

---

190 See also *Jones v Chief Adjudication Officer* [1990] IRLR 533, CA, where, in the context of a very complex claim alleging indirect discrimination in the operation of social security provisions, Mustill LJ observed: 'I think it is essential when considering proportionality in the context of the Directive to be very clear about the issue which the national court is called upon to decide. What the court does not have to decide is whether it represents a sensible and moderate way of giving effect to a general legislative policy. Those general questions fall within the purview of the national legislature and of the national constitutional court, if the Member State possesses one, and are not the concern of European law. What the national court must do is to identify with precision those features of the measure under attack which discriminate against members of one sex either directly by their terms or indirectly by their effect. The court must then consider whether *those features* are the unavoidable consequence of a justifiable policy, not in itself of a sexual discriminatory nature.

The task is not to assess the general merits of [the] regulation ... but to consider whether those features of it which are sexually discriminatory can be validated on the grounds of a sexually neutral social policy.'

191 *Arbeiterwohlfahrt der Stadt Berlin eV v Monika Botel* Case C-360/90 [1992] IRLR 423, ECJ.

employer concerned. Where a difference in treatment arises directly from national legislation and it is alleged that it is justified by reasons of social policy, it is less likely that the specific circumstances of the employees and of the employer concerned will be of decisive influence. In such a case, it may be possible for this Court to give more detailed guidance to the national court.

[T]he difference in treatment of part-time workers is inherent in the nature of part-time work and any disadvantage which part-time workers suffer as a result of the measures is only an accidental consequence of the principle of compensation for loss of earnings.

The tenor of the judgment is probably meant as an indication to the German courts that they will be safe in finding the policy is justified. The case shows again that, while for analytical purposes it is important to divide them into their component parts, it is also important to view indirect discrimination cases in the round. The employer's argument is undoubtedly strengthened by the fact that the challenged payment only came within Art 119 (now Art 141) on a wide reading of that provision,[192] and that, while there was indirect discrimination, the impact on an individual part-time employee was rather marginal.

R v Secretary of State for Employment ex p Seymour-Smith, ECJ and HL[193]

The Unfair Dismissal (Variation of Qualifying Period) Order 1985 (the Order) extended the qualification period for unfair dismissal rights to two years.[194] Ms Seymour-Smith challenged this as being contrary to Art 119 (now Art 141) of the EC Treaty because it discriminated against women, who are more transient in the workforce than men.[195] The House of Lords referred the case to the ECJ for a ruling on several matters, including the meaning of justification in a case concerning a State's social policy. The case then returned to the House of Lords, who, by a majority, found that the Order, although adversely affecting women, was justified.

ECJ judgment:

69. It is settled case law that if a member state is able to show that the measures chosen reflect a necessary aim of its social policy and are suitable and necessary for achieving that aim, the mere fact that the legislative provision affects far more women than men at work cannot be regarded as a breach of art 119 of the Treaty (see esp the judgments in *Megner v Innungskrankenkasse Vorderpfalz* Case C-444/93 [1996] All ER (EC) 212, [1995] ECR I-4741 (para 24) and *Freers* [1996] ECR I-1165 (para 28)).

70. In this case, the UK government contends ... that extension of the qualifying period for protection against dismissal would stimulate recruitment.

71. It cannot be disputed that the encouragement of recruitment constitutes a legitimate aim of social policy.

72. It must also be ascertained, in the light of all the relevant factors and taking into account the possibility of achieving the social policy aim in question by other

---

192 See below, Chapter 14, pp 381–84.

193 Case C-167/97; [1999] All ER (EC) 97; [1999] 3 WLR 460; [1999] ICR 447; [1999] IRLR 253; [1999] 2 CMLR 273, ECJ; [2000] 1 All ER 857; [2000] 1 WLR 435; [2000] ICR 244; [2000] IRLR 263, HL.

194 Now reduced to one year where the effective date of termination is after 1 June 1999: Unfair Dismissal and Statement of Reasons for Dismissal (Variation of Qualifying Period) Order 1999, SI 1999/1436.

195 The detail statistics are set out above, p 270.

means, whether such an aim appears to be unrelated to any discrimination based on sex and whether the disputed rule, as a means to its achievement, is capable of advancing that aim.

73.   In that connection, the UK government maintains that a member state should merely have to show that it was reasonably entitled to consider that the measure would advance a social policy aim. It relies to that end on *Nolte v Landesversicherungsanstalt Hannover* Case C-317/93 [1996] All ER (EC) 212, [1995] ECR I-4625.[196]

74.   It is true that in the judgment in *Nolte* [1996] All ER (EC) 212, [1995] ECR I-4625 (para 33) the court observed that, in choosing the measures capable of achieving the aims of their social and employment policy, the member states have a broad margin of discretion.

75.   However, although social policy is essentially a matter for the member states under Community law as it stands, the fact remains that the broad margin of discretion available to the member states in that connection cannot have the effect of frustrating the implementation of a fundamental principle of Community law such as that of equal pay for men and women.

76.   Mere generalisations concerning the capacity of a specific measure to encourage recruitment are not enough to show that the aim of the disputed rule is unrelated to any discrimination based on sex nor to provide evidence on the basis of which it could reasonably be considered that the means chosen were suitable for achieving that aim.

77.   Accordingly ... if a considerably smaller percentage of women than men is capable of fulfilling the requirement of two years' employment imposed by the disputed rule, it is for the member state, ... to show that the said rule reflects a legitimate aim of its social policy, that that aim is unrelated to any discrimination based on sex, and that it could reasonably consider that the means chosen were suitable for attaining that aim.

House of Lords: [2000] 1 All ER 857

Lord Nicholls (at pp 872–75):

The Divisional Court and the Court of Appeal held that the Secretary of State had failed to discharge the burden of proving that the 1985 order was objectively justified ... the test applied by the Court of Appeal was whether the threshold of two years had been 'proved to result' in greater availability of employment than would have been the case without it. The Court of Appeal declined to incorporate into this formulation any margin of appreciation: [1996] All ER (EC) 1 at 29, [1995] ICR 889 at 95.

The answer given by the Court of Justice ... has now shown that this test was too stringent. The burden placed on the government in this type of case is not as heavy as previously thought. Governments must be able to govern ... Governments must be able to take into account a wide range of social, economic and political factors. The Court of Justice has recognised these practical considerations. If their aim is legitimate, governments have a discretion when choosing the method to achieve their aim. National courts, acting with hindsight, are not to impose an impracticable burden on governments which are proceeding in good faith. Generalised assumptions, lacking any factual foundation, are not good enough. But governments are to be afforded a broad measure of discretion. The onus is on the member state to show (1) that the allegedly discriminatory rule reflects a legitimate aim of its social policy, (2) that this aim is unrelated to any discrimination based on sex, and (3) that

---

196 See above, p 293.

the member state could reasonably consider that the means chosen were suitable for attaining that aim.

The object of the 1985 order was to encourage recruitment by employers. This was a legitimate aim of the government's social and economic policy, and this aim was unrelated to any sex discrimination. Whether the third requirement was satisfied ... is more debatable. ...

The requirements of Community law must be complied with at all relevant times. A measure may satisfy Community law when adopted, because at that stage the minister was reasonably entitled to consider the measure was a suitable means for achieving a legitimate aim. But experience of the working of the measure may tell a different story. In course of time the measure may be found to be unsuited for its intended purpose. The benefits hoped for may not materialise. Then the retention in force of a measure having a disparately adverse impact on women may no longer be objectively justifiable. In such a case a measure, lawful when adopted, may become unlawful.

Accordingly, if the government introduces a measure which proves to have a disparately adverse impact on women, the government is under a duty to take reasonable steps to monitor the working of the measure. The government must review the position periodically. The greater the disparity of impact, the greater the diligence which can reasonably be expected of the government. Depending on the circumstances, the government may become obliged to repeal or replace the unsuccessful measure.

In the present case the 1985 order had been in operation for six years when the two claimants were dismissed from their jobs. The Divisional Court and the Court of Appeal noted there was no evidence that the extension of the qualifying period in 1985 led to an increase in employment opportunities. ...

As time passed, the persistently adverse impact on women became apparent. But, as with the broad margin of discretion afforded to governments when adopting measures of this type, so with the duty of governments to monitor the implementation of such measures: the practicalities of government must be borne in mind. The benefits of the 1985 order could not be expected to materialise overnight, or even in a matter of months. The government was entitled to allow a reasonable period to elapse before deciding whether the order had achieved its objective and, if not, whether the order should be replaced with some other measure or simply repealed. Time would then be needed to implement any decision. I do not think the government could reasonably be expected to complete all these steps in six years, failing which it was in breach of Community law. The contrary view would impose an unrealistic burden on the government in the present case. Accordingly I consider the Secretary of State discharged the burden of showing that the 1985 order was still objectively justified in 1991.

Connolly, M, 'Commentary, *R v Secretary of State for Employment, ex parte Seymour-Smith*' [2000] 5(2) J Civ Lib 212, pp 220–21:

In the House of Lords, Lord Nicholls cited only [the] ... last part (the formula) of the ECJ's views on justification. The absence of the word 'necessary' in the formula was enough for Lord Nicholls to conclude that the test was no longer as stringent as previously thought.

Read as a whole the ECJ's judgement clearly envisages that the measure must be 'necessary' to achieve an aim. It also makes clear that the Order, supported by no more than a generalisation (that if employers have less fear of Unfair Dismissal claims, they will employ more people), was not justified. Even on his less stringent test, Lord Nicholls' decision was surprising. The Government offered no evidence that, after six years, the Order had made any difference to recruitment. If such a policy failed for six years, the Government could cling to no more than hope and political dogma as justification. In these circumstances the Order was not even 'suitable' to encourage recruitment, let alone necessary.

Without Unfair Dismissal rights, a worker can be fired, with proper notice, for no reason. It can be on the whim of the employer. For some fourteen years,[197] hundreds of thousands of British women worked without the protection of Unfair Dismissal rights, which were meanwhile being enjoyed by men. That was solely because of a useless law that achieved nothing bar making a huge number of the female workforce insecure in their jobs. This decision recognised the Government's discretion to maintain such laws.

---

197 The qualification period is now one year, where the effective date of termination is after 1 June 1999. For the statistics, see above, p 270.

CHAPTER 11

VICTIMISATION

1   INTRODUCTION

It is clearly necessary to provide legal protection for people who take legal action under anti-discrimination law or assist others to do so.[1]

Bourn, C and Whitmore, J, *Anti-Discrimination Law in Britain*, 3rd edn, 1996, London: Sweet & Maxwell, p 83:[2]

In reality, adverse employer reaction is not uncommon, as is shown by [Leonard's] survey of the experiences of successful claimants undertaken by the EOC. The existence of the section on victimisation was not effective in preventing the fact of having taken action under the sex discrimination legislation from having an adverse effect on the careers and working experience of many of the applicants who had ... been successful in the tribunals, partly because the pressures to which they were subject were often subtle and informal.

'Victimisation is discrimination' (1990) 30 EOR 23, p 23:

Jeanne Gregory in her study of 106 unsuccessful applicants found that more than half experienced a deterioration in working relationships, particularly with employers and managers, as a result of their bringing the case ... Forty five stated that their conditions of employment were adversely affected. Many reported that their chances of promotion had deteriorated to nil; some claimed that they had received smaller pay increases than their fellow workers and others that they were demoted ... Twenty applicants stated that they had left their job as a direct result of the case. Four made redundant said their selection was related to the case.

The victimisation provisions are defined in the legislation as the fourth instance of discrimination, along with harassment, and direct and indirect discrimination. The issue of discrimination 'after the relationship has ended' – typically, victimising ex-workers – is discussed in Chapter 12.[3]

2   THE ELEMENTS OF VICTIMISATION

Race Directive 2000/43/EC[4]

Article 9 Victimisation

Member States shall introduce into their national systems such measures as are necessary to protect individuals from any adverse treatment or adverse consequence

---

1   'Whistleblowers' may also gain protection from the Public Interest Disclosure Act 1998.
2   See also Gregory, J, *Picking Up the Pieces: Managing the Aftermath of Harassment Complaints*, 2002, Ware: Wainwright Trust. Available at www.wainwrighttrust.org.uk; click on 'catalogue'.
3   See below, p 327.
4   See also Equal Treatment Directive (76/207/EC), Art 7 (amended by the Equal Treatment Amendment Directive (2002/73/EC), due for implementation 5 October 2005) and the Equal Treatment in Employment Directive (2000/78/EC), Art 11.

as a reaction to a complaint or to proceedings aimed at enforcing complying with the principle of equal treatment.

Race Relations Act 1976

2 Discrimination by way of victimisation[5]

(1)   A person ('the discriminator') discriminates against another person ('the person victimised') in any circumstances relevant for the purposes of any provision of this Act if he treats the person victimised less favourably than in those circumstances he treats or would treat other persons, and does so by reason that the person victimised has—

   (a)   brought proceedings against the discriminator or any other person under this Act; or

   (b)   given evidence or information in connection with proceedings brought by any person against the discriminator or any other person under this Act; or

   (c)   otherwise done anything under or by reference to this Act in relation to the discriminator or any other person;[6] or

   (d)   alleged that the discriminator or any other person has committed an act which (whether or not the allegation so states) would amount to a contravention of this Act,

   or by reason that the discriminator knows that the person victimised intends to do any of those things, or suspects that the person victimised has done, or intends to do, any of them.

(2)   Subsection (1) does not apply to treatment of a person by reason of any allegation made by him if the allegation was false and not made in good faith.

Section 2(1)(a)–(d) define what have become known generally as 'protected acts'. It is necessary to prove that there has been a protected act and that the defendant treated the complainant less favourably *by reason that* the complainant did the protected act.

(1)   The Protected Acts

Beyond the obvious examples of bringing a claim or giving evidence in support of a claim, the sections have also been held to cover reporting that particular employers were attempting to induce the Manpower Services Commission to discriminate, action held to be within s 2(1)(c), though not (a) or (b),[7] and the making of secret tape recordings in an attempt to establish discrimination by a taxi cab association, which was covered by the same sub-section.[8] Section 2(1)(a) includes claims made if an employer has rejected an application for employment because the applicant has previously sued an employer for discrimination. The Court of Appeal has taken a narrow approach to the question of what amounts to an allegation under s 2(1)(d) of a contravention of the Act.

---

5   SDA 1975, s 4; Religion or Belief, or Sexual Orientation, Regulations 2003 (in force since 2 December 2003 and 1 December 2003, respectively) provide similar definitions.

6   There must here be limits: hitting the discriminator or damaging his property is literally within the section but cannot amount to a protected act.

7   *Kirby v Manpower Services Commission* [1980] 1 WLR 725; [1980] ICR 420; [1980] IRLR 229, EAT. See further, below, pp 302–04.

8   *Aziz v Trinity Street Taxis Ltd* [1989] QB 463; [1988] ICR 534; [1988] IRLR 204, CA. See further, below, p 303.

Waters v Commissioner of Police of the Metropolis **[1997] IRLR 589; [1997] ICR 1073, CA**

Miss Waters, a police officer, alleged that she was the victim of rape and buggery by a fellow officer while they were both off duty. No action was taken against the alleged assailant. She testified that as a result of making the complaint she was aggressively treated, ostracised by colleagues and senior officers, transferred to civilian duties, denied proper time off, refused placements, told she should leave, subjected to pornography by colleagues, threatened with violence by her chief superintendent, and required to take a psychological analysis to verify she was fit for duty. Further, her complaints were not properly investigated and confidences were broken. The Employment Appeal Tribunal (EAT) and the Court of Appeal (CA) both rejected the complaint on the ground that she had not alleged that the Act had been contravened.[9]

Mummery J (EAT [1995] IRLR 531, p 534):

[There would not be] a contravention of the 1975 Act unless [the act] was done by the police officer 'in the course of his employment' ... As the tribunal decided that ... the alleged assault was not done in the course of the police officer's employment, the Commissioner is not treated as having done that act. It follows that Miss Waters has not alleged that the Commissioner has done an act which would amount to a contravention of the 1975 Act.

Waite LJ (CA, p 597):

[It was argued] that Parliament must have intended, if the prohibition against victimisation was to have any real value at all, that protection should arise from the making of the complaint, and should not depend on the terms in which it is articulated.

Charges of race or sex discrimination are hurtful and damaging and not always easy to refute. In justice, therefore ... it is vital that discrimination (including victimisation) should be defined in language sufficiently precise to enable people to know where they stand before the law. Precision of language is also necessary to prevent the valuable purpose of combating discrimination from being frustrated or brought into disrepute through the use of language which encourages unscrupulous or vexatious recourse [to the law]. The interpretation proposed ... would involve an imprecision of language leaving employers in a state of uncertainty as to how they should respond to a particular complaint, and would place the machinery of the Acts at serious risk of abuse. It is better, and safer, to give the words of the sub-section their clear and literal meaning. The allegation relied on need not state explicitly that an act of discrimination has occurred ... All that is required is that the allegation relied on should have asserted facts capable of amounting in law to an act of discrimination ... The facts alleged by the complainant in this case were incapable in law of amounting in law to an act of discrimination by the Commissioner because they were not done by him [and] because the alleged perpetrator was not acting in the course of his employment.

This conclusion is dubious on both policy and linguistic grounds. At the time the complaint is made, it may be difficult for the complainant to know whether an allegation is protected. The policy should be to protect allegations whether or not they

---

9   Waters won her appeal to the House of Lords against the decision to strike out her claim on grounds of negligence. She did not appeal against the s 4 aspect of the court's decision. See [2000] 1 WLR 1607; [2000] IRLR 720; [2000] ICR 1064, HL.

necessarily turn out to be well-grounded, especially as the vast majority will never be brought to court. In addition, the phrase 'which would amount to a contravention' only appears in s 2(1)(d); in the other sub-sections, there is no requirement that the claim needs to be well-founded in order to form the basis of a successful victimisation complaint. It seems that the result may have been different had the complaint been, not under s 2(1)(d), but under s 2(1)(c), that the victimisation was for doing something 'under or by reference to' the Act 'in relation to the discriminator or any other person'. Finally, it is specifically provided in s 4(2) that the protection does not apply 'if the allegation was false and not made in good faith';[10] a false allegation which was made in good faith *will* thus be protected. It should make no difference whether the complaint failed on factual or on legal grounds.[11]

(2)   Treated Less Favourably

(a)   What is 'less favourable'?

In *Chief Constable of West Yorkshire v Khan*,[12] Sergeant Khan was refused, by his current employer, a reference in support of a job application elsewhere, because he was pursuing a claim of racial discrimination against his current employer. Nonetheless, the Norfolk Police invited him for an interview, which he failed. It was common ground that had a reference been given, containing the Yorkshire Police's low assessment of Sergeant Khan's managerial skills, he would have stood *less* chance of being short-listed for an interview. Accordingly, in Khan's action for victimisation, the Yorkshire Police argued that he had been treated *more*, not less, favourably. The House of Lords rejected that argument. Lord Scott concluded: 'It cannot ... be enough for s 2(1) purposes simply to show that the complainant has been treated differently ... I think it suffices if the complainant can reasonably say that he would have preferred not to have been treated differently.'[13] This approach has echoes of the direct discrimination case *R v Birmingham CC ex p EOC*.[14] It would seem that the courts should not be too pedantic about this element. There must be more than just *different* treatment, but it is enough if the complainant perceives – reasonably – that he has been treated less favourably.

(b)   The comparison – treated less favourably than whom?

In *Kirby v Manpower Services Commission*,[15] an employee at a job centre was moved to less desirable work because he disclosed confidential information regarding suspected discrimination by some employers. The EAT rejected his claim of victimisation

---

10   Sexual Orientation and Religion or Belief Regulations 2003 (in force since 1 December 2003 and 2 December 2003 respectively); reg 4(2) of each provides 'if the allegation, evidence or information was false and not made (... or given) in good faith'.

11   See Townshend-Smith, R, 'Casenote on *Waters v Commissioner of Police of the Metropolis*' [1995] IRLR 531, EAT; (1996) 2 IJDL 137.

12   [2002] 1 WLR 1947; [2001] 4 All ER 834, HL. See further, below, p 306.

13   *Ibid*, at para 76.

14   [1989] 1 AC 1156. See Chapter 7, p 182 *et al*. The statutory definition of direct discrimination also uses the phrase 'treats less favourably'.

15   [1980] ICR 420, [1980] IRLR 229, EAT.

because any person disclosing confidential information of *any nature* would have been moved to other work. Thus ,the EAT held that that treatment was not less favourable. The Court of Appeal in *Aziz* overruled *Kirby* and held that the comparison should *not* include any element of the protected act.

Aziz v Trinity Street Taxis Ltd [1988] IRLR 204; [1988] ICR 534; [1989] QB 463, CA

The complainant was an Asian taxicab proprietor and a member of an association of taxicab operators. When the association required him to pay £1,000 to have a third taxi admitted to its radio system, he felt he was being unfairly treated on racial grounds. He secretly recorded conversations with other taxi drivers, and made an unsuccessful complaint to a tribunal about the additional fee. During the hearing of that complaint, the existence of the recordings was revealed. As a result, he was expelled from the association on the ground that the making of the recordings was an unjustified intrusion and a serious breach of the trust which had to exist between members. He complained of victimisation. The Court of Appeal found against Aziz, holding that his expulsion was not caused by the protected act (see below), although it found for Aziz on the issue of the comparison.

Slade LJ (pp 210–11):

A complaint made in reliance on s 2 necessarily presupposes that the complainant has done a protected act ... If the doing of such an act itself constituted part of the relevant circumstances, a complainant would necessarily fail to establish discrimination if the alleged discriminator could show that he treated or would treat all other persons who did the protected act with equal intolerance. That would be an absurd result.

So, the correct comparison was to be made with a non-Asian member of the taxi company who had not made secret tape recordings. The House of Lords, in *Chief Constable of West Yorkshire v Khan*,[16] endorsed this approach, but perhaps not with the certainty to banish the *Kirby* comparator entirely, as noted in the following commentary on *Khan*.

Connolly, M, 'The House of Lords retreat from the causative approach announced in *Nagarajan* and leave claimants in a "Khan's Fork"' [2002] 31 ILJ 161, pp 163–64:

For Lord Nicholls it boiled down to a choice between *Kirby* and *Aziz*. He concluded (at para 27): 'There are arguments in favour of both approaches. On the whole I see no sufficient reason for departing from the ... approach adopted by Slade, LJ in the Aziz case'. Lord Scott was more trenchant. He rejected the *Kirby* approach, stating (at para 72) 'That cannot be right ... It would enable employers to victimise employees who brought race discrimination proceedings against them provided they, the employers, were prepared similarly to victimise any employee who had the temerity to sue them for anything.' Lord Hoffman rejected *Kirby* with equal certainty (at para 48).

The point is that the approach in *Kirby* ensures that virtually no claim could succeed. This is because a '*Kirby* comparator' has done the protected act except for the RRA element. Thus, any employer could testify 'I treat all complainants the same, whether or not the complaint is one of discrimination.' Further, if one removes only the RRA element from the protected act, a tribunal is then effectively trying to identify less favourable treatment on grounds of race, which is covered by section 1, [RRA] not section 2, thus rendering section 2 meaningless.

---

16 [2002] 1 WLR 1947; [2001] 4 All ER 834, HL. See further, below, p 306.

It is surprising that this argument – that was apparently settled in *Aziz* back in 1988 – is still being raised by employers. They may have been encouraged by the Court of Appeal's reluctance to overrule its own decision on this element in *Cornelius v University College of Swansea* [1987] IRLR 141 where it held (at para 33) that an employer's refusal to grant a transfer request or allow the grievance procedure, after the claimant had issued (sex) discrimination proceedings, was not less favourable treatment. (See further [2000] 29 ILJ 304.) Since then, in a number cases, counsel for the defendant has cited *Cornelius* in support of using a '*Kirby* comparator,' only for the Court of Appeal to reject *Kirby* but 'distinguish' *Cornelius*. This occurred in *Aziz* (at 872), *Khan* [2000] ICR 1169, (at para 28) and *Brown v TNT Express Worldwide* [2001] ICR 182 (at para 33).

Employers may have also been encouraged by some sentiments expressed by the judiciary. For instance, Lord Nicholls' comment (above) that 'There are arguments in favour of both approaches' is not the language to reject a case absolutely. In the same case in the Court of Appeal,[17] Lord Woolf, MR stated (at para 24): 'I would like to look favourably on [the] submission that you should ask whether the respondent was treated any differently from anyone else who brought proceedings'. But he 'felt driven' by precedent and his interpretation of section 2 to reject the '*Kirby* comparator'. In *Khan*, only Lords Scott and Hoffman echoed the certainty of Slade, LJ in *Aziz*. All the same, it must be assumed that now the House of Lords has rejected *Kirby*, no matter how reluctantly, it is bad law.

(3)   'By Reason That'

The third element in proving a case of victimisation is causation, or, in the statutory language, 'by reason that'. This is the most controversial aspect of the formula. It is possible to introduce an element of intention, or discriminatory motive, in the link between the protected act and the less favourable treatment. The debate parallels that for the 'causative' element 'on the ground of', in the definition of direct discrimination;[18] the same dichotomy – between 'strict liability' and 'discriminatory intent' – has underpinned the confusion in the precise meaning of this element, as the next two House of Lords decisions illustrate.

Nagarajan v London Regional Transport [2000] AC 501; [1999] 3 WLR 425; [2000] 4 All ER 65, HL

The claimant, a man of Indian origin, was interviewed for a job with London Regional Transport (LRT), against whom, in the past, he had brought several complaints of racial discrimination. LRT did not offer Mr Nagarajan a job and he won a claim of victimisation in the industrial tribunal. They supported their decision with three findings. First, all three members of the interviewing panel were aware of the previous proceedings. Secondly, Mr Nagarajan was given one out of 10 for 'articulacy' [*sic*] by the panel, despite him having been a transport information assistant for four months without complaint; the mark was 'plainly ridiculous and unrealistically low', the tribunal found. Thirdly, the tribunal found that one of the panellists considered that Mr Nagarajan was 'very anti-management'.

The tribunal concluded that the interviewers 'were consciously or subconsciously influenced by the fact that the applicant had previously brought industrial tribunal

---

17   [2000] ICR 1169.
18   See Chapter 7, p 182 *et al*.

proceedings against LRT'.[19] LRT appealed on the basis that a defendant must be shown to have been 'consciously motivated' by the protected act; as the tribunal failed to distinguish between *conscious* and *subconscious* motivation, no case of *conscious* motivation had been made out. A majority of the House of Lords dismissed LRT's appeal.

> *Lords Browne-Wilkinson (dissenting), Nicholls, Steyn, Hutton and Hobhouse*
> *Lord Nicholls (pp 510–12):*
>
> Section 2 should be read in the context of section 1. Section 1(1)(a) is concerned with direct discrimination, to use the accepted terminology ... This is the crucial question. Was it on grounds of race? Or was it for some other reason ...?
>
> For the purposes of direct discrimination under section 1(1)(a) ... the reason why the alleged discriminator acted on racial grounds is irrelevant. Racial discrimination is not negatived by the discriminator's motive or intention or reason or purpose (the words are interchangeable in this context) in treating another person less favourably on racial grounds ...
>
> This law, which is well established, was confirmed by your Lordships in *R v Birmingham City Council ex p EOC* ... The same point was made in *James v Eastleigh Borough Council* ...[20]
>
> I can see no reason to apply a different approach to section 2. 'On racial grounds' in section 1(1)(a) and 'by reason that' in section 2(1) are interchangeable expressions in this context ... A variety of phrases, with different shades of meaning, have been used to explain how the legislation applies in such cases: discrimination requires that racial grounds were a cause, the activating cause, a substantial and effective cause, a substantial reason, an important factor. No one phrase is obviously preferable to all others, although in the application of this legislation legalistic phrases, as well as subtle distinctions, are better avoided so far as possible. If racial grounds or protected acts had a significant influence on the outcome, discrimination is made out.
>
> *Lord Steyn (p 521):*
>
> The purpose of section 2(1) is clear. Its primary purpose is to give to persons victimised on account of their reliance on rights under the Act effective civil remedies, thereby also creating a culture which may deter individuals from penalising those who seek to enforce their rights under the Act. Despite valiant efforts counsel for LRT was unable to point to any plausible policy reason for requiring conscious motivation under section 2(1) but not under section 1(1)(a). On the contrary, counsel for LRT accepted that victimisation is as serious a mischief as direct discrimination. In these circumstances policy considerations point towards similar interpretations.
>
> For my part it is not the logic of symmetry that requires the two provisions to be given parallel interpretations. It is rather a pragmatic consideration. Quite sensibly in section 1(1)(a) cases the tribunal simply has to pose the question: Why did the defendant treat the employee less favourably? ... That is a straightforward way of carrying out its task in a section 1(1)(a) case. Common sense suggests that the tribunal should also perform its functions in a section 2(1) case by asking the equally straightforward question: Did the defendant treat the employee less favourably because of his knowledge of a protected act?

---

19   [2000] 1 AC 501, at p 513.
20   See above, Chapter 7, pp 182–83.

Lord Browne-Wilkinson (dissenting, p 510):

I accept that to treat both section 1(1)(a) and section 2(1) as requiring the court to determine the reason activating the defendant means that the court is led into the minefield of investigating an individual's mental processes ... What is quite clear is that Parliament has, in introducing legislation to outlaw discrimination on grounds of sex or race, expressly required the court to investigate the reasons which have led the alleged discriminator to take the steps which he did. This is not surprising since this was pioneering legislation designed to produce a social, as much as a legal, change. The only yardstick (in the field of direct discrimination) must be the mental state of the alleged discriminator. To dismiss somebody who comes from an ethnic minority is not, *per se*, unlawful ... There is no escape from the difficulties inherent in examining the minds of the parties ...

I find it regrettable that LRT and the members of the interviewing committee should be found to have been guilty of victimisation, a most serious charge, if the relevance (if any) of the applicant's earlier proceedings was not present to their conscious minds when they took the decision ... To introduce something akin to strict liability into the Acts which will lead to individuals being stamped as racially discriminatory or victimisers where these matters were not consciously in their minds when they acted as they did is unlikely to recommend the legislation to the public as being fair and proper protection for the minorities that they are seeking to protect.

Chief Constable of West Yorkshire v Khan [2002] 1 WLR 1947; [2001] 4 All ER 834, HL

In September 1996, Sergeant Khan applied to become an Inspector within his force. However, his Chief Constable failed to support the application. That failure led Khan to issue proceedings under the Race Relations Act 1976. Then, in October, Khan applied to be an Inspector with the Norfolk Police. Acting on legal advice, the Chief Constable refused to provide the Norfolk Police with a reference. Following that, Khan brought separate proceedings, claiming that he had been victimised. The Chief Constable argued that the reason for withholding a reference was to avoid prejudicing his own case in the discrimination proceedings brought by Khan. The House of Lords, reversing all the decisions below, allowed the Chief Constable's appeal. Lords Nicholls, Mackay of Clashfern, Hoffmann and Scott each made separate speeches. Lord Hutton agreed with Lords Nicholls and Hoffmann.

Lord Nicholls:

[29] Contrary to views sometimes stated, the third ingredient ('by reason that') does not raise a question of causation as that expression is usually understood. Causation is a slippery word, but normally it is used to describe a legal exercise. From the many events leading up to the crucial happening, the court selects one or more of them which the law regards as causative of the happening. Sometimes the court may look for the 'operative' cause, or the 'effective' cause. Sometimes it may apply a 'but for' approach. For the reasons I sought to explain in *Nagarajan's* case,[21] ... a causation exercise of this type is not required either by s 1(1)(a) or s 2. The phrases 'on racial grounds' and 'by reason that' denote a different exercise: why did the alleged discriminator act as he did? What, consciously or unconsciously, was his reason? Unlike causation, this is a subjective test. Causation is a legal conclusion. The reason why a person acted as he did is a question of fact.

---

21 [2000] 1 AC 501, pp 510–12. See extract above, pp 304–06

[30] A situation, closely comparable to that in the present case, arose in *Cornelius v University College of Swansea* [1987] IRLR 141 [CA] ... Like the present case, *Cornelius'* case concerned steps taken by employers to preserve their position pending the outcome of proceedings. A college declined to act on an employee's transfer request or to operate their grievance procedure while proceedings under the 1975 [SDA] ..., brought by the employee against the college, were still awaiting determination. Giving the only reasoned judgment, Bingham LJ said (at 145–146 (para 33)):

> There is no reason whatever to suppose that the decisions of the [College] ... on the applicant's requests for a transfer and a hearing under the grievance procedure were influenced in any way by the facts that the appellant had brought proceedings or that those proceedings were under the Act. The existence of proceedings plainly did influence their decisions. No doubt, like most experienced administrators, they recognised the risk of acting in a way which might embarrass the handling or be inconsistent with the outcome of current proceedings. They accordingly wished to defer action until the proceedings were over. But that had ... nothing whatever to do with the appellant's conduct in bringing proceedings under the Act. There is no reason to think that their decision would have been different whoever had brought the proceedings or whatever their nature, if the subject matter was allied. If the appellant was victimised, it is not shown to have been because of her reliance on the Act.

Two strands are discernible in this passage. One strand is that the reason why the officers of the college did not act on the complainant's two requests was the *existence* of the pending proceedings, as distinct from the complainant's conduct in *bringing* the proceedings. They wished to defer action until the proceedings were over. The second strand is that the college decisions had nothing to do with the complainant's conduct in bringing proceedings against the college *under the 1975 Act*. The decisions would have been the same, whatever the nature of the proceedings, if the subject matter had been allied to the content of the employee's requests.

[31] ... Employers, acting honestly and reasonably, ought to be able to take steps to preserve their position in pending discrimination proceedings without laying themselves open to a charge of victimisation. This accords with the spirit and purpose of the Act. Moreover, the statute accommodates this approach without any straining of language. An employer who conducts himself in this way is not doing so because of the fact that the complainant has brought discrimination proceedings. He is doing so because, currently and temporarily, he needs to take steps to preserve his position in the outstanding proceedings. Protected act (a) ('by reason that the person victimised has—(a) brought proceedings against the discriminator ... under this Act') cannot have been intended to prejudice an employer's proper conduct of his defence, so long as he acts honestly and reasonably. Acting within this limit, he cannot be regarded as discriminating by way of victimisation against the employee who brought the proceedings.

Lord Scott:

[77] Was the reference withheld 'by reason that' Sgt Khan had brought the race discrimination proceedings? In a strict causative sense it was. If the proceedings had not been brought the reference would have been given. The proceedings were a *causa sine qua non*. But the language used in s 2(1) is not the language of strict causation. The words 'by reason that' suggest, to my mind, that it is the real reason, the core reason, the *causa causans*, the motive, for the treatment complained of that must be identified.

[78]   In *Cornelius v University College of Swansea* ... Bingham LJ put his judicial finger on the critical distinction for s 2(1) purposes between the bringing of discrimination proceedings and the existence of the proceedings ...

Lord Hoffmann:

[54]   ... This raises a question of causation: was the fact that he brought proceedings a reason why the West Yorkshire police treated him less favourably.

[55]   Of course, in one sense the fact that he had brought proceedings was a cause of his being treated less favourably. If he had not brought proceedings, he would have been given a reference. In some contexts, a causal link of this kind will be enough. For example, in *R v Birmingham City Council, ex p EOC* ...

[56]   There are parallels between the purposes of ss 1 and 2 of the 1976 Act ... see *Nagarajan* ... But the causal questions which they raise are not identical.

[59]   ... the treatment need not be, consciously or unconsciously, a response to the commencement of proceedings. It may simply be a reasonable response to the need to protect the employer's interests as a party to the litigation. It is true that an employee who had not commenced proceedings would not have been treated in the same way. Under s 1, one would have needed to go no further. Under s 2, however, the commencement of proceedings must be a reason for the treatment and in *Cornelius'* case it was not.

These two House of Lords decisions, made within a two-and-a-half year period, appear to contradict each other. The next extract examines the judgments in detail, concludes that *Khan* was wrongly decided and suggests an alternative approach to this question.

Connolly, M, 'The House of Lords retreat from the causative approach announced in *Nagarajan* and leave claimants in a "Khan's Fork"' [2002] 31 ILJ 161, p 166:

There is obviously confusion over the precise meaning of the phrase *by reason that*. [In *Khan*] Lord Nicholls says it is not causative, Lord Hoffman said that it was. Lord Hutton's position is unclear because he concurred with *both* Lord Nicholls and Lord Hoffman. Meanwhile Lord Scott said the phrase was one of not *strict* causation.

The reasoning becomes more obscure when read alongside the majority's speeches in *Nagarajan*. Lord Nicholls – the only judge common to both cases – said in *Khan* (at para 29) that he explained in *Nagarajan* why the causative approach was not required. In fact, in *Nagarajan*, Lord Nicholls approved the 'objective and not subjective' approach applied to section 1 in *EOC v Birmingham City Council*, and again in *James v Eastleigh BC*, where Lord Goff specifically applied the 'but for' test. Lord Nicholls concluded in *Nagarajan* (at 71) 'I can see no reason to apply a different approach to section 2'. ...

The appeal in *Nagarajan* turned on whether it was enough that the employer's motivation (in reacting to previous proceedings) was *sub*conscious. The House of Lords, applying the 'straightforward' causative test, held that it was. Nothing said in *Khan* upsets the *ratio decidendi* of *Nagarajan*, which was that motivation could be either conscious or subconscious. The speeches in *Khan* at best side-stepped, and at worst ignored, the wider statements in *Nagarajan* concerning causation. Nevertheless, a unanimous House of Lords clearly rejected the 'straightforward' causative approach. And so, following *Khan*, that is what the law is *not*. The 'but for' test is not suitable for cases of victimisation. But it is less easy to say what the law *is*.

The key to understanding that, so far as it is possible, lies in the decision of the whole House depending upon a fine distinction, between the *bringing* and *existence* of proceedings. To this end Lords Nicholls, Hoffman and Scott drew support from *Cornelius v University College of Swansea* ...

Lords Nicholls, Hoffman and Scott noted that the feature of this [case] ... was that College had acted on the *existence* of the proceedings, not the *bringing* of them ...

The fine distinction between the *bringing* and *existing* of proceedings shows a drift away from the 'straightforward' approach adopted by the House of Lords in *Nagarajan*, where Lord Nicholls himself said (at 71): '... in the application of this legislation legalistic phrases, as well as subtle distinctions, are better avoided so far as possible.' Khan may have defeated this distinction by adding a second protected act to his claim: under section 2(1)(c), RRA, he had 'otherwise done anything under or by reference to this Act.' As well as having *brought* proceedings, he was 'otherwise' *maintaining* them in existence.

Thus far it could be ventured that the *ratio decidendi* of *Khan* is that a defendant who acted by reason of the *existence*, and not the *bringing*, of the proceedings cannot be liable under section 2(1)(a), RRA (by reason that the person has 'brought proceedings...'). Standing alone, this proposition sabotages the purpose of the House's own rejection of the *Kirby* comparator for proving less favourable treatment. Employers could simply argue that they responded to all proceedings in this way, whatever their nature. So long as the employer acted when proceedings were pending, virtually no claim of victimisation could succeed under section 2(1)(a).

However, Lord Nicholls added a further dimension when concluding (at para 31) that 'Employers, acting reasonably and honestly, ought to be able to take steps to preserve their position in pending proceedings without laying themselves open to a charge of victimisation.' Similar sentiments were expressed in the other speeches. Lord Mackay noted (at para 44) that the Chief Constable 'acted in accordance with perfectly understandable advice.' Lord Scott said (at para 80) that this approach still allowed for the case where the employer 'singled out' a worker for less favourable treatment but allowed 'justice to be done to an employer who ... would otherwise be placed ... in an unacceptable Morton's fork'. And Lord Hoffman observed (at para 59) that the Chief Constable's act may have been 'a reasonable response to the need to protect the employer's interests as a party to litigation.'

It is now possible to qualify the *ratio* as being that there is no liability under section 2(1)*(a)*, RRA, where the defendant acted, *reasonably and honestly*, by reason of the existence, and not the bringing, of proceedings. The qualification appears to safeguard the decision from abuse by employers who may otherwise use it, for example, to 'single out' workers. However the qualification carries a series of problems.

First and most obviously, there is no such requirement in the legislation that for liability, the defendant *does not* act reasonably and honestly. Second, focusing on the predicament of the 'reasonable and honest' employer undermines the policy of the provisions, which is the removal of deterrents to enforcing the anti-discrimination legislation. The Law Lords' speeches are littered with statements sympathetic to the employers' dilemma. Nowhere did a judge express sympathy for the worker who – as well as having acted just as 'reasonably and honestly' as their employer – will have his or her career frozen for the duration (conceivably several years) of the proceedings, simply because they used anti-discrimination legislation. This decision places the worker in an unacceptable 'Khan's fork', suffering either discrimination or a frozen career.

Whilst both the employer and the worker will find themselves in a difficult position, the provisions on victimisation are not aimed at resolving the employer's predicament. Empirical research shows that victimisation is a serious problem in the workplace.[22] ... Accordingly Lord Steyn pronounced in *Nagarajan* (at 79) that victimisation was as serious a mischief as discrimination itself. It is now inconceivable, one hopes, that a tribunal would embark on such a diversion from the statutory wording and purpose in a case of discrimination under section 1, no matter how 'reasonably and honestly' the defendant had acted.

Third, this 'extra element' of acting reasonably and honestly actually does little to save the decision from sabotaging the purpose of rejecting *Kirby*. It will be recalled (see above) that Lord Scott rejected *Kirby* because (at para 72) 'It would enable employers to victimise employees who brought race discrimination proceedings ... provided ... the employers were prepared similarly to victimise any employee who had the temerity to sue them for anything.' In most cases though, employers will prove that they acted 'reasonably and honestly' by showing that the company normally treats in the same way, any worker who brings *any* proceedings. Indeed, that was the defence in *Khan*. And so the qualification does little to prevent this decision subverting the rejection of *Kirby*. Accordingly, employers can escape liability (once again) when, for example, suspending a worker on full pay, or refusing a transfer, promotion, access to a grievance procedure, or the usual – but discretionary – incremental pay rise or bonus. So long as all workers are equally 'victimised' pending the outcome of proceedings, a claim of victimisation will fail and Lord Scott's words on the *Kirby* comparator count for little.

The fourth problem with the sentiments expressed is that they carry an indication that a tribunal should look for an *intent* to victimise – or simple vengeance – on the part of the employer. Under the provisions, an employer who acted reasonably and honestly, on 'understandable advice' and did *not* 'single out' a worker for treatment, *can* be liable for victimisation. For instance, where several months into discrimination proceedings the employer announces, 'I've had enough of this trial, it's gone on far too long. All the claimant's transfer requests are to be refused.' Such an employer would rely on *Khan* stating that he reacted to the *existence*, not the *bringing*, of proceedings. If a tribunal then demands honest and reasonable behaviour, it must find the employer liable. Yet the only difference between this example and *Khan* is vengeance, which should not be an ingredient for liability.

Lord Nicholls' speech appeared to go further than that by including a *racial* motive. After approving *Cornelius*, he identified a 'second strand' to the case, noting that (at para 30) 'the College's behaviour had nothing to do with the bringing of proceedings *under the 1975* [Sex Discrimination] Act. The decisions would have been the same, whatever the nature of the proceedings, if the subject matter had been allied to the content of the employee's requests.' (Lord Nicholls' emphasis.) In other words, to be liable, the employer's reason for acting has to be related to the discrimination legislation aspect of the protected act. This approach is wrong because it is actually identifying race, or sex, discrimination, and not victimisation. If, to prove a case of victimisation a claimant has to prove racial discrimination, then section 2 would be redundant ...

None of this is to say that intention, or motivation, *per se* should not be a factor. After all, the employer is part of the causal chain, or link between the protected act and the less favourable treatment. What goes through the employer must, presumably, go

---

22 See above, p 299.

through his mind. But the real issue is, motivated by *what*? In *Aziz*[23] it was held that the defendants were motivated by the breach of trust, even though the tape recordings were part of the protected act. In *Cornelius* and *Khan* the employer was motivated by the *existence* of the proceedings. These cases did not turn on an employer's clean conscience or benign motive, but the *dividing* (in *Aziz*), or the *distinguishing* (in *Cornelius* and *Khan*), of the protected act.

Thus, an element of motivation per se need not curtail the simple causative approach expressed in *Nagarajan* and *James*. So long as the cause of the less favourable treatment is the protected act, taken without division or fine distinctions, motivation is a harmless ingredient. This does not impose a 'strict liability' upon defendants, where all that would be required is the less favourable treatment and the protected act. There remains a link between the two. So, for example, an employer, who knows that a worker has brought a complaint of sexual harassment, sacks that worker for an entirely separate incident of theft, would not liable for victimisation.

With respect, in making a fine distinction between the existence and bringing of proceedings and focussing on the 'honest and reasonable' employer's predicament, the House of Lords in *Khan* have strayed from the wording and the purpose of the legislation.

... At present, the law on victimisation appears to be thus. For establishing less favourable treatment, the claimant must be compared with a person who has *not* done the protected act, even in a partial sense. It is not enough that the claimant was treated *differently* from that person, but it is sufficient if the claimant *perceived*, reasonably, that the treatment was less favourable. However, on the 'causative' element, an employer may argue that he reacted, reasonably and honestly, to the *existence* – not the *bringing* – of proceedings in order to protect his position. And so a claimant may be treated less favourably for the duration of the proceedings. This places a victim of discrimination in a 'Khan's Fork'. It may be that the employer's argument will be defeated if the claim includes a section 2(1)(c) protected act, which should cover the *existence* of proceedings. An employer may also argue that he reacted to a particular part of the protected act, eg a breach of confidence (*Aziz*). It is probable that the ECJ would take a different, purposive, approach and protect the worker in such cases, irrespective of the technicalities.

---

23 See above, p 303.

CHAPTER 12

DISCRIMINATION IN EMPLOYMENT

1 QUALIFYING REQUIREMENTS

(1) Employment

Under the legislation, 'employment' means 'employment under a contract of service or of apprenticeship or a contract personally to execute any work or labour'.[1] The definition is wider than most employment protection legislation, such as the law of unfair dismissal, which only covers employees – those who work under a contract of employment. Most self-employed workers are thus entitled to bring a complaint if they are rejected for work on one of the protected grounds, such as the self-employed sales assistant in *Quinnen v Hovells*.[2] Waite J said that 'those who engage, however cursorily, the talents, skills or labour of the self-employed' must ensure there is no discrimination in their appointment, terms or dismissal. The position of purely commercial contracts, where a sole trader or practitioner, or partner of a firm, is contracted to provide services, is less certain. It would seem that tribunals should look for the 'dominant purpose' of the contract to see if it is personal or not. These matters were discussed by the House of Lords in *Loughran*.

Loughran & Kelly v Northern Ireland Housing Executive **[1999] 1 AC 428, HL**[3]

These joined appeals arose from appointments made by the defendants for solicitors to sit on a panel to defend public liability claims. Loughran was a sole practitioner and Kelly was one of a two-partner firm. They were not appointed and brought a claim of discrimination under the Fair Employment (Northern Ireland) Act 1976, which carries the same definition of 'employment' as the other discrimination legislation. The defendants contended that the claimants were not employed for the purposes of the Act. The House of Lords, by a bare majority in each case, found for the claimants, although Lord Griffiths found for Kelly on different grounds than Lords Steyn and Slynn.

Lord Slynn (p 435):

In [*Mirror Group Newspapers Ltd v Gunning* [1986] 1 WLR 546[4] ... an application was made by a woman to have transferred to her her father's agency for the wholesale distribution of Sunday newspapers. She said that this application was refused in breach of section 6 of the Sex Discrimination Act 1975 ... Oliver LJ ruled, at p 551h, that 'what is contemplated by the legislature in this extended definition is a contract the dominant purpose of which is the execution of personal work or labour.' In that case it was not, since 'here the dominant purpose was simply the regular and efficient distribution of newspapers:' ... There was, moreover, no evidence that the agent was

---

1   SDA 1975, s 82(1), RRA 1976, s 78(1), and the Religion or Belief, or Sexual Orientation, Regulations 2003, reg 9 (in force since 2 December 2003 and 1 December 2003, respectively).
2   [1984] ICR 525; [1984] IRLR 227, EAT.
3   See also, [1998] ICR 828, [1998] 3 WLR 735; [1998] IRLR 593. Applied in *Patterson v Legal Services Commission* [2003] All ER (D) 306 (Feb), EAT.
4   See also [1986] ICR 145; [1986] 1 All ER 385, CA.

required personally to carry out the work though his personality was important and his personal involvement might be regarded as desirable. The dominant purpose of the contract was to ensure that newspapers were efficiently distributed ...

(pp 437–38):

[I]n respect of Mr Loughran. The definition of employment is clearly wide enough to cover the provision of services by a professional man, as was held in *Mirror Group Newspapers Ltd v Gunning* ... Whatever he called himself he was the individual seeking employment in the sense of someone offering to enter into a 'contract personally to execute any work or labour.' He was the person undertaking to do the work and he would be liable for any breach of the contract that was made. On the form he was said to be 'mainly responsible for carrying out the panel work.' So far as 'responsible' means legally responsible he was solely responsible. In so far as it means 'would mainly in fact carry out the work' he was such a person even if he was entitled to delegate some part of it to his assistant. Plainly it does not cease to be a contract 'personally to execute any work' because his secretary types and posts the executive's defence to any claim or that his assistant solicitor goes along to file such a defence ...

Mrs Kelly's case raises different issues ... I start with the provision of the Interpretation Act 1978 that 'unless the contrary intention appears' 'person' includes a body of persons unincorporate. I do not think that any such contrary intention is to be deduced from the Fair Employment (Northern Ireland) Act 1976. The intention of the statute it seems to me is in favour of the wider definition applying for two reasons in particular. In the first place the intention of the Act of 1976 is clearly to outlaw discrimination on the grounds of religious or political opinion in the employment sphere. It would be wrong to ignore the object and purpose of the Act as seen in the long title to, and in Part III of, the Act. It is factually possible to discriminate against the partners of a firm or against the firm itself as it is against a sole practitioner. *Prima facie* one would expect the Act to outlaw both.

In the second place the Act of 1976 clearly and deliberately adopts a wide definition of employment so as to include a contract to provide services and a firm can contract to provide services. If the definition had included only 'workman' or 'artificer' or 'a contract of service' the position might well be different but with the extended definition of employment I consider that a contract by a firm to provide services is capable of being a contract 'personally to execute any work or labour.' Is it such a contract here? In my view it is. The contract is for the firm itself, ie, personally, to execute work. The firm as such will be legally responsible for the doing of the work and will be liable for breach of the contract. The firm which contracts and is legally responsible consists of all the partners but clearly all the partners do not have to do all the work. It is sufficient that one or more of the partners is intended to and does execute the work subject to delegation of some activities by the firm in the same way as a sole practitioner can delegate. What is required is that the dominant purpose of the contract is that the firm undertakes to do, and by one of its partners is responsible for and does, the work undertaken to be done.

Lord Griffiths (pp 442–43):

I turn now to the case of Bernadette Kelly ... [I]f a firm of solicitors had designated an assistant solicitor, to defend the claims of the executive, that assistant solicitor would have no claim for unlawful discrimination, as he would not be a contracting party, nor in my view would the firm have any claim. This may be considered unfortunate, but is the inevitable consequence of the drafting of the statute. But Bernadette Kelly, as a partner in the firm of 'John Hoy, Son & Murphy',. was a contracting party. A firm of solicitors has no legal existence, independent of the partners of the firm ... Bernadette

Kelly was seeking to enter into a contract personally to execute work within the meaning of section 57, and is entitled to pursue her claim for discrimination.

I cannot, however, agree that the Interpretation Act 1978 should be applied to achieve the same result. It seems to me that the language of the statute is aimed at giving protection to individuals and not to companies or unincorporated corporations ... Furthermore I foresee that the most formidable difficulties in the practical application of the Act of 1976 would be likely to arise if tribunals were called upon to decide on the religious beliefs or political opinions of companies or corporations.

Lord Lloyd (dissenting, pp 444–46):

So the only question is whether the contracts which would have been made in these cases were made with the persons who would have performed the personal services covered by the contracts. In the case of Mrs Kelly the answer must surely be no. The application form draws a clear distinction between the firm and the designated solicitor. It is the firm which takes overall responsibility. But it is the designated solicitor who is responsible for carrying out the work.

Had Mrs Kelly's firm been successful in the application for appointment to the panel, the contract would have been with the firm, but the actual work would have been performed by Mrs Kelly as the designated solicitor. If one assumes for a moment that Mrs Kelly had been an assistant solicitor, and not a partner, it seems clear enough that she could not have complained. The contract would not have been with her. Nor could the firm have complained, since a firm (as distinct from an individual) cannot agree to execute work personally.

As for Mr. Loughran, the Court of Appeal drew a distinction between his case and that of Mrs Kelly on the ground that Mr Loughran was 'in substance' seeking to have himself appointed to the panel. Parliament cannot have intended the application of section 17 to depend on the number of partners in the firm.

Lord Griffiths' different grounds for his decision means that there is no majority to say that firms or companies could be protected under the legislation.

Under s 85 of the SDA 1975, s 75 of the RRA 1976 and reg 36 of the Religion or Belief, or Sexual Orientation, Regulations 2003,[5] Crown employees are protected on the same basis as other employees.[6] The recent legislation has extended the coverage of office-holders.[7] In the past, magistrates have been outside the scope of the legislation,[8] although in *Perceval-Price v NI Civil Service*,[9] an employment tribunal ruled that tribunal chairs were 'workers' within Art 141 (equal pay) of the EC Treaty.

While an illegal contract, such as one where the tax and national insurance authorities are defrauded, may well preclude a claim for wrongful dismissal (that is,

---

5 Respectively, SI 2003/1660, in force since 2 December 2003; SI 2003/1661, in force since 1 December 2003.

6 For exceptions, see below, p 357, 'Public Bodies'.

7 RRA 1976, s 76ZA, (in force 19 July 2003); and the Sexual Orientation, or Religion or Belief, Regulations 2003, reg 10.

8 *Knight v AG* [1979] ICR 194, EAT; *Department of the Environment v Fox* [1979] ICR 736, EAT; *Arthur v AG* [1999] ICR 631, EAT. The new legislation does not cover posts without remuneration and so lay magistrates remain unprotected (RRA 1976, s 76ZA (7); Sexual Orientation, or Religion or Belief, Regulations 2003, reg 10(8)).

9 [2000] IRLR 380; 41 EOR DCLD (1999), ET.

breach of contract),[10] it was held in *Leighton v Michael and Charalambous*[11] that an employee under such a contract was nevertheless entitled to sue for sexual harassment. This was approved by the Court of Appeal in *Hall v Woolston Hall Leisure*.[12] The reasoning is that discrimination is a statutory tort, and the right arises separately from the employment contract, although the illegality could be of such a nature that it would be against public policy to enforce the action.

(2)   In Great Britain

With one exception (below), a complainant must be employed at an establishment in Great Britain,[13] a condition which is satisfied 'if the employee does his work wholly or partly in Great Britain'.[14] This is a question of fact. The specific problem areas have arisen in relation to seafarers. In *Deria v The General Council of British Shipping*,[15] the claim failed despite the fact that the ship unexpectedly docked in Southampton, on the ground that when the employment commenced, it was contemplated that the work would be done wholly outside Great Britain. The justification was that the parties would know for certain at the outset of the voyage whether or not the legislation applied, an explanation which will work in favour of the employer far more often than the worker.

Marleasing tells us that domestic legislation must be interpreted in the light of the policy of European law,[16] and there is a strong argument of principle that a person who works all or most of the time within the EC must be protected under EC law if the employer is subject to the law of any Member State.[17] A further example of primacy of EC law was shown in *Bossa v Nordstress Ltd*,[18] where an Italian national claimed that he had been discriminated against on ground of nationality contrary to the RRA 1976. Despite the fact that the job entailed working wholly or mainly outside Great Britain,[19] it was held that the claim could proceed; Art 39 (formally 48) of the EC Treaty, which provides for free movement of workers of Member States and thus

---

10   *Napier v National Business Agency* [1951] 2 All ER 264; [1950] TR 201; 44 R&IT 413; [1951] WN 392, CA. The Court of Appeal, in *Hewcastle Catering v Ahmed and Elkanah* [1991] IRLR 473 allowed a claim of *unfair* dismissal to succeed, despite the claimant workers participating, but not profiting, in the employer's tax fraud. The special circumstances were that the workers were sacked for giving evidence against the employer regarding the fraud.

11   [1995] ICR 1091; [1996] IRLR 67, EAT.

12   [2001] 1 WLR 225; [2001] ICR 99; [2000] IRLR 578.

13   In 1987, both statutes were extended so as to cover the offshore oil industry: see the Sex Discrimination and Equal Pay (Off-Shore Employment) Order SI 1987/930, made under the SDA 1975, s 10(5); and the Race Relations (Off-Shore Employment) Order SI 1987/920, made under the RRA 1976, s 8(5).

14   Religion or Belief Regulations 2003, SI 2003/1660, or the Sexual Orientation Regulations 2003 SI 2003/1661, reg 9; RRA 1976, s 8 (inserted by reg 11, SI 2003/1626, in force since 19 July 2003). SDA 1975, s 10, still uses the phrase 'unless the employee does his work wholly outside Great Britain'. Until 16 December 1999, the exception was for work 'wholly or *mainly* outside Great Britain'. The words 'or mainly' were repealed by SI 1999/3163.

15   [1986] 1 WLR 1207; [1986] ICR 172; [1986] IRLR 108, CA. Decided under the earlier definition: unless work is done 'wholly or mainly outside Great Britain'.

16   See further, Chapter 5, pp 111–12.

17   See *Murray v NAAFI*, unreported, IT, Case No 3100459/96, see 34 DCLD 11.

18   [1998] IRLR 285; [1998] ICR 694, EAT.

19   That was the statutory definition at the time. See further, fn 14 above.

protects against discrimination on the ground of nationality, meant that the territorial restriction of the RRA 1976 had here to be disapplied.

Exceptionally, work wholly outside Great Britain is covered if the discrimination or harassment is on the ground of sexual orientation, race or ethnic or national origins, religion or belief, and:

(a)   the employer has a place of business at an establishment in Great Britain;

(b)   the work is for the purposes of the business carried on at that establishment; and

(c)   the employee is ordinarily resident in Great Britain:

    (i)   at the time when he applies for or is offered the employment, or

    (ii) at any time during the course of the employment.[20]

2   UNLAWFUL EMPLOYMENT DISCRIMINATION

(1)   Hiring Employees

Sex Discrimination Act 1975

Section 6(1)

It is unlawful for a person, in relation to employment by him at an establishment in Great Britain, to discriminate against a woman:

(a)   in the arrangements he makes for the purpose of determining who should be offered that employment; or

(b)   in the terms on which he offers her that employment; or

(c)   by refusing or deliberately omitting to offer her employment.

The parallel provisions in s 4(1) of the RRA 1976 and reg 6(1) are materially the same. The Codes of Practice issued by the Commission for Racial Equality and the Equal Opportunities Commission provide guidance on how to comply with the law and how to promote equal opportunities. Much of the guidance concerns the actual processes of how to avoid discrimination in recruitment. Failure to observe a provision of the Codes is not in itself automatically unlawful, but is evidence which may be taken into account in determining whether discrimination has occurred.[21]

Section 6 of the SDA 1975 and its parallel provisions are concerned with all aspects of the recruitment process, from the drawing up of the job specification to the actual decision on who will be offered a job and on what terms.[22] If the *effect* of the procedures is discriminatory, it is irrelevant that they are not intended to operate in such a fashion. In *Brennan v JH Dewhurst Ltd*,[23] a manager was responsible for the filtering out of some applicants even though he would not be involved in the final selection; his role was clearly part of the arrangements. Those filtered out would have

---

20   RRA, 1976, s 8(1A); and Sexual Orientation, or Religion or Belief, Regulations 2003, reg 9.

21   See further below, and especially pp 321–23.

22   It was held in *Ministry of Defence v Fair Employment Agency* (1988) Belfast Recorder's Court, unreported, 355 IRLIB 14, to be discriminatory to require references only on Catholic candidates. All arrangements concerned with the taking up of references are clearly covered by the legislation.

23   [1993] IRLR 357, EAT.

had a claim whether or not they would have been offered the job if the procedures had operated in a non-discriminatory fashion or even if no one had been appointed. There is a right not to be discriminated against even if the plaintiff was unlikely to have been appointed.[24]

The Codes of Practice demonstrate how recruitment and interview practices may operate in a discriminatory manner and give examples of good practice. Word-of-mouth hiring[25] may give rise to discrimination, although one suspects that it is still commonplace, especially where there is an urgent need to fill a vacancy. It is a cheap and convenient method, often thought to be at least as reliable as more formal methods, whereas complying to the letter with the Codes of Practice imposes costs on the employer.[26] It is very important to ensure that recruitment knowledge is widely and generally available; even sports clubs and other networks may be a source of job information, sources which could work to the disadvantage of those from the protected groups.

We have seen[27] that many selection criteria may be indirectly discriminatory: mobility, experience, ability in English, education in the UK, etc. The Codes recommend – and the law may insist – that employers ensure that such requirements are actually necessary.[28] The combined impact of the law, the Code of Practice and more general pressure on behalf of women has certainly contributed to a reduction in the utilisation of criteria seen to disadvantage women. For example, it is probable that the use of mobility requirements is declining as employers fear that their utilisation has reduced the ability of employers to recruit and retain well-qualified women.

However, the ability of the Codes and the law to counter direct discrimination is problematic; stereotypes may be unspoken or unacknowledged. It is safe to assume that discriminatory attitudes and behaviour may flourish more easily where employers do not operate their recruitment procedures with any degree of formality; it would *not* be safe to assume that formal procedures can necessarily prevent discriminatory attitudes and behaviour from being manifested. This is especially true for jobs where recruitment is based on attitude rather than ability – where decisions are based on subjective rather than objective criteria.[29] In addition, the subjective criteria themselves may be affected by racial or gender issues. These may range from ideas that women do not want to build a career; that some jobs such as sales require

---

24 For discussion of compensation in such cases, see below, Chapter 17, p 536.

25 See the discussion of 'subjective hiring practices' in Chapter 10, p 249 *et al*; and for where word-of-mouth recruitment led to a segregated workforce, see *Pel Ltd v Modgill* [1980] IRLR 142, EAT, discussed in Chapter 7, pp 173–75.

26 Two formal investigations carried out by the Commission for Racial Equality castigated employers who adopted word-of-mouth recruitment. A policy of requiring drivers to be recommended by an existing employee had the result that the only black employee was the brother-in-law of one of the drivers; see *F Broomfield and London Drivers Supplied Services Ltd, Employment Agency*, 1980, London: CRE; Massey Ferguson in Coventry did not advertise for vacancies, but relied on unsolicited applications. This benefited those who could obtain information from current employees, and, as a result, there were six black employees in a total workforce of 5,500. This is precisely the type of case where a formal investigation is potentially so valuable, as an individual is unlikely to be able to make a successful claim for a failure to advertise; see *Massey Ferguson Perkins Ltd*, 1982, London: CRE.

27 Chapter 10, pp 249–51.

28 See the discussion on justification of indirect discrimination, Chapter 10, pp 273–82.

29 See Jenkins, R, *Racism and Recruitment: Managers, Organisations and Equal Opportunity in the Labour Market*, 1986, Cambridge: CUP, pp 18–21. For a discussion 'subjective hiring practices' as *indirect* discrimination, see Chapter 10, p 249 *et al*.

an aggressive personality women do not possess; for other jobs that 'femininity' will give a more effective job performance; that members of a particular racial group might antagonise clients or fellow employees or would not 'fit in';[30] or take long periods of leave to visit relatives. In many such cases, discrimination remains concealed and impossible for applicants to prove, especially where these and other similar criteria are used to distinguish between candidates who, on paper, appear relatively equally qualified. The impact of the law in these marginal and subjective cases is extremely difficult to determine.[31]

It may be possible to establish discrimination purely from the way in which an interview was conducted. In *Saunders v Richmond BC*,[32] amongst other questions put to a female golf professional was: 'Do you think men respond as well to a woman golf pro as to a man?' It was clear that such a question would not have been put to a man; the question whether she could teach men really meant whether they could accept being taught by her, but it was held that asking such gender-related questions was not of itself discriminatory and that on the facts discrimination had not been established. Such questions, though, usually reflect discriminatory attitudes and are strongly discouraged by the Code of Practice. Thus, it may be that nowadays not a great deal more evidence will be needed to support a finding of discrimination where an interview panel has persistently and intrusively questioned a female candidate about family responsibilities and childcare arrangements. The EAT also expressed the rather more controversial view that such questions may be entirely appropriate if related to capacity to do the job. The facts of *Saunders* have some parallels to those concerning jobs entailing the counselling of people of a different sex, and here questions to establish appropriate empathy – which may not be asked in precisely the same way of both genders – are justified. However, such argument is less convincing as regards questions designed to establish empathy with the needs of members of a different race.

(a)   Advertising and recruitment[33]

Section 29(1) of the RRA 1976 makes it unlawful to publish 'an advertisement[34] which indicates, or might reasonably be understood as indicating, an intention by a person to do an act of discrimination' even if in fact any subsequent act of discrimination would be lawful. The equivalent provision of the SDA 1975, s 38(1), is weaker, being limited to those advertisements which 'indicate an intention' to do an unlawful act.[35]

---

30 See, eg, *Noone v North West Thames RHA* [1988] ICR 813; [1988] IRLR 195, CA, where a Sri Lankan consultant microbiologist, who was by far the best candidate on paper, was rejected for this reason.

31 On proving *direct* discrimination, see above, Chapter 7, p 188.

32 [1978] ICR 75; [1977] IRLR 362, EAT. See also *Adams v Strathclyde Regional Council* (1989), unreported, EAT, Case 456/88; *Woodhead v Chief Constable of West Yorkshire Police* (1990), unreported, EAT, Case 285/89.

33 See 'Job advertising and the SDA' (1993) 52 EOR 12.

34 'Advertisement' is widely defined and need not necessarily be to the public; internal staff communications are thus included. Other examples include postcards in shop windows and house-to-house circulars.

35 An advertisement to discriminate in a lawful way is protected by s 38(2), enabling an employer to specify that a female is wanted in circumstances where being female is a genuine occupational qualification for the job being advertised. There are no parallel advertisement provisions in the Religion or Belief, or Sexual Orientation, Regulations 2003.

However, s 38(3) creates a presumption that job titles with a sexual connotation (postman, waitress, etc) indicate an intention to discriminate unless the contrary specifically appears in the wording of the advertisement. The test for determining intention is objective, based on what an ordinary reasonable person, without any special knowledge, would understand by the advertisement. What the employer intended is irrelevant.[36]

It is clear that both the publisher and the advertiser may be liable for discriminatory advertising. The right to take action is placed primarily in the hands of the Equal Opportunities Commission and the Commission for Racial Equality. All a person offended by a discriminatory advertisement who is not interested in the position advertised can do is to inform the relevant Commission of the facts. However, it was long thought that advertising forms part of the arrangements made under s 6(1) or s 4(1) for the purpose of determining who will be offered employment, and thus someone directly affected in such a way had a right to claim.[37] Furthermore, unlike actions instigated by the Commissions, individual actions are not limited to complaints about the wording. It might, for example, be argued that it was indirectly discriminatory to place an advert in a magazine predominantly read by women or a part of a factory predominantly frequented by men. While in such a case the disparate impact would be difficult if not impossible to establish, and an employer should not be liable if reasonable efforts have been made to ensure that the applicant pool is representative, it should in theory be possible for a claim to be brought by, for example, someone who never saw an advertisement because of where it was placed.

This view of the law was altered by *Cardiff Women's Aid v Hartup*,[38] where Smith J said that: 'it is only the Commission for Racial Equality which can bring ... proceedings. We also accept the construction of s 29 ... that "an intention by a person to do an act of discrimination" should be contrasted with "an act of discrimination" itself ...' As a result, individuals may not sue if they are affected by a discriminatory advertisement; they have to rely on the appropriate Commission to take action. The individual right to sue is dependent on the *individual* being discriminated against; thus, the person must apply, wait to be rejected, and then sue, when presumably the wording of the advert may be used as part of the evidence that discrimination has occurred. The incentive for individuals to go through such a process is decidedly limited. Such a restriction is particularly inappropriate where it concerns internal company advertisements: there is no fear of intermeddlers commencing litigation and the effect on excluded individuals is more likely to be immediate and significant.

The Code of Practice on racial equality recommends that 'employers should not confine advertisements unjustifiably to those areas or publications which would exclude or disproportionately reduce the numbers of applicants of a particular racial group' and that: '[i]n order to demonstrate their commitment to equality of

---

36   In *Equal Opportunities Commission v Robertson* [1980] IRLR 44, the industrial tribunal held that the words 'craftsman', 'ex-policeman or similar', 'bloke', 'manageress' (but not 'manager' and 'carpenter/handyman') all had sexual connotations and so it would need to be specifically stated in the advertisement that the job was open to people of either sex.

37   *Brindley v Tayside Health Board* [1976] IRLR 364, IT.

38   [1994] IRLR 390, EAT.

opportunity it is recommended that where employers send literature to applicants, this should include a statement that they are equal opportunity employers.'[39]

Cases on discriminatory advertising have been few; the Commissions have preferred to proceed by way of advice and explanation and have sought as much voluntary co-operation as possible. The cases themselves have usually involved flagrant and obvious breaches of the law, which have understandably become less common, though non-discriminatory advertising in no way guarantees that the remainder of the recruitment process will be free from direct or indirect discrimination. In practice, the greater problem with discriminatory advertisements concerns keeping the wording of a positive action advert within the boundary of what the law permits.

(2)   Discriminatory Terms of Employment.

Offers which are on different terms are potentially caught by sub-s (1)(b) of the parallel provisions.[40] Once the offer becomes part of the contract, any sex discrimination claim must then be under the Equal Pay Act 1970 rather than the SDA 1975; the complex interrelationship between the two pieces of legislation is explained in Chapter 14.[41]

(3)   Discrimination Within Employment.

Under s 6(2)(a) of the SDA 1975, it is unlawful for an employer to discriminate against a woman 'in the way he affords her access to opportunities for promotion, transfer or training, or to any other benefits, facilities or services, or by refusing or deliberately omitting to afford her access to them ...'. Section 4(2)(b) of the RRA 1976 is effectively identical. The parallel provisions in the Religion or Belief, or Sexual Orientation, Regulations[42] are materially the same, but spread over sub-paras 6(2)(a), (b) and (c). Sections 6(2)(b) of the SDA 1975, 4(2)(c) of the RRA 1976 and reg (2)(d) of the Religion or Belief, or Sexual Orientation, Regulations render unlawful discrimination by dismissal, or by subjection 'to any other detriment'.

(a)   *Access to opportunities for promotion, etc*

EOC Code of Practice

25   It is ... recommended that:

(a) where an appraisal system is in operation, the assessment criteria should be examined to ensure that they are not unlawfully discriminatory and the scheme monitored to assess how it is working in practice;

---

39 Paragraphs 1.6, 1.7; see also EOC Code of Practice, paras 19 and 20. Advertising may be very important as part of a strategy of positive action, as will be seen in Chapter 18. It is not unlawful to target a particular group in the hope of attracting applicants, for that in itself does not discriminate against members of the non-targeted group, assuming, of course, that actual applicants are judged solely on merit.

40 That is, SDA 1975, s 6 (set out above, p 317); RRA 1976, s 4; and Religion or Belief, or Sexual Orientation, Regulations 2003, reg 6.

41 See below, p 379.

42 In force since 2 December 2003 and 1 December 2003, respectively.

(b) when a group of workers predominantly of one sex is excluded from an appraisal scheme, access to promotion, transfer and training and to other benefits should be reviewed, to ensure there is no unlawful indirect discrimination;

(c) promotion and career development patterns are reviewed to ensure that the traditional qualifications are justifiable requirements for the job to be done ...;

(d) when general ability and personal qualities are the main requirements for promotion to a post, care should be taken to consider favourably candidates of both sexes with differing career patterns and general experience;

(e) rules which restrict or preclude transfer between certain jobs should be questioned and changed if they are found to be unlawfully discriminatory. Employees of one sex may be concentrated in sections from which transfers are traditionally restricted without justification;

(f) policies and practices regarding selection for training, day release and personal development should be examined for direct and indirect discrimination. Where there is found to be an imbalance in training as between sexes, the cause should be identified to ensure that it is not discriminatory ...

30   It is ... recommended that:

(a) particular care is taken to ensure that an employee who has in good faith taken action under the Sex Discrimination Act or the Equal Pay Act does not receive less favourable treatment than other employees, for example, by being disciplined or dismissed;

(b) employees should be advised to use the internal procedures, where appropriate, but this is without prejudice to an individual's right to apply to an Industrial Tribunal within the statutory time limit ...

(c) particular care is taken to deal effectively with all complaints of discrimination, victimisation or harassment. It should not be assumed that they are made by those who are over-sensitive.

The guidance on promotion is especially significant where an organisation operates an internal labour market (which places added weight on the original recruitment decision). It is not uncommon for there to be favoured pathways to promotion, whether by accident or design, benefiting those hired to certain lower level entry jobs. If these are predominantly male, women will be disadvantaged. Just as with initial hiring, the Code works on the assumption that there is less scope for discrimination if there is open competition through advertising rather than promotion by simple selection; if the latter is the case, formal appraisal procedures should be in place.[43]

As promotion opportunities need to be open to all, irrespective of the protected grounds, it follows that there is no *obligation* on employers to give special training to women or minorities to equip them for promotion.[44] However, such special training may be *permissible* as being positive action to remedy situations where there is under-

---

43 Even objective promotion criteria may be indirectly discriminatory, especially if dependent primarily on length of service. However, it is arguable that women stand to gain more by the use of objective criteria, such as seniority, than they stand to lose because they have lower average lengths of service. Such criteria, after all, remove the need for subjective decision making where unspoken discriminatory assumptions may operate to women's disadvantage. See above, pp 249–51.

44 *Mecca Leisure Group Ltd v Chatprachong* [1993] ICR 668; [1993] IRLR 531, where the EAT held that there was no obligation to provide special language training which would have better equipped the plaintiff for the relevant promotion examination.

representation of women or minorities.[45] Where this is done, the actual decision on who to hire must continue to be made solely on the basis of merit.

The Codes emphasise that all training opportunities should be checked to ensure the absence of direct or indirect discrimination. Length-of-service requirements, exclusion of part-time employees and preference to those with technical qualifications are examples of criteria which may disadvantage women. Day release has often only been available in the immediate post-school years, which may disadvantage women returners to the labour market and limit retraining opportunities.

Discrimination is also prohibited as regards access to fringe benefits. The most important of these is pension provision,[46] but discrimination could occur in access to sick pay schemes, mortgage subsidy, company car arrangements and so on, especially against part-time employees. The effect of *Bilka-Kaufhaus v Weber von Hartz*[47] is that any provision which disadvantages part-time employees will need to be justified according to objective criteria which by definition will not include long standing traditional arrangements. Recreational benefits are within the definition, so it might be possible to argue that the employer discriminates by providing facilities and subsidy for predominantly male sports rather than female, or predominantly white or European cultural activities rather than those more likely to be of interest to minority employees.

(b) Discriminatory dismissals

Discriminatory dismissals are made unlawful by s 6(2)(b) of the SDA 1975, s 4(2)(c) of the RRA 1976 and reg 6(2)(d) of either the Religion or Belief, or Sexual Orientation, Regulations.[48] There is overlap with the general unfair dismissal provisions now contained in the Employment Rights Act 1996, which provide that 'dismissal' includes constructive dismissal.[49] A statutory definition, belatedly, has been introduced into the sex and race legislation.[50] *Weathersfield* decided that the RRA 1976 (before the introduction of the statutory definition) covered constructive dismissal. A further issue was the communication, by the worker, of her reason for leaving. The Court of Appeal saw no reason to depart from the established contract principles of acceptance of a repudiatory breach, for the purposes of the discrimination legislation.

Weathersfield Ltd (t/a Van & Truck Rentals) v Sargent **[1999] IRLR 94; [1999] ICR 425, CA**[51]

Mrs Sargent, a white European, was appointed as a receptionist by the defendants. On her first day she was told: 'We do have a special policy regarding coloured and Asians.

---

45 See below, Chapter 18, pp 574–78.

46 See Chapter 15.

47 Case 170/84 [1986] ECR 1607; [1986] 2 CMLR 701; [1987] ICR 110; [1986] IRLR 317. See now the Part-Time Workers (Prevention of Less Favourable Treatment) Regulations 2000, SI 2000/1551, in force since 1 July 2000, implementing Directive 97/81/EC, set out in Chapter 10, p 283.

48 In force since 2 December 2003 and 1 December 2003, respectively.

49 Employment Rights Act 1996, s 95(1)(c).

50 SDA 1975, s 82(1A) (introduced by the SDA 1986, s 2(3)); RRA 1976, s 4A (by the Race Relations Act 1976 (Amendment) Regulations 2003, reg 5(2)(c), in force since 19 July 2003). See also reg 6(5) of either the Religion or Belief, or Sexual Orientation, Regulations 2003 (in force since 2 December 2003 and 1 December 2003, respectively).

51 Applied in *Derby Specialist Fabrication Ltd v Burton* [2001] 2 All ER 840, EAT.

We have got to be careful who we hire the vehicles to. If you get a telephone call from any coloured or Asians you can usually tell them by the sound of their voice. You have to tell them that there are no vehicles available.' She was stunned and a few days later resigned, without giving her reason. She brought a claim of racial discrimination, claiming that she had been constructively dismissed on the ground of race. The Court of Appeal held, following *Showboat v Owens*[52] that it was possible to be discriminated against on the grounds of another's race. The next issue was whether 'dismissal' in s 4(2)(c) of the RRA 1976 included constructive dismissal and, if it did, was it a requirement that the worker give her reasons for resigning? The court found for Mrs Sargent on both points.

Pill LJ (paras 21–22):

I reject as a proposition of law the notion that there can be no acceptance of a repudiation unless the employee tells the employer, at the time, that he is leaving because of the employer's repudiatory conduct. Each case will turn on its own facts and, where no reason is communicated to the employer at the time, the fact-finding tribunal may more readily conclude that the repudiatory conduct was not the reason for the employee leaving. In each case it will, however, be for the fact-finding tribunal, considering all the evidence, to decide whether there has been an acceptance ...

In *Heyman v Darwins Ltd* [1942] AC 356, Viscount Simon LC stated at pp 361–62:

'But repudiation by one party standing alone does not terminate the contract. It takes two to end it, by repudiation, on the one side, and acceptance of the repudiation, on the other. ...' Thus, in *General Billposting Company Ltd v Atkinson* [1909] AC 118, ... Lord Collins ... said (p 122): "I think the true test applicable to the facts of this case is that which was laid down by Lord Coleridge CJ in *Freeth v Burr* [1874] LR 9 CP 208, ... that the true question is whether 'the acts and conduct of the party evince an intention no longer to be bound by the contract'."'

Acceptance of a repudiation of a contract of employment will usually take the form of the employee leaving and saying why he is leaving but it is not necessary in law for the reason to be given at the time of leaving. The fact-finding tribunal is entitled to reach its own conclusion, based on the 'acts and conduct of the party', as to the true reason ...

In the present case, the industrial tribunal were amply justified in holding that there was a constructive dismissal. In the first days of her employment, the employers had put Mrs Sargent in an outrageous and embarrassing position. It was understandable that she did not want immediately to confront the employers with her reason for leaving. In the event, and having taken advice, she did so within a matter of days. No other reason why she may have left the employment became apparent in the evidence.

For many employees, the more outrageous or embarrassing are the instructions given to them, or suggestions made to them, the less likely they may be to argue the point there and then. They may reasonably wish to remove themselves at the first opportunity and with a minimum of discussion. Leaving the employment without notifying the reason does not preclude a finding of constructive dismissal, though it will usually make it more difficult to obtain such a finding ... Moreover, there is no suggestion in this case that the employers would have changed their policy had she asked them to do so. Industrial tribunals will, on the other hand, be astute to discover the true reason for the employee leaving and reject those claims in which alleged conduct by the employer is no more than a pretext or cover for leaving on other grounds.

The two key differences between unfair dismissal and discriminatory dismissal concern qualifying conditions and compensation. There is a one-year[53] qualification period for unfair dismissal rights. The weekly hours threshold, which used to exist for unfair dismissal and other purposes, was abolished as, contrary to European law, it indirectly discriminatory against women.[54] Unfair dismissal compensation remains subject to a statutory maximum limit on compensation. At the time of writing, the maximum compensatory award for unfair dismissal was £52,600.[55] An equivalent statutory maximum limit in both race and sex discrimination cases was swept away as a result of the decision of the European Court in *Marshall (No 2)*.[56] A claimant who can establish that the dismissal was discriminatory, therefore, may benefit, depending on the amount of compensation due.[57] It is possible to combine the two allegations in one statement of claim.[58]

(c) Any other detriment

This final phrase of s 6(2) of the SDA 1975, or the parallel provisions, ensures that claims are not restricted to those situations specified, such as access to promotion or dismissal. The phrase has often been defined over the years, yet recently, its meaning was in question again, this time before the House the Lords.

---

53 Reduced from two years, where the effective date of termination is after 1 June 1999: Unfair Dismissal and Statement of Reasons for Dismissal (Variation of Qualifying Period) Order 1999, SI 1999/1436. The previous two-year period was challenged unsuccessfully as being contrary to EC discrimination law: see *R v Secretary of State for Employment ex p Seymour-Smith and Perez* [2000] 1 All ER 857; [2000] 1 WLR 435; [2000] ICR 244; [2000] IRLR 263, HL, discussed in Chapter 10, p 270 and pp 295–98.

54 *R v Secretary of State for Employment ex p EOC* [1995] 1 AC 1; [1994] ICR 317; [1994] 1 All ER 910; [1994] IRLR 176, HL. The Employment Protection (Part-time Employees) Regulations 1995, SI 1995/31 repealed the relevant provisions in the Employment Protection (Consolidation) Act 1978, which has been superseded by the Employment Rights Act 1996.

55 Employment Rights Act 1996, s 124. In 1998, the Government proposed to abolish this limit: *Fairness at Work*, Cm 3968, 1998, London: HMSO, para 3.5.

56 *Marshall v Southampton and South West Hampshire AHA* Case C-271/91 [1993] ECR I-4367; [1994] AC 530; [1994] QB 126; [1994] ICR 242; [1993] IRLR 445. See below, Chapter 15, p 440.

57 The abolition of the limit on compensation proved crucial in the cases where the armed forces admitted a long standing policy of dismissing those who became pregnant. As the claim was against an organ of the State, damages could be awarded for losses arising in respect of any period after the UK's failure to implement the Equal Treatment Directive. The Government was forced to concede the unlawfulness of its policy, so the litigation concerned the proper approach to compensation in such cases. See, eg, *Ministry of Defence v Cannock* [1994] ICR 918; [1995] 2 All ER 449; [1994] IRLR 509, EAT; Arnull, A, 'EC law and the dismissal of pregnant servicewomen' [1995] 24 ILJ 215; and now the Sex Discrimination Act 1975 (Application to Armed Forces, etc) Regulations 1994, SI 1994/3276.

58 The Employment Appeal Tribunal pointed out in *Clarke v Eley (IMI) Kynoch Ltd* [1983] ICR 165; [1982] IRLR 482, that an indirectly discriminatory dismissal will not automatically be unfair as the facts which made it discriminatory might not have been known to the employer at the time of the decision to dismiss; whether or not the dismissal is unfair will depend on the employer's knowledge and purpose at that time.

Shamoon Appellant v Chief Constable of the Royal Ulster Constabulary **[2003]**
UKHL 11; [2003] 2 All ER 26, HL

Joan Shamoon, a police inspector, carried out, as one of her duties, appraisals of
officers. Following complaints by officers, she was relieved of the appraisal duty. She
brought claim of discrimination under the Sex Discrimination (Northern Ireland)
Order 1976. Article 8(2)(b) is set out in identical terms to s 6(2)(b) of the SDA 1975. The
Northern Ireland Court of Appeal[59] held that Shamoon has not suffered a detriment
because: 'She did not have a "right" to carry out appraisals, and it was at most a
practice that this work was entrusted to her. There was no loss of rank and no
financial consequence when the function was removed from her.' The House of Lords
reversed that finding although, for other reasons, it dismissed her appeal.[60] Lord
Hope cited *Khan v Chief Constable of West Yorkshire*,[61] a case concerning similar
provisions on victimisation, where Khan was refused a reference, in circumstances
where he was better off without one.

33.   At p 1951A–B, para 14 in *Khan's* case Lord Nicholls of Birkenhead said:

> I accept Sergeant Khan's claim that the refusal to provide a reference for him
> constituted a detriment ... even though, as matters turned out, this did not
> cause him any financial loss. Provision of a reference is a normal feature of
> employment.

Lord Hoffmann ... pointed out, at p 1959G-1960A, that being subjected to detriment ...
is an element of the statutory cause of action additional to being treated 'less
favourably' which forms part of the definition of discrimination:

> A person may be treated less favourably and yet suffer no detriment. But,
> bearing in mind that the employment tribunal has jurisdiction to award
> compensation to injury to feelings, the courts have given the term
> 'detriment' a wide meaning. In *Ministry of Defence v Jeremiah* [1980] QB 87,
> 104 Brightman LJ said that 'a detriment exists if a reasonable worker would
> or might take the view that the [treatment] was in all the circumstances to
> his detriment'.

35.   But once this requirement is satisfied, the only other limitation that can be read
      into the word is that indicated by Lord Brightman. As he put it in *Ministry of
      Defence v Jeremiah* [1980] QB 87, 104B, one must take all the circumstances into
      account. This is a test of materiality. Is the treatment of such a kind that a
      reasonable worker would or might take the view that in all the circumstances it
      was to his detriment? An unjustified sense of grievance cannot amount to
      'detriment': *Barclays Bank plc v Kapur and Others (No 2)* [1995] IRLR 87. But,
      contrary to the view that was expressed in *Lord Chancellor v Coker and Osamor*[62]
      on which the Court of Appeal relied, it is not necessary to demonstrate some
      physical or economic consequence. ...

37.   ... There was evidence that the appellant had carried out as many as thirty five
      appraisals since she was promoted to the rank of chief inspector. Once it was
      known, as it was bound to be, that she had had this part of her normal duties
      taken away from her following a complaint to the Police Federation, the effect
      was likely to be to reduce her standing among her colleagues. A reasonable

---

59   [2001] IRLR 520.
60   Because she had not been treated less favourably than a male officer would have been, in the
     same circumstances. See further Chapter 7, pp 170–77.
61   [2002] 1 WLR 1947; [2001] 4 All ER 834; see further, Chapter 11, p 306.
62   [2001] IRLR 116, CA; see further, Chapter 10, p 261.

employee in her position might well feel that she was being demeaned in the eyes of those over whom she was in a position of authority. ... In my opinion the appellant was entitled to a finding that she was subjected to a detriment within the meaning of article 8(2)(b).

(4) Discrimination After Employment

Race Relations Act 1976

Relationships that have come to an end

Section 27A

(1) In this section a 'relevant relationship' is a relationship during the course of which, ...

    (a) an act of discrimination by one party to the relationship ("the relevant party") against another party to the relationship, on grounds of race or ethnic or national origins, or

    (b) harassment of another party to the relationship by the relevant party, is unlawful.

(2) Where a relevant relationship has come to an end it is unlawful for the relevant party -

    (a) to discriminate against another party, on grounds of race or ethnic or national origins, by subjecting him to a detriment, or

    (b) to subject another party to harassment,

    where the discrimination or harassment arises out of and is closely connected to that relationship.

(3) In subsection (1) reference to an act of discrimination or harassment which is unlawful includes, in the case of a relationship which has come to an end before 19th July 2003, reference to such an act which would, after that date, be unlawful.

This section was inserted[63] to implement the Race Directive[64] and so only covers areas within the scope of that Directive. It does not cover, for instance, discrimination solely on grounds of colour or nationality,[65] nor does it cover post-relationship acts of discrimination or harassment occurring before s 27A came into force (on 19 July 2003). Similar provisions are given in reg 21 of either the Religion or Belief, or Sexual Orientation, Regulations 2003[66] and s 20A of the SDA.[67]

The position for cases pre-dating these new provisions, and for the residual race cases, is much the same, following *Relaxion v Rhys-Harper*.[68] The issue was the

---

63 By the Race Relations Act 1976 (Amendment) Regulations 2003, SI 2003/1626, reg 15, in force since 19 July 2003.

64 Council Directive 2000/43/EC.

65 See further, Chapter 6, pp 137–38 and 140–42.

66 In force since 2 December 2003 and 1 December 2003, respectively.

67 Inserted by the Sex Discrimination Act 1975 (Amendment) Regulations 2003, SI 2003/1657, reg 3. Regulation 3 also inserted a new parallel s 35C, which covers barristers, advocates and vocational training. The definition in the SDA differs slightly in that it does not specify 'harassment'. This is because the SDA does not yet provide free-standing definition of harassment. Harassment is unlawful under the SDA when it amounts to 'discrimination': see further, Chapter 9, especially pp 219–24.

68 The collective appeals of *Relaxion Group plc v Rhys-Harper, D'Souza v Lambeth LBC, Jones v 3M Healthcare Ltd* [2003] UKHL 33, overruling *Post Office v Adekeye* [1997] ICR 110; [1997] IRLR 105, CA.

interpretation of s 6(2) of the SDA 1975 (or s 4(2) of the RRA), which provides: 'It is unlawful for a person, in the case of a woman employed by him ... to discriminate against her ...' In *Coote v Granada*,[69] Mrs Coote sued her employer following her dismissal for being pregnant. Subsequently, and after those proceedings were dead, the employer refused to give her a reference and Mrs Coote sued again, this time for victimisation. An industrial tribunal ruled that s 6 of the SDA extended discrimination only so far as persons *employed* by the defendant. As Mrs Coote no longer worked for Granada when they refused the reference, she was not protected by the Act. The ECJ, under the Equal Treatment Directive, took a different view, holding that: 'Fear of such measures ... might deter workers who considered themselves the victims of discrimination from pursuing their claims ... and would consequently ... seriously ... jeopardise implementation of the aim pursued by the Directive.'[70] Following the ECJ's ruling, the Employment Appeal Tribunal held that s 6(2) covered ex-workers.[71] In *Relaxion v Rhys-Harper*,[72] the House of Lords confirmed this approach for discrimination, as well as victimisation, under the RRA, as well as the SDA.[73]

3   PERMISSIBLE DISCRIMINATION WITHIN EMPLOYMENT

This section brings together a range of situations where discrimination in employment continues, to a greater or lesser extent, to be permissible. It does not consider discrimination in pension provision or permissible discrimination within the non-employment context, which are considered elsewhere. In addition, a number of exceptions or possible exceptions relating to issues of pregnancy, maternity and paternity leave have been specifically considered in Chapter 8.

The most significant general exception in all the legislation is what is known as a 'genuine occupational qualification' (GOQ). For instance, Art 4 of the Race Directive[74] provides an exception where a: 'characteristic related to racial or ethnic origin ... constitutes a genuine and determining occupational requirement, provided that the objective is legitimate and the requirement is proportionate.' Article 2(2) of the Equal Treatment Directive carries, at present, a less strict formula, which allows exclusion where 'by reason of their nature or the context in which they are carried out, the sex of the worker constitutes a determining factor'. A stricter formula, in line with the Race Directive, is due for implementation by 5 October 2005.[75] The definitions given in the domestic legislation generally reflect the EC definitions, but, of course, they apply only as far as the scope of the Directives. This leaves a class of residual cases which are

---

69   Case C-185/97 [1998] All ER (EC) 865.

70   *Ibid*, at para 24. This decision led to the amendment of the SDA.

71   *Coote v Granada Hospitality Ltd (No 2)* [1999] ICR 942; [1999] IRLR 452; [1999] 3 CMLR 334.

72   The collective appeals of *Relaxion Group plc v Rhys-Harper, D'Souza v Lambeth LBC, Jones v 3M Healthcare Ltd* [2003] UKHL 33, overruling *Post Office v Adekeye* [1997] ICR 110; [1997] IRLR 105, CA.

73   And also the DDA. Except where the act complained of does not arise from the employment relationship, such as a refusal to implement an employment tribunal's reinstatement order, for which there is a free-standing remedy (under the Employment Rights Act 1996, ss 112, 113, 114 and 117): *ibid*, in the case of *D'Souza*, at paras 49–53, 124–25, 159–60, 205 and 221.

74   Council Directive 2000/43/EC. The Equal Treatment in Employment Directive (2000/78/EC), Art 4 provides the same formula for religion or belief, sexual orientation, (implemented on 2 December 2003 and 1 December 2003, respectively) and age and disability.

75   Equal Treatment Amendment Directive 2002/73/EC.

not covered by the new formula in the RRA 1976, for instance, cases arising before the definition came into force[76] or discrimination solely on the grounds of colour or nationality.[77]

(1)   Genuine Occupational Qualifications – Sex and Race

Under the British legislation, there have been many more GOQs concerning sex than race. This reflects the underlying social and moral reality that segregation of the sexes is, in many circumstances, regarded as appropriate and necessary, whereas segregation of the races is seen, because of its historical connotations, as a moral evil and a practice which was used to reinforce white power over other races.

The defence can be raised where only *some* of the job duties fall within the scope of the exception.[78] This is subject to two limits. First, the defence will fail if the duties of the job were reorganised with the express purpose of bringing it within the scope of the defence.[79] Secondly, under s 7(4) of the SDA 1975 and s 5(4) of the RRA 1976, the defence will fail where other employees are 'capable of carrying out the duties', that it would be reasonable to employ them on such duties, and where this can be done without undue inconvenience. In *Lasertop Ltd v Webster*,[80] it was held that these 'other employees' to whom the duties may be re-allocated must already exist at the time, so s 7(4) did not apply where the employer was hiring for a job in a health club which was not yet open. Thus, the GOQ applied even though it might well not do so once other employees had been hired.[81] In *Etam plc v Rowan*,[82] the defence of GOQ in relation to a job in a ladies' clothing shop failed because reorganisation was possible. The only parts of the job which fell within the defence involved work in the fitting room and measuring customers, but there were some 16 employees normally in the shop – all women. A man would have been able to carry out the bulk of the job and the remainder could easily have been done by other sales assistants without causing any inconvenience or difficulty for the employers. It follows that, to an extent at least, the tribunal in effect has power to require the employer to reorganise the business, or at least to conclude that the defence will fail unless such reorganisation has been carried out.

Where the defence applies, it is lawful for the employer to discriminate in the arrangements made for determining who should be offered a job, in determining that someone may not be offered a job, or in denying opportunities for promotion or transfer. These all concern aspects of management pertaining to the obtaining of

---

76   19 July 2003.

77   See further, Chapter 6, pp 137–38 and 140–42.

78   SDA 1975, s 7(3); RRA 1976, s 5(3); see *Tottenham Green* below, p 334.

79   *Timex Corp v Hodgson* [1982] ICR 63; [1981] IRLR 530, EAT.

80   [1997] IRLR 498, EAT.

81   Such a construction may well be contrary to the Equal Treatment Directive; again, no attempt was made to apply the *Marleasing* principle in order to avoid such a conflict.

82   [1989] IRLR 150, EAT. A different result was reached in *Lasertop Ltd v Webster* [1997] IRLR 498, EAT, where it was held to be permissible to restrict to women a job of selling membership of a women-only health club, as the man would have to hand over to a woman whenever the changing area was reached. The industrial tribunal found this aspect of the job did not involve a great deal of time and that arrangements could have been made without undue inconvenience. The EAT, accepting the employer's argument rather easily and reversing a finding largely of fact, held that the defence was made out.

employment, but the defence is not available in relation to the terms on which employment is offered, to dismissal or to the imposition of any other detriment on an employee. The defence is only concerned with the process of offering employment in situations where jobs may legitimately be restricted to one race or gender; if members of more than one race or gender are performing a job, there is no logic or policy justification for allowing the defence. Thus, an employer may not, after an employee has been hired, retrospectively decide that a GOQ applies to a job in question. It is, however, permissible, to dismiss someone following a reorganisation if the new job involves a GOQ where the incumbent's previous job did not do so. According to *Timex Corp v Hodgson*,[83] the GOQ defence is permissible because in such circumstances it affixes to the failure to offer the reorganised new job rather than dismissal from the old job.

The new s 4A of the RRA 1976, reflecting the Directive, provides only a general principle for the courts to apply. As with the existing definition (s 5 of the RRA 1976, below), it exempts employers from the Act in recruitment, promotion, training and transfer matters only.[84]

Race Relations Act 1976

Section 4A

(2)   ... having regard to the nature of the employment or the context in which it is carried out—

    (a) being of a particular race or particular ethnic or national origins is a genuine and determining occupational requirement; and

    (b) it is proportionate to apply that requirement in the particular case; and

    (c) either—

       (i) the person to whom that requirement is applied does not meet it, or

       (ii) the employer is not satisfied, and in all the circumstances it is reasonable for him not to be satisfied, that that person meets it.[85]

The word 'proportionate' gives this section its EC flavour. However, the section omits the word 'legitimate' from the Directive, which may lead to a conflict with EC law. However, where the Directive is not directly effective, it should be possible for domestic tribunals to read 'legitimate' into the word 'genuine' under the *Marleasing* principle of indirect effect.[86] So long as they comply with the principles of 'legitimacy' and 'proportionality', it is likely that the courts will follow the 'old' detailed examples provided in the RRA 1976, which, strictly speaking, only apply to residual cases. As the SDA 1975 has yet to be amended[87] with the new formula, the provisions there apply as ever.

Section 5(2) of the RRA 1976 specifies four GOQs:

Being of a particular racial group is a genuine occupational qualification for a job only where:

---

83 [1982] ICR 63; [1981] IRLR 530, EAT.
84 That is, those covered by s 4(1)(a) and (b), and (2)(b).
85 For a commentary on s 4A(2)(c)(ii), see below, p 342.
86 See Chapter 5, pp 111–12.d
87 The Equal Treatment Amendment Directive (2002/73/EC) is due for implementation by 5 October 2005.

(a)   the job involves participation in a dramatic performance or other entertainment in a capacity for which a person of that racial group is required for reasons of authenticity; or

(b)   the job involves participation as an artist's or photographic model in the production of a work of art, visual image or sequence of visual images for which a person of that racial group is required for authenticity; or

(c)   the job involves working in a place where food or drink is (for payment or not) provided to and consumed by members of the public or a section of the public in a particular setting for which, in that job, a person of that racial group is required for authenticity; or

(d)   the holder of the job provides persons of that racial group with personal services promoting their welfare, and those services can most effectively be provided by a person of that racial group.

The provisions of the Sex Discrimination Act 1975 which directly match these are in s 7(2):

Being a man is a genuine occupational qualification for a job only where:

(a)   the essential nature of the job calls for a man for reasons of physiology (excluding strength and stamina) or, in dramatic performances or other entertainment, so that the essential nature of the job would be materially different if carried out by a woman ...;

(e)   the holder of the job provides individuals with personal services promoting their welfare or education, or similar personal services, and those personal services can most effectively be provided by a man ...

In addition, s 4(3) of the RRA 1976 once provided an exception where the employment was in a private household. Within the structure of the legislation it is not a GOQ, although it parallels one of the GOQs relating to gender. The provision was repealed, so far as discrimination on grounds of race, ethnic or nation origins, but not for nationality or colour.[88] This is because the amendment merely implements the Race Directive.

(a)   Physiology and authenticity

At first sight it appears that there are, in these provisions, two types of GOQ, one based on *physical* differences between the races or the genders, and the other based on social or cultural expectations of what is most appropriate or beneficial. However, the first category, based on physical differences, is itself entirely based on a conventional *social* or *cultural* response to such differences.

It is permitted to hire a black person or a white person in all branches of the entertainment industry, if this is read widely to include modelling in all its forms, and in the catering industry. For example, it is permitted to restrict applications for the role of Hamlet to white people and Othello to black people. Such action is *permissible*; it is not *mandatory*. Directors may cast a white person as Othello. The suspicion may be that the practical result of the law does little to enhance opportunities for minority

---

88   Race Relations Act 1976 (Amendment) Regulations 2003, SI 2003/1626, reg 6(2), in force since 19 July 2003.

group members working in the performing arts.[89] While the RRA 1976 is more detailed than the SDA 1975, it appears that the same criteria as to authenticity will apply when restricting candidates to members of one sex. However, it does have to be shown that the essential nature of the job would be *materially* different if carried out by a woman. This gives scope to tribunals to make value judgments about what is appropriate or necessary. The problems are epitomised by advertising, as certain types of commercials are normally cast with women or with men – washing powder and beer, for example. It is highly likely that opportunities are restricted by gender, yet it is perhaps unlikely that tribunals, even if it could be demonstrated that such practices exist, would hold them to be unlawful, even though it could hardly be argued that the job of 'starring' in a soap powder commercial would be materially different if performed by a man.

The physiology exception – the more appropriate word would be anatomy – seems restricted to wet-nurses and those working in the sex industry.[90] 'There is a thin but important line between sex as a GOQ where the essential nature of the job requires a woman, and the case where the job can more effectively be performed by a woman because of customer reaction.'[91]

(b)   Personal services

This defence raises directly the issue of when customer reaction or customer preference may provide a defence; the very existence of the defence is based on the assumption that in some limited circumstances these factors may justify discrimination. It has to be shown that the relevant services can 'more effectively' be provided by a person of the same race or gender as the recipient. The main difference between the two statutes is that the SDA 1975 refers to 'welfare or education', while the RRA 1976 is restricted to 'welfare'. The line between the two may be hard to distinguish, (see *Tottenham Green* below), as university tutors could no doubt testify, but it is contended that it is very unlikely that a court would accept that, in a normal case, education could most effectively be provided by someone of the same sex as the pupils. Only if the education has a significant welfare component might the defence apply. As a general rule, therefore, teaching jobs in single-sex schools must be open to both men and women. In Muslim schools, however, it may be regarded as appropriate that girls should only be taught by female teachers, though if this GOQ were interpreted strictly, it is arguable that such a restriction would be unlawful.[92]

The services provided must be 'personal'.

London Borough of Lambeth v Commission for Racial Equality [1990] IRLR 231; [1990] ICR 768, CA

The council advertised two jobs in the housing benefit department, one for the assistant head and the other for group manager. More than half of tenants dealt with

---

89 See Pitt, G, 'Madam Butterfly and Miss Saigon: reflecting on genuine occupational qualifications', in Dine, J and Watt, B (eds), *Discrimination Law: Concepts, Limitations and Justifications*, 1996, Harlow: Addison Wesley Longman, Chapter 15.

90 In *Cropper v UK Express Ltd* (1992) unreported (but see EOC.org.UK) that sex was a GOQ for working on a telephone sex chat-line.

91 Pannick, D, *Sex Discrimination Law*, 1985, Oxford: OUP, p 238.

92 Related arguments may arise under the Religion or Belief Regulations 2003; see below, pp 342–44.

by the department were of Afro-Caribbean or Asian origin. The council therefore decided that the employees should also be Afro-Caribbean or Asian. The advertisement specifically referred to s 5(2)(d) of the RRA 1976 – the personal services defence.

The Commission for Racial Equality considered that these were managerial and administrative posts not covered by the defence. The council argued that the restriction was justified so as to ensure that housing benefit officers trained by the jobholders would have a particular empathy with black claimants.

The defence failed.

Balcombe LJ (p 234):

I am wholly unpersuaded that one of the two main purposes of the Act is to promote positive action to benefit racial groups ... It is true that ss 35, 37 and 38 do allow for limited acts of positive discrimination which would otherwise be unlawful, but that does not constrain us to give to s 5(2)(d) a meaning which its words do not naturally bear. If s 5(2)(d) had been intended to provide for positive action in the particular field to which it relates, one would have expected to find it grouped together with ss 35, 37 and 38 ...

I agree with the EAT when they say that the Act appears to contemplate direct contact between the giver and the recipient – mainly face to face or where there could be susceptibility in personal, physical contact. Where language or a knowledge and understanding of cultural and religious background are of importance, then those services may most effectively be provided by a person of a particular racial group.

[The tribunal also held that the racial group of the jobholder and of the recipient were not sufficiently identified so as to establish that the holder and the recipient were of the same racial group. The Industrial Tribunal took the view that an advertisement which purported to designate persons from at least two racial groups was not consistent with the statutory language.]

If a person is providing persons of a racial group defined by colour (for example, black people) with personal services promoting their welfare ... it will be open to an Industrial Tribunal ... to find that those services can most effectively be provided by a person of that colour, from whatever ethnic group she (or he) comes, and even though some of her (or his) clients may belong to other ethnic groups.

Three points arise from this decision. First, the Court of Appeal was surely correct to interpret the phrase 'personal services' narrowly and as requiring direct contact between provider and client. Secondly, these provisions cannot be used as a substitute for the provisions on positive action in order to ensure that a team of workers have a balanced representation of races and sexes. Maintaining such a balance, while it probably happens rather frequently, is *never* a defence to discrimination. This reflects the individualistic focus of the legislation; each act of hiring has to be individually justified under the GOQ provisions. Thirdly, the EAT rejected the argument that the defence under the RRA 1976 can only apply if the provider of the defence is from precisely the same racial group as the recipient. This is realistic, given the range of ethnic backgrounds from which a particular clientele may originate. One may surmise, however, that rather more will be needed to convince a tribunal that the services can more effectively be provided by someone from a *different*, albeit minority, group than by a white person. In a sense, such a tribunal will be required to take judicial notice of common aspects of discrimination and stereotyping experienced by members of minority ethnic groups.

Tottenham Green Under Fives' Centre v Marshall **[1989] IRLR 147; [1989] ICR 214,
EAT**

The policy of a day care centre was to maintain a balance between ethnic backgrounds
both among the children and the staff. When an Afro-Caribbean nursery worker left, it
was decided to replace her with another Afro-Caribbean. At the time, the centre had
four white staff, one Greek Cypriot and one other Afro-Caribbean. The advertisement
stated that the post was for an Afro-Caribbean worker and said that the successful
applicant would need 'a personal awareness of Afro-Caribbean culture' and 'an
understanding of the importance of anti-racist and anti-sexist childcare'.

The complainant was a white male and the issue was whether the GOQ defence
under s 5(2)(d) of the RRA 1976 applied. The centre contended that the personal
services related to four areas: maintaining the cultural background link for children of
Afro-Caribbean background; dealing with the parents and discussing those matters
with them; reading and talking where necessary in dialect; and generally looking after
their skin and health, including where necessary plaiting their hair.

The industrial tribunal said that, save for the requirement of reading a book in
West Indian patois, there was 'no evidence that a nursery worker of any ethnic origin
would not be able to carry out the requirements of caring for the child at the nursery
equally well'.

The EAT allowed the appeal.

Wood J (p 149):

We would make the following points:

(a)   The particular racial group will need to be clearly and, if necessary, narrowly
      defined because it will have to be that of the holder of the post and also that of
      the recipient of the personal services.

(b)   The holder of the post must be directly involved in the provision of the services
      – to direct others so to do is insufficient as the service must be personal. It does
      not seem to us that it need necessarily be on a one to one basis.

(c)   If the post holder provides several personal services to the recipient, then
      provided one of those genuinely falls within the sub-section, the defence is
      established.

(d)   'Promoting their welfare' is a very wide expression. The facts of each case are
      likely to vary enormously and different considerations will apply. It would be
      undesirable to seek to narrow the width of those words.

(e)   [T]he words are not 'must be provided' nor 'can only be provided'. The Act
      assumes that the personal services could be provided by others, but can they be
      'most effectively provided?' Would they be less effective if provided by others?
      Welfare of a child will include the broad understanding and handling of a child,
      and in the present circumstances an understanding of the background of the
      culture and the ways of the family. This is a matter of fact for the tribunal, and in
      so deciding the tribunal will need to carry out a delicate balancing exercise
      bearing in mind the need to guard against discrimination and the desirability of
      promoting racial integration. However, it seems to us that if a tribunal accepts
      that the conscious decision of a responsible employer to commit an act of
      discrimination and rely upon s 5(2)(d) is founded upon a genuinely held and
      reasonably based opinion that a GOQ will best promote the welfare of the
      recipient, then considerable weight should be given to that decision when
      reaching a conclusion whether or not the defence succeeds.

[The case was sent back to an industrial tribunal as too high a fence had been placed in the path of the appellants.]

***Tottenham Green Under Fives' Centre v Marshall (No 2)* [1991] IRLR 162; [1991] ICR 320, EAT**

An industrial tribunal again held that the defence failed. The tribunal accepted that one of the personal services required for the post was reading and talking where necessary in dialect and that an Afro-Caribbean would most effectively provide this service. However, they concluded: 'this particular requirement was the least emphasised of the four. We believe than an applicant who fulfilled the other requirements listed and who had no ability to speak or read the dialect would not have been precluded from getting the post ... Also this requirement is not mentioned in the advertisement or in the job description. It is in the nature of a desirable extra and no more.'

The EAT allowed the appeal and held that the defence succeeded.

Knox J (p 165):

[I]t is not the correct view of the meaning of this paragraph that the Industrial Tribunal can make an evaluation of the importance of the duty in question and disregard it although it is satisfied that it is something that is not so trivial that it can properly be disregarded altogether. It seems to us that sub-s (3) indicates clearly that one of the duties of the job, if it falls within any of the relevant paragraphs ... will operate to make the exception available.

[Reading and talking in dialect is] one of the duties of the job and in those circumstances, it not being trivial and it being genuine, it seems to us that the exception necessarily did apply.

The principles underlying the defence are clearly and correctly stated in this case – until the final point. The EAT assumes that only an Afro-Caribbean will be able to read and talk in the appropriate dialect. This is a stereotype which is no different from assuming that men are stronger than women. A white person who had the necessary abilities should have the right to be considered for such a job. That a higher proportion of Afro-Caribbean applicants would have been able to satisfy the requirements goes to justified indirect discrimination and not to the existence of a GOQ.

Neither of these cases, important as they are, do much to explore the key issue of what kinds of service are potentially within the scope of the defence. Examples often given include rape crisis centres, refuges for battered women and birth control clinics on the one hand, and dealing with the victims of racial attack or abuse on the other. It is contended that, strictly speaking, most legal and other advice centres for minority ethnic groups would not come under this section unless specifically concerned with the experience of being black or a victim of discrimination. However, it may well be that, by analogy with *Tottenham Green*, the section will not be interpreted so rigidly. This may be all very well where the issue is of providing services to a member of a minority group, but when, if ever, can a white person argue that personal services can most effectively be provided by another white person? Given that discrimination against white people is dealt with in exactly the same way as discrimination against black people, a wide reading of this defence is potentially problematic. Tribunals have to balance two arguably conflicting approaches to discrimination law: first, that the law should aim to be colour-blind and gender-blind, under which approach the characteristics of the provider of the service should be irrelevant; secondly, the approach be based on recognition of differences, under which an assumption is made that there are differences which arise from culture,[93] background and experience, and of which the law should take note. The personal services defence is a limited acceptance of the latter approach. The extent to which such a defence *ought* to be accepted is very controversial. Of course, the strategy whereby as much as possible is left to be decided on the facts by tribunals means that issues of principle and theory are unlikely to be resolved in litigation.

There is also here a potentially complex interaction of religion, race and gender. For example, it is contended that most cases of medical treatment do not fall within the sections, because the cultural norm allows and expects medical treatment to be carried out by members of either sex. This becomes progressively less true as the medical treatment involves a greater element of counselling, as with birth control clinics. However, some racial and religious groups, especially Muslim women, may object to medical examination and treatment, not necessarily intimate, by a man. If a school or a factory which was predominantly Muslim hired a female nurse, it is probable that the defence would apply. It is contended that all medical treatment comes within the meaning of the term 'personal services'; whether the services can most effectively be provided by a woman will then turn on the tribunal's evaluation of the depth and appropriateness of the objection. Furthermore, there is a clear overlap between the issue under this section of whether the services can more effectively be provided by a woman and the issue under s 7(2)(b) of whether a woman might reasonably object to such procedures on the grounds of privacy or decency.

The remainder of the GOQs apply only to gender.

(2)   Genuine Occupational Qualifications – Sex Only

(a)   *Privacy or decency*

Section 7(2)(b) provides a defence:

... where the job needs to be held by a man to preserve privacy or decency because:

(i)   it is likely to involve physical contact with men in circumstances where they might reasonably object to its being carried out by a woman; or

(ii)   the holder of the job is likely to do his work in circumstances where men might reasonably object to the presence of a woman because they are in a state of undress or are using sanitary facilities ...

Examples of physical contact[94] include measurements for clothing,[95] medical procedures and perhaps instruction in sports such as gymnastics. The nature of the physical contact must potentially involve an issue of privacy or decency – dentistry and shoe fitting are outside the section. No guidance is given as to when objections are to be regarded as reasonable. The section states that it is enough if men or women '*might*' reasonably object. The question arises at the point of hiring; the employer will

---

93   These are not necessarily based on race. The definition of racial group allows for reference to be made to what are in effect cultural differences. See above, Chapter 10, especially pp 138–40.

94   The industrial tribunal in *Sisley v Britannia Security Systems Ltd* [1983] IRLR 404, EAT (see below), in an aspect of the decision which was not appealed, correctly held that physical contact means what it says and that proximity is insufficient.

95   *Etam plc v Rowan* [1989] IRLR 150, EAT.

be refusing employment on the basis of anticipated objections and whether they will be regarded as reasonable. Given the wide variety of attitudes in society, and the fact that norms may be changing, it is impossible to be definitive on what objections will be accepted as reasonable and, just as important, what evidence employers will be required to produce to demonstrate their belief in the existence of such objections.

This GOQ also applies to the provision of goods, facilities and services, where admitting both sexes to certain facilities simultaneously would be likely to cause serious embarrassment.[96] The EOC is concerned that the provision of women-only sports and leisure sessions does not clearly fall within this defence, as the degree of embarrassment may be insufficiently substantial, yet many women might be unwilling to participate in mixed sessions. The reason for the embarrassment may vary as between women of different cultural and religious traditions, though male sexism may cause difficulty for all different groups of women. The law needs to be clarified and perhaps widened.[97]

The second limb of the defence is where the jobholder is in a state of undress or is using sanitary facilities.

Sisley v Britannia Security Systems Ltd [1983] IRLR 404; [1983] ICR 628, EAT

The employers operated a security control station. The employees worked in shifts, the longest of which was 12 hours, in a part of the premises described as 'a building within a building'. When the unit was opened, it was felt that there would be problems if men and women worked together and shared the facilities provided in such a confined space. Therefore, only women were hired.

Tudor Evans J (p 408):

We read [s 7(2)(b)(ii)] as dealing with the situation where the holder of a particular job is likely to do his work, and all matters reasonably incidental to it, in circumstances where the holder might reasonably object ... because the holder is ... in a state of undress ... We do not read the sub-section as being confined to cases where the job itself requires the holder to be in a state of undress ... We think that the sub-section covers the situation where the employer says that he has to have a man (or a woman) to do the job because working conditions are such that if the holder is in a state of undress or is using sanitary facilities, he or she might object to the presence of a member of the opposite sex at the place of work ... We construe the reference to 'the duties of the job' as encompassing not only the duties of the job but all matters reasonably incidental to it ... It seems to us to be reasonably incidental to that necessary part [of taking a rest] for the women to remove their clothing.

The EAT held that, literally, the section only applied where the jobholder is in a state of undress, but that there were good policy arguments for not so restricting it and that it should also cover situations where members of the public, customers or fellow employees are in a state of undress. Otherwise, the section would not cover the cleaning of showers or work in a sauna because the actual jobholder may not be undressed while performing the duties. However, the decision is problematic in that the EAT went beyond work in a state of undress to cover rest periods. There is no warrant for this and, in addition, no consideration was given as to whether the

---

96 SDA 1975, ss 35(1)(c), 35(2).
97 See *Equality in the 21st Century: A New Approach*, 1998, Manchester: EOC, paras 64–65.

women had to be undressed during the rest periods and whether there were alternative methods available to preserve decency.

If an employer refuses to employ both men and women on the ground that it is impracticable to provide separate toilet facilities, two questions will arise. First, is it truly impracticable? This raises similar issues to that of the provision of separate sleeping accommodation and will be considered there. Secondly, when will objection be considered reasonable? There are different tribunal decisions on whether a unisex lockable lavatory ensures enough privacy.[98] Equally, it may be contended that it is not reasonable to object to a lavatory cleaner of a different sex as long as individual cubicles are private, though some would argue that there is a difference between female cleaners in male facilities and vice versa. Who can predict what objections a tribunal would view as reasonable?

(b)   Work in a private home

Section 6(3) of the original SDA 1975 provided exceptions in all cases where the number of employees did not exceed five, and also where the employment was for the purposes of a private household. These wide exceptions were held to be contrary to the Equal Treatment Directive in *Commission of the European Communities v UK*.[99] The ECJ reasoned that, as regards small undertakings with not more than five employees, it was not the case that in any undertaking of that size the sex of the worker would be a determining factor for the purposes of Art 2(2) of the Directive. However, it was recognised that the law must reconcile the principle of equal treatment with the fundamental principle of respect for private life. The SDA 1986 therefore repealed the provisions held unlawful by the European Court and introduced a new s 7(2)(ba) to the 1975 Act which is couched in far more restrictive terms. It provides a defence where:

... the job is likely to involve the holder of the job doing his work, or living, in a private home and needs to be held by a man because objection might reasonably be taken to allowing to a woman:

(i)   the degree of physical or social contact with a person living in the home; or

(ii)   the knowledge of intimate details of such a person's life,

which is likely, because of the nature or circumstances of the job or of the home, which is allowed to, or available to, the holder of the job ...

For example, personal companions and nurses may be the same sex as the client; those working outside the home are not covered. For those with a large coterie of domestic servants, most, such as butlers or cooks, surely do not provide a sufficiently personal or intimate service.[100] Actual physical contact is not required; a very close working relationship may suffice as long as it provides intimate knowledge of the client's life, knowledge which must be personal rather than, say, financial.

---

98 See 'Genuine occupational qualification' (1988) 18 EOR 24, p 28.

99 Case 165/82 [1984] ECR 3431; [1984] ICR 192; [1984] 1 All ER 353; [1984] IRLR 29.

100 The employee covered need not be working for the actual employer; she could be working directly with a parent or children. It is, however, unlikely that employment as a nanny, governess or private tutor will be covered, though in *Neal v Watts* (1989) unreported, IT, the rejection of a professionally qualified male nanny was held not to be unlawful because the job duties would include bathing the child and the mother liked to bath with her baby.

(c) Live-in jobs

Section 7(2)(c) of the SDA 1975, provides a defence where:

> ... the nature or location of the establishment makes it impracticable for the holder of the job to live elsewhere than in premises provided by the employer, and:
>
> (i) the only such premises which are available ... are lived[101] in, or normally lived in, by men, and are not equipped with separate sleeping accommodation for women and sanitary facilities which could be used by women in privacy from men; and
>
> (ii) it is not reasonable either to equip those premises with such accommodation and facilities or to provide other premises for women ...

This defence applies to jobs such as on oil rigs or building sites. It is contended that there is no need to provide separate sleeping *blocks*. Just as the provision of individually separate toilet facilities should suffice, so should the provision of individually separate rooms or separate dormitories. Such an interpretation would greatly limit the scope for a successful defence under this section. This is important as many such jobs, often short term and moving from place to place, are in areas where the proportion of women workers is extremely low. While it is not suggested that this interpretation will cause an influx of women into such jobs, the law should not make it easier for employers to resist *any* female entrants at all. The section is a rare example under the legislation of a cost defence being admissible. Clearly, what is reasonable expenditure will depend on the total size of the workforce, the numbers of men and women, and the likely duration of the work in that location. Tribunals will have to balance the right to be free from discrimination against a plea of financial hardship, which places them in what is potentially an uncomfortable position.

(d) Hospitals, prisons, etc

Section 7(2)(d) of the SDA 1975 provides a defence where:

> ... the nature of the establishment, or the part of it within which the work is done, requires the job to be held by a man because:
>
> (i) it is, or is part of, a hospital, prison, or other establishment for persons requiring special care, supervision or attention; and
>
> (ii) those persons are all men (disregarding any women whose presence may be exceptional); and
>
> (iii) it is reasonable, having regard to the essential character of the establishment or that part, that the job should not be held by a woman.

This defence is additional to, and not dependent on, the provision of personal services or issues of privacy or decency. Certain jobs in prisons and hospitals may well come within one or both of those defences, but it must be assumed that some jobs are covered by this and only this GOQ. The emphasis here is on the essential character of the establishment rather than simply on the particular job being performed. The section is based on the assumption that it is permissible for staff in an all-female hospital or prison to be female – medical or custodial staff dealing with patients or

---

101 In *Sisley* (above, p 337), this was interpreted as requiring actual residence rather than the mere provision of rest facilities.

inmates, not support or domestic staff. In the case of hospitals, this may provide a defence for a medical job which would not be within any other GOQ. The emphasis on the nature and function of the establishment rules out an argument that, for example, women prison staff would be more vulnerable to attack by male prisoners than their male counterparts.[102]

(e)   Duties to be performed abroad by men or by women

Section 7(2)(g)[103] of the SDA 1975 provides a defence where a job involves the performance of some duties outside the UK[104] 'in a country whose laws or customs are such that the duties could not, or could not effectively, be performed by a woman'. The defence recognises that women may be culturally unacceptable for some jobs in some countries; there is no equivalent defence in the RRA 1976. A defence based on the racism of another country is not permissible; a defence based on the sexism of that self-same country may be. There are no cases: it is assumed that the defence would apply to, for example, women seeking jobs as salespeople where the duties involve travelling to some Middle Eastern countries or where a man would be unable to deal with female customers in similar situations. It would be difficult for an employment tribunal to gainsay an employer's assertion that a particular job could not be effectively performed by a man or a woman, as the case may be. The lack of cases is probably more because of an absence of complaints than because this kind of discrimination does not occur.

(f)   Married couples

The final GOQ is s 7(2)(h) of the SDA 1975, which provides a defence where the 'job is one of two to be held by a married couple'. As there is no general prohibition against discrimination against single people, it is perfectly lawful to require a married couple to perform two jobs. It seems to follow that the only activity legitimated by this GOQ is to specify which of the couple is to perform which job.

(3)   Genuine Occupational Qualifications – Gender Reassignment

Section 7A of the SDA 1975,[105] provides an exception where being a man, or being a woman, is a genuine occupational qualification, if 'the employer can show that the treatment is reasonable in view of the circumstances described in the relevant paragraph of section 7(2)[106] and any other relevant circumstances'. Section 7B lists 'supplementary exceptions':

> (2)   Subject to subsection (3), there is a supplementary genuine occupational qualification for a job only if—

---

102 In *Dothard v Rawlinson* 433 US 321 (1977), the US Supreme Court accepted the validity of just such a defence. A similar argument was rejected in *Secretary of State for Scotland v Henley* (1983), unreported, EAT, Case 95/83.

103 Section 7(2)(f) was repealed by the Employment Act 1989; see above, Chapter 8, pp 212–15.

104 If the work is to be done wholly outside the UK, the SDA 1975 is inapplicable by virtue of s 10.

105 Inserted by SI 1999/1102, reg 4(1). Date in force: 1 May 1999: see SI 1999/1102, reg 1(2).

106 Discussed above.

(a) the job involves the holder of the job being liable to be called upon to perform intimate physical searches pursuant to statutory powers;

(b) the job is likely to involve the holder of the job doing his work, or living, in a private home and needs to be held otherwise than by a person who is undergoing or has undergone gender reassignment, because objection might reasonably be taken to allowing to such a person—

(i) the degree of physical or social contact with a person living in the home, or

(ii) the knowledge of intimate details of such a person's life,

which is likely, because of the nature or circumstances of the job or of the home, to be allowed to, or available to, the holder of the job;

(c) the nature or location of the establishment makes it impracticable for the holder of the job to live elsewhere than in premises provided by the employer, and—

(i) the only such premises which are available for persons holding that kind of job are such that reasonable objection could be taken, for the purpose of preserving decency and privacy, to the holder of the job sharing accommodation and facilities with either sex whilst undergoing gender reassignment, and

(ii) it is not reasonable to expect the employer either to equip those premises with suitable accommodation or to make alternative arrangements; or

(d) the holder of the job provides vulnerable individuals with personal services promoting their welfare, or similar personal services, and in the reasonable view of the employer those services cannot be effectively provided by a person whilst that person is undergoing gender reassignment.

(3) Paragraphs (c) and (d) of subsection (2) apply only in relation to discrimination against a person who—

(a) intends to undergo gender reassignment, or

(b) is undergoing gender reassignment.

These are exceptions to s 2A, which was inserted in response to an ECJ decision[107] that the Equal Treatment Directive covered discrimination against transsexuals. As they are peculiar to gender reassignment, their compliance with the European Convention on Human Rights and the Equal Treatment Directive has been thrown into doubt by the decision of the European Court of Human Rights (EctHR),[108] that transsexuals are entitled to a birth certificate in their new sex. Accordingly, a male-to-female transsexual must be treated as a woman, and vice versa, which makes the exceptions rather meaningless.[109] Of course, the ECtHR allows for a 'margin of appreciation'. However, the ECJ is likely to follow the principles of 'legitimate aim' and 'proportionality' expressed in the other Directives[110] and only allow a margin of appreciation where the exception is in pursuit of a social policy.[111]

107 *P v S and Cornwall CC* Case C-13/94 [1996] ECR I-2143; [1996] ICR 795; [1996] IRLR 347, ECJ. See Chapter 6, p 153.

108 *Goodwin v UK* Application No 28957/95, Judgment, 11 July 2002; (2002) EHRR 447; [2002] 2 FCR 577; see above, Chapter 6, p 158.

109 See the discussion in *A v Chief Constable of West Yorkshire* [2002] EWCA 1584; [2002] All ER (D) 50, CA; see above, Chapter 5, pp 116–17.

110 See above, pp 328–29.

111 See Chapter 10, p 290 *et al*.

(4)   Genuine Occupational Requirements – Sexual Orientation and Religion or Belief

Council Directive 2000/78/EC

Article 4

1.   ... Member States may provide that a difference of treatment which is based on a characteristic related to any of the grounds referred to in Article 1[112] shall not constitute discrimination where, by reason of the nature of the particular occupational activities concerned or of the context in which they are carried out, such a characteristic constitutes a genuine and determining occupational requirement, provided that the objective is legitimate and the requirement is proportionate.

2.   Member States may maintain national legislation in force at the date of adoption of this Directive or provide for future legislation incorporating national practices existing at the date of adoption of this Directive pursuant to which, in the case of occupational activities within churches and other public or private organisations the ethos of which is based on religion or belief, a difference of treatment based on a person's religion or belief shall not constitute discrimination where, by reason of the nature of these activities or of the context in which they are carried out, a person's religion or belief constitute a genuine, legitimate and justified occupational requirement, having regard to the organisation's ethos. This difference of treatment shall be implemented taking account of Member States' constitutional provisions and principles, as well as the general principles of Community law, and should not justify discrimination on another ground.

Provided that its provisions are otherwise complied with, this Directive shall thus not prejudice the right of churches and other public or private organisations, the ethos of which is based on religion or belief, acting in conformity with national constitutions and laws, to require individuals working for them to act in good faith and with loyalty to the organisation's ethos.

Regulation 7 in either the Sexual Orientation, or the Religion or Belief, Regulations 2003 apply to recruitment, promotion, transfer, training or dismissal. As with the new s 4A of the RRA 1976, this formula omits the word 'legitimate' provided by the Directive.[113] Another point common to both pieces of legislation is that sub-para (c)(ii) takes the exceptions beyond the normal definition. Regulation 7 does not only operate where, say, the worker is not of a required sexual orientation; it also applies where the employer *perceives* that he is not, although that perception must be reasonable, so it is not entirely subjective. The only use for this paragraph is where the employer makes a mistake as to the sexual orientation (or religion or belief) of the worker or applicant. That mistake will often be based on widely held, but stereotypical, views. Litigation over this issue will come to this: was the employer's perception reasonable by the standards of mainstream society, or by the standards of legislation solely intended to combat the standards of mainstream society? For the legislation to retain integrity, tribunals must opt for the latter.

---

112 That is, religion or belief, disability, age and sexual orientation.
113 Discussed above, p 330.

(a)   Sexual orientation

The Employment Equality (Sexual Orientation) Regulations 2003[114]

Regulation 7

Exception for genuine occupational requirement etc

(2)   This paragraph applies where, having regard to the nature of the employment or the context in which it is carried out—

    (a) being of a particular sexual orientation is a genuine and determining occupational requirement;

    (b) it is proportionate to apply that requirement in the particular case; and

    (c) either—

        (i) the person to whom that requirement is applied does not meet it, or

        (ii) the employer is not satisfied, and in all the circumstances it is reasonable for him not to be satisfied, that that person meets it,

and this paragraph applies whether or not the employment is for purposes of an organised religion.

(3)   This paragraph applies where—

    (a) the employment is for purposes of an organised religion;

    (b) the employer applies a requirement related to sexual orientation—

        (i) so as to comply with the doctrines of the religion, or

        (ii) because of the nature of the employment and the context in which it is carried out, so as to avoid conflicting with the strongly held religious convictions of a significant number of the religion's followers; and

    (c) either—

        (i) the person to whom that requirement is applied does not meet it, or

        (ii) the employer is not satisfied, and in all the circumstances it is reasonable for him not to be satisfied, that that person meets it.

At once it can be seen that the domestic version is more extensive than the Directive. There are, in effect, two exceptions. The second, in reg 7(3), gives churches a free reign to discriminate against homosexuals, even where the only objection is by *some* of the congregation.[115] So, for instance, even where the leaders (or majority of members) have no objection to homosexuality, discrimination may lawfully persist or, in some cases, *commence*, under the authority of reg 7(3)(b)(ii).[116] In such cases there is clearly no 'legitimate' aim and as such reg 7(3) goes beyond the wording of Art 4(1) of the Directive. Secondly, to ban gay men because of the opinion of a minority would be disproportionate and, again, in breach of the Directive. It may be argued that Art 4(2) of the Directive allows for this exception, but the underlying principle of that paragraph is *religious* discrimination and it does not legitimise discrimination on different grounds. It would be akin to allowing a church with racist views to indulge in racial discrimination.

---

114 In force since 1 December 2003.

115 A similar formula is used by SDA 1975, s 19.

116 This is contrary to the non-regression principle in Art 8 of the Directive.

(b)   Religion or belief

The Employment Equality (Religion or Belief) Regulations 2003[117]

Regulation 7

(2)   This paragraph applies where, having regard to the nature of the employment or the context in which it is carried out—

     (a)   being of a particular religion or belief is a genuine and determining occupational requirement;

     (b)   it is proportionate to apply that requirement in the particular case; and

     (c)   either—

         (i)   the person to whom that requirement is applied does not meet it, or

         (ii)   the employer is not satisfied, and in all the circumstances it is reasonable for him not to be satisfied, that that person meets it,

   and this paragraph applies whether or not the employer has an ethos based on religion or belief.

(3)   This paragraph applies where an employer has an ethos based on religion or belief and, having regard to that ethos and to the nature of the employment or the context in which it is carried out—

     (a)   being of a particular religion or belief is a genuine occupational requirement for the job;

     (b)   it is proportionate to apply that requirement in the particular case; and

     (c)   either—

         (i)   the person to whom that requirement is applied does not meet it, or

         (ii)   the employer is not satisfied, and in all the circumstances it is reasonable for him not to be satisfied, that that person meets it.

Regulation 7(2) applies whether or not the employer holds an ethos based on religion or belief, but can only be used where a particular religion or belief of the worker or applicant is a *determining* factor. Regulation 7(3) can only be used by an employer with a religion or belief, but otherwise it offers a more general defence. Here the religion or belief of the worker or applicant need no be a *determining*, or decisive, factor, although it must be a genuine 'requirement'. Finally, note that reg 26 provides an exception for Sikhs wearing turbans, instead of safety helmets, on construction sites.

4   GENERAL DEFENCES

There are two defences which are potentially of general application but are of particular relevance in the employment context. These concern acts done under statutory authority and acts done for the purpose of safeguarding national security.

(1)   Statutory Authority

This general defence now only applies to residual cases under the RRA 1976, outside of EC competence. In this context, these will be cases brought purely on grounds of nationality or colour. Otherwise, it is not for a Member State, except where specifically

---

117   In force since 2 December 2003. Discussed by Vickers, L, 'The Draft Employment Equality (Religion or Belief) Regulations' [2003] 32(1) ILJ 23, at pp 26–35.

provided,[118] to pass legislation having the effect of reducing the scope of Community discrimination law. However, the cases of *Hampson and Nabadda* demonstrate that residual race cases will continue to arise. For this reason, s 41 of the RRA 1976, now of limited scope, and two major cases under it are reproduced.[119]

Section 41(1) of the RRA 1976 provides that:

Nothing shall render unlawful any act of discrimination done:

(a)   in pursuance of any enactment or Order in Council; or

(b)   in pursuance of any instrument made under any enactment made by a minister of the Crown; or

(c)   in order to comply with any condition or requirement imposed by a minister of the Crown (whether before or after the passing of this Act) by virtue of any enactment.

The key phrase is in sub-s (1)(c): the defence applies to acts done 'in order to comply with' any statutory requirement, though in paras (a) and (b) the equivalent phrase is 'in pursuance of'.

Hampson v Department of Education and Science **[1990] IRLR 202, HL**[120]

A Hong Kong Chinese woman was refused qualified teacher status in England. She had taken a two-year course in Hong Kong. Eight years later, she took a third year. She came to England and claimed qualified teacher status. The Secretary of State had power to make regulations under which the key phrase was 'approved as comparable'. Her application was rejected on the grounds that her initial training was two rather than three years and because the content did not meet Department of Education standards.

She claimed that this rule was indirectly discriminatory on the ground of nationality. The EAT held that the Secretary of State had a defence under s 41(1)(b) by reason of it being an act done 'in pursuance of any instrument made under any enactment by a minister of the Crown'. The Court of Appeal, by a majority (Balcombe LJ dissenting), upheld this aspect of the EAT decision.[121]

The House of Lords allowed the appeal.

Lord Lowry (pp 305–07):

(1)   The Act binds the Crown, which, apart from the prerogative, discharges its duties and exercises its powers by virtue of a multitude of statutes and regulations ...

(2)   The acts not only of the Crown but of local authorities and a large number of statutory bodies, including the governing bodies of some (but not all) universities, would achieve virtual immunity under the wide construction.

---

118 Equal Treatment Directive, Art 2(3) and SDA 1975, s 51 allow for specific legislation for the protection of women, particularly regarding pregnancy. See further, Chapter 8, pp 212–15.

119 Section 41 no longer applies to discrimination on grounds of race or ethnic or national origins: Race Relations Act 1976 (Amendment) Regulations 2003, reg 35.

120 See also [1991] 1 AC 171; [1990] ICR 551; [1990] 2 All ER 513.

121 Balcombe LJ, in reasoning subsequently approved by the House of Lords, said that Parliament 'could not have intended that the Secretary of State should be entitled to ignore altogether the racial implications of what he was doing ... If what is done is not necessary to comply with a statutory requirement, there is no valid reason why it should not have to be justified before an Industrial Tribunal': [1989] IRLR 69, p 74.

(3)   The most important weapons contained in Parts II and III of the Act would be irretrievably blunted and, indeed, would not make sense.

To adopt the Balcombe principle, if I may so describe it, will mean that racial discrimination is outlawed (or at least needs to be justified ...) unless it has been sanctioned by Parliament, whereas, if the respondent's argument were correct, a wide and undefined area of discrimination would exist, immune from challenge save, in very exceptional circumstances, through the medium of judicial review ...

[W]hen one reflects that almost every discretionary decision, such as that which is involved in the appointment, promotion and dismissal of individuals in, say, local government, the police, the NHS and the public sector of the teaching profession, is taken against a statutory background which imposes a duty on someone, just as the regulations of 1982 imposed a duty on the Secretary of State. It seems to me that to apply the reasoning of the majority here to the decisions I have mentioned would be to give them the protection of s 41 and thereby to achieve results which no member of the Court of Appeal would be likely to have thought acceptable.[122]

Arguably, this is one of the most important decisions ever handed down on the interpretation of the discrimination legislation. It does not define discrimination or bring additional people within the scope of the legislation. What it does is to confirm that the legislation applies even where the activity challenged is founded upon statutory duties or powers. In other words, those acting under statutory authority are not immune from the general duty to take into account the anti-discrimination legislation in formulating policy and acting upon it. That this point should ever have been doubted may be a matter of some wonderment; that it was roundly rejected in *Hampson* was essential if the legislation was to have any significant impact at all in the public sector.[123]

Since *Hampson*, legislation has to comply with the Human Rights Act 1998[124] and with the greatly increased amount of EC discrimination legislation. This EC legislation, of course, did not affect Mrs Hampson's case, as she was not a national of an EC Member State. That was unlike the next claim, which provoked a detailed discussion of the relationship between s 41 and EC law.

Nabadda and Others v Westminster CC; Gomilsek v Haringey London BC [2000] ICR 951, CA

Swedish students, on courses in England, were denied grants under the Education (Mandatory Awards) Regulations 1997 because the Regulations provided that Swedish students (but not English ones) were to be means-tested. (That provision was later repealed.) The students brought a claim of discrimination, relying on the prohibition of discrimination on grounds of nationality by Art 6 of the EC Treaty, which provides: 'Within the scope of application of this Treaty, and without prejudice to any special provisions contained therein, any discrimination on grounds of nationality shall be prohibited.' They claimed damages only for injury to feelings under the RRA 1976. The defendants relied on s 41(1)(b). The Court of Appeal dismissed the students' claims.

---

122 The same approach was adopted by the EAT in *General Medical Council v Goba* [1988] ICR 885; [1988] IRLR 425.

123 It follows that, for areas to be excluded from the legislation, specific statutory provision must have been made. Immigration law and family law are obvious examples.

124 See Chapter 5, p 114.

Buxton LJ:

7.   ... The next and crucial step in the students' case is, however, that they are by reason of such discrimination entitled to damages within the English system under the Race Relations Act 1976. To the extent that (as is the case) certain provisions of the Act of 1976 stand in the way of granting the remedy sought in this case in respect of the breach of article 6 of the Treaty, those provisions must be disapplied or ignored, in deference to the primacy of Community law. ...

8.   The Act of 1976 in its relationship to Community law is thus crucial to this case. It is important also at this stage to note that the claim is deliberately not made under what might be called the general mechanisms required of national law for recovery of reparation for breaches of directly effective Community provisions that have been recognised by the Court of Justice, in such cases as *Francovich* ... (Case C-6/90) [1995] ICR 722 ... The most convenient summary of that jurisprudence is to be found in the most recent case in the Court of Justice, *Norbrook Laboratories Ltd v Ministry of Agriculture, Fisheries and Food* (Case C-127/97) [1998] ECR I-1531, 1598, 1599, paras 106–107. I shall refer to the relief envisaged by that jurisprudence as '*Norbrook* damages'. To ground recovery for such damages it has to be established, *inter alia*, that the breach of Community law was 'sufficiently serious' to justify a claim for compensation. No such allegation is made in this case ...

The rules of Community law on reparation

10.   In some instances provisions of Community law, notably Directives, contain requirements as to the penalties or compensation to be provided by member states in the event of breach of the transposing provisions in the national legal order. Damages provided for by such provisions are *sui generis* in Community law and are governed by rules different from those applying to *Norbrook* damages: see the observations of this court in *Matra Communications SAS v Home Office* [1999] 1 WLR 1646, 1655B-D. Where such requirements are contained in a Directive, their meaning and effect, and the obligation that they impose on the member state, are a question of interpretation of the Directive: see for instance *Marshall v Southampton and South West Hampshire Health Authority (Teaching) (No 2)* (Case C-271/91) [1993] ICR 893. However, where, as will be the case with articles of the EC Treaty such as article 6 in our case, no specific provisions exist in respect of reparation, then the claimant for damages rather than for a purely public law remedy must rely in the national legal order on the jurisprudence of *Norbrook* ...

11.   It will be apparent that the claim made in this case falls under neither of those two categories of entitlement to damages. ...

18.   It is easy to see why section 41 was enacted. Acts done in pursuit of policies approved, either at first or at second hand, by Parliament are not to be proceeded against as discriminatory, even if they are in fact such. It will be immediately seen that this is another clear reason why the Act of 1976 is inept as an instrument to enforce Community law. Breaches of Community law are not excused or exempted simply on the ground that they are committed by the national government of a member state, or simply because they have legislative approval. That, amongst other things, was decided by the *Factortame* litigation. But if the Act of 1976 were indeed the chosen instrument for the enforcement of breaches of article 6 of the EC Treaty, it could none the less not be deployed against breaches committed by the national government, as I understood Mr Allen [for the students] to accept. As Miss Richards [for the defendants] pointed out in an intervention that was as effective as it was economical, it is therefore

the singular result of the students' argument that a legislative act could only be the subject of a damages claim if it met the *Norbrook* criterion of sufficiently serious breach: whereas the authorities, by acting in obedience to that legislation, make themselves subject to liability free of any such limitation.

19.   The significance of section 41 is, however, not only for the further light that it sheds on the students' basic position, but also more directly because the local authorities contend that section 41 provides them with a complete defence to the claims. Mr Allen sought to meet that contention by two arguments.

20.   The first was that by normal principles of Community law any provision in national legislation that was inconsistent with Community law must be ignored or disapplied. Section 41 fell into that category precisely because it had the effect of depriving the students of the remedy that they sought for a breach of article 6. This argument is difficult to grapple with, because it depends on the assumption that Community law does have a legitimate interest in the terms and operation of the Act of 1976: an assumption that, as I have already demonstrated, is unfounded. One may, however, add that the rules of Community law relied on for this purpose (eg, in *Amministrazione delle Finanze dello Stato v Simmenthal SpA* (Case 106/77) [1978] ECR 629) have been concerned with national provisions affecting the substantive application of Community law, rather than with reparation for breaches of that substantive law. The reason for that is not far to seek. The relationship between Community and national law in respect of damages is governed by the specific jurisprudence set out earlier in this judgment. That jurisprudence applies to the national legal order directly, and not through the medium of national provisions drawn for different purposes.

21.   Mr Allen's second riposte ... was that section 41 must be read as only protecting a person who acts lawfully in pursuance of an enactment, etc. The Regulations of 1997 being, as was admitted, unlawful in the sense of being in breach of article 6 of the EC Treaty, the local authorities when acting in pursuit of them could not be acting under section 41, and therefore were not protected by it.

22.   ... First, the construction, depriving the local authorities of protection if the legislation under which they acted was in fact unlawful, breached both the literal wording of the provision and the general expectation of English law. Second, there was nothing in Community law that rendered section 41 invalid. Community law only required the national legal order to provide adequate remedies for a breach of a Community provision. The English system, including section 41 of the Act of 1976, still provided the remedies of judicial review, and of *Norbrook* damages, albeit in the latter case against the national government. It was of no concern to Community law which organ of the state was held liable, provided that reparation in *Norbrook* terms was available somewhere within the national legal order: see *Konle v Republic of Austria* (Case C-302/97) [1999] ECR I-3099, 3140, para 63 of the judgment of the Court of Justice. And it was for the national legal order to decide which heads of damage (including, in this case, damages for injury to feelings) were recoverable: see *Brasserie du Pêcheur SA v Federal Republic of Germany* (Case C-46/93) [1996] QB 404 ...

24.   In dismissing the appeal for the reasons set out above, it is necessary to do no more than declare that the acts of discrimination alleged in the various particulars of claim were, by reason of the provisions of section 41(1)(b) of the Race Relations Act 1976, not unlawful.

(2)   National Security

Section 52 of the SDA 1975 and s 42 of the RRA 1976 provide that nothing in the respective Acts 'shall render unlawful an act done for the purpose of safeguarding national security'. Section 52(2) of the SDA 1975, now repealed, provided that a ministerial signature was to be conclusive proof that an act was done for that purpose. The ECJ in *Johnston* held that the conclusive nature of such a certificate was contrary to Art 6 of the Equal Treatment Directive, which gives a right to 'all persons who consider themselves wronged by failure to apply ... the principle of equal treatment ... to pursue their claims by judicial process'. In other words, domestic law may not prevent an individual having access to the courts, even on the purported ground of national security, as there is no national security exception within the terms of the Equal Treatment Directive.[125] The Fair Employment (Northern Ireland) Act 1989 had a similar defence, which has been similarly repealed following the ECtHR decision in *Tinnelly v UK*.[126] The blocking, on national security grounds, of a complaint that Catholics were refused public works contracts because of their religious beliefs or political opinions, was in breach of the Convention because it deprived the applicants of their right to 'a fair and public hearing ... by an independent and impartial tribunal' under Art 6 of the Convention. Section 42 of the RRA 1976 was amended accordingly with the rider, '... if the doing of the act was justified by that purpose'.[127] The Sexual Orientation, and Religion or Belief, Regulations 2003[128] each contain this modified formula.

5   DISCRIMINATION BY OTHER BODIES

(1)   Contract Workers[129]

The employer of contract workers is liable in the normal way, under s 6 of the SDA 1975, s 4 of the RRA 1976, or reg 6 of either the Religion or Belief, or Sexual Orientation, Regulations 2003.[130] Section 9 of the SDA 1975, s 7 of the RRA 1976 and reg 8 of either of the 2003 Regulations deal with the liability of the principal for whom the work is actually performed, such as the business for whom an agency secretary is working, or a construction worker supplied to the site under a labour-only subcontract. The legislation applies by analogy, bearing in mind that the employer

---

125 It followed that the only exceptions were those within the terms of the Equal Treatment Directive itself. The employers failed on Art 2(3), the pregnancy and maternity defence, but the Court held that the Art 2(2) defence, where the sex of the worker constitutes a determining factor for the job in question, was satisfied.

126 *Tinnelly & Sons Ltd and Others & McElduff and Others v UK*, Cases 62/1997/846/1052–53.

127 Added by the Race Relations (Amendment) Act 2000, s 7(1), in force since 2 April 2001 (SI 2001/566, Art 2(1)).

128 Regulation 24. In force since 2 December 2003 and 1 December 2003, respectively.

129 Discriminatory terms in collective agreements are now covered by the RRA 1976, ss 72A and 72B (inserted by SI 2003/1626, in force since 19 July 2003); the Employment Equality (Sexual Orientation) Regulations 2003, SI 2003/1661; or the Employment Equality (Religion or Belief) Regulations 2003, SI 2003/1660, reg 35 and Sched 4. These new provisions are in similar terms to the existing sex discrimination scheme, which is discussed in Chapter 14, p 432, below.

130 In force since 2 December 2003 and 1 December 2003, respectively.

continues to control many aspects of selection, hiring and dismissal.[131] Thus, the principal may not discriminate in relation to the terms of the employment; by not permitting the worker to carry on working; in relation to any benefits, facilities or services which are provided; and finally, the usual provision applies which prevents the imposition of any other detriment: here, this includes a duty on employers to prevent harassment by their own employees of agency workers. As like must be compared with like, the necessary comparison is with how the principal treats the complainant *as compared with other contract workers.* Two important issues have arisen in case law: the first deals with who is a principal, and the second with what discrimination is prohibited. *Harrods Ltd v Remick*[132] concerned three employees of employers who had concessions to work within the Harrods store: a pen consultant, a cosmetics consultant and a florist. Such workers are required to have 'store approval'; in each case it was withdrawn, leading to their dismissal. They were held to be entitled to pursue claims of race discrimination against Harrods; what was done within the store amounted to doing 'work for' Harrods; the sub-section was not limited to situations where the principal had direct control over the work being done. The scope of the statutory definition of a contract worker is wider than that. In *Abbey Life v Tansell,*[133] the Court of Appeal held that a worker, who operated through a company wholly owned by him, which in turn supplied him to an agency, which in turn supplied him to Abbey Life, was a 'contract worker' within the similar definition in s 12 of the Disability Discrimination Act 1995, even though there was no contract between the company employing the worker (that is, his own company) and Abbey Life.

In *BP Chemicals v Gillick and Roevin Management Services Ltd,*[134] the applicant complained of discrimination when BP, the principal for whom she had worked for three years while the agency remained her direct employers, refused to allow her to return to the same job after maternity leave. Her claim succeeded on the basis that the prohibition against discrimination in s 9 is not limited to discrimination when the contract worker is actually working for the principal, but includes the decision on who will work for the principal and when. It follows that the principal can be liable if the selection from among the candidates supplied by the agency is carried out in a discriminatory manner.

(2)   Partnerships

By s 10 of the RRA 1976, small partnerships (those with less than six partners) were exempt from the Act, but this exemption no longer applies where the discrimination comes within Community law competence,[135] which will be in most cases. However, the s 10 exemption may still be used where, for instance, the harassment or discrimination is purely on grounds of colour, or nationality.[136] Otherwise, there are

---

131 The provisions will also apply if the person supplied to perform the work does so on a self-employed basis.

132 [1997] IRLR 583, CA.

133 *Abbey Life Assurance Co Ltd v Tansell (MHC Consulting Services Ltd v Tansell)* [2000] IRLR 387; [2000] ICR 789, CA

134 [1995] IRLR 128, EAT. Applied by the Northern Ireland Court of Appeal in *Patefield v Belfast CC* [2000] IRLR 664.

135 RRA 1976, s 10(1A) and (1B), inserted by reg 12, SI 2003/1626, in force since 19 July 2003.

136 See Chapter 6, especially pp 137–38.

no exemptions for small partnerships. By parallel with the standard provisions on employment, the law covers arrangements for who should be offered a partnership, the actual offer, its terms, expulsion from a partnership or any other detriment.[137] The genuine occupational qualification defence applies by analogy.

(3)   Trade Organisations

These are defined in all the legislation as 'an organisation of workers, or ... of employers, or any other organisation whose members carry on a particular profession or trade for the purposes of which the organisation exists'. The relevant provisions are s 12 of the SDA 1975, s 11 of the RRA 1976, and reg 15 of either the Sexual Orientation, or Religion or Belief, Regulations 2003.[138] The law covers access to and conditions of membership – as opposed to employment – as well as benefits, facilities and services conditional upon such membership, and expulsion and the imposition of any other detriment. Depending on its tactics in collective bargaining, a union might also be liable for pressure to discriminate or for aiding the unlawful acts of an employer. A union is normally vicariously liable for the actions of its *paid* officials, but as shop stewards are unpaid agents rather than paid employees, liability is dependent on general principles applicable to liability for the actions of agents – whether the actions of the shop stewards had been taken within the scope of the authority conferred upon them by the trade union.[139] The provisions extend to discrimination and, save for the SDA 1975, harassment.[140] This does not mean that sexual *harassment* by trade organisations is lawful, as the courts have recognised sexual harassment as a form of direct discrimination, it is just that there is now a statutory definition, which, for sex, is not due for implementation until 5 October 2005. Trade organisations are permitted to engage in two limited forms of positive action, which are discussed in Chapter 18.[141]

Unions may be placed in a difficult situation where an allegation of harassment is made by one union member against another, as occurred in *Fire Brigades Union v Fraser*.[142] It was the union's stated policy to support a person (of whatever sex) in a claim of harassment and not to support the accused. The union chose to support a women who had complained of harassment and consequently declined to provide the accused, Mr Fraser, with assistance and representation in the disciplinary hearing. The Court of Session held that as the policy was conduct-related, rather than gender-related, it did not infringe s 12 of the SDA 1975, and so the accused lost his claim against the union for sex discrimination.

Legally, the principles applicable to trade unions apply equally to employers' organisations, though these are bodies which may have a far looser relationship with their members than trade unions. In *National Federation of Self-Employed and Small*

---

137 SDA 1975, s 11 and reg 14 of the Religion or Belief Regulations 2003, or the Sexual Orientation Regulations 2003.

138 In force since 1 December 2003 and 2 December 2003, respectively. See further, Chapter 5, pp 162 and 150.

139 *Heatons Transport (St Helens) Ltd v T and GWU* [1973] AC 15; [1972] ICR 308, HL.

140 See further, Chapter 9, especially pp 217–19.

141 At pp 574–78.

142 [1998] IRLR 697, CS.

Businesses Ltd v Philpott,[143] it was held that the appellant was 'an organisation of employers', even though it was partly a campaigning group and not all its members were employers. As a result, the tribunal had jurisdiction to hear the respondent's claim of expulsion from the organisation.

(4)   Qualifying Bodies

Section 13 of the SDA 1975, s 12 of the RRA 1976 and reg 16 of either the Religion or Belief, or Sexual Orientation, Regulations 2003[144] deal with discrimination by bodies which confer authorisation or qualification necessary for entry into employment, such as the Law Society, the various Institutes of Professional Engineers, or sporting bodies such as the British Boxing Board of Control, a licence from whom is necessary in order to box professionally.[145] In parallel with the basic employment provisions, the sections cover the grant of the relevant qualification, its terms and its withdrawal.

In *British Judo Association v Petty,*[146] the defendant refused to grant Ms Petty a certificate to referee in men's judo competitions, arguing that their job was to uphold refereeing standards rather than to award a qualification. The EAT held that the issue was whether entry into the occupation was *in fact* facilitated – or not – by their activities, even if not specifically intended to do so, and on that basis the claim was permitted to proceed. In *Patterson v Legal Services Commission,*[147] the EAT held that the provision of a legal aid franchise to a sole practitioner solicitor 'facilitated' her entry into and continuing practice, and so came within s 12 of the RRA 1976. However, in *Tattari v Private Patients Plan Ltd,*[148] the Court of Appeal held that the rejection by the defendants, who underwrite private health care, of the plaintiff's application to be added to their list of accredited specialists was outside s 12 of the RRA 1976. The defendants were not authorising her to practise in her profession. They simply required that those wishing to enter commercial agreements with them should have a recognised UK qualification.

A number of cases have arisen over whether the selection of candidates by a political party for election is caught under these provisions. In *Jepson and Dyas-Elliott v The Labour Party,*[149] an industrial tribunal held that it was. Consequently, the Labour Party's policy of all-women shortlists was held to be unlawful. Recently, the effect of the decision was reversed by the introduction of s 42A into the SDA 1975,[150] allowing for arrangements 'adopted for the purpose of reducing inequality in the numbers of men and women elected, as candidates for the party'. This applies for elections to the

---

143 [1997] IRLR 340; [1997] ICR 518, EAT.

144 In force since 2 December 2003 and 1 December 2003, respectively. In line with the GOR in reg 7(3) of the Sexual Orientation Regulations, reg 16 does apply to an organised religion requiring a particular sexual orientation to comply with its doctrine or the strongly held religious convictions of a significant number of its followers. See above, p 343.

145 Refusing women such a licence was held to be unlawful in *Couch v British Boxing Board of Control* (1998) *The Guardian,* 31 March, IT.

146 [1981] ICR 660; [1981] IRLR 484, EAT.

147 [2003] All ER (D) 306 Feb, EAT.

148 BMLR 24; [1998] ICR 106; [1997] IRLR 586, CA.

149 [1996] IRLR 116.

150 Inserted by the Sex Discrimination (Election Candidates) Act 2002, s 1. The provision will expire at the end of 2015, unless renewed by statutory instrument: s 3.

UK, European and Scottish Parliaments, as well as the Welsh Assembly and local government. *Jepson* was applied in *Sawyer v Ahsan*,[151] a case under the RRA 1976. However, the Court of Appeal in *Triesman v Ali*[152] held that *Sawyer* was wrongly decided and that the nomination of candidates for local government elections was *not* a matter within s 12 of the RRA 1976. This was because, first, the Labour Party was not a body 'which can confer a qualification or authorisation' and, secondly, in this case the nomination of a candidate did not, in any meaningful sense, confer any status on the nominee, whose name merely went into a pool for selection. However, the court did hold that a claimant may have a case under s 25 of the RRA 1976, regarding associations.[153]

Section 13(2) of the SDA 1975 – there is no equivalent in the other discrimination legislation – requires such bodies, in assessing whether someone is of a proper character to enter the relevant profession, to take account of evidence that they have engaged in unlawful discrimination. It is not clear whether this covers both direct and indirect discrimination and how it might be enforced.

(5)   Vocational Training Bodies

Section 14 of the SDA 1975, s 13 of the RRA 1976 and reg 17 of either the Religion or Belief, or Sexual Orientation, Regulations 2003[154] deal with discrimination by bodies which offer training to help fit people for employment. By analogy with the situation of employers, discrimination is prohibited in relation to offers, terms and terminations. However, there is an important exception, to deal with the fact that in some circumstances such bodies are permitted to offer special training to members of a particular race or gender in order to remedy under-representation.[155]

(6)   Employment Agencies

These are defined as bodies which, whether or not for profit, 'provide services for the purpose of finding employment for workers or supplying employers with workers'. This definition includes the careers service of a school[156] and the activities of a trade union branch which supplies workers – if any still have that power. Under s 15 of the SDA 1975, s 14 of the RRA 1976 and reg 18 of either the Religion or Belief, or Sexual Orientation, Regulations 2003,[157] discrimination is prohibited in relation to the terms and methods in which services are provided, and refusal to provide services. There is a defence if the employer states that a job falls within one of the exceptions and it is reasonable for the agency to rely on that statement.

---

151 [1999] IRLR 609, EAT.
152 *Triesman (sued on his own behalf and on behalf of all other members of the Labour Party) v Ali and Another* [2002] EWCA Civ 93; [2002] ICR 1026; [2002] IRLR 489, CA.
153 See below, Chapter 13, pp 365–67.
154 In force since 2 December 2003 and 1 December 2003, respectively.
155 See Chapter 18, pp 574–78.
156 *CRE v Imperial Society of Teachers of Dancing* [1983] ICR 473; [1983] IRLR 315, EAT.
157 In force since 2 December 2003 and 1 December 2003, respectively.

6   SPECIAL PROVISIONS FOR CERTAIN EMPLOYMENTS

(1)   The Police

Section 16, now repealed, of the RRA 1976 provided that a constable was an employee, whilst s 32 provides that 'Anything done by a person in course of his employment shall be treated ... as done by his employer as well'. In *Chief Constable of Bedfordshire Police v Liversidge*,[158] the Court of Appeal held that ss 16 and 32 combined did not make the Chief Constable, as employer, vicariously or constructively liable for discrimination by one police officer to another. Ironically, the court was influenced by concurrent passing of the Race Relations (Amendment) Act 2000, which expressly remedied this problem. For the Court of Appeal, the new Act was evidence that Parliament had not intended the old definition to cover such situations. Of course, for those police officers complaining of racial discrimination or harassment from colleagues, there is now a remedy.[159] More recently, the Sex Discrimination Act has been amended in the same way.[160] There will also be a remedy under the Sexual Orientation, or Religion or Belief, Regulations 2003.[161]

Section 17(2)(a) of the SDA 1975 permits discrimination between men and women police officers 'as to requirements, relating to height, uniform or equipment ...'. This legitimises different height requirements, and prevents a claim that different uniforms are discriminatory. It would not prevent a claim, for example, that women but not men were required to wear uniforms in a particular context. It is the different rules which are protected, not necessarily the way in which those rules are operated. Different equipment is more problematic: *Johnston v Chief Constable of the Royal Ulster Constabulary*[162] only legitimised differential firearms rules in the particular context of Northern Ireland,[163] and any differentiation must be interpreted according to European law. It is submitted that equipment must be read as analogous to clothing rather than referring to special operational policing equipment. For example, it cannot be lawful under this provision to allow male but not female officers to drive specially modified police vehicles.[164]

---

158 [2002] IRLR 15, CA.

159 The 2000 Act replaced s 16 with ss 76A and 76B.

160 Sex Discrimination Act 1975 (Amendment) Regulations 2003, SI 2003/1657, reg 2 inserting s 17(1A) into the SDA 1975.

161 Regulation 11(2) of either Regulations. In force since 1 December 2003 and 2 December 2003, respectively.

162 Case 222/84 [1986] IRLR 263; [1986] ECR 1651; [1987] QB 129; [1986] 3 All ER 135, ECJ. See further, Chapter 8, p 214.

163 See Chapter 8, p 214.

164 Under the Pregnant Workers Directive (92/85/EEC) OJ L348/1, 1992, as incorporated into domestic law by the Employment Rights Act 1996, s 99(1), it is unfair to dismiss a woman 'for any reason connected with her pregnancy'. But as police officers may not complain of unfair dismissal, any such claim must be on the ground of unlawful discrimination rather than unfair dismissal.

(2)   The Prison Service

Unlike the police, the only specifically permissible discrimination concerns height requirements.[165] A challenge would still be permissible if the rules excluded disproportionately more men than women. The absence of reference to clothing means that different rules for men and women on dress must be tested according to the normal employment case law, which at present gives employers substantial discretion to impose different requirements.[166]

(3)   Religion

Employment by religious groups is excluded from the SDA 1975 'where the employment is limited to one sex so as to comply with the doctrines of the religion or to avoid offending the religious susceptibilities of a significant number of its followers'.[167] The formula is repeated for cases of gender reassignment[168] and on similar terms for sexual orientation.[169] There is no parallel provision in the RRA 1976. The protection covers not only employment, but also the obtaining of relevant qualifications for the purposes of employment by that religious group. Such employment is not restricted to ministers. It could cover administrators and, for example, could permit teachers in a Muslim girls' school to be restricted to women. There are, of course, specified GORs for cases under the Religion or Belief Regulations.[170]

(4)   Midwives

The original s 20 of the SDA 1975 permitted discrimination against men in the context of employment as a midwife. In *Commission of the European Communities v UK*,[171] the Court rejected the argument that this exception contravened the Equal Treatment Directive. It was stated that 'personal sensitivities may play an important role in relations between midwife and patient. In those circumstances ... the UK had not exceeded the limits of the power granted to the Member States by Art 2(2) ... which permits Member States to exclude from the application of the Directive occupational activities where the sex of the worker constitutes a determining factor'. In any event, the Government had already decided to change the law; men may now become midwives on the same terms as women.[172] However, the defence of genuine occupational qualification relating to 'decency or privacy' may still be applicable. How many women must object, whether such objection would be reasonable, and indeed how many men are practising as midwives are all unclear.

---

165 SDA 1975, s 18.
166 See above, Chapter 7, pp 177–82.
167 SDA 1975, s 19(1).
168 SDA 1975, s 19(3).
169 Sexual Orientation Regulations 2003, reg 7. Discussed above, p 343.
170 See above, pp 342–44.
171 Case 165/82 [1983] ECR 3431; [1984] 1 All ER 353; [1984] ICR 182; [1984] IRLR 29.
172 Sex Discrimination Act (Amendment of s 20) Order 1983, SI 1983/1202.

(5)   The Armed Forces

There are no exceptions for the armed forces,[173] except under the SDA. However, the Government might argue such an exception under 'national security', discussed above.[174] Section 85(4) of the original SDA 1975 provided a blanket immunity as regards employment discrimination carried out by the armed services. Such justification could only relate, tenuous as it might be, to national security. *Johnston v Chief Constable of the Royal Ulster Constabulary*[175] made it clear that a defence of national security had to be tested according to the facts of individual cases – blanket exclusions were impermissible. As from 1995, s 85(4) only provides exemption for acts 'done for the purpose of ensuring the combat effectiveness' of the armed forces.[176]

Sirdar v Secretary of State for Defence **Case C-273/97 [2000] ICR 130, ECJ**[177]

A female chef challenged the policy of the Royal Marines not to permit women to serve. The Ministry of Defence relied, successfully, on s 85(4). The ECJ endorsed s 85(4) only so far as it is necessary, with a margin of discretion, to guarantee public security.

Judgment:

26.   In determining the scope of any derogation from an individual right such as the equal treatment of men and women, the principle of proportionality, one of the general principles of Community law, must also be observed ... That principle requires that derogations remain within the limits of what is appropriate and necessary in order to achieve the aim in view ...

27.   However, depending on the circumstances, national authorities have a certain degree of discretion when adopting measures which they consider to be necessary in order to guarantee public security in a member state (see *Leifer's* case[178] (para 35)) ...

29.   ... the reason given for refusing to employ the applicant ... a chef with the Royal Marines is the total exclusion of women from that unit by reason of the 'interoperability' rule established for the purpose of ensuring combat effectiveness.

30.   ... the organisation of the Royal Marines differs fundamentally from that of other units in the British armed forces, of which they are the 'point of the arrow head'. They are a small force and are intended to be the first line of attack. It has been established that, within this corps, chefs are indeed also required to serve as frontline commandos, that all members of the corps are engaged and trained for that purpose, and that there are no exceptions to this rule at the time of recruitment. ...

---

173 Expressly stated by the RRA 1976, s 75. See also reg 36(2)(c) of the Sexual Orientation, or Religion or Belief, Regulations 2003. However there are restrictions on bringing a complaint until it has been dealt with internally; see respectively, s 75(9) and reg 36(8).

174 See p 349.

175 Case 222/84 [1986] IRLR 263; [1986] ECR 1651; [1987] QB 129; [1986] 3 All ER 135, ECJ. See further, Chapter 8, p 214.

176 Sex Discrimination Act 1975 (Application to Armed Forces, etc) Regulations 1994, SI 1994/3276.

177 See also [1999] All ER (EC) 928; [2000] IRLR 47.

178 Case C-83/94 [1995] ECR I-3231.

32.   ... the exclusion of women from service in special combat units such as the Royal Marines may be justified under art 2(2) of the directive by reason of the nature of the activities in question and the context in which they are carried out.

(6)   Barristers

It became apparent that barristers fell outside the legislation because they work neither under a contract nor under a partnership agreement. In consequence, new sections were inserted into the SDA 1975 and RRA 1976 and now ss 35A and 35B, and ss 26A and 26B, respectively,[179] make the legislation applicable to barristers. The Sexual Orientation, and Religion or Belief, Regulations 2003 cover barristers and advocates as well.[180] Proceedings under the SDA 1975 and 'residual' cases[181] under the RRA 1976 are, however, brought in county courts rather than before employment tribunals.

(7)   Public Bodies

Under s 75(5) of the RRA 1976, there is an exemption in relation to employment in the service of the Crown or certain public bodies which are permitted to restrict employment to persons of a particular birth, nationality, descent or residence. The number of such bodies has been greatly reduced by the Race Relations (Prescribed Public Bodies) (No 2) Regulations 1994.[182]

7   OTHER UNLAWFUL ACTS

(1)   Employer Responsibility for the Actions of Employees

Under s 41 of the SDA 1975, s 32 of the RRA 1976 and reg 22 of the Religion or Belief, or Sexual Orientation, Regulations 2003,[183] the employer is made liable for actions done by employees in the course of their employment.[184] Generally, employers are not liable for the discriminatory acts (including harassment) of third parties.[185]

---

179 Inserted by the Courts and Legal Services Act 1990, ss 64 and 65.
180 Regulations 12 and 13.
181 Those not covered by the Race Directive (2000/43/EC), for these purposes, discrimination solely on grounds of colour, or nationality.
182 SI 1994/1986. The schedule lists as bodies exempt from the Act: Bank of England, Board of Trustees of the Armouries, British Council, House of Commons, House of Lords, Metropolitan Police Office, National Army Museum, National Audit Office, Natural Environment Research Council, United Kingdom Atomic Energy Authority. See (1994) 54 EOR 7.
183 In force since 2 December 2003 and 1 December 2003, respectively.
184 Sub-sections 41(2), 32(2) and reg 26(2) respectively provide for the liability of a principal for the actions of an agent.
185 *Pearce v Governing Body of Mayfield Secondary School* [2003] UKHL 34; [2003] All ER (D) 259 (Jun), HL, discussed in Chapter 9, p 232.

(2)   Instructions and Pressure to Discriminate[186]

For unlawful instructions, the instructor must either have authority over the person subject to the instructions, or the latter must be accustomed to act in accordance with his wishes. For pressure, there must either be the provision or offer of a benefit, or the imposition or threat of a detriment.

In *CRE v Imperial Society of Teachers of Dancing*,[187] the defendant's secretary told a careers service that she would 'rather the school did not send anyone coloured'. It was held that there were no unlawful instructions to discriminate, as the secretary had no authority over the school, even though the school might normally have complied with her requests. However, pressure to discriminate was established because of the implied suggestion that the defendants would no longer deal with the school.

A person who is instructed, or pressured, to discriminate does not, without more, have a right to bring an action. The power to bring proceedings lies, in sex and race cases, with the Equal Opportunities Commission or the Commission for Racial Equality, respectively. However, the person being instructed to discriminate may refuse and face disciplinary action, or some other detriment. This will amount to direct discrimination under the legislation, save the SDA 1975, and the *individual* affected will be able to bring an action. Under the RRA 1976, it is unlawful to treat a person less favourably on the ground of *another person's* race.[188] The same will be possible under the Religion or Belief, and Sexual Orientation, Regulations 2003.[189] However, under the SDA 1975, the less favourable treatment must be on the ground of the gender of the actual complainant. It might nevertheless be possible to argue that there has been victimisation under s 4(1)(c) or (d). If a person complains that he has been instructed to discriminate, he has effectively alleged that an unlawful act has been committed. There is no requirement either that there must be a victim of the unlawful act or that the person victimised is aware that the act is unlawful.[190] The Equal Treatment Amendment Directive[191] brings the Equal Treatment Directive[192] into line by deeming instructions to discriminate to be 'discrimination'.[193] Hence, in due course, the SDA 1975 should be amended to give an individual remedy. A further point flows from the EC definition, which states that the instructions alone amount to discrimination. No related less favourable treatment (such as a dismissal for a refusal to comply with an instruction) is necessary. Hence, it is arguable that the domestic definition of direct discrimination does not implement fully the EC definition. One solution could be for the courts to interpret 'less favourable treatment' to cover an instruction to discriminate.

---

186 SDA 1975, ss 39, 40; RRA 1976, ss 30, 31.

187 [1983] ICR 473; [1983] IRLR 315, EAT.

188 *Showboat Entertainment Centre Ltd v Owens* [1984] 1 WLR 384; [1984] ICR 65; [1984] IRLR 7, EAT (see above, Chapter 7, p 187). In *Weathersfield Ltd v Sargent* [1999] IRLR 94, CA, it was held to amount to less favourable treatment on racial grounds where, in response to instructions not to rent vehicles to black people, the complainant resigned. See above, p 323.

189 In force since 2 December 2003 and 1 December 2003, respectively.

190 See Chapter 11, especially p 300.

191 2002/73/EC, due to be implemented by 5 October 2005.

192 76/270/EEC.

193 *Ibid*, Art 2(4).

(3)   Aiding Unlawful Acts

Section 42 of the SDA 1975, s 32 of the RRA 1976, and regulation 23 of either the Religion or Belief, or Sexual Orientation, Regulations,[194] make it unlawful 'knowingly' to aid another person to do an act of unlawful discrimination. Under s 42(2), s 32(2) or reg 23(2), the individual discriminator is deemed to aid the doing of the act by the employer. This means that individual liability for aiding an unlawful act depends upon the direct liability of the employer. This is particularly problematic in harassment cases, as it means that the individual harasser can only be liable under anti-discrimination legislation if the employer is also deemed to be liable. Where the employer is liable, the individual employee may also be personally liable.[195] There is, however, a defence if the alleged aider has reasonably relied on an assurance from the person alleged to be being aided that the act in question does not amount to unlawful discrimination.[196]

---

194 In force since 2 December 2003 and 1 December 2003, respectively.
195 *Read v Tiverton DC and Bull* [1977] IRLR 202, IT.
196 SDA 1975, ss 39, 40 and 42 only apply to contravention of that Act. It follows that it is not unlawful to instruct, pressure or aid a breach either of the Equal Pay Act or European law, eg, instructions to manipulate the outcome of a job evaluation study to favour male workers. In principle, this needs changing, although there is no evidence that problems have arisen.

CHAPTER 13

DISCRIMINATION IN FIELDS OTHER THAN EMPLOYMENT

1   EDUCATION

(1)   Types of Education Covered

The sex and race discrimination legislation applies to state, independent and special schools, as well as further and higher education colleges and universities.[1] The Employment Equality (Religion or Belief) Regulations 2003 (the 'Religion or Belief Regulations') or the Employment Equality (Sexual Orientation) Regulations 2003 (the 'Sexual Orientation Regulations') cover only further and higher education.[2]

(2)   Unlawful Discrimination in Education

(a)   Discrimination

The educational provisions of the Sex Discrimination Act (SDA) 1975 have three main objectives: first, to define which actions are unlawful; secondly, to reconcile the non-discrimination principle with the fact that single-sex education remains relatively commonplace; and thirdly, to impose various duties on bodies concerned with the provision of education, such as local education authorities and funding councils. There is no parallel to the second of these objectives in the other legislation.

> **Sex Discrimination Act 1975**
>
> **Section 22**
>
> It is unlawful in relation to an educational establishment ... to discriminate against a woman:
>
> (a)   in the terms on which it offers to admit her to the establishment as a pupil; or
>
> (b)   by refusing or deliberately omitting to accept an application for her admission to the establishment as a pupil; or
>
> (c)   where she is a pupil of the establishment:
>
>   (i)   in the way it affords her access to any benefits, facilities or services, or by refusing or deliberately omitting to afford her access to them; or
>
>   (ii)   by excluding her from the establishment or subjecting her to any other detriment.

Section 17 of the Race Relations Act (RRA) 1976 and reg 20 of either the Religion or Belief, or Sexual Orientation, Regulations 2003[3] are in substantially similar terms. Both sections deal only with discrimination in the way in which a particular educational establishment operates. Under this head, no comparison is permitted between

---

1   See respectively tables in the SDA 1975, s 22 and the RRA 976, s 17.

2   Regulations 20(3) and (4) of either the Religion or Belief, or Sexual Orientation, Regulations 2003, in force since 2 December 2003 and 1 December 2003, respectively.

3   In force since 2 December 2003 and 1 December 2003, respectively.

different schools or universities, even if the schools are within the same local education authority. St George's Hospital Medical School at one time operated an admissions system with a deliberate built-in bias against women and ethnic minorities. A formal investigation by the Commission for Racial Equality uncovered this practice, which was enshrined in a computer programme and thus demonstrable.[4] Bias on the part of university admissions tutors or interviewers is clearly unlawful, but may be impossible to demonstrate in practice.

Harassment is specifically outlawed by RRA 1976 and the Religion or Belief, or Sexual Orientation, Regulations, although the statutory definition of racial harassment is restricted to grounds of race, ethnic or national origins.[5] Sexual harassment is yet to be specifically outlawed by the SDA 1975. However, it is recognised by the courts as a form of sex discrimination, although there are some problems associated with this approach.[6]

(b)   Other discrimination by education authorities

Section 23 of the SDA 1975 (or s 18 of the RRA 1976) places an added duty on Local Education Authorities (LEAs), Further Education (FE) and Higher Education (HE) funding councils and teacher training agencies. This section allows for comparisons between different institutions under the control of one of these bodies. This duty may, in effect, entail an obligation to take corrective measures to overcome disadvantage caused by the fact that, for example, specialist extra facilities are only available, within the LEA, in single-sex establishments.[7] The claim in *Birmingham CC v EOC*,[8] a challenge to the council's policy of allocating grammar school places in favour of boys, was brought under s 23. In *R v Secretary of State for Education & Science ex p Keating*,[9] parents challenged the policy of closing an all-boys' school, whilst maintaining two all-girls' schools.

(c)   Relationships that have come to an end

The SDA, the RRA and the Sexual Orientation, and Religion or Belief, Regulations provide that discrimination or harassment[10] after the 'relationship has come to an end' is unlawful.[11] This statutory definition, deriving from EC Directives, has some limits. For instance, in the SDA, it covers only employment matters, and so impinges on the education provisions only so far as they apply to vocational training. The statutory definition in the RRA does not extend to discrimination purely on the grounds of

---

4   *Medical School Admissions: St George's Hospital*, 1988, London: CRE.
5   RRA 1976, s 17(2) (in force since 19 July 2003), and reg 20(2) of either the Religion or Belief, or Sexual Orientation, Regulations 2003, in force since 2 December 2003 and 1 December 2003, respectively.
6   See generally, Chapter 9, and especially pp 219–24.
7   Bourn, C and Whitmore, J, *Anti-Discrimination Law in Britain*, 3rd edn, 1996, London: Sweet & Maxwell, p 271.
8   [1989] AC 1155, HL. See further, Chapter 7, pp 170 and 182.
9   [1985] LGR 469, QBD.
10   For the definitions of harassment, see above, and in more detail, Chapter 9, p 217.
11   SDA 1975, s 35C; RRA 1976, s 27A, (both in force since 19 July 2003), reg 21 of either Regulations, in force since 1 December 2003 and 2 December 2003, respectively. The definition is discussed above, Chapter 12, pp 327–28.

colour or nationality. However, recent case law suggests that these residual cases will be treated in much the same way. The House of Lords held in *Relaxion v Rhys-Harper*[12] that the phrase 'whom he employs' in s 6 of the *employment* provisions of the SDA extends to discrimination against ex-workers.[13] A case under the education provisions of the SDA will turn on the parallel phrase in s 22(c)(ii) 'where she is a pupil'[14] and is likely to be given an equally broad interpretation.

(3)   Exceptions

(a)   *General occupational requirements – religion or belief, sexual orientation*

Regulation 20(3) of either the Religion or Belief, or Sexual Orientation, Regulations[15] provides that para (1) (recruitment) 'does not apply if the discrimination only concerns training which would help fit a person for employment which, by virtue of [the GORs in] reg 7, the employer could lawfully refuse to offer ...'[16]

(b)   *Single-sex schools*

Section 26 of the SDA 1975 provides an exception for a single-sex educational establishment, with s 27 providing a parallel transitional exception for establishments which are in the process of becoming co-educational.[17] Section 26(2) further provides that a school which is not a single-sex establishment may nevertheless choose to offer boarding facilities and the benefits and services consequent upon such facilities to members of one sex only. Differential provision within the individual educational establishment will automatically be unlawful if it is based on race, as racial segregation amounts to discrimination.[18]

(c)   *Physical training and sport*

Sex Discrimination Act 1975

44 Sport etc

Nothing in Parts II to IV shall, in relation to any sport, game or other activity of a competitive nature where the physical strength, stamina or physique of the average

---

12   The collective appeals of *Relaxion Group plc v Rhys-Harper, D'Souza v Lambeth LBC, Jones v 3M Healthcare Ltd* [2003] UKHL 33, overruling *Post Office v Adekeye* [1997] ICR 110; [1997] IRLR 105, CA. Discussed briefly, above, Chapter 12, pp 327–28.
13   Except where the act complained of does not arise from the employment relationship, such as a refusal to implement an employment tribunal's reinstatement order, for which there is a free-standing remedy (under the Employment Rights Act 1996, ss 112, 113, 114 and 117): *ibid*, in the case of *D'Souza*, at paras 49–53, 124–25, 159–60, 205 and 221.
14   Or the RRA 1976, s 17(c): 'where he is a pupil.'
15   In force since 2 December 2003 and 1 December 2003, respectively.
16   For a discussion of these GORs, see Chapter 12, pp 342–44.
17   A 'single-sex establishment' is defined by SDA 1975, s 26(1), as one which 'admits pupils of one sex only, or which would be taken to admit pupils of one sex only if there were disregarded pupils of the opposite sex (a) whose admission is exceptional, or (b) whose numbers are comparatively small and whose admission is confined to particular courses of instruction or teaching classes'.
18   RRA 1976, s 1(2); see Chapter 7, p 173–75.

woman puts her at a disadvantage to the average man, render unlawful any act related to the participation of a person as a competitor in events involving that activity which are confined to competitors of one sex.

Not only does this legitimise, for example, teaching athletics in single-sex groups, it also appears to legitimise the common practice whereby boys are taught one sport while girls are taught another – football and hockey, basketball and netball are common examples.[19] Section 28 provides a further exception for physical education courses in FE and HE only. Segregation of physical education lessons by race, or by other protected grounds, is unlawful.

2   GOODS, FACILITIES AND SERVICES

Sex Discrimination Act 1975

Section 29

(1)   It is unlawful for any person concerned with the provision (whether for payment or not) of goods, facilities or services to the public or a section of the public to discriminate against a woman who seeks to obtain or use those goods, facilities or services:

    (a) by refusing or deliberately omitting to provide her with any of them; or

    (b) by refusing or deliberately omitting to provide her with goods, facilities or services of the like quality, in the like manner or on the like terms as are normal in his case in relation to male members of the public ...

(2)   The following are examples of the facilities and services mentioned in sub-s (1):

    (a) access to and use of any place which members of the public or a section of the public are permitted to enter;

    (b) accommodation in a hotel, boarding house or other similar establishment;

    (c) facilities by way of banking or insurance or for grants, loans, credit or finance;

    (d) facilities for education;

    (e) facilities for entertainment, recreation or refreshment;

    (f) facilities for transport or travel;

    (g) the services of any profession or trade, or any local or other public authority.

(3)   For the avoidance of doubt ... where a particular skill is commonly exercised in a different way for men and for women it does not contravene sub-s (1) for a person who does not normally exercise it for women to insist on exercising it for a woman only in accordance with his normal practice or, if he reasonably considers it impracticable to do that in her case, to refuse or deliberately omit to exercise it.[20]

Section 20 of the RRA 1976 is substantially the same. There are no equivalent provisions in the Religion or Belief, or Sexual Orientation, Regulations. It is now specifically provided, by s 20(3) of the RRA 1976,[21] that harassment is unlawful under

---

19   The argument is not clear cut: the section refers to 'any sport, game or other activity of a competitive nature'. There is a strong case to be made that it is unlawful for school to deny girls the opportunity at least to try their hand at, eg, football, rugby and cricket. See also below, p 372–73.

20   There is no equivalent to this sub-section in RRA 1976.

21   Inserted by SI 2003/1626, reg 22, in force since 19 July 2003.

the RRA 1976, in the provision of goods, facilities and services. Sexual harassment is yet to be specifically outlawed by the SDA 1975.[22] However, it is recognised by the courts as a form of sex discrimination, although there are some problems associated with this approach.[23] Harassment will most likely fall within the phrase in s 29(1)(b) of the SDA 1975, 'in the like manner'. It might be easier to succeed in a claim than in the employment context, especially where the harassment concerns a single incident, as there is no requirement that the harassment be to the complainant's detriment, although that will clearly be relevant in assessing the degree of injury to feelings.

(1)   The Public or a Section of the Public

This part of the legislation is concerned with activities which potentially lie at the margin of acceptable legal intervention. The law has to determine which activities should be controlled and which should remain unregulated in the interests of personal autonomy.[24] It would be too great an infringement of personal liberty to allow a claim of race discrimination if a black person was not invited to a birthday party.[25] A key way in which the law seeks to avoid controls on essentially private behaviour is by insisting that the provision be to the public or a section of the public. We should not be surprised to discover that the dividing line is not at all clear, and may be different in different contexts where regulation is under consideration.

(a)   Clubs

The leading case on the meaning of the phrase 'section of the public', *Charter v Race Relations Board*,[26] arose under the Race Relations Act 1968. The House of Lords held that a Conservative club was outside the scope of the legislation as membership was not offered to a section of the public. The issue depends on whether the right to become a member is effectively automatic or whether genuine discretion is exercised in selecting candidates for membership. This was extended to associate club members in *Dockers Labour Club and Institute Ltd v Race Relations Board*,[27] where the House of Lords held that a working men's club was outside the scope of the legislation, even though there was a national organisation linking all the various such clubs. Lord Diplock set the test: 'Would a notice, "Public not admitted" exhibited on the premises ... be true?'[28]

---

22 A specific definition for employment matters is due by 5 October 2005, under the recently amended Equal Treatment Directive. See further Chapter 9, pp 217–18.

23 See generally, Chapter 9, pp 219–24.

24 See Gardner, J, 'Private activities and personal autonomy: at the margins of anti-discrimination law', in Hepple, B and Szyszczak, E (eds), *Discrimination: The Limits of Law*, 1992, London: Mansell, Chapter 9.

25 It makes no difference if the party is held, eg, in a hotel for which a room has been booked. The hotelier can only be liable if there is discrimination in the letting arrangements. Even if there is knowledge that there has been discrimination in the invitations, the hotelier is not liable: there has been no refusal or deliberate omission to provide the relevant service. It is for this reason that there is no breach of the legislation if facilities are provided to a known racist organisation.

26 [1973] AC 885; [1973] 1 All ER 512, HL.

27 [1976] AC 285; [1974] 3 All ER 592, HL.

28 *Ibid*, at 297G.

Section 25 of the RRA 1976 specifically brought such clubs with 25 or more members within the ambit of *that* legislation. No such equivalent was introduced into the SDA 1975. Section 26 provides an exception from s 25 if the main object of the association is to enable the benefits of membership to persons of a particular racial group, defined otherwise than by reference to colour. This enables organisations to offer membership to groups defined by, say, nationality, such as a Swansea Bangladeshi association or a London Welsh society.

Membership criteria may be directly or indirectly discriminatory; the equivalent to word-of-mouth hiring in the employment context is where applicants for membership are required to be sponsored by an existing member.[29] On the assumption that such a practice would in most cases be *prima facie* indirectly discriminatory, the question arises whether such a practice could ever be justified. It is contended that the answer must be 'no', either if the club is comparatively large, or if it a local club with rather general purposes; the answer *might* – no more than might – be different if the club was a small one with specific objectives, such as to pursue an interest in war games or white-knuckle rides at theme parks around the country.

By contrast with s 20 of the RRA 1976, s 25 only applies to clubs, although that is broadly defined. It does not apply generally to 'any person concerned with the provision ... of goods, facilities or services'. By s 25(1)(b), the section applies if 'membership is ... so conducted that the members do not constitute a section of the public within the meaning of section 20(1)'. Consequently, the narrow definition given in *Charter* and *Dockers Labour Club* is still relevant. In *Triesman v Ali*,[30] the claimant was suspended from the Labour Party, pending a disciplinary investigation. The consequence for Ali was that he could not be nominated for re-selection as a candidate for the local elections. He brought his claim, *inter alia*, under s 25, but not under s 20. As Peter Gibson LJ noted, 'it is far from obvious'[31] that the Labour Party were offering goods, facilities or services. Noting Lord Diplock's '*Public Not Admitted* notice' test (from *Dockers Labour Club*), the Court of Appeal held that s 25 was 'capable'[32] of applying to the Labour Party. It was a question of fact for the county court under s 25(1)(b).

Private clubs whose membership is restricted by gender are not within the legislation.[33] While understandable, this may have unfortunate consequences. Such clubs may be nominally private, but given the degree of networking and decision making to which some are privy, they may be said to exercise a quasi-public function. Arguably, the law should cover such clubs unless, perhaps, their total membership is below a certain figure. This would bring, for example, London clubs within the legislation. In addition, certain clubs, of which some golf clubs are prime example,

---

29 The Commission for Racial Equality issued a non-discrimination notice (see Chapter 17, pp 550–62) to a social club whose rules stated that new members had to be sponsored by two members and approved by committee. No non-white had ever applied for membership in an area of just 40% white population. See *Handsworth Horticultural Institute Ltd v CRE* (unreported). See *Ruled Out*, F Invest 1992, Appendix C.

30 [2002] IRLR 489; [2002] EWCA 93; [2002] ICR 1026, CA.

31 *Ibid*, at p 497.

32 *Ibid*.

33 Of course, such clubs cannot discriminate in respect of their employees on grounds of race or gender. See, eg, *Hayes v Malleable Working Men's Club and Institute* [1985] ICR 703; [1985] IRLR 367.

adopt differential membership criteria for men and women under which, for example, only men have the right to full voting membership and where only full membership carries a right to reciprocal membership of other such clubs. There can be no justification for such stereotyped differentiations which should be removed by law.

(b)   Care of children

In *Applin v Race Relations Board*,[34] the House of Lords held that children who had been taken into the care of a local authority were a section of the public and that therefore the provision of fostering facilities was covered by the legislation. In consequence, there could be no discrimination in the way in which fostering arrangements were organised, making it impermissible for foster parents to specify the race of the child they wished to foster. Section 23(2) of the RRA 1976 reverses this position, removing from the ambit of the Act situations where someone 'takes into his home, and treats as if they were members of his family, children, elderly persons, or persons requiring a special degree of care and attention'. The exception only covers acts of discrimination by the putative foster parents; it will thus only absolve actions by the local authority in so far as they respond to the declared wishes of potential fosterers. Accordingly, in *Conwell v Newham LBC*,[35] the Employment Appeal Tribunal held that provision of care *by the local authority* came within s 20 of the RRA 1976, despite s 22(5) of the Children Act 1989.

(2)   Goods, Facilities or Services

Most of the situations covered by these sections are clear. A few examples will suffice. It is unlawful to discriminate in relation to admission charges for, for example, stately homes, hotels or sporting facilities;[36] it is unlawful to refuse to serve women or black people when men or white people would be served;[37] it is unlawful to apply different rules of behaviour to men and women in places of public entertainment;[38] it is unlawful to apply different criteria to men and women, or black people and white people, in relation to the provision of facilities or services such as credit facilities or the offer of a mortgage. It is unlawful to refuse the service on ground of race and gender, to grant the service on different conditions, and if the service is not provided 'in like manner'.

(a)   Exception – s 29(3) of the SDA 1975

Section 29(3) of the SDA 1975 deals with the question of where the clientele for the service may be self-selecting on ground of gender: examples include a ladies'

---

34 [1975] AC 259; [1974] 2 All ER 73, HL.
35 [2000] ICR 42, [1999] 1 All ER 696; [1999] 3 FCR 625; [2000] 1 FLR 595; [2000] LGR 370, EAT.
36 *James v Eastleigh BC* [1990] 2 AC 751; [1990] 2 All ER 607; [1990] IRLR 208. In *R v Secretary of State for Health ex p Richardson* Case C-137/94 [1996] ICR 471; [1996] All ER (EC) 865 the European Court held that it was a breach of the Social Security Directive 79/7 to grant, on the ground of different pensionable ages, free medical prescriptions for women aged 60 whereas men only obtained the concession at age 65. The scope of the Directive is limited to matters concerning social security.
37 *Gill v El Vino Co Ltd* [1983] QB 425; [1983] 1 All ER 398; [1983] IRLR 206, CA.
38 *McConomy v Croft Inns Ltd* [1992] IRLR 561, High Ct of NI. See further, Chapter 7, p 178.

hairdresser or fashion shop. It is clearly discrimination to refuse to serve a person of a different gender from the usual clientele, but there is no obligation to alter the range of the services provided to make them more attractive to people of a different gender. The sections assume that the services being provided are genuinely comparable. There is nothing to prevent, for example, differential pricing for male and female hair care, if it can be shown that there is a fundamental difference in the service being provided.[39] For reasons of commercial convenience, it is probably acceptable to have a single price for women which is higher than for men, even though in some particular instances the hair care being provided could not be regarded as involving a different service.

(b)   When provided by public authorities

It is clear that commercial services provided by public bodies or local authorities are within the sections. The position with respect to non-commercial activities is much less straightforward. The answer to the question will determine the extent to which many of the major policy and administration functions of government are brought within the scope of the legislation. While judicial review may be available as an alternative, it is by no means automatic and under that route there is no possibility of compensation as a remedy. It seems clear that an activity of government which is primarily *detrimental* to individuals is outside the scope of the section. In *Savjani v IRC*,[40] the Court of Appeal held that the Inland Revenue was not providing a service to members of the public in collecting tax from them. It is perfectly consistent to argue that some of the activities of the Inland Revenue may be within the section: the giving of advice or information entails the provision of a service and must be carried out in a non-discriminatory fashion. Similarly, the prison department does not provide a service to the prisoners it incarcerates, but it does provide a service or a facility to prisoners in respect of work allocation within a prison.[41]

> **R v Entry Clearance Officer Bombay ex p Amin [1983] 2 AC 818; [1983] 2 All ER 864, HL**

The plaintiff was a British Overseas Citizen whose right to enter the UK depended on a voucher scheme which, by assuming that men were normally the heads of households, discriminated between men and women. This was not a challenge to the operation of immigration legislation based on race, which was specifically excluded, but on ground of gender. The majority of the House of Lords held that the scheme fell outside s 29 of the SDA 1975.

> *Lord Fraser of Tullybelton (pp 834–35):*

> Section 29 as a whole seems to me to apply to the direct provision of facilities or services, and not to the mere grant of permission to use facilities ... The example in para (d) refers, in my view, to the actual provision of schools and other facilities for education, but not to the mere grant of an entry certificate or a special voucher to enable a student to enter the United Kingdom in order to study here ... In the present

---

39   *Waldock v Whitney and Prosser* (1984) unreported, county court.
40   [1981] QB 458; [1981] 1 All ER 1121.
41   *Alexander v Home Office* [1988] 2 All ER 118; [1988] ICR 685; [1988] IRLR 190. Work in a prison falls outside the statutory definition of employment; the case can only be argued on the basis of the provision of a facility or a service.

case the entry clearance officer in Bombay was in my opinion not providing a service for would-be immigrants; rather he was performing his duty of controlling them ...

[Section 85(1) of the 1976 Act] puts an act done on behalf of the Crown on a par with an act done by a private person, and it does not in terms restrict the comparison to an act of the *same kind* done by a private person. But in my opinion it applies only to acts done on behalf of the Crown which are of a kind similar to acts which might be done by a private person. It does not mean that the Act is to apply to any act of any kind done on behalf of the Crown by a person holding statutory office ...

Lord Scarman (dissenting) (p 843):

In my view the granting of leave to enter the country by provision of a special voucher or otherwise is the provision of a facility to a section of the public. Indeed, I have no doubt that some see it as a very valuable facility. Section 29(1) is wide enough, therefore, to cover the special voucher scheme which, in my judgment, is properly described as offering a facility to some members of the public, ie, United Kingdom passport holders, who seek access to this country for the purposes of settlement but have no lawful means of entering other than by leave.

If the first reason relied on by Lord Fraser is correct, it would mean that merely permitting someone to do something was outside the scope of the legislation. That cannot be right. It is much more natural to view *James v Eastleigh BC*[42] as the granting of a permission through the issue of a ticket to use the swimming pool rather than, say, ensuring that the water was warm and germ-free. *Amin* itself is almost a case concerning the denial of a ticket or an equivalent facility. Furthermore, the need to restrict the meaning of the section to activities similar to those which might be provided by non-public bodies is never explained. It cannot be the case that whether any activities of the prison department are covered depends on whether private prisons were in existence at the time of the alleged breach.

Gardner, J, 'Section 20 of the Race Relations Act 1976: "facilities" and "services"' (1987) 50 MLR 345, pp 347, 351:

[T]here is no necessary relationship between a person's primary function under statute and his subjection or non-subjection to s 20. Nor is there any necessary relationship between public conceptions of his role and his subjection or non-subjection to s 20. A government officer may conceive of himself as primarily an agent of control. The general public (even those who are successful in extracting some favourable decision from him) may also view him as an agent of control. Nevertheless, he may provide 'facilities' to the public for the purpose of s 20 if, for example, he accepts applications for some advantage or concession; he also provides 'services' by advertising the facility, advising on it, and accepting applications ...

[E]ven if it were plausible to claim that the 1975 Act and the 1976 Act only bind the Crown in respect of actions which are 'similar' to those of private persons, we need to provide a criterion of similarity. In some respects the process of considering an application for leave to settle is very similar to process of considering whether to grant a gratuitous licence to another to reside on one's land. In other respects the process of considering whether to grant leave does seem peculiar to governments. Unless the criterion of similarity is spelled out, we cannot tell whether Lord Fraser is right to treat the grant of a clearance voucher as being a purely governmental power. It is really only peculiarly governmental in the obvious sense in which all statutory powers of the Crown are peculiarly governmental.

42 [1990] AC 751; see further, Chapter 7, p 182.

The theme persisted in *Farah v Commissioner of Police for the Metropolis*,[43] where a Somali refugee and her 10-year-old cousin were set upon by white teenagers with a dog. She called the police, who arrested *her* for affray and causing suffering to the dog. The police offered no evidence and she was acquitted. She sued the police, *inter alia*, under the RRA 1976 and the Court of Appeal found her claim fell within s 20, but only because the police duties of giving assistance and protection were capable of being carried out by a private security company.

A reversal of *Amin* was urged by the Commission for Racial Equality (CRE): 'It is very particularly in areas such as the exercise of police powers, immigration controls, the treatment of prisoners and the licensing and enforcement functions of local authorities that discrimination can cause the greatest damage to race relations.'[44] The catalyst for change was the Stephen Lawrence Inquiry, which recommended that the police become fully subject to the RRA 1976.[45] The change that followed opened the scope of the Act to all public authorities. The Race Relations (Amendment) Act 2000 introduced ss 19B to 19F into the Act. Section 19B provides simply that: 'It is unlawful for a public authority in carrying out any functions of the authority to do any act which constitutes discrimination.' This covers the police,[46] among others. Moreover, 'public authorities' includes private companies carrying out public functions, such as running prisons.[47] In line with this theme, public authorities have no liability under the section if 'the nature of the act is private'.[48]

Despite all this, *Amin* remains good law for the Sex Discrimination Act, although new arguments are now available under the Human Rights Act 1998.[49]

3   HOUSING AND OTHER PREMISES

Race Relations Act 1976

21 Discrimination in disposal or management of premises

(1)   It is unlawful for a person, in relation to premises in Great Britain of which he has power to dispose, to discriminate against another:

    (a) in the terms on which he offers him those premises; or

    (b) by refusing his application for those premises; or

    (c) in his treatment of him in relation to any list of persons in need of premises of that description.

---

43   [1997] 1 All ER 289, CA.

44   *Reform of the Race Relations Act 1996: Proposals from the Commission for Racial Equality*, 1998, London: CRE, p 12.

45   See Chapter 1, pp 11–16, 23–24 and especially 31–33.

46   Decisions not to prosecute are exempted by s 19F. Further, in practice, liability may be difficult to prove because investigations that may lead to a decision to prosecute are specifically exempted (contrary to the Macpherson recommendation) from the Freedom of Information Act 2000 (s 30(1)).

47   Exempted public authorities include: either House of Parliament; the security and secret intelligence services; Government Communications Headquarters (s 19B(3)); and, for grounds of nationality, national or ethnic origins only, immigration and nationality officials (s 19D).

48   RRA 1976, s 19B(4).

49   See generally, Chapter 5, p 114.

(2)   It is unlawful for a person, in relation to premises managed by him, to discriminate against a person occupying the premises:

(a) in the way he affords him access to any benefits or facilities, or by refusing or deliberately omitting to afford him access to them; or

(b) by evicting him, or subjecting him to any other detriment.[50]

(3)   Subsection (1) does not apply to [discrimination on grounds other than those or race or ethnic or national origins by] a person who owns an estate or interest in the premises and wholly occupies them unless he uses the services of an estate agent for the purposes of the disposal of the premises, or publishes or causes to be published an advertisement in connection with the disposal.[51]

The potential defendants under these provisions are primarily owners and managers; the likely claimants, potential purchasers and potential tenants. Others involved in the transaction, such as estate agents and accommodation agencies, are covered by the section concerning the provision of facilities or services. Harassment on grounds of race or ethnic or national origins is outlawed by s 21(4). In any case, racial or sexual harassment should come within the meaning of 'discrimination' in s 21, although there are some problems associated with this approach.[52]

It had become unclear whether the planning functions of local and other authorities were within the scope of the legislation, because of the difficulties associated with identifying when a public authority was bound not to discriminate (discussed above). For this reason, the Housing and Planning Act 1986 added s 19A to the RRA 1976, so it is now unlawful for a planning authority to discriminate.

(1)   Exemptions – Sex, Colour and Nationality Only

There are two exemptions, which for many purposes were repealed in deference to the Race Directive.[53] Accordingly, what follows only applies under the SDA 1975, and the residual race cases[54] outside the scope of the Directive, for instance, discrimination purely on the grounds of colour or nationality.

By s 21(3),[55] individual owner-occupiers are exempt when disposing (typically, selling or renting) of their premises, unless they either use the services of an estate agent or advertise in a discriminatory fashion. Accordingly, the exemption is a narrow one. One example might be word-of-mouth letting. It seems to follow that if such an owner harassed a potential purchaser, on grounds of sex or nationality or colour, there would be no liability under this section, but if the harassment was by an estate agent the situation would be different.

Section 22 of the RRA 1976 and s 32 of the SDA 1975 provide an exception from this provision[56] for small dwellings. If the owner or a close relative lives in the

---

50   SDA 1975, s 30, is substantially identical.

51   Words in brackets inserted by the Race Relations Act 1976 (Amendment) Regulations 2003, SI 2003/1626, reg 23. In force since 19 July 2003.

52   See generally, Chapter 9, especially pp 219–24.

53   Council Directive 2000/43/EC, implemented by the Race Relations Act (Amendment) Regulations 2003, SI 2003/1626, in force 19 July 2003.

54   See further, Chapter 6, especially pp 137–38.

55   RRA 1976, s 21(3); SDA 1975, s 30(3). For a discussion on whether racist covenants are unlawful, see Cretney, S (1968) 118 NLJ 1094; Garner, JF (1972) 35 MLR 478; Brooke-Taylor, JDA (1978) 42 Conv(ns) 24.

56   And RRA 1976, s 20 and SDA 1975, s 29 ('Goods, facilities and services').

premises, and shares a significant part of the premises with others, discrimination is permitted as long as no more than six people occupy the property in addition to the landlord's household. Thus, a landlord or landlady who rents accommodation to students may not discriminate if the students are in exclusive accommodation, but may do so, on grounds either of sex, or nationality or colour, if the accommodation is shared. For example, a resident landlord may conclude that male students are rowdier than female students, which is the kind of stereotyping which is normally unlawful.

4   OTHER PROVISIONS

There are a number of other provisions where special or differential treatment is permitted under one or both pieces of legislation. Only the first two examples are covered by both the SDA 1975 and the RRA 1976.

(1)   Sex and Race

(a)   Charities

Section 34 of the RRA 1976 legitimises discriminatory provisions in charitable instruments unless the ground of the discrimination is colour, in which case the restriction is disregarded, thereby bringing a wider class of beneficiary within the scope of the instrument. The effect is to exclude charities defined by race, but to permit those defined by nationality or religion. However, s 34(3A)[57] removes this exemption for charities to discriminate in employment. Section 43 of the SDA 1975 provides a similar exception for charitable instruments which only benefit members of one sex.[58] If the purpose of the charity is itself to provide employment or, more likely, education – such as to the sons of Swansea solicitors – discrimination is permissible, but ss 78 and 79 provide a way of altering educational charities which discriminate on the basis of sex. Such charities may not, of course, discriminate as regards their own employees.

(b)   Sports

Section 44 of the SDA 1975 (set out at 1(3)(c) above in the context of education) legitimises most unequal or discriminatory treatment in the context of the playing of sports and games, though not of course in relation to employment as teachers, coaches, physiotherapists, etc, unless the particular circumstances are covered by one of the genuine occupational qualifications.[59] Section 39 of the RRA 1976 legitimises discrimination on the basis of nationality, place of birth or length of residence for the purpose of selecting sporting teams, and for the purpose of eligibility to compete in a

---

57   In force since 19 July 2003.

58   Inserted by SI 2003/1626, reg 33. See *Hugh-Jones v St John's College Cambridge* [1979] ICR 848, EAT.

59   It was held in *British Judo Association v Petty* [1981] ICR 660; [1981] IRLR 484, EAT, that preventing a female judo referee from refereeing bouts between men was unlawful. Section 13 of the SDA 1975, which covers discrimination by qualifying bodies, applied; s 44 did not; that section only covers participants. It was irrelevant that such referees are not paid.

sporting competition. It is therefore permissible to pick only Welshmen or women to play rugby for Wales, and permissible to restrict eligibility to compete in the Welsh Junior Gymnastics Championships to those resident in Wales. In *The Football Association v Bennett*,[60] it was held to be lawful to refuse to register an 11-year-old girl as a soccer player. It was irrelevant that she might have been under no disadvantage as compared with her opponents; the question was whether, taken as a whole, the average woman would be at a disadvantage. In *French v Crosby*,[61] the court rejected an argument that women would be at a disadvantage in playing snooker against men. While this case concerned casual snooker in a pub, in which context it is far more difficult to satisfy the defence than in a competitive context, it is far from clear what is the legal basis for continuing to differentiate between men and women in sports such as snooker, table tennis, bowls and darts. The defence is on its face permissive, that is, there is no *obligation* to segregate men and women for the purposes of sport, though if there were no such segregation it might be possible for a woman to argue that she had been treated less favourably than a man by being forced to compete against men.

A more liberal approach to discrimination in women's sports is reflected in *Couch v British Boxing Board of Control*.[62] It was held to be unlawful to refuse a licence to a female boxer to fight other women. It was held that there was no medical basis for regarding women's boxing as more dangerous to the participants than male boxing, especially as one of the purported reasons for denying a licence was that, during menstruation, women would be too unstable to be permitted to box. The real reason was probably that a dead or seriously injured woman boxer might lead to unstoppable demands for the total outlawing of boxing.

(2)   Race Only

(a)   Education and training

The next exception applies to discriminatory education and training and only appears in the RRA 1976; it is closely linked with what positive action is permissible as discriminatory training.[63] Section 35 provides a defence: 'for any act done in affording persons of a particular racial group access to facilities or services to meet the special needs of persons of that group in regard to their education, training or welfare ...' This legitimises, for example, literacy campaigns targeted at immigrant groups, or assisting minority ethnic groups with housing or employment problems, assuming that the particular needs of the group targeted were sufficiently 'special'. Section 36 legitimised the provision of education or training to people not ordinarily resident in Great Britain and who do not intend to remain afterwards; language schools are the obvious example. However, this exemption no longer applies to discrimination on grounds of race or ethnic or national origins.[64]

---

60   (1978) unreported, CA.
61   (1982) unreported, county court.
62   (1998) *The Guardian*, 31 March.
63   RRA 1976, ss 37, 38. Discriminatory training is also permissible under the other legislation. See below, Chapter 18, pp 574–78.
64   Race Relations Act 1976 (Amendment) Regulations 2003, SI 2003/1626, reg 34.

(3)   Sex Only

There are five exceptions peculiar to the SDA 1975.

(a)   *The actuarial exception*

Sex Discrimination Act 1975

45.   Nothing ... shall render unlawful the treatment of a person in relation to an
annuity, life insurance policy, accident insurance policy, or similar matter
involving the assessment of risk, where the treatment:
   (a) was effected by reference to actuarial or other data from a source on which it
        was reasonable to rely; and
   (b) was reasonable having regard to the data and any other relevant factors.

This provision is unaffected by developments at the European level concerning
pensions, which are primarily dependent on the interpretation of 'pay' in Art 119 of
the Treaty of Rome.[65] In any event, the European Court has approved the use of
actuarial tables in some forms of pension arrangements.[66] In *Pinder v Friends Provident
Life Office*,[67] it was held to be reasonable for the defendants to charge a female self-
employed dentist 50% more than men for permanent health insurance. As the
available statistics for private insurance lacked detail, considerable reliance was
placed on National Insurance statistics, even though they had been prepared for a
different purpose. Furthermore, the county court held that the 50% loading was
reasonable, even though by its own admission it was on the high side. They
considered the amount of the weighting to be in the end a matter of commercial
judgment. There is no rigorous examination of the policy, great deference to the
company being manifested. The lack of subsequent litigation on this issue is perhaps
surprising and there is a strong case for the repeal of this provision.

(b)   *Political parties*

Section 33 of the SDA 1975 permits political parties to make 'special provision for one
sex only in [their] constitution, organisation or administration'. Thus, political parties
may have special women's groups and may reserve places for women on, for
example, the national executive of the party. Without this provision, many of the
activities of political parties would come within the definition of 'facilities and
services' in s 29.[68] Recently, s 42A, inserted into the SDA 1975,[69] has extended the
exception to the selection of candidates for election. It appears to follow that black
groups within a political party will normally be unlawful unless they can be regarded
as meeting the special needs of that racial group under s 35 of the RRA 1976.

---

65   See Chapter 15, pp 442–47.
66   See Chapter 15, pp 457–60.
67   (1985) *The Times*, 16 December, county court.
68   See, eg, *Triesman v Ali*, [2002] ICR 1026; [2002] IRLR 489, CA, discussed briefly above, p 353.
69   Inserted by the Sex Discrimination (Election Candidates) Act 2002, s 1. See further, Chapter
     12, pp 352–53.

(c)   Voluntary bodies

There are three exceptions from the section concerning the provision of goods, facilities and services which closely mirror the defence of genuine occupational qualification for employment. Under s 34 of the SDA 1975, voluntary bodies may restrict their membership to persons of one sex only, and may likewise restrict the benefits or facilities which they provide. This provision is needed because many such bodies may cast their net sufficiently wide that their benefits are conferred upon a section of the public. For example, a centre for victims of female domestic violence is permitted to restrict employment to women under s 7(2)(e) of the SDA 1975 and may, under this provision, restrict its benefits to women.

(d)   Special facilities or services

This exception, which is closely linked with the previous one, enables the provision of single-sex facilities for 'persons requiring special care, supervision or attention' where the facilities are provided for members of one sex for religious reasons, and where segregation is needed for reasons of privacy.[70]

(e)   Communal accommodation

Section 46 of the SDA 1975 permits, for reasons or privacy or decency, discrimination in relation to the provision of communal accommodation. However, the providers of such accommodation must ensure that 'the accommodation is managed in a way which, given the exigencies of the situation, comes as near as may be to fair and equitable treatment of men and women'.

5   ADVERTISEMENTS

Race Relations Act 1976

29 Discriminatory advertisements

(1)   It is unlawful to publish or to cause to be published an advertisement which indicates, or might reasonably be understood as indicating, an intention by a person to do an act of discrimination, whether the doing of that act by him would be lawful or, by virtue of Part II or III, unlawful.

(2)   Subsection (1) does not apply to an advertisement—

(a) if the intended act would be lawful by virtue of any of sections 5,[71] 6,[72] 7(3) and (4),[73] 10(3),[74] 26,[75] 34(2)(b),[76] 35 to 39[77] and 41;[78] or

---

70 SDA 1975, s 35.
71 GOQs in employment.
72 Employment outside GB.
73 GOQs and employment outside GB, re contract workers.
74 GOQs for partnerships.
75 Exempt associations.
76 Charities.
77 Special cases re training, education, welfare and sport.
78 Acts done under statutory authority.

(b) if the advertisement relates to the services of an employment agency (within the meaning of section 14(1)) and the intended act only concerns employment which the employer could by virtue of section 5, 6 or 7(3) or (4) lawfully refuse to offer to persons against whom the advertisement indicates an intention to discriminate.

(3)   Subsection (1) does not apply to an advertisement which indicates that persons of any class defined otherwise than by reference to colour, race or ethnic or national origins are required for employment outside Great Britain.

(4)   The publisher of an advertisement made unlawful by subsection (1) shall not be subject to any liability under that subsection in respect of the publication of the advertisement if he proves—

(a) that the advertisement was published in reliance on a statement made to him by the person who caused it to be published to the effect that, by reason of the operation of subsection (2) or (3), the publication would not be lawful; and

(b) that it was reasonable for him to rely on the statement.

(5)   A person who knowingly or recklessly makes a statement such as is mentioned in subsection (4)(a) which in a material respect is false or misleading commits an offence, and shall be liable on summary conviction to a fine not exceeding [level 5 on the standard scale].

Sex Discrimination Act 1975

38 Discriminatory advertisements

(1)   It is unlawful to publish or cause to be published an advertisement which indicates, or might reasonably be understood as indicating, an intention by a person to do any act which is or might be unlawful by virtue of Part II or III.

(2)   Subsection (1) does not apply to an advertisement if the intended act would not in fact be unlawful.

(3)   For the purposes of subsection (1), use of a job description with a sexual connotation (such as 'waiter', 'salesgirl', 'postman' or 'stewardess') shall be taken to indicate an intention to discriminate, unless the advertisement contains an indication to the contrary.[79]

There are no parallel provisions for religion or belief, or sexual orientation. The main difference here, between the SDA 1975 and RRA 1976, is that the RRA 1976 covers (subject to a number of exceptions) advertisements 'which might be reasonably understood' to convey an intention to discriminate in way that is *lawful*. An example would be letting accommodation with a nationality requirement, under the small premises exception. In the White Paper, the Government said: 'the public display of racial prejudices and preferences is inherently offensive and likely to encourage the spread of discriminatory attitudes and prejudices.'[80]

Section 82 of the SDA 1975 and s 78 of the RRA 1976 offer a common definition of an advertisement:

'Advertisement' includes every form of advertisement or notice, whether to the public or not, and whether in a newspaper or other publication, by television or radio, by display of notices, signs, labels, showcards or goods, by distribution of samples, circulars, catalogues, price lists or other material, by exhibition of pictures, models or

---

79 Sub-sections (4) and (5) are substantially the same as RRA 1976, s 29.
80 *Racial Discrimination*, Cmnd 6234, p 19.

films, or in any other way, and references to the publishing of advertisements shall be construed accordingly;

This covers a notice in a house window 'For sale to English family'[81] and a notice at a public house 'No travellers'.[82] Only the CRE or the EOC can bring an action for a discriminatory advertisement.[83]

81   *Race Relations Board v Relf*, county court, RRB Report 1975, p 56.
82   *CRE v Dutton* [1989] QB 783; [1989] 1 All ER 306; [1989] IRLR 8, CA. See Chapter 6, p 146.
83   *Cardiff Women's Aid v Hartup* [1994] IRLR 390, EAT. See also Chapter 12, pp 320–21.

CHAPTER 14

THE LAW OF EQUAL PAY

1   INTRODUCTION

The Equal Pay Act (EqPA) 1970 enables a woman to claim equality with a man where she is engaged on 'like work',[1] work 'rated as equivalent' under a job evaluation scheme[2] and, since 1983, where her work is of equal value with that of her male comparator.[3] The employer has a defence where the difference in pay is 'genuinely due to a material factor which is not the difference of sex'.[4] The Act applies to employees, the self-employed[5] and the Crown service.[6] In addition, both the Equal Opportunities Commission (EOC) and the European Commission have issued Codes of Practice on equal pay.[7]

Article 141 (formerly Art 119) of the Treaty of Rome guarantees the application of 'the principle of equal pay for male and female workers for equal work or work of equal value'. This is directly effective.[8] In other words, public and private employers are bound. Both schemes apply to both men and women. Of course, it is possible to mount a claim based on Art 141 even if the claim falls outside the provisions of the EqPA 1970.

2   RELATIONSHIP WITH THE SEX DISCRIMINATION ACT[9]

Despite the fact that the two pieces of legislation took effect on the same date in 1975, the relationship between them is unnecessarily complex and confusing.[10] While it is clear that as far as possible they are complementary and should be construed as one Code, courts have not always found this to be practicable or appropriate. Especially

---

1   EqPA 1970, s 1(2)(a), (4).
2   EqPA 1970, s 1(2)(b), (5).
3   EqPA 1970, s 1(2)(c).
4   EqPA 1970, s 1(3)(a).
5   EqPA 1970, s 1(6)(a): '"employed" means employed under a contract of service or of apprenticeship or a contract personally to execute any work or labour.'
6   EqPA 1970, s 1(8).
7   Respectively, *Equal Opportunities Commission Code of Practice on Equal Pay*, 1997, Manchester: EOC, in force since 26 March 1997; see (1996) 70 EOR 36 (at the time of writing a revised Code was – see www.eoc.org.uk); *A Code of Practice on the Implementation of Equal Pay for Work of Equal Value for Women and Men*, Commission of the European Communities COM(96) 336 final; see (1996) 70 EOR 43.
8   *Defrenne v SABENA* Case 43/75 [1976] ECR 455; [1976] 2 CMLR 98; [1976] ICR 547; *Jenkins v Kingsgate (Clothing Productions) Ltd* Case 96/80 [1981] ECR 911; [1981] ICR 592; [1981] 1 WLR 972; [1981] IRLR 228. See generally, Chapter 5, p 109.
9   Claims of victimisation under both statutes are dealt with by the SDA 1975, s 4. See Chapter 11.
10 See arguments for a single Equality Act, Chapter 5, p 130 *et al.*

where the application of the principles of indirect discrimination are concerned, the approach under one Act will not always mirror that under the other.[11]

The Equal Pay Act is something of a misnomer. The Act governs 'terms (whether concerned with pay or not) of a contract under which a woman is employed ...'.[12] It follows that a claim may be brought in respect of inequality in any matter which is regulated by the contract of employment, such as hours, holidays, fringe benefits, etc. The Sex Discrimination Act (SDA) 1975 deals with matters not regulated by the contract, such as job offers (including promotions), dismissals, etc. It is therefore important for claimants to know whether or not a particular issue is part of the contract; it is especially important to bear in mind that contracts do not necessarily have to be in writing and that terms of contracts may be derived from external sources, such as a collective agreement between employer and trade union.

If something is done under the contract of employment, whether the payment of money or the provision of other benefits, the first question is whether the EqPA 1970 applies.[13] If, for some reason, that Act does not apply, a claim may still be brought under the SDA 1975 *except* where the benefit consists of the payment of money.[14] An offer of a contractual term is governed by the SDA 1975, but the EqPA 1970 will apply when that offer is accepted and becomes part of the contract.[15] Thus, an allegation of discrimination in relation to fringe benefits must first consider whether the case falls within the area of comparison mandated by the EqPA 1970; only if does not do so is a claim under SDA 1975 permissible.

The determination of the issue under which Act a claim may be brought can be crucial. Under the SDA 1975, a claim may allege discrimination as regards how a man was or *'would have been'* treated. Under the EqPA 1970, a claim may only proceed if there is an *actual* male comparator; the courts have rejected claims to permit comparison with the so called 'hypothetical man'.[16] In fact, the complexity of the interrelationship between the two statutes has not led to the litigation which might have been expected, but nevertheless the need for consolidation is impossible to oppose; the current distinction on serves no practical purpose and is simply the result of the fact that the two pieces of legislation were passed separately, and that their origins and philosophy are significantly different from each other.[17]

---

11   Thus, in *Bhudi v IMI Refiners Ltd* [1994] ICR 307; [1994] IRLR 204, EAT, it was held that the claimant, in an indirect discrimination claim (based on selection for redundancy) under the SDA 1975, had to establish that a requirement or condition (now provision, criterion or practice; see Chapter 10, p 243 *et al*) was applied, thus adopting a different approach from that adopted in the equal pay context by the European Court in *Enderby v Frenchay AHA and Secretary of State for Health* Case C-127/92 [1993] ECR I-5535; [1994] ICR 112; [1994] 1 All ER 495; [1993] IRLR 591. Similarly, the approach to the defence of genuine material factor taken by the House of Lords in *Ratcliffe v North Yorkshire DC* [1995] ICR 837; [1995] 3 All ER 597; [1995] IRLR 439 differs markedly from the approach to justification in cases of indirect discrimination.

12   EqPA 1970, s 1(2).

13   SDA 1975, ss 6(2)(a), 8(5).

14   SDA 1975, ss 6(2), 6(5).

15   SDA 1975, s 8(3).

16   See below, p 386.

17   See generally above, Chapter 2, p 35.

3   THE MEANING OF PAY

The coverage of the legislation has been transformed by European law. Article 141 provides:

> For the purposes of this article, 'pay' means the ordinary or minimum wage or salary and or any other consideration whether in cash or in kind which the worker receives, directly or indirectly, in respect of his employment from his employer. Equal pay without discrimination based on sex means:
>
> (a)   that pay for the same work[18] at piece rates shall be calculated on the same unit of measurement;
>
> (b)   that pay for the same work at time rates shall be the same for the same job.

Clearly, all fringe benefits are covered, such as mortgage interest allowance,[19] voluntary Christmas bonus,[20] and removal expenses.[21] But the effect of jurisprudence from the European Court has been to give the concept a far wider meaning. *Garland v British Rail Engineering*[22] extended the law in two ways. First, it applied the concept of pay to travel concessions granted after retirement to the dependants of male employees but not to the dependants of female employees. That the benefits were not received by the employee personally did not prevent them from being pay. Secondly, the benefits were granted by the employer as a concession rather than pursuant to a contractual obligation. Under English law that means that any claim would fall within the SDA 1975 rather than the EqPA 1970, but the European Court held that their non-contractual nature did not prevent them being 'pay' within Art 141.

Payments made to third parties are an essential component of pension benefits, so *Garland* was a key step in the reasoning which eventually held that pensions were within the scope of Art 141. *Bilka-Kaufhaus v Weber von Hartz*[23] had decided that indirectly discriminatory rules governing membership of pension schemes were contrary to Art 141, and this implied that the payment of benefits under such schemes amounted to deferred pay, an approach subsequently confirmed in *Barber v Guardian Royal Exchange*.[24]

There are many other components of a wage packet which clearly fall within the concept of pay. These include overtime,[25] performance-related pay, piece rates,[26] sick

---

18 It was held in *Royal Copenhagen* Case C-400/93 [1995] IRLR 648, p 657, that this provision applies to piece work in the context of an equal value claim (see below, p 385), even though there the work is not the same. In such circumstances, the system 'must be objectively capable of ensuring that the total individual pay for workers in the two groups is the same'.

19 *Sun Alliance and London Insurance Ltd v Dudman* [1978] ICR 551; [1978] IRLR 169, EAT.

20 *Lewen v Denda* [2000] IRLR 67, ECJ.

21 *Durrant v North Yorkshire HA* [1979] IRLR 401, EAT.

22 Case C-12/81 [1983] 2 AC 751; [1982] ECR 359; [1982] 2 All ER 402; [1982] IRLR 111.

23 Case C-170/84 [1986] ECR 1607; [1986] 2 CMLR 701; [1987] ICR 110; [1986] IRLR 317.

24 Case C-262/88 [1990] ECR I-1889; [1991] 1 QB 344; [1990] ICR 616; [1990] IRLR 240. In logic, the detailed rules on the application of Art 141 to pensions should be explored here, for they are significantly dependent on working out what is entailed in treating pensions as deferred pay. However, pension issues are complex and raise peculiar problems; for practical purposes it makes sense to consider them in the separate, following chapter.

25 But employers may set an hours threshold (eg, 38 hours per week), common to full- and part-time workers, above which overtime may be paid: *Stadt Lengerich v Helmig* Case C-399/92 [1994] ECR I-5725; [1996] ICR 35; [1995] IRLR 216, ECJ.

26 See *Handels- og Kontorfunktionaerernes Forbund i Danmark v Dansk Arbejdsgiverforening* Case 109/88 [1989] ECR 3199; [1991] 1 CMLR 8; [1989] IRLR 532, ECJ; *Royal Copenhagen* Case C-400/93 [1995] IRLR 648, ECJ.

pay[27] and maternity pay.[28] Similarly, payment for time off to attend training courses falls within the ambit of Art 141, as established in *Botel* and applied by the EAT in *Davies*.

Arbeiterwohlfahrt der Stadt Berlin Ev v Botel **Case C-360/90 [1992] IRLR 423**[29]

German law provided that workers attending training courses (necessary in this case to work on staff councils) should be released without loss of pay. Ms Botel worked 29.5 hours per week, but her attendance at a training course exceeded that time. She received no pay for time in excess of 29.5 hours spent on the course. However, full-time workers were compensated up to 50.3 hours per week. The European Court of Justice (ECJ) held that this compensation constituted 'pay' for Art 119 (now Art 141).

Judgment:

12   As the Court has consistently held (see the judgment in Case 171/88 *Rinner-Kuehn v FWW Spezial-Gebaeudereinigung* [1989] ECR 2743 and in Case C-262/88 *Barber v Guardian Royal Exchange Assurance Group* [1990] ECR I-1889), the concept of pay, within the meaning of the second paragraph of Article 119, comprises any consideration, whether in cash or in kind, whether immediate or future, provided that the worker receives it, albeit indirectly, in respect of his employment from his employer, and irrespective of whether the worker receives it under a contract of employment, by virtue of legislative provisions or on a voluntary basis. ...

14   Although [this] compensation ... does not derive as such from the contract of employment, it is nevertheless paid by the employer by virtue of legislative provisions and under a contract of employment. Staff council members are necessarily employees of the undertaking and are entrusted with the task of safeguarding staff interests, thus promoting harmonious working relationships within the undertaking, which is in its interests.

15   The compensation paid under legislation ... is also intended to ensure that staff council members receive income even where during periods of training they are not performing any work as stipulated in their contracts of employment.

Botel was distinguished in *Manor Bakeries v Nazir*,[30] where the Employment Appeal Tribunal (EAT) held that a female part-time worker was not doing 'work' within Art 119 (now Art 141), by attending her trade union's annual conference. However, the EAT in *Davies* said that *Nazir* was erroneously decided and should be followed.

---

27   In *Rinner-Kuhn v FWW Spezial-Gebäudereinigung* Case C-171/88 [1989] ECR 2743; [1989] IRLR 493, the fact that the German *statute* provided that sick pay from the employer need not be paid to those working less than 10 hours a week did not prevent the payment in question from constituting pay.

28   The problem is with whom should a comparison be made in order to show that its amount is discriminatory – a man still at work, or a man off work for another reason? In *Gillespie v Northern Health and Social Services Board* Case C-342/93 [1996] ICR 498; [1996] IRLR 214 (see above, p 210), it was held not discriminatory to cease paying a woman her normal salary while on maternity leave.

29   The facts were very similar in *Kuratorium für Dialyse und Nierentransplantation Ev v Lewark* Case C-457/93 [1996] IRLR 637. Here, the complainant worked four days a week; the training course in question, for which the employers refused to pay, was on the fifth day. It was held that the national court might be able to conclude that the rule was justified; the court would have to balance the social policy objective of ensuring the independence of such representatives against the fact that the rule might make it more difficult to ensure adequate representation of part-time employees. See above, p 294.

30   [1996] IRLR 769, EAT.

Davies v Neath Port Talbot County Borough Council **[1999] IRLR 769, EAT**

Mrs Davies was employed part-time on a 22-hour week. As her union's (GMB) Health and Safety representative, she attended two five-day courses run by her union, which lasted 40 and 32.5 hours respectively. Her employer paid her compensation for only 22 hours. She brought a claim under Art 119 (now Art 141).

Morison J:

14.   In relation to the European judgment in *Botel*, the tribunal in *Nazir* found that the decision was dependent on its own facts, in particular the fact that staff committees are an important feature of German labour law and, therefore, the duties of a staff committee member promoted the employer's interests. Attendance at a trade union annual conference, on the other hand, could be distinguished from the duties of a German staff committee as it did not benefit the employer ...

20.   It is our view that the decision in *Nazir* should not be followed. It was an error of law to distinguish 'pay' and 'work' as they did and to distinguish *Botel*. 'Pay' within Article 119 is 'pay for work' within Article 119. *Botel* decided that training for staff council functions was 'work' for the employer, in the broad sense that staff committees safeguard staff interests and promote harmonious working relationships in the interests of the business. Whilst trade union work is not strictly comparable to German staff committees and there are important differences between them, they are analogous, and we do not consider that any of the differences would be so significant so as to bring the GMB training course outside the scope of *Botel*. Attending a training course organised by a recognised trade union is still related to the employment relationship and is safeguarding staff interests, which is ultimately beneficial to the employer. Health and safety representatives require training for the better performance of their duties. Training may be made available either by the union or the employer. In each case the training of the representative facilitates the execution of the health and safety representatives' duties, which is of direct benefit to the employer and fellow-employees. Such a representative must be an employee and their functions and training stem wholly from their employment relationship. Attendance at the training courses is work within the meaning of Article 119 because it was by reason of the existence of an employment relationship. The tribunal therefore failed properly to apply the principles expounded in *Botel* and followed in *Lewark*[31] that part-time female workers should be paid on the same basis as their full-time counterparts when attending training courses away from work. Any other approach would be in contradiction to the expressed purpose of Article 119.

Where the EAT went wrong in *Nazir* was in applying the literal words of Art 119 (now Art 141) without consideration of how they have been interpreted in other contexts. That definition extends to payment received from an employer, directly or indirectly, in respect of employment. It is difficult to see how payment from an employer to reimburse an employee for what has not been earned because the person concerned is not at work falls outside this definition of pay. As Morison J said, any money paid because of the attendance at the conference was paid because of the existence of the employment relationship. The fact that there is no direct benefit to the employer from making the payment is irrelevant: that is true of many fringe benefits, such as sick pay

---

31   See above, fn 29.

and holiday pay, where the employee receives 'pay' even though not actually 'at work'. Finally, the question at this stage is simply whether the payment is 'pay'; as in *Lewark*, the employer still has the opportunity to justify the disparity.

Redundancy pay is within Art 141, as held by the European Court in *Barber*[32] and the House of Lords in *R v Secretary of State for Employment ex p Equal Opportunities Commission*.[33] This is clearly correct; even though the criteria are laid down by statute, the amount of the payment depends both on pay level and length of service. It is thus clearly referable to the employment in much the same way as pension provision. The same approach has been taken with unfair dismissal compensation.

R v Secretary of State for Employment ex p Seymour-Smith [1999] IRLR 253, ECJ[34]

Judgment:

24   The Court has also held that the fact that certain benefits are paid after the termination of the employment relationship does not prevent them from being in the nature of pay, within the meaning of Article 119 of the Treaty [*Barber*,[35] ... paragraph 12].

25   As regards, in particular, the compensation granted by an employer to an employee on termination of his employment, the Court has already stated that such compensation is a form of deferred pay to which the worker is entitled by reason of his employment but which is paid to him on termination of the employment relationship with a view to enabling him to adjust to the new circumstances arising from such termination [see *Barber*, cited above, paragraph 13, and Case C-33/89 *Kowalska* [1990] ECR I-2591, paragraph 10].[36]

26   In this case, the compensation awarded to an employee for unfair dismissal, which comprises a basic award and a compensatory award, is designed in particular to give the employee what he would have earned if the employer had not unlawfully terminated the employment relationship.

27   The basic award refers directly to the remuneration which the employee would have received had he not been dismissed. The compensatory award covers the loss sustained by him as a result of the dismissal, including any expenses reasonably incurred by him in consequence thereof and, subject to certain conditions, the loss of any benefit which he might reasonably be expected to have gained but for the dismissal.

28   It follows that compensation for unfair dismissal is paid to the employee by reason of his employment, which would have continued but for the unfair dismissal. That compensation therefore falls within the definition of pay for the purposes of Article 119 of the Treaty.

29   The fact that the compensation at issue in the main proceedings is a judicial award made on the basis of the applicable legislation cannot, of itself, invalidate that conclusion. As the Court has already stated in this connection, it is irrelevant that the right to compensation, rather than deriving from the contract of employment is, for instance, a statutory right [see, to that effect, *Barber*, cited above, paragraph 16].

---

32 Case C-262/88 [1990] ECR I-1889; [1991] 1 QB 344; [1990] ICR 616; [1990] IRLR 240.
33 [1995] 1 AC 1; [1994] ICR 317; [1994] 1 All ER 910; [1994] IRLR 176.
34 See also [1999] All ER (EC) 97; [1999] 3 WLR 460; [1999] ICR 447; [1999] 2 CMLR 273, ECJ. See further, Chapter 10, p 295.
35 *Barber v Guardian Royal Exchange* Case C-262/88 [1990] ECR I-1889; [1991] 1 QB 344; [1990] ICR 616; [1990] IRLR 240, ECJ, see further, below, Chapter 15, p 445.
36 See further, below, p 433 and in more detail, Chapter 10, p 287.

4   CHOOSING A COMPARATOR

(1)   Who Chooses the Comparator?

The claimant may choose with which employee she is claiming equality.[37] However, EAT authority that an employment tribunal may not substitute a more suitable or 'representative' comparator[38] had doubt put upon it by a *dictum* of Balcombe LJ in *British Coal Corp v Smith*.[39] He commented that it: 'is necessary that the selected male comparator should be representative of the class, or group, of male employees from whom he is selected ...'[40] He argued that this limitation is implicit in the somewhat more collective and less individualistic approach to issues of equal pay which has been taken by the European Court. This is especially the case where the claim is based on equal value, and true most of all where based on a difference in average pay between a group of men and a group of women. Here the selection of the appropriate group is crucial to the claim, and, according to the European Court in the *Royal Copenhagen*[41] case, must: 'encompass groups each comprising all the workers who, taking account of a set of factors such as the nature of the work, the training requirements and the working conditions, can be considered to be in a comparable situation. [Such] comparison ... must cover a relatively large number of workers in order to ensure that the differences found are not due to purely fortuitous or short term factors or to differences in the individual output of the workers concerned.'[42] Even if an English court does permit a totally untrammelled choice of an individual comparator, use of a 'rogue' comparator may be of no avail to a female applicant, as the employer will normally be able to rely on the genuine material factor defence under s 1(3) to explain the inequality of pay.

(2)   Need the Comparator be an Existing Worker?

In *Macarthys Ltd v Smith*,[43] the ECJ held that it was possible to use predecessor in the same job as a comparator. In *Diocese of Hallam Trustee v Connaughton*,[44] Miss Connaughton, an organist, was paid £11,138 per annum down to her leaving in September 1994; her male successor got £20,000 per annum from January 1995. The EAT held that whilst using a predecessor posed evidential problems, it did not preclude Miss Connaughton's claim; she was able to advance a case to the effect that the male successor's contract was so proximate to her own as to render him as effective a comparator as an 'actual' one. Although Holland J noted: 'Absent an actual

---

37   *Ainsworth v Glass Tubes and Components Ltd* [1977] ICR 347; [1977] IRLR 74. The EAT held that a tribunal could not use its own comparator instead of that chosen by the claimant.

38   *Thomas v National Coal Board* [1987] ICR 757; [1987] IRLR 451, EAT.

39   [1994] ICR 810; [1994] IRLR 342, CA. The case was subsequently reversed by the House of Lords [1996] ICR 515; [1996] 3 All ER 97; [1996] IRLR 404 (see below, p 389) where the *dictum* was cited but not commented upon.

40   *British Coal Corp v Smith* [1994] IRLR 342, p 358.

41   *Specialarbejderforbundet i Danmark v Dansk Industri (acting for Royal Copenhagen A/S)* Case C-400/93 [1995] IRLR 648, ECJ.

42   *Ibid*, p 658.

43   Case C-129/79 [1980] IRLR 210; [1980] ICR 672; [1980] ECR 1275, ECJ.

44   [1996] ICR 860; [1996] IRLR 505, EAT.

comparator, whether contemporaneous or immediately preceding, then inevitably proof of inequality of pay becomes more difficult, not in principle but in practice ...'[45]

(3)   Real or Hypothetical Comparator?

Although predecessors or successors may be used, the comparator must be a real person. This is a major limitation on the potential effectiveness of the Act. There is a close correlation between low pay and the proportion of female employees in a firm; in many of the lowest paying firms, the workforce is 100% female. In such firms, claims under the EqPA 1970 can effectively never be brought; therefore, the Act cannot be viewed as the spearhead of an attack against poverty and low pay generally. For this, minimum wage legislation is a far more direct and immediate weapon. In 1988, the Government calculated that the proposed minimum wage rate of £3.60 would benefit 1.4 million women and 1.3 million part-time workers.[46]

However, there are situations where such claims using a hypothetical comparator may succeed. Discrimination in salary setting may contravene the SDA 1975, where of course comparison with how a man *would have* been treated is permissible. This might occur not only when a woman is paid less than a hypothetical man would be paid, but possibly also where the pay differential is not commensurate with the differences in the value of the work done by the man and the woman. In the American case of *County of Washington v Gunther*,[47] it was held to be unlawful to pay men 95% of their evaluated worth under a job evaluation study whereas the women were only paid 70%. In British terms, there is no question that the women were treated less favourably on the ground of their gender.[48] Proving that a pay structure was tainted by direct discrimination is never likely to be straightforward. Proving that it was tainted by indirect discrimination brings into play all the various factors which lead to the relative underpayment of women, and is conceptually very close to the entitlement to be paid equally for work of equal value. Pannick considers the case for allowing a hypothetical comparator into equal pay claims generally.

Pannick, D, *Sex Discrimination*, 1985, Oxford: Clarendon, p 96:

Can a woman claim equal pay to that of a hypothetical male worker by showing that, if she were a man, she would be paid more by her employer? In *Macarthys*[49] the ECJ suggested that a comparison with 'a hypothetical male worker' could not be made as it would be 'indirect and disguised discrimination, the identification of which' would require 'comparative studies of entire branches of industry'. Therefore, the direct application of Article [141] is 'confined to parallels which may be drawn on the basis of concrete appraisals of the work actually performed by employees of different sex within the same establishment or service'. The ECJ here seems to have confused two different concepts. It is understandable that Article [141] should not entitle a woman to compare her pay with that of a man in a different industry. But the practical

---

45   *Ibid*, para 5.
46   Department of Trade and Industry Press Release, P/98/489, 18 June 1998, London: DTI. See further, Chapter 2, pp 40–41.
47   452 US 161 (1981).
48   Along similar lines, it has been argued that discrimination in collective bargaining and in resulting collective agreements is unlawful under the SDA 1975 irrespective of the position under the EqPA 1970. See Lester, A and Rose, D, 'Equal value claims and sex bias in collective bargaining' [1991] 20 ILJ 163.
49   Case C-129/79 [1980] IRLR 210; [1980] ICR 672; [1980] ECR 1275, ECJ.

difficulties there involved are not raised where the woman is able to prove that her employer would pay her more if she were male. The reference to the hypothetical male worker is merely one means of proving that she has been less favourably treated on the ground of her sex.

The notion of the hypothetical male comparison is central to the concept of discrimination in the Sex Discrimination Act 1975. Direct discrimination is there defined as treating the complainant, on the ground of her sex, less favourably than one treats, or would treat, a man. The absence of this express concept in the Equal Pay Act is one indication of its lack of sophistication. Since the 1970 and 1975 Acts form an interlocking code and since the mischief aimed at by the 1970 Act cannot be removed unless the statute prohibits an obvious form of sex discrimination, it may well be that the 1970 Act can be interpreted as covering this case.

(4)   Multiple Comparators

It is possible to claim equality with more than one comparator at the same time; in theory, losing a claim for equality with one comparator does not preclude a future claim utilising a different, more appropriate, comparator, but such a course is both practically and psychologically difficult. In *Hayward v Cammell Laird Shipbuilders Ltd (No 2)*,[50] the applicant claimed equality with a painter, a decorator and a thermal insulation engineer. This made practical and legal sense, as an applicant may have only a rough idea of what potential comparators earn, especially when fringe benefits are taken into account. It may be possible to use the discovery procedure to find out the details of the pay of comparators, but this can only be done after the commencement of a claim. In principle, even if a claim fails, there could be a further allegation involving the same comparator based on an argument that the nature of the work had changed since rejection of the first claim, but the tribunal will need to be convinced that there has been a significant change either in the work or in the pay and conditions of at least one of the two jobs being compared.[51] A successful claim in relation to one comparator may generate subsequent claims seeking to use the successful claimant as the new comparator. The fact that there is, in theory, nothing to stop a series of leap-frogging claims, and nothing to guarantee the representativeness of the comparator chosen, demonstrates the need for collective rather than individualistic solutions.

(5)   The Scope of the Comparison

Normally, a claimant chooses a work colleague as a comparator, but s 1(6) of the EqPA 1970 allows a claimant to choose a comparator who works for an 'associated employer'. However, according to *Defrenne v Sabena (No 2)*,[52] Art 141 goes further than that, allowing a comparator (a) whose terms originate from the same legislative provisions, or collective agreement, or (b) who is in the same 'service'.

---

50   [1988] AC 894; [1988] 2 All ER 257; [1988] IRLR 257, HL.
51   *McLoughlin v Gordons (Stockport) Ltd* [1978] IRLR 127, EAT.
52   Case C-43/75 [1976] ECR 455; [1976] 2 CMLR 98; [1976] ICR 547.

(a)   Section 1(6) of the EqPA 1970 – associated employer

Equal Pay Act 1970

Section 1

(6)   ... (c) two employers are to be treated as associated if one is a company of which
the other (directly or indirectly) has control or if both are companies of which a
third person (directly or indirectly) has control

[and men shall be treated as in the same employment with a woman if they are men
employed by her employer or any associated employer at the same establishment or
at establishments in Great Britain which include that one and at which common terms
and conditions of employment are observed either generally or for employees of the
relevant classes.][53]

There are a number of elements in this somewhat complex formula. There are two
limbs to the first part of the sub-section. Under the first limb, two employers are to be
treated as associated if one (employer) is a company of which the other (employer –
not necessarily a company) has control. The second limb applies where both
employers are companies under the control of a third person (not necessarily a
company).[54] Local authorities and public bodies, as statutory bodies corporate, are not
'companies' within this definition.[55]

A claimant can only use a comparator from a different establishment (of the same
or associated employer), if 'common terms of employment are observed between the
two establishments'.[56] In the next two cases, the House of Lords have avoided a strict
comparison of the terms.

Leverton v Clwyd CC [1989] IRLR 28; [1989] AC 706; [1989] 1 All ER 78, HL

A nursery nurse claimed that her work was of equal value to that of other staff
employed by the local authority, none of whom worked at the same place as her, but
whose pay was regulated by the same collective agreement.

The majority of the Court of Appeal held that the difference in working hours and
holidays was a radical difference in the 'core terms' of the respective contracts of
employment which prevented the comparison from satisfying the statutory test.

Lord Bridge of Harwich (pp 31–32):

It seems to me, first, that the language of the sub-section is clear and unambiguous. It
poses the question whether the terms and conditions of employment 'observed' at
two or more establishments ... are 'common', being terms and conditions of
employment observed 'either generally or for employees of the relevant classes'. The
concept of common terms and conditions of employment observed generally at
different establishments necessarily contemplates terms and conditions applicable to a
wide range of employees whose individual terms will vary greatly *inter se* ... Terms
and conditions of employment governed by the same collective agreement seem to

---

53   Words in square brackets inserted by the SDA 1975, s 8(6), Sched 1, Pt I.
54   See comments in *Hasley v Fair Employment Agency* [1989] IRLR 106, NICA.
55   *Gardner v London Borough of Merton* [1980] IRLR 472, CA; *Hasley v Fair Employment Agency*
     [1989] IRLR 106, NICA.
56   In *Lawson v Britfish Ltd* [1988] IRLR 53, EAT, it was held that there is no need to show
     employment under common terms and conditions if the comparator works at the same
     establishment as the applicant.

me to represent the paradigm, though not necessarily the only example, of the common terms and conditions of employment contemplated by the sub-section ...

The purpose [of the sub-section] is to enable a woman to eliminate discriminatory differences between the terms of her contract and those of any male fellow employee doing like work, work rated as equivalent or work of equal value ... With all respect to the majority view which prevailed below, it cannot in my opinion possibly have been the intention of Parliament to require a woman claiming equality with a man in another establishment to prove an undefined substratum of similarity between the particular terms of her contract and his as the basis of her entitlement to eliminate any discriminatory differences ...

The effect of this undoubtedly correct decision is that the tribunal must ask itself whether the applicant would have been under the same terms and conditions of employment had she been doing her job at the comparator's establishment. The question then arose how great a degree of similarity must there be between the terms and conditions observed at the establishments in question for them to be regarded as 'common'.

British Coal Corp v Smith [1996] 3 All ER 98, [1996] ICR 515; [1996] IRLR 404, HL

Canteen workers and cleaners claimed that they were employed on work of equal value with surface mineworkers and clerical workers. The claimants were employed at 47 different establishments, the comparators at 14. The industrial tribunal held that s 1(6) applied and the claim could proceed on the basis that, no matter at which establishment they worked, they were governed by national terms and conditions of employment. This was despite the fact that there were local variations resulting from differences in underground mineworkers' pay. The House of Lords upheld the industrial tribunal's decision.

Lord Slynn of Hadley (pp 105–09):

Your Lordships have been referred to a number of dictionary definitions of 'common' but I do not think that they help. The real question is what the legislation was seeking to achieve. Was it seeking to exclude a woman's claim unless, subject to *de minimis* exceptions, there was complete identity of terms and conditions for the comparator at his establishment and those which applied or would apply to a similar male worker at her establishment? Or was the legislation seeking to establish that the terms and conditions of the relevant class were sufficiently similar for a fair comparison to be made, subject always to the employers' right to establish a 'material difference' defence under s 1(3) of the 1970 Act?

If it was the former then the woman would fail at the first hurdle if there was any difference (other than a *de minimis* one) between the terms and conditions of the men at the various establishments since she could not then show that the men were in the same employment as she was. The issue as to whether the differences were material so as to justify different treatment would then never arise.

I do not consider that this can have been intended. The purpose of requiring common terms and conditions was to avoid it being said simply 'a gardener does work of equal value to mine and my comparator at another establishment is a gardener'. It was necessary for the applicant to go further and to show that gardeners at other establishments and at her establishment were or would be employed on broadly similar terms. It was necessary, but it was also sufficient.

Whether any differences between the woman and the man selected as the comparator were justified would depend on the next stage of the examination under s 1(3). I do not consider that the s 1(3) inquiry, where the onus is on the employer, was intended to be excluded unless the terms and conditions of the men at the relevant establishments were common in the sense of identical. This seems to me to be far too restrictive a test.

[In] *Leverton v Clwyd CC* ... the critical question was between whose terms and conditions should the comparison be made. In the present case the question is, having established the persons between whom the comparisons should be made, whether there was a sufficient identity between the respective terms and conditions for them to be 'common'. ...

If, as I consider, the terms and conditions do not have to be identical, but on a broad basis to be substantially comparable, then it seems to me that the industrial tribunal did not err in law in ... its finding that the applicants and their comparators were in the same employment.

The outcome is appropriate, adopting a far less technical approach than that taken by the Court of Appeal. Yet such comparisons are only likely to prove possible where the employer operates a centralised collective bargaining structure. Plant bargaining, fragmented bargaining, or no collective bargaining at all are all likely to prevent cross-establishment comparisons being permissible.

(b)   Article 141 – same service, or legislative or collective bargaining

As noted above, s 1(6) does not reflect fully Art 141, as interpreted in *Defrenne*. The most obvious difference is that there is no restriction that one of the associated employers must be a 'company'. Unlike s 1(6), Art 141 covers the situation where both the claimant's, and comparator's, employers are not companies. Among others, this allows many claims from the public sector, as *Morton* illustrates. The limit of Art 141 is that there must be a single source of the difference in pay, as shown in *Lawrence*.[57]

South Ayrshire Council v Morton [2002] IRLR 257; [2002] ICR 956, CS

In Scotland, the salary scales for primary school head teachers (75% women), is lower than it is for secondary school head teachers (75% men). Both salary scales were set by the Scottish Joint Negotiating Committee (SJNC), a quasi-autonomous body set up by the Education (Scotland) Act 1980 under the general control of the Secretary of State. There are 32 local authorities in Scotland and each is obliged to implement the salary scale, but each has autonomy, as an employer, on how to do this. Stella Morton, a primary school head teacher employed by South Ayrshire Council, brought an equal pay claim, using a male comparator, a secondary school head teacher, employed by Highland Council.

Gill LJC (pp 261–62):

The comparator has been put forward on the basis that the teacher in question is male and is being paid at a higher rate for work that is like work or work of equal value. We are not concerned with the question whether the comparator is a good one. That would have to be decided on the facts. We are asked simply to decide whether, as a matter of law, it is admissible at all. ...

---

57 *Lawrence* was relied on in the Opinion of Advocate-General Geelhoed in *Allonby v Accrington College*, C-256/1, 2 April 2003, where the claimant worked at the same establishment as her comparator, but was employed by a supply agency and so the pay difference could not be attributed to a single source.

The key text on Article 141 is the decision of the European Court in *Defrenne v Sabena (No 2)*[58] ... *Defrenne* was a case of direct discrimination. It bears to state general principles of interpretation of the article.

In our view, the essential parts of the decision, so far as it affects this case, are these:

18.   For the purposes of the implementation of these provisions a distinction must be drawn within the whole area of application of Article 119 between, first, direct and overt discrimination which may be identified solely with the aid of the criteria based on equal work and equal pay referred to by the article in question and, secondly, indirect and disguised discrimination which can only be identified by reference to more explicit implementing provisions of a Community or national character ...

21.   Among the forms of direct discrimination which may be identified solely by reference to the criteria laid down by Article 119 must be included in particular those which have their origin in legislative provisions or in collective labour agreements and which may be detected on the basis of a purely legal analysis of the situation.

22.   This applies even more in cases where men and women receive unequal pay for equal work carried out in the same establishment or service, whether public or private.

Paragraph 18 makes the important distinction between direct and indirect discrimination. It is agreed that the present case, like *Defrenne*, involves direct discrimination.[59] That therefore takes us to paragraphs 21 and 22, which in our view must be read together.

From these paragraphs we conclude that in determining whether men and women receive unequal pay for equal work, the scope of the enquiry is not always confined to the claimant's own workplace or to his own employer ...

In paragraph 21 of *Defrenne*, the Court of Justice says that there can be direct discrimination where the discrimination originates in legislation or in a collective labour agreement. In our view, paragraph 22 merely sets out a specific case falling within the generality of paragraph 21, namely where there is unequal pay for equal work carried out in the same establishment or service.

If that is correct, it follows that the requirements of paragraph 22 do not put a limitation on the right to found on a comparator such as we are considering. Instead, if the case falls within paragraph 21, such a comparator is at once admissible, whatever its evidential value may be found to be, and there is no need to apply the further test set out in paragraph 22 as to whether the work is carried out in the same establishment or service ...

The present case is a good example of what Article 141 envisages. The respondent contends that there is an objective and meaningful comparison to be made between her work and that of her comparator. ...[W]e consider that an SJNC settlement conducted under statutory authority and under overall governmental control constitutes a national collective agreement of the kind contemplated in *Defrenne* ... It is agreed that the SJNC settlements do not set different rates for men and women; but the complaint is that, so far as headteachers are concerned, that in practice is the

---

58   Case 43/75 [1976] ECR 455; [1976] 2 CMLR 98; [1976] ICR 547. For the facts, see above, p 109.

59   This surely, is incorrect, but it makes little difference to the issue, as, since *Defrenne*, the ECJ has held Art 119 to apply, with direct effect, to indirect discrimination (see, eg, *Jenkins v Kingsgate* Case 96/80 [1981] ECR 911; [1981] ICR 692; [1981] 1 WLR 972; [1981] IRLR 228, paras 17–18).

result. In our view, it is logical and reasonable to suggest that in a uniform statutory regime governing pay and conditions in the public sector of education, comparisons may be made across the boundaries of the authorities that are statutorily obliged to give effect to it. We conclude therefore that a comparator employed by another education authority is admissible in this case ...

On the view that we have taken, it is unnecessary for us to decide whether the public sector of education constitutes a 'service' in the sense in which that expression is used in *Defrenne* ...

In our view, the material considerations are that the applicant and her comparators are in the same branch of public service and are subject to a uniform system of national pay and conditions set by a statutory body whose decision is binding on their employers. It seems reasonable to us to refer to them as being engaged in the same service ...

Lawrence and Others v Regent Office Care Ltd Case C-320/00 [2002] IRLR 822, ECJ

In some districts, North Yorkshire county council contracted out its school cleaning and catering services. In other districts, the council carried on providing the service itself. The workers affected by the contracting-out were made redundant and re-employed by Regent, who paid them less than the council's rates. These workers brought a claim of equal pay, using an existing council worker as a comparator.

Judgment:

15.   Three features distinguish the present case. First, the persons whose pay is being compared work for different employers, that is to say, on the one hand, the council and, on the other, the respondent undertakings. Second, the work which the appellants perform for those undertakings is identical to that which some of them performed for the council before the transfer of undertakings. Finally, that work has been recognised as being of equal value to that performed by the chosen comparators employed by the council and continues to be so recognised.
       ...

17.   There is, in this connection, nothing in the wording of Article 141(1) EC to suggest that the applicability of that provision is limited to situations in which men and women work for the same employer. The Court has held that the principle established by that article may be invoked before national courts, in particular in cases of discrimination arising directly from legislative provisions or collective labour agreements, as well as in cases in which work is carried out in the same establishment or service, whether private or public (see, *inter alia*, *Defrenne (No 2)*, paragraph 40; case 129/79 *Macarthys* [1980] IRLR 210, paragraph 10; and case 96/80 *Jenkins* [1981] IRLR 228, paragraph 17).

18.   However, where, as in the main proceedings here, the differences identified in the pay conditions of workers performing equal work or work of equal value cannot be attributed to a single source, there is no body which is responsible for the inequality and which could restore equal treatment. Such a situation does not come within the scope of Article 141(1) EC. The work and the pay of those workers cannot therefore be compared on the basis of that provision.

5   LIKE WORK – SECTION 1(2)(a)

Section 1(4) provides that:

> A woman is to be regarded as employed on like work with men if, but only if, her work and theirs is of the same or a broadly similar nature, and the difference (if any) between the things she does and the things they do are not of practical importance in relation to terms and conditions of employment; and accordingly in comparing her work with theirs regard shall to be had to the frequency or otherwise with which any such differences occur in practice as well as to the nature of the differences.

This is the first and most obvious manifestation of the equal pay principle. It is also the most limited in its scope and impact. Unsurprisingly, there were, in the years immediately after the Act took effect, many cases under this section, as employers came to terms with the fact that they were no longer permitted to have separate men's rates and women's rates for people doing the same work. One response was to move either women or men to ensure that the like work provision could not be applied.[60] Pay inequalities continue, despite the fact that men and women routinely receive the same pay for the same work; the problem is that women do not routinely do the same work as men, and the work that women do may be undervalued compared with the work that men do.

In deciding whether there is 'like work', the first question is whether the jobs are *broadly* similar. The wording clearly shows that they are not required to be absolutely identical, and thus tribunals must disregard minor differences which are, in the real world, not likely to be reflected in different terms and conditions of employment.[61] The second stage, which is conceptually very close to the first and difficult to keep separate from it, is that the differences must be of practical importance in relation to terms and conditions of employment. Attention must be focused not simply on what the contract says but on what actually happens in practice. In *Shields v E Coomes (Holdings) Ltd*,[62] male employees in a betting shop were paid more because they had special responsibility for security in shops considered particularly vulnerable to burglary. This differentiation was unlawful for two reasons: first, all the men received the higher pay irrespective of whether in fact they carried out the additional function – they were paid for what the employers said would happen rather than for what actually happened in practice; secondly, the employers allocated the extra responsibilities to men simply because they were men. There was no proper individual selection of employees to exercise these functions and thus the whole payment structure was based on sex discrimination. The concept of what is done is to be viewed widely. For example, two employees may in a physical sense do precisely the same work, but one may be in a position of responsibility over the other. They are clearly not engaged on like work.[63] Flexibility and availability to do other work may also be relevant, depending on its frequency and duration.[64]

---

60 Snell, M, Glucklich, P and Povall, M, *Equal Pay and Opportunities: A Study of the Implementation and Effects of the Equal Pay Act and the Sex Discrimination Act in 26 Organisations*, 1981, London: Department of Employment.

61 *Capper Pass Ltd v Lawton* [1977] QB 852; [1977] 2 All ER 11; [1976] IRLR 366, EAT.

62 [1978] ICR 1159; [1979] 1 All ER 456; [1978] IRLR 263, CA.

63 *Eaton Ltd v Nuttall* [1977] ICR 272; [1977] 3 All ER 1131; [1977] IRLR 71, EAT.

64 *Maidment v Cooper and Co (Birmingham) Ltd* [1978] ICR 1094; [1978] IRLR 462, EAT; *Electrolux Ltd v Hutchinson* [1977] ICR 252; [1976] IRLR 410, EAT.

However, the time when work is performed is irrelevant to the like work issue.[65] The fact that the comparator works at night and the applicant works days is thus irrelevant *unless* the nature of the work changes if done at night, for example, because of greater responsibility or risks.[66] This does not mean, however, that people who work days earn as much as those doing the same job at night. While the work is like work, the fact of night work attracts and justifies an additional premium – often in the order of 20% – which constitutes a genuine material factor which is not the difference of sex and thus provides a defence to an equal pay claim. However, if the night shift premium is excessive, the tribunal can, according to the EAT in *Sherwin v National Coal Board*,[67] increase the applicant's basic pay so that the difference between her pay and that of her comparator becomes no more than an appropriate night shift premium would make permissible. The problem with this approach is that it may conflict with another principle: if the like work principle is not satisfied, there is no remedy, however great the pay disparity – if the jobs are 90% the same, there is no entitlement to 90% of the pay. Arguably, if the night shift premium is excessive, the whole amount should be disallowed. The *Sherwin* approach virtually entails the tribunal acting as a rate fixing body, which is beyond their jurisdiction. In policy terms, the outcome is undoubtedly correct and whether or not it can be supported by the strict wording of the Act matters less now that the European Court in *Enderby v Frenchay AHA*[68] has approved such an approach.

6   WORK RATED AS EQUIVALENT – SECTION 1(2)(b)[69]

Under s 1(2)(b) of the Equal Pay Act 1970, an equality clause comes into operation if the woman's work has been 'rated as equivalent' to that of a man. What this means is defined by s 1(5):

> A woman is to be regarded as employed on work rated as equivalent with that of any men if, but only if, her job and their job have been given an equal value, in terms of the demand made on a worker under various headings (for instance effort, skill, decision), on a study made with a view to evaluating in those terms the jobs to be done by all or any of the employees in an undertaking or group of undertakings, or would have been given an equal value but for the evaluation being made on a system setting different values for men and women on the same demand under any heading.

The section raises two issues: (a) what is meant by such a scheme?; and (2) when will two jobs be regarded as having been rated as equivalent?

---

65   *Dugdale v Kraft Foods Ltd* [1977] ICR 48; [1977] 1 All ER 454; [1976] IRLR 368, EAT.
66   *Thomas v National Coal Board* [1987] ICR 757; [1987] IRLR 451, EAT.
67   [1978] ICR 700; [1978] IRLR 122, EAT.
68   Case C-127/92 [1993] ECR I-5535; [1994] ICR 112; [1994] 1 All ER 495; [1993] IRLR 591.
69   See generally: Ghobadian, A, 'Job evaluation: trade union and staff association representatives' perspectives' (1990) 12(4) Employee Relations; Biman, D and Garcia-Diaz, A, 'Factor selection guidelines for job evaluation: a computerised statistical procedure' (2001) 40(3) Computer and Industrial Engineering 259; Lofstrom, A, 'Can job evaluation improve women's wages?' (1999) 31(9) Applied Economics 1053.

(1)   Evaluating a Job

McCrudden, C, 'Equal pay for work of equal value: the Equal Pay (Amendment) Regulations 1983' [1983] 12 ILJ 197, pp 201–02:

The value of the job might have been assessed in at least three ways. First, market value might have been taken. This would consider the value of the job to be that which is actually paid for it in the market ... This is clearly not the meaning of value which is intended by the principle of 'equal pay for work of equal value' ... though its relevance has not been rejected, as we shall see in examining the scope of the material factor defence.

A second idea of value is that of marginal productivity. What is the value which 'the work adds to the total output of the enterprise'? An oversimplified example may help to explain the approach. Suppose that widgets are manufactured by first stamping them from sheets of widgetstock, then polishing them. A widget stamper and a widget polisher can each process 100 widgets per day. If widgetstock costs 10p per widget, and if stamped but unpolished widgets are worth 50p and if polished widgets are worth £3.00 each, the work of the polisher is worth £25 per day, and the work of the stamper is worth £4 per day. This method is not chosen, either, though, again, it is relevant as an aspect of the material factor defence. Instead a third method has been adopted ... which imposes an obligation to assess job content, ie, a form of job evaluation.

Job evaluation is primarily a management technique used to relate jobs to one another, both to develop and implement a fair pay structure and to persuade the employees of the merits of the structure thus produced, in the hope, for example, of reducing employee discontent and turnover. The definition of value which is used is based on the input of the worker to the job, rather than any other possible criteria which might have been utilised. The same approach is used to the assessment of value where it is claimed that a woman's work is equal in value to that of a man. In *Eaton Ltd v Nuttall*,[70] the EAT, in an appendix to the decision, briefly summarised the principal methods of job evaluation:

• *Job ranking*. This is commonly thought to be the simplest method. Each job is considered as a whole and is then given a ranking in relation to all other jobs. A ranking table is then drawn up and the ranked jobs grouped into grades. Pay levels can then be fixed for each grade.

• *Paired comparisons*. This is also a simple method. Each job is compared as a whole with other jobs in turn and points (0, 1 or 2) awarded according to whether its overall importance is judged to be less than, equal to or more than the other. Points awarded for each job are then totalled up and a ranking order produced.

• *Job classification*. This is similar to ranking except that it starts from the opposite end; the grading structure is established first and individual jobs are fitted into it. A broad description of each grade is drawn up and individual jobs considered typical of each grade are selected as 'benchmarks'. The other jobs are then compared with these benchmarks and the general description and placed in their appropriate grade.

• *Points assessment*. This is the most common system in use. It is an analytical method which, instead of comparing whole jobs, breaks down each job into a

---

70 [1977] ICR 272; [1977] 3 All ER 1131; [1977] IRLR 71.

number of factors – for example, skills, responsibility, physical and mental requirements and working conditions. Each of the factors may be analysed further. Points are awarded for each factor according to a predetermined scale and the total points decide a job's place in the ranking order. Usually, the factors are weighted so that, for example, more or less weight may be given to hard physical conditions or to a high degree of skill.

• *Factor comparison.* This is also an analytical method, employing the same principles as points assessment but using only a limited number of factors, such as skill, responsibility and working conditions. A number of 'key' jobs are selected because their wage rates are generally agreed to be 'fair'. The proportion of the total wage attributable to each factor is then decided and a scale produced showing the rate for each factor for each key job. The other jobs are then compared with this scale, factor by factor, so that a rate is finally obtained for each factor of each job. The total pay for each job is reached by adding together the rates for its individual factors.

The first three methods can be summarised as being 'non-analytical' methods, the latter two as 'analytical'. The basic distinction is that non-analytical methods compare the whole job being assessed, whereas analytical methods break down the jobs into component elements. The next case explores the significance of this distinction.

Bromley v H and J Quick Ltd [1988] IRLR 249; [1988] ICR 623, CA

Female clerical workers claimed that their work was equal in value to that of male managers. The employers claimed that the jobs in question had been given different values under a job evaluation study. If there had been such evaluation, the tribunal would, under s 1(5) of the EqPA 1970, not have had jurisdiction to hear the equal value claim. The EAT held that such a scheme was not required to be analytical in nature.

The method used was a form of paired comparisons. The panel was permitted to change the ranking of the benchmark jobs on a 'felt fair' basis, ie, in accordance with the general level of expectation as to the value of the jobs.

The Court of Appeal reversed the decision of the EAT and held that only analytical schemes could satisfy the requirements of s 1(5).

Dillon LJ (pp 253–54):

One has to be a little careful ... in considering what is meant by 'objective' since ... there are no universally accepted external criteria for measuring how much of a factor or quality is involved in a particular job or for measuring what relative weights ought to be attached to different factors or qualities involved, to differing extents, in various jobs. Every attempt at job evaluation will ... inevitably at some stage involve value judgements, which are inherently to some extent subjective or 'felt fair' ...

In my judgment, [the word 'analytical'] conveniently indicates the general nature of what is required by the section, *viz*, that the jobs of each worker covered by the study must have been valued in terms of the demand made on the worker under various headings ... It is not enough ... that the 23 benchmark jobs were valued ... on the factor demand basis required by s 1(5) if the jobs of the appellants and their comparators were not.

Bromley reaches the correct result. A job evaluation study may be the basis of a successful claim under s 1(5) and may defeat an equal value claim under s 2A(2). No one contends that such studies are completely objective – a fact that Dillon LJ acknowledges – but that is no reason for not requiring them to be as objective as is reasonably possible. Analytical methods have a potential to do this in a way that non-analytical methods do not. Objectivity contributes to the attainment of appropriate and defensible results and, more particularly, to the avoiding of sex bias creeping into the way in which schemes operate, even though rooting out such bias is not straightforward even in relation to analytical schemes.

(2)   Rated as Equivalent

The second question is when can it be said that two jobs have been 'rated as equivalent'. In *O'Brien v Sim-Chem Ltd*,[71] it was held to be sufficient if the evaluations under the scheme had been completed. There was no need for the scheme to be implemented; complaints under this section are most likely to be because a completed scheme was, for some reason, not implemented. However, in *Arnold v Beecham Group Ltd*,[72] it was held that a scheme cannot be regarded as having been completed before it had been accepted by the parties. This must include the employer; whether it includes the union, where there has been union involvement in conducting the study, is unclear.[73]

7   EQUAL VALUE – SECTION 1(2)(c)[74]

The purpose of a job evaluation study is to compare the value of different jobs. Section 1(5) only applies where the employer has voluntarily undertaken a job evaluation study; the law provided no compulsion and little impetus for this to occur, although general developments in the management of industrial relations meant that such schemes were being utilised more frequently. As we shall see, the law and procedure are lengthy, complex and hard to follow.

Section 1(2)(c) of the EqPA 1970 provides:

> ... where a woman is employed on work which, not being work in relation to which para (a) [like work] or (b) [work rated as equivalent] above applies, is, in terms of the demands made on her (for instance under such headings as effort, skill and decision) of equal value to that of a man in the same employment ...

The phrase in this section 'not being work in relation to which para (a) or (b) applies' proved troublesome. It was argued in *Pickstone v Freemans plc*[75] that the words prevented an equal value claim from being brought in any situation where a man was engaged on like work or work rated as equivalent with the female comparator, for in that situation there would be work to which (a) or (b) applied. This meant that a claim could not have been brought if there was *any* man engaged on like work with the

---

71 [1980] ICR 573; [1980] 3 All ER 132; [1980] IRLR 373, HL.

72 [1982] ICR 744; [1982] IRLR 307, EAT.

73 As long as the scheme satisfies s 1(5), it is not possible to argue that a different scheme would have produced a different result more favourable to the female applicant; see *England v Bromley London BC* [1978] ICR 1, EAT. The only exception is where it can be shown that there has been a fundamental error in operating the scheme, such as basing judgments on a wrong job description; see *Green v Broxtowe DC* [1977] ICR 241; [1977] IRLR 34, EAT. Given the complexity involved, it seems clear that only very significant errors would invalidate a scheme in this way.

74 See Gregory, J, 'Dynamite or damp squib – an assessment of equal value law' (1997) 2 IJDL 167.

75 [1989] AC 66; [1988] 2 All ER 803; [1988] IRLR 357, HL.

applicant, however much her work might have been undervalued in comparison with other men. There is little doubt that this is the best literal meaning of the phrase. Had it been accepted, the only women who could have utilised the procedure would have been those whose job categories were 100% female. Such a construction would undoubtedly have led to a finding of failure properly to implement the decision of the European Court. To avoid the problem, the House of Lords construed the section in a manner designed to achieve its avowed purpose, that a woman should be able to claim that her work was equal in value to that of *any* man in the same establishment. In a technical sense, this was achieved by notionally adding the words 'as between the woman and the man with whom she claims equality' *after* the words 'not being work to which para (a) or (b) applies'.[76]

As with other equal pay and discrimination cases, claims may be referred to the Advisory Conciliation and Arbitration Service (ACAS) to investigate the possibility of a conciliated settlement,[77] though in equal value claims, such an outcome is most unlikely. Assuming no settlement or withdrawal, there is a preliminary hearing before an employment tribunal at which the tribunal either determines the equal value question itself or adjourns the hearing for a so called 'independent expert' to prepare a report on whether the applicant's work is equal in value to that of her comparator. The tribunal hearing is then reconvened and the final decision is made in the light of the expert's report and other evidence. In addition, the employer may argue that the pay difference was explained and justified by a genuine material factor. The procedure has been notorious for delay[78] and many of the modifications have been introduced to shorten cases. Delay is especially damaging in this context because the law does no more than take a snapshot of the pay relationship between an applicant and a comparator at one moment. A proper picture of pay structures requires a moving picture to take account of inevitable changes over time and a broad screen to include a fully representative group of workers.

(1)   The Preliminary Hearing

Equal Pay Act 1970

Section 2A

(1)   Where ... a dispute arises as to whether any work is of equal value ... the tribunal may either:

   (a) proceed to determine that question;[79] or

   (b) unless it is satisfied that there are no reasonable grounds for determining that the work is of equal value as so mentioned, require a member of the panel of independent experts to prepare a report with respect to that question.

Under s 2A(1), tribunals have power to determine the equal value issue *without* first referring the claim to an independent expert. Section 2A(1)(b) gives a tribunal the

---

76   *Pickstone v Freemans plc* [1988] IRLR 357, p 362, *per* Lord Templeman.

77   See Chapter 17, p 525.

78   'Industrial Tribunals have now ruled on equal pay following referral to an independent expert in 39 cases ... The total average time taken is 20 months, ranging from five months to 49 months.' Where issues needed to be resolved by appeal courts before the expert even started work, some cases have taken more than a decade to resolve. 'Equal value update' (1997) 76 EOR 18, p 19.

79   The power in the tribunal to determine the claim for itself and not refer the case to an independent expert was introduced by the Sex Discrimination and Equal Pay (Miscellaneous Amendments) Regulations 1996, SI 1996/438, reg 3, in force since 31 July 1996.

right to strike out a claim where it considers that there were 'no reasonable grounds' that the work was of equal value. The problem with this rule is that tribunals can act on stereotypes. For instance, a tribunal may assume that a cook could not possibly compare herself with an electrician and, without more, strike out the claim.[80]

The tribunal may, if it considers it appropriate to do so, hear evidence at the preliminary hearing concerning the defence of genuine material factor.[81] If the defence succeeds at this stage, the complaint is dismissed with no reference being made to the independent expert.

(2)   Job Evaluation Schemes

Under s 1(5), a complainant may allege that her job has been given the *same* rating as that of a man under such a scheme. Thus, the scheme provides the basis for a successful claim. Under s 2A(2), on the other hand, a job evaluation scheme where a man's job and a woman's job have been given *different* values may operate to defeat that woman's claim that her work is equal in value to that man's. Unfortunately, the convolutions of the drafting make unravelling the principles a grim task.

Equal Pay Act 1970

Section 2A

(3)   An evaluation ... is made on a system which discriminates on grounds of sex where a difference, or coincidence, between values set by that system on different demands under the same or different headings is not justifiable irrespective of the sex of the person on whom those demands are made.[82]

What this contorted language is attempting to say is that discrimination in a scheme may exist either where the same demands have been given different values, or where different demands have been given the same value.

McCrudden, C, 'Equal pay for work of equal value: the Equal Pay (Amendment) Regulations 1983' [1983] 12 ILJ 197, pp 207–08:

Suppose a JES has been set up and has resulted in different values for job x and job y. Suppose further that the factors, sub-factors, maximum points and weightings are as follows

Factors and Subfactors	*Maximum Points*
1 Responsibility	40
(i) Cost of replacement of machine	30
(ii) Amount of supervision required	10
2 Physical requirements	40
3 Mental requirements	30

---

80   In 2003, the Government dropped a proposal to remove the right to strike out a claim in favour of a more general reform of tribunal procedure. Consultation began in Autumn 2003, with legislation due in Autumn 2004. See www.dti.gov.uk/er/individual/ etregs_consult.htm.

81   Employment Tribunals (Constitution and Procedure) Regulations 2001, SI 2001/1171, r 11(2E).

82   Inserted by SI 1983/1794, reg 3(1).

Factors and Subfactors	Maximum Points
4 Working conditions	40
(i) Outside work	20
(ii) Noise	20

The Regulations allow each of the elements in this scheme to be challenged. The different weightings for physical and mental requirements constitute a difference between values set by that system on different demands under different headings. The same weightings for responsibility and physical requirements constitute a coincidence between values set by that system on different demands under different headings. The different weightings given the responsibility subfactors constitute a difference in values set by that system on different demands under the same heading. The same weightings given the working conditions subfactors constitute a coincidence in valued set by that system on difference demands under the same heading. Last, the omission of a relevant factor, say 'skill', may be regarded as giving it a nil value and thus as constituting a difference in values set by that system on different demands under different headings.

Dibro Ltd v Hore[83] establishes, perhaps surprisingly, that the study relied on by the employer need not be in existence at the date of a claim. The employer may conduct and complete a study right up to the date of the reconvened hearing, and if it is a properly conducted analytical scheme, it will have the effect of blocking the equal value claim 'provided it related to facts and circumstances existing at the time when the proceedings were initiated'. The policy behind this approach is that 'encouragement should be given to employers to carry out such schemes'. Such an approach has much to commend it: one argument is that a major purpose of the equal value law is to act as a spur to voluntary job evaluation. Whether the employer should be allowed to trump the applicant's claim with a belated scheme largely depends on the degree of confidence felt in the ability of tribunals to detect schemes which are tainted with discrimination or disadvantage. It is strongly arguable that employer schemes, whether conducted before or after the initiation of a claim, should *never* operate as a complete defence, but should be part of the evidence which the tribunal considers in deciding whether the jobs in question are indeed of equal value.

The employer has the burden of establishing that there is no basis for supposing that the scheme is tainted by discrimination. If there is any doubt, the case must go forward for the equal value issue to be resolved. In *Bromley v H and J Quick Ltd*,[84] Dillon LJ said that the employer must: 'explain how any job evaluation study worked and what was taken into account at each stage ... [I]t must be possible to see through to what actually happened ... [The tribunal] may not be satisfied on the evidence in a particular case if the evidence offers no explanation of the basis on which some apparently wholly subjective decision was made ...'[85] Employers will naturally contest vigorously any suggestion that the scheme has discriminatory elements. Such a finding will stigmatise a scheme and make it very difficult for the employer to continue its operation. The finding at this stage need not necessarily show that the scheme affected the complainant or her comparator in a discriminatory fashion; discrimination anywhere in the scheme's operation will defeat the employer's argument. However, the resolution of the equal value issue will focus simply on the

---

83 [1990] ICR 370; [1989] IRLR 129, EAT.
84 [1988] ICR 623; [1988] IRLR 249, CA.
85 [1988] IRLR 249, p 254.

two individuals and will not necessarily resolve the doubts cast upon the scheme by the preliminary hearing.

There has been little litigation concerning job evaluation. The most significant case came before the European Court.

Rummler v Dato-Druck GmbH **Case 237/85 [1987] IRLR 32; [1986] ECR 2101; [1987] ICR 774, ECJ**

The case concerned a job evaluation system at a German printing firm. The scheme provided for seven pay grades, with jobs classified according to previous knowledge required, concentration, effort and exertion, and responsibility. The claimant's job was classed in pay grade III, requiring medium and sometimes high muscular effort. She claimed that she should be in grade IV, arguing that, for her, the job entailed heavy physical work.

Judgment (pp 33–34):

[The first] question ... is directed fundamentally at ascertaining whether a job classification system which is based on criteria of muscular effort and exertion and the degree to which the work is physically heavy is compatible with the principle of equal pay ...

The principle of equal pay ... requires fundamentally that the nature of the work to be done must be considered objectively ... If a job classification system is used in determining pay, then on the one hand it must be based on the same criteria regardless of whether the work is to be done by a man or by a woman, while on the other it may not be so designed overall as to lead in fact to general discrimination ...

It is compatible with the prohibition of discrimination to apply a criterion in setting differentiated pay grades which takes account of the objectively measurable level of physical strength needed to do the job or the objective degree to which the work is physically heavy.

Even if a particular criterion, such as that of the muscular exertion needed, may in fact favour male employees on the grounds that it may be assumed that they generally have greater physical strength than female employees, then that particular criterion should be considered along with the others which play a part in determining pay within the overall job classification system when assessing whether that criterion is discriminatory. A system is not discriminatory solely because one of its criteria is based on characteristics more commonly found among men. If a job classification system is not to be discriminatory overall and is to be in accordance with the principles of the Directive, it must, however, be so designed that, if the nature of the work under discussion so permits, it includes as 'work to which equal value is attributed', work in which other criteria are taken into account for which female employees may show particular aptitude.

It is the task of the national courts to decide ... whether the ... system in its entirety permits fair account to be taken of all the criteria on the basis of which pay is determined ...

The claimant argued that, in determining whether the work was 'heavy' work, account should have been taken of the fact of women's lower average strength. This was properly rejected for sound reasons of both principle and policy. She was seeking to *require* the employers to introduce an element of direct discrimination – in a sense, affirmative action – into the scheme. Furthermore, if job evaluation is to have any chance of benefiting women, it must operate and be seen to operate on objective criteria. The 'argument that typically female criteria are undervalued in some aspects of a scheme is not assisted by arguments that elsewhere in the scheme special allowance should be made for the fact that women score relatively badly. To say that an employer is not permitted to favour factors found more frequently in jobs of one sex is tantamount to saying that he is not permitted to value aspects of the job which he might legitimately regard as of value, simply because it happens that they are more associated with men's jobs than women's jobs'.[86]

However, *Rummler* does make clear that a scheme must be *representative* of the skills and attributes of both sexes. It must not be 'designed' to lead to discrimination and must take proper account of any different attributes of both sexes. In other words, a scheme can be challenged as being either directly or indirectly discriminatory. The concern here is with the outcomes which result from a scheme; challenge to the scheme at an earlier stage for being discriminatory in operation might also be possible.[87] It was held in *Handels v Danfoss*[88] – a case concerning a merit rating system – that the employer will not be able to justify using a pay structure unless its criteria and methodology are made clear.[89]

(3)   Parallels with Voluntary Evaluation

While the procedures are significantly different, there are close parallels between what is involved in voluntary job evaluation and the resolution of an equal value claim by an independent expert. It must be borne in mind that voluntary job evaluation costs an employer money; additional checks and balances in the interests of gender neutrality can only add to the costs, at least in the short term.

The first stage of voluntary job evaluation is to produce accurate descriptions of the jobs to be evaluated. At the next stage, the most important issues arise. This encompasses the choice of factors, the assigning of a maximum score to each of those factors, and then deciding how much each job is worth on each of the factors. The factors of effort, skill, responsibility and working conditions are those most frequently employed in schemes, and may be subdivided, such as into physical and mental effort. The evaluators must decide how important each of these factors is in the job to be evaluated, and then determine a maximum score for each factor. This is a matter of judgment and experience in which awareness of the possibilities of gender bias is vital. It is more likely that gender bias will be present in relation to the choice of factors and the maximum values attached to each rather than to the process of giving each job a value under each factor. The latter is so subjective that, unless gender differentiation has been explicitly mentioned, it will be very hard even to show reasonable suspicion that discrimination has occurred.

There is a danger that evaluators will overlook important characteristics of female-dominated jobs, especially those associated with skills needed to run a family. They may be regarded not as job-related skills but rather as qualities intrinsic to being a

---

86   Rubenstein, M, *Equal Pay for Work of Equal Value*, 1984, London: Macmillan, p 94.

87   See Lester, A and Rose, D, 'Equal value claims and sex bias in collective bargaining' [1991] 20 ILJ 163.

88   Case C-109/88 [1989] ECR 3199; [1991] 1 CMLR 8; [1989] IRLR 532.

89   The EOC consider that it is 'unrealistic and unfair to expect an employee to be able to challenge effectively an employer's study for evidence of a sex-based system'. See 'Equal pay law: paradise for lawyers – hell for women' (1991) 35 EOR 30, p 31.

woman. Examples of characteristics of female jobs which are frequently ignored include doing the same job over and over for a long time; working around people who are sick and disabled with no hope of recovery; physically handling sick or injured people; and showing new workers who make more money how to do their job. Working with mentally ill or retarded persons may be overlooked as a stressful working condition, while working with noisy machinery may not. Poor working conditions such as lifting heavy weights or working out of doors may be given a high point value, while the eye strain associated with working on VDUs may be entirely ignored; nurses who supervise employees and care for patients only receive points for supervision, because the way 'human relations know-how' is defined largely excludes skills necessary in working with people other than those supervised.

'Making the invisible visible: rewarding women's work' (1992) 45 EOR 23, p 28:

According to the [Ontario] Pay Equity Commission, the following are some of the job requirements frequently overlooked or ignored:

Skill

- operating and maintaining several different types of office, manufacturing, treatment/diagnosis or monitoring equipment;
- manual dexterity required for giving injections, typing, or graphic arts;
- writing correspondence for others, and proofreading and editing others' work;
- establishing and maintaining manual and automated filing systems, or records management and disposal;
- training and orienting new staff;
- deciding the content and format of reports and presentations to clients.

Effort

- adjusting to rapid changes in the office or plant technology;
- concentrating for long periods at computer terminals, lab benches and manufacturing equipment;
- performing complex sequences of hand-eye co-ordination in industrial jobs;
- providing service to several people or departments, working under many simultaneous deadlines;
- developing work schedules; and
- frequent lifting (office or medical supplies, retail goods, injured or sick people).

Responsibility

- caring for, and providing emotional support to children and institutionalised people;
- protecting confidentiality;
- acting on behalf of absent supervisors;
- representing the organisation through communications with clients and the public;
- supervising staff;
- shouldering consequences of error to the organisation;
- preventing possible damage to equipment; and
- co-ordinating schedules for many people.

Working conditions

- stress from noise in open spaces, crowded conditions; and production of noise;
- exposure to disease and stress from caring for ill people;
- dealing with upset, injured, irate or irrational people;
- cleaning offices, stores, machinery or hospital wards;
- frequent bending or lifting of office or medical supplies, retail goods;
- stress from answering complaints; and
- long periods of travel and/or isolation.[90]

It is impossible to say that one system of job evaluation or one conclusion as to the weight of appropriate factors can ever be found. The law must thus focus on the *procedures* rather than the *outcome*. Yet, the independent experts are given no detailed guidance as to how to go about their task and what factors to consider. All that is stated that is that they must compare the jobs 'for instance under the headings of effort, skill and decision'.

After the jobs have been evaluated and the points tallied, pay levels must be resolved. There is no necessary connection between job evaluation and high pay; indeed, job evaluation may be associated with an increase in differentials and, if this is the case, might even make the position of female employees worse. Pay levels need to be resolved by negotiation or other methods. There is no direct correlation between a points score and the amount of pay. If a job scored twice as much for responsibility than another job, it does not follow that in respect of that factor the former job would receive twice the pay of the latter. From an administrative perspective, it is sensible to have a wide spread of points. The normal practice is to band points for salary purposes, so that, for example, those who score 151–175 might be on a basic rate of £200 per week, with those scoring 176–200 on a basic rate of £220.

(4)   The Report of the Independent Expert and the Reconvened Hearing

One of the major criticisms of the equal value procedure has been the time taken by experts to prepare reports. This has recently been tackled in two ways, first, by providing that tribunals may decide the issue for themselves[91] and, secondly, by requiring tribunals to set a date by which the expert must have completed the report.

Employment Tribunals (Constitution and Rules of Procedure) Regulations 2001, SI 2001/1171

Rule 10A

(5)   The requirement [for a report] shall stipulate that the expert shall—

---

90   'A particular problem with skill and knowledge factors is the emphasis on formal qualifications. There are many schemes ... whose measure of knowledge depend entirely on formal qualifications and take no account of knowledge obtained through experience either within the workplace or in, for example, the domestic environment ... Experience [factors may also] have an adverse impact on women. [Hastings] gave the example of a UK health service trust which has an experience factor with a number of levels which at the top level would suggest that there are jobs requiring 20 years of experience in order to perform them competently. What the factor is actually measuring ... is a particular career progression through the organisation, which is one usually followed by men ...' 'Making the invisible visible: rewarding women's work' (1992) 45 EOR 23, p 26.

91   See above, 'The Preliminary Hearing', p 398.

(a) take account of all such information supplied and all such representations made to him as have a bearing on the question;

(b) before drawing up his report, produce and send to the parties a written summary of the said information and representations and invite the representations of the parties upon the material contained therein;

(c) make his report to the tribunal in a document which shall reproduce the summary and contain a brief account of any representations received from the parties upon it, any conclusion he may have reached upon the question and the reasons for that conclusion or, as the case may be, for his failure to reach such a conclusion;

(d) take no account of the difference of sex and at all times act fairly.

The only guidance given to experts is that the jobs shall be compared under such heads as 'effort, skill and decision'.[92] This clearly mirrors a points-factor job evaluation study.[93] However, it focuses only on the applicant and the comparator or comparators, rather than attempting to fix the criteria for determining a more general pay structure. Experts must ignore the impact which a particular decision might have on pay elsewhere in the enterprise, especially if it is considered that a particular finding might generate consequential equal value claims. Furthermore, voluntary job evaluation aims at fixing a hierarchy of jobs. There is no claim under the equal value law if it is concluded that the jobs are not equal in value, however great the disparity in pay which ensues. The fact that the expert is directed to 'take no account of the difference of sex'[94] means that if the approach to the assessment of value was tainted by gender in any way, such as the potential defects identified earlier in connection with voluntary job evaluation,[95] the tribunal may, at the reconvened hearing, decide not to admit the report.[96] Finally, the expert must compare the value of the jobs as they were at the date the claim was submitted rather than at the date they are observed or the date of the reconvened hearing. In contrast, a well-designed voluntary job evaluation system will have procedures for dealing with changes in content over time, and will always look to the future rather than to the past.

At the reconvened hearing the tribunal may either admit the report into evidence, reject it, or commission a new one. In reaching this decision, the expert may be called for cross-examination, and each party has the right to call one witness to give evidence on the equal value question.[97] The report must be admitted in evidence unless defective in one of a number of stated ways.[98] The most likely reason for contending that a report should not be admitted is that it was prepared under a fundamental

---

92 EqPA 1970, s 1(5).

93 See above, 'Job Evaluation Schemes', p 399.

94 Employment Tribunals (Constitution and Rules of Procedure) Regulations 2001, SI 2001/1171, r 10A(5)(d).

95 See above, 'Job Evaluation Schemes', p 399.

96 Employment Tribunals (Constitution and Rules of Procedure) Regulations 2001, SI 2001/1171, r 10A(18).

97 *Ibid*, r 11(2B).

98 *Ibid*, r 10A(18): 'Where the tribunal, on the application of one or more of the parties or otherwise, forms the view— (a) that the expert has not complied with a stipulation in paragraph (5) [in text, above], or (b) that the conclusion contained in the report is one which, taking due account of the information supplied and representations made to the expert, could not reasonably have been reached, or (c) that for some other material reason (other than disagreement with the conclusion that the applicant's work is or is not of equal value or with the reasoning leading to that conclusion) the report is unsatisfactory, the tribunal may, if it thinks fit, determine not to admit the report ...'

misapprehension of fact, such as that the work observed had changed significantly since the claim was submitted, or that one aspect of a job was either not taken into account or was over-emphasised.

It is now clear that the findings of the independent expert are not conclusive. In *Tennants Textile Colours Ltd v Todd*,[99] a laboratory assistant claimed equal value with technicians. The expert said that the work was equal in value with one of her chosen comparators. The tribunal decided to admit the report. The employers then sought an adjournment to obtain a report from their own expert witness. This was granted by the tribunal which, however, observed that the findings of fact contained in the expert's report would be binding as the report had already been admitted. On re-hearing, the tribunal held that once the report was admitted, the expert's conclusions should only be rejected if it were shown that they were so plainly wrong that they could not be accepted. The Northern Ireland Court of Appeal allowed the employer's appeal, holding that it was wrong to conclude that the findings of fact, once admitted, were binding on both parties, as although r 8(2C)[100] restricted the rights of parties, it did not prevent a party from making submissions to contradict the conclusions of the independent expert, or inhibit the tribunal from asking questions. Furthermore, while the burden of proof is on the applicant, it does not become heavier if the report is against the applicant, nor is the burden of proof transferred to the employer if the report is in favour of the applicant. Finally, it was wrong to conclude that the report could only be rejected if the evidence were such as to show that it was so plainly wrong that it could not be accepted. Given that it has been held that the report is not conclusive, it is preferable, in order to avoid further delay, to admit the report and then reach a finding contrary to that of the expert.[101]

It is arguable that there is no need for independent experts and that tribunals should be able to determine all claims.[102] The relatively new power to resolve claims without reference to the expert can be seen as an experiment along these lines, yet the Equal Opportunities Commission is worried about the potential effects.

'Equal pay law: paradise for lawyers – hell for women' (1991) 35 EOR 30, p 32:

First, an equal value case involves the measurement of work against a variety of factors, which in the EOC's view cannot be 'carried out sensibly during a tribunal hearing'. Secondly, the measurement of work inevitably involves skill and experience in work measurement techniques. Thirdly, independent experts are completely

---

99 [1989] IRLR 3, NICA.
100 The equivalent is now in the Employment Tribunals (Constitution and Rules of Procedure) Regulations 2001, SI 2001/1171, r 11(2C): 'Except as provided in rule 10A(19) or by paragraph (2D), no party may give evidence upon, or question any witness upon, any matter of fact upon which a conclusion in the report of the expert is based.'
101 The procedures are discussed in more detail by Bourn, C and Whitmore, J, *Anti-Discrimination Law in Britain*, 3rd edn, 1996, London: Sweet & Maxwell, pp 245–51.
102 Beddoe, R, 'Independent experts' (1986) 6 EOR 13, an article written soon after the procedure came into effect, highlighted instances where experts had failed to follow best practice: (a) by highlighting unreal differences between jobs, which would be unlikely to have any practical impact in the real world; (b) by failing to provide adequate definitions of the factors taken into account; (c) by providing inadequate job descriptions; and (d) by insisting on 100% parity in a way which would be unlikely to occur in the real world. It is probable that since 1986, matters have improved somewhat. However, given the inevitable delay and cost which the independent expert procedure entails, it is defensible only if the outcomes are more reliable than would occur if tribunals decided the matter for themselves. There is little reason for believing this to be the case. See also 'Evaluating the work of independent experts' (1989) 24 EOR 17.

detached from the responsibility to present the case for either party. Finally, the EOC fears that applicants could find themselves in a very difficult position in practice as regards the burden of proof if independent experts are removed from the proceedings. 'In the absence of an independent expert, and given the choice of competing evaluations commissioned by the parties, where both evaluations seem reasonable we consider that an Industrial Tribunal would very probably be driven to dismiss a claim, particularly in the light of the special nature of equal value, namely its tendency to challenge and upset established pay arrangements.'

(5)   The Meaning of Equal Value

The applicant needs to establish that her work is of equal value to that of her comparator. She also succeeds if she establishes that her work is of *greater* value than his.[103] It is a question of fact whether relatively minor points differences will at the end of the process support a conclusion that the work is not of equal value. Two industrial tribunal decisions point in different directions. In *Wells v F Smales and Son (Fish Merchants)*,[104] the tribunal held that applicants who scored between 79% and 95% of the comparator's score were employed on work of equal value as the differences were too small to be material and substantial. However, in *Brown and Royle v Cearns and Brown*,[105] a different tribunal found that an applicant who was scored at 95% of her comparator's score was not employed on work of equal value. Given that a percentage difference in score cannot be translated into a percentage pay difference, this tribunal was surely relying on technical and minor differences which most employers would regard as of no practical relevance.

8   THE DEFENCE OF 'GENUINE MATERIAL FACTOR'

It is logical that direct discrimination is not justifiable and, as such, has no defence. The *'Bilka'* defence for cases under Art 141 (formerly Art 119) arose from a case of indirect discrimination. The domestic equivalent, however, is worded with no distinction between direct and indirect discrimination.[106]

> *Bilka-Kaufhaus v Weber von Hartz* **Case 170/84 [1986] IRLR 317, ECJ**[107]
>
> *Judgment (pp 321):*
>
> If the national court finds that the means chosen ... correspond to a real need on the part of the undertaking, are appropriate with a view to attaining the objectives pursued and are necessary to that end, the fact that the measures in question affect a far greater number of women than men is not sufficient to show that they constitute an infringement of Art 119 ...

---

103 *Murphy v Bord Telecom Eireann* Case 157/86 [1988] ECR 673; [1988] ICR 445; [1988] IRLR 267.
104 (1985) unreported, Hull IT.
105 (1985) unreported, Liverpool IT.
106 For a discussion on the compatibility between the two defences, see Chapter 10, pp 275–79.
107 [1986] ECR 1607, [1986] 2 CMLR 701; [1987] ICR 110. See further above, p 275.

Equal Pay Act 1970

Section 1(3)

An equality clause shall not operate in relation to a variation between the woman's contract and the man's contract if the employer proves that the variation is genuinely due to a material factor which is not the difference of sex and that factor

(a)   [where the claim is based on like work or work rated as equivalent] must be a material difference between the woman's case and the man's; and

(b)   [in equal value claims] may be such a material difference.[108]

The operation of the defence assumes that the applicant has proved that she is employed on like work, work rated as equivalent or work of equal value. It was held in *Davies v McCartneys*[109] that there was no limit on the range of factors which could be considered as relevant to the defence.[110] This goes too far: matters relevant to the question whether there is a *prima facie* case of equal pay, such as relative job content, cannot logically be relevant to this defence, which is concerned with distinctions apart from the nature of the jobs themselves.[111] It is especially important that tribunals bear this in mind where the defence is being considered in a preliminary hearing before consideration of the equal value question.

(1)   The Basis of the Defence

The explanation for the difference in wording between (a) and (b) is only comprehensible in the light of judicial decisions on the interpretation of the sub-section before the equal value amendment was introduced. It is nevertheless a good example of legislation aimed at giving rights to and imposing obligations on ordinary people which is expressed in a manner which in most cases will be quite beyond their capacity to grasp. The wording is a disgrace.

Its origin is the decision of the Court of Appeal in *Clay Cross (Quarry Services) Ltd v Fletcher*.[112] The question was whether it was a defence that a male employee hired to do the same job as an existing female employee could be paid more than her, as otherwise he would not have been prepared to accept the job. As Lord Denning MR pointed out: 'If any such excuse were permitted, the Act would become a dead letter.

---

108   The equivalent authority for European equal pay cases is *Bilka-Kaufhaus v Weber von Hartz* Case 170/84 [1986] ECR 1607; [1986] 2 CMLR 701; [1987] ICR 110; [1986] IRLR 317, where it was held that the practice or policy being challenged must meet a real need of the enterprise, must be necessary for that purpose and must be appropriate for attaining the purpose pursued (see above, p 407). European law thus imposes the same test for discrimination cases as for equal pay cases. As English law has two different tests, the interrelationship between English and European law is far from straightforward.

109   [1989] ICR 707; [1989] IRLR 439, EAT.

110   Such factors must continue to operate at the time the claim is made. In *Benveniste v University of Southampton* [1989] ICR 617; [1989] IRLR 122, CA, because of financial constraints, the plaintiff was appointed on a salary scale below that to which her age and qualifications entitled her. After the constraints ended, she was awarded normal annual increments but remained underpaid for a lecturer of her age and qualifications. It was held that the defence failed as, when the constraints ended, she should have been placed in the salary position in which she would have been had they never existed.

111   Cf *McGregor v GMBATU* [1987] ICR 505, where the EAT wrongly accepted the view of the tribunal that the pay difference was attributable to the man's skills, knowledge, responsibilities and experience. This totally confuses factors relevant to the nature of the job with personal factors relevant to the establishment of the defence.

112   [1979] 1 All ER 374; [1979] ICR 1; [1978] IRLR 361.

Those are the very reasons why there was unequal pay before the statute. They are the very circumstances in which the statute was intended to operate.' However, rather than holding that the employer failed because the difference alleged was in reality a difference of sex, Lord Denning concentrated on the words 'between her case and his' and held that only distinctions based on differences between the 'personal equation' of the woman and the man could provide a defence. Market forces, such as relied on here, were outside the personal equation and thus were no defence.

The approach taken by Lord Denning failed to survive for two reasons. First, it proved impossible to decide what was part of the personal equation and what was not. After all, the fact that the man would not work for less pay was very personal to him and arguably within the concept. Secondly, the European Court in *Bilka-Kaufhaus* held that business efficiency considerations, which *Fletcher* had held to be outside the scope of the defence, were potentially justifiable. In consequence, the House of Lords in *Rainey v Greater Glasgow Health Board*[113] refused to follow *Fletcher*.

These developments occurred after the passing of the equal value amendment, the philosophy of which clearly permits challenges to wage levels set by the principles of market economics. The Government had been forced by European developments to concede the applicability of the equal value principle, but were anxious to ensure that market forces should remain a potential defence where two jobs were held to be of equal value, contrary to the view of Lord Denning in *Fletcher*. The wording applicable to equal value claims was that the defence 'may' relate to the personal equation, but by implication need not do so. Following *Bilka* and *Rainey*, the distinction ceases to be relevant; the remainder of this section assumes that there is now no practical difference between s 1(3)(a) and s 1(3)(b).

The explanation for the pay differential must be 'genuine', 'material' and 'not the difference of sex'. 'Genuine' means that the employer's purported reason for the pay differential must be the real reason. As the employer will never put forward gender as the explanation for the pay differential, an ungenuine explanation will often be one that is directly discriminatory, but a reason which is 'not the difference of sex' may also be one which operates to the practical disadvantage of women even if not intended to do so. Thus, a genuine material factor may be a factor which operates to justify what would otherwise be an indirectly discriminatory pay criterion.

(a)   Equal pay and fair pay

A debate has arisen in number of cases as to whether an employer is obliged to justify a difference in pay, when it is not tainted with sex discrimination. The first cases involved the employer overpaying a man, by reason of an administrative error. In all but one of these cases, the EAT accepted this reason as a genuine material factor.[114] These decisions were approved by the House of Lords in two recent cases, where the

---

113 [1987] AC 224; [1987] 1 All ER 65; [1987] IRLR 26.
114 In *Yorkshire Blood Transfusion Service v Plaskett* [1994] ICR 74, EAT, the court accepted that such a defence amounted to a genuine material factor, whereas in *McPherson v Rathgael Centre for Children and Young People* [1991] IRLR 206, NICA, the opposite result was reached. *McPherson* was overruled in *Wallace* (below). Other cases to adopt a similar approach to *Plaskett* are *Tyldesley v TML Plastics Ltd* [1996] ICR 356; [1996] IRLR 385, EAT; and *Barber v NCR Manufacturing* [1993] IRLR 95, EAT.

debate resurfaced. The House of Lords characterised the claims as fair pay, rather than equal pay.

Strathclyde Regional Council v Wallace [1998] 2 WLR 259; [1998] 1 All ER 394, HL

The nine female applicants were 'unpromoted' teachers doing the work of principal teachers, but not paid as such. (Lord Browne-Wilkinson explains why, below). They claimed equality with men who were *employed* as principal teachers and thus were paid more. The House of Lords held that it was sufficient to show that the pay disparity was genuinely due to a material factor which was not the difference of sex; there was no need to show that it was justified according to the *Bilka* test.

Lord Browne-Wilkinson (pp 262–66):

Over the years there have been changes in the demand for certain subjects such as computing, for which demand has increased, or Latin, for which the demand has decreased. However, in terms of the relevant conditions of employment, the respondents were obliged to preserve the existing structure of promoted posts, with the result that if a principal teacher of Latin had been appointed then, even if the number of pupils taking Latin fell to a fraction of what it had been, the principal teacher was entitled to continue to hold that appointment and to receive the appropriate salary. On the other hand, the respondents were not free simply to create new promoted posts to meet the demand for new subjects because they were restrained by the Scottish Office Education Department circulars relating to staffing standards ...

Finally, I must state an agreed fact of the greatest importance. The disparity in pay between the appellants and principal teachers has nothing to do with gender. Of the 134 unpromoted teachers who claimed to be carrying out the duties of principal teachers, 81 were men and 53 women. The selection by the appellants in this case of male principal teachers as comparators was purely the result of a tactical selection by these appellants: there are male and female principal teachers employed by the respondents without discrimination. Therefore the objective sought by the appellants is to achieve equal pay for like work regardless of sex, not to eliminate any inequalities due to sex discrimination. There is no such discrimination in the present case. To my mind it would be very surprising if a differential pay structure which had no disparate effect or impact as between the sexes should prove to be unlawful under the Equal Pay Act 1970 ...

To establish a subsection (3) defence, the employer has to prove that the disparity in pay is due to a factor 'which is not the difference of sex', ie is not sexually discriminatory ...

Under the Sex Discrimination Act 1975, direct sexual discrimination is always unlawful. But, both under the Sex Discrimination Act 1975 and under article 119, indirect discrimination is not unlawful if it is 'justified': ... Indirect discrimination can be 'justified' if it is shown that the measures adopted by the employer which cause the adverse impact on women 'correspond to a real need on the part of the [employer], are appropriate with a view to achieving the objectives pursued and are necessary to that end': *Rainey v Greater Glasgow Health Board* ...

The cases establish that the Equal Pay Act 1970 has to be construed so far as possible to work harmoniously both with the Sex Discrimination Act 1975 and article 119. ... It follows that the words 'not the difference of sex' where they appear in section 1(3) of the Equal Pay Act 1970 must be construed so as to accord with the Sex Discrimination Act 1975 and article 119 of the EC Treaty, ie an employer will not be able to demonstrate that a factor is 'not the difference of sex' if the factor relied upon is sexually discriminatory whether directly or indirectly. Further a sexually discriminatory practice will not be fatal to a subsection (3) defence if the employer can 'justify' it applying the test in the *Bilka-Kaufhaus* case ...

The correct position under section 1(3) of the Equal Pay Act 1970 is that, even where the variation is genuinely due to a factor which involves the difference of sex, the employer can still establish a valid defence under subsection (3) if he can justify such differentiation on the grounds of sex, whether the differentiation is direct or indirect. I am not aware as yet of any case in which the European Court of Justice has held that a directly discriminatory practice can be justified in the *Bilka* sense. However, such a position cannot be ruled out since, in the United States, experience has shown that the hard and fast demarcation between direct and indirect discrimination is difficult to maintain.

From what I have said, it is apparent that, in considering section 1(3) of the Equal Pay Act 1970, the only circumstances in which questions of 'justification' can arise are those in which the employer is relying on a factor which is sexually discriminatory. There is no question of the employer having to 'justify' (in the *Bilka* sense) all disparities of pay. Provided that there is no element of sexual discrimination, the employer establishes a subsection (3) defence by identifying the factors which he alleges have caused the disparity, proving that those factors are genuine and proving further that they were causally relevant to the disparity in pay complained of.

Glasgow CC v Marshall [2000] 1 WLR 333, HL[115]

The local authority employed instructors and teachers in special schools for children with learning difficulties. Although they did like work, instructors were paid less than teachers. This was because each profession was paid according to respective national agreements, although the local authority had flexibility on the pay of instructors. Eight female and one male instructors brought claims of equal pay, using teachers of the opposite sex as comparators. The House of Lords held that the difference in pay was not discriminatory and therefore did not need to be justified.

Lord Nicholls (339-40):

It is a curious result in a sex discrimination case that, on the same facts, claims by women and a claim by a man all succeed.

I do not believe the Act of 1970 was intended to have this effect. ... The variation between her contract and the man's contract is presumed to be due to the difference of sex. The burden passes to the employer to show that the explanation for the variation is not tainted with sex. In order to discharge this burden the employer must satisfy the tribunal on several matters. First, that the proffered explanation, or reason, is genuine, and not a sham or pretence. Second, that the less favourable treatment is due to this reason. The factor relied upon must be the cause of the disparity. In this regard, and in this sense, the factor must be a 'material' factor, that is, a significant and relevant factor. Third, that the reason is not 'the difference of sex'. This phrase is apt to embrace any form of sex discrimination, whether direct or indirect. Fourth, that the factor relied upon is or, in a case within section 1(2)(c), may be a 'material' difference, that is, a significant and relevant difference, between the woman's case and the man's case.

---

115 See also [2000] IRLR 272; [2000] ICR 196; [2000] LGR 229; 2000 SC (HL) 67.

When section 1 is thus analysed, it is apparent that an employer who satisfies the third of these requirements is under no obligation to prove a 'good' reason for the pay disparity. In order to fulfil the third requirement he must prove the absence of sex discrimination, direct or indirect. If there is any evidence of sex discrimination, such as evidence that the difference in pay has a disparately adverse impact on women, the employer will be called upon to satisfy the tribunal that the difference in pay is objectively justifiable. But if the employer proves the absence of sex discrimination he is not obliged to justify the pay disparity.

Some of the confusion which has arisen on this point stems from an ambiguity in the expression 'material factor'. A material factor is to be contrasted with an immaterial factor. Following the observations of Lord Keith of Kinkel in *Rainey v Greater Glasgow Health Board* [1987] AC 224, 235, the accepted synonym for 'material' is 'significant and relevant.' This leaves open the question of what is the yardstick to be used in measuring materiality, or significance and relevance. One possibility is that the factor must be material in a causative sense. The factor relied on must have been the cause of the pay disparity. Another possibility is that the factor must be material in a justificatory sense. The factor must be one which justifies the pay disparity. As already indicated, I prefer the former of these two interpretations. It accords better with the purpose of the Act.

The distinction may not greatly matter in practice when an employer is having to justify the disparity in pay. But the matter stands differently when sex discrimination is not under consideration. Then the distinction may be of crucial importance, as the present case exemplifies.

In *Wallace*, Lord Browne-Wilkinson noted that the majority of the claimants' group (unpromoted teachers) were men. This may have been evidence that there was no direct discrimination (being paid less because she is a woman). So far as indirect discrimination is concerned, this was a superfluous observation in the absence of information about the comparators' group. It may well have been that the comparators' group, of principal teachers, contained an even higher proportion of men, in which case, there was a *prima facie* case of indirect discrimination to justify.[116] Lord Browne-Wilkinson's comment that the defence may be available in cases of direct discrimination was *obiter*, and at odds with the view of the House in *Ratcliffe*, below.

The Equal Opportunities Review offered the following commentary on *Marshall*.

(2000) 91 EOR 44

The House of Lords reduces the issues in this case to a simple proposition: if there is no sex discrimination, the EqPA 1970 does not require an employer to justify a pay differential ...

Section 1(3) requires the employer to prove that the variation between the woman's contract and the man's contract 'is genuinely due to a material factor which is not the difference of sex'. In our view, the natural reading of these words suggests that there are four ingredients to this test: (1) the explanation must be genuine, (2) it must explain the difference in a causative sense, (3) the factor relied on must be 'material' in the sense of not being of minor or trivial significance, and (4) there must be no taint of direct or indirect sex discrimination.

---

116 In *Enderby v Frenchay AHA* Case C-127/92 (see below, p 420), the *comparators'* group was predominantly *female*: speech therapists (98% female) and pharmacists (63% female).

The House of Lords reduces the ingredients of the test to three elements, and possibly even to one. According to Lord Nicholls's leading opinion, the requirement that the factor must be 'material', means that it must be significant and relevant in a 'causative' sense, rather than in a 'justificatory' sense. This makes the language of s 1(3) read that the variation must be 'genuinely and significantly due' to a factor which is not the difference of sex. In truth, it renders the word 'material' unnecessary. The test would be no different if the word was omitted.

This removes an element in the statutory test which served an important function. The orthodox understanding amongst commentators has been that the word 'material' required the employer to do more than merely narrate, as a matter of history, how the differential came about. 'Material' is used later in s 1(3), where the statute provides that the 'material factor' in a like work case 'must be', and in an equal value case 'may be', a 'material' difference between the woman's case and the man's. The use of the word 'material' twice in s 1(3) in such close succession appeared to suggest that the word's purpose was to ensure that any explanation for the pay difference was relevant to the circumstances of the particular case. On the reasoning of the House of Lords, this is not required unless there is a taint of sex discrimination.

Does the *Marshall* decision go even further? Lord Nicholls declares that 'if the employer proves the absence of sex discrimination he is not obliged to justify the pay disparity'. Does this mean there must be a finding of sex discrimination in order for an equal pay claim to succeed? Where sex discrimination is not at issue, it is a misuse of the EqPA 1970 to try to call it into aid to challenge a pay disparity. But where does this leave the other ingredients of the test identified, even as interpreted by the House of Lords?

Suppose, for example, the employer puts forward a sham explanation which is found by the tribunal to be not the genuine reason, but it is not a pretext for sex discrimination? What if the material factor put forward is found not be causative of the pay differential? If such a finding can result in an employer not discharging the burden under s 1(3) even where there is no hint of sex discrimination, then why shouldn't 'material' be given its natural meaning of 'significant or relevant' in the sense of 'substantial', as the concept was widely understood after the decision of the House of Lords in *Rainey*[117] ...?

Conversely, if it suffices under s 1(3) to show that there was no sex discrimination, that not only renders 'material' otiose, it renders 'genuinely' and 'due' meaningless as well.

This is not an arid semantic debate. Twenty-five years after the EqPA came into force, it is increasingly less common for women to be paid less than men on equal work merely because they are women. If one were to bet on the most common explanation that would be given for why a man is paid more than a woman, it would be that the employer, or the parties to the collective agreement, would say that they genuinely thought that the work the man was doing was worth more than the work of the woman.

This is just another way of expressing what is termed a 'good faith' defence. Discrimination law traditionally has not accepted this as being a sufficient explanation, in part because a 'bad faith' test would be tantamount to requiring the employer to have a discriminatory motive.

---

117 *Rainey v Greater Glasgow Health Board* [1987] AC 224, HL (see below, p 422).

It is true that the House of Lords, as it is bound to do in light of the *Enderby*[118] decision, acknowledges that the employer must prove the absence of sex discrimination, direct or indirect ... This means that an ostensibly gender-neutral reason can be tested both for whether it is a pretext for sex discrimination and for whether it has an adverse impact on women.

After *Glasgow City Council v Marshall* ... however, it is questionable whether an equal pay claim can be successfully brought against an employer who can satisfy the tribunal that the genuine reason why the man was paid more was because the employer thought the man's work was worth more, even if this was objectively mistaken and the two jobs, in the event, had been found to be of equal value.

(b)   Direct and indirect discrimination

The question whether the distinction between direct and indirect discrimination should be incorporated into equal pay law is not free from difficulty, especially when considering a defence.

Ratcliffe v North Yorkshire CC [1995] IRLR 439, HL[119]

School catering assistants claimed equal pay with men in jobs such as road sweepers and gardeners, with whom they had been rated as equivalent under the local government revaluation scheme. Because of compulsory competitive tendering, they were given notices of dismissal and re-employed at lower rates of pay, being told that unless the rates were lower, the authority would have lost the school meals contract to a cheaper private contractor.

The Court of Appeal allowed the defence. The employers did not directly discriminate against women. Further, the 'material factor' which led to the lower pay was genuinely due to the operation of market forces and the need to compete with a rival bid. It was not in any way based on the difference of sex.

The House of Lords allowed the appeal.

Lord Slynn of Hadley (p 442):

In my opinion the Act of 1970 must be interpreted ... without bringing in the distinction between so called 'direct' and 'indirect' discrimination.

By a majority [the industrial tribunal] were satisfied that the employers had failed to show that the [defence was made out] ... In my opinion it is impossible to say that they were not entitled on the evidence to come to that conclusion ...

The women could not have found other suitable work and were obliged to take the wages offered if they were to continue with this work. The fact that two men were employed on the same work at the same rate of pay does not detract from the conclusion that there was discrimination between the women involved and their male comparators. It means no more than that the two men were underpaid compared with other men doing jobs rated as equivalent ...

---

118 *Enderby v Frenchay AHA* Case C-127/92 ECJ (see below, p 420).
119 See also [1995] 3 All ER 597; [1995] ICR 837.

> The fact that [they] paid women less than their male comparators because they were women constitutes direct discrimination and *ex hypothesi* cannot be shown to be justified on grounds 'irrespective of the sex of the person' concerned.[120]

This is a difficult case, not least because of the brevity of the single judgment. The House found it unnecessary to 'review the many decided cases ... [nor] to consider Art 119 of the Treaty of Rome and the decisions of the European Court on that article ...' It is not clear what the case *did* decide. While rejecting the relevance to the issue of 'genuine material factor' of the distinction between direct and indirect discrimination, the House stressed that here, the employers were guilty of direct pay discrimination. Even if they were not, the tribunal were entitled to conclude that the defence had not been made out. As no reference is made to other cases, one can only guess at the appropriate criteria for establishing the defence. It is contended that where it is alleged that a salary structure on average operates to disadvantage women, it will be impossible to resolve such a claim without reference to the concepts of adverse impact and justification.

One may also question the conclusion that the facts established direct discrimination. For that, the reason they were paid less must be on the ground of gender. The fact that all but two of those who were underpaid were female is evidence of that fact, but it is not conclusive evidence. In *Bullock v Alice Ottley School*,[121] the fact that all the female employees had to retire at 60 did not establish that they were victims of discrimination: they retired at 60 not because of their gender, but because of the job they did. That logically impeccable reasoning seems equally applicable here. The House of Lords accepted the reasoning of the tribunal that the pay differential arose 'out of the general perception ... that a woman should stay at home and look after the children and if she wants to work it must fit in with that domestic duty and a lack of facilities to enable her, easily, to do otherwise'. However, the perception and lack of facilities do not affect all woman; it would have been preferable to analyse this as a situation where the utilisation of market forces failed to operate in a gender-neutral way and so was unjustifiable on that basis. It *would* have been theoretically possible to argue that the way in which the tendering process operated was tainted by gender, but as the tendering requirement applied to all manual jobs, such argument would be hard to establish.

It is not being contended that the claim should have failed, rather that the sketchiness of the judgment both glosses over the issues and decides the case on an inappropriate basis. What was at issue was a clash between the values of public service, which emphasises national pay rates covering a wide range of different types of job, and the values of pure market forces, where employers may pay no more than is necessary in order to attract workers and remain in business. Of course, that process affects many women in a qualitatively different way from men, but the real issue is the extent to which reliance on market forces can be justified. It would have better for the future had the House's commendable awareness of the problems lower paid part-time women face in the labour market been translated into suitably sceptical rules on when employers are permitted to rely on market forces.

---

120 For a discussion as to whether direct discrimination should be justifiable, see Bowers, J and Moran, E, 'Justification in direct sex discrimination law: breaking the taboo' [2002] 31 ILJ 307.

121 [1993] ICR 138; [1992] IRLR 564, CA.

Despite *Ratcliffe*, it is clear from the decisions of the House of Lords in *Rainey* and the European Court in *Enderby*[122] that indirect discrimination doctrine is applicable to pay as well as other areas of discrimination, and the House of Lords in *Wallace* stated that the view in *Ratcliffe* – denying the relevance of the distinction – 'must not be carried too far'.[123] However, Lord Browne-Wilkinson also stated that 'where the variation [in pay] is genuinely due to a factor which involves the difference of sex, the employer can still establish a valid defence ... if he can justify such discrimination, whether the differentiation is direct or indirect'.[124] The suggestion that direct discrimination can be justified is contrary to principle, has the capacity seriously to undermine the Equal Pay Act, was unnecessary to the decision in the case, and should not be regarded as binding.

(c)   Proportionality, discovery and the questionnaire

The next question is what facts the employer must establish in order to explain the variation in pay. However, payment structures and levels have often developed piecemeal and it may be difficult or impossible for the employer to show the extent to which particular factors contribute to overall pay. It is this fact which explains and justifies the approach of the European Court in *Enderby*:[125] it may be impossible to explain *why* women are paid less than men by a particular employer, but the differential average in effect raises a case to answer that the factors are discriminatory. Whatever, the original position taken by the courts was not helpful to claimants and has been retrieved somewhat by the recent introduction of a questionnaire, which will be discussed at the end of this section.

Byrne and Others v The Financial Times Ltd [1991] IRLR 417, EAT[126]

In an equal value claim, the employer's defence relied on factors such as different responsibilities, different hours of work or rotas, total flexibility, red-circling, and collective bargaining.

The applicants sought a breakdown of the difference between their salaries and those of their male comparators and an allocation of a specific sum or a specific fraction of that difference to a particular fact in the work record or history of each comparator.

The tribunal chair refused the application for discovery: 'The pay of the woman and the pay of the comparator have got to be looked at as one sum – it is not permissible to split them.'

The EAT dismissed the appeal.

Wood J (p 418):

[The lay members] stress that in realistic industrial situations, it was impossible to attribute a particular weight to a particular factor when fixing a wage ... [T]he

---

122 *Enderby v Frenchay AHA* Case C-127/92 [1993] ECR I-5535; [1994] ICR 112; [1994] 1 All ER 495; [1993] IRLR 591.
123 [1998] 1 WLR 259, p 262.
124 [1998] 1 All ER 394, p 400.
125 Where the employer could only explain part of the difference in pay being unrelated to sex. See further, below, p 420.
126 Affirmed by the Court of Appeal in *Financial Times v Byrne*, unreported, 14 July 1992.

situation quite often occurs where it is impossible to attribute a particular percentage or amount to a specific part of the variation and that more than the variation may ultimately be proved.

This does not even require the employer to show that it is impossible to break down the pay so that a particular sum of money cannot be applied to a particular factor; it assumes this to be the case and denies the employee the information necessary to disprove it. The burden of lack of knowledge falls entirely on the employee;[127] this cannot be consistent with *Handels- og Kontorfunktionaererernes Forbund i Danmark v Dansk Arbejdsgiverforening (acting for Danfoss)*,[128] where the European Court held that 'where an undertaking applies a pay system which is characterised by a total lack of transparency, the burden of proof is on the employer to show that his pay practice is not discriminatory, if a female worker establishes that, by comparison with a relatively high number of employees, the average pay of female workers is lower than that of male workers'.

> **Townshend-Smith, R, 'Economic defences to equal pay claims', in Hervey, T and O'Keeffe, D (eds),** *Sex Equality Law in the European Union*, **1996, Chichester: John Wiley, pp 42–43:**
>
> [T]he law should exercise reasonable deference to the payment *choices* made by employers, even those which have an adverse impact on women, though the *degree* of adverse impact will be significant. A key caveat to this point is that they should indeed be choices. The labour market is characterised by ill-thought out and ill-planned behaviour, where payment strategies may simply reflect long standing tradition or what other similarly situated employers habitually do. It is central to the operation of an appropriately balanced equal value law that employers are not permitted to engage in *ex post facto* rationalisations or justifications for their payment strategies.[129] Deference should be paid to choices, but the employer should face the burden of showing that such a choice was indeed made. This approach prevents women from continuing to be victims of historically discriminatory structures reproduced without thought, while at the same time permitting innovative approaches to pay.
>
> Employers should therefore be required to produce evidence of how such decisions were taken and why. That this may require them to disclose the internal workings of the firm, internal memoranda, etc, is inevitable. This goes beyond ... *Danfoss*, which concerned openness in the implementation of decisions rather than in the prior decision to utilise particular criteria. Indeed, greater openness in pay is essential to enable courts to make, and to be seen to make, a fair assessment of an equal value claim, given that in the end such decisions are impressionistic rather than scientific or purely logical. The detailed facts on pay are necessary for a strict scrutiny, in a literal sense, to occur.

---

127 [I]t is difficult to see how equal value proceedings can be fairly disposed of without revealing information that may hitherto have been regarded by the employer as confidential.' Rubenstein, M, *Equal Pay for Work of Equal Value*, 1984, London: Macmillan, p 68.

128 Case C-171/88 [1989] ECR 3199; [1991] 1 CMLR 8; [1989] IRLR 532.

129 It is for this reason that, in *Hayward v Cammell Laird Shipbuilders Ltd* [1988] AC 894; [1988] 2 All ER 257; [1988] IRLR 257, HL, the House of Lords rejected the argument that the woman's greater fringe benefits adequately compensated for her lower rate of basic pay. As the distinction was based on history, the employers would not have been able to produce evidence to show that the one was introduced specifically to compensate for the other.

McColgan, A, 'Legislating equal pay: lessons from Canada' [1993] 22 ILJ 269, p 271:

The existing law requires a woman to perceive a disparity between her wages and the wages of a man who is engaged in work of equal value to hers. Given the secrecy which surrounds the issue of wages, particularly in non-unionised workplaces, many potential complainants will have no idea what other employees earn. Further, even if such information were available, a woman must choose as a comparator a man engaged in work of less than or equal value to hers. The evaluation of jobs is an immensely complex task from which fortunes have been made by firms of management consultants. Such evaluation is impossible without detailed analyses of the skill, knowledge and responsibilities demanded by each job, and the working conditions under which it is performed. This information is not readily available to fellow workers; nor can they know the weights which an expert might ascribe to each category under which value could be assessed. To attempt to redress the collective underpayment of women by requiring such improbable feats from individuals, and by failing to ensure the extension of any wage increase to those performing the same or similar work to the claimant, is to condemn the whole enterprise to failure.

The *Byrne* approach is especially problematic for an applicant where an employer proves the existence of a factor which explains *some* but not necessarily all of the variation.[130] Originally, in *Enderby*,[131] the EAT held that, where market forces account for some of the difference in pay, the whole of the difference is justified, as to hold otherwise would involve the tribunal in a wage fixing role. This approach was rejected by the ECJ.[132] A similar approach was adopted in *Calder v Rowntree Mackintosh Confectionery Ltd*,[133] where Balcombe LJ observed that 'the fact that some indeterminate part of the shift premium was attributable to unsociable hours did not mean that the IT was in error in finding that the difference in pay was due to a genuine material factor'. The court felt able to reach this conclusion despite the fact that the employer abandoned reliance on the other factors which had been put forward to explain the differential, namely, market forces and collective bargaining. Thus, even though the employer all but admitted that the whole of the differential was *not* attributable to the unsocial hours premium, the defence nevertheless succeeded. The deference shown to employer reasoning processes on pay – or lack of them – is quite inconsistent with the ECJ decisions in *Enderby* and *Danfoss*. To say that it cannot *always* be established precisely how a pay level is made out does not mean that employers should be not required to make the attempt, to be as transparent as is reasonably practicable, and to justify the components which can be observed, even if such justification, as in *Sherwin*, can be no more than what is commonplace.

---

130 In *Sherwin v National Coal Board* [1978] ICR 700; [1978] IRLR 122, EAT, it was held that the differential for night shift work was too great, that 20% was appropriate, and that the applicant's basic pay should be increased so that the remaining differential was appropriate. While this approach permits analysis of the components which make up total pay, the court is not deciding that 20% is the appropriate differential for night shift work for any other reason than that is what is conventionally paid.

131 *Enderby v Frenchay AHA* [1991] ICR 382, [1991] IRLR 44, [1991] 1 CMLR 626, EAT (see further, below, p 420, and above, p 276).

132 Case C-127/92 [1993] ECR I-5535; [1994] ICR 112; [1994] 1 All ER 495; [1993] IRLR 591, at para 27. (See further, below, p 420.)

133 [1993] ICR 811; [1993] IRLR 212, CA.

Section 7B[134] now provides the right of an employee deciding whether or not to bring a claim, to send a questionnaire to her employer, asking for the pay of potential comparators *and* any reasons explaining any disparity. The employer's answer will be admissible in any subsequent litigation. If the employer refuses to answer questions, or answers them evasively or equivocally, the tribunal may make such inferences as is just and equitable. This should go some way to resolving the problems outlined above.

(2)   The Defence in Operation

In Chapter 10, we considered, *inter alia*, the question of when first, seniority and, secondly, part-time work can justify unequal pay. We now turn to other specific examples of the defence in operation.

(a)   *Market forces/collective bargaining cases*

Cases where market forces are put forward as a defence are critical for the conceptual aim and practical effectiveness of equal pay – especially equal value – legislation. There is a clear philosophical clash between determining wages according to the input of the individual worker – equal value – and determining them according to the operation of supposedly impersonal and external market forces. If the latter is permitted to trump the former, the potential cutting edge of the law will be severely blunted.

We examined earlier[135] the causes of pay inequality and concluded, first, that the market, being no more than a sum of its component actors, does not operate in an impersonal and gender-neutral fashion, and, secondly, that there are ideological, historical, structural and organisational explanations for women's lower average pay than men.

> **Townshend-Smith, R, 'Economic defences to equal pay claims', in Hervey, T and O'Keeffe, D (eds),** *Sex Equality Law in the European Union,* **1996, Chichester: John Wiley, pp 40–42:**
>
> The concept of the market is fundamentally ambiguous. At one level it refers to those factors regarded by employers as worthy of reward, such as seniority, qualifications and individual performance. In a sense there is a 'market' in these qualities, yet the second meaning relates to the supply of and the demand for workers, irrespective of their personal qualities. A third meaning, hardly discussed in litigation but significant in governmental thinking, relates pay to the employer's ability to pay, which may be affected by profitability or by cash limits. Each argument may become the defence to an equal pay claim, and each must be tested by the objective standard outlined above. Labelling a defence based on 'market forces' does not change the applicable legal rules, both because the very concept is ambiguous and because in policy terms the defence should be tested by the same standard.
>
> The unspoken assumption appears to be that there is a uniformity in the way wages are fixed based on the universal, immutable economic laws of supply and demand. In

---

134 Inserted by the Employment Act 2002, s 42, in force since 6 April 2003 (SI 2002/2866, Art 2(3), Sched 1, Pt 3).
135 Above, Chapter 2.

reality, systems vary at three levels at least, between Member States, within Member States, and within individual enterprises.

First, payment strategies tend to differ between Member States. For example, Germany tends to value qualifications, while France places greater weight on seniority.[136] The concept of the single market in goods and services entails that the market should operate in the same way, valuing the same features, in each Member State. Even if that could be attained for the labour market, it is not self-evident that such objective is desirable for payment structures, given the variation in the social meaning of wage structures between different countries. Equal value law needs to work within such social expectations and not against them.

Not only are there differences between countries, there are also significant differences within countries, even between similar employers. One employer might operate an internal labour market characterised by high investment and training and a well established career structure; another might invest less in training and prefer to 'buy in' already trained employees.[137] At a level of individual litigation it would be inappropriate to describe one policy as better than the other.

Thirdly, employers frequently have different approaches to pay covering different areas of the workforce. 'Most organisations have several different pay structures and each pay structure tends to be dominated by either male or female-dominated jobs.'[138] Again it is contended that it is both undesirably interventionist and beyond the objective of equal value legislation to require uniformity of approach. For this reason, enterprise-wide job evaluation schemes, even gender-sensitive ones, are not a universal panacea.

Enderby v Frenchay AHA Case C-127/92 [1993] IRLR 591, ECJ[139]

The EAT held that either market forces or the existence of different collective bargaining structures could amount to a defence. The standard of justification imposed was relatively lax, and included 'objectively justified grounds which are other than economic, such as administrative efficiency in a concern not engaged in commerce or business'.

Judgment (p 595):

The fact that the rates of pay at issue are decided by collective bargaining processes conducted separately for each of the two professional groups concerned, without any discriminatory effect within each group, does not preclude a finding of *prima facie* discrimination where the results of those processes show that two groups with the same employer and the same trade union are treated differently.

The state of the employment market, which may lead the employer to increase the pay of a particular job in order to attract candidates, may constitute an objectively justified economic ground ...

If ... the national court has been able to determine precisely what proportion of the increase in pay is attributable to market forces, it must necessarily accept that the pay

---

136 Rubery, J and Fagan, C, *Social Europe: Wage Determination and Sex Segregation in Employment in the European Community*, 1993, Luxembourg: Office for Official Publications of the European Communities, pp 111–13; Rubery, J, *The Economics of Equal Value*, 1992, Manchester: EOC, p 68.

137 Rubery, J, *The Economics of Equal Value*, 1992, Manchester: EOC, p 41.

138 *Ibid*, p 104.

139 See also [1993] ECR I-5535; [1994] ICR 112; [1994] 1 All ER 49. For the facts, see above, p 276.

differential is objectively justified to the extent of that proportion. When national authorities have to apply Community law, they must apply the principle of proportionality.

Advocate General (pp 599–600):

If a *pro rata* justification is to be permitted, the effect of the objective criterion on the level of pay must be quantifiable. The EAT, the UK and the defendant were all of the opinion that a series of factors go to determine the level of pay and it is not possible to ascribe a particular amount of pay to any one of those factors. But elsewhere it is asserted that the requirements of the labour market justify a difference in pay of at most 10%. On that basis it would appear to be quantifiable. The very fact that several factors influence the level of pay ought to make it possible to ascribe part of the pay to each of the factors.

[If] it can also be established that only part of the difference between job A and job B is attributable to the need to attract suitable candidates to job B, only that part of the difference which is attributable to the need to attract suitable candidates to job B is objectively justified.[140]

British Coal Corp v Smith [1994] IRLR 342; [1994] ICR 810, CA[141]

The facts are set out above, p 389. The defence was based on separate wage structures and a policy of removing the link between the pay of mineworkers and all other workers for economic reasons. Over the years, some ancillary workers had been transferred to the category of surface mineworkers – all such employees were male. The Court of Appeal rejected the defence.

Balcombe LJ (pp 300–02):

[D]oes the appellant show that a group which is predominantly female is treated less favourably than a group doing like work or work of equal value, of whom a majority are men? If so, then the burden shifts to the employer to show the difference is 'objectively justified' on a non-discriminatory basis ... If 'market forces' are relied upon, [the employer] must show that these are gender-neutral.

The canteen workers and the cleaners are predominantly female – thus [there is] a *prima facie* case of discrimination within *Enderby*. But if they should be regarded as part of the larger group of ancillary workers, no such case is made out, because there is no preponderance or even a majority of women employees in that larger group.

The appellants are separately classified as regards their terms and conditions of employment, and the fact that their classes form part of a larger group does not alter that fact ...

[T]he variation in the rates of pay ... is the result of separate collective bargaining processes which themselves are untainted by sex.

The question is not whether the policy of disassociation was capable of objective justification [we agree that it was], but whether its application to these particular classes of employees was shown to be objectively justified.

The tribunal said that they were not satisfied that there was any economic justification for paying surface mineworkers – some of whom did work which on a superficial

---

140 Dr Enderby's claim was lodged in March 1986. Following a Government concession, it was finally settled in April 1997. See (1997) 73 EOR 2. However, other claims from that litigation persisted. See, eg, *Evesham*, below, p 431.
141 See also [1994] ICR 810.

comparison was no more arduous, strenuous or difficult than the work of cleaners – at a higher rate.

It seems to us likely that the difference was due to an ingrained approach based upon sex, which meant that women, whatever they did, would not be classed or categorised as surface mineworkers.

[The House of Lords[142] dismissed the appeal on this point, without examining the legal issues in great detail. They accepted that the existence of separate bargaining structures was not in itself a defence, reasoned that the question was primarily one of fact for the tribunal and concluded that the employers had not discharged their burden of proof.]

There are few cases where the facts have been subject to a detailed examination to show when market forces may be a defence. In *Lord v Knowsley BC*,[143] the pay of home carers, almost all women, was reduced in order to compete with outside contractors. Male refuse drivers and school caretakers, on the other hand, continued to be paid at the same local government rate. The industrial tribunal rejected the employers' market forces defence. The employers were in effect saying to the women: 'Yours, we realise, is work predominantly done by women. We need to compete against others who pay less than we do for it. We will therefore pay you less.' The tribunal concluded that it is the vulnerability of women workers such as these in the labour market outside the local government service that enabled them to pay less to home carers. That was not 'a factor which is not the difference of sex. The women were paid less than the men because their equivalent work attracts lower pay for the women who do it elsewhere'. Thus, the 'market forces' defence failed: it was not operated in a gender-neutral fashion, both because the same criteria and approach were not applied to male employees and because the application of market forces had a disparate impact on women which could not be justified.

Rainey v Greater Glasgow Health Board [1987] IRLR 26, HL[144]

It was decided to set up an NHS prosthetic service in Scotland and to discontinue the existing arrangement under which prosthetic services were provided by private contractors. Private sector prosthetists who wished to transfer to the new service were able to remain on the rates of pay and service that they were then receiving, subject to future changes as negotiated by their union. However, new entrants were paid at significantly lower rates based on the Whitley scale for ancillary health service staff. The 20 prosthetists previously employed by private contractors were all men. Female new entrant prosthetists claimed equal pay with these men, there being no question that they were employed on like work.

Lord Keith of Kinkel (pp 28–31):

The Secretary of State for Scotland decided, as a matter of general policy. that the Whitley Council scale ... was appropriate. It was also decided that the appropriate part of the scale ... was that applicable to medical physics technicians ...

[W]here there is no question of intentional sex discrimination, whether direct or indirect (and there is none here) a difference which is connected with economic factors

---

142 [1996] 3 All ER 97; [1996] ICR 515; [1996] IRLR 404, HL.
143 Unreported, Liverpool IT – see (1996) 70 EOR 23.
144 See also [1987] AC 224; [1987] 1 All ER 65.

affecting the efficient carrying on of the employer's business or other activity may well be relevant.

I consider that, read as a whole, the ruling of the European Court [in *Bilka*] would not exclude objectively justified grounds which are other than economic, such as administrative efficiency in a concern not engaged in commerce or business ...

[A] new prosthetic service could never have been established within a reasonable time if [they] had not been offered a scale of remuneration no less favourable than that which they were then enjoying. That was undoubtedly a good and objectively justified ground for offering ... that scale of remuneration.

[As far as paying the women less is concerned] from the administrative point of view it would have been highly anomalous and inconvenient if prosthetists alone ... were to have been subject to a different salary scale and different negotiating machinery ... There is no suggestion that it was unreasonable to place them on the particular point on the Whitley Council scale ... It was not a question of the appellant being paid less than the norm but of [the comparator] being paid more. He was paid more because of the necessity to attract him and other privately employed prosthetists into forming the nucleus of the new service.

The *general* operation of market forces cannot be a defence, as the fact of women's lower average pay is the mischief at which the law is aimed. The defence must be confined to situations where it is argued that, in a *particular* job situation, pay levels need to be *above* the rate paid for a job of equal value in order to counteract, for example, staff shortages. It is this approach which leads, for example, to offering higher pay to teachers of mathematics and physics than English and French. The operation of the defence is necessary to prevent other groups of employees comparing themselves with the higher paid group. Employers who seek to use market forces as a defence must, as a minimum, show how they discover the market rate. They must also show that the same criteria are applicable to grades which are predominantly female as well as to grades which are predominantly male. 'An employer who pays 10% above the market rate for all jobs except those mainly occupied by women may be said to be treating the women less favourably on grounds of sex.'[145]

'The system of collective bargaining has a dual role in the determination of gender pay differentials: it provides a form of protection against low pay and is the major vehicle through which changes in gender pay differentials have been achieved; yet it acts to codify and reinforce customary payment practices, including gender pay differentials.'[146] It is clearly no defence for an employer to argue that he had to pay a male bargaining group more than a female group because of the former's greater industrial strength. The employer is responsible for the pay outcome and, just as under the SDA 1975, cannot hide behind discriminatory behaviour or attitudes, direct or indirect, manifested by the workforce. Unions have traditionally been more successful in recruiting men and in serving their interests. There may be no difference of substance between a market forces defence and one based on the operation of collective bargaining. It is unclear when a collective bargaining outcome, jointly

---

145 'Market forces and the equal value material factor defence' (1986) 5 EOR 5, p 8.
146 Rubery, J and Fagan, C, *Social Europe: Wage Determination and Sex Segregation in Employment in the European Community*, 1993, Luxembourg: Office for Official Publications of the European Communities, Pt V.

negotiated by employer and union, could ever satisfy the defence.[147] It is tentatively suggested that one example might be where the employer operates collective bargaining in one part of the enterprise and, say, job evaluation in another. A successful claim might thus cause stresses and dissatisfaction with the differing pay structures. The difficulty is the extent to which a court will permit any comparison across payment structures. This may depend partly on the degree of occupational segregation within the enterprise and the degree of pay disparity between primarily male and primarily female grades.

Many argue that an important way forward for pay equity is to increase the number of women in trade unions and the coverage of collective bargaining. However, strong and effective bargaining has been associated with the widening of gender differentials.[148] Typically, male workplaces may be easier to organise, and atypical workers, predominantly female, may fall outside the coverage of collective bargaining. On the other hand, women benefit through their over-representation in the public sector, as collective bargaining there is both wider in its coverage and more regulatory in its nature, especially where the bargaining is conducted nationally.

(b)   Premium, merit and service payments

We are concerned here with controls over decisions to base pay on individual factors, such as payments based on qualifications, merit or productivity. Like other payment systems, they may operate to the advantage or disadvantage of women, depending on the criteria and the way in which they are operated, and they are most unlikely to be justifiable under the stringent *Bilka* criteria. The advantage for women is that performance within the current job may be recognised and rewarded, and that performance pay may be associated with less emphasis, so far as pay is concerned, on position in a job hierarchy. The disadvantage is clearly that reliance may be placed on subjective criteria and managerial discretion. In addition, performance pay often benefits most those in higher grades, which might widen differentials between average pay of men and women. It may also be used as a signal to attract men, and the emphasis on competition rather than co-operation may also benefit men.[149]

> *Handels- og Kontorfunktionaerernes Forbund i Danmark v Dansk Arbejdsgiverforening (acting for Danfoss)* **Case C-109/88 [1989] IRLR 532**[150]

A collective agreement allowed the employer to make additional payments to individuals within a grade on the basis of the employee's 'flexibility', which was defined to including an assessment of their capacity, quality of work, autonomy of work and responsibilities. In addition, pay could be increased on the basis of the employee's vocational training and seniority. The average pay of women was 6.85% less than that of men.

---

147 In *Royal Copenhagen* Case C-400/93 [1995] IRLR 648, the Court held that collective bargaining 'may be taken into account' in determining whether differences in average pay can be explained by objective factors. This approach is less stringent than that adopted in *Enderby*, but no specific examples were given.

148 Rubery, J and Fagan, C, *Social Europe: Wage Determination and Sex Segregation in Employment in the European Community*, 1993, Luxembourg: Office for Official Publications of the European Communities, p 99.

149 *Ibid*, p 149.

150 See also [1989] ECR 3199; [1991] 1 CMLR 8.

Employees did not actually know what were the criteria for the increases which applied to them and how they were applied. They were only informed of the amount of their increased wages, without being able to determine the effect of each of the criteria for the increases. Those who came within a particular pay grade were, therefore, unable to compare the different components of their pay with those of the pay of their fellow employees within the same grade.

Judgment (pp 536–37):

[W]here an undertaking applies a pay system which is characterised by a total lack of transparency, the burden of proof is on the employer to show that his pay practice is not discriminatory, if a female worker establishes that, by comparison with a relatively high number of employees, the average pay of female workers is lower than that of male workers.

In order to demonstrate that his pay practice is not systematically unfair to female workers, the employer is bound to show how he has applied the incremental criteria, thereby making his pay system transparent.

[A] distinction is to be made according to whether the criterion of flexibility is used to reward the quality of the work carried out by the employee or whether it is used to reward the adaptability of the employee to variable work schedules and places of work.

In the first case, the criterion of flexibility is indisputably totally neutral from the point of view of sex. Where it results in systematic unfairness to female workers, that can only be because the employer has applied it in an abusive manner. It is inconceivable that the work carried out by female workers would be generally of a lower quality. The employer may not therefore justify the use of the criterion of flexibility so defined where its application shows itself to be systematically unfavourable to women.

If it were understood as referring to the adaptability of the worker to variable work schedules and places of work, the criterion of flexibility may also operate to the disadvantage of female workers who ... may have greater difficulty than male workers in organising their working time in a flexible manner.

[To such a result the *Bilka* test applies.]

The employer may justify payments for such adaptability by showing that it is of importance in the performance of the specific duties entrusted to the worker concerned.

[T]he employer may justify rewarding specific vocational training by demonstrating that that training is of importance for the performance of the specific duties entrusted to the worker.

This approach is clearly inconsistent with and preferable to prior English authority. In *Reed Packaging Ltd v Boozer and Everhurst*,[151] hourly paid employees earned more than those on staff grades. It was held that there were 'objectively justified administrative reasons' for the distinction, despite the fact that the majority of hourly paid workers were men. It should be impossible to justify a scheme such as this, which originates in

---

151 [1988] ICR 391; [1988] IRLR 333, EAT. A similar approach based largely on the fact that subjectively there was no intention to discriminate exonerated the employer in *Calder v Rowntree Mackintosh Confectionery Ltd* [1993] ICR 811; [1993] IRLR 212, CA (approved in *Strathclyde RC v Wallace* [1998] 1 WLR 259, p 267, HL).

tradition and convenience. If jobs are of equal value, their being placed in different grades may be due to different bargaining structures, or simply to the fact that the employer considered one employee to be more worthy than another. Neither defence can provide objective justification in the face of a finding that jobs are of equal value.

The *Danfoss* approach requires the employer to explain and justify the criteria used to reward individual performance. On the facts, if this led to a lower average pay for women than men, that would be clear evidence of discrimination, at least where the numbers were sufficiently large to eliminate the possibility of chance results. Flexibility defined by reference to adaptability and vocational training are both potentially justifiable.

Townshend-Smith, R, 'Economic defences to equal pay claims', in Hervey, T and O'Keeffe, D (eds), *Sex Equality Law in the European Union*, 1996, Chichester: John Wiley, p 45:

[T]he employer must show that employees knew the applicable criteria in advance in order to establish a correlation with increased performance. Beyond that, there must be a system for measuring performance which is both objectively and consistently applied, which may cause problems especially in relation to higher level jobs where accurate measurement of performance is often not possible. Employers should be required to produce statistics where these are logically relevant. If it is claimed that productivity would be improved, the methods used for its assessment must be demonstrated. Similarly, the employer should be required to show how, for example, qualifications and work performance, or bonus payments and absenteeism, are linked. To reiterate, this cannot be done at a scientifically satisfactory level of proof, but, where appropriate, the reasonable effort must be made. It is especially important in relation to performance-related pay, which carries an obvious risk that subjectivity may perpetuate gender pay inequalities.

However, if this approach were applied literally, employers would be unable to introduce changes to their payment systems which had an adverse impact until those changes had been shown to be effective in attaining the required purpose. This is to impose an unrealistic, often impossible, standard. Reference to the experience of other employers is neither necessary nor sufficient proof of the causal connection. Employers must be permitted to innovate, without proof of effectiveness, if the possible adverse impact is considered and if it can be shown that the attainment of the objective is a reasonably plausible consequence.

Rubery, J and Fagan, C, *Social Europe: Wage Determination and Sex Segregation in Employment in the European Community*, 1993, Luxembourg: Office for Official Publications of the European Communities, p 43:

It may ... be possible to state, as an argument against its introduction, that performance-related pay causes the pay structure to become opaque: the pay structure may therefore be protected from an examination as to whether the principle of equal value has been implemented ... It is, however, much more difficult to argue that a firm must adopt a detailed job evaluation system and detailed pay grading by job in order to implement equal value, if it is at the same time moving towards more flexible deployment of labour. Equally, it is difficult to maintain that a firm should not relate pay to the qualifications of its employees and only to their current jobs, when it wishes to encourage employees to acquire qualifications.

Benefits rewarding service have potential to discriminate because women are more likely to have had an interrupted work record and spent more time working part-time hours. The ECJ in *Hill* suggested that such discrimination would be difficult to justify.

Hill v Revenue Commissioners **Case C-243/95 [1998] ECR I-3739; [1998] IRLR 466, ECJ**

A criterion for pay was the *amount* of service given. Accordingly, a (predominantly female) group who in the past had job-shared were penalised.

Judgment:

37 In the view of the Revenue Commissioners ... a method of pay progression based on the duration of work actually performed is objectively justified by criteria which satisfy the conditions laid down by the Court in its case-law.

38 In this connection, neither the justification provided by the Revenue Commissioners ... to the effect that there is an established practice within the Civil Service of crediting' only actual service, nor that stating that this practice establishes a reward system which maintains staff motivation, commitment and morale, is relevant. The first justification is no more than a general assertion unsupported by objective criteria. With regard to the second, the system of remuneration for employees working on a full-time basis cannot be influenced by the job-sharing scheme.

39 So far as concerns the justification that, if an exception were to be made in favour of job-sharing, this would result in arbitrary or inequitable situations or would amount to impermissible discrimination in favour of women, it should be pointed out, ... that to grant to workers who convert to full-time employment the same point as that which they had under their job-sharing contract does not constitute discrimination in favour of female workers.

40 So far as the justification based on economic grounds is concerned, it should be noted that an employer cannot justify discrimination arising from a job-sharing scheme solely on the ground that avoidance of such discrimination would involve increased costs.

41 It must be borne in mind that all the parties to the main proceedings, and the national tribunal, agree that almost all job-sharing workers in the Irish public sector are women. It is apparent from the case-file that approximately 83% of those who chose that option did so in order to be able to combine work and family responsibilities, which invariably involve caring for children.

42 Community policy in this area is to encourage and, if possible, adapt working conditions to family responsibilities. Protection of women within family life and in the course of their professional activities is, in the same way as for men, a principle which is widely regarded in the legal systems of the Member States as being the natural corollary of the equality between men and women, and which is recognised by Community law.

43 The onus is therefore on the Revenue Commissioners ... to establish before the Labour Court that the reference to the criterion of service, defined as the length of time actually worked, in the assessment of the incremental credit to be granted to workers who convert from job-sharing to full-time work is justified by objective factors unrelated to any discrimination on grounds of sex.

(c)   Red-circle cases

The *principle* of what has come to be known as red-circling is entirely fair. It is commonplace that a person who, for example, is unable to continue with a job for reasons of illness or redundancy, but for whom there is an alternative job in the workplace, nevertheless continues to be paid at the old rate so that no reduction in pay is experienced. Furthermore, it is normal for the 'red-circled' employee, at least in sickness cases, to receive the pay increases that would have been received in the old job had that been continuing. A particular problem with the practice from an equal pay perspective is that a successful claim of equality with a red-circled employee may lead to a substantial increase for the applicant, and consequential claims from those on like work or work of equal value with that applicant, claims which may undermine a whole pay structure.

It must be shown that the employee received the higher rate because he had been red-circled and not because it was the rate for the job. This may be problematic where some jobs have a tradition of being filled by those who, for health reasons, are unable to continue in their old job.[152] It should also be permissible for an applicant to argue that she is doing like work or work of equal value with the job the comparator would have been doing but for the red circle. This may be important if there is no other potential comparator, though comparing the value of the applicant's job which has disappeared through redundancy may not be straightforward.[153]

Like any other pay practice, there must be no direct discrimination in the way in which it operates.

Snoxell v Vauxhall Motors Ltd; Charles Early and Marriott (Witney) Ltd v Smith and Ball [1977] IRLR 123, EAT[154]

In the first case, a male warehouseman was transferred to the lesser paid job of ticket writer. In the second case, the employers had graded men and women on separate wage scales, but in 1970 they reorganised their pay structure, and machine part inspectors in a protected all-male grade were red-circled. No women had been in the protected grade and no women were red-circled.

In both cases, the defence failed.

Phillips J (pp 126–29):

[I]t is relevant to consider: whether the red-circling is permanent or temporary, being phased out; whether the origin of the anomaly enshrined in the red-circling is to be found in sex discrimination; whether the group of red-circled employees is a closed group; whether the red-circling has been the subject of negotiations with the representatives of the workpeople, and the views of the women taken into account; or whether the women are equally with the men able to transfer between grades.

[The argument is that] although the immediate cause of the discrimination lay in the fact that the male inspectors were red-circled whereas [the applicants] were not, and although they were red-circled to preserve their status for reasons unconnected with sex, it was necessary to look to see why [the applicants] were not also within the red circle. The answer was that, because they were women, they were not able to enter grade X2, and so did not qualify.

---

152 *Methven and Musiolik v Cow Industrial Polymers Ltd* [1979] ICR 613; [1979] IRLR 276, EAT; [1980] ICR 463; [1980] IRLR 289, CA.

153 As this is not a claim of current equal value, it would be more appropriate for the tribunal to resolve the claim directly rather than refer it to an independent expert; there may not even be power to do the latter. It is possible to use a predecessor as a comparator (*McCarthy's v Smith* Case C-129/79, ECJ), but not a hypothetical person. (See generally, above, pp 385–87.) Cases such as these would involve a real comparator and should not therefore fail for want of an existing post.

154 See also [1978] 1 QB 11; [1977] 3 All ER 770.

[T]he employer can never establish ... that the variation ... is genuinely due to a material difference ... when it can be said that past sex discrimination has contributed to the variation.

Does it make any difference that the red-circling is continued, even continued indefinitely? In principle, we do not see why it should. Assuming that there are no additional factors, and that in other respects affairs are operated on a unisex, non-discriminatory basis, the situation will continue to be that the variation is genuinely due to a material difference other then the difference of sex. The red circle will persist, ageing and wasting until eventually it vanishes.

The defence failed because the history of discrimination prevented women from having access to the red-circled grade. However, the defence should be satisfied if the employer's criteria for red-circling have no adverse impact on female grades.

Outlook Supplies v Parry,[155] as well as *Snoxell*, make it clear that there is no rule requiring the elimination of a red circle as soon as is practicable, though its duration is an element in the decision on its acceptability. It is especially problematic where the beneficiaries receive pay increases which would have been received had they continued in their old job. If there is no discrimination in such a policy apart from the fact that the applicant is receiving lower pay than a man on like work or work of equal value, the employer should have the burden of establishing that giving the increases in this manner accorded with good industrial relations practice.

9   THE EFFECT OF THE EQUALITY CLAUSE

Section 1(1) provides that if 'the terms of a contract under which a woman is employed ... do not include ... an equality clause they shall be deemed to include one'. Of course, the vast majority of contracts, without this, contain no such clause, so equal pay legislation operates by way of a compulsory modification of the contract of employment. Section 1(2) provides that any term of the contract which is less favourable than the man's is modified to provide equivalence, and where there is no such equivalent term, such term is in effect created by the tribunal. A new or modified term introduced to accord with the equality clause remains part of the contract in the normal way. So, for example, it cannot be 'undone' should the comparator cease to do like work.[156]

This approach caused problems when the law was extended to enable a woman to claim that her work was of equal value to that of a man, as the terms and conditions of employment which had to be equalised might be very different, some more favourable to the man and some more favourable to the woman.

Hayward v Cammell Laird Shipbuilders Ltd [1988] IRLR 257; [1988] AC 894; [1988] 2 All ER 257, HL[157]

A female canteen cook in a shipyard claimed equality with a painter, a joiner and an insulation engineer. The employers argued that there was no obligation to pay her the same basic pay as the men because she had a paid meal break, additional holidays

---

155 [1978] ICR 388; [1978] IRLR 12, EAT.
156 *Sorbie v Trust House Forte Hotels* [1976] IRLR 371, EAT.
157 See Ellis, E, 'A welcome victory for equality' (1988) 51 MLR 781.

and better sickness benefits which compensated for her lower basic pay. The issue was whether pay should be considered as a whole or whether there is entitlement to equality in relation to each and every term. The latter approach prevailed.

Lord Goff of Chieveley (pp 262–63):

> If a contract contains provisions relating to (1) basic pay, (2) benefits in kind such as the use of a car, (3) cash bonuses, and (4) sickness benefits, it would never occur to me to lump all these together as one 'term' of the contract, simply because they can all together be considered as providing for the total 'remuneration' ... under the contract ...

> I fully appreciate that this construction ... will always lead ... to enhancement of the relevant term in the woman's contract. Likewise, it will in the converse case lead to the enhancement of the relevant term in the man's contract ... I also appreciate that this may, in some cases, lead to what has been called mutual enhancement or leap-frogging, as terms of the woman's contract and the man's contract are both, so to speak, upgraded to bring them into line with each other. It is this effect which was found to be so offensive by the Employment Appeal Tribunal and the Court of Appeal. They viewed with dismay the possibility of equality being achieved only by mutual enhancement, and not by an overall consideration of the contractual terms of both the man and the woman ... considering that mutual enhancement transcended the underlying philosophy of the 1970 Act and that it could have a profoundly inflationary effect.

> To these fears there are, I consider, two different answers on two different levels. The first answer is that ... the employer must, where he can, have recourse to s 1(3)[158] [which] could ... have the effect, in appropriate cases, of preventing the mutual enhancement which was so much feared by the Court of Appeal ...

> [T]he second answer ... is that, if the construction of s 1(2) which I prefer does not accord with the true intention of Parliament, then the appropriate course for Parliament is to amend the legislation ...

Not only does this decision accord with the literal meaning of the statute,[159] but it also accords with the underlying policy of the legislation. It would be extremely difficult to assess the value of a fringe benefit as compared with basic pay; how great a reduction in basic pay would be appropriate to compensate for the granting of contractual sick pay? There could be no right answer and the issue would inevitably generate litigation. There has been no evidence since *Hayward* that leap-frogging claims have been a significant issue. The solution is for employers to create a unified and coherent pay structure so that different groups do not have their pay and benefits determined according to radically different criteria. Trends in pay determination are in this direction, and it is doubtful if *Hayward* is more than a gentle nudge towards a development that was occurring in any event.[160]

---

158 The employers' 'genuine material factor' defence. See above, pp 407–08.
159 A factor which concerned the House of Lords very much less in *Pickstone v Freemans plc* [1989] AC 66; [1988] 2 All ER 803; [1988] IRLR 357, which was decided around the same time.
160 Although s 1(3) might provide a defence to leap-frogging claims, it is only likely to do so in very limited circumstances, requiring the employer to show that one element in a compensation package has been specifically introduced to counterbalance a more favourable element granted to other employees, rather than, as is usually the case, the different packages having arisen through historical accident.

The same approach was taken by the ECJ in *Jamstalldhetsombudsmannen v Orebro Lans Landsting*,[161] where the comparison was between the basic salaries of midwives and a clinical technician, and excluded an 'unsocial-hours' payment to the midwives. Whether such an approach was adopted in the next decision is debatable.

Evesham v North Hertfordshire Health Authority [2000] IRLR 257; [2000] ICR 612, CA

Mrs Evesham, a speech therapist,[162] was on level five of her incremental pay scale (reflecting five years' service) and, at the time of her claim, received £14,592 per annum. Her comparator, Dr Mollon, a clinical psychologist, was on level one of his pay scale, and received £22,667 per annum. Mrs Evesham argued that she should be paid *as if* she were on level seven of the clinical psychologists' pay scale, which would have been £26,624. The Court of Appeal dismissed her appeal.

Roch LJ (p 261):

In my judgment, the issue in this appeal is to be resolved by examining first if the finding that the work done in 1987 by Mrs Evesham was of equal value to the work done in that year by Dr Mollon was dependent upon the length of service and experience of Mrs Evesham and the length of service and experience of her chosen comparator. [Evesham] ... maintain[s], correctly, that the annual salary increment does not depend on the employee's performance. It depends solely upon length of service and is, in effect, a reward for loyal service. Nevertheless, if the finding that the work that Mrs Evesham did in 1987 was the equivalent of the work Dr Mollon did in that year depended upon the fact that Mrs Evesham with her five years of experience was in her sixth year contributing work of greater value than she would have contributed in the first year of her employment, ... and if her chosen comparator in his sixth year would have been contributing work of greater value than the work he actually contributed in his first year, then to allow Mrs Evesham to receive in respect of 1987 not merely the salary that Dr Mollon received in that year, but Dr Mollon's salary plus four annual increments, would be to allow Mrs Evesham to double-count her experience. Such an approach would also disregard additional value to work done by her chosen comparator which the extra years of experience in post would bring to that comparator's work.

... [T]hese factors did play a significant part in Mrs Evesham establishing that she was doing work of equal value to that of Dr Mollon in 1987. Further, ... were Mrs Evesham to enter, at the relevant date, the pay scale enjoyed by her comparator but at an incremental level higher than her comparator, the effect would be that from that date she received pay at a level in excess of that received by her comparator with whom she had established equal value, and commensurate with the pay scale of somebody with whom she had not established equal value.

It was a term of Mrs Evesham's contract to be paid according to the speech therapists' pay scale. A simple modification of that term would have put her on the clinical psychologists' scale. All other terms remaining the same (as they should, under *Hayward*, above), should she not be put on level five of her comparator's scale? The court's decision is largely based on the comparison presented by Dr Evesham, which included her experience as a factor in the establishing that she did work of equal value

---

161 Case C-236/98 [2000] ECR I-2189; [2000] IRLR 421. See also *Brunhöfer v bank der Osterreichischen Postsparkasse* Case C-381/99 [2001] ECR I-4961; [2001] IRLR 571; [2001] All ER (EC) 693, ECJ.

162 This is part of the *Enderby* litigation. See above, p 420 and Chapter 10, p 276.

to her comparator. Should that not be a factor, such a remedy may be possible. As Rubenstein commented, 'In hindsight ... it is apparent that [the claimants'] path would have been easier had greater care been taken in 1987 as to the choice of comparator'.[163]

10   EQUAL PAY AND COLLECTIVE BARGAINING

(1)   History

The story here is an unhappy one, both in a technical legal sense and in a policy sense. It is a story of total failure to get to grips with the issues.[164]

The Equal Pay Act 1970 originally contained, in s 3, a limited provision aimed at remedying discrimination in collective agreements. If a provision of an agreement referred 'specifically to men or women only', it could be referred to the Central Arbitration Committee (CAC), which had the power to alter the terms of the agreement so as to eliminate discrimination. By virtue of the normal contractual effect of collective agreements, any such amendment would have become incorporated into the contract of employment of the individual employee. The problem with the law, of course, was that the likelihood of finding agreements, which referred *expressly* to men or women only, rapidly disappeared once the Act came into force. The *real* equality issue came to be seen as agreements which had a discriminatory effect, in particular where occupational segregation meant that different agreements *in practice* applied to women or men only. The CAC took jurisdiction over such situations, but, in *R v Central Arbitration Committee ex p Hy-Mac*,[165] the Divisional Court held that such activity and activism was beyond their powers. The decision in effect made s 3 a dead letter.

The original s 77 of the SDA 1975 provided that any contractual term which required a contracting party to perform an act of unlawful discrimination should be void. This was assumed to be irrelevant to British collective agreements, which are normally not enforceable as contracts.[166] However, the European Court held in *Commission of the European Communities v UK*[167] that s 77 was in breach of the Equal Treatment Directive because it provided no means of regulating discriminatory clauses in collective and other agreements which were not enforceable as contracts.

---

163 Rubenstein, M, commentary to *Evesham*, [2000] IRLR 222.

164 'Women are more likely to fall outside the net of collective bargaining for several reasons. First, these agreements may exclude some atypical workers where women are dominant (homeworkers and short part time work); second, in some countries agreements exclude certain feminised occupations such as clerical or cleaning work (by omission rather than design in some cases, but this itself is evidence of the invisibility of women in the collective bargaining system); third, women are often over-represented in industries where enforcement of collective agreements is weak, for example in textiles and clothing, retail and catering.' Rubery, J and Fagan, C, *Social Europe: Wage Determination and Sex Segregation in Employment in the European Community*, 1993, Luxembourg: Office for Official Publications of the European Communities, p 100.

165 [1979] IRLR 451, DC.

166 Trade Union and Labour Relations (Consolidation) Act 1992, s 179; *Ford v AEF* [1969] 2 QB 303, QBD.

167 Case 165/82 [1983] ECR 3431; [1984] ICR 192; [1984] 1 All ER 353; [1984] IRLR 29.

Section 6 of the Sex Discrimination Act 1986 repealed s 3 of the 1970 Act and amended s 77 of the 1975 Act by extending it to non-binding collective agreements. A discriminatory non-binding collective agreement is void. However, the section cannot be invoked by an individual claimant. The legal effect of declaring a non-binding provision to be void is nil and, perhaps more importantly, provides no deterrent against discriminatory terms in such collective agreements. Once such an agreement becomes a part of an individual contract, there will be a normal EqPA 1970 claim, but such claims are not automatically extended to all members of the group covered by the same agreement, which is the great procedural advantage of taking action in respect of the agreement itself.

(2) The Current Position

Discriminatory terms in collective agreements are covered also by ss 72A and 72B of the RRA 1976 (inserted by SI 2003/1626, in force since 19 July 2003); the Employment Equality (Sexual Orientation) Regulations 2003, SI 2003/1660; or the Employment Equality (Religion or Belief) Regulations 2003, SI 2003/1661 (in force since 1 December 2003 and 2 December 2003, respectively), reg 35 and Sched 4.

The 1993 Trade Union Reform and Employment Rights Act added a new s 6(4A) into the 1986 Sex Discrimination Act. An individual may now claim before an employment tribunal that a term of a collective agreement[168] that is discriminatory *against her* is void. Further, the tribunal may take action, not simply against rules which have a present discriminatory effect, but also against those which may have such effect in the future, even though they bring about no present detriment which would support a claim under s 6 of the SDA 1975.[169] It remains the case that there is no mechanism whereby the outcome of a successful equal pay claim can be automatically extended to all other employees in the same position as the successful applicant. As a matter of practice, though, employers are likely take such a step in order to avoid consequential claims from being brought. Perhaps more importantly, having a discriminatory term declared void goes only part of the way to conform with a principle of equal pay. Section 6(4A) offers no mechanism for *extending* benefits to women. For example, in *Kowalska v Freie und Hansestadt Hamburg*,[170] a collective agreement provided for severance pay for full-time workers. The European Court held that workers covered by a discriminatory collective agreement are entitled to the terms and conditions of employment that they would have had if the agreement had not been discriminatory. Thus, the (predominantly female) part-time workers were entitled to severance pay as well. Consequently, there is an argument that current English law is defective in failing to provide a specific mechanism to enable this to be done.

Section 77 of the SDA 1975 appears to be geared towards direct discrimination. However, in *Meade-Hill v British Council*,[171] it was held to be potentially applicable to

---

168 The provision also applies to rules made by employers, trade unions, employers' organisations, professional organisations or qualifying bodies.

169 *Meade-Hill v National Union of Civil and Public Servants and British Council* [1995] ICR 847; [1996] 1 All ER 79; [1995] IRLR 478, CA.

170 Case C-33/89 [1990] ECR I-2591; [1992] ICR 29; [1990] IRLR 447.

171 *Meade-Hill v National Union of Civil and Public Servants and British Council* [1995] ICR 847; [1996] 1 All ER 79; [1995] IRLR 478, CA.

an indirectly discriminatory clause in a collective agreement which had been incorporated in the applicant's contract of employment, in this case a mobility clause which might potentially require employees to serve anywhere in the UK. However, for it to be void, it would have to be shown that there were no possible circumstances in which the application of such a clause to the applicant could be justified. Proving a negative such as this is likely to be an almost impossible task.

11   EQUAL PAY REMEDIES

Two procedural rules for equal pay claims were challenged as being contrary to Art 119 (now Art 141) in the cases of *Levez v Jennings*[172] and *Preston v Wolverhampton Healthcare NHS Trust*.[173] The first rule, s 2(4) of the EqPA, required claims be brought, at the latest, within six months of the termination of employment ('the qualifying date'). The second rule, s 2(5) of the EqPA, provided that arrears or damages in respect of unequal pay could only be awarded in respect of the period of two years before the proceedings were instituted; tribunals had no discretion. These rules have now been amended[174] to accord with the judgments of the two cases. The amendments came into force on 19 July 2003.

(1)   The Qualifying Date

Under the new s 2ZA of the EqPA 1970,[175] the general (six month) rule still applies, but with three exceptions. The first (s 2ZA(4)) is where a worker is employed on a series of temporary contracts. Before the amendment, she would have to make a claim in respect of each contract, but now, where the series of contracts could be defined by as 'stable employment case', the time limit will not begin to run until the end of the stable employment. The second one (s 2ZA(5)) arises where, for instance, the employer lies about the pay of a comparator (a 'concealment case'). The qualifying date is six months after the claimant discovered (or *ought* to have discovered) the truth. This scenario occurred in *Levez*, below. The third exception (s 2ZA(6)) arises where the woman falls under a disability during the six month period following employment. The qualifying date is six months after she ceased to be under a disability.[176] In case of concealment *and* disability, the qualifying date is the later of those given by sub-ss (5) and (6).

(2)   Award of Arrears or Damages

The general thrust of the new ss 2ZB (England and Wales) and 2ZC (Scotland)[177] is to bring the law into line with a claim for breach of contract. So, the arrears date is now

---

172 Case C-326/96; [1998] ECR I-7835; [1999] IRLR 36, ECJ.
173 [2000] All ER (EC) 714; [2001] 2 WLR 408; [2000] ICR 961; [2000] IRLR 506, ECJ. See further Chapter 15, p 456.
174 By the Equal Pay (Amendment) Regulations 2003, SI 2003/1656. Note that slightly different rules apply to the armed forces.
175 Inserted by SI 2003/1656, reg 4.
176 England and Scotland have slightly different definitions of 'disability': EqPA 1970, s 11(2A).
177 Both sections inserted by SI 2003/1656, reg 5.

six years for England and Wales, and five years for Scotland. In concealment[178] or disability cases, arrears can be claimed for the *whole* period of unequal pay, although for Scotland, this is limited to a 20 year maximum. These new sections arose from the cases of *Preston* and *Levez*.

> *Levez v Jennings (Harlow Pools) Ltd* **Case C-326/96 [1998] ECR I-7835; [1999] IRLR 36, ECJ**

In February 1991, Mrs Levez began work as betting shop manager, at £10,000 per annum. In December, her employer falsely told her that another manager, doing like work, earned £10,800 per annum, and raised her salary accordingly. In fact, the male manager had earned £11,400 per annum. On leaving her job in March 1993, Mrs Levez discovered the truth. In September, she began proceedings for equal pay, claiming arrears from February 1991. The employer argued that by the then s 2(5) of the EqPA 1970, it was only liable for arrears going back two years from the date the claim was made, that is September 1991. The ECJ held that s 2(5), by (a) providing a general two-year limit, and (b) allowing an employer to profit from his deceit (even though Mrs Levez could bring a claim of fraud in the county court), was incompatible with Community law.

Judgment:

18   The first point to note is that, according to established case-law, in the absence of Community rules governing the matter it is for the domestic legal system of each Member State to designate the courts and tribunals having jurisdiction and to lay down the detailed procedural rules governing actions for safeguarding rights which individuals derive from Community law, provided, however, that such rules are not less favourable than those governing similar domestic actions (the principle of equivalence) and do not render virtually impossible or excessively difficult the exercise of rights conferred by Community law (the principle of effectiveness) ...

20   Consequently, a national rule under which entitlement to arrears of remuneration is restricted to the two years preceding the date on which the proceedings were instituted is not in itself open to criticism.

21   However, with respect to the main proceedings, it is clear ... that Jennings misinformed Mrs Levez ...

22   In such circumstances, according to Mrs Levez, the rule at issue manifestly precludes the possibility of either full compensation or an effective remedy in cases of failure to comply with the principle of equal pay, ... Mrs Levez also points out that the national court has no discretion to extend the limitation period on account of the conduct of the defendant, who deceived her ... nor does it have a general discretion to extend the time-limit on the ground that it would be just and equitable to do so. ...

30   As the Commission rightly pointed out, even though, in the present case, only part of the plaintiff's claim is affected, in a different case and in similar circumstances, the whole of a claim might be excluded by the operation of the rule at issue. ...

32   In short, to allow an employer to rely on [section 2(5)] ... would ... be manifestly incompatible with the principle of effectiveness ... Application of [section 2(5)] ...

---

178 See above, '(1) The Qualifying Date'. In Scotland, fraud, or error induced by the employer: EqPA 1970, s 2ZC(2)(a).

is likely, in the circumstances of the present case, to make it virtually impossible or excessively difficult to obtain arrears of remuneration in respect of sex discrimination. It is plain that the ultimate effect of this rule would be to facilitate the breach of Community law by an employer whose deceit caused the employee's delay in bringing proceedings for enforcement of the principle of equal pay.

33 Furthermore, it does not appear that application of [section 2(5)] ... in the circumstances of the case before the national court can reasonably be justified by principles such as legal certainty or the proper conduct of proceedings.

[On the issue of an alternative county court remedy]

45 [The UK argued] ... Since the Act applies to a whole series of claims concerned with enforcing compliance with the rule of equality of contractual terms, whether or not in relation to pay, it is reasonable for all claims to be subject to the same limitation period. Thus, according to the United Kingdom, the principle of equivalence is complied with.

47 ... the fact that the same procedural rules – namely, the limitation period laid down by section 2(5) of the Equal Pay Act – apply to two comparable claims, one relying on a right conferred by Community law, the other on a right acquired under domestic law, is not enough to ensure compliance with the principle of equivalence, as the United Kingdom Government maintains, since one and the same form of action is involved ...

51 ... it is appropriate to consider whether, in order fully to assert rights conferred by Community law before the County Court, an employee in circumstances such as those of Mrs Levez will incur additional costs and delay by comparison with a claimant who, because he is relying on what may be regarded as a similar right under domestic law, may bring an action before the Industrial Tribunal, which is simpler and, in principle, less costly.

53 ... Community law precludes the application of a rule of national law which limits an employee's entitlement to arrears of remuneration or damages for breach of the principle of equal pay to a period of two years prior to the date on which the proceedings were instituted, even when another remedy is available, if the latter is likely to entail procedural rules or other conditions which are less favourable than those applicable to similar domestic actions. It is for the national court to determine whether that is the case.

In *Preston*, the ECJ held that s 2(5), in preventing pensionable service to be credited before the two years preceding an initial claim of equal pay, contravened Community Law. When the case returned to the House of Lords,[179] it was held, following *Fisscher*,[180] that credit should be backdated to 8 April 1976 (the date when the ECJ held, in *Defrenne v Sabena*[181] that Art 119 (now Art 141) had direct effect). As we have seen, the Government responded to the ECJ judgment by replacing the two-year rule with the six- (or for Scotland, five-) year rule, which brings such claims into line with breach of contract. But the House of Lord's judgment reveals that, in cases of pensions at least, even the amended rule, may contravene Community law.

179 [2001] All ER (D) 99 (Feb), HL.
180 *Fisscher v Voorhuis Hengelo BV and Stichting Bedrijfspensioenfonds voor de Detailhandel* Case C-128/93 [1994] ECR I-4583; [1995] ICR 635; [1994] IRLR 662, ECJ. See further, below, Chapter 15, pp 455–57.
181 *Defrenne v Sabena* Case C-43/75, [1976] ICR 547, ECJ.

12   CONCLUSION: THE FUTURE FOR EQUAL PAY LAW[182]

Despite many recent developments, there remain two serious defects of current equal pay law: first, its failure to recognise the collective element in pay determination and, secondly, the fact that employers may wait for a claim to be brought rather than being under an obligation to take positive steps in the direction of equal value. As the legislation in force in Ontario purports to deal with both these issues, it provides a possible model for future British developments.

> **McColgan, A, 'Legislating equal pay: lessons from Canada' [1993] 22 ILJ 269, pp 273–77, 283:**
>
> The aim of Ontario's legislation is far from unique. What differentiates it from legislation in the UK and in the rest of Europe is the method chosen to achieve that aim. Rather than ... leaving it to individual employees to complain of perceived wage inequalities, the Act goes a step further and obliges employers to take the initiative in eliminating sex-based wage differentials. Employers are required to determine the relative value of female and male 'job classes' within each 'establishment' and to correct any disparity between female and male job classes of equal or comparable value, unless the disparity is shown to result from one of a number of permissible factors, such as a formal non-discriminatory seniority system or a skills shortage in a particular area. A 'job class' is defined as 'those positions ... that have similar duties and responsibilities and require similar qualifications, are filled by similar recruiting procedures, and have the same compensation schedule, salary grade or range of salary grades'. A job class is 'female' where 60% or more of its incumbents are female or where it has been designated 'female' by the employer, through collective bargaining or by the Pay Equity Commission. Gender predominance may also be determined by reference to the historical incumbency and gender stereotype of work ...
>
> Once a suitable job comparison system has been chosen and applied, the Act requires that public employers and private employers of 100 or more workers post a 'pay equity plan' for the establishment or, where one or more unions are recognised, for each bargaining unit within the establishment and for the non-unionised workforce. The plans must describe the comparison system chosen and its application to the job classes covered by the pay equity plan, and detail the pay equity adjustments to be made, together with a timetable for necessary wage adjustments in accordance with the Act. No more than 1% of the previous year's payroll need be spent on pay equity adjustments in any year, although the adjustments must be continued until each female job class has the same job rate as that of its chosen comparator ...
>
> The potential of Ontario's legislation lies in its effective reversal of the burden of proving discrimination. Rather than encouraging employers to ignore issues of equal pay save in the unlikely event of an individual's complaint, the Pay Equity Act obliges them, in co-operation with any bargaining agent, to scrutinise their own pay practices for evidence of discrimination and eliminate it. The success of the Act, then, must depend in the first instance upon the good faith of the employers and the strength and commitment to pay equity of any bargaining agent, and thereafter upon the effectiveness of any enforcement mechanisms ... The legislation takes a 'self-managed' approach, providing for intervention by the Commission generally only upon the request of one of the parties. This approach is most apparent in the failure of the legislation to provide for the systematic monitoring of pay equity plans, making it

---

182 See also McColgan, A, *Just Wages for Women*, 1997, Oxford: Clarendon.

possible that many employers who claim to have 'done' pay equity are in fact very far from having eradicated the effects of gender discrimination on their compensation practices. The 'self-management' ethos is perhaps one of the reasons why the impact of pay equity in Ontario has been rather more in the nature of a whimper than a bang ...

There is a strong argument ... for legislation to support unions in bargaining for better pay for women, and to prod into action those unions which might otherwise not place pay equity high on their bargaining agenda. Even unions which are committed to improving women's pay have to deal with the conflict thrown up by male members who fear that such an improvement will damage their own earnings. The potentially inflationary effects of equalising men's and women's pay are enormous, the relatively low costs of the legislation in Ontario being proof of the inadequacies of the Pay Equity Act rather than of the possibility of achieving true pay parity without a significant increase in the wage bill. Employers in the UK are unlikely to capitulate readily to union demands for action unless those demands have strong legislative backing. The cost of achieving equal pay cannot be viewed as a valid argument against it, but renders legislation necessary. To use an argument borrowed from one leading proponent of pay equity: 'If one were honestly to believe economists and employers who cry out that equal value will be disastrous for the economy, causing inflation and widespread unemployment, then it appears that the ongoing health of the Canadian economy depends mainly on the exploitation of working women ... I cannot think of any other area of human rights legislation where it is a legitimate point of discussion to debate whether society can afford the costs of eliminating discrimination.'

No one knows the true cost of a full commitment to equal value principles. Even if a legislative commitment to such equality were introduced, other factors may militate against a significant reduction in the male/female pay gap.

Rubery, J and Fagan, C, *Social Europe: Wage Determination and Sex Segregation in Employment in the European Community,* **1993, Luxembourg: Office for Official Publications of the European Communities, p 43:**

The principle of equal value requires a systematic evaluation of jobs, a removal of systematic gender bias in the evaluation of jobs and greater integration of pay structures between and within organisations. Some of the problems in Britain in the implementation of these principles arise from the general movement in institutions away from these principles to more fragmented pay between organisations and between workers within organisations. Other problems relate to the fact that, in some societies or organisations, pay determination based on training, qualifications, or potential skill might be considered to be as valid as payment according to current job content; however, where there are gender differences in the acquisition of training, experience and qualifications, such systems may in fact be used to evade the implications of the equal value principle. Until, or unless, there is institutional or legal change, the only effective way of implementing equal value within a specific organisation may be to engage in detailed job evaluation. This is the conclusion that unions have tended to reach in Britain and the USA, despite all the inherent problems of job evaluation and despite the fact that there are many other ways in which pay structures can be formulated.

Given the inevitable problems involved in the effective use of the law, can voluntary Codes of Practice be expected to contribute to reducing the pay gap? Here again, proactive steps are needed; it is dubious whether employers can be encouraged or persuaded to take the steps which the Equal Opportunities Commission would like to see.

CHAPTER 15

RETIREMENT AND PENSIONS

1   INTRODUCTION[1]

Pensions law is exceedingly complex but of fundamental importance in relation to issues of equality and to the more general issue of maintaining a proper standard of living for the growing proportion of the population which has ceased to work. For many years, it was conventional in the UK for men to retire at 65 and women to retire at 60. The original Sex Discrimination Act adopted the conservative stance of not wishing to upset these traditional arrangements, and thus s 6(4) permitted discrimination 'in relation to death or retirement'. The Court of Appeal in *Garland v British Rail Engineering Ltd*[2] held that the section should be interpreted widely, and consequently any discrimination in pension provision and retirement ages continued to be lawful despite the Sex Discrimination Act (SDA) 1975.

The fact that women conventionally retired earlier than men was perhaps slightly curious given that women, on average, live longer than men. It followed that women would, on average, be contributing towards pension provision for a shorter period and yet receiving benefits for a longer period than men. As a result, on average, it costs more to provide the same periodic pension for women than for men. In the same way, schemes which accumulate a capital sum which is used on retirement to purchase an annuity which will cover the period between retirement and death will, if averages are used, necessarily lead to a man's annuity being larger than a woman's. This use of average behaviour goes against the general thrust of the SDA 1975.[3] It is, however, fundamental and essential to the operation of any pension scheme, for the amount of contributions which must be collected depends on an actuarial assessment of the amount of benefits which must one day be paid out, which in turn depends on the average life expectancy of the beneficiaries under the scheme. There is, however, no *logical* need for a scheme to differentiate between men and women; it might be equally rational to differentiate, say, between smokers and non-smokers. The attraction of differentiation by gender is that it is cheap and, unlike smoking, for example, cannot be faked and does not normally change over time.

There are also difficulties in determining what is meant by equality. To allow a woman to retire earlier than a man may look like discrimination against the man; to *require* her to retire at 60 where a man may work until 65 and thus, among other

---

1   See generally, Kingsford Smith, D, 'Superannuating the second sex: law, privatisation and retirement income' (2001) 64 MLR 519.
2   [1979] ICR 558; [1979] IRLR 244. The case subsequently went to the European Court: Case 12/81 [1982] ECR 359; [1983] 2 AC 751; [1982] 2 All ER 402; [1982] IRLR 11.
3   SDA 1975, s 45, permits insurance companies to quote different rates for men and women, provided that these derived from appropriate and commonly used statistics.

things, earn a higher pension, may look like discrimination against her.[4] In times when many take early retirement, the terms of which will be more beneficial the closer to pension age at which it occurs, the increase in women's pension age from 60 to 65 will disadvantage large numbers of women.

Pension arrangements in the UK are divided between occupational pensions and the State retirement pension scheme. Every employee is entitled to a flat-rate State pension on reaching retirement age.[5] For employees who are not members of an occupational scheme, the Second State Pension[6] provides additional benefits. There are two types of occupational pension scheme. In final salary schemes, the level of pension is normally a defined fraction of the final salary, such as one-sixtieth or one-eightieth, for each year of service. In money purchase schemes, the contributions are put into a fund which is used, on retirement, to purchase an annuity. Both types of schemes may be contributory, where the fund is built up from contributions from both employer and employee, or non-contributory, where the employer provides the whole income for the scheme.

The conservative, non-interventionist stance of the original SDA 1975 has been totally transformed and swept aside by EC law. The current law remains in some aspects problematic, as regards the precise legal rules currently in place, the procedures to enforce them, and the extent to which they will bring a substantial improvement in the financial position of women – and maybe some men – post-retirement.[7]

2   RETIREMENT AGE

Marshall v Southampton and South West Hampshire AHA **Case C-152/84, ECJ**[8]

This was a straightforward allegation that to require women to retire at 60 whereas men could work until 65 contravened the Equal Treatment Directive,[9] even though it was clearly permitted by the SDA 1975. The case concerned the dismissal as such rather than the financial consequences of that dismissal, such as pensions. The defence was that such a differentiation depended on the difference in State pension age, which continued to be lawful under the Social Security Directive.[10]

---

4   This may depend on economic circumstances. In 1996, Fredman observed: 'Soaring unemployment and compulsory early retirement has meant that the lower pension age for women has come to be seen as a coveted advantage. Currently, as many as 43% of men and 68% of women have already retired by the age of 60. Pension age crucially affects the terms of such retirement: redundancy within sight of pension age usually attracts a more advantageous package than a redundancy earlier on in a worker's life.' Fredman, S, 'The poverty of equality: pensions and the ECJ' [1996[25 ILJ 91, p 96.

5   For the ways in which the assumption of men as workers and women as dependants led to the State scheme operating to women's disadvantage, see Fredman, S, *Women and the Law*, 1997, Oxford: Clarendon, pp 336–39.

6   This replaced the 'SERPS' (State Earnings Related Pension Scheme) on 6 April 2001.

7   The changes wrought by European law have in many respects been consolidated by the Pensions Act 1995, though the primary purpose of this Act was to reform the general operation of pensions law in the light of the Maxwell scandal.

8   [1986] IRLR 140; [1986] ECR 723; [1986] 1 QB 401; [1986] ICR 335.

9   Directive 76/207/EEC, OJ L39/40, 1976.

10   Directive 79/7/EEC, OJ L6/24, 1979.

Judgment (p 148):

> The Court observes in the first place that the question ... does not concern access to a statutory or occupational retirement scheme, that is to say the conditions for payment of an old age or retirement pension, but the fixing of an age limit with regard to the termination of employment pursuant to a general policy concerning dismissal. The question therefore relates to the conditions governing dismissal and falls to be considered under Council Directive 76/207 EEC.

> [A]n age limit for the compulsory dismissal of workers pursuant to an employer's general policy concerning retirement falls within the term 'dismissal' ... even if the dismissal involves the grant of a retirement pension ...

> [I]n view of the fundamental importance of the principle of equal treatment ... Art 1(2) of Directive No 76/207, which excludes social security from the scope of that Directive, must be interpreted strictly. Consequently, the exception to the prohibition of discrimination on grounds of sex provided for in Art 7(1)(a) of Directive No 79/7 applies only to the determination of pensionable age for the purposes of granting old age and retirement pensions ...

> [W]hereas the exception contained in Art 7 of Directive No 79/7 concerns the consequences which pensionable age has for social security benefits, this case is concerned with dismissal within the meaning of Art 5 of Directive No 76/207.

> [A] general policy concerning dismissal involving the dismissal of a woman solely because she has attained the qualifying age for a State pension, which age is different under national legislation for men and for women, constitutes discrimination on grounds of sex ...[11]

Had the facts been treated as a matter of social security, the discrimination would have been permissible. It was the construction of the situation as concerning working conditions that brought the case within the Equal Treatment Directive. In British terms, the consequence of that decision was the Sex Discrimination Act 1986, as a result of which it is now unlawful to discriminate against a woman in relation to retirement with regard to access to opportunities for promotion, transfer or training, or by subjecting her to any detriment, demotion or dismissal. The employer is no longer permitted, therefore, to discriminate in relation to employment on the basis of retirement age. This is true even though the State retirement provision is still based on a man retiring at 65 and a woman at 60. The Government has opted to equalise the State pension age at 65 by the year 2025; this will mean that women who would previously have retired at 60 will take substantially less by way of pension than would formerly have been the case.[12]

3   PENSION PROVISION

The main legal issues which need to be addressed are as follows:

(a) To what extent do pension arrangements constitute 'pay' within the meaning of Art 141 (formerly Art 119) of the Treaty of Rome and to what extent may pension

---

11 See also *Beets-Proper v Van Lanschot Bankiers NV* Case C-262/84 [1986] 2 ECR 773; [1986] ICR 706.

12 See Department of Works and Pensions booklet 'Pensions for Women – Your Guide' (PM6, ISBN 1-84388-002-4) or www.thepensionservice.gov.uk/pdf/pm6april03.pdf.

provision be outside the scope of Art 141 and governed by the Social Security Directive?

(b) If pensions constitute pay, do the rules governing equality in pension schemes apply only to employer and employee, or will they apply to others, such as the employee's spouse, and the scheme trustees, who may be affected by the operation and administration of the scheme?

(c) If pensions are in principle within the scope of equality law, which discrimination is prohibited? In particular, does the law apply to access to schemes and to benefits under schemes?

(d) Given that for many years it has been the accepted practice that differentiation between men and women was permissible in relation to pension provision, a belief which was fortified by the provisions of the Occupational Social Security Directive,[13] should there be transitional arrangements before full equality becomes mandatory?

(e) How should the law deal with the issue of equality so far as pensionable age – as opposed to retirement age – is concerned and should it continue to be permissible to take account of the fact that, on average, women live longer than men?

(f) What remedies should be available for the failure to provide past equality in pensions?

(1)   Are Pensions Pay?

Article 141 (formerly Art 119) provides that 'pay' is 'the ordinary minimum wage or salary and any other consideration, whether in cash or in kind, which the worker receives, directly or indirectly, in respect of his employment from his employer'. In the context of pension provision, the wording has received an extremely broad interpretation, an interpretation which has been the basis of the dramatic changes in the law wrought by the European Court.

Bilka-Kaufhaus v Weber von Hartz **Case 170/84 [1986] IRLR 317**[14]

Under the company's occupational scheme, part-time employees could obtain pensions only if they had worked full-time for 15 out of a total period of 20 years. The claim was that to differentiate in this way was indirectly discriminatory against women. Breach of Art 119 (now Art 141) could be established only if the employer's pension arrangements fell within the definition of 'pay'.

Judgment (pp 319–21):

In *Defrenne v Belgium* [Case 80/70 [1971] ECR 445 the Court took] the view that, although pay within the meaning of Art 119 could in principle include social security benefits, it did not include social security schemes or benefits, in particular retirement pensions, directly governed by legislation which do not involve any element of agreement within the undertaking or trade concerned and are compulsory for general categories of workers. [The contributions to such a scheme are] determined less by the

---

13   Directive 86/378/EEC, OJ L225/40, 1986. This Directive was subsequently amended by Directive 96/97/EEC, OJ C218/5, 1997.
14   See also [1986] ECR 1607; [1986] 2 CMLR 701; [1987] ICR 110.

employment relationship between the employer and the worker than by considerations of social policy, so that the employer's contribution cannot be regarded as a direct or indirect payment to the worker ...[15]

[T]he occupational pension scheme at issue [here], although adopted in accordance with the provisions laid down by German legislation for such schemes, is based on an agreement between *Bilka* and the staff committee representing its employees and has the effect of supplementing the social benefits paid under national legislation of general application with benefits financed entirely by the employer ... Benefits paid to employees under the scheme therefore constitute consideration received by the worker from the employer in respect of his employment, as referred to in the second paragraph of Art 119.

[The Court went on to hold that the exclusion of part-time workers was indirectly discriminatory against women, and to lay down criteria against which national courts should judge whether such policy could be justified.][16]

[The applicant also argued] that the disadvantages suffered by women because of the exclusion of part-time workers ... must at least be mitigated by requiring the employer to regard periods during which women workers have had to meet family responsibilities as periods of full time work.

[T]he scope of Art 119 is restricted to questions of pay discrimination between men and women. Problems relating to other conditions of work and employment, on the other hand, are covered generally by other provisions of Community law ... with a view to the harmonisation of the social systems of Member States and the approximation of their legislation in that area.

The imposition of an obligation such as that envisaged ... goes beyond the scope of Art 119 and has no other basis in Community law as it now stands.[17]

What is critical about this case is that denial of *access* to the pension scheme is held to be pay discrimination by treating it as equivalent to discriminatory *benefits under* the scheme.[18] The case decides that, in principle, Art 141 may be applicable to occupational pension schemes. The exclusion of part-time employees will normally be unlawful, at least where the number of hours worked per week is substantial,[19] but qualification rules for pension schemes will be subject to the normal rules concerning justification of an indirectly discriminatory practice. Assuming that they will have a disparate impact – which is by no means self-evident – the employer may have to

---

15 In *Defrenne v Belgium*, entitlement did not depend on the particular employment, and benefit did not depend on the level of employer contributions.

16 See further, Chapter 10, p 275 and Chapter 14, p 407.

17 In response to this, Fredman, *op cit*, fn 4 above, p 110, observes that 'structural considerations such as the division of labour within the family are explicitly disregarded. The refusal to neutralise the effects of breaks in continuity of employment leaves uncorrected a crucial factor contributing towards women's disadvantage in old age'.

18 See also *Worringham v Lloyds Bank Ltd* Case 69/80 [1981] ECR 767; [1981] ICR 558; [1981] IRLR 178; *Liefting v Directie van het Academish Ziekenhuis* Case 23/83 [1984] ECR 3225.

19 The reasoning in *R v Secretary of State for Employment ex p Equal Opportunities Commission* [1994] ICR 317; [1995] AC 1; [1994] 1 All ER 910; [1994] IRLR 176, HL, might suggest that an eight-hour threshold would not be regarded as too high. *Dietz v Stichting Thuiszorg Rotterdam* Case C-435/93 [1996] IRLR 692 concerned a claim for retroactive membership of a scheme by a female cleaner who had worked seven hours a week for 18 years. The Court held that the limitation in *Barber v Guardian Royal Exchange Insurance Group* Case C-262/88 [1990] ECR I-1889; [1991] 1 QB 344; [1990] ICR 616; [1990] IRLR 240 to claims from the date of judgment onwards did not apply to the denial of access to a scheme, and did not consider whether on the facts such denial might have been justified.

justify, for example, requiring employees to work for a year to qualify for a pension scheme, or excluding temporary and fixed-term workers. In no sense does the case establish a universal right to join a pension scheme. Nor is an employer required to extend pension provision to all grades of employee, even if the lower grades are predominantly female. In fact, it is arguable that *Bilka* might encourage employers to abandon pension provision for lower grade employees where a substantial proportion of such employees work part-time. High turnover might well be accepted as a justification for not establishing pension provision for particular grades, and high turnover is associated with lower grade employment.

It remained unclear after *Bilka* precisely which schemes were subject to Art 119, especially as the nature of schemes varies so enormously among the Member States. *Defrenne v Belgium*[20] decided that pure social security schemes were outside the scope of Art 119. In *Beune*, the ECJ had to consider a scheme where the degree of legislative control was far greater than in *Bilka*.

Bestuur van het Algemeen Burgerlijk Pensioenfonds v Beune Case C-7/93 [1995] IRLR 103[21]

This case concerned the applicability of Art 119 (now Art 141) to the Dutch Civil Service pension scheme (ABPW) and its interrelationship with the general State old age pension scheme (AOW). The applicant, a married man, retired in 1988, having worked in the public service for 40 years. The set off from his ABPW pension was 16,286 guilders per year. Had he been a female civil servant with the same length of service the set off would have only been 11,300 guilders per year. The European Court of Justice (ECJ) held that the Civil Service scheme was governed by Art 119, rather than Directive 79/7 (Equal Treatment in Social Security).

Judgment (pp 116–17):

On the basis of the situations before it, the Court has developed, *inter alia*, the following criteria: the statutory nature of a pension scheme, negotiation between employers and employees' representatives, the fact that the employees' benefits supplement social security benefits, the manner in which the pension scheme is financed, its applicability to general categories of employees and, finally, the relationship between the benefit and the employees' employment ...

[T]he possibility of relying on Art 119 before a national court cannot depend on whether the unequal treatment in respect of pay allegedly suffered by the employee derives from legislation or regulations or from a collective agreement.

It follows that in classifying pension schemes, the Court has not confined itself to a formal finding of statutory origin. It has given precedence to the criterion of whether there is an agreement rather than the criterion of statutory origin ...

However, the negotiation between the employers and the employees' representatives must ... be such as results in a formal agreement. In most of the Member States, even in the Civil Service, there are various kinds of consultation between employers and employees, which take different forms and are more or less binding on the parties, without thereby necessarily culminating in agreements properly so called ...

No doubt a pension fund like the Netherlands fund is almost entirely funded by contributions paid by the various Civil Service employers and deductions from civil

20 Case 80/70 [1971] ECR 445.
21 See also [1994] ECR I-4471.

servants' salaries and is managed independently in accordance with rules similar to those applicable to occupational pension funds. But those characteristics do not substantially distinguish it from certain social security schemes covered by Directive 79/7 which, under laws or regulations governing contributions and benefits, may also be funded by contributions from employers and employees and be managed jointly by employers and employees.

Moreover ... by contrast with the scheme in *Ten Oever*[22] ... the ABP may, exceptionally, have recourse to the budget of the Netherlands State if the pension fund is unable to discharge the obligations imposed on it by the ABPW. It is also apparent that the scheme reimburses to the ABP the additional costs associated with the elimination of discrimination between widows and widowers. The scheme is not therefore financed exclusively by the public employers and their employees ...

[C]onsiderations of social policy, of State organisation, of ethics or even budgetary preoccupations which influenced, or may have influenced, the establishment by the national legislature of a scheme such as the scheme at issue cannot prevail if the pension concerns only a particular category of workers, if it is directly related to the period of service and if its amount is calculated by reference to the civil servant's last salary. The pension paid by the public employer is therefore entirely comparable to that paid by a private employer to his former employees.

This apparently arcane case is of great significance.[23] Much of the judgment, focusing on the State involvement in legislative and even in fiscal terms, appears to be pointing to a conclusion that Art 119 would not apply. Yet, the final section of the judgment shows that these considerations do not prevail, because the scheme concerned only particular categories of worker, and the benefits were related to length of service and final salary. It follows that schemes, however established, which relate only to the employees of a particular employer – even if that employer is the Civil Service – will be within the scope of Art 119. It may even follow that the result in *Defrenne v Belgium* would be different today, although in that case there was no element of consultation with the workers concerned. It is unclear whether agreement is necessary or whether it is sufficient that the scheme covers workers employed by one particular employer.

Barber v Guardian Royal Exchange Case C-262/88 [1990] IRLR 240[24]

The employer's non-contributory pension scheme provided that workers should receive a pension but the payment of the pension was deferred until a man reached the age of 62 and a woman 57. A number of employees were being made redundant and the severance terms agreed provided for an immediate pension if the employee made redundant was a man aged 55 or a woman aged 50. The employee was made redundant compulsorily at the age of 52 and therefore he was entitled only to a deferred pension under the scheme, whereas a woman of the same age would have received an immediate pension.

The questions for the ECJ were whether benefits received under a private, contracted-out, non-contributory scheme by a group of employees made compulsorily redundant were 'pay'; whether the principle of equal pay was infringed if a man and a woman of the same age were made redundant but only the woman received an

---

22 *Ten Oever v Stichting Bedrijfspensioenfonds Voor het Glazenwassers – en Schoonmaakbedrijf* Case C-109/91 [1993] ECR I-4879; [1995] ICR 74; [1993] IRLR 601.

23 See also *Moroni v Firma Collo GmbH* Case C-110/91 [1993] ECR I-6591; [1995] ICR 137; [1994] IRLR 130.

24 See also [1990] ECR I-1889; [1991] 1 QB 344; [1990] ICR 616.

immediate pension, or the total value of the benefits received by the woman was greater than the man's.

Judgment (pp 257–58):

[T]he fact that certain benefits are paid after the termination of the employment relationship does not prevent them from being in the nature of pay ...

[T]he schemes in question are the result either of an agreement between workers and employers or the result of a unilateral decision taken by the employer. They are wholly financed by the employer or by both the employer and the workers without any contribution being made by the public authorities in any circumstances. Accordingly, such schemes form part of the consideration offered to workers by the employer.

[S]uch schemes are not compulsorily applicable to general categories of workers. On the contrary, they apply only to workers employed by certain undertakings, with the result that affiliation to those schemes derives of necessity from the employment relationship with a given employer. Furthermore, even if the schemes in question are established in conformity with national legislation and consequently satisfy the conditions laid down by it for recognition as contracted out schemes, they are governed by their own rules ...

[I]t is contrary to Art 119 to impose an age condition which differs according to sex in respect of pensions paid under a contracted out scheme, even if the difference between the pensionable age for men and that for women is based on the one provided by the national statutory scheme ...[25]

[G]enuine transparency, permitting an effective review, is assured only if the principle of equal pay applies to each of the elements of remuneration granted to men or women.[26]

Whereas *Bilka* had implied that benefits under occupational schemes were 'pay', this case decided the point. Moreover, it did so in the face of the fact that the differentiation here depended on the differential retiring age for women and men, which itself depended on the different State pension age. Furthermore, it did so in the face of Art 9 of Directive 86/378 EEC – the Occupational Social Security Directive – which provided that 'Member States may defer compulsory application of the principle of equal treatment with regard to: (a) determination of pensionable age for the purposes of granting old age or retirement pensions, and the possible implications for other

---

25 In *Burton v British Railways Board (No 2)* Case 19/81 [1982] ECR 554; [1982] 1 QB 1080; [1982] IRLR 116, the employers had offered early retirement to all employees within five years of normal retirement age, so women were eligible for early retirement at 55 while men had to wait until they were 60. It was held by the ECJ that the case concerned discriminatory working conditions and was therefore governed by the Equal Treatment Directive 76/207 rather than Art 119. Had this approach been adopted in *Barber*, the Directive would not have had direct effect, as the defendant was a private employer. In *Barber*, the Advocate General distinguished the cases on the basis that *Burton* concerned differential ages for dismissal, and so no issue of pay was involved; see *Barber v Guardian Royal Exchange Insurance Group* Case C-262/88 [1990] IRLR 240, pp 248–50. No mention was made of *Burton* in the judgment of the Court in *Barber*.

26 The case was decided on 17 May 1990. Subsequent cases showed that rights in respect of benefits accruing after that date differed from those in respect of benefits accruing before that date. See p 452 below, and Chapter 14, pp 381–84, above.

benefits ...'[27] Not surprisingly, this had been taken to authorise the continued payment of different benefits where these were dependent on the different pensionable age under State social security systems – a different issue from that in *Bilka*. However, the Court decided that the principle of equal pay enshrined in Art 119 took precedence over Directive 86/378; the exception contained in that Directive was therefore of no application.

(2) Equality in Pension Provision

(a) Who may claim and against whom?

In determining what is meant by equality in pension arrangements, the first question concerns who is entitled to claim equality and against whom may equality be claimed. A wide interpretation has consistently been given to these issues. First, in *Barber* itself, it was stated that the 'interpretation of Art 119 [now Art 141] is not affected by the fact that the private occupational scheme in question has been set up in the form of a trust and is administered by trustees who are technically independent of the employer, since Art 119 also applies to consideration received indirectly from the employer'.[28] In *Coloroll Pension Trustees Ltd v Russell*[29] the ECJ held that 'employers and trustees cannot rely on the rules of their pension scheme, or those contained in the trust deed, in order to evade their obligation to ensure equal treatment in the matter of pay. In so far as the rules of national law prohibit them from acting beyond the scope of their powers or in disregard of the provisions of the trust deed, employers and trustees are bound to use all the means available under domestic law to ensure compliance with the principle of equal treatment, such as recourse to the national courts to amend the provisions of the pension scheme or the trust deed'.[30] Furthermore, *Coloroll* also decided that:[31]

> in the event of the transfer of pension rights from one occupational scheme to another owing to a worker's change of job, the second scheme is obliged, on the worker reaching retirement age, to increase the benefits it undertook to pay him when accepting the transfer so as to eliminate the effects, contrary to Art 119, suffered by the worker in consequence of the inadequacy of the capital transferred, this being due in turn to the discriminatory treatment under the first scheme, and it must do so in relation to benefits payable in respect of periods of service subsequent to 17 May 1990.

The second issue was also clarified in *Coloroll*, where the Court held that 'since the right to payment of a survivor's pension arises at the time of the death of the employee affiliated to the scheme, the survivor is the only person who can assert it. If

---

27 The temporary derogation for social security schemes found in Directive 79/7, Art 7(1)(a) was mirrored in this provision for occupational schemes.

28 [1990] IRLR 240, p 258.

29 Case C-200/91 [1994] ECR I-4389; [1995] ICR 179; [1994] IRLR 586. See also *Fisscher v Voorhuis Hengelo BV and Stichting Bedrijfspensioenfonds voor de Detailhandel* Case C-128/93 [1994] ECR I-4583; [1995] ICR 635; [1994] IRLR 662.

30 [1994] IRLR 586, p 596. As a result of this ruling trustees were given powers, by the Pension Act 1995, s 65, to make alterations to pension schemes, in defined circumstances, in order to ensure conformity with the principle of equal treatment.

31 [1994] IRLR 586, p 600. This ruling has led to the widespread practice in the pensions industry of refusing to accept such transfers. See McCrudden, C, 'Third time lucky? The Pensions Act 1995 and equal treatment in occupational pensions' [1996] 25 ILJ 28, p 39.

the survivor were to be denied this possibility, this would deprive Art 119 of all its effectiveness so far as survivors' pensions are concerned'.[32]

(b)   The meaning of equality

The second aspect of equality concerns the issue of what is meant by equality in the context of pensions, and how that equality is to be achieved. There are two issues: equality as regards access to a scheme, and equality as regards the benefits under the scheme.

Smith v Advel Systems Ltd Case C-408/92 [1994] IRLR 602[33]

Until 1 July 1991, the employers' normal retirement age was 65 for men and 60 for women. At that date the age for women was increased to 65. This change was applied both to benefits earned in respect of years of service after 1 July 1991 and service before that date. This reduced the pension payable to women retiring between 60 and 65 by up to 20%, as if a woman were to retire at age 60, her pension would be reduced by 4% per year for each year that her retirement preceded age 65, whereas previously she would have received a pension at the full rate. The same rule was applied to benefits earned in a previous pensionable employment on the basis that retirement would be at 60. Furthermore, if she were to leave the scheme before age 65, the pension rights which could be transferred or used to purchase an insurance policy would be calculated on the basis that her normal pension date was her 65th birthday.

It was claimed that all three of these rules contravened Art 119 (now Art 141).

Judgment (pp 614–15):

[O]nce the Court has found that discrimination in relation to pay exists and so long as measures for bringing about equal treatment have not been adopted by the scheme, the only proper way of complying with Art 119 is to grant to the persons in the disadvantaged class the same advantages as those enjoyed by the persons in the favoured class.

Application of this principle to the present case means that, as regards the period between 17 May 1990 [the date of the *Barber* judgment] ... and 1 July 1991 the pension rights of men must be calculated on the basis of the same retirement age as that for women ...

As regards periods of service completed after the entry into force, on 1 July 1991, of rules designed to eliminate discrimination, Art 119 of the Treaty does not preclude measures which achieve equal treatment by reducing the advantages of the persons previously favoured ...

[T]he step of raising the retirement age for women to that for men, which an employer decides to take in order to remove discrimination in relation to occupational pensions as regards benefits payable in respect of future periods of service, cannot be

---

32   [1994] IRLR 586, p 596. The same point was made in *Ten Oever*, Case C-109/91 [1993] ECR I-4879; [1995] ICR 74; [1993] IRLR 601. Fredman, *op cit*, fn 4, p 99, comments that these decisions mean that the 'assumption of men as providers and women as dependants [is] punctuated. It is worth noting, perhaps cynically, that this is one context in which men are the direct beneficiaries of equality for women'. This is because the decisions hold that pension schemes must provide for *women's* survivor-dependants on the same terms as *men's*.

33   See also [1994] ECR I-4435; [1995] ICR 596.

accompanied by measures, even if only transitional, designed to limit the adverse consequences which such a step may have for women ...

Even assuming that it would, in this context, be possible to take account of objectively justifiable considerations relating to the needs of the undertaking or of the occupational scheme concerned, the administrators of the occupational scheme could not reasonably plead, as justification for raising the retirement age for women [during the period between 17 May 1990 and 1 July 1991] financial difficulties as significant as those of which the Court took account in the *Barber* judgment, since the space of time involved is relatively short and attributable in any event to the conduct of the scheme administrators themselves.[34]

This judgment provides that equality may be brought about by the process of so called 'levelling down' – benefits for the advantaged group may be *reduced* so long as equality is attained. This is despite the fact that the Court in *Defrenne v SABENA (No 3)*[35] held that Art 119 necessitated raising the lower salary to the level of the higher 'in view of connection between Art 119 and the harmonisation of working conditions while maintaining improvement'. Not only that, the Court requires that this notion of equality be achieved immediately, with no transition period permissible to cushion those disadvantaged by the change.

This approach is a fundamental challenge to the view that anti-discrimination legislation is designed to improve the living standards of previously disadvantaged groups rather than simply concerned with a formal notion of equality.

Fredman, S, 'The poverty of equality: pensions and the ECJ' [1996] 25 ILJ 91, pp 96–97:

While the earlier cases demonstrate a clear commitment to the improvement of living and working standards, the Court has rapidly moved away from the notion that equality is allied to distributive justice. Instead, a formal conception has emerged, one which is fully satisfied by consistent treatment, even if this means depriving women of their existing benefits or vested expectations. Indeed, the Court has gone further and insisted that, once a decision has been made to 'level down', equality requires that this be achieved immediately and without any transitional measures protecting women's vested interests. Only in cases where women have already received benefits does equality require the extension of such benefits to men. The result is a notion of equality which is fully consistent with an increase in disadvantage ...

It was only in respect of discrimination between the date of the *Barber* decision and the equalisation of pensions that it was necessary to extend women's benefits to men. Three factors seem to have influenced this limiting choice of 'levelling up': a practical recognition of the impossibility of withdrawing benefits already granted to women; the fact that the financial consequences for employers would be limited and well defined; and a gesture towards fault-based fairness, which requires that compensation be payable because the employer was at fault in failing to introduce equality speedily.[36]

---

34 The Court ruled in the same way in *Van den Akker v Stichting Shell Pensioenfonds* Case C-28/93 [1994] ECR I-4527; [1995] ICR 596; [1994] IRLR 616. These cases do not overturn the principle that changing the terms of a employee's pension may give rise to remedies against the employer for breach of the employment contract; it is also possible that there may be remedies in trust against the trustees.

35 Case C-149/77 [1978] ECR 1365; [1978] 3 CMLR 312, ECJ.

36 According to the 1993 survey conducted by the National Association of Pension Funds, at least 90% of UK occupational pension schemes had equalised pensionable ages by that date, of which 63% had chosen equality at 65. Generally, see www.napf.co.uk.

(c)   Interaction with State schemes

Because of the fact that State pension arrangements – as well as ages – often differentiated between male and female benefits, it is not uncommon for occupational pension schemes to make adjustments in an attempt to ensure overall fairness. While equality of benefits is now mandatory for benefits applicable to periods of service after the date of the *Barber* judgment, these cases raise the problem of whether consideration of equality permits the level of benefits under the State scheme to be taken into consideration.

Birds Eye Walls Ltd v Roberts Case C-132/92 [1994] IRLR 29[37]

Mrs Roberts retired aged 57 on grounds of ill-health after 17 years' service. She received an annual pension of £383 from the Unilever Superannuation Fund. In addition, she received £919 (making a total of £1,302) as a 'bridging pension' from a discretionary scheme operated by companies in the Unilever Group.

These additional payments were made where the employee was not yet entitled to a State pension and where the entitlement to an occupational pension was at a reduced rate. The objective was to place the employees in the position they would have been in had they not been forced to retire. The additional sum was paid to make up the difference between what was actually received by way of pension and what would have been received had the employee continued to work until the State pension age.

Thus, until age 60, there was no substantial difference between the bridging pension paid to women and to men, since neither qualified for a State pension. From the age of 60, however, the bridging pension for a woman was reduced by the amount of the State pension she received or was deemed to have received, but no such reduction was made in respect of a man until age 65. Her pension was reduced by £749 (£919 to £170) from age 60 when it was assumed that she would start to receive an old age pension from the State. She argued that a man in her position would have been entitled to receive the pension at the full rate until age 65.

An industrial tribunal rejected her claim on the basis that the difference in payment stemmed from the difference in State pension provision.

Barber was decided after that decision. Allowing her appeal, the Employment Appeal Tribunal (EAT) held that by deducting her State pension from her occupational pension, the employers would be depriving her of her entitlement to the same 'pay' from her employer as a man would receive, even though the result would be that she would receive, when the State provision was added on, £749 per year more in total than a male comparator between 60 and 65.

Judgment (pp 31–32):

> While sharing Mrs Roberts' view as to the existence of direct discrimination, the Commission considers, however, that this does not mean that because the discrimination is direct it cannot be justified, since the very concept of discrimination, whether direct or indirect, involves a difference of treatment which is unjustified ... Birds Eye Walls is attempting to achieve substantive equality between the sexes by

---

37 See also [1993] ECR I-5579; [1994] ICR 338. Applied in *Trustees of Uppingham School Retirement Benefits Scheme for Non-Teaching Staff and Another v Shillcock* [2002] EWHC 641; [2002] IRLR 702, ChD.

compensating for an inequality arising from the difference in pensionable ages in a particular set of circumstances where such inequality would cause considerable hardship ...

[A]lthough until the age of 60 the financial position of a woman taking early retirement on grounds of ill-health is comparable to that of a man in the same situation, neither of them as yet entitled to the payment of the State pension, that is no longer the case between the ages of 60 and 65 since that is when women, unlike men, start drawing that pension. That difference as regards the objective premise, which necessarily entails that the amount of the bridging pension is not the same for men and women, cannot be considered discriminatory.

What is more, given the purpose of the bridging pension, to maintain the amount for women at the same level as that which obtained before they received the State pension would give rise to unequal treatment to the detriment of men who do not receive the State pension until the age of 65 ...

It is not contrary to Art 119 ... when calculating the bridging pension, to take account of the full State pension which a married woman would have received if she had not opted in favour of paying contributions at a reduced rate ...

This case purports to focus on the justice of the substantive outcome rather than on a more formal notion of inequality. Normally, such a process of reasoning might be thought to favour women. It is ironic that what is said to be substantive equality here reduces the total amount of post-retirement income available to women. Moreover, the case assumes entitlement to a State pension, even though the plaintiff was not entitled to one since she had elected to pay National Insurance contributions at the reduced married woman's rate. Her decision and the consequences flowing from it were said to depend on her free choice and could not affect the Court's reasoning.

However, the Court took a different, more formalistic approach in *Bestuur van het Algemeen Burgerlijk Pensioenfonds v Beune*.[38] Here, when equality was introduced into the Dutch Civil Service pension scheme, it was decided to protect the expectations of married women rather than opt for absolute immediate equality. The upshot was that the operation of the State scheme caused married men to face a greater deduction from their occupational scheme than did married women. A male plaintiff was successful in his argument that he should be treated no less favourably than a woman. *Roberts* decided that an occupational scheme may take into account the benefits received under a statutory scheme in order to ensure overall equality. It is the only recent case in which differentiation in private pension arrangements dependent upon a different State pensionable age has been found compatible with European law. There may be a distinction in that in *Roberts*, there was no differentiation as to the age at which benefits became payable; rather, the differentiation concerned the level of such benefits; on the other hand, in *Beune*, it seems that the differentiation was based upon and perpetuated the permitted distinction in State pensionable ages. Whether or not this is convincing – it may simply be that the cases are in conflict – it is clear that *Roberts* is out of line with the trend of more recent authority.

---

38   Case C-7/93 [1994] ECR I-4471; [1995] IRLR 103.

Whiteford, E, 'Occupational pension schemes and European law: clarity at last?', in Hervey, T and O'Keeffe, D (eds), *Sex Equality Law in the European Union,* **1996, Chichester: John Wiley, pp 32–33:**

[The Court in *Roberts* appeared] to acquiesce in account being taken of sources of income (the statutory pension) falling outside the scope of Art 119. The total income received from both sources may well have been equal as a result of the scheme operated by Birds Eye Walls, but the 'pay' (the amounts paid by the occupational scheme) of male and female employees between the ages of 60 and 65 was different. A discrimination in the statutory scheme which is generally seen to favour women was used in this case to justify a discrimination in the occupational scheme which favours men, because the outcome was seen to be neutral. Two wrongs do apparently make a right.

(d)   The retrospective effect

Barber v Guardian Royal Exchange Insurance Group Case C-262/88 [1990] IRLR 240[39]

Judgment (at p 259):

[M]ember States [are authorised] to defer the compulsory implementation of the principle of equal treatment with regard to the determination of pensionable age for the purposes of granting old age pensions and the possible consequences thereof for other benefits ...

In the light of [the provisions of the Occupational Pensions Directive] the Member States and the parties concerned were reasonably entitled to consider that Art 119 did not apply to pensions paid under contracted out schemes and that derogations from the principle of equality between men and women were still permitted in that sphere.

In those circumstances, overriding considerations of legal certainty preclude legal situations which have exhausted all their effects in the past from being called in question where that might upset retrospectively the financial balance of many contracted out pension schemes. It is appropriate, however, to provide an exception in favour of individuals who have taken action in good time in order to safeguard their rights. Finally, it must be pointed out that no restriction of the effects of the aforesaid interpretation can be permitted as regards the acquisition of entitlement to a pension as from the date of this judgment.

It must therefore be held that the direct effect of Art 119 of the Treaty may not be relied upon in order to claim entitlement to a pension with effect from a date prior to that of this judgment, except in the case of workers or those claiming under them who have before that date initiated legal proceedings or raised an equivalent claim under applicable national law.

In other words, the *Barber* decision was only to apply as from the date of the judgment, 17 May 1990, but given the fact that pension entitlement builds up gradually over a period of years, it was unclear what was the precise effect of this temporal limitation. There were four possible views as to the persons who could rely on *Barber*:

(a) those who began to contribute to a pension after 17 May 1990 (a very narrow interpretation);

---

39   See also [1990] ECR I-1889; [1991] 1 QB 344; [1990] ICR, 616.

(b) those in receipt of pension benefits which were applicable only in respect of periods of employment after 17 May 1990 (arguably a middle position and the one eventually adopted);

(c) those beginning to receive pension benefits after 17 May 1990, whether referable to periods of employment before or after that date (a fairly wide interpretation);

(d) those receiving any pension payment after 17 May 1990, whether referable to periods of employment before or after that date (the widest interpretation).

Moore, S, 'Justice doesn't mean a free lunch: the application of the principle of equal pay to occupational pension schemes' (1995) 20 EL Rev 159, pp 165–66:

The financial balance of a pension scheme depends upon a number of premises, including pension lifetimes and the survival probabilities of men and women but, in particular, upon the correlation between the pension contributions paid in respect of a period of pensionable service and the subsequent pension benefit which is derived from that same period of service. An interpretation of *Barber* which had raised pension benefits in respect of service before 17 May 1990 would therefore have led to an increase in liabilities without a corresponding change in assets and thereby upset the financial balance of the scheme. It would also have failed to respect the legitimate expectations of the parties by imposing upon the pension funds, and/or the employer, retrospective liabilities.

[T]he actual cost to the industry and the reserves which it had on hand to meet that cost were a matter of fierce controversy. For example, the estimated bill ranged from £45 billion, on the part of the UK Government, to £6–12 billion spread over a period of 10–15 years ... Furthermore, it was argued that the real cost of implementing *Barber* pursuant to the third or fourth interpretation was less than the pension industry claimed because it was necessary to deduct the costs of payments made to men aged 60–65 which would no longer have to be made if men were to receive pensions at the same age as women. Two benefits identified as yielding reductions were death-in-service benefits and ill-health pensions. In addition, it was suggested that it was legitimate to take account of the extent to which pension schemes had built up a surplus of capital assets over the years which could be used to fund the cost of equalisation.

[The] Court has held on many occasions that Art 119 is intended to guarantee a fundamental right ... The Court has also consistently recognised that it is appropriate to draw inspiration from international treaties designed to protect human rights and from the constitutional traditions of Member States in order to determine what constitutes a fundamental human right ... Any restriction on the temporal effect of Art 119 should therefore have taken account of the fundamental nature of the rights guaranteed by Art 119 and should have been construed as narrowly as possible with due regard to the social policy which it reflects.

There was widespread unease at the potential width – which really means cost – of *Barber*. As a result, before the European Court clarified the law, a protocol was attached to the Treaty of European Union – the Maastricht Treaty:

For the purposes of Art [141] ... benefits under occupational social security schemes shall not be considered as remuneration if and in so far as they are attributable to periods of service prior to 17 May 1990, except in the case of workers or those claiming under them who have before that date initiated legal proceedings or raised an equivalent claim under applicable national law.

In any event, the issue soon came before the European Court.

Ten Oever v Stichting Bedrijfspensioenfonds Voor het Glazenwassers – en Schoonmaakbedrijf Case C-109/91 [1993] IRLR 601, p 603[40]

[I]t must be made clear that equality of treatment in the matter of occupational pensions may be claimed only in relation to benefits payable in respect of periods of employment subsequent to 17 May 1990, the date of the *Barber* judgment, subject to the exception prescribed therein for workers or those claiming under them who have, before that date, initiated legal proceedings or raised an equivalent claim under the applicable national law.[41]

Coloroll Pension Trustees Ltd v Russell Case C-200/91 [1994] IRLR 586, p 598

[T]he national court asks whether, and how, the limitation of the effects in time of the *Barber* judgment applies to benefits payable under occupational social security schemes which are not linked to length of actual service ... such as a lump sum payment in the event of an employee's death during his employment.

Since such a benefit is payable solely by reason of an employment relationship existing at the time of the event triggering payment of the benefit, irrespective of the length of previous periods of service, the limitation of the effects in time of the *Barber* judgment applies only where the operative event occurred before 17 May 1990. After that date, such benefits must be granted in accordance with the principle of equal treatment without any need to distinguish between periods of service prior to the *Barber* judgment and periods of service subsequent to that judgment.

Thus, equal treatment was required in respect of one-off payments such as a death-in-service lump sum, whereas benefits which were dependent on length of service accrued over time would only be equalised gradually as the period since *Barber* increased.

Vroege v NCIV Institut voor Volkshuisvesting BV and Stichting Pensioenfonds NCIV Case C-57/93[42]

From 1 May 1975, the applicant worked 25.9 hours per week for NCIV. Until 1 January 1991, their pension scheme rules allowed only men and unmarried women working at least 80% of the normal full working day to be members, a rule which excluded the applicant. From 1 January 1991, when the rules were changed, she began to accrue pension rights. However, under the transitional arrangements adopted, she was not allowed to purchase years of membership in respect of her service prior to 1991.

She claimed that the fund rules contravened Art 119 (now Art 141) in that she had no right to be a member of the scheme in respect of periods of service prior to 1 January 1991. She claimed membership with retrospective effect as from 8 April 1976, the date of the decision in *Defrenne v SABENA*,[43] in which the ECJ held that Art 119 (now Art 141) had direct effect.

The argument was based on *Bilka-Kaufhaus*, which held that an hours requirement for membership of a pension scheme was indirectly discriminatory against women. The UK Government argued that the terms of the post-*Barber* Protocol were

40   See also [1993] ECR I-4879; [1995] ICR 74.
41   The same approach was adopted in *Neath v Hugh Steeper Ltd* Case C-152/91 [1994] ECR I-6935; [1995] ICR 118; [1994] IRLR 91.
42   See also [1994] IRLR 651; [1994] ECR I-4541; [1995] ICR 635.
43   Case C-43/75 [1976] ECR 455; [1976] 2 CMLR 98; [1976] ICR 547, ECJ.

sufficiently wide that *Bilka* was impliedly overruled and that therefore retrospective membership of schemes could not be claimed in respect of periods before the *Barber* judgment. The ECJ disagreed.

Judgment (p 661):

[T]he limitation of the effects in time of the *Barber* judgment concerns only those kinds of discrimination which employers and pension schemes could reasonably have considered to be permissible owing to the transitional derogations for which Community law provided and which were capable of being applied to occupational pensions.

It must be concluded that, as far as the right to join an occupational scheme is concerned, there is no reason to suppose that the professional groups concerned could have been mistaken about the applicability of Art 119 ...

[I]f the court had considered it necessary to impose a limit in time on the rule that the right to be a member of an occupational pension scheme is covered by Art 119, it would have done so in the *Bilka* judgment.

Protocol No 2 [of the Maastricht Treaty] ... relates only to benefits – being all that is mentioned in Protocol No 2 – and not to the right to belong to an occupational social security scheme.[44]

This decision gave the right to retrospective pension schemes, in theory back to 1976.[45] Its enormous potential was, however, significantly curtailed by the following case.

Fisscher v Voorhuis Hengelo BV and Stichting Bedrijfspensioenfonds voor de Detailhandel Case C-128/93 [1994] IRLR 662[46]

Here again, a part-time worker claimed retrospective membership of the relevant scheme.

Judgment (p 665):

[A] worker cannot claim more favourable treatment, particularly in financial terms, than he would have had if he had been duly accepted as a member [when he started work].

[T]he fact that a worker can claim retroactively to join an occupational pension scheme does not allow the worker to avoid paying the contributions relating to the period of membership concerned.[47]

---

44 In *Quirk v Burton Hospital NHS Trust* [2002] IRLR 353, the claimant, a male nurse, challenged the National Health Service Pension Scheme Regulations 1995, which permitted nurses to retire at age 55, as opposed to age 60. However, reg 2(4) provided: 'Where ... a member becomes entitled to receive a pension before age 60, the amount payable shall — (a) in the case of a female member, be calculated by reference to all of her pensionable service under the scheme; and (b) in the case of a male member, be calculated only by reference to pensionable service in or after 17 May 1990' (the date of the *Barber* decision). The Court of Appeal held that the claim concerned the level of benefit, rather than access to the scheme, and as such fell under *Barber* and the regulation did not infringe Community law.

45 This probably means that the six- (or, in Scotland, five-) year limit for an arrears award, contained in the EqPA 1970, s 2ZB or 2ZC (respectively), is contrary to Community law. See further, Chapter 14, pp 434–36.

46 See also [1994] ECR I-4583; [1995] ICR 635.

47 Followed in *Preston v Wolverhampton Healthcare NHS Trust* [2001] 2 AC 415; [2000] All ER (EC) 714; [2001] 2 WLR 408; [2000] ICR 961; [2000] IRLR 506, ECJ. See, further, below, p 456; also, Chapter 14, p 434.

To obtain retrospective membership of a contributory scheme, the worker will have to pay the contributions which would have been paid during the relevant period. Thus, the employer avoids having to pay contributions in respect of any previous years the backdated contributions for which the employee cannot now afford to buy. The decision has been the subject of powerful criticism, in terms both of its reasoning and its practical impact.

Fredman, S, 'The poverty of equality: pensions and the ECJ' [1996] 25 ILJ 91, p 105:

[*Fisscher* held that contributions were payable retrospectively by the women.] In practice ... this functions as an effective bar to married or part-time women making use of their rights to retrospective membership, given the fact that employee contributions are worth an average of £550 per annum. This is a good example of the fluidity of equality justifications: a focus on the requirement to pay contributions yields a diametrically opposite decision to a focus on whether pension benefits will in fact be available. Moreover, the Court in this case takes a static view of equality, ignoring the very real continuing effects of past discrimination. Instead, the Court has clearly been influenced by the expense likely to be incurred by employers to make good their denial of membership.

Whiteford, E, 'Lost in the mists of time: the ECJ and occupational pensions' (1995) 32 CML Rev 801, pp 813–15:

It appears to have been considered beyond doubt by the parties to the [Fisscher] litigation that where an individual wishes to claim retroactive membership the employer will be bound to pay the backdated retroactive contributions. However, merely requiring that employer and employee to pay the contributions which they would have had to pay in the past will not suffice to ensure that the level of benefit obtained by the wrongfully excluded employee is equal to that which has been accrued by the formerly advantaged employee. This is because pensions are funded not only through employer and employee contributions, but the funds invest their income which, in turn, all being well, yields investment income which also funds the future benefits. So in ensuring that all the consequences of the past discrimination are eradicated, someone must pay the interest. It is suggested that the employer must be held responsible for making good any interest which has been lost ...

If an employer chooses to require that someone in Ms Fisscher's position pay all backdated contributions in one lump sum – which does not appear to be precluded by the Court's judgment – the financial barrier to the individual seems likely to prove insurmountable in most cases.

There have been, in the UK, some procedural barriers to retrospective claims. In *Preston v Wolverhampton Healthcare NHS Trust*,[48] the ECJ held that s 2(5) of the EqPA 1970, in preventing pensionable service to be credited before the two years preceding an initial claim of equal pay, contravened Community law. When the case returned to the House of Lords,[49] it was held, following *Fisscher*,[50] that credit should be backdated to 8 April 1976 (the date when the ECJ held in *Defrenne v Sabena*[51] that Art 119 (now

---

48 [2001] 2 AC 415; [2000] All ER (EC) 714; [2001] 2 WLR 408; [2000] ICR 961; [2000] IRLR 506, ECJ.
49 [2001] 2 AC 455; [2001] All ER (D) 99 (Feb), HL.
50 *Fisscher v Voorhuis Hengelo BV and Stichting Bedrijfspensioenfonds voor de Detailhandel* Case C-128/93 [1994] ECR I-4583; [1995] ICR 635; [1994] IRLR 662, ECJ.
51 *Defrenne v Sabena* Case C-43/75; [1976] ICR 547, ECJ.

Art 141) had direct effect). The Government responded to the ECJ judgment by replacing the two-year rule with the six- (or for Scotland, five-) year rule, which brings such claims into line with breach of contract.[52] However, the House of Lords' judgment reveals that, in cases of pensions at least, even the amended rule may contravene Community law.

(e)   Actuarial considerations

The issue is the extent to which it is permissible for pension arrangements to take into account the fact that, on average, women live longer than men. This could be done by increasing female employee contributions relative to men, or by differentiating between employer contributions in respect of male and female employees. There is no *logical* need to do either of these: the total potential liabilities of a scheme may be calculated actuarially, but the level of contributions could be averaged out between men and women. The issue is also relevant to the level of benefits to be reimbursed to an early leaver from a scheme.[53]

Neath v Hugh Steeper Ltd **Case C-152/91 [1994] IRLR 91, ECJ**[54]

The applicant was employed from January 1973 to 29 June 1990, when he was made redundant when aged 54. He was a member of a pension scheme where employee contributions were the same for men and women. A woman could retire on full pension at 60, whereas a man could not do so until 65. The method of calculating the pension varied according to the sex of the worker and the circumstances of the case. An employee could retire early and take a reduced pension at any time after age 50, with the consent of the employee and the trustees. The reduction took account of the length of the period between actual retirement date and normal retirement date. If the employer and the trustees did not consent to early retirement, a member leaving the scheme after 50 was entitled only to a deferred pension or a transfer payment to another scheme. The transfer payment varied according to the sex of the worker based on actuarial factors. As the cost of providing a pension for a woman was greater than for a man, the transfer value for a woman's accrued pension contributions was therefore considered to be greater than for a man.

The applicant was allowed to take an immediate pension when made redundant. He was offered the choice of a deferred pension or a transfer payment; if he opted for the latter, its value would be £30,672.59. This calculation was based on the assumption that he received his pension at 65, except as regards benefits attributable to his period of employment after 17 May 1990, in relation to which the calculation was based on a retirement age of 60 in accordance with one view of the effect of *Barber*. If he were assumed to have a normal retirement age of 60 in relation to his entire pensionable service, the transfer payment would have been £39,934.56 using male actuarial factors and £41,486.25 using female actuarial factors.

---

52   See Chapter 14, pp 434–36.
53   Under Directive 86/378, money purchase schemes were permitted different benefit levels where this represented actuarial differences, employee contributions had to be equal after 30 July 1999 – a point rendered irrelevant by *Barber* – but employer contributions could continue to differentiate. Final salary schemes required equal benefits, equal employer contributions, and equal employee contributions after 30 July 1999.
54   See also [1994] ECR I-6935; [1995] ICR 118.

He also argued that he would have to wait five more years than a woman in order to receive a deferred pension, but also that if he then wished to exercise his right to exchange part of his pension for cash, he would receive £17,193.94 rather than the £21,029.02 that would be received by a woman in similar circumstances. That difference was also based on actuarial tables.

Judgment (pp 94–95):

The employer's contributions ... vary over time, so as to cover the balance of the cost of the pensions promised. They are ... higher for female than for male employees.

This variability and inequality is due to the use of actuarial factors in the mechanism for funding the scheme. The aim of an occupational retirement pension scheme being to provide for the future payment of periodic pensions, the scheme's financial resources, accrued through funding, must be adjusted according to the pensions which, according to the forecasts, will have to be paid. The assessments needed to give effect to this system are based on a number of objective factors, such as the return on the scheme's investments, the rate of increase in salaries and demographic assumptions, in particular those relating to the life expectancy of workers.

The fact that women live on average longer than men is one of the actuarial factors taken into account in determining how the scheme in question is to be funded. This is why the employer has to pay higher contributions for his female employees than for his male employees ...

It must be determined whether transfer benefits and lump sum options constitute pay ...

The Commission claims that this is indeed the case and that consequently any difference in treatment based on sex would be permissible only if it were objectively justified. Statistical data based on the life expectancy of the two sexes do not, in its view, constitute an objective justification because they reflect averages calculated on the basis of the entire male and female population, whereas the right given to equal treatment in the matter of pay is a right given to employees individually and not because they belong to a particular class ...

The assumption underlying this approach is that the employer commits himself, albeit unilaterally, to pay his employees defined benefits or to grant them specific advantages and that the employees in turn expect the employer to pay them those benefits or to provide them with those advantages. Anything that is not a consequence of that commitment and does not therefore come within the corresponding expectations of the employees falls outside the concept of pay.

In the context of a defined-benefit occupational pension scheme such as that in question ... the employer's commitment to his employees concerns the payment, at a given moment in time, of a periodic pension for which the determining criteria are already known at the time when the commitment is made and which constitutes pay under Art 119. However, that commitment does not necessarily have to do with the funding arrangements chosen to secure the periodic payment of the pension, which thus remain outside the scope of application of Art 119.

The amount of contributions must be the same for all employees, male and female, which is indeed so in the present case. That is not so in the case of the employer's contributions, which ensure the adequacy of the funds necessary to cover the cost of the pensions promised, so securing their payment in the future, that being the substance of the employer's commitment. It follows that, unlike periodic payment of pensions, inequality of employer's contributions paid under funded defined-benefit schemes, which is due to the use of actuarial factors differing according to sex, is not struck at by Art 119.

Coloroll Pension Trustees Ltd v Russell Case C-200/91 [1994] IRLR 586, pp 599–600[55]

The essence of the High Court's fourth question is whether Art 119 precludes actuarial factors ... from being taken into account in occupational pension schemes and, if so, how the limitation of the effects in time of the *Barber* judgment applies in this context.

Article 119 applies to all benefits payable to an employee by an occupational pension scheme, irrespective of whether the scheme is contributory or non-contributory. Whether contributions are payable by the employer or the employees has no bearing on the concept of pay when applied to occupational pensions ...

However, the situation is different in the case of additional voluntary contributions paid by employees to secure additional benefits such as, for example, an additional fixed pension for the member or the member's dependants, an additional tax-free lump sum or additional lump sum benefits on death.

The order for reference shows that these additional benefits are calculated separately, solely on the basis of the value of the contribution paid, which are credited to a special fund managed by the trustees as a distinct fund ...

[S]uch benefits cannot be regarded as pay ...

Thus, the situations in which the use of actuarial factors remains permissible are: first, in respect of the transfer value of a scheme or its conversion into a capital sum; secondly, in respect of additional voluntary contributions; and, thirdly, where a reduced pension is paid on early retirement, where the reduction is due to actuarial factors. The device used to ensure their continued lawfulness is to exclude them from the definition of 'pay' in Art 141.

Moore, S, 'Justice doesn't mean a free lunch: the application of the principle of equal pay to occupational pension schemes' (1995) 20 EL Rev 159, p 176:

The rationale [of *Neath*] appears to be [that] since contributions made by the employer do not fall within Art 119 [now Art 141], differences in those contributions due to actuarial factors are not prohibited by Art 119 and, consequently, differences in benefits payable under the scheme which are the direct result of the differences in the contributions paid by the employer are not prohibited by Art 119 either. If this is indeed the reasoning behind the judgment, it is surprising that the Court did not distinguish between differences in the *funding arrangements* which are due to actuarial factors and similar differences in the *benefits* paid ... [Such benefits are clearly pay and] there is no reason why Art 119 should cease to apply to discriminatory benefits simply because the discrimination is the result of the funding arrangements chosen by the employer to operate the scheme. First, as a matter of practice, there seems to be no necessity for an employer to use sex-based actuarial factors to calculate his liabilities ... Secondly ... a prohibition of the use of sex-based actuarial tables to calculate benefits paid out under a pension scheme would not have affected the ability of the pension fund to acquire an accurate picture of the life expectancy of the scheme members in order to assess outstanding and future liabilities because the internal actuarial methods of administration, used to calculate the funds needed in order to maintain a financial balance between contributions and benefits, do not, in any event, fall within Art 119.

---

55 See also [1994] ECR I-4389; [1995] ICR 179; [1994] IRLR 586.

This permitted continued use of actuarial factors arises from the interpretation given by the Court to Art 141.[56] This case law was codified in Directive 96/97, which amended the Equal Treatment in Occupational Social Security Schemes Directive, 86/378. An exception is provided for defined-contribution schemes which may continue to take account of actuarial factors based on sex.[57] In the case of funded defined-benefit schemes, certain elements may continue to be unequal where such inequality is dependent upon actuarial factors.[58] Examples given in an annex to the Directive include the conversion into a capital sum of part of a periodic payment, the transfer of pension rights, and a reduced pension where the worker opts to take early retirement. In other words, the case law of the ECJ, which gave a limited green light to the continued use of actuarial factors, is confirmed by subsequent legislation. It is arguably permissible for employers to grant their employees low basic occupational pensions which are then topped up with substantial additional contributions, voluntary in theory but perhaps less so in practice, to which, because they are outside the definition of 'pay', Art 141 is inapplicable. Such schemes may continue to utilise gender-based actuarial factors.

---

56 The Pensions Act 1995, s 64(3), allows for the continued use of actuarial factors when calculating the level of employer contributions.

57 Directive 86/378, Art 6(1)(h).

58 *Ibid*, Art 6(1)(i).

CHAPTER 16

DISABILITY DISCRIMINATION

1 INTRODUCTION

After many years of political pressure, the anti-discrimination principle was finally extended to disabled people through the Disability Discrimination Act (DDA) 1995.[1] The Act is similar in some ways to the Sex Discrimination Act (SDA) 1975 and the Race Relations Act (RRA) 1976, and its procedural and remedial provisions are almost identical. The major differences of substance are, first, that direct discrimination is potentially justifiable and, secondly, that there is no explicit outlawing of indirect discrimination; rather, there is a duty to make reasonable adjustments to the needs of disabled people, a duty which fulfils many of the same functions as the concept of indirect discrimination. Another difference is that far more details of the law are given in the form of Regulations and Guidance. The reason is that the many different forms and varying severity of disabilities make it more difficult to deal with every issue through primary legislation. The technical complexities of the Act were noted by Mummery LJ in *Clark v TGD t/a Novacold*:[2]

> It is certainly more ambitious in its aim and scope than the system of registered disabled persons and quotas in the Disabled Persons (Employment) Act 1944, now repealed [see below]. And it is without doubt an unusually complex piece of legislation which poses novel questions of interpretation. It is not surprising that different conclusions have been reached at different levels of decision.

> This state of affairs should not be taken as a criticism of the Act or of its drafting or of the judicial disagreements about its interpretation. The whole subject presents unique challenges to legislators and to tribunals and courts, as well as to those responsible for the day-to-day operation of the Act in the workplace. Anyone who thinks that there is an easy way of achieving a sensible, workable and fair balance between the different interests of disabled persons, of employers and of able-bodied workers, in harmony with the wider public interests in an economically efficient workforce, in access to employment, in equal treatment of workers and in standards of fairness at work, has probably not given much serious thought to the problem.

There is now another dimension to this law to consider. The Equal Treatment at Work Directive[3] will be implemented on October 2004, by amending the 1995 Act extensively. The effect of the amendments will be discussed near the end of this chapter.

(1) Previous Legislation

The previous legal framework regulating the employment of disabled people was provided by the Disabled Persons (Employment) Act 1944. The Act required all employers employing 20 or more employees to have a quota whereby 3% of

---

1   See Doyle, B, 'Enabling legislation or dissembling law? The Disability Discrimination Act 1995' (1997) 60 MLR 64.
2   [1999] IRLR 318, at p 320, CA.
3   Council Directive 2000/78/EC.

employees should be registered disabled. Employing a non-disabled person where an employer was below quota was a criminal offence. Two classes of employment, passenger electric lift attendant and car park attendant, were reserved for registered disabled people.

There is no doubt that the quota system failed to meet the aspirations and expectations of disabled people and, by the time of its abolition, it had come close to falling into disuse. The Act allowed for employers to apply for a permit exempting them from responsibilities under the quota legislation; permits were issued straightforwardly in bulk, an approach which contributed to the view that, in effect, compliance was voluntary. Evidence suggested that employer awareness of the scheme was low and did not in practice influence employment decisions.[4] Only those who were registered as disabled counted towards fulfilment of quota; registration was voluntary and, for many disabled people, unnecessary and stigmatising. It became mathematically impossible for all employers to achieve their quota requirements. In these circumstances, perhaps not surprisingly, enforcement was so lax that there were only eight successful prosecutions throughout the operational period of the quota legislation.

Thus, the scheme failed for practical reasons. Whether it is objectionable in principle and whether a different approach is appropriate is less obvious. The advantages are a potential guarantee of employment opportunities irrespective of the individual merit of a disabled applicant, a recognition that it is society's responsibility through employers to provide meaningful work for disabled people, and the possibility of linking a quota system with employment subsidies. But the disadvantages are many. First, it provides no guarantee of employment at a level commensurate with the abilities of the individual, and indeed the two jobs reserved for the disabled only served to entrench a view that low-level menial tasks were the best that could be aspired to. Secondly, it imposes a solution on the disabled, rather than empowering individuals by the granting of rights, and it is thus paternalistic in nature. Thirdly, the enforcement mechanisms are taken out of the hands of individuals and given to some kind of enforcement agency. Experience with this kind of regulatory legislation suggests that there will always be a great willingness to find reasons not to prosecute. Finally, a quota system reinforces a belief that the disabled are an entirely separate category from the able-bodied and pays no heed to the fact that what is regarded as a disability depends in large measure on society's response to particular situations.

(2)   Progress Towards Legislation

Even if the view is taken that a quota system is inappropriate, it does not follow that anti-discrimination legislation is the right solution. Throughout most of the 1970s and 1980s, the preferred Government response was an entirely voluntary approach by way of education and assistance, both of employers and the disabled, in the belief that goodwill towards the disabled was present, with only the means to implement it lacking.[5]

---

4   Doyle, B, *New Directions Towards Disabled Workers' Rights*, 1994, London: Institute of Employment Rights, p 11.

5   *Ibid*, pp 13–17.

The pressure for anti-discrimination legislation, strong as it was in its own terms, developed a momentum from the fact that other jurisdictions, especially the USA and Australia, had themselves enacted such legislation.[6] In America, legislation was a response to the growing political power and social awareness of disabled people, especially disabled war veterans, who were able to argue that the cause of their disability imposed obligations of fair treatment on the State, and who were able to extend that reasoning to other groups of disabled people.

Proponents of anti-discrimination legislation had to face up to the fact that the experience of the SDA 1975 and the RRA 1976 was somewhat disappointing, a fact that many critics attributed to the individualism of the legislation, with the enforcement emphasis firmly based on the victim's claim before an employment tribunal. Some, indeed, regarded the emphasis on individual rights as wholly misplaced and as apt to deflect attention from the real political and social changes necessary to improve the lot of women and ethnic minorities. Gooding answered the argument in the following terms.[7]

Gooding, C, *Disabling Laws, Enabling Acts*, 1994, London: Pluto, p 43:

[A] rights-based discourse has a great capacity for empowering disabled people and for beneficially shaping broader social discourse ... [While] rights do not resolve problems [their value is] in transposing the problem into one which is defined as having a legal solution ...

[T]he subordination of disabled people has been located by society in the incapacities of their own bodies. Casting access requirements in the framework of rights discourse locates disabled people's subordination in the public rather than the private sphere. It therefore promotes a sense of collective identity among disabled people who, despite the vast differences in their individual disabilities, share a common experience of exclusion and stigmatisation by society ...

[T]his contradicts the common argument that because law reduces people to isolated individuals it runs counter to the only possible basis for radical change – collective action. Rights discourse promotes the development of an individual's sense of self and a group's collective identity most powerfully through the process in which these rights are asserted. The act of claiming a right is itself an assertion of moral self-worth. The advocacy process itself, for a group like disabled people who have historically been excluded from public life, combats this exclusion ...

It is a paradox, in no way unique to disabled people, that the anti-discrimination approach requires that in order to assert their right to full and equal participation in society, they must continue to assert their differences. The price of being heard, and achieving some control over the consequences of disability, is to accept the label.

However, to accept that rights are appropriate does not resolve the question of what kind of rights. Disability may have an impact upon capacity and qualifications, especially in relation to work, that race and gender do not have. That there are a few exceptions to this point, in the form of the genuine occupational qualification defences

---

6   See Doyle, B, *Disability, Discrimination and Equal Opportunity: A Comparative Study of the Employment Rights of Disabled People*, 1995, London: Mansell.

7   See also, Davies, J and Davies, W, 'Reconciling risk and the employment of disabled persons in a reformed Welfare State' (2000) 29 ILJ 347. At the time of writing, the Government plans to impose general duties on public authorities. See further below, p 520.

under the SDA 1975 and the RRA 1976, does not destroy its main thrust. It is further arguable that disabilities vary so greatly in their nature and impact that to the utilisation of one overarching anti-discrimination principle is flawed in theory and unworkable in practice.

These points can be answered. There is a clear parallel with the historical exclusion of women, which, while often purporting to be for physical reasons, in reality had a social explanation. Arguments that there are 'real' differences between the disabled and the able-bodied collapse in the face of social explanations in much the same way as explanations that there are differences between men and women. They collapse even more obviously, as disability is clearly not a status, but a relative position on a sliding scale of different abilities. The fact that there are exceptions within the SDA 1975 and the RRA 1976 merely demonstrates that rights are rarely absolute. That the DDA 1995 accepts the possibility of a defence for the employer based on excessive cost – adjustments need only be 'reasonable' – does not destroy the argument based on rights, but merely indicates that the employer has rights as well, albeit of a different nature. After all, cost may be relevant under the SDA 1975 and the RRA 1976 as a potentially relevant factor to the question of justified indirect discrimination. Finally, we have already stressed the symbolic importance of rights. Discrimination is now generally acknowledged to be 'wrong'; this attitude, while a huge generalisation, has been wrought by previous legislation. For both symbolic and practical reasons, it is appropriate for those wishing to counter disadvantages experienced by the disabled to utilise the anti-discrimination strategy.

The legislation was passed by the Conservative Government, a fact that might be thought somewhat surprising. The explanation is that, having ensured that a previous – and arguably stronger – Private Member's Bill – was prevented from passing through Parliament, the Government felt under a moral obligation to legislate. Several Codes of Practice have been issued.[8] They cover employment,[9] the definition of disability,[10] trade organisations,[11] rights of access to goods, facilities and services,[12] and education.[13] While their legal effect is the same, they are noticeably more comprehensive and detailed than the equivalent race and gender Codes, because of the greater variety of situations with which disability issues are concerned. The detail provided in the Codes, and especially the many specific examples, suggest that tribunals may be encouraged to refer to and rely on this Code more than has been the case with the gender and race Codes.

8 Available at www.drc-gb.org.uk; click on 'The Law'.
9 *Code of Practice for the Elimination of Discrimination in the Field of Employment Against Disabled Persons or Persons who have had a Disability*, 1996, London: HMSO. Issued on 25 July 1996 under the DDA 1995, s 53, by the Secretary of State (SI 1996/1996) with statutory effect from 2 December 1996.
10 *Guidance on Matters to be Taken into Account in Determining Questions Relating to the Definition of Disability*, London: HMSO. (ISBN 0 11 270 955 9). Issued on 25 July 1996 under the DDA 1995, s 3 by the Secretary of State (SI 1996/1996) with statutory effect from 31 July 1996.
11 *Duties of Trade Organisations to their Disabled Members and Applicants*, 1999, London: HMSO. (ISBN 0 11 271071 9).
12 *Code of Practice (Revised): Rights of Access; Goods, Facilities, Services and Premises.* Issued by the Disability Rights Commission (DRC) (ISBN No 011 702860 6). Effective from 27 May 2002 (SI 2002/720). It replaced the 1996 version, itself revised in 1999.
13 The DRC has issued two Codes: one for schools (ref COPSH July 2002) and one for post-16 education (COPP16 July 2002). Both were effective from 1 September 2002 (SI 2002/2216).

2   THE DEFINITION OF DISABILITY

(1)   Defining Disability

The definition of who is protected by the legislation – the definition of disability – is more complex than in relation to gender and race.

Gooding, C, *Disabling Laws, Enabling Acts*, 1994, London: Pluto, p 15:

To understand the full operation of discrimination on disabled people's lives we need to extend our understanding of that process to include the socio-economic and political forces which shape not only our attitudes towards disability but also the very meaning of that term. In a very real sense society disables individuals by constructing a disabled identity into which individuals are fitted ... [For example] the labels 'blind' or 'deaf' are relative ones, based on the percentage of 'full' vision' which a person possesses ...

[C]lassifications of disability have varied historically. In part, these historical variations result from shifts in technology and the social conditions in which that technology is disseminated ... [For example] visually impaired people ... by wearing glasses can possess a 'normal' range of vision. Often these people would be unable to read or distinguish objects without their visual aids. Yet they will not be considered 'disabled' both because this impairment is sufficiently widespread not to be stigmatised and because in our society such corrective aids are readily available.

The technological level of society can reduce disabilities by 'curing' physical impairments or by reducing their impact ... However it can also, paradoxically, increase them. Medical advances can increase the numbers of disabled people, prolonging the lives of people who would previously have died. Less positively, society can disable more individuals by increasing the level at which individuals are expected to function in society, and hence magnifying the disabling effects of impairments. One example of this is the invention of the telephone, which has had a detrimental effect on the ability of deaf people to function socially ...

Stone suggests that the concept of disability has been used to resolve the issue of distributive justice. This issue is created by the presence in the modern world of two distributive systems – one of which distributes on the basis of waged labour and the other on the basis of need. There is a potential conflict between the two systems, since if people can acquire goods through the need system they will not need to engage in waged work ... This conflict has historically been resolved by the creation of rigid categories of need – the elderly, children, the disabled – to determine who will be allowed to claim public assistance. Hence, disability becomes synonymous with dependence and inability to work.

(2)   The Legal Definition of Disability[14]

Disability discrimination is governed by the Disability Discrimination Act 1995.[15] The amending Regulations[16] do not affect the existing definition of discrimination. The

14 See 'Interpreting the DDA – part 1: the meaning of disability' (1998) 79 EOR 13.
15 The Disability Rights Commission Act 1999 established the Commission.
16 Disability Discrimination Act 1995 (Amendment) Regulations 2003, due in force 1 October 2004. However, at the time of writing, the Government plans to extend the definition regarding HIV and cancer. See below, p 520.

definition of disability is key to the scope of the legislation, even though the vast majority of claimants or potential claimants will be disabled under any definition. More than under any other discrimination legislation, the boundary between the protected and unprotected groups is unclear. 'The definition of disability must be both inclusive and exclusive: embracing individuals outside the limited popular perception of "disability", yet excluding idiosyncrasies, human traits and transient illness. A distinction must be drawn between chronic or handicapping conditions and temporary or minor maladies.'[17] The statutory definition is provided by s 1, as amplified by Sched 1. In addition, the meaning is further expanded by Regulations[18] and Guidance[19] on matters to be taken into account in interpreting the definition.

Disability Discrimination Act 1995

Section 1

(1)   Subject to the provisions of Schedule 1, a person has a disability for the purposes of this Act if he has a physical or mental impairment which has a substantial and long term adverse effect on his ability to carry out normal day-to-day activities.

In general, the Act adopts the 'medical' model of disability. This is in contrast to the 'social' model, which identifies the infrastructure of society and social barriers as the cause of disability, rather than a condition or impairment of the claimant. There are four criteria which must be satisfied: there must be (a) a physical or mental impairment, (b) it must affect ability to carry out everyday activities, and such effect must be both (c) long-term and (d) substantial. Before looking them in turn, we should note the general approach adopted by the Employment Appeal Tribunal (EAT).

Goodwin v The Patent Office [1999] ICR 302; [1999] IRLR 4, EAT

The facts are set out below, p 484.

Morison J (p 307):

The role of the industrial tribunal contains an inquisitorial element, as rule 9[20] of their Rules of Procedure indicates. The interventionist role which they have in relation to equal value claims, and which is more clearly set out in the rules contained in Schedule 2 of the procedural rules, might be thought a good model for disability cases. There is a risk of a genuine 'Catch-22' situation. Some disabled persons may be unable or unwilling to accept that they suffer from any disability; indeed, it may be symptomatic of their condition that they deny it. Without the direct assistance of the tribunal at the hearing, there may be some cases where the claim has been drafted with outside assistance but which the applicant, for some reason related to his disability, is unwilling to support. Whilst we are sure that tribunals would be alert to such cases, some might feel constrained not to intervene perhaps as much as they would wish ...

---

17   Doyle, B, 'Employment rights, equal opportunities and disabled persons: the ingredients of reform' [1993] 22 ILJ 89, p 91.

18   Disability Discrimination (Meaning of Disability) Regulations 1996, SI 1996/1455.

19   *Guidance on Matters to be Taken into Account in Determining Questions Relating to the Definition of Disability*, London: HMSO (ISBN 0 11 270 955 9). Issued on 25 July 1996 under the DDA, s 3 by the Secretary of State (SI 1996/1996) with effect from 31 July 1996.

20   See now, r 11, Sched 1 of the Employment Tribunals (Constitution and Rules of Procedure) Regulations 2001, SI 2001/1171.

The tribunal should bear in mind that with social legislation of this kind, a purposive approach to construction should be adopted. The language should be construed in a way which gives effect to the stated or presumed intention of Parliament, but with due regard to the ordinary and natural meaning of the words in question. With this legislation, tribunals are given explicit assistance ... which should detract from the need to adopt a loose construction of the language: Guidance ...

The EAT repeats what it has said on a previous occasion, namely that, at least during the early period of the Act's operation, reference should always be made, explicitly, to any relevant provision of the Guidance ... which has been taken into account in arriving at its Decision.

... [I]n addressing the substantial and long-term conditions, [see below] ... a tribunal 'shall' take such guidance into account. But, as the Guide makes clear, in many cases the question whether a person is disabled within the meaning of the Act can admit of only one answer. In such clear cases it would be wrong to search the Guide and use what it says as some kind of extra hurdle over which the applicant must jump.

Morison J made two points: that the tribunal had an inquisitorial role and the legislation should be interpreted purposively. However, in more recent cases, Morison's J enthusiasm was not repeated. The first point was received soberly in the later EAT case of *Rugamer*, which was upheld by the Court the Appeal as a 'valuable judgment'.[21] The second point was simply ignored by the Court of Appeal, when discussing interpretation.

Rugamer v Sony Music; McNicol v Balfour Beatty Rail Maintenance [2001] IRLR 644; ICR 381, EAT

The facts are set out below, p 471.

Mr Commissioner Howell QC:

47   ... the observations of Morison J relied on are shown by their context to mean no more than that the Tribunal is obliged, as indeed is expressly recorded in r 9[20] of the Tribunal Procedure Rules, to conduct the hearing in a fair and balanced manner, intervening and making its own enquiries in the course of the hearing ... so as to ensure due consideration of the issues raised ... However the role of the Tribunal is not thereby extended so as to place on it the duty to conduct a free standing inquiry of its own, or require it to attempt to obtain further evidence beyond that placed in front of it on the issues raised by the parties, or to cause the parties to raise additional issues they have not sought to rely on at all.

McNicol v Balfour Beatty Rail Maintenance [2002] EWCA Civ 1074; [2002] IRLR 711, CA

Mummery LJ:

17.   The approach of the tribunal should be that the term 'impairment' in this context bears its ordinary and natural meaning. It is clear from Schedule 1 to the 1995 Act [see below] that impairment may result from an illness or it may consist of an illness, provided that, in the case of mental impairment, it must be a 'clinically well-recognised illness'. Apart from this there is no statutory description or definition of physical or mental 'impairment'. The Guidance [see below] issued under s 3 of the 1995 Act ... states in the introduction section in Part 1 that 'it is not necessary to consider how an impairment was caused' and

---

21   [2002] EWCA Civ 1074; [2002] IRLR 711, at para 1.

some examples of physical and mental impairment are given (eg, sensory impairments affecting sight or hearing), but no general definition or description of 'impairment' is attempted ...

It is left to the good sense of the tribunal to make a decision in each case on whether the evidence available establishes that the applicant has a physical or mental impairment with the stated effects. Such a decision can and should be made without substituting for the statutory language a different word or form of words in an ambitious and unnecessary attempt to describe or to define the concept of 'impairment'. The essential question in each case is whether, on sensible interpretation of the relevant evidence, including the expert medical evidence and reasonable inferences which can be made from all the evidence, the applicant can fairly be described as having a physical or mental impairment. The ordinary meaning of the statutory language and of the Guidance issued by the Secretary of State under s 3(1) is sufficiently clear to enable the tribunal to answer the question on the basis of the evidence.

This judgment suggests several times that words in the legislation and Guidance should be given their 'ordinary' meaning. 'Purposive' does not appear once in the judgment. On the contrary, tribunals were told not to be 'ambitious'. The view that a tribunal should adopt an inquisitorial role in Disability Discrimination Act cases was developed by counsel in *Woodrup v London Borough of Southwark*.[22] He argued that, in providing a service to the public, tribunals were obliged under Pt III of the Act to make 'reasonable adjustments' when dealing with disabled people. However, the Court of Appeal called this notion 'far fetched'.[23]

(a) Impairment

Disability Discrimination Act 1995

Schedule 1, para 1(1)

'Mental impairment' includes an impairment resulting from or consisting of a mental illness only if the illness is a clinically well-recognised illness.

Disability Discrimination (Meaning of Disability) Regulations 1996, SI 1996/1455

3 Addictions

(1)   Subject to paragraph (2) below, addiction to alcohol, nicotine or any other substance is to be treated as not amounting to an impairment for the purposes of the Act.

(2)   Paragraph (1) above does not apply to addiction which was originally the result of administration of medically prescribed drugs or other medical treatment.

4 Other conditions not to be treated as impairments

(1)   For the purposes of the Act the following conditions are to be treated as not amounting to impairments:
   (a) a tendency to set fires;
   (b) a tendency to steal;
   (c) a tendency to physical or sexual abuse of other persons;
   (d) exhibitionism; and
   (e) voyeurism.

---

22 [2002] EWCA Civ 1716.
23 *Ibid*, para 16.

(2)   Subject to paragraph (3) below for the purposes of the Act the condition known as seasonal allergic rhinitis (eg, hay fever) shall be treated as not amounting to an impairment.

(3)   Paragraph (2) above shall not prevent that condition from being taken into account for the purposes of the Act where it aggravates the effect of another condition.

Guidance[24]

10.   The definition requires that the effects which the person may experience arise from a physical or mental impairment. In many cases there will be no dispute whether a person has an impairment. Any disagreement is more likely to be about whether the effects of the impairment are sufficient to fall within the definition. Even so, it may sometimes be necessary to decide whether a person has an impairment so as to be able to deal with the issues about its effects.

11.   It is not necessary to consider how an impairment was caused, even if the cause is a consequence of a condition which is excluded. For example, liver disease as a result of alcohol dependency would count as an impairment.

12.   *Physical or mental impairment* includes sensory impairments, such as those affecting sight or hearing.

13.   Mental impairment includes a wide range of impairments relating to mental functioning, including what are often known as learning disabilities (formerly known as 'mental handicap'). However the Act states that it does not include any impairment resulting from or consisting of a mental illness unless that illness is a clinically well-recognised illness (Sched 1, para 1).

14.   A clinically well-recognised illness is a mental illness which is recognised by a respected body of medical opinion. It is very likely that this would include those specifically mentioned in publications such as the World Health Organisation's International Classification of Diseases.

There are a number of problems with this definition. First, there must be an actual impairment.[25] Someone who is wrongly perceived as having an impairment is not within the statutory definition. This excludes, for example, a person who is misdiagnosed as being dyslexic or as suffering from a mental illness and, for instance, sacked as a result. It also excludes someone who does have an impairment, but one which has no substantial[26] effect on everyday activities. This might apply to cases of epilepsy or mild mental illness, where the prejudiced employer might still wish to exclude employees. It is possible in such cases that a sympathetic tribunal might find it rather easy to conclude that there was a substantial degree of impairment, but that depends upon the discretion of a particular tribunal rather than the certainty of the law. This is in contrast with the Americans with Disabilities Act 1990, which defines

---

24   *Guidance on Matters to be Taken into Account in Determining Questions Relating to the Definition of Disability*, London: HMSO. (ISBN 0 11 270 955 9) Issued on 25 July 1996 under the DDA 1995, s 3 by the Secretary of State (SI 1996/1996) with effect from July 1996.

25   In *Howden v Capital Copiers (Edinburgh) Ltd* (1997) unreported, IT, Case S/400005, 33 DCLD 1, it was held that severe abdominal pain was an impairment even though its exact cause could not be diagnosed; in *O'Neill v Symm and Co Ltd* (1997) unreported, IT, Case 2700054, 33 DCLD 2, ME, it was held to be a disability on the basis that it is classified by the World Health Organisation as a separate and recognisable disease of the central nervous system. The employer's successful appeal to the EAT, [1998] IRLR 233, did not contradict the correctness of this conclusion, though it was stressed that all will depend on the applicant's particular impairments.

26   There is an exception for progressive conditions where there must be only some effect: DDA 1995, Sched 1, para 8 (see below, p 487).

disability as: '(A) a physical or mental impairment that substantially limits one or more of their major life activities ... or (C) [they are] regarded as having such an impairment.'[27]

> **Doyle, B, 'Employment rights, equal opportunities and disabled persons: the ingredients of reform' [1993] 22 ILJ 89, p 93:**
>
> In the US, the protected class includes a person whose disability represents no handicap to employment but is treated by employers as if it did; or whose disability is a handicap to employment but only as a result of attitudes of others towards it; or who has no disability at all but is erroneously treated by employers as disabled. As the Supreme Court has explained in *School Board of Nassau County, Florida v Arline* 480 US 273 (1987): an impairment might not diminish a person's physical or mental capabilities, but could nevertheless substantially limit that person's ability to work as a result of the negative reactions of others to the impairment ... Congress acknowledged that the society's accumulated fears about disability and disease are as handicapping as are the physical limitations that flow from actual impairment.

Boyle's comment has proved optimistic regarding the American position. In *Sutton v United Air Lines*,[28] the Supreme Court held that the United Airlines, in barring two seriously short-sighted pilots from global routes, were not 'regarding' the pilots as a having an impairment, as they allowed them to fly local routes.[29]

The second problem with the definition in the DDA 1995 is that mental illness[30] is only covered if it is a clinically well-recognised illness.[31] There are potential problems both in defining what is meant by an 'illness' and in deciding how much recognition is needed for an illness to be well-recognised. The recent controversy in criminal law as to whether 'battered woman syndrome' amounts to an 'abnormality of mind' for the purposes of the law of diminished responsibility shows that 'new' mental illnesses remain discoverable or classifiable. Thirdly, the exclusion of substance addictions and conditions with extreme anti-social or criminal consequences shows a desire to exclude conditions for which the individual is responsible and which, if within the definition, carry the potential for bringing the law into disrepute. Smokers, for example, will not be able to claim that they are victims of discrimination if a no-smoking policy is introduced in their workplace. This approach is applied to mental conditions; it is not carried through to physical conditions, even if the physical condition resulted from an addiction. If somebody becomes physically disabled as a result of a failed suicide attempt, or has a liver disease resulting from alcoholism, they are clearly within the statutory definition.

(i)   Cases on the meaning of 'impairment'

Goodwin v The Patent Office **[1999] ICR 302; [1999] IRLR 4, EAT**

The facts are set out below, p 484.

---

27   42 USCS 12101 (2).

28   *Karen Sutton And Kimberly Hinton v United Air Lines* 527 US 471 (1999), at pp 489–94.

29   *Ibid*, at pp 489–94.

30   Although, strictly speaking, this is a sub-category of mental impairment, leaving scope for non-orthodox mental impairments. See *Morgan v Staffordshire University* [2002] ICR 475, below at p 472.

31   DDA 1995, Sched 1, para 1.

Morison J (p 308):

The applicant must have either a physical or mental impairment. Mental impairment includes an impairment which results from or consists of a mental illness provided that the mental illness is 'a clinically well-recognised illness' – see para 1 of Schedule 1 [above] – but mental illness does not have the special meaning attributed to it in other legislation. Not all mental impairments will inevitably satisfy the impairment test, and some impairments (eg, due to alcoholism or tobacco or kleptomania) are excluded: see paragraph 8 of the Guidance. On the other hand, persons whose names appear on the Disabled Persons Register both on 12 January 1995 and 2 December 1995 are to be treated as having a disability without further inquiry, until 2 December 1998. Thereafter, they are to be treated as a person who had a disability in the past, and tribunals will note in that connection the provisions of Schedule 2, headed 'Past disabilities'.[32]

As the Guidance makes clear, a sensory impairment such as blindness (complete or partial) or loss of hearing (complete or partial) falls within the definition of a physical or mental impairment. If there is doubt as to whether the impairment condition is fulfilled in an alleged mental illness case, it would be advisable to ascertain whether the illness described or referred to in the medical evidence is mentioned in the WHO's International Classification of Diseases. That Classification would very likely determine the issue one way or the other: see paragraph 14 of the Guidance.

Rugamer v Sony Music; McNicol v Balfour Beatty Rail Maintenance [2001] IRLR 644; [2001] ICR 381, EAT

Daniel McNicol was employed as a trackman. During the course of his work, he was in a vehicle that went over a pothole, causing him to be jolted. From that day he was off work, reporting a continuing injury to his neck and spine. He and his employer disagreed what, if any, work to which he could return. Finally, he brought a claim under the DDA 1995, arguing that he suffered from a physical impairment, but there was no evidence of any physical injury. The only explanation was that he suffered from a functional or psychological 'overlay', where the cause of his suffering was either a subconscious mental psychological or psychiatric impairment, or that the symptoms were consciously produced or exaggerated. The industrial tribunal held that McNicol had neither a physical or mental impairment, within the meaning of the DDA 1995. The EAT and Court of Appeal upheld that decision. (The EAT heard a similar appeal of *Rugamer* at the same time.)

Mr Commissioner Howell QC (for the EAT):

45 ... What is we think clear is ... that short of satisfactory medical evidence of a diagnosed or diagnosable clinical condition or other mental disorder of a recognised type, evidence simply of a restriction on a person's level of function or activity accompanied by a general suggestion that this is (or may be) a manifestation of some psychological state will not meet the statutory threshold for establishing mental impairment. In neither of the present cases was there any attempt to produce evidence to demonstrate the presence of any identified condition meeting the very specific diagnostic criteria for generally recognised mental disorders in either the World Health Organisation's International Classification of Diseases 1996 (ICD-10) or the American Psychiatric Association's Diagnostic and Statistical Manual of Mental Disorders 4th Edn

---

32 See below, p 488.

1994 (DSM-IV) which we understand to be the two systems in general medical use: and it is significant that in neither system of classification does 'functional overlay' or 'psychogenic overlay' appear as a recognised illness or disorder in its own right.

Morgan v Staffordshire University [2002] ICR 475; [2002] IRLR 190, EAT

Samantha Morgan suffered 'anxiety', 'stress' and 'depression' following an assault on her at work. She made a claim against her employer under the DDA 1995. The employment tribunal summarised her evidence thus:

[H]er life was adversely affected from the date of the assault ... She stated that before the incident she would mop the kitchen floor and vacuum her carpets every single morning. After the incident she only reluctantly did this on a Sunday with moral pressure from her husband. She would often get the vacuum out in the morning, do virtually nothing all day, and put it away in the evening without using it. She would mix up the children's sandwiches and sometimes fail to give them the correct sandwiches or any sandwiches at all, and sometimes only gave them a drink. She sometimes omitted to include a spoon so that they could eat their yoghurt. She had problems with making up their sandwiches about three times out of five every week. She would walk the children to school and her head would be full of thoughts about the incident at work, she failed to listen to what her children were saying and talking to her about, and she would take an extraordinary long time to cross the road. She hardly ever slept. Before the incident she used to read books from the library every month and afterwards she did not read at all. She used to do some embroidery before the incident but did not do so afterwards. Prior to the incident she used to enjoy going out with her family at the weekend, including visiting National Trust properties, shopping and having picnics etc. After the incident she was just not interested in going out anywhere at all with the family at weekends. There were a couple of times when she had a panic attack, once in a public house and once in Woolworths where she just had to leave the premises and go home for no apparent reason. Although she was prescribed medication on one occasion by the doctor, for most of the period she was not on any medication. She had counselling. She had problems with the physical relationship with her husband. She wished to embark on an NVQ course. She started, but she had to give it up. She could not concentrate. Normally she would have enjoyed doing it.

The EAT upheld the employment tribunal's decision that Morgan did not suffer from a mental impairment.

Lindsay J:

9   ... [I]n general there will be three or possibly four routes to establishing the existence of 'mental impairment' within the DDA, namely:

   (i)   proof of a mental illness specifically mentioned as such in the World Health Organisation's International Classification of Diseases ('WHOICD');

   (ii) proof of a mental illness specifically mentioned as such in a publication 'such as' that classification, presumably therefore referring to some other classification of very wide professional acceptance;

   (iii) proof by other means of a medical illness recognised by a respected body of medical opinion.

   A fourth route, which exists as a matter of construction but may not exist in medical terms, derives from the use of the word 'includes' in para 1(1), Schedule 1 to the Act. If, as a matter of medical opinion and possibility, there may exist a state recognisable as mental impairment yet which neither results from nor consists of a mental illness, then such state could be accepted as a mental impairment within the Act because the statutory definition is inclusive only, rather than purporting to exclude anything not expressly described by it. This fourth category is likely to be rarely if ever invoked and could be expected to require substantial and very specific medical evidence to support its existence ...

Whilst the words 'anxiety', 'stress' and 'depression' could be dug at intervals out of the copies of the medical notes put before the tribunal, it is not the case that their occasional use, even by medical men, will, without further explanation, amount to proof of a mental impairment within the Act, still less as its proof as at some particular time ...

There was no evidence from any doctor to explain what he had meant at the time his note was made, nor to assert that Mrs Morgan was at any time mentally impaired within the Act. Without our here setting out further extracts from the WHOICD, we notice that the work shows at many parts of its classification that specific symptoms, often required to be manifest over a minimum specified periods or with a minimum specified frequency, are required if a claimant relies upon falling within it. For Mrs Morgan to have pointed, as happened below, to the occasional references in the medical notes and then to the indices in the WHOICD, without any informed medical evidence beyond those notes, was to invite failure.

By asserting that the fourth category will be 'rarely if ever invoked', Lindsay J highlighted that the law is less willing to recognise mental impairments than it is physical impairments. In *College of Ripon & York St John v Hobbs*,[33] the same judge upheld an employment tribunal's decision that the applicant had a *physical* impairment, even though expert evidence said that there was no organic disease causing the symptoms (muscle twitching and cramps, walking with the aid of a stick).

(b) Ability to carry out normal day-to-day activities.

The DDA 1995 demands that the impairment has an adverse effect on the claimant's ability to carry out day-to-day activities. This is a variation on the Americans with Disabilities Act 1990, which demands that the impairment 'limits one or more of [their] major life activities'. The American definition is potentially wider by including those who are restricted in just one activity,[34] but both models are in marked contrast to the Australian Disability Discrimination Act 1992, which has no demand for a limitation of activities. It simply demands an impairment.[35] For the purposes of the DDA 1995, day-to-day activities can only be limited in the following ways.

---

33 [2002] IRLR 185, EAT.

34 But see the narrow construction given by the Supreme Court in *Sutton v United Air Lines* 527 US 471 (1999). Cf 'Guidance C2', below.

35 By s 4 of the Australian Disability Discrimination Act 1992, 'Disability' means: (a) total or partial loss of the person's bodily or mental functions; or (b) total or partial loss of a part of the body; or (c) the presence in the body of organisms causing disease or illness; or (d) the presence in the body of organisms capable of causing disease or illness; or (e) the malfunction, malformation or disfigurement of a part of the person's body; or (f) a disorder or malfunction that results in the person learning differently from a person without the disorder or malfunction; or (g) a disorder, illness or disease that affects a person's thought processes, perception of reality, emotions or judgment or that results in disturbed behaviour; and includes a disability that: (h) presently exists; or (i) previously existed but no longer exists; or (j) may exist in the future; or (k) is imputed to a person.

Disability Discrimination Act 1995

Schedule 1, para 4

(1)   An impairment is to be taken to affect the ability of the person concerned to carry out normal day-to-day activities only if it affects one of the following—

(a) mobility;

(b) manual dexterity;

(c) physical co-ordination;

(d) continence;

(e) ability to lift, carry out or otherwise move everyday objects;

(f) speech, hearing or eyesight;

(g) memory or ability to concentrate, learn or understand; or

(h) perception of the risk of physical danger.

Disability Discrimination (Meaning of Disability) Regulations 1996, SI 1996/1455

6   [W]here a child under six years of age has an impairment which does not have [a relevant] effect ... that impairment is to be taken to have a substantial and long term adverse effect ... where it would normally have a substantial and long term adverse effect on the ability of a person aged six years or over to carry out normal day-to-day activities.[36]

Guidance[37]

C2   The term 'normal day-to-day activities' is not intended to include activities which are normal only for a particular person or group of people. Therefore ... account should be taken of how far [an activity] is normal for most people and carried out by most people on a daily or frequent and fairly regular basis.

C3   [It] does not, for example, include work of any particular form, because no particular form of work is 'normal' for most people. In any individual case, the activities carried out might be highly specialised. The same is true of playing in a particular game, taking part in a particular hobby, playing a musical instrument, playing sport, or performing a highly skilled task. Impairments which effect only such an activity and have no effect on 'normal day-to-day activities' are not covered ...

C6   Many impairments will, by their nature, adversely effect a person directly in one of the [relevant] respects ... An impairment may also indirectly affect a person in one or more of these respects, and this should be taken into account when assessing whether the impairment falls within the definition. For example:

• medical advice: where a person has been professionally advised to change, limit or refrain from a normal day-to-day activity on account of an impairment or only to do it in a certain way or under certain conditions;

• pain or fatigue: where an impairment causes pain or fatigue in normal day-to-day activities, so that the person may have the capacity to do something but suffer pain in doing do; or the impairment might make the activity more than usually fatiguing so that the person might not be able to repeat the task over a sustained period of time.

---

36 While this has little if any relevance to employment discrimination, it is relevant for the provision of goods, services and education.

37 *Guidance on Matters to be Taken into Account in Determining Questions Relating to the Definition of Disability*, London: HMSO (ISBN 0 11 270 955 9). Issued on 25 July 1996 under the DDA 1995, s 3 by the Secretary of State (SI 1996/1996) with effect from 31 July 1996.

C7   Where a person has a mental illness such as depression, account should be taken
      of whether, although that person has the physical ability to perform a task he or
      she is, in practice, unable to sustain an activity over a reasonable period.

The Guidance lists examples of day-to-day activities, which are specifically stated not
to be exhaustive. Included are examples of activities that it would be reasonable to
regard as having a substantial adverse effect, and those which it would not. For
example, in relation to mobility, ability to walk is not mentioned because it is obvious;
rather, the examples of a substantial adverse effect which are given include 'inability
to walk other than at a slow pace or with unsteady or jerky movements' and
'difficulty in going up or down stairs, steps or gradients'; those not having such effect
are 'difficulty walking unaided a distance of about ... a mile without discomfort or
having to stop ...' and 'inability to travel in a car for a journey lasting two hours
without discomfort'.[38] It is, though, important to note that indirect effects are
included, as where a person can no longer perform a day-to-day activity because of
medical advice or where such activity causes abnormal pain or fatigue.

Below, Morison J in *Goodwin* sets out the general approach to 'day-to-day
activities,' which was applied in *Ekpe*.

Goodwin v The Patent Office [1999] ICR 302; [1999] IRLR 4, EAT

The facts are set out below, p 484.

Morison J (pp 308–10):

The adverse effect condition

In many ways, this may be the most difficult of the four conditions to judge ... The fact
that a person can carry out such activities does not mean that his ability to carry them
out has not been impaired. Thus, for example, a person may be able to cook, but only
with the greatest difficulty. In order to constitute an adverse effect, it is not the doing
of the acts which is the focus of attention but rather the ability to do (or not do) the
acts ...

Experience shows that disabled persons often adjust their lives and circumstances to
enable them to cope for themselves. Thus a person whose capacity to communicate
through normal speech was obviously impaired might well choose, more or less
voluntarily, to live on their own. If one asked such a person whether they managed to
carry on their daily lives without undue problems, the answer might well be 'yes', yet
their ability to lead a 'normal' life had obviously been impaired ...

Furthermore, disabled persons are likely, habitually, to 'play down' the effect that
their disabilities have on their daily lives ...

What is a day-to-day activity is best left unspecified: easily recognised, but defined
with difficulty. What can be said is that the inquiry is not focused on a particular or
special set of circumstances. Thus, it is not directed to the person's own particular
circumstances, either at work or home. The fact that a person cannot demonstrate a
particular skill, such as playing the piano, is not an issue before the tribunal, even if it
is considering a claim by a musician ...

It will be borne in mind that the effect of a disability on a person's ability to conduct
his daily life might have a cumulative effect, in the sense that more than one of the

---

38   This exercise is repeated for each of the specifically listed day-to-day activities; there is not
     the space to discuss them all in detail. See 'Disability Discrimination Act Regulations and
     Guidance' (1996) 68 EOR 29, pp 36–38.

capacities had been impaired. It is not necessary for the tribunal to go further, if satisfied that one 'capacity' has been impaired ...

During argument, an example was given of a person whose hearing was exceptionally acute. One might say that this was not likely to be regarded as a handicap to the person's ability to carry out his normal day-to-day activities. Certainly, one might say that there was no adverse effect upon his hearing: quite the contrary. However, such a condition could well adversely affect other capacities: for example, such a person might find it impossible or difficult to cope with conversation in a group of people or to go to a busy shop or to concentrate.

Ekpe v Commissioner of Police of the Metropolis [2001] IRLR 605; [2001] ICR 1084, EAT

Mrs Ekpe was required by the Metropolitan Police to move to a job which involved keyboard duties. She felt that she could not do such a job because she had a physical impairment, which consisted of a wasting of the intrinsic muscles of her right hand. The evidence was that Mrs Ekpe could not carry heavy shopping, scrub pans, peel, grate, sew or put rollers in her hair. She said that sometimes she had to apply her makeup, as well as feeding herself, with her left hand. The employment tribunal concluded that the Mrs Ekpe's impairment did not have a substantial adverse effect on her ability to carry out normal day-to-day activities because, *inter alia*, it was only heavy shopping with which she was unable to cope, she could cook normally and she could still apply makeup with her left hand. Further, applying make-up and putting in hair-rollers were not normal day-to-day activities because 'they are activities carried out almost exclusively by women'. The EAT allowed Mrs Ekpe's appeal because the tribunal had erred in law by focussing on each activity, rather than making an overall assessment.

Mr Recorder Langstaff QC (at paras 21–29):

Accordingly, thus far, following the statutory provisions without recourse to authority the enquiry as to whether an impairment affects the ability of the person concerned to carry out normal day-to-day activities becomes an enquiry into whether or not any of the abilities (or, as they have been termed, 'capacities') listed in para 4(1)(a) to (h) has been affected ...

The opening words of [s 3(2) of the DDA 1995] make it clear that what is to be provided [by the Guidance] is by way of example only, and is not intended to provide a determinative test of whether there is an impairment which has a substantial effect on normal day-to-day activities: it is in the nature of examples that they are illustrative rather than conclusive.

So far as manual dexterity is concerned, paragraph C15 of the Code says that it would be reasonable to regard as having a substantial adverse effect the ability to press the buttons on keyboards or keypads but only much more slowly than is normal for most people.

So far as the ability to lift, carry or move everyday objects is concerned, paragraph C18 regards it as reasonable to regard the inability to carry a moderately loaded tray steadily as having a substantial adverse effect ...

In answering the question whether the effect is substantial, regard may be had to the examples given by the Guidance – but it needs to be emphasised that they are examples only. To focus upon the detail of an example may be to exclude the broader picture of which the detail is only part – yet it is that broader picture (implied in a question such as 'is manual dexterity affected?') that has to be considered. In colloquial terms, it may constitute an inability to see the wood for the trees ...

Authority serves only to confirm it. [Citing *Goodwin*, above and *Vicary*, below][39] ...

This proposition has been put beyond doubt by *Leonard v Southern Derbyshire Chamber of Commerce* [2001] IRLR 19. The EAT criticised an employment tribunal for taking an approach that took examples of what the appellant could do – such as being able to eat, drink and catch a ball – and weighed them against what she could not do – such as negotiate a pavement edge safely. Mr Justice Nelson noted that the Guidance was only illustrative, accepted that a tribunal must look at the matter in the round, considering the evidence as a whole, but added (at para 27):

> Whilst it is essential that a tribunal considers matters in the round and makes an overall assessment of whether the adverse effect of an impairment on an activity or capacity is substantial, it has to bear in mind that it must concentrate on what the applicant cannot do or can only do with difficulty rather than on the things that they can do. This focus of the Act avoids the danger of a tribunal concluding that as there are still many things that an applicant can do the adverse effect cannot be substantial.

(i) Work as a day-to-day activity

The most important, and, arguably, most illogical exclusion from day-to-day activities is that of work.[40] Despite the legislation being concerned with employment discrimination, work is not treated as a normal day-to-day activity. The explanation is to prevent an argument that someone is disabled merely by virtue of the fact that they are unable to pursue a particular occupation. So, for example, if a back condition prevents someone from performing a job involving heavy lifting, the definition of disability would only be satisfied if their ability to lift ordinary objects outside work were also affected.[41] However, the outcome may be different where the work itself is a cause of the impairment.

Cruickshank v Vaw Motorcast Ltd [2002] IRLR 24; [2002] ICR 729, EAT

Cruickshank suffered severe breathing difficulties ('occupational asthma') at work because of the fumes in the works foundry. When away from work, on sick leave, and at the tribunal hearing following his dismissal, the symptoms cleared up, and so, out of work, he could carry out normal day-to-day activities.[42]

Judge J Altman (at 28–29):

'Normal day-to-day activities' in s 1 are included, it seems to us, as a way of deciding whether the impairment is serious enough to qualify for protection under the Act. They are there as a yardstick, but only as a yardstick. It follows that in assessing whether a disability has a significant and long-term effect on the ability to do everyday tasks, it is not appropriate to confine the evaluation to the extent to which the applicant is disabled only in a 'normal day-to-day' environment. In this case when the appellant is away from work he can obviously accomplish most everyday tasks,

---

39 See p 484, below.
40 Paragraph C3 of the Guidance, above. For a debate on this issue in the USA, see *Sutton v United Air Lines* 527 US 471 (1999), at pp 489–94.
41 'Interpreting the DDA – part 1: the meaning of disability' (1998) 79 EOR 13, p 15.
42 See *Law Hospital NHS Trust v Rush* [2001] IRLR 611, CS, where the claimant, a nurse, could perform work duties, but was held to have a disability.

on the findings of the employment tribunal. But the position of the 'everyday tasks' test is as a measure of seriousness, it is not dictating the actual environment in the particular case in which such symptoms are to be judged. Accordingly if, whilst at work, an applicant's symptoms are such as to have a significant and long-term effect on his ability to perform day-to-day tasks, such symptoms are not to be ignored simply because the work itself may be specialised and unusual, so long as the disability and its consequences can be measured in terms of the ability of an applicant to undertake day-to-day tasks. The Act is not restricted to the period when people who are only doing day-to-day activities; those activities are rather a 'barometer' or test of the degree of severity of the impairment.

In these circumstances, where an employee's ability to carry on day-to-day activities may vary depending on his general pattern of life at the time, in this case on whether or not he is at the work from which he was dismissed, there is a stage of enquiry that should precede the examination of ability to perform day-to-day activities. That stage is to identify the particular circumstances in and background against which the ability to perform those activities is to be judged. Was it whilst he was at work, in employment but on sick leave, or some time later after dismissal?

... [T]he allegation is that the discrimination acts on the disability and therefore the disability that falls for consideration must be that which exists before the act of discrimination complained of, and not the other way around. Accordingly the employment tribunal should ask whether there was the substantial and long-term adverse effect whilst the employee was still in employment.

The dismissal is then an intervening cause that changes the effect of the impairment – it is the disability before the act complained of that must be looked at. We see no reason why, in examining the ability to perform day-to-day activities, a tribunal should preclude itself from considering, amongst other evidence, such ability whilst the employee is actually at his work. This enquiry may lead to factual questions such as, 'how long did this effect continue?' 'Did it take a few days, or weeks to improve, or could you resume normal activity the minute you walked out of the factory gate?' 'What day-to-day activities could you perform in the evenings after work, at the weekends, after two weeks' break, whilst you were off sick?' It seems to us that it is only with that sort of picture that a tribunal can assess the extent of adverse effect. Whilst we agree that the 'snapshot' must be taken from the vantage point of the employer when he decides to dismiss, we consider that the narrow picture at that moment may be too restrictive. It is the general condition, the condition as it manifested itself in the circumstances which the employer considered in acting as he did, that must be looked at.

(ii)   Disfigurements

There is an exception under the British legislation where the disability is a 'severe disfigurement'. Here, the disability need not adversely affect the person's day-to-day activities. This exception resembles the 'social' (rather than the, medical) model of disability.

Disability Discrimination Act 1995

Schedule 1, para 3

(3)   An impairment which consists of a severe disfigurement is to be treated as having a substantial adverse effect on the ability of the person concerned to carry out normal day-to-day activities.

Disability Discrimination (Meaning of Disability) Regulations 1996, SI 1996/1455

5   For the purposes of para 3 ... a severe disfigurement is not to be treated as having a substantial adverse effect ... if it consists of:

(a) a tattoo (which has not been removed); or

(b) a piercing of the body for decorative or other non-medical purposes, including any object attached through the piercing for such purposes.

Guidance[43]

A17 Examples of disfigurements include scars, birthmarks, limb or postural deformation or diseases of the skin. Assessing severity will be mainly a matter of the degree of the disfigurement. However, it may be necessary to take account of where the feature in question is (for example, on the back as opposed to on the face).

The assumption is that such disfigurements may cause no functional impairment but may lead to social disadvantage or discrimination, although the effect of the disfigurement must be long-term.

(c)   Long-term effects

Disability Discrimination Act 1995

Schedule 1, para 2

(1)   The effect of an impairment is a long term effect if:

(a) it has lasted at least 12 months;

(b) the period for which it lasts is likely to be at least 12 months; or

(c) it is likely to last for the rest of the life of the person affected.

(2)   Where an impairment ceases to have a substantial adverse effect ... it is to be treated as continuing to have that effect if that effect is likely to recur.

Guidance[44]

B2   It is not necessary for the effect to be the same throughout the relevant period. It may change, as where activities which are initially very difficult become possible to a much greater extent. The main adverse effect might even disappear – or it might disappear temporarily – while ... other effects ... continue or develop. Provided the impairment continues to have, or is likely to have, such an effect throughout the period, there is a long term effect.

B3   Conditions which recur only sporadically or for short periods (for example, epilepsy) can still qualify [see para 2(2) above] ... *Regulations specifically exclude* ... hayfever ... except where it aggravates the effect of an existing condition.

B5   Likelihood of recurrence should be considered taking all the circumstances of the case into account. This should include what the person could reasonably be expected to do to prevent the recurrence [for example, avoiding substances to which there is an allergy] ... In addition, it is possible that the way in which a person can control or cope with the effects of a condition may not always be successful because, for example, a routine is not followed or the person is in an unfamiliar environment. If there is an increased likelihood that the control will

---

43 *Guidance on Matters to be Taken into Account in Determining Questions Relating to the Definition of Disability*, London: HMSO (ISBN 0 11 270 955 9). Issued on 25 July 1996 under the DDA 1995, s3 by the Secretary of State (SI 1996/1996) with effect from 31 July 1996.

44 *Ibid*.

break down, it will be more likely that there will be a recurrence. That possibility should be taken into account when assessing the likelihood of a recurrence.

The most problematic issue here concerns fluctuating conditions. First note that if the effects are likely to recur 12 months after the last occurrence, then they are treated as long-term, for the DDA 1995.[45] Under para 2(2) of Sched 1, a tribunal must decide whether the impairment was likely to recur. The difficulty is at what point in time should that assessment be made, for instance, at the time of the discriminatory act, or the time of the hearing, (probably several months later)? There is an apparent tension between the DDA 1995 and the Guidance here. The DDA 1995 supposes, for many purposes, that it should be at the time of the discriminatory act complained of, but the Guidance suggests otherwise:

Guidance[46]

B8.   In assessing the likelihood of an effect lasting for any period, account should be taken of the total period for which the effect exists. This includes any time before the point when the discriminatory behaviour occurred as well as time afterwards.

In *Goodwin v The Patent Office*,[47] Morison J stated no more than that reference to the Guidance was 'necessary'.[48] The matter was explored by the EAT in *Greenwood, Collet* and *Cruickshank*.

Greenwood v British Airways [1999] ICR 969; [1999] IRLR 600, EAT

Greenwood was employed as a senior cargo assistant. Between 1993 and March 1997, he was absent from work on several occasions, suffering from depression. By May 1997, following treatment, his condition had apparently ceased. He then applied for promotion and was rejected – in June 1997 – partly because of his sickness record. This rejection triggered another bout of depression. He brought a claim under the DDA 1995. By the time of the hearing – some nine months later, in March 1998 – the employment tribunal found that at the time of the rejection, it was reasonable to assume that Greenwood no longer suffered from depression and therefore he had no disability for the purposes of the DDA 1995. The EAT allowed Greenwood's appeal.

Judge Peter Clark (at p 977):

In our judgment, the tribunal fell into error by considering the question of disability only as at the date of the alleged discriminatory act. We are quite satisfied, as the Guidance makes clear, that the tribunal should consider the adverse effects of the applicant's condition up to and including the employment tribunal hearing. By disregarding its findings of fact as to the actual recurrence of the adverse effects of the applicant's condition which led him to go off work by reason of depression on 16 August 1997 and to continue off work until the date of the tribunal hearing the tribunal's approach was fatally flawed.

Even if we accept ... that the applicant had had a disability, but no longer had a disability as at June 1997, ... the fact that the adverse effect did recur and became

---

45   *Ibid.*
46   *Ibid.*
47   [1999] ICR 302; [1999] IRLR 4, EAT.
48   *Ibid*, at p 310.

worse ... leads us to the conclusion that ... the applicant made out his case on s 2 ['Past'] disability.

In these circumstances it is not strictly necessary for us to determine the question whether, on the basis of those factual findings, the substantial adverse effect of the impairment was likely to last for at least 12 months for the purposes of s 1 and Schedule 1 paragraph 2(1)(b).

So, whatever the merits of the decision on para 2(1)(b) issue, the case could be decided in Greenwood's favour under s 2 of the DDA 1995, because it was clear that he had a 'past disability'.[49] This point was picked up in the next case.

Collet v Diocese of Hallam Trustee (2001) unreported, 17 December, EAT[50]

At the time of her dismissal, the claimant suffered a back problem that, on the evidence, was not likely to recur. However, after the dismissal, it did recur. The industrial tribunal, assessing the facts at the time of the dismissal, decided that she did not have a disability, even though, by the time of the hearing some 14 months later, they accepted that she did.

Judge D Pugsley:

10   ... It is argued that because it did not construe Part IIB [above], the paragraph for guidance, and referred to the case of *Greenwood v British Airways* ... the Tribunal fell into error.

11.   We do not accept, if we may say so, that that case is an authority for saying that we should substitute our view and make a finding of disability. We think that is a tempting but fallacious interpretation of the *Greenwood* case. On closer analysis of the words of His Honour Judge Clark, the appeal was allowed and they declared the Applicant was a person who had a disability within the meaning of Section 2 ... It was not therefore necessary for them to determine the question on the factual findings ...

Cruickshank v Vaw Motorcast Ltd [2002] ICR 729; [2002] IRLR 24, EAT

Cruickshank suffered severe breathing difficulties ('occupational asthma') at work because of the fumes in the works foundry. When on sick leave, the symptoms cleared up. He was dismissed and sometime later, at the hearing of his DDA 1995 claim, his symptoms had of course ceased.

Judge J Altman (at p 27):

We turn first to consider the point in time to be looked at ... when evaluating disability. The time at which the existence of a disability is to be assessed has been considered by the EAT, for instance in the cases of *Goodwin and Greenwood v British Airways* and the conclusion appears to be that the 'material' time at which to assess the disability is at the time of the alleged discriminatory act, in this case the dismissal ...

Much depends in our judgment on the starting point under the Act ...

[W]e consider that the starting point is the cause of action, or the basis of proceedings, under the Act. Section 4(2) provides: 'It is unlawful for an employer to discriminate against a disabled person whom he employs ... (d) by dismissing him ...'Section 5

---

49   See below, p 488.
50   EAT/1400/00 (transcript) 17 December 2001, revised 25 May 2002. Available at www.employmentappeals.gov.uk.

provides '... an employer discriminates against a disabled person if – for a reason which relates to the disabled person's disability, he treats him less favourably ...'

It seems to us that a claim against an employer for breach of duty under these sections must involve an examination of the actions of the employer towards the employee at the time ... To make sense of this process must of necessity mean looking at the disabled person at the time of the actions complained of. Section 1[51] is simply a definition section that provides the meaning to attach to disability where it arises in the many parts of the Act. The fact that it uses the present tense does not alter the meaning of ss 4 and 5, but rather it provides the meaning of the word to be applied in the context of those sections. What is being asked is whether 'an employer discriminates against a disabled person ...' To answer that question requires an examination of how the employer treated the employee as he was at that time ... This is confirmed, on an examination of other provisions of the Act. For instance, in s 6, which imposes on an employer an obligation to make reasonable adjustments, subsection 6 provides: 'Nothing in this section imposes any duty on an employer in relation to a disabled person if the employer does not know, and could not reasonably be expected to know— ... (b) ... that that person has a disability.'

That which requires examination is that which was, or should have been, in the mind of the employer at the time, and that must require an examination of whether there was a disability at that time. Indeed, in s 1 itself, subsection (4) provides: '... the question whether a person had a disability at a particular time ("the relevant time") shall be determined, for the purposes of this section, as if the provisions of, or made under, this Act in force when the act complained of was done had been in force at the relevant time.'

Here again the Act seems to require any examination of whether there was a disability, to involve examination of the employee's impairment at the time of the act complained of, in this case the dismissal.

Cruickshank offers perhaps the most detailed and persuasive judgment on the issue. It contains some anomalies though. First, neither *Goodwin* nor *Greenwood* suggests that the time for assessment was at the time of dismissal. In fact, *Greenwood* is to the contrary. Secondly, the judgment omits any mention of the Guidance – the one thing that challenges the interpretation given. However, the issue should not be as polarised as these cases suggest. The Guidance only states that the time for assessment includes 'any time before the point when the discriminatory behaviour occurred as well as time afterwards',[52] and so tribunals are free to take account of facts before, at the time of, and after the discriminatory act to assess whether, at the time of the alleged act of discrimination, the claimant had a disability. That is what was suggested in *Greenwood*. In *Cruickshank* Judge Altman makes the seemingly logical connection between the definitions of disability and discrimination, concluding that, say, an employer could not be held to discriminate for a reason related to disability if, at that time, the disability was unlikely to recur. The problem with this reasoning is exposed by the facts in *Greenwood*. One of the reasons Greenwood was refused promotion was his sickness record. On the facts, this fear was irrational: the condition was unlikely to recur. So, in contrast to Judge Altman's logic, it *is* possible to treat a person less favourably for a reason related to the claimant's disability, even if, at the time, there was no objective evidence of that disability. Of course, if the claimant *did not* have a

---

51 See above, p 466.
52 Paragraph B8, *op cit*, fn 43.

disability at the time, then the Act will not cover him.[53] In other words the definition of discrimination includes subjective or irrational reasons by the defendant, but the definition of disability does not.[54]

(d)   Substantial

The statute contains no definition on what this concept entails, as in most instances it will be a question of fact. It is fleshed out through examples given by way of guidance.

Guidance[55]

A1   A 'substantial' effect is more than would be produced by the sort of physical or mental conditions experienced by many people which have only minor effects ...

A2   The time taken by a person with an impairment to carry out a normal day-to-day activity should be considered when assessing whether the effect of that impairment is substantial ...

A4   An impairment might not have a substantial effect on a person in any one [of the relevant respects], but its effects in more than one of these respects taken together could result in a substantial adverse effect ...

A5   For example, although the great majority of people with cerebral palsy will experience a number of substantial effects, someone with mild cerebral palsy may experience minor effects ... which together could create substantial adverse effects ... fatigue may hinder walking, visual perception may be poor, co-ordination and balance may sometimes cause difficulties. Similarly, a person whose impairment causes breathing difficulties may experience minor effects in a number of respects but which overall have a substantial adverse effect ... For some people, mental illness may have a clear effect in one ... respect ... However, for others ... there may be effects in a number of different respects which, taken together [amount to a substantial adverse effect].

A6   A person may have more than one impairment, any one of which alone would not have a substantial effect. In such a case, account should be taken of whether the impairments together have a substantial effect overall ... For example, a minor impairment which affects physical co-ordination and an irreversible but minor injury to a leg which affects mobility, taken together, might have a substantial effect ...

A7   Account should be taken of how far a person can reasonably be expected to modify behaviour to prevent or reduce the effects of an impairment ...

A10   Whether adverse effects are substantial may depend on environmental conditions which may vary; for example, the temperature, humidity, the time of day or night, how tired the person is or how much stress he or she is under may have an impact ...

In *Goodwin*, Morison J explains the general approach. We can see that approach applied in *Goodwin* and *Vicary*.

---

53   Consequently, Cruickshank would win the point under this approach as well. A person would be covered if he had a disability in the past; see below, p 488.

54   Of course, the DDA 1995 defines some limited circumstances where mere stigmatism may be actionable, for instance, disfigurements and past disabilities. But in each case the 'impairment' must have existed.

55   *Guidance on Matters to be Taken into Account in Determining Questions Relating to the Definition of Disability*, London: HMSO (ISBN 0 11 270 955 9). Issued on 25 July 1996 under the DDA 1995, s 3 by the Secretary of State (SI 1996/1996) with effect from 31 July 1996.

Goodwin v The Patent Office **[1999] ICR 302; [1999] IRLR 4, EAT**

Matthew Goodwin was dismissed from his post as a patent examiner after complaints from female staff of disturbing behaviour. He is a paranoid schizophrenic and he had auditory hallucinations – that is, he heard voices – which interrupted his concentration. He brought a complaint under the DDA 1995. The employment tribunal held that he failed to come within the definition of a 'disabled person', finding that he was able to 'perform his domestic activities without the need for assistance, to get to work efficiently and to carry out his work to a satisfactory standard'. The EAT reversed that decision.

Morison J (pp 310–11):

The substantial condition

On the assumption that the impairment and adverse effect conditions have been fulfilled, the tribunal must consider whether the adverse effect is substantial. This is a word which is potentially ambiguous. 'Substantial' might mean 'very large' or it might mean 'more than minor or trivial'. Reference to the Guide shows that the word has been used in the latter sense: see paragraph A1.

The tribunal may, where the applicant still claims to be suffering from the same degree of impairment as at the time of the events complained of, take into account how the applicant appears to the tribunal to 'manage', although tribunals will be slow to regard a person's capabilities in the relatively strange adversarial environment as an entirely reliable guide to the level of ability to perform normal day-to-day activities.

The decision in this case

It seems to us that the industrial tribunal have not looked at the effect which the applicant's disability had on his abilities. They appeared to have moved from the finding that the applicant was able to cope at home to the conclusion that, therefore, he fell outwith the provisions of the Act. A close scrutiny of the [pleadings] ... would inevitably have led them to the conclusion that the applicant was simply unable to carry on a normal day-to-day conversation with work colleagues. Furthermore, the employers produced a memorandum recording the fact that the manager was complaining that the applicant was unable to hold a normal conversation. This was good evidence of the fact that the applicant's capacity to concentrate and communicate had been adversely affected in a significant manner. It seems to us that in this case the question whether the applicant was, at the relevant time, disabled within the meaning of the Act admitted only one conclusion: he was.

Vicary v British Telecommunications **[1999] IRLR 680, EAT**

The claimant had a disability relating to the use of her right arm and hand. She suffered pain when doing repetitive light work, for example, typing or cutting vegetables, or when she was doing more physical work on a one-off basis, such as shifting a chair at home when sitting down or getting up from a table. The EAT reversed the employment tribunal's decision that the effects were not substantial. In doing so, the EAT held that (a) 'substantial' means more than trivial; (b) it is only necessary to refer to the Guidance in 'marginal cases'; (c) a tribunal should look at what activities the claimant cannot, rather can, do; and (d) it is for the tribunal, not expert medical witnesses, to assess whether or not the effects are 'substantial'.[56]

Morison J (at p 682):

[T]he employment tribunal has not considered the interpretation of the word 'substantial'. It seems to us clear that they must have approached the case on the basis that 'substantial means more than what the word means in this context. Paragraph 6 of Annex 1 of the Code of Practice issued by the Secretary of State[57] ... provides:

> A substantial adverse effect is something which is more than a minor or trivial effect. The requirement that an effect must be substantial reflects the general understanding of disability as a limitation going beyond the normal difference in ability which might exist among people ...

Paragraph 1 of Part 1 [of the Guidance] goes on to say:

> In the vast majority of cases there is unlikely to be any doubt whether or not a person has or has had a disability, but this guidance should prove helpful in cases where it is not clear.

The Guidance, therefore, will only be of assistance in what might be described as marginal cases ... [I]n this case there was in fact no need for the employment tribunal to refer to the Guidance once they had properly understood the meaning of the word 'substantial'. Having concluded that the ability of the applicant to do the activities specified in paragraph 7(3) of the decision was impaired, the tribunal inevitably should have concluded that the applicant was a person suffering from a disability within the meaning of the Act. Instead, the employment tribunal appears to have used the Guidance in a somewhat literal fashion so as to arrive at the surprising conclusion that the applicant was not substantially impaired in her ability to carry out normal day-to-day activities.

... [T]he employment tribunal assert that a loss of strength cannot be equated to a loss of function. We do not understand what is being said. A loss of strength may well have a substantial adverse effect on the applicant's manual dexterity. They then refer to the things that she was able to do which in our view is not the right focus of attention. Their conclusion that the applicant's lack of ability to cut up meat and roast potatoes could not 'as an isolated example' make the impairment substantial. That seems to us to show a misunderstanding of the task in hand. It is clear that an ability to prepare vegetables, cut up meat and carry a meal on a tray would all be regarded as examples of normal day-to-day activities. An inability to carry out those functions would, in our view, obviously be regarded as a substantial impairment of an ability to carry out normal day-to-day activities.

Furthermore, the tribunal's conclusion in that paragraph that DIY tasks, filing nails, tonging hair, ironing, shaking quilts, grooming animals, polishing furniture, knitting and sewing and cutting with scissors were not normal day-to-day activities 'as set out in the Guidance' misunderstands the nature of the guidance given. Paragraph C9 of the guidance makes it plain that the lists of examples which follow 'are not exhaustive; they are only meant to be illustrative'. It seems to us obvious that making beds, doing housework (polishing furniture), sewing and cutting with scissors would be regarded as normal day-to-day activities as would minor DIY tasks, filing nails, curling hair and ironing. These are all activities which most people do on a frequent

---

56 In *Vyas v Camden LBC* [2003] All ER (D) 116 (Mar), (EAT/1153/01/RN, see www. employmentappeals.gov.uk), the EAT held that where an employment tribunal faced a straight conflict between two experts, it was entitled to prefer one or the other.

57 For Education and Employment on 25 July 1996, issued under s 53(1)(a) of the DDA 1995.

or fairly regular basis. Yet the tribunal has dismissed the applicant's inability to carry out these functions without pain on the grounds that they are not normal day-to-day activities.

... The fact that the medical adviser had been told on some disability discrimination course or seminar that something was or was not a normal day-to-day activity is not of relevance to the tribunal's determination. It is not for a doctor to express an opinion as to what is a normal day-to-day activity. That is a matter for them to consider using their basic common sense. Equally, it was not for the expert to tell the tribunal whether the impairments which had been found proved were or were not substantial. Again that was a matter for the employment tribunal to arrive at its own assessment. What, of course, a medical expert was entitled to do was to put forward her own observations of the applicant carrying out day-to-day activities and to comment on the case or otherwise with which she was performing those functions.

There are two situations for which the law makes specific provision on the issue of 'substantial'.

(i)   Deducting the effect of medical treatment

Disability Discrimination Act 1995

Schedule 1, para 6

(1)   An impairment which would be likely to have a substantial adverse effect ... but for the fact that measures are being taken to treat or correct it, is to be treated as having that effect.

(3)   Sub-paragraph (1) does not apply:
   (a) in relation to a person's sight, to the extent that the impairment is, in his case, correctable by spectacles or contact lenses ...

Guidance[58]

A11   [The effect of Sched 1, para 6 is] that where an impairment is being treated or *corrected* the impairment is to be treated as having the effect it would have without the measures in question.

A12   This applies even if the measures result in the effects being completely under control or not at all apparent.

A13   For example, if a person with a hearing impairment wears a hearing aid the question ... is to be decided by reference to what the hearing level would be without the hearing aid. And in the case of someone with diabetes, whether or not the effect is substantial should be decided by reference to what the condition would be if he or she was not taking medication.

A14   [But with sight impairments] the only effects ... to be considered are those which remain when spectacles or contact lenses are used.

Goodwin v The Patent Office [1999] ICR 302; [1999] IRLR 4, EAT

The facts are set out above, p 484.

Morison J (p 310):

The tribunal will wish to examine how the applicant's abilities had actually been affected at the material time, whilst on medication, and then to address their minds to

---

58   *Op cit*, fn 55.

the difficult question as to the effects which they think there would have been but for the medication: the *deduced* effects. The question is then whether the actual and deduced effects on the applicant's abilities to carry out normal day-to-day activities is *clearly more than trivial.*

In many cases, the tribunal will be able to reach a conclusion on these matters without reference to the statutory Guidance (which is there to illuminate what is not reasonably clear) ...

It should thus be clear that a person may be within the definition even if there are no current adverse effects. It is the potential for such effects in the absence of the controls which provides the foundation for satisfaction for the definition. Apart from diabetes and hearing impairments mentioned in the Guidance, other examples might be asthma and epilepsy. This may be particularly significant for those suffering from mental illness which is controlled by medication; the test is what would be the effects of the condition in the absence of that medication. In *Kapadia v Lambeth LB*[59] the EAT held that counselling sessions for a man with depression constituted 'medical treatment'.

(ii) *Progressive conditions*

Disability Discrimination Act 1995

Schedule 1, para 8

(1)   Where:

(a) a person has a progressive condition (such as cancer, multiple sclerosis or muscular dystrophy or infection by the human immunodeficiency virus),

(b) as a result of that condition, he has an impairment ...; but

(c) that effect is not (or was not) a substantial adverse effect,

he shall be taken to have an impairment which has such a substantial adverse effect if the condition is likely to result in his having such an impairment.

Guidance[60]

A15   Where a person has a progressive condition, he or she will be treated as having an impairment which has a *substantial* adverse effect from the moment any impairment resulting from that condition first has *some* effect ... The effect need not be continuous and need not be substantial.

The effect of this provision is that the sufferer is protected as from the moment that there is any effect on normal day-to-day activities as defined. It follows that someone diagnosed as HIV positive is *not* protected merely by virtue of that fact;[61] the protection only comes into effect when some symptom of the illness is manifest. In consequence of this approach, the definition excludes someone who is wrongly thought by the employer to be disabled when in fact there is no actual impairment. Equally, those with a genetic disorder which is latent are outside the statutory

---

59   [2000] IRLR 14. Confirmed by the Court of Appeal, 57 BMLR 170; [2000] IRLR 699.

60   *Op cit*, fn 55.

61   On HIV generally, see Napier, B, 'AIDS, discrimination and employment law' [1989] 18 ILJ 84. The Government, in *Towards Inclusion – Civil Rights for Disabled People* (available www.dwp.gov.uk), has stated that it will extend the DDA 1995 to cover HIV from the time of diagnoses, and cancer, from when diagnosed as likely to require substantial treatment. (See s 3, para 3.11.) See also HL Deb Col 587, 28 Feb 2003, *per* Lord McIntosh.

protection. It is thus not permissible to discriminate against someone who has a diagnosed impairment, even though the currents effects may be relatively minor, whereas it is lawful to discriminate against someone who is likely to develop precisely the same condition in the future.

The meaning of Sched 1, para (8)(1) was debated in *Mowat-Brown v University of Surrey*.[62] Counsel argued that the phrase 'if the condition is likely to result' referred to the condition, rather than the particular claimant. Otherwise, the argument went, many sufferers would be removed from protection for want of proof that the effect of the condition would become substantial. However, for the EAT, Judge Reid QC stated:

> The question to be asked is whether, on the balance of probabilities, the claimant has established that the condition in his case is likely to have a substantial adverse effect. It is not enough simply to establish that he has a progressive condition and that it has or has had an effect on his ability to carry out normal day-to-day activities. The claimant must go on and show that it is more likely than not that at some stage in the future he will have an impairment which will have a substantial adverse effect on his ability to carry out normal day-to-day activities. How the claimant does this is up to him. In some cases, it may be possible to produce medical evidence of his likely prognosis. In other cases, it may be possible to discharge the onus of proof by statistical evidence.[63]

(3)   Past Disabilities

Disability Discrimination Act 1995

Section 2

(1)   The provisions of this Part and Parts II to IV apply in relation to a person who has had a disability as they apply in relation to a person who has that disability

    ...

(4)   In any proceedings under Part II, III or IV of this Act, the question whether a person had a disability at a particular time ('the relevant time') shall be determined, for the purposes of this section, as if the provisions of, or made under, this Act in force when the act complained of was done had been in force at the relevant time.

(5)   The relevant time may be a time before the passing of this Act.

A person is treated as being presently disabled if he or she is at present symptom-free but such symptoms are likely to recur. This does not include someone who has recovered from a past disability. This is particularly important as regards mental illness, even though the person will still be treated as *currently* disabled if the condition is only controlled rather than cured.[64] Section 2 therefore provides that a person who has had a disability in the past is equally protected. This important provision allows for consideration of potentially long-term social consequences of disability as well as its current effects. For instance, an employer who dismisses a worker, upon discovering that the worker once had a mental illness, can be liable under the Act. Of course, in these cases, proving that the less favourable treatment 'related to' the disability may be more difficult. Section 2(4) ensures that a person who

---

62   [2002] IRLR 235, EAT.

63   *Ibid*, para 21

64   See above, p 486.

had a disability before the Act came into force, but suffers discrimination after it came into force, is protected.

Schedule 2 modifies Sched 1, para 2, which covers fluctuating effects, so that where, in the past, the effects have ceased and recurred (rather than being *likely* to recur), the effects will be regarded as continuing.[65]

(4)   Those Previously in the Register of Disabled Persons

The legislation abolished the previous protection available through the quota system. While such protection was very limited, it was considered to be inappropriate to exclude anyone who might previously have been classified, rightly or wrongly, as disabled, but who, but for this section, would fall outside the new definition. The effect of Sched 1, para 7 is to grant the protection to those who were registered as disabled both in January 1995, when the Bill was introduced, and in December 1996, when the employment provisions came into effect. Such a person is classed as having a disability for an initial period of three years. From then on, of course, they can be classed as having a disability in the past, and benefit from s 2 of the DDA 1995.[66]

3   DISCRIMINATION IN EMPLOYMENT

(1)   Introduction

The most important point concerning the coverage of the legislation is that the employment provisions apply only to employers who had 15 or more employees at the time of the alleged discriminatory act.[67] Section 7 of the DDA 1995 allows for a statutory instrument to reduce, but not to increase, the threshold, although it may only be reduced to two employees rather than abolished altogether,[68] which would require fresh legislation.[69]

Application of the provision will not always be straightforward. It is not always precisely clear when a discriminatory act occurs. While part-time, temporary and casual workers come within the Act's definition of employment and so must be counted, the same is not true where work is contracted out. Even an employee working for an enterprise may be unsure of the exact employment status of some workers; for a rejected applicant, the problems are even greater. It may be necessary to expend considerable time and money in order to rebut an employer's defence that at the relevant time there were fewer than 15 employees on the books. Employers may move in and out of the legislation as circumstances change.[70]

---

65   See *Greenwood v British Airways* [1999] ICR 969; [1999] IRLR 600, EAT, above, p 480.

66   See above, p 488.

67   DDA 1995, s 7.

68   In 1998, it was reduced from 20 to 15; SI 1998/2618.

69   This is due to happen on 1 October 2004. See further below, p 516.

70   In *Burton v Higham (t/a Ace Appointments)* [2003] All ER (D) 113 (Mar), the defendant employed six workers permanently, and many others on a 'Temporary Workers Contract'. The EAT held that the temporary workers fell within the definition of employment in the DDA 1995, s 68, and so one of the six permanent workers could bring a claim under the DDA 1995.

The qualifications provisions are similar to those under the other anti-discrimination statutes. 'Employment' has the same extended meaning, not being restricted to those employed under contracts of service. It follows that the Act applies to those who hire contractors to do work and, strictly speaking therefore, the duty to make reasonable accommodation applies also. It is difficult to imagine that a tribunal would often impose such a duty where the person being hired was genuinely self-employed.

Section 4(6) excludes employment outside 'Great Britain', although in contrast with the other statutes, the DDA 1995 applies directly in Northern Ireland rather than having specific separate legislation.[71] There are significant exceptions from the coverage of the legislation: the police are excluded, as they have no contract, and there is no specific inclusion as is the case with the SDA 1975 and RRA 1976; prison officers, fire fighters, employment in the armed services, and employment on board a ship, hovercraft or aeroplane are also excluded. While it is clear that many people with particular categories of disability would be unable to perform some such jobs, blanket exceptions are unnecessary and unacceptable. Many jobs in the services are desk jobs, and many disabilities would not hinder combat effectiveness; the legislation would permit airlines to refuse to employ cabin staff with disfigurements or who require a hearing aid. Once again, the instinctive reaction of the Government appears to have been to exclude its own employees rather than to give a lead to the private sector.[72]

Section 13 covers discrimination by trade organisations – trade unions,[73] employers' organisations, etc – in similar terms to that prohibited by the RRA 1976 and the SDA 1975. The duty to make reasonable adjustments also applies. This is potentially a source of considerable expense for unions. Meetings may need to be at a time and place suitable for those with mobility impairments, and union literature will need to be accessible to those with visual impairments.[74] There is, however, no specific prohibition, as in the other legislation, against discrimination by partnerships, qualifying bodies, bodies concerned with vocational training[75] and employment agencies, although in many situations employment agencies will be covered by the provision concerning discrimination against contract workers.[76] In many of these examples, reliance could be placed on the prohibition of discrimination in relation to the provision of goods and services.

Some unlawful acts are regulated by the DDA 1995 in much the same way as under the SDA 1975 and the RRA 1976. Victimisation is outlawed by s 55, whilst s 58 provides the same test for the liability of the employer for acts of employees, and s 57 prohibits the aiding of unlawful acts. There is no equivalent to the sections dealing with instructions to discriminate and pressure to discriminate.[77] The different

71   DDA 1995, s 70(6).
72   The exceptions in this paragraph are due to be covered from 1 October 2004. See below, p 516.
73   See 'Trade unions and the DDA' (1998) 77 EOR 23.
74   *Ibid*. The Code of Practice (*op cit*, fn 9) suggests many instances where Braille or audio tape should be used. Cf s 21(4), where service providers, and s 28T, post-16 education providers, are obliged to offer 'auxiliary aids'. (In force, respectively, 1 October 1999: SI 1999/1190, Arts 3, 5(g); 1 September 2003: Special Educational Needs and Disability Act 2001 (Commencement No 5) Order 2002, SI 2002/2217, Art 6, Sched 2.).
75   These exceptions are due to be covered from 1 October 2004. See below, p 516.
76   For a discussion on the meaning of 'contract worker', see Chapter 12, p 349.
77   This is due for remedy in October 2004. See below, p 516.

approach concerns discriminatory advertising; under the SDA 1975 and the RRA 1976 the Commissions have responsibility for enforcement.

Section 4 of the DDA 1995 directly parallels the equivalent provisions of the SDA 1975 and the RRA 1976, making it unlawful to discriminate before someone obtains a job, while they are in employment, and in relation to dismissal.[78] The specific reference to subjecting an employee to 'any other detriment'[79] means that harassing someone on the ground of their disability will be unlawful on the same basis as racial and sexual harassment.[80]

(2)   The Legal Definition

Section 5 provides two separate and overlapping forms of disability discrimination: *less favourable treatment* and a *failure to make reasonable adjustments*.

Disability Discrimination Act 1995

Section 5

(1)   ... [A]n employer discriminates against a disabled person if:

   (a) for a reason which relates to the person's disability, he treats him less favourably than he treats or would treat others to whom that reason does not or would not apply; and

   (b) he cannot show that the treatment in question is justified.

(2)   ... [A]n employer also discriminates against a disabled person if:

   (a) he fails to comply with a section 6 duty [to make reasonable adjustments] imposed on him in relation to the disabled person; and

   (b) he cannot show that his failure to comply with that duty is justified.

Under the RRA 1976, a white person may claim to have been the victim of discrimination; under the SDA 1975, a man may claim to have been the victim. However, under the DDA 1995, a non-disabled person does not have the right to make a claim. Conceptually, this is a very important difference, for it means that positive action to benefit disabled people normally will be lawful. Quotas, special training and so on are all presumptively lawful; this is inevitable and correct given that the foundation stone of the Act is the duty to make reasonable accommodation for the needs of disabled people. But the general point is subject to an exception. A disabled person may argue that he or she has been treated less favourably *than another disabled person* has or would have been treated. It thus appears that positive action beyond that mandated by the reasonable accommodation principle may not be targeted at any particular group of the disabled. Section 10(2)(a) protects those who provide 'supported employment'[81] for a particular group of the disabled – such as Workshops for the Blind – from falling foul of the anti-discrimination principle. However, what might be described as open market employers may not specifically target particular

---

78 DDA 1995, s 12, covers discrimination against contract workers. The duty of reasonable adjustment may therefore be placed on the principal/hirer rather than, or in addition to, the employer of the contracted worker. However, what that duty requires will vary greatly according to the circumstances, especially where the hiring is only for a short period.

79 DDA 1995, s 4(2)(d).

80 See Chapter 9. Harassment is due to be specifically outlawed in 1 October 2004. See below, p 519.

81 This is defined by s 10(3) as where there are 'facilities provided, or in respect of which payments are made, under s 15 of the Disabled Persons (Employment) Act 1944'.

groups of the disabled. This may be especially problematic where reasonable accommodation is provided in advance, so to encourage and enable particular groups to apply for and perform a job. A person from another group may have a case that such accommodation was only provided on a selective basis.

Two other consequences follow from this definition. First, discrimination on the grounds of *another's* disability is not covered. For instance, where a manager shuns a person for associating with a disabled person. Secondly, 'perceived discrimination' is not covered, for instance, where a manager treats a worker less favourably because he wrongly perceives that the worker has AIDS.[82] In this respect, the Act differs from the RRA 1976, but resembles the SDA 1975. Of course, the provisions on victimisation may catch some instances.

This definition shows how the DDA 1995 is substantially different from the SDA 1975 and the RRA 1976. There is no formalised distinction between direct and indirect discrimination and, furthermore, direct discrimination is potentially justifiable.[83] Nevertheless the differences may be more apparent than real. The functional equivalent of indirect discrimination is the s 6 duty to make reasonable adjustments. Failure to make such adjustments means that unnecessary and unjustifiable barriers are being placed in the way of equal employment opportunities for disabled people in much the same way as unjustifiable employment conditions may disadvantage women and minority ethnic groups. However, as we shall see, it may be that cases of indirect discrimination can fall also under s 5(1).

(3)   Less Favourable Treatment

(a)   *The comparison and the reason for the treatment*

It is clear from *Clark v Novacold* that the comparison cannot be made until the reason for the treatment is identified.

> **Clark v TGD Ltd t/a Novacold [1999] ICR 951; [1999] IRLR 318; 48 BMLR 1, CA**

In August 1996, Clark suffered a back injury at work and was diagnosed as having soft tissue injuries around the spine. He was unable to work and absent from September 1996 until his dismissal, in January 1997. He made a complaint under the DDA 1995. Novacold argued that they would have dismissed any person unable to work for that long. The Court of Appeal held that that was the wrong approach. Clark should have been compared with a person who was able to work.

Mummery LJ (at pp 323–24):

> [T]he 1995 Act adopts a significantly different approach [from the Sex Discrimination Act 1975 and Race Relations Act 1976] to the protection of disabled persons against less favourable treatment in employment. The definition of discrimination in the 1995 Act does not contain an express provision requiring a comparison of the cases of different persons in the same, or not materially different, circumstances. The statutory focus is narrower: it is on the 'reason' for the treatment of the disabled employee and

---

the comparison to be made is with the treatment of 'others to whom that reason does not or would not apply'. The 'others' with whom comparison is to be made are not specifically required to be in the same, or not materially different, circumstances: they only have to be persons 'to whom that reason does not or would not apply'.

This is to be contrasted not only with the different approach in the 1975 and the 1976 Acts, but also with the express requirement of comparison with the treatment of other persons 'whose circumstances are the same' stipulated in victimisation cases by s 55(1)(a) of the 1995 Act.

The result of this approach is that the reason would not apply to others even if their circumstances are different from those of the disabled person. The persons who are performing the main functions of their jobs are 'others' to whom the reason for dismissal of the disabled person (ie inability to perform those functions) would not apply.

In the context of the special sense in which 'discrimination' is defined in s 5 of the 1995 Act it is more probable that Parliament meant 'that reason' to refer only to the facts constituting the reason for the treatment, and not to include within that reason the added requirement of a causal link with disability: that is more properly regarded as the cause of the reason for the treatment than as in itself a reason for the treatment. This interpretation avoids the difficulties which would be encountered in many cases in seeking to identify what the appeal tribunal referred to as 'the characteristics of the hypothetical comparator'. It would avoid the kind of problems which the English (and Scottish) courts and the tribunals encountered in their futile attempts to find and identify the characteristics of a hypothetical non-pregnant male comparator for a pregnant woman in sex discrimination cases before the decision of the European Court of Justice in *Webb v EMO Air Cargo (UK) Ltd* ...[84] This interpretation is also consistent with the emphasis on whether the less favourable treatment of the disabled person is shown to be justified. That defence is not available in cases of direct discrimination under the other discrimination Acts.

... Consider his[85] example. If no dogs are admitted to a cafe, the reason for denying access to refreshment in it by a blind person with his guide dog would be the fact that no dogs are admitted. That reason 'relates to' his disability. His guide dog is with him because of his disability.

On the Novacold interpretation of the comparison to be made, the blind person with his guide dog would not be treated less favourably than the relevant comparator, ie 'others', to whom that reason would not apply, would be sighted persons who had their dogs with them. There could not therefore be any, let alone *prima facie*, discrimination ... It could only be a case of less favourable treatment and therefore a *prima facie* case of discrimination, if the comparators are 'others' without dogs: 'that reason' for refusing access to refreshment in the cafe would not apply to 'others' without dogs.

The same point can be made on the example given in the Code of Practice on Rights of Access issued by the Secretary of State at para 2.12:

> A waiter asks a disabled customer to leave the restaurant because she has difficulty eating as a result of her disability. He serves other customers who have no difficulty eating. The waiter has therefore treated her less favourably than other customers. The treatment was for a reason related to her disability – her

---

84 [1995] IRLR 645; see Chapter 8, p 199.
85 Minister of State for Social Security and Disabled People, 253 HC Official Report (6th series) Col 150, 24 Jan 1995.

difficulty when eating. And the reason for her less favourable treatment did not apply to other customers. If the waiter could not justify the less favourable treatment, he would have discriminated unlawfully.

It is clear from this example that the comparison to be made is with other diners who have no difficulty in eating and are served by the waiter, and not with other diners who may be asked to leave because they also have difficulty eating, but for a non-disability reason, eg, because the food served up by the waiter is disgusting. This interpretation of s 20(1) provides support for Mr Clark's interpretation of s 5(1). The reason for his dismissal would not apply to others who are able to perform the main functions of their jobs; he has been treated less favourably than those others. He was dismissed for not being able to perform the main functions of his job. The 'others' would not be dismissed for that reason.

There is still some confusion. In *Hood v London Clubs Management*,[86] the claimant's sick pay was withdrawn under a policy to cut sick pay to all workers. The EAT held, apparently applying *Clark*, that the reason for the treatment was the general policy, and not the claimant's disability (migraines). Therefore, the claimant was not treated less favourably than other workers who may have been off sick. Of course, this outcome is wrong. The first problem is distinguishing sick pay from ordinary pay,[87] a triumph of form over substance. For the parties it was pay, no matter what the label. Taken this way, the treatment, withdrawing pay, was related to the claimant's disability, and he was treated less favourably than those workers who able to work and were paid. As Mummery LJ said in *Clark*: 'The reason for his dismissal would not apply to others who are able to perform the main functions of their jobs.' Equally, in *Hood*, the reason for the withdrawal of pay would not apply to those who could work. The 'sick-pay policy' argument should have been a matter for the defence of justification, not the comparison.

(b)   Knowledge of the disability

Another issue related to defining discrimination is whether or not the alleged discriminator must have knowledge of the claimant's disability. This is often expressed as *subjective* or *objective* interpretation of the legislation. In *Heinz*, the EAT held that the test was an objective one, in other words, knowledge of the disability is not required for liability.

Heinz v Kendrick [2001] IRLR 144, EAT

Lindsay J:

22   ... Firstly, [the subjective interpretation] would, we fear, lead in many cases to hair-splitting medical evidence ... One can readily imagine cases in which, if detailed knowledge were to be relevant, there would need to be medical evidence as to the labels which could be attached to this or that symptom or aggregation of symptoms as a person's condition deteriorated or improved. We cannot think such an approach was within the legislature's broad intendment ...

24.   Thirdly ... without being, we hope, too far-fetched, one can imagine, for example, a postman or messenger who, at his engagement and for a while afterwards, successfully conceals the fact that he has an artificial leg and can

---

86   [2001] IRLR 719, EAT.
87   Fault here lies with the claimant's pleadings, on which the law was applied.

walk only for short distances at a time. He may later be dismissed for a conduct or capability ground, namely that he had proved to be unacceptably slow in making his rounds, but still without his disability being spotted. His slowness could have been taken by the employer to have been by reason of idleness or absenteeism. If, however, the employee were then able to show that his slowness was by reason of his having an artificial leg then, as it seems to us, he would, in such a case, have been treated less favourably 'than others to whom that reason does not apply' (namely, as *Clark v Novacold* [see above] requires, less favourably than other employees who did their rounds at an acceptable pace). Moreover he would have been so treated for a reason – unacceptable slowness – which related to his disability. That, it seems to us, would be the case whether or not the employer ever knew before the dismissal that the reason for the slowness was that the employee was disabled. The employee would, as it seems to us, have been discriminated against within the Act even if the employer had assumed that the slowness was attributable only to laziness or absenteeism. As another example, one might imagine a secretary dismissed because he or she, despite repeated training, persisted in typing hopelessly misspelt letters, yet without the employer or, perhaps, even the employee knowing that the reason for the errors was not ignorance or carelessness but dyslexia.

(c)   *Indirect discrimination and s 5(1)*

Mummery LJ warned in *Clark v Novacold*[88] that the DDA 1995 adopts a considerably different approach from the established definitions in the race and sex discrimination legislation. The phrase, 'related to' – especially as interpreted in *Heinz* – suggests that there is scope in the statutory definition for *indirect* discrimination. The Government were unsure of this. The 1994 Green Paper stated that the inclusion of indirect discrimination would be 'more difficult to tackle effectively where disabled people are involved because disability occurs in many forms'.[89] The White Paper stated that 'a general prohibition on indirect discrimination ... could have unforeseen consequences which were mainly unfairly burdensome for business'.[90] However, on the second reading of the Bill, the Minister for Social Security and Disabled People stated:

> The Bill is drafted in such a way that indirect as well as direct discrimination can be dealt with ... A situation where dogs are not admitted to a cafe, with the effect that blind people would be unable to enter it, would be a *prima facie* case of indirect discrimination against blind people and would be unlawful.[91]

However, the phrase 'related to' is quite different language from any traditional definition of indirect discrimination, such 'applying a neutral practice that adversely affects the protected group'. As the 'no-dogs' example given by the Minister illustrates, the definitions will often overlap. The DDA 1995 definition embraces indirect discrimination, it does not replicate it. The new Regulations[92] support this view, as the new s 3A(3) will abolish justification for less favourable treatment so far as

---

88 Above, p 492.
89 *A Consultation on Government Measures to Tackle Discrimination Against Disabled People*, 1994, London: Disability Unit, Department of Social Security, para 4.11.
90 *Ending Discrimination Against Disabled People*, 1995, Cm 2729, London: HMSO, para 4.5.
91 253 HC Official Report (6th series) Col 150, 24 January 1995.
92 The Disability Discrimination (Amendment) Regulations 2003, due in force 1 October 2004; see below, p 516.

it amounts to direct discrimination, thus envisaging cases other than direct discrimination coming within the definition.

Further, it may well be that, with a purposive interpretation, the present definition is *wider* than the conventional direct/indirect discrimination approach.[93] As the facts of *Hambidge* illustrate, not all instances of disability discrimination fall neatly into the conventional analysis.

R v Powys CC ex p Hambidge (No 2) [2000] 2 FCR 69; 54 BMLR 133; [2000] LGR 564, CA

The council charged for home help by means testing. Service users were divided into three bands. Band A received income support only. Band B, consisting of persons with more serious disabilities, received a disability allowance of £49.50 as well. Those in band C were not poor enough to receive income support. For those in band A, the council charged nothing, for band B £32.70 per week, and band C £49.50 per week. Ms Hambidge, who fell into band B, argued that the charge indirectly discriminated against her under the DDA 1995.

Laws LJ:

20. The argument advanced ... for the appellant, is a simple and elegant one. It is to the effect that the appellant is charged more for her care than those who are in Band A, who are charged nothing, because she has more money, but the reason she has more money is and is only that she receives disability living allowance. That is accordingly a reason which relates to her disability. Thus she is charged more and therefore discriminated against for a reason which relates to her disability within the meaning of s 20(1)(a). He emphasises the fact that those in Band B, like his client, are by definition more disabled than those in Band A yet that very fact has promoted these differential charges so that the more disabled person pays, the less disabled person does not.

21. If Mr Gordon's argument were right on the statute, I have to say I would look for a different interpretation even if it were strained. I do not think that his construction of s 20(1)(a) in relation to the facts of this case is a construction which the legislator may reasonably be thought to have had in mind ...

23. The judge below, accepting a submission made to him by Mr Lewis for the respondent, said:

    Mr Lewis submits that whatever the difference in treatment between Mrs Hambidge and someone in Band A it is not because of her disability. She is required to pay because she has the money to pay. The reason why she has the money is not part of the reason for the difference in treatment. In my judgment this submission is correct and I accept it.

24. More particularly here, as Mr Lewis submitted to us this morning, the charging regime is based on the possession or otherwise of resources by the persons in Bands A–C. It is simply a form of means testing; and there is no causal link in my judgment between the rate charged to persons in Band B and their disability. The local authority are, as Mr Gordon rightly said himself, indifferent to the appellant's receipt of disability living allowance as such. What concerns them is the level of resources in the hands of those in receipt of care whether or not the presence of disability lies behind the receipt of cash in any particular case. The point is very well-illustrated by the situation applying in relation to those in

---

93   Although these are concepts employed (with some modification for disability) by the Equal Treatment at Work Directive 2000/78/EC, which covers disability. See generally below, p 516.

Band C. A person in Band C could not rely on Mr Gordon's arguments. Such a person's disability is either irrelevant to or at most coincidental with his receipt of resources though his disability may be exactly the same as that of someone in Band A. Mr Gordon drew attention to an example given by the minister promoting the 1995 Act [the 'no-dogs' example, above] ...

25. If the case were, however, that some dogs were admitted and some dogs were not admitted, such indirect discrimination would not arise. Here the charges bear differentially on persons with the same disability: persons in Band C and persons in Band B. The disability, in my judgment, is categorically not the reason for the differential charges. That, if Aldous and Henry LJJ agree, would dispose of the appeal. For my part I do not find it necessary to go into questions which would otherwise arise, namely whether after all Mrs Hambidge is treated differently from those in Band A and, last, if she is whether the council may put forward a justification under s 20. My view of this case is that the Disability Discrimination Act 1995 does not bite on it at all and I would dismiss the appeal for those reasons.

The EAT here has applied the traditional analysis of direct and indirect discrimination. Consequently, it found no direct discrimination because the charges were made according to income, not disability; so there was no *direct* relationship between the treatment and disability. Although the decision was couched in terms of 'related to', this is the only explanation. Clearly the charge was related to disability, although it may not have been *directly* related to it. It also found no *indirect* discrimination because the charges were not neutral, in that they did not apply across the range of bands A and B. These facts may fall through the net of the conventional analysis quite neatly,[94] but it is clearly a case of disability discrimination. The council's charging policy was a matter for justification.

(d) Justifying less favourable treatment

Disability Discrimination Act 1995

Section 5

[F]or the purposes of sub-s (1) treatment is justified if, but only if, the reason for it is both material to the circumstances of the particular case and substantial.

Unlike race and sex discrimination, 'direct' discrimination on ground of disability is potentially justifiable.[95] Where a disabled person is not appointed on merit, the treatment will be justified.[96] However, the legislation contemplates that, despite merit, there may still be circumstances where it is permissible to discriminate. It is specifically provided that this defence cannot succeed where the employer has failed to make a reasonable adjustment as required by s 6 but, in circumstances falling

---

94 It may be possible to argue that the means testing policy, intended to be neutral in its effect, was a neutral practice.

95 This is due for repeal on 1 October 2004, see below, pp 517–18. For a discussion of the authorities, see *Murray v Newham CAB* [2003] All ER (D) 138 (Mar) (EAT/554/01/ST, see www.employmentappeals.gov.uk), paras 23–33.

96 In *Fozard v Greater Manchester Police Authority*, unreported, IT, Case 2401143/97, see 33 DCLD 2, a person with learning difficulties applied for a job as a word processor operator, but was rejected as the application form contained a number of errors. The tribunal held that the rejection was related to her disability, but was justified, as accuracy in written work was an important element in the job.

outside the scope of that section, justified discrimination is a possibility. Safety is likely to be a common factor in such defences.[97] The less favourable treatment may be justified if it is both material and substantial.[98] Quite what these each of these terms mean was discussed in *Jones v Post Office*.

Jones v Post Office [2001] EWCA Civ 558; [2001] IRLR 384; [2001] ICR 805, CA

Mr Jones was employed as a mail delivery driver from 1977. He was diagnosed with diabetes and, following a heart attack in June 1997, his treatment was altered from tablets to insulin. As a result, and following their medical advice, the Post Office restricted Jones to two-hours per day driving duties. He brought a case under the DDA 1995. The tribunal heard expert evidence for Jones that the deterioration in his condition signalled by his reliance on insulin made no material difference to the existing risk that he would experience a hypoglycaemic episode while driving a Post Office van. The tribunal preferred this evidence to the Post Office's expert and found that the Post Office were not justified in restricting Jones' driving so. The Court of Appeal held that it was not for the tribunal to decide such matters.

Pill LJ (at para 10):

... Miss Tether's [counsel for Jones] submission is that the justification turns upon medical evidence which the respondent had, or ought to have had, at the date of the decision. If, by the standards applying at that date, the medical evidence relied on can be shown, to the satisfaction of the employment tribunal, to be wrong, justification under s 5(3) is not established.

... Miss Tether submits that, when the 'reason' relied on by the employer for the purposes of the subsection is a belief about the effects of a disability, the subsection requires an employment tribunal to determine objectively whether that belief is correct. If the employer wrongly believes that the disability constitutes a safety risk, the reason is not 'material' for the purposes of the subsection [s 5(3)] ...

In support of her submission, Miss Tether relies upon the ordinary meaning of the words used, the consistency of her construction with the purpose of the Act, the use of terminology different from that applying to providers of services and the circumstances in which the subsection resulted from an amendment to the Bill during its passage through Parliament.

In relation to the words used, Miss Tether submits that the 'reason' must be material and substantial. The subsection does not merely provide that it is sufficient if the employer reasonably believes it is material and substantial ...

Miss Tether distinguishes the language now under consideration from that employed in s 20 of the Act, which deals with providers of services ...

'(b) it is reasonable in all the circumstances of the case, for him to hold that opinion.'

---

97 In *Smith v Carpets International UK plc*, unreported, IT, Case 1800507/97, see 34 DCLD 2, it was held to be justified on safety grounds to suspend a person with epilepsy from work which involved driving a fork-lift truck. However, a similar defence in a case of a labourer working in a forge was rejected in *Holmes v Whittingham and Porter*, unreported, IT, Case 1802799/97, see 34 DCLD 4, as specialist medical advice should have been taken before the employee was dismissed rather than relying on the recommendation of a general practitioner.

98 For specific examples, see Code of Practice (*op cit*, fn 9), para 4.6.

That test expressly provides that it is only the reasonableness of the opinion of the provider of services which is to be tested. In the draft bill, a similar justification subsection appeared in s 5.

In moving an amendment to that clause, the Minister of State stated that: 'the fact that the justifications would be subject to an employer's opinion, albeit one which must be shown to have been reasonably held, has caused concern.' The minister stated that the amendment 'substitutes for a fixed list of specific justifications a principle that can be applied much more easily in the wide and varied range of circumstances that can arise in the field of employment. Less favourable treatment of a disabled person would thus be justified if the reason for it were both material to the circumstances and substantial . . . the new provisions will be clear to understand and to operate.' ...

The 1995 Act is plainly intended to create rights for the disabled and to protect their position as employees, but those intentions must be considered in the context of the employer's duties to employees generally and to the general public. I cannot accept, in a case such as the present, involving an assessment of risk, that Parliament intended in the wording adopted to confer on employment tribunals a general power and duty to decide whether the employer's assessment of risk is correct. The issue is a different one from whether a person has a disability, within the meaning of s 1 of the Act, which is to be determined by the employment tribunal (*Goodwin v Patent Office* [1999] IRLR 4).

...Where a properly conducted risk assessment provides a reason which is on its face both material and substantial, and is not irrational, the tribunal cannot substitute its own appraisal ...

The present problem will typically arise when a risk assessment is involved. I am not doubting that the employment tribunal is permitted to investigate facts, for example as to the time-keeping record of the disabled person or as to his rate of productivity, matters which would arise upon some of the illustrations given in the Code of Practice ... Thus if no risk assessment was made or a decision was taken otherwise than on the basis of appropriate medical evidence, or was an irrational decision as being beyond the range of responses open to a reasonable decision-maker ... the employment tribunal could hold the reason insufficient and the treatment unjustified ...

The limited function of the employment tribunal ... is different but not very different from the task employment tribunals have to perform in cases of unfair dismissal. Under [s 98 of the Employment Rights Act 1996] ... the tribunal's task is to consider the reasonableness of the employer's response and, under the present section, it is to consider the materiality and substantiality of his reason. In both cases, the members of the tribunal might themselves have come to a different conclusion on the evidence, but they must respect the opinion of the employer, in the one case if it is within the range of reasonable responses and in the other if the reason given is material and substantial.

Arden LJ (at para 37):

... Mr Griffith-Jones [counsel for the Post Office] submits that 'material' means 'relevant'. As to this, it is often said that there are degrees of relevance. In this context, I would add to Mr Griffith-Jones's submission the rider that it is not sufficient that the connection is an extenuated one. The use of the word 'material' rather than 'relevant' or 'applicable' indicates to me that there must be a reasonably strong connection between the employer's reason and the circumstances of the individual case. The strength of this connection involves largely a factual enquiry. It ought not to involve an enquiry into medical evidence since such an enquiry is relevant, if at all, only to the second limb of s 5(3).

An example may help throw light on the function of the word 'material' in s 5(3). Suppose that it is shown that diabetes (of either type) leads to diminished night-time vision and the employer of an employee with diabetes prohibits that employee from doing night-time shifts for the reason that he has diabetes. In this example there would be a material connection between the employer's reason and the circumstances of the particular case. Miss Tether sought to argue that materiality also involved correctness. However, in my judgment, if the employer in the example last given believed that diabetes diminished night-time vision but was entirely wrong in that belief; the requirement for materiality in the example which I have given would still be met. However, there would be difficulty in the employer meeting the second requirement of substantiality ...

The second requirement in s 5(3) is that the reason should be 'substantial'. This means, in my judgment, that the reason which the employer adopted as his ground for discrimination must carry real weight and thus be of substance.

Pill LJ discussed the issue (of the correctness of the Post Office's opinion) under 'material', whilst Arden LJ stated that it was an issue for 'substantial'. As Pill LJ pointed out, a tribunal is obliged to make its own judgment on the medical issue of whether or not a person has a disability. The same applies under 'reasonable adjustments'.[99] Is there any reason for this anomaly, apart from a policy one of giving employers some leeway? Perhaps Pill LJ hinted at this when saying the Act's intentions 'must be considered in the context of the employer's duties ...'.

(i)   Justification without knowledge of the disability

Can an employer who is ignorant of the claimant's disability at the time of the less favourable treatment rely on the defence? The matter was addressed in *Callaghan*.

Callaghan v Glasgow CC [2001] IRLR 724, EAT

Lord Johnston (at p 726):

It is also important to note, in our opinion, given that the discriminatory act relates to treatment, that is to say how the employer treats the employee, knowledge of disability is not necessarily an essential element. Accordingly, in so far as this tribunal may have suggested in *Quinn v Schwarzkopf*[100] ... that justification can never occur if the employer is ignorant of the fact of disability at the relevant time, that goes too far. That case was primarily concerned with an attempt by the employer to claim justification *ex post facto* which had not featured at the time of the relevant discriminatory act, which was in fact a dismissal. Obviously, the fact the employer did not know that disability exists might affect the justification issue but does not preclude it. It follows that we do not consider that Quinn assists the appellant in this case. What matters, therefore, is to analyse the treatment meted out by the employer.

---

99 *Morse v Wiltshire CC* [1998] IRLR 352, EAT. See below, p 506.
100 [2001] IRLR 67, EAT.

(4)   The Duty to Make Adjustments

This section is the key to the legislation. It imposes a duty to take positive action in a way entirely unknown to the SDA 1975 and the RRA 1976, reflecting the truths that disabilities do affect ability to perform a job, but to a far lesser extent than is often supposed and in a way which can often be overcome with effort and imagination. Section 5(2) (set out above) defines this as discrimination and so provides a separate possible claim.

Disability Discrimination Act 1995

Section 6

(1)   Where:

    (a) any arrangements made by or on behalf of an employer; or

    (b) any physical feature of premises occupied by an employer,

    place the disabled person concerned at a substantial disadvantage in comparison with persons who are not disabled, it is the duty of the employer to take such steps as it is reasonable, in all the circumstances of the case, for him to have to take in order to prevent the arrangements or feature having that effect.[101]

(3)   The following are examples of steps which have to take ... in order to comply with sub-s (1):

    (a) making adjustments to premises;

    (b) allocating some of the disabled person's duties to another person;

    (c) transferring him to fill an existing vacancy;

    (d) altering his working hours;

    (e) assigning him to a different place of work;

    (f) allowing him to be absent during working hours for rehabilitation, assessment or treatment;

    (g) giving him, or arranging for him to be given, training;

    (h) acquiring or modifying equipment;

    (i) modifying instructions or reference manuals;

    (j) modifying procedures for testing or assessment;

    (k) providing a reader or interpreter;

    (l) providing supervision.[102]

(4)   In determining whether it is reasonable for an employer to have to take a particular step ... regard should be had, in particular, to:

    (a) the extent to which taking the step would prevent the effect in question;

    (b) the extent to which it is practicable for the employer to take the step;

    (c) the financial and other costs which would be incurred by the employer in taking the step and the extent to which taking it would disrupt any of his activities;

    (d) the extent of the employer's financial and other resources;

---

101 In *Morse v Wiltshire CC* [1998] IRLR 352, EAT, (below, p 506), it was held that this covered the making of reasonable adjustments so as to avoid the need to dismiss an employee who would otherwise have been dismissed, in this case on ground of redundancy.

102 For specific examples of how these might operate, see Code of Practice (*op cit*, fn 9), paras 4.7 and 4.20.

(e) the availability to the employer of financial or other assistance with respect to taking the step.

(5) In this section 'the disabled person concerned' means:

    (a) in the case of arrangements for determining to whom employment should be offered, any disabled person who is, or who has notified the employer that he may be, an applicant for that employment;

    (b) in any other case, a disabled person who is:

        (i) an applicant for the employment concerned; or

        (ii) an employee of the employer concerned.

(6) Nothing in this section imposes any duty on an employer in relation to a disabled person if the employer does not know, and could not reasonably be expected to know:

    (a) in the case of an applicant or potential applicant, that the disabled person is, or may be, an applicant for the employment; or

    (b) in any case, that the person has a disability and is likely to be affected in any way mentioned in sub-s (1).

A claim may be based on a failure to make adjustment in addition to, or instead of, a claim for less favourable treatment under s 5(1). An employer may refuse to hire a disabled person, either out of pure prejudice or from a lack of belief that a disabled person could be competent to do the job, or the rejection might be on the basis that, while disabled people are considered on merit, in the circumstances it would be impracticable for the particular applicant to perform the job. At the outset, the basis of claim may be unclear: it will frequently be sensible to argue both alternatives. The duty is triggered where the disabled person is placed at a 'substantial disadvantage'. This includes factors affecting the actual performance of the job, factors affecting safe access to and from the place of work, and any other factor affecting the safe performance of the job. If a reasonable adjustment would enable the job to be performed safely, the duty may be triggered.

The duty is personal in nature, being triggered by some action on the part of an individual disabled person. It follows that there is no general obligation to make a workplace more accessible or work practices more amenable to disabled people. It would be extremely difficult for an employer to predict in advance the wide range of disabilities in respect of which prospective adjustments would otherwise have to be made.[103] However, where the disability is relatively commonplace, and where clear steps to overcome it are possible, failure to plan ahead may constitute failure to make reasonable adjustments.[104]

The duty only arises when the employer has sufficient knowledge as to the situation of the disabled applicant or potential applicant. This may include current employees, for while the employer may normally be expected to be aware of the current situation of members of the workforce, many people become disabled while in

---

103 However, para 3.4 of the Code of Practice (*op cit*, fn 9) states that 'when planning for change it could be cost-effective to consider the needs of a range of possible future disabled employees and applicants. There may be helpful improvements that could be built into plans. For example, a new telecommunications system might be made accessible to deaf people even if there are currently no deaf employees'.

104 Eg, in *Williams v Channel 5 Engineering Services Ltd*, unreported, IT, Case 2302136/97, see 34 DCLD 3, the employers were held liable for organising a training course which included a video with no subtitles, which meant that the deaf complainant was unable to complete the course.

employment – whether or not through a workplace incident. In the past, it might have been in the interests of disabled people to conceal their situation from the employer; that is no longer the case. One of the practical and psychological difficulties with the legislation is that a disabled person will be best advised to be as frank and explicit as possible. There is a fine line between giving information necessary to trigger the employer's duty to make reasonable adjustments, and making the situation appear so bad as to suggest that no adjustment may be practicable.[105]

The duty can only arise where the employer has become aware of the disability. Under normal principles, knowledge held by any employee should be imputed to the employer. For example, if an employer instructs a secretary to discard application forms of applicants without degrees, and on checking the forms, the secretary becomes aware that an applicant without a degree has a disability, the employer will be treated as aware of that fact. If the form is discarded before anyone appreciates that the applicant is disabled, no duty can arise – subject of course to any informal communications between applicant and employer – but once there is any knowledge of a disability, the employer must be taken to be aware of all the information contained in the form concerning any necessary adjustments.

The example itself shows the limitations, inevitable perhaps, of the legislation. While reasonable adjustments must be within the scope of the employer, the question of what is reasonable is an objective one for the tribunal, upon which it is legitimate and, in some cases, necessary for the tribunal to substitute its own view of what is reasonable for that of the employer.[106] However, employers cannot be expected to make up for the fact that the applicant's disability may have contributed to educational under-achievement or lack of experience. An employer is still permitted to require applicants to possess an engineering degree, even though, on average, this may operate to the disadvantage of disabled people. The requirement itself cannot be challenged as being indirectly discriminatory if it is justifiable, and nothing by way of adjustment could reasonably be expected of all but the very biggest employers. Furthermore, maintenance of pay levels is not required by way of reasonable adjustment: if an employee becomes disabled, even in a workplace accident, such that the old job becomes impossible, the employer is under a duty to make reasonable efforts to find alternative work, if necessary by making adjustments to that work, but there is no obligation to keep paying the employee the same pay as was being earned before the disability struck.[107]

Section 6(3) shows how potentially wide the duty may be. There is a large body of knowledge and experience as to what adjustments are *capable* of being made in the interests of a disabled person, and disabled people themselves are often the best sources of what can be done in the most cost-effective manner. The key issue, however, is what degree of adjustment will tribunals consider to be reasonable.[108]

Adjustments to the job application process can be used as an example.

---

105 See also Code of Practice (*op cit*, fn 9), paras 4.57–4.63.
106 *Morse v Wiltshire CC* [1998] IRLR 352, EAT.
107 See, eg, *British Gas Services Ltd v McCaull* [2001] IRLR 60, below. The obligation to transfer a disabled employee provides greater protection than is provided by the law of unfair dismissal to victims of ill-health, even apart from the fact that the latter has at present a one-year qualifying period and the DDA 1995 none at all. Victims of long-term ill-health will receive greater protection if the problem can be classed as a disability. It is contended that most such cases will be within the definition.
108 See, Code of Practice (*op cit*, fn 9), paras 4.21–4.34.

'Adjusting the workplace: employers' duty under the Disability Discrimination Bill' (1995) 61 EOR 11, p 13:

The Cornell Program on Employment and Disability in the USA [has given the following] examples of possible accommodation to the selection process:

- For people with cognitive disabilities: simplifying and minimising wording on the job applications; clarification and assistance in completing information needed on the job application; describing job requirements clearly, concisely and simply and showing the person the job; adjustment of the length of interview to maximise a person's ability to remain attentive and decrease stress level.

- A person who does not see well enough to read an application form may be discouraged from applying for a job, even if the job itself requires minimal vision. Ask the applicant how he or she would prefer to meet the requirements of the process. If you require applicants to complete an application form, ask which would be the most convenient; mail the application to the candidate who requests it; offer the walk-in applicant the opportunity to take the form, have someone help complete it, and return it by mail or in person; offer the services of someone in the office to assist in completing the form.

- For applicants who are deaf or hard or hearing: minimally, interviews should be sensitive to the range of communication abilities of [such] persons ... Simple accommodations may include conducting the interview in a quiet, well lit environment that minimises visual distractions. The interviewer must be willing to use the interviewee's assistive listening device, if one is used ... Avoid sitting in front of bright lights or windows which make it difficult to speech read. If requested, use an effective professional sign language interpreter.

[T]he 'simplest' strategy is to ask the applicant what appropriate accommodations are needed.

It will also be necessary for employers to review any tests or examinations to ensure that they do not discriminate against disabled people. In the USA, the ADA requires that tests be given to people who have sensory, speaking or manual impairments in a format that does not require the use of the impaired skill, unless that is the job-related skill the test is designed to measure. The EEOC gives as an example: 'An applicant who has dyslexia, which causes difficulty in reading, should be given an oral rather than a written test, unless reading is an essential function of the job. Or, an individual with a visual disability or a learning disability might be allowed more time to take a test, unless the test is designed to measure speed required on the job.'

British case law in this area has been concerned with the finer details and implications of the 'test' of reasonable adjustment being objective.[109]

British Gas Services Ltd v McCaull [2001] IRLR 60, EAT

Mr McCaull was employed as a service engineer servicing central heating systems at customers' homes. He has epilepsy. The job involved driving a van and in November 1996, he blacked out as a result of an epileptic fit and had an accident, leaving the van a write-off. Mr McCaull remained off work from the time of the accident. After a medical consultation, the employers' occupational health service advised that he should only work subject to a number of restrictions, including no driving, no work without supervision and no work with electrical equipment. His employer offered

---

109 For a case where no adjustments at all were made, see *HM Prison Service v Beart* [2003] All ER (D) 191 (Jan), CA.

him alternative clerical work which would have meant a large reduction in salary. He declined and made a claim, *inter alia*, under s 5(2) of the DDA 1995. The employment tribunal found that as the employer had not 'considered' making adjustments, they could not argue that they had done so in offering the alternative job. The EAT allowed the employer's appeal.

Keene J (at para 38):

[The tribunal] ... then went on to consider the step which the appellant had taken, namely offering transfer to an existing vacancy. It commented that the appellant had had no regard to the fact that Mr McCaull was a disabled person, to the DDA or to s 6 thereof or to the Code. It noted that the company had sought to justify its action by reference to the fifth example in para 6.20 of the Code which it quoted as follows:

> In many cases where no reasonable adjustment would overcome a particular disability so as to enable the disabled person to continue with similar terms or conditions, it might be reasonable for the employer to have to offer a disabled employee a lower-paying job, applying the rate that would apply to such a position under his usual practices.

The tribunal commented that at no time before his dismissal did the company consider this or discuss it with Mr McCaull. It then found that 'it was not reasonable' for the company to offer him a job paying between 23% and 30% less than his existing job ...

... Upon analysis the tribunal seems to be running together a number of separate points. First, it seems to be saying that an employer must consciously consider what steps it should take in the context of its s 6 duty; in other words, it will be in breach of that statutory duty if it is unaware of the existence of that duty. In so far as the tribunal was saying that, it was wrong in law ...

The tribunal also seems to be making an associated but separate point, to the effect that an employer cannot argue *post hoc* that a s 6(3) step was not a reasonable one which he should have taken, if he did not consider taking it at the time. We can see no basis for such an interpretation of the statute. The test of reasonableness as set out in s 6(4) does not relate to what the employer considered but to what he did and did not do ...

Any other approach would deprive the employer of his entitlement to rely on s 6(4) of the Act, under which he can seek to show that, for example, there were no particular steps which it was reasonable for him to have to take in all the circumstances. If Parliament had intended an employer to be in breach of statutory duty because he failed to consider what steps he might reasonably take, it would have so provided in the Act, and it has not done so.

Of course, the reason for the employer's failure to comply with his s 6 duty may come into play under s 5(4) [justification] and it will no doubt be very difficult for an employer to justify the failure to take reasonable steps if he has not considered what steps should be taken. But that provision only comes into play once a breach of duty has been established ...

We conclude therefore that the tribunal did go wrong in law when dealing with the claim of discrimination under s 5(2) of the Act.

The EAT held that the approach should be objective. In *McCaull*, that favoured the employer, who did not consider adjustments for the claimant's disability, but nonetheless made some.

Morse v Wiltshire CC [1998] IRLR 352; [1998] ICR 1023; 44 BMLR 58, EAT

Mr Morse, a road worker, had limited movement and grip in his right hand, stiffness in his right leg and a susceptibility to blackouts. Accordingly, he was not allowed to drive. The council decided to cut the workforce to save money and required that all staff should be able to drive. Accordingly, they made Morse redundant. Morse made a claim under s 5(2) of the DDA 1995, but the industrial tribunal dismissed it, saying: 'if a driving licence is essential, and that discriminates against persons with a disability which makes them unable to hold a licence, then that is unfortunate, but it is hard to see how it can be avoided.' The tribunal added: 'As to adjustments, it is hard to see what they could be. Nothing was suggested on the applicant's behalf, and anything we could speculate upon would inevitably involve the respondent in considerable expense, in having to have a team effectively "carry" the applicant, which was precisely a situation which the respondent could not afford.' The EAT allowed Morse's appeal.

Bell J (p 356):

In our judgment, ss 5(2) and (4), and 6(1), (2), (3) and (4) of the Act require the industrial tribunal to go through a number of sequential steps when dealing with an allegation of s 5(2) discrimination.

Firstly, the tribunal must decide whether the provisions of s 6(1) and s 6(2) impose a s 6(1) duty on the employer in the circumstances of the particular case.

If such a duty is imposed, the tribunal must next decide whether the employer has taken such steps as it is reasonable, in all the circumstances of the case, for him to have to take in order to prevent the s 6(1)(a) arrangements or s 6(1)(b) feature having the effect of placing the disabled person concerned at a substantial disadvantage in comparison with persons who are not disabled.

This in turn involves the tribunal enquiring whether the employer could reasonably have taken any steps including any of the steps set out in paragraphs (a) to (1) of s 6(3). The purpose of s 6(3) is to focus the mind of the employer on possible steps which it might take in compliance with its s 6(1) duty, and to focus the mind of the tribunal when considering whether an employer has failed to comply with a s 6 duty.

At the same time, the tribunal must have regard to the factors set out in s 6(4) paragraphs (a) to (e).

If, but only if, the tribunal (having followed these steps) finds that the employer has failed to comply with a s 6 duty in respect of the disabled applicant, does the tribunal finally have to decide whether the employer has shown that its failure to comply with its s 6 duty is justified, which means deciding whether it has shown that the reason for the failure to comply is both material to the circumstances of the particular case and substantial (see s 5(2) and (4)).

In taking these steps, the tribunal must apply ... an objective test, asking for instance whether the employer has taken such steps as were reasonable, whether any of the steps in s 6(3) were reasonably available in the light of the actual situation so far as the factors in s 6(4) were concerned; and asking whether the employer's failure to comply with its s 6 duty was in fact objectively justified, and whether the reason for failure to comply was in fact material to the circumstances of the particular case and in fact substantial.

No doubt, in carrying out these exercises, the tribunal will pay considerable attention to what factors the employer has considered or failed to consider, but it must scrutinise the explanation for selection for redundancy, for instance, put forward by the employer, and it must reach its own decision on what, if any, steps were reasonable and what was objectively justified, and material and substantial.

This approach contrasts with that taken in *Clark v Novacold*,[110] on the issue of justification, where a tribunal may not substitute its judgment for the reasonable judgment of the employer.

(a)   Treat more favourably

Disability Discrimination Act 1995

Section 6

(7)   Subject to the provisions of this section, nothing in this part [Pt II Employment] is to be taken to require the employer to treat a disabled person more favourably than he treats or would treat others.

In *Archibald v Fife Council*,[111] the EAT held that an employer did not breach his s 5(2) duty by failing to waive the 'well-established' competitive interview for the alternative vacancy. This was because, *inter alia*, as the practice was applied to all, there was no substantial disadvantage and it was justified. Further, allowing the claimant to skip the interview would be treating her more favourably, contrary to s 6(7). The EAT seemed unaware[112] of the opening phrase of this sub-section that excludes s 6 from its ambit. The result is that the employer was obliged to make no adjustments whatsoever, which seems contrary to ss 5 and 6.

(5)   Victimisation[113]

The provision for victimisation in the Act is materially the same as that given in the RRA 1976 and the SDA 1975. The case law under those Acts should be 'informative' according to the Government.[114] Recently, the House of Lords in *Jones v 3M Healthcare*[115] held that the phrase in s 4(2) of the DDA 1995, 'a disabled person whom he employs', extends to victimisation (and discrimination) after the employment relationship has ended,[116] thus upsetting existing case law on the issue.[117] The proposed amendments will confirm this position, specifying liability where 'the

---

110 [1999] IRLR 318, CA, at p 320. See above, p 492.
111 [2003] All ER (D) 13 (Jan), EAT, EATS/0025/02.
112 In the judgment s 6(7) is cited without its opening phrase (at para 2). Nowhere else in the judgment is the opening phrase of s 6(7) mentioned.
113 For discussion of the elements of victimisation, see Chapter 11.
114 HC Deb Standing Committee E, cols 425–26. The case law appears in Chapter 11.
115 The collective appeals of *Relaxion Group plc v Rhys-Harper, D'Souza v Lambeth LBC, Jones v 3M Healthcare Ltd* [2003] UKHL 33.
116 Except where the act complained of does not arise from the employment relationship, such as a refusal to implement an employment tribunal's reinstatement order, for which there is a free-standing remedy (under the Employment Rights Act 1996, ss 112, 113, 114 and 117): *ibid*, in the case of *D'Souza*, at paras 49–53, 124–25, 159–60, 205 and 221.
117 Reversing *sub nom, Kirker v Ambitious Personnel Ltd* [2002] All ER (D) 372 (Feb); [2002] EWCA Civ 304, CA; overruling *Post Office v Adekeye* [1997] ICR 110; [1997] IRLR 105, CA.

relationship has come to an end' in the fields of employment and vocational training.[118]

Disability Discrimination Act 1995

Section 55 Victimisation

(1)   For the purposes of Part II or Part III, a person ('A') discriminates against another person ('B') if—

       (a) he treats B less favourably than he treats or would treat other persons whose circumstances are the same as B's; and

       (b) he does so for a reason mentioned in subsection (2).

(2)   The reasons are that—

       (a) B has—

           (i) brought proceedings against A or any other person under this Act; or

           (ii) given evidence or information in connection with such proceedings brought by any person; or

           (iii) otherwise done anything under this Act in relation to A or any other person; or

           (iv) alleged that A or any other person has (whether or not the allegation so states) contravened this Act; or

       (b) A believes or suspects that B has done or intends to do any of those things.

(3)   Where B is a disabled person, or a person who has had a disability, the disability in question shall be disregarded in comparing his circumstances with those of any other person for the purposes of subsection (1)(a).

(4)   Subsection (1) does not apply to treatment of a person because of an allegation made by him if the allegation was false and not made in good faith.

The reasons in s 55(2) are generally known as 'protected acts'. As s 55(3) implies, this provision may also be used by a person without a disability. So where, for instance, a non-disabled person is demoted for giving evidence in a claim by a disabled colleague, that person may use this section to sue his employer.[119] Section 55(3) also reiterates that for this section the less favourable treatment is *not* for a reason of disability. That is why the comparison should not involve anyone's disability. The reason for the less favourable treatment should the *protected act*, not disability.

(6)   Occupational Pension Schemes and Insurance Services

While s 4 already covers the actions of employers as regards membership and terms of pension schemes, s 17 imposes an obligation on the trustees and managers of a scheme not to discriminate against disabled people, and s 17(1) implies a non-discrimination rule into the terms of such schemes. The purpose of the provisions is to ensure that decisions relating to pension schemes are taken in the light of the particular health, personal circumstances and life expectancy of the individual – as will continue to be permissible – rather than on the mere fact of that person's disability, a fact which may carry no necessary consequences for pension scheme membership.

---

118 DDA, s 16A inserted by the Disability Discrimination Act 1995 (Amendment) Regulations 2003, SI 2003/1673, reg 15, due in force 1 October 2004. See below, p 519.

119 For other examples, see Code of Practice on Employment (*op cit*, fn 9), paras 4.53–4.54 and Access (*op cit*, fn 12), paras 10.3–10.5.

Section 18 adopts a similar approach to situations where the employer arranges with a private insurer for the provision of benefits – such as private health insurance – for employees. The insurance company will be acting unlawfully if it acts in a way that would be unlawful in the case of the provision of such services to members of the public. Again, the objective is to ensure that the criteria adopted relate to health, etc, and not to the mere fact of being disabled.

The duty of reasonable adjustment does not apply either to occupational pension schemes or to private insurance arrangements. 'Therefore, neither the employer nor the scheme's trustees or managers will need to make any adjustment for a disabled person who will be justifiably denied access either to such a scheme or to a benefit under the scheme. Nor will they receive an adjustment for someone receiving less benefit because they justifiably receive a lower rate of pay.'[120] However, the employer may need to make an adjustment in order to ensure that an insurance company would continue to provide cover, for example, where an epileptic person is removed from contact with valuable items so that the insurance company will continue to provide cover in respect of those items.[121]

4   DISCRIMINATION IN OTHER FIELDS

For many disabled people, discrimination and disadvantage in employment are but one of a litany of problems that may be experienced. A substantial proportion of the disabled do not seek work: many are over retirement age and others will be unable to work in other than sheltered surroundings. Even if discrimination in employment is removed, a non-driving disabled person may either be unable to use public transport or be greatly restricted as to the physical range of employment opportunities. It is not being suggested that the non-employment provisions of the SDA 1975 and the RRA 1976 are unimportant – though they have been litigated relatively little – but the non-employment provisions of the DDA 1995 have developed a higher public profile.

(1)   Goods, Facilities and Services

Section 19 deals with discrimination as regards goods, facilities and services and in this regard is similar to the RRA 1976 and the SDA 1975, in particular the need for the service to be provided to 'members of the public'. By contrast with the employment provisions in the DDA 1995, the provisions apply even if the service provider has

---

120 Code of Practice (*op cit*, fn 9), para 6.16.
121 Code of Practice (*op cit*, fn 9), para 6.18.

fewer than 15 employees.[122] The section applies whether or not the service is paid for.[123] Transport is regulated elsewhere.[124]

As with employment, discrimination may take the form either of less favourable treatment or of a failure to make reasonable adjustments. A defence of justification is available for both types of discrimination. As well as refusing a service to a disabled person, s 19 specifically covers the standard, manner and terms of the service provided. The Code of Practice observes that: '[b]ad treatment is not necessarily the same as less favourable treatment although, where a service provider acts unfairly or inflexibly, a court might draw inferences that discrimination has occurred.'[125] It also notes that '[a] service provider does not have to stock special products for disabled people to avoid providing a worse standard of service (although as a matter of good practice it might consider doing so). However, if the service provider would take orders from other customers for products which it does not normally stock, it would be likely to be unlawful to refuse to take such an order from a disabled person.'[126]

In this part of the Act, what amounts to justification is spelt out.

Disability Discrimination Act 1995

Section 20

(3)   ... [T]reatment is justified only if:

    (a) in the opinion of the provider of the services, one or more of the conditions satisfied in sub-s (4) is satisfied; and

    (b) it is reasonable, in all the circumstances of the case, for him to hold that opinion.

(4)   The conditions are that:

    (a) in any case, the treatment is necessary in order not to endanger the health and safety of any person (which may include that of the disabled person);[127]

---

122 This exception is due to be repealed on 1 October 2004; see below, p 516.
123 Section 19(3) provides that the 'following are examples of services ...
    (a) access to and use of any place which members of the public are permitted to enter;
    (b) access to and use of means of communication;
    (c) access to and use of information services;
    (d) accommodation in a hotel, boarding house or other similar accommodation;
    (e) facilities by way of banking or insurance or for grants, loans, credit or finance;
    (f) facilities for entertainment, recreation or refreshment;
    (g) facilities provided by employment agencies ...
    (h) the services of any profession or trade, or any local or other public authority.
124 See below, p 514.
125 *Code of Practice (Revised): Rights of Access; Goods, Facilities, Services and Premises.* Issued by the DRC (ISBN 011 702860 6). Effective from 27 May 2002 (SI 2002/720), at para 3.5.
126 *Ibid*, para 3.21.
127 'An amusement park operator refuses to allow a person with muscular dystrophy onto a physically demanding, high speed ride. Because of her disability, the disabled person uses walking sticks and cannot stand unaided. The ride requires users to brace themselves using their legs. The refusal is based on genuine concerns for the health or safety of the disabled person and other users of the ride. This is likely to be justified. ... Health or safety reasons which are based on generalisations and stereotyping of disabled people provide no defence. For example, fire regulations should not be used as an excuse to place unnecessary restrictions on wheelchair users based on the assumption that wheelchair users would be an automatic hazard in a fire.' *Ibid*, paras 7.11–7.12.

(b) in any case, the disabled person is incapable of entering into an enforceable agreement, or of giving an informed consent ...[128]

(c) [in a case of refusal to provide the service] the treatment is necessary because the provider of services would otherwise be unable to provide the service to members of the public;[129]

(d) [in a case relating to the standard or manner of the service or the terms on which it is provided] the treatment is necessary in order for the provider of services to be able to provide the service to the disabled person or to other members of the public;[130]

(e) [in a case relating to different terms of service] the difference in the terms on which the service is provided to the disabled person and those on which it is provided to other members of the public reflects the greater cost to the provider of the services in providing the service to the disabled person.[131]

The principal difference between this and the duty in employment is under *justification*, in s 20(3)(b). The emphasis placed on the opinion of the service provider means that there is a risk that courts might be too deferential to arguments based on subjective considerations.[132] This should not happen for two reasons. First, the reason given to the court for the discrimination must be the actual reason that operated at the time and not a subsequent rationalisation; secondly, the duty to make reasonable adjustments in s 21 to some extent requires a proactive approach to the provision of services to disabled people.

---

128 'A person with senile dementia applies for a mortgage loan from a building society to finance the purchase of a house. Although he has the means of keeping up with the mortgage loan repayments, the building society has sound reasons for believing that the disabled person does not understand the nature of the legal agreement and obligations involved. The building society refuses his application. This is likely to be justified.

A long-term patient in a psychiatric hospital wishes to open a bank account. The bank wrongly assumes that because she is in a hospital she is incapable of managing her affairs. It refuses to open an account unless it is provided with an enduring power of attorney. The bank continues with its refusal despite being provided with good evidence that the person has full capacity to manage her own affairs. This is unlikely to be justified.' *Ibid*, para 7.15. See also the Disability Discrimination (Services and Premises) Regulations 1996, SI 1996/1836.

129 'A tour guide refuses to allow a person with a severe mobility impairment on a tour of old city walls because he has well-founded reasons to believe that the extra help the guide would have to give her would prevent the party from completing the tour. This is likely to be justified.

Disabled customers with a speech impairment or a learning disability may have difficulty in explaining to a bank cashier what their service requirements are. If the cashier asks the disabled customers to go to the back of the queue so as not to delay other customers waiting to be served, this is unlikely to be justified.' *Ibid*, paras 7.18–7.19.

130 'A hotel restricts a wheelchair user's choice of bedrooms to those with level access to the lifts. Those rooms tend to be noisier and have restricted views. The disabled person would otherwise be unable to use the hotel. The restriction is necessary in order to provide the service to the disabled guest. This is likely to be justified ... A public fitness centre restricts the times a customer who has AIDS is allowed to use its facilities. The other users have objected to his presence and use of the centre's facilities because of a groundless fear that they might become infected with HIV by normal contact with him. Despite his reassurances, the centre has bowed to the pressure of the other customers. This is unlikely to be justified.' *Ibid*, paras 7.21–7.22.

131 Charging more can be justified only where the service is individually tailored to the needs of the customer and the disabled person's particular requirements increase costs – one example given is that of an orthopaedic bed. *Ibid*, para 7.24.

132 Briefly discussed in *Jones v Post Office* [2001] IRLR 384; [2001] ICR 805, CA. See above, p 498.

The duty to make adjustments, with one exception, came into force on 1 October 1999.[133] It applies where there is a 'practice, policy or procedure which makes it impossible or unreasonably difficult' for a disabled person to make use of a service. Section 21(2) applies where 'a physical feature (for example, one arising from the design or construction of a building or the approach or access to premises)' has the same effect, but the only duty here is to 'provide a reasonable alternative'.[134] The more ambitious part of s 21 regarding buildings does not come into force until 1 October 2004.[135] The duty here will be 'to take such steps as is reasonable' to remove or alter the feature, or provide a reasonable means of avoiding it.[136]

Much of what is required in practice will be spelt out by Regulations.[137] In particular, it is envisaged that a maximum limit will be set on necessary expenditure under this section, thereby avoiding county courts having to decide what is appropriate to spend to make such services more user-friendly for disabled people; no such limit has yet been set and many of the details of the practical implementation of these provisions remain to be finalised.

(2)   Housing

24 Meaning of 'discrimination'

(1)   For the purposes of section 22 [disposal and management of premises], a person ('A') discriminates against a disabled person if—

    (a) for a reason which relates to the disabled person's disability, he treats him less favourably than he treats or would treat others to whom that reason does not or would not apply; and

    (b) he cannot show that the treatment in question is justified.

(2)   For the purposes of this section, treatment is justified only if—

    (a) in A's opinion, one or more of the conditions mentioned in subsection (3) are satisfied; and

    (b) it is reasonable, in all the circumstances of the case, for him to hold that opinion.

---

133 SI 1999/1190, Arts 3, 5(g).

134 DDA 1995, s 21(d).

135 SI 2001/2030, Art 3(a).

136 DDA 1995, s 21(2)(a)–(c).

137 See, eg, Disability Discrimination (Services and Premises) Regulations 1999, SI 1999/1191 (made under s 21(5)(e), (h)) and the Disability Discrimination (Providers of Services) (Adjustment of Premises) Regulations 2001 SI 2001/3253 (made under s 21(5)(a), (b)).

(3) The conditions are that—

    (a) in any case, the treatment is necessary in order not to endanger the health or safety of any person (which may include that of the disabled person);[138]

    (b) in any case, the disabled person is incapable of entering into an enforceable agreement, or of giving an informed consent, and for that reason the treatment is reasonable in that case;[139]

    (c) in a case falling within section 22(3)(a), the treatment is necessary in order for the disabled person or the occupiers of other premises forming part of the building to make use of the benefit or facility;

    (d) in a case falling within section 22(3)(b), the treatment is necessary in order for the occupiers of other premises forming part of the building to make use of the benefit or facility.[140]

This part of the Act deals with the disposal and management of premises. Sections 22 and 23 follow the format used in the SDA 1975,[141] including the exception for small dwellings. The definition of discrimination is limited to unjustifiable less favourable treatment. There is no duty to make reasonable adjustments. In a similar fashion to s 20 of the DDA 1995 ('goods, facilities and services'), justification is limited to reasons specified in s 24(3), *so long as* the defendant held an opinion that a specified reason existed, and that it was reasonable for him to do so.[142] In *North Devon Homes Ltd v Brazier*,[143] the tenant suffered from paranoid psychosis, which caused her to be 'disagreeable and aggressive'. She was, accordingly, in breach of her tenancy

---

138 'A landlord refuses to let a third floor flat to a disabled person who has had a stroke resulting in mobility problems and who lives alone. The disabled person is clearly unable to negotiate the stairs in safety or use the fire escape or other escape routes in an emergency. The landlord believes that there is a health or safety risk to the disabled person. Provided it is reasonable for the landlord to hold that opinion, the refusal to let is likely to be justified.

A landlord refuses to let a flat to someone with AIDS, believing him to be a health risk to other tenants. The prospective tenant provides the landlord with government literature confirming that AIDS is not a health risk, but the landlord continues to refuse to let the flat. The landlord's opinion that the prospective tenant is a health risk is unlikely to be a reasonable one for the landlord to hold. The refusal to let is unlikely to be justified.' *Code of Practice (Revised): Rights of Access; Goods, Facilities, Services and Premises*. Issued by the DRC (ISBN No 011 702860 6). Effective from 27 May 2002 (SI 2002/720), para 9.35.

139 'The owner of a lock-up garage refuses to rent it to a person with a learning disability. Despite the owner attempting to explain that she expects to be paid a weekly rent for the garage, the disabled person appears incapable of understanding the legal obligation involved. The garage owner believes that the disabled person is incapable of entering into an enforceable agreement. This is likely to be a reasonable opinion for the garage owner to hold and the refusal to rent the garage is therefore likely to be justified. However, if the disabled person ... offers to pay rent monthly in advance, or if his friend is able to act as guarantor for payment of the rent, the refusal to rent the garage is unlikely to be reasonable and would therefore not be justified.' *Ibid*, para 9.36.

140 'A disabled tenant with a mobility impairment is prevented by the management agency of a block of flats from parking in front of the main entrance to the block. The agency requires him to park in the car park at the back of the block. Although this causes the disabled tenant inconvenience and difficulty, the reason for the agency's decision is that there is insufficient space at the front of the building and the disabled tenant's car frequently causes an obstruction to other tenants. The decision is likely to be justified.

A landlord refuses to allow a disabled tenant with a learning disability to use the shared laundry facilities in a block of flats because the disabled tenant frequently breaks the washing machines. She does not understand the instructions. The landlord's refusal is likely to be justified.' *Ibid*, para 9.37.

141 Discussed in Chapter 13, pp 370–72.

142 Sections 24(4) and 24(5) allow for Regulations to be made regarding the definition of justification.

143 [2003] EWHC 574, QB.

agreement and, as such, s 7 of the Housing Act 1988, gave a court discretion to grant the landlord possession where it was 'reasonable' to do so. The recorder's decision to grant the landlord possession under s 7 was reversed by the High Court. David Steel J held that the eviction of a disabled person had to be justified according to the DDA 1995, rather than by the standards of the Housing Act 1998.

(3)   Transport

The 'use' of means of transport is excluded from the general principle of non-discrimination in relation to the provision of services.[144] In consequence, the range of facilities provided to the public, such as information about times, waiting rooms, etc, are covered under s 19 and, again, the employment provisions clearly apply to transport operators in the same way as to other employers. Aircraft and sea-going vessels are excluded from the Act altogether.[145] The basic principle, which applies to taxis, buses and trains, gives the Secretary of State power to make regulations to control the design, manufacture and mode of operation of such vehicles, as well as to ensure that they comply with standards of accessibility for those who are disabled.[146]

(4)   Education

The Special Educational Needs and Disability Act 2001 removed the 'education' exemption from Pt III of the DDA 1995 (provision of facilities and services).[147] Part IV of the Act is dedicated to 'education' and originally conferred no individual right to claim unlawful discrimination in relation to education. The basic obligations, imposed on schools by s 29, and institutes of further and higher education by s 30, were no more than to publish information concerning their polices in relation to the education of disabled persons. These sections have now been replaced by the 2001 Act, with extensive obligations and individual rights. Sections 28A–28Q of the DDA 1995 cover school pupils and outlaw less favourable treatment[148] and a failure to take reasonable

---

144 DDA 1995, s 19(5)(6).

145 There could be no claim paralleling the Australian case of *Waters v Public Transport Corp* (1991) 173 CLR 349, where the High Court of Australia upheld a claim of indirect discrimination against a transport company which had, *inter alia*, removed conductors from trams and introduced 'scratch' tickets. The claim was brought by nine individuals and 29 community groups, which represented people suffering a wide range of physical and intellectual impairments. (See Thornton, M, 'Domesticating disability discrimination' (1997) 2 IJDL 183, p 190.)

146 Part V of the Act allows the Government to set access standards for buses, coaches, trains, trams and taxis. The Government has produced regulations on access standards for rail vehicles and these apply to vehicles entering service from 1 January 1999 (SI 1998/2456). Regulations on access standards for certain buses and coaches, which are used on local or scheduled services, have applied to new vehicles from the end of 2000 (SI 2000/1970, as amended SI 2000/3318). Since April 2001, it has been unlawful, by DDA 1995, s 37, for licensed taxis in England and Wales to refuse to carry, or to make any extra charge for, disabled passengers who are accompanied by a guide or assistance dog. It has also been unlawful not to allow the dog to remain with the passenger. A driver who fails to comply with this duty may be guilty of a criminal offence and subject to a fine (SI 2000/2989).

147 Special Educational Needs and Disability Act 2001, ss 38(1), (5)(a), 42(6), Sched 9, in force since 1 September 2002 (SI 2002/2217, Art 3, Sched 1, Pt 1). *The Guardian* reported on 15 January 2003 that, in response to the Act, Cambridge University has introduced a 'special access scheme' and consequently offered, provisionally, a place to a deaf student.

148 DDA 1995, s 28B.

steps so that pupils are not placed at a substantial disadvantage.[149] Parents may take claims (in England and Wales to a Special Educational Needs and Disability Tribunal or (in Scotland) to a sheriff court.[150] Sections 28R to 28V provide for post-16 students on a similar basis. In addition, students are entitled to auxiliary aids and services, such as information in Braille or by audio.[151] Post-16 students in England, Wales and Scotland may bring complaints as a statutory tort.[152] The Disability Rights Commission has issued two Codes of Practice, one for schools and one for post-16 education.[153]

5   THE HUMAN RIGHTS ACT AND DISABILITY DISCRIMINATION

Daw, R, *The Impact of the Human Rights Act on Disabled People*, The Royal National Institute for Deaf People:[154]

Interpretation

The notions of the dignity and integrity of the individual inherent in the HRA may influence the interpretation of the DDA in subtle ways as the court itself must comply with Convention rights.

Under the ... DDA service providers must make reasonable adjustments ... In deciding what is 'reasonable' for a government department in providing its publications for people with visual impairments, the court may need to take into account that a disabled person has a right to freedom of information.

Part III of the Act requires reasonable adjustments to be made by service providers but imposes no hierarchy of approaches. So, if a physical feature of premises excludes disabled people the service provider may choose to eliminate the feature, change it or introduce an alternative. A wheelchair user may for instance be given access to a building from the side entrance or tradesman's entrance rather than expect a ramp at the front door. There is little doubt that notions of dignity or physical integrity inherent in Article 3 and Article 8 will bolster arguments about what is reasonable as an adjustment or what is impossible or unreasonably difficult for a disabled person to put up with – (this being the threshold which must be reached before a reasonable adjustment can be demanded).

It may also be that concepts of proportionality will influence the development of jurisprudence on an employer's justification of a 'material and substantial' reason for discriminating, at least where the employer is a public authority.

---

149 DDA 1995, s 28C.

150 DDA 1995, ss 28N and 28H respectively.

151 DDA 1995, s 28T. (In force, 1 September 2003: Special Educational Needs and Disability Act 2001 (Commencement No 5) Order 2002, SI 2002/2217, Art 6, Sched 2.)

152 DDA 1995, s 28V.

153 Respectively, re COPSH July 2002 and COPP 16 July 2002. Both were effective from 1 September 2002 (SI 2002/2216).

154 A report prepared for the Disability Rights Commission and the Royal National Institute for Deaf People, September 2000. Published by DRC, available at www.drc-gb.org.

Exemptions

Some employers and some occupations are exempted from the DDA. For instance, a disabled person turned down on medical grounds from a job in the military forces or the prison service has no redress.[155] A person with asymptomatic HIV who suffers discrimination on grounds of that disability has no redress. That person may be able to use Article 6 to argue a denial of their civil right to be free of discrimination. They would need also to argue that the exemption was too broad to be justified as pursuing a legitimate aim – the efficiency and standards of the military for instance – and as proportionate to that end.[156] ...

Employment cases

... A limited right to privacy might protect the disabled employee who needs to discuss issues relating to his/her disability through private phone calls at work.[157] A right to family life might assist a person dismissed for requesting flexible hours or a job share in order to tend the needs of a disabled family member. At present UK law focuses on employee's rights in relation to their children, not their elderly dependents.

6   AMENDMENTS DUE OCTOBER 2004[158]

(1)   Introduction

In response to the Equal Treatment at Work Directive,[159] the DDA 1995 will be substantially amended by the Disability Discrimination Act (Amendment) Regulations 2003,[160] which come into force on 1 October 2004. As the Regulations are implementing the Directive, they can only modify the DDA in matters of employment and vocational training. Consequently, the changes to Pt II of the DDA 1995 will be comprehensive and relatively straightforward. However, the scope of the Directive spills over into Pt III (provision of services). The result is a complicated dual-class set of definitions. If the service relates to vocational training or other employment matters, then the new definitions apply. Otherwise, the old ones persist.

(2)   Fields Covered

Part II, 'Employment', is renamed 'Employment Field', which reflects the wider scope. It removes the previous exclusions of employers with less than 15 workers,[161]

---

155 Prison officers are due to be included in the Act from 1 October 2004. See below, pp 516–17.

156 Maybe a similar argument could be used to challenge the employment threshold of 15 employees, which in any case, is due for repeal on 1 October 2004, see below.

157 The leading case is *Halford v UK* (1997) 24 EHRR 523.

158 See generally, *Equality and Diversity: The Way Ahead*. Government Response to the consultation document, *Towards Equality and Diversity* – contains Government proposals for taking this work forward. URN 02/1164. Published 24 October 2002. See also *Towards Inclusion – Civil Rights for Disabled People* (available www.dwp.gov.uk), Section 3, para 3.44; and HL Deb Col 587, 28 February 2003, *per* Lord McIntosh.

159 Council Directive 2000/78/EC.

160 SI 2003/1673.

161 *Ibid*, reg 7, will repeal DDA 1995, s 7.

employment on ships, planes and hovercraft,[162] fire-fighters, prison officers and specialised police forces.[163] Part II now extends to cover police, barristers, advocates and their pupils,[164] partnerships,[165] qualification bodies, and practical work experience.[166] For employment matters, the definition of discrimination will vary slightly. For instance, the defence of justification will no longer be available for direct discrimination or a failure to make reasonable adjustments.

(3)   Definition of Discrimination in Employment Matters

(a)   Less favourable treatment and justification

Section 5 is replaced by a new s 3A.[167] The old definitions of 'less favourable treatment' and justification ('material' and 'substantial') have been replicated by ss 3A(1)(a) and 3A(3) respectively, except that so far as less favourable treatment amounts to direct discrimination, the justification defence is no longer available (s 3A(4)). Section 3A(5) defines direct discrimination thus:

> A person directly discriminates against a disabled person if, on the ground of the disabled person's disability, he treats the disabled person less favourably than he treats or would treat a person not having that particular disability whose relevant circumstances, including his abilities, are the same as, or not materially different from, those of the disabled person.

The Government envisaged this definition covering the following instances, which are hardly likely to be justifiable in any case:[168]

(a) an employer, on learning that a job applicant has diabetes, summarily rejects the application without giving any consideration of the applicant's circumstances or whether the person concerned would be competent to do the job (with or without a reasonable adjustment);

(b) a disabled employee is refused access to the employer's sports and social club simply on the basis that the club does not allow disabled members, and without any consideration of whether the employee might benefit from membership, and even though they could access the club with a reasonable adjustment;

(c) without any consideration of whether he will be able to work for as many years as other employees, a newly recruited disabled person is required to pay the same contributions to an occupational pension scheme even though he is denied access to ill-health retirement benefits available to other members of the scheme.

The key difference between this definition and s 3A(1) is the use of the phrase 'on the ground of' instead of 'related to'. The comparator must have the same 'abilities' as the claimant. This drafting is attempting to draw a line between the person's disability

---

162 *Ibid*, reg 27.
163 *Ibid*, regs 24–26.
164 *Ibid*, reg 8, inserting ss 7A–7D.
165 *Ibid*, reg 6, inserting ss 6A–6C.
166 *Ibid*, reg 13, inserting ss 14A–14D.
167 SI 2003/1673, reg 4.
168 Explanatory Notes to the *pre-consultation draft* Regulations, para 32.

and the consequences of that disability. For instance, an employer may state: 'Do not hire her as a driver. She cannot drive safely.' He believes this because the applicant has epilepsy. The refusal to hire was 'related to' the applicant's epilepsy, but 'on the ground of' an inability to drive safely, which of course, in itself, is not actionable. A claim could only be made under s 3A(1) and the employer would be given an opportunity to justify the treatment.

Both definitions cover only the claimant's disability. Consequently, two forms of discrimination remain outside the legislation: discrimination on the grounds of *another's* disability and 'perceived discrimination'.[169] The Equal Treatment at Work Directive covers these two forms of discrimination by prohibiting discrimination on the grounds of *disability*. Here the lack of amendment leaves the DDA 1995 inconsistent with the Directive.

The defence of justification remains for less favourable treatment which does not amount to direct discrimination. Here, the case of *Jones v Post Office*[170] sets the standard of justification in domestic law. Under the parent Directive, indirect discrimination is permissible (in disability cases only) if taking 'appropriate measures' would place an 'disproportionate burden on the employer'.[171]

(b)   Permissible discrimination

As things stood, direct discrimination was permissible under s 59, which allows for discrimination in order to comply with any legislation. Section 59 has been amended, for employment matters only, so that an act done for the purpose of national security must be justified to be lawful under the DDA 1995.[172] Originally, the Government was 'considering' narrowing more substantially the effect of s 59.[173] A new sub-section would have narrowed the scope for legislation permitting direct discrimination only where it concerned (a) health and safety, (b) public order and the prevention of crime, and (c) the protection of rights and freedoms of others. That proposal was abandoned.

(c)   Reasonable adjustment

The new definition (s 4A) is similar,[174] except that the defence of justification is removed. The Government's thinking is that the adjective 'reasonable' gives an employer the opportunity to 'justify' not making adjustments, in any case.[175] However, the new definition still carries the defence of 'no knowledge'.

---

169 See above, pp 491–92 and 468–70.

170 [2001] EWCA Civ 558; [2001] IRLR 384; [2001] ICR 805, CA. See above, p 498.

171 Equal Treatment in Employment Directive, 2000/78/EC, Art 5.

172 The Disability Discrimination Act 1995 (Amendment) Regulations 2003, SI 2003/1673, reg 23, inserting s 59(2A).

173 Explanatory Notes to the *pre-consultation draft* Regulations, paras 193–98.

174 Guidance for the meaning of 'reasonable adjustments' is given by the new S18B, inserted by SI 2003/1673, reg 17 (in force 1 October 2004).

175 Explanatory Notes to the *pre-consultation draft* Regulations, para 33.

(d)   Harassment

In line with the Directive, a new s 3B[176] will provide a uniform free-standing right against harassment. It differs slightly in principle from the other free-standing definitions (in relation to race, sexual orientation and religion or belief), in that the harassment must be related to the *victim's* disability. So, for example, harassing a colleague because of a spouse's disability, or in the mistaken belief that the colleague has a disability (for example, AIDS) will remain lawful under s 3B. According to the Government, s 3 is intended to replicate the approach taken to sexual harassment by the EAT in *Driskel v Peninsula Bus Services*.[177]

(e)   Victimisation

The only minor change is to extend the definition of the protected act in s 55(2)(a)(iii). Instead of 'otherwise done anything under this Act ...', it will read 'otherwise done anything under or *by reference* to this Act ...'.[178] This applies to employment matters only, and brings it into line, for the employment field, with the SDA 1975 and RRA 1976. In addition, the definition of discrimination in employment and vocational training has been extended, with a new s 16A,[179] to cover discrimination after the relationship has come to an end. Therefore, for instance, an employer who refuses to provide a reference for a former worker because, in the past, that worker had brought a claim of disability discrimination, will be liable.

(4)   Part III and Employment Matters

Part III of the DDA 1995 covers the provision of goods, facilities and services. In some cases, this will cover employment matters, such as vocational training, the definition of discrimination given in s 20 is modified so far as it covers the provision of 'employment services'. This is to comply with the parent Directive,[180] and so the whole range of activities covered by Pt III of the DDA 1995 cannot uniformly be modified by statutory instrument. A new s 21A modifies the existing definitions of discrimination in Pt III to bring them into line with those in Pt II (see above). So, for example, less favourable treatment cannot be justified if it amounts to direct discrimination.[181] The trigger for the duty to make reasonable adjustments under s 21(1) (in relation to 'practices, policies or procedures') is lowered. The duty did arise when the 'practices, policies or procedures' made it 'impossible or unreasonably difficult' for disabled persons to use the service. Now, it will arise when it puts the disabled person at a 'substantial disadvantage'.[182] Harassment will be specifically

---

176 Inserted by SI 2003/1673, reg 4 (due in force 1 October 2004).
177 [2000] IRLR 151, EAT; see Chapter 9, p 223. Explanatory Notes to the *pre-consultation draft* Regulations, para 40.
178 Inserted by SI 2003/1673, reg 21 (due in force 1 October 2004).
179 Inserted by the Disability Discrimination Act 1995 (Amendment) Regulations 2003, SI 2003/1673, reg 15.
180 Equal Treatment in Employment Directive, 2000/78/EC.
181 SI 2003/1673, reg 19, inserting s 21A(5)(c) (due in force 1 October 2004).
182 *Ibid*, inserting s 21A(6).

outlawed in Pt III, but only so far as it covers employment services. The new definition is the one used for Pt II (above).[183]

(5)   The Disability Rights Commission

The amendments will give the Commission power (s 17B) to take action in relation to instructions and pressure to discriminate (s 16C) and discriminatory advertisements (s 16B).[184]

7   PROPOSED REFORM

At the time of writing, the Government was planning to pass through Parliament new primary legislation further extending the scope of disability law. Amongst other things, it proposed to extend the definition of disability to include HIV from the time of diagnoses, and cancer from when diagnosed as likely to require substantial treatment.[185] A draft Bill was published in December 2003. Secondly, it was planning to impose upon local authorities duties to eliminate disability discrimination and pursue to equality of opportunity for disabled persons.[186] This was expected to work on similar lines to the duties imposed on public authorities by s 71 of the Race Relations Act 1976.[187]

---

183 *Ibid*, inserting s 21A(2).
184 *Ibid*, inserted by regs 15 and 16.
185 See *Towards Inclusion – Civil Rights for Disabled People* (available www.dwp.gov.uk), Section 3, para 3.11; and HL Deb Col 587, 28 February 2003, *per* Lord McIntosh.
186 Disabled People (Duties of Public Authorities) Bill 2003; *Towards Inclusion – Civil Rights for Disabled People* (available www.dwp.gov.uk), Section 3, para 3.44; and HL Deb Col 587, 28 February 2003, *per* Lord McIntosh.
187 Discussed in Chapter 17, pp 564–66.

CHAPTER 17

ENFORCEMENT OF ANTI-DISCRIMINATION LEGISLATION

1   INTRODUCTION

Effective implementation of anti-discrimination legislation requires, first, a system of procedural law which readily permits the presentation of serious claims; secondly, a definition of unlawful practices which includes those which actually bar job progress; thirdly, remedies which provide incentive for voluntary compliance and effective means for change; and fourthly, the availability of adequate resources both in the legal profession and in the government to implement the law.[1] Lustgarten in effect adds a fifth: that the judiciary must show a sensitivity to the underlying moral force of the legislation.[2] All but the second criterion focus on procedure and remedies, and they provide a helpful framework by which to evaluate the procedural and remedial provisions of the legislation.

The legislation provides two forms of enforcement: individual and strategic. The strategic enforcement is entrusted to the respective Commissions: the Equal Opportunities Commission (EOC), the Commission for Racial Equality (CRE) and the Disability Rights Commission (DRC). There are no commissions yet under the Employment Equality (Sexual Orientation) Regulations 2003 (the 'Sexual Orientation Regulations') and the Employment Equality (Religion or Belief) Regulations 2003 (the 'Religion or Belief Regulations'). The individual remedies are substantially the same under the legislation and will be considered together, save for equal pay claims, where the complex procedures are set out in Chapter 14.[3] The burden of proof for direct discrimination is discussed in Chapter 7.[4] The powers afforded to the EOC and the CRE are substantially the same and will be considered together. The DRC varies slightly and is considered separately.

2   INDIVIDUAL REMEDIES

The legislation directs employment claims to employment tribunals and other claims to the county court. Most litigation occurs in employment. County court claims are considered in Chapter 13.

(1)   Employment Tribunals

Employment tribunals – formerly known as industrial tribunals – are statutory bodies established to resolve disputes concerning the individual employment relationship.

---

1   See Chambers, J and Goldstein, B, 'Title VII: the continuing challenge of establishing fair employment practices' (1986) 49 Law and Contemporary Problems 9.
2   Lustgarten, L, 'The new meaning of discrimination' [1978] PL 178, p 198. On the judiciary, see Chapter 5, p 117.
3   See above, p 434–36. For equal value claims, see pp 397–407.
4   See above, p 188 *et al*.

They are locally based and consist of a panel of three people, a legally qualified chair and two lay people. Appointments to serve as panel members are taken from lists supplied by employers' organisations and trades unions, though it cannot be said that the panel members directly *represent* their constituency. The tribunals were established in 1964 to handle disputes about levies under the Industrial Training Act of that year, a jurisdiction long since disappeared. Their powers were extended to deal with, *inter alia*, disputes under the Redundancy Payments Act 1965 and claims of unfair dismissal under the Industrial Relations Act 1971; since then, unfair dismissal cases have always formed the bulk of their case load.[5] It was seen as inevitable that employment discrimination cases should be resolved in the same way, partly because the same facts might generate a claim of unlawful discrimination and unfair dismissal. The EOC recommends that all discrimination cases, both employment and non-employment, should be heard by a specialist division within the industrial tribunal system.[6]

(a)   Inquisitorial or adversarial?[7]

There was, however, little planning or forethought as to the way in which the tribunals would operate.[8] In particular, it was assumed that the normal 'judicial' accusatorial approach would operate, rather than an 'administrative' inquisitorial approach. This assumption has done no favours for the enforcement of anti-discrimination law. Tribunals are rightly perceived as courts, albeit lacking some of the pageantry and formality. Cases proceed by the normal method of examination and cross-examination of witnesses, so legal and forensic skills are hugely significant. The degree of assistance which the tribunal chair will provide to an unrepresented applicant is variable but tends to be very limited, because the impartiality and distance of the court are key features of the distinction between inquisitorial and accusatorial techniques. The assumption, which may be an *ex post facto* rationalisation rather than the original notion, that tribunals will provide a cheap, speedy and relatively informal dispute resolution mechanism is highly dubious throughout their jurisdiction. It is at its weakest in relation to anti-discrimination law, where the cases tend to be factually and legally complex, often to the tribunal as well as to the parties and their representatives.

Two attempts have been made to introduce an inquisitorial element into tribunals. The first was based on the rules of procedure.

Employment Tribunals (Constitution and Rules of Procedure) Regulations 2001, SI 2001/1171, Sched 1:

11(1) The tribunal shall, so far as it appears to it appropriate, seek to avoid formality in its proceedings and shall not be bound by any enactment or rule of law relating to the admissibility of evidence in proceedings before the courts of law. The tribunal shall make such enquiries of persons appearing before it and

---

5   The statutory basis of these jurisdictions is now the Employment Rights Act 1996, Pts XI and X respectively.

6   *Equality in the 21st Century: A New Approach*, 1998, Manchester: EOC, para 96.

7   See Clark, J, 'Adversarial and investigative approaches to the arbitral resolution of dismissal disputes: a comparison of South Africa and the UK' [1999] 28 ILJ 319.

8   Davies, P and Freedland, M, *Labour Legislation and Public Policy*, 1993, Oxford: Clarendon, pp 161–64.

> witnesses as it considers appropriate and shall otherwise conduct the hearing in
> such manner as it considers most appropriate for the clarification of the issues
> before it and generally to the just handling of the proceedings.

In *Goodwin v The Patent Office*,[9] a case under the DDA 1995, Morison J stated: 'The role
of the industrial tribunal contains an inquisitorial element, as rule [11] of their Rules of
Procedure indicates.'[10] However, in *Rugamer v Sony Music*,[11] Mr Commissioner
Howell QC, stated:

> ... the observations of Morison J relied on are shown by their context to mean no more
> than that the Tribunal is obliged, as indeed is expressly recorded in r [11] of the ...
> Rules, to conduct the hearing in a fair and balanced manner, intervening and making
> its own enquiries in the course of the hearing ... so as to ensure due consideration of
> the issues raised ... However the role of the Tribunal is not thereby extended so as to
> place on it the duty to conduct a free standing inquiry of its own, or require it to
> attempt to obtain further evidence beyond that placed in front of it on the issues
> raised by the parties, or to cause the parties to raise additional issues they have not
> sought to rely on at all.[12]

The Court of Appeal upheld this as a 'valuable judgment',[13] thus rebuffing further
Morison's J view. The second, less specific, attempt was based on the Human Rights
Act 1998. Counsel in *Woodrup v London Borough of Southwark*,[14] again a case under the
DDA 1995, argued that tribunals, in providing a service to the public, were obliged
under Pt III of the Act to make 'reasonable adjustments' when dealing with disabled
people. However, the Court of Appeal called this notion 'far fetched'.[15]

(b)   State-funded legal assistance

State funded legal assistance in currently not available for employment tribunal
hearings in England and Wales.[16] McCrudden's research concluded that prospects for
'success are considerably better for applicants with legal representation than others;
while this is partly due to selection effects (strong cases attract representation) it does
probably indicate that legal representation gives applicants better chances of success.
Indeed, legal representation seems to be almost a prerequisite of a successful outcome:
at only 12% of full hearings that upheld the applicant's case was the applicant not
represented by a lawyer, compared with 32% of hearings where the applicant was not

---

9   [1999] ICR 302; [1999] IRLR 4, EAT. See further, Chapter 16, pp 466, 470, 475, 484 and 486.

10 *Ibid*, at p 307.

11 *Rugamer v Sony Music; McNicol v Balfour Beatty Rail Maintenance* [2001] IRLR 644; ICR 381,
    EAT. See further, Chapter 16, pp 467 and 471.

12 *Ibid*, para 47.

13 [2002] EWCA Civ 1074; [2002] IRLR 711, at para 1.

14 [2002] EWCA Civ 1716.

15 *Ibid*, para 16.

16 There have been two Government-led reports recently: *Moving Forward*, by the Employment
    Tribunal System Taskforce (2002) (see www.dti.gov.uk/er/ individual/ taskforce.htm); and
    *Report of the Review of Tribunals by Sir Andrew Leggatt: Tribunals for Users – One System, One
    Service*, 2001 (see www.tribunals-review.org.uk/leggatthtml/leg-04.html#4.21). The latter
    proposed extending public funding in employment tribunals only for 'exceptional cases'
    (paras 4.21–4.28).

successful'.[17] This is undoubtedly still a major problem, despite growing expertise among specialist practitioners.[18] 'It can be argued that representation, and especially representation which is provided through the assistance of the EOC, is effective because the applicant is enabled through skilled advocacy to counter the explanations of the employer and improve his or her chances of winning the case. In addition, the applicant is enabled through reasoned argumentation and analysis to elucidate and expose the practices in which the particular act was grounded. In this way, the employer's failings become more readily apparent both to the employer himself (whose understanding of the issues may in consequence be better developed), and to the tribunal panel which is more likely to make constructive suggestions and to give pointers for follow-up action.'[19] However, access to affordable and effective legal services is hardly a problem confined to discrimination law: it may be that there is no longer a significant gap in availability between discrimination and other branches of law. In Scotland, since 15 January 2001, complainants to employment tribunals are entitled to State-funded legal assistance where: the claimant is unable to fund or find alternative representation elsewhere; the case is arguable; and the case is too complex to allow the applicant to present it to a minimum standard of effectiveness.

Advice and Assistance (Assistance by Way of Representation) (Scotland) Regulations 1997, SI 1997/3070[20]

Regulation 13

(2)   The Board shall only approve the provision of assistance by way of representation in relation to ... [employment tribunal] proceedings ... where it is satisfied that—

   (a) the case is arguable;

   (b) it is reasonable in the particular circumstances of the case that assistance by way of representation be made available; and

   (c) the case is too complex to allow the applicant to present it to a minimum standard of effectiveness in person.

(3)   The factors to be taken into account by the Board in determining whether paragraph (2)(c) above applies shall include—

   (a) the determination of the issue may involve procedural difficulty or consideration of a substantial question of law, or of evidence of a complex or difficult nature;

---

17 McCrudden, C, Smith, D and Brown, C, *Racial Justice at Work: Enforcement of the Race Relations Act 1976 in Employment*, 1991, London: Policy Studies Institute, p 147.

18 '[U]se of the law involves skills which large-scale employers may be expected to command far more readily than complainants ... [This] goes a long way towards explaining both the relative ease with which discrimination claims have been defeated, and also the fact that individual complainants are more likely to be successful if they obtain aid from the CRE ... The element of skill also means that each potential loophole will be explored in depth ... delaying tactics adopted, and the like. This is standard practice for good lawyers ... [y]et short of forbidding discriminators to defend themselves in a legal forum, these tactics cannot be curbed.' Lustgarten, L, 'Racial inequality and the limits of law' (1986) 49 MLR 68, pp 77–78.

19 Chambers, G and Horton, C, *Promoting Sex Equality: The Role of Industrial Tribunals*, 1990, London: Policy Studies Institute, pp 171–72.

20 Inserted by reg 5 of the Advice and Assistance (Assistance by Way of Representation) (Scotland) Amendment Regulations 2001, SI 2001/2. In force since 15 January 2001.

(b) the applicant may be unable to understand the proceedings or to state his own case because of his age, inadequate knowledge of English, mental illness, other mental or physical disability, or otherwise.

The Scottish Ministers took the view that this measure was necessary to comply with the Human Rights Act 1998.[21] Article 6 of the European Convention on Human Rights guarantees a right to a fair trial. Implicit in this is access to court and a fair hearing. Legal assistance obviously plays a part in this. The European Court on Human Rights has found the lack of public funding to be a breach of Art 6 in cases of complexity.[22] The Court has stated: 'The Convention is intended to guarantee not rights that are theoretical or illusory but rights that are practical and effective ... It must therefore be ascertained whether [the applicant's] appearance ... without the assistance of a lawyer would be effective in the sense of whether she would be able to present her case properly and satisfactorily.'[23]

(c)   Alternatives to tribunal hearings

Trade Union and Labour Relations (Consolidation) Act 1992

Section 210 Conciliation

(1)   Where a trade dispute exists or is apprehended ACAS may, at the request of one or more parties to the dispute or otherwise, offer the parties to the dispute its assistance with a view to bringing about a settlement.

(2)   The assistance may be by way of conciliation or by other means, and may include the appointment of a person other than an officer or servant of ACAS to offer assistance to the parties to the dispute with a view to bringing about a settlement.

(3)   In exercising its functions under this section ACAS shall have regard to the desirability of encouraging the parties to a dispute to use any appropriate agreed procedures for negotiation or the settlement of disputes.

As with other employment tribunal matters, individual claims of discrimination are referred to the Advisory, Conciliation and Arbitration Service (ACAS) in an attempt to promote settlement.[24] Conciliation may be problematic in unfair dismissal cases, but the consensus is that it is even more problematic in the field of discrimination, so much so that it is arguable that it may do more harm than good.[25] First, 'conciliation

---

21   The HRA and discrimination is discussed above, p 114 and for disability, p 515.

22   See *Airey v Ireland* (1979) 2 EHRR 305 (access) and *Granger v UK* (1990) 12 EHRR 469 (fair hearing).

23   *Airey v Ireland* (1979) 2 EHRR 305, at para 24.

24   The normal rule is that a contractual term which attempts to prevent an employee utilising the legislation is void; SDA 1975, s 77(3); RRA 1976, s 72(3); Sexual Orientation, or Religion or Belief, Regulations 2003, reg 35 (the Regulations came into force on 1 December and 2 December, 2003, respectively.); DDA 1995, s 9 (due to be replaced s 17C and Sched 3A on 1 October 2004): SI 2003/1673, regs 10 and 16. This rule does not apply to a proper settlement drawn up under the auspices of a conciliation officer, to settlements achieved without such assistance as long as the applicant has received legal advice, nor to cases where a dispute is settled by arbitration; see, eg, SDA 1975, s 77(4A)–(4C); RRA 1976, s 72(4A)–(4C), inserted by the Trade Union Reform and Employment Rights Act 1993 and amended by the Employment Rights (Dispute Resolution) Act 1998, s 8. This exception is repeated in the Regulations and the DDA 1995.

25   See, especially, Graham, C and Lewis, N, *The Role of ACAS Conciliation in Equal Pay and Sex Discrimination Cases*, 1985, Manchester: EOC.

officers will pursue a settlement. That is their goal. They will not be deflected by the broader issues of principle which an application raises, for it is the immediate interests of the person before them which they have to address'.[26] It is not their function to determine what a case is worth or to point the applicant in the direction of independent expert legal advice. Secondly, there is no guarantee whatever that a monetary settlement will reflect what an applicant might have been awarded had the case reached a tribunal; a significant offer inevitably generates pressure to settle and thereby avoid the psychological and financial costs of proceeding to a hearing. Thirdly, an intransigent employer who refuses all suggestion of settlement may convey the message that fighting on is unwise and thereby lead to withdrawal; this may partly explain the surprisingly high proportion of claims which are initiated but withdrawn in advance of a hearing. Fourthly, it may be more difficult than in a relatively straightforward unfair dismissal case for the employer to accept the possibility that there has been unlawful discrimination; a finding of unlawful discrimination implies a moral condemnation possibly absent from a finding of unfair dismissal. Fifthly, the variations in the level of compensation mean that it is more difficult to predict what a case would be 'worth' should it go to tribunal, especially as such a high proportion of compensation is for injury to feelings; this makes the process of conciliation more uncertain.[27] Sixthly, 'compared with unfair dismissal ... discrimination complaints are more likely to lead to considerable argument over the facts. When this is combined with less access to hard evidence on the part of the complainant, it is harder to give sensible advice while abstaining from giving an opinion on the merits of the case'.[28]

Hunter, R and Leonard, A, 'Sex discrimination and alternative dispute resolution: British proposals in the light of international experience' [1997] PL 298, pp 304–11:[29]

[A] major advantage of mediation as opposed to adjudication – or arbitration – is its potential for enabling parties to work out a mutually acceptable solution rather than submit to a decision in favour of one or the other of them. Moreover, the range of outcomes that may be agreed in mediation is much broader than is available in the ITs or the county court, or that might result from arbitration. For example, terms of settlements agreed in the [Equal Employment Opportunity Commission] mediation pilot programme and in the conciliation of Australian sex discrimination complaints included, in addition to compensation: apologies; the provision of references; assistance in searching for a new job; reconsideration for a position; making a casual employee permanent; promotion; adjustment to seniority; transfer to a different position; the provision of training; an employee responsible for discrimination penalised or removed from the workplace; the clarification of duties or policies; review of management structure; a voluntary departure package; and the dropping of criminal charges against the complainant. In some ... cases ... respondents also agreed to institute an EEO programme and/or EEO training.

[But the authors highlight several potential problems with private forms of dispute resolution. The first is the removal of issues from the public agenda, so that the

---

26   *Ibid*, p 61.
27   McCrudden, C, Smith, D and Brown, C, *Racial Justice at Work: Enforcement of the Race Relations Act 1976 in Employment*, 1991, London: Policy Studies Institute, p 190.
28   *Ibid*.
29   See also Thornton, M, 'Equivocation of conciliation: the resolution of discrimination complaints in Australia' (1989) 52 MLR 733.

educational/deterrent impact of the law is weakened, as well as reducing the scope for the clarification of legal rules and responsibilities. They continue.]

A second potential problem with mediation of sex discrimination cases is that it fails to even out, and therefore reproduces, financial, informational, skill, status and personal power imbalances between the parties. There are suggestions in the literature that alternative methods of dispute resolution work best when the parties are in more or less equal power positions. When this is not the case, outcomes of mediation will be the product of power relations rather than of the free agreement of each party ...

If power imbalances are to be addressed ... the role played by the mediator becomes crucial. A mediator who remains strictly impartial, who sees his or her role as merely to facilitate negotiations between the parties, and who is prepared to accept any outcome the parties agree, can only reflect power imbalances, not rectify them.

[If these disadvantages can be overcome, the advantages of mediation are considerable.]

[M]ediation may be very attractive to sex discrimination complainants who cannot produce documentary or other strong evidence to support their claim ... Early referral of weaker cases to mediation might also help to reduce the withdrawal rate for sex discrimination cases, which to date has remained around 30% ...

[M]any disputes are largely factual ... These kinds of differences might again be suitable for mediation, where the parties are encouraged to listen to each other's point of view rather than harden their own position about what did or did not occur and what it did or did not mean ...

In the US mediation pilot project, 21% of settlements included changes in employer policies and practices ... The lowest figure [in Australia] came from the agency which was most determinedly neutral as to the outcomes agreed by the parties, while the highest figure came from the agency which included institutional change as one of the objectives of conciliation ...

Mediation as a method of dispute resolution must be integrated with the substantive provisions of the SDA. It must reflect the aims of and ensure compliance with the legislation. The Act must be treated not merely as a set of guidelines within which parties may or may not choose to operate, but as a source of binding behavioural norms, legal rights and entitlements ... We would argue that the experience of conciliation by ACAS and by Australian complaint-handling agencies illustrates the limitations and inappropriateness of an interest-based approach – [where parties are assisted to arrive at a solution which enhances their mutual interests] – to the resolution of discrimination cases. Arbitration based on general industrial relations standards of fairness ... would also fail to achieve the aims of sex discrimination legislation.

By contrast, rights-based mediation would be an appropriate dispute resolution method for sex discrimination cases. This model prioritises legal rights and the elimination of discrimination. It also intervenes in the power balances between the parties by allowing an otherwise less powerful complainant to assert legal entitlements which have 'an existence and legitimacy separate from the relationship' between herself and the respondent. This model of mediation ... involves certain requirements about the role of the mediator and/or other professionals.

Under s 212A of the Trade Union and Labour Relations (Consolidation) Act 1992[30] ACAS has drawn up an arbitration scheme, the aim of which is that more claims should be settled by arbitration and fewer proceed to a tribunal hearing. The scheme will apply in the first instance to unfair dismissal and so will exclude discrimination claims. If both are alleged, the discrimination claim must be pursued separately. The arbiter may decide, if appropriate or convenient, to postpone the hearing pending the outcome of the employment tribunal proceedings.

(2)   Individual Claims Before Employment Tribunals

(a)   Before the hearing

Under the Sex Discrimination Act (SDA) 1975, the Race Relations Act (RRA) 1976, Sexual Orientation, and Religion or Belief, Regulations 2003, individuals may complain to an employment tribunal of a breach of the employment part of the legislation.[31] A potential applicant may question the employer concerning the alleged discriminatory acts, when deciding whether to issue proceedings.[32]

(b)   Commission assistance – the SDA, RRA and DDA only

Both the CRE and the EOC have the legal power to assist applicants with individual cases. There are far more requests for assistance with proceedings than can be met from available resources, but the Commissions provide some forms of preliminary and general assistance in many other cases.[33] The requests that are received are necessarily dependent on the applicant's knowing that such a power exists. This cannot be taken for granted. The statutory criteria for deciding whether or not to provide assistance are if:

(a)   the case raises a question of principle; or

(b)   it is unreasonable, having regard to the complexity of the case or the applicant's position in relation to the respondent or other person involved or any other matter, to expect the applicant to deal with the case unaided; or

(c)   by reason of any other special consideration.[34]

The forms of assistance may include:

(a)   giving advice;

(b)   procuring or attempting to procure the settlement of any matter in dispute;

---

30   Inserted by s 7 of the Employment Rights (Dispute Resolution) Act 1998. For details of the scheme, see www.acas.org.uk/publications/pdf/acassche.pdf. See also Clark, J, 'Adversarial and investigative approaches to the arbitral resolution of dismissal disputes: a comparison of South Africa and the UK' [1999] 28 ILJ 319.

31   Non-employment matters go to county courts.

32   In the context of equal pay claims, see Chapter 14, pp 416–19.

33   'As regards representation at tribunal or in the county court and higher, the EOC is only able to assist approximately 100 individuals per year. Several thousands of individuals, however, are given information and advice.' *Equality in the 21st Century: A New Approach*, 1998, Manchester: EOC, para 92.

34   SDA 1975, s 75(1); RRA 1976, s 66(1); DRCA 1999, s 7(2).

(c)   arranging for the giving of advice or assistance by a solicitor or counsel;

(d)   arranging for representation by any person including all such assistance as is usually given by a solicitor or counsel in the steps preliminary or incidental to any proceedings ...[35] [This may include taking over a case at the appeal stage.]

It is not normal practice for the Commissions to give reasons for refusing to provide assistance in any given case. As a matter of *logic*, refusal says nothing about the merits of the case, but in practice, such refusal may be followed by abandonment of the claim, for financial or other reasons:[36]

> Applicants who are granted assistance by the CRE have a substantially better chance of success than other claimants under RRA 1976, for at least three reasons: first, the CRE tries to select the stronger cases; secondly, it is likely to provide more effective advice and representation than any other body; thirdly, and perhaps more important, it provides moral support to the applicant throughout the earlier stages, thus greatly reducing the chance that he or she will withdraw. Because the minority of applicants who are granted CRE assistance have a substantial advantage, the determining factor becomes the CRE's decision about whether or not to assist. This means that the CRE retains a dominant and quasi-judicial function. Another consequence is that there has been no development of campaigning organisations which sponsor individual complaints.

(c)   Time limits

The normal rule in sex, race, sexual orientation and religion or belief discrimination cases[37] is that an application must have been presented within three months of the commission of the acts of discrimination of which complaint is made.[38] The tribunal has discretion to permit a claim which is out of time 'if, in all the circumstances of the case, it considers that it is just and equitable to do so'.[39] There are two linked problem areas with the limitation period: first, when will the tribunal exercise its discretion to permit a claim to proceed, despite more than three months having elapsed? Secondly, when does the act of discrimination occur so as to start time running?

---

35   SDA 1975, s 75(2); RRA 1976, s 66(2). The DRCA 1999, s 7(3) is slightly different: 'If the Commission grants an application, it may—(a) provide or arrange for the provision of legal advice; (b) arrange for legal or other representation (which may include any assistance usually given by a solicitor or counsel); (c) seek to procure the settlement of any dispute; (d) provide or arrange for the provision of any other assistance which it thinks appropriate.'

36   McCrudden, C, Smith, D and Brown, C, *Racial Justice at Work: Enforcement of the Race Relations Act 1976 in Employment*, 1991, London: Policy Studies Institute, p 155.

37   For time limits in equal pay cases, see Chapter 14, pp 434–36.

38   SDA 1975, s 76(1); RRA 1976, s 68(1); Sexual Orientation Regulations, or Religion or Belief, Regulations 2003, reg 34(1); DDA 1995, Sched 3, para 3(1).

39   SDA 1975, s 76(5); RRA 1976, s 68(6); Sexual Orientation Regulations, or Religion or Belief, Regulations 2003, reg 34(3); DDA 1995, Sched 3, para 3(2). This is a more lenient test than that which normally applies in employment tribunal proceedings, such as unfair dismissal and redundancy payment claims, where the tribunal must be satisfied that it was not reasonably practicable for the complaint to be presented within the three-month period.

(i)   The meaning of 'just and equitable'

British Coal Corporation v Keeble and Others [1997] IRLR 336, EAT

Mrs Keeble was made redundant and paid according to a scheme which was more favourable to men. Her union advised her, incorrectly, that the scheme was lawful, but later took Counsel's opinion and advised her instead to claim. Consequently, her claim was made 22 months after her dismissal for redundancy. She was allowed to pursue her claim by the Employment Appeal Tribunal (EAT), which issued the following guidance.

Smith J (at p 338):

... the industrial tribunal should adopt as a checklist the factors mentioned in s 33 of the Limitation Act 1980. That section provides a broad discretion for the Court to extend the limitation period of three years in cases of personal injury and death. It requires the court to consider the prejudice which each party would suffer as the result of the decision to be made and also to have regard to all the circumstances of the case and in particular, *inter alia*, to —

(a)   the length of and reasons for the delay;
  (b)   the extent to which the cogency of the evidence is likely to be affected by the delay;
  (c)   the extent to which the party sued had cooperated with any requests for information;
  (d)   the promptness with which the plaintiff acted once he or she knew of the facts giving rise to the cause of action;
  (e)   the steps taken by the plaintiff to obtain appropriate professional advice once he or she knew of the possibility of taking action.

In *London Borough of Southwark v Afolabi*,[40] however, Peter Gibson LJ, in the Court of Appeal, said:

Nor do I accept that the ET erred in not going through the matters listed in s 33(3) of the 1980 Act. Parliament limited the requirement to consider those matters to actions relating to personal injuries and death. Whilst I do not doubt the utility of considering such a check-list ... in many cases, I do not think that it can be elevated into a requirement on the ET to go through such a list in every case, provided of course that no significant factor has been left out of account by the ET in exercising its discretion.[41]

In *Hawkins v Ball and Barclays Bank plc*,[42] an applicant only presented a claim of sexual harassment five months after an incident of verbal harassment, having originally been advised by a solicitor that the incident was trivial. The EAT held that in the circumstances, it was just and equitable to permit the claim to proceed. Similar cases reaching a different outcome under the more stringent unfair dismissal law were of no relevance.

---

40   [2003] EWCA Civ 15, CA.
41   *Ibid*, at para 33. Peter Gibson LJ dissented on a separate issue. The wide discretion afforded to a tribunal was emphasised by the Court of Appeal in *Robertson v Bexley Community Centre (t/a Leisure Link)* [2003] All ER (D) 151 (Mar). It held that that a decision should not be reversed unless it was plainly wrong in law.
42   [1996] IRLR 258, EAT.

This question arises commonly where the worker awaits the outcome of a grievance of disciplinary procedure, before issuing proceedings. In *Aniagwu v London Borough of Hackney*,[43] Morison J said: '... unless there is some particular feature about the case or some particular prejudice which employers can show every tribunal would inevitably conclude that it is a responsible and proper attitude for someone to seek to redress a grievance through the employer's grievance procedure before embarking on legal proceedings.' However, in *Robinson v Post Office*,[44] Lindsay J, in a response later approved by the Court of Appeal,[45] made it clear that delay due to an internal, or 'domestic,' process, was just one factor in the balance:

> That is not, and does not purport to be, a proposition of broad applicability such that wherever and so long as there is an unexhausted internal procedure, then delay to await its outcome necessarily furnishes an acceptable reason for delaying the presentation of an IT1[46] such as would, of itself and without more, lead to relief under s 68(6) of the Race Relations Act or by analogy, s 76(5) of the Sex Discrimination Act or, as we are concerned with, para 3 of Sched 3 of the Disability Discrimination Act. Parliament could so easily have so provided in any one of those three Acts. ...

> We can only conclude that Parliament has quite deliberately not provided that invariably the running of time against an employer should be delayed until the end of domestic processes. According, when delay on account of an incomplete internal appeal is relied upon as a reason for delaying an IT1 or failing to lodge it in time, and where that is not merely alleged but upheld as a matter of fact, if that allegation and that fact is fairly considered by the Employment Tribunal and put into the balance when the justice and equity of the matter is considered, that ordinarily will suffice for the Employment Tribunal to escape error of law as to that issue.[47]

(ii)   When time starts running

In relation to the second issue, it is provided that:

(a)   where the inclusion of any term in a contract renders the making of the contract an unlawful act, that act shall be treated as extending throughout the duration of the contract; and

(b)   any act extending over a period shall be treated as done at the end of that period; and

(c)   a deliberate omission shall be treated as done when the person in question decided upon it ...[48]

There is a difference between a continuing act of discrimination and a single act of discrimination with continuing consequences. This distinction may be crucial in determining when the three months' limitation period commences. It is not at all easy to determine which side of the line a particular case falls.

---

43 [1999] IRLR 303, EAT.

44 [2000] IRLR 804, EAT.

45 *Apelogun-Gabriels v London Borough of Lambeth* [2001] EWCA Civ 1853; [2002] ICR 713; [2002] IRLR 116, CA.

46 The claim form for unfair dismissal.

47 [2000] IRLR 804, EAT, at paras 29–31.

48 SDA 1975, s 76(6); See also RRA 1976, s 68(7); Sexual Orientation, or Religion or Belief, Regulations 2003, reg 34(4); DDA 1995, Sched 3, para 3(3).

Barclays Bank plc v Kapur [1991] IRLR 136, HL[49]

The case concerned East African Asians who had come to the UK in the early 1970s and had become employees of predecessors of the defendants. The bank had refused to take account of previous service with East African banks in computing their pension entitlement. The question was whether the complaints were time barred; the House of Lords held that the refusal was continuing discrimination, rather than a one-off act.

Lord Griffiths (pp 138–39):

> The applicants ... say that the term upon which they are credited with a pension is to be classified as an act extending over a period, namely the length of their employment, and therefore to be treated as done at the end of the period of employment ...

> Calder v James Finlay Corporation[50] [concerned the] refusal of a mortgage subsidy. The EAT said that there was continuing discrimination against her so long as she remained in their employment. The rule of the scheme constituted a discriminatory act extending over the period of her employment and is therefore to be treated as having been done at the end of her period of employment.

> [The position is the same here. In substance here there is no] real difference to the continued payment of lower wages.

On the other side of the line are cases such as a re-grading or downgrading which will have continuing consequences in the form of lower pay and benefits, but is not in itself an act of continuing discrimination.[51] However, an act extends over a period of time if it is sufficiently entrenched in the organisation to amount to a practice or policy which governs decisions on a particular issue.[52] Which side of the line a particular case falls may not be at all obvious. Furthermore, there may be problems both in identifying precisely when an individual act of discrimination has occurred and whether there is a single act of discrimination or more than one such act.

In *Rovenska v General Medical Council*,[53] the claimant had made repeated requests for registration as a doctor. Following her final request and refusal, the CRE wrote on her behalf, but the defendants wrote back confirming the refusal. The Court of Appeal was held that each refusal was a separate act of discrimination and that the letter to the CRE was itself a refusal constituting an act of discrimination. In *Cast v Croydon College*,[54] the claimant, after becoming pregnant, was refused permission to return to work on a part-time basis after giving birth. She did in fact return on what was theoretically a full-time basis, but accrued holiday entitlement meant that in practice she only worked part-time. Further requests to transfer to a part-time contract were refused and eventually she resigned. The Court of Appeal, reversing the EAT's decision, held that the application of a discriminatory policy here amounted to an act extending over a period, so that the effects of the first decision were continuing. In addition, each subsequent refusal was a separate act of discrimination; further

---

49   See also [1991] 2 AC 355; [1991] 1 All ER 646.
50   [1989] ICR 157; [1989] IRLR 55.
51   Eg, *Sougrin v Haringey HA* [1992] ICR 650; [1992] IRLR 416, CA.
52   *Owusu v London Fire and Civil Defence Authority* [1995] IRLR 574, EAT.
53   [1997] IRLR 367, CA.
54   [1997] IRLR 14, EAT; [1998] IRLR 319; [1998] ICR 500, CA.

consideration was given to the matter rather than mere reference back to the prior decision. There is no doubt that the Court of Appeal's decision is right both in law and policy. The effect of the EAT's decision was to require her either to make a complaint of discrimination close to the time the baby was born, or to make the request on return from maternity leave, in which case the employer might be able to argue that there was insufficient advance warning to be able to accede to the request. Neither is a satisfactory outcome. These are specific examples. The Court of Appeal in *Hendricks* offered some more general guidance.

> *Hendricks v Metropolitan Police Commissioner* **[2002] EWCA Civ 1686; [2003] 1 All ER 654, CA**

Joy Hendricks, a black woman police constable, specified a large number of discriminatory acts, committed by her employer, spanning the whole of her 11-year career. She argued that these amounted to a continuing act of discrimination under the SDA 1975 and RRA 1976. The Court of Appeal allowed her appeal.

Mummery LJ:

[48] On the evidential material before it, the tribunal was entitled to make a preliminary decision that it has jurisdiction to consider the allegations of discrimination made by Miss Hendricks. The fact that she was off sick from March 1999 and was absent from the working environment does not necessarily rule out the possibility of continuing discrimination against her ... Her complaints are not confined to less favourable treatment of her in the working environment from which she was absent after March 1999. They extend to less favourable treatment of Miss Hendricks in the contact made with her by those in the Service (and also in the lack of contact made with her) in the course of her continuing relationship with the Metropolitan Police Service: she is still a serving officer, despite her physical absence from the workplace. She is, in my view, entitled to pursue her claim beyond this preliminary stage on the basis that the burden is on her to prove, either by direct evidence or by inference from primary facts, that the numerous alleged incidents of discrimination are linked to one another and that they are evidence of a continuing discriminatory state of affairs covered by the concept of 'an act extending over a period.' I regard this as a legally more precise way of characterising her case than the use of expressions such as 'institutionalised racism', 'a prevailing way of life', a 'generalised policy of discrimination', or 'climate' or 'culture' of unlawful discrimination. ...

[50] I appreciate the concern expressed about the practical difficulties that may well arise in having to deal with so many incidents alleged to have occurred so long ago; but this problem often occurs in discrimination cases, even where the only acts complained of are very recent. Evidence can still be brought of long-past incidents of less favourable treatment in order to raise or reinforce an inference that the ground of the less favourable treatment is race or sex.

[51] In my judgment, the approach of both the Employment Tribunal and the Appeal Tribunal to the language of the authorities on 'continuing acts' was too literal. They concentrated on whether the concepts of a policy, rule, scheme, regime or practice, in accordance with which decisions affecting the treatment of workers are taken, fitted the facts of this case: see *Owusu v London Fire & Civil Defence Authority* [1995] IRLR 574 at 576–577 (paras 21–23); *Rovenska v General Medical Council* [1997] IRLR 367 at 371, [1998] ICR 85 at 96; *Cast v Croydon College* [1998] IRLR 318 at 322, [1998] ICR 500 at 509 (cf the approach of the Appeal Tribunal in *Derby Specialist Fabrication Ltd v Burton* [2001] 2 All ER 840 at 846, [2001] ICR 833 at 841 (para 20) where there was an

'accumulation of events over a period of time' and a finding of a 'climate of racial abuse' of which the employers were aware, but had done nothing. That was treated as 'continuing conduct' and a 'continuing failure' on the part of the employers to prevent racial abuse and discrimination, and as amounting to 'other detriment' within s 4(2)(c) of the 1976 Act.

[52] The concepts of policy, rule, practice, scheme or regime in the authorities were given as examples of when an act extends over a period. They should not be treated as a complete and constricting statement of the indicia of 'an act extending over a period'. I agree with the observation made by Sedley LJ, in his decision on the paper application for permission to appeal, that the Appeal Tribunal allowed itself to be sidetracked by focusing on whether a 'policy' could be discerned. Instead, the focus should be on the substance of the complaints that the Commissioner was responsible for an ongoing situation or a continuing state of affairs in which female ethnic minority officers in the Service were treated less favourably. The question is whether that is 'an act extending over a period' as distinct from a succession of unconnected or isolated specific acts, for which time would begin to run from the date when each specific act was committed.

A somewhat similar issue arises in relation to internal procedures. If the employee is dismissed, and an (internal) appeal against that dismissal fails, it can either be concluded that the confirmation of the dismissal is a separate act of discrimination, or that the original dismissal is the only act of discrimination, but that in such circumstances it would be just and equitable to extend the time limit. In *Littlewoods Organisation plc v Traynor*,[55] the employee complained of racial abuse, was promised by the employer that the situation would be remedied, but in the event nothing happened. The claim was brought more than three months after the original incident. While the claim was correctly permitted to proceed, the argument that there was here a continuing act of discrimination fails to convince. While the employer might have been liable for the abuse, failing to remedy it is discrimination of a different form from the original discrimination, and is more appropriately regarded as a 'deliberate omission'.

It has proved remarkably difficult to determine when a single 'act' of discrimination occurs. In *Clarke v Hampshire Electro-Plating Co Ltd*,[56] it was not the date of a dismissive interview – the date on which the claimant *felt* he had suffered discrimination – but the subsequent date on which someone else was appointed, because only then could it be said that the cause of action had 'crystallised'. In *Swithland Motors plc v Clarke*,[57] Swithland were negotiating a take-over of Colmore Ltd, and interviewed a number of Colmore's salesmen. Swithland decided then not to employ those salesmen, but did not (upon request of Colmore's receivers) communicate this decision until the take-over, some two to three weeks later. The EAT held, interpreting s 76(6)(c) of the SDA 1975,[58] that the act of discrimination occurred not when the decision was made, but when it was communicated to the salesmen, because it was only then (after the take-over) that they were in a position to make the decision. Before then, the decision was merely 'hypothetical'. But as in some instances, such as a failure to upgrade, discrimination can occur with no communication with

---

55   [1993] IRLR 154, EAT.

56   [1992] ICR 312; [1991] IRLR 490, EAT.

57   [1994] ICR 231; [1994] IRLR 275, EAT. The claimants' allegation was that the defendant had an 'all-female' policy.

58   Set out above, p 531.

the victim, it would have been preferable to conclude that the discrimination occurred when the action was taken, but to extend the time limit on the basis that it was just and equitable to do so.

These cases are highly technical but highly important. The three-month period is so short that any problem with its application has potential for injustice. While tribunals have discretion to extend the time limit, there is no guarantee that they will exercise it appropriately. Many potential complainants may be disadvantaged by the shortness of the period; there is a strong case for its extension.[59]

(3)   Employment Tribunal Remedies

There are three remedies available to the tribunal if a claim succeeds: a declaration, an award of compensation, and a recommendation for action.[60] The remedies apply only to the successful applicant, reflecting the individualistic philosophy of the legislation. The failure to make the remedies more collective and wide-ranging is one of the major failings of the legislation, and contrasts sharply with the class action procedure available in the USA.[61]

(a)   Declaration

A declaration is 'an order declaring the rights of the complainant and the respondent in relation to the act to which the complaint relates'.[62] Such an order follows naturally upon a conclusion that the complaint is well-founded, but in most cases is accompanied by one or both of the other available remedies, both of which are of more direct practical significance.

(b)   Compensation

Unlawful discrimination is treated as a statutory tort and, as such, the method of assessment is the same as it would be in a tort case,[63] although, as we shall see, this includes compensation for injury to feelings.[64] There is no upper limit for

---

59 For amendments to the six-month time limit in equal pay claims, see Chapter 14, pp 434–36.

60 SDA 1975, s 65; RRA 1976, s 56; Sexual Orientation, or Religion or Belief, Regulations 2003, reg 30(1); DDA 1995, s 8 (due to be renumbered s 17A on 1 October 2004: SI 2003/1673, reg 9(1)).

61 See Pannick, D, *Sex Discrimination Law*, 1985, Oxford: OUP, pp 284–301.

62 SDA 1975, s 65(1)(a); RRA 1976, s 56(1)(a); Sexual Orientation, or Religion or Belief, Regulations 2003, reg 30(1)(a); DDA 1995, s 8(2)(a) (due to be renumbered s 17A on 1 October 2004: SI 2003/1673, reg 9(1)).

63 The measure is based on all losses caused by the discrimination, rather than just reasonable foreseeable losses: *Essa v Laing Ltd* [2003] All ER (D) 215 (Feb), applying *dictum* of Stuart-Smith LJ in *Sheriff v Klyne Tugs (Lowestoft) Ltd* [1999] IRLR 481, CA.

64 DDA 1995, s 8(4) (renumbered 17A on 1 October 2004); SDA 1975, s 66(4); s 65(1)(b) (employment tribunals) refers to s 66 (county courts) for the basis of compensation. The other legislation uses the same arrangement: RRA 1976, s 57(4); Sexual Orientation, or Religion or Belief, Regulations 2003, reg 31(3).

compensation in discrimination cases in employment tribunals.[65] Compensation may be obtained for pecuniary losses, non-pecuniary losses (in the form of injury to feelings) and aggravated damages. In the current state of the law, exemplary damages may not be awarded. In some cases, compensation is not available for indirect discrimination.

(i)   Pecuniary losses

The principles are the same as in tort;[66] the application of the principles may be far from straightforward, especially where it is unclear whether, but for the discrimination, the applicant would have been appointed to the job in question. Where the discrimination is the 'arrangements' for selection, a claimant may prove easily that she lost a *chance* of appointment, but rarely will prove that, but for the discrimination, she would have been appointed.

If the tort principles were applied properly and thoroughly, the approach to compensation for loss of earnings should be as follows. First, the tribunal should determine the net annual loss for the job in question. Secondly, it should estimate a reasonable period into the future in which the employee would be performing the job. This is similar to, but may be even more difficult than, the process of determining the likely effect of future possible ill-health and redundancy on the plaintiff's earning capacity. Thirdly, the tribunal should make any deduction which is appropriate if the plaintiff has failed to mitigate her loss. Fourthly, the tribunal may have to discount for the chance that the employee would not have been appointed or would not have remained in the job.[67] This approach based on 'loss of a chance' was held applicable to past pecuniary losses in *Ministry of Defence v Cannock*[68] and the same logic must apply to the assessment of future losses. Estimating the chance will be a process fraught with difficulty, and appears rarely, if ever, to be attempted in discrimination cases, but there is no doubt in principle that it *ought* to be attempted. For the applicant to convince a tribunal that he or she might well have been appointed in the face of employer denial will, however, almost never be straightforward. Finally, earnings in the period up to trial, and in the (post-trial) period for which damages are being calculated, should be deducted.

---

65   The ECJ ruling in *Marshall v Southampton and South West Hampshire AHA (No 2)* Case C-271/91 [1993] IRLR 445 led to the Sex Discrimination and Equal Pay (Remedies) Regulations 1993, SI 1993/2798. Had the law been left there, there would have been an anomaly between gender cases and race cases. In consequence, the statutory limit in race cases was removed by the Race Relations (Remedies) Act 1994. This is an excellent example of the piggybacking effect of European law in relation to race discrimination.

66   SDA 1975, s 66(1); RRA 1976, s 57(1); Sexual Orientation, or Religion or Belief, Regulations 2003, reg 31(1); DDA 1995, s 8(3) (due to be renumbered s 17A on 1 October 2004: SI 2003/1673, reg 9(1)). But see *Mangera v Ministry of Defence* [2003] All ER (D) 245 (May), where the Court of Appeal held that the RRA 1976, s 4(2) (discrimination against employees) provided an employment right in contrast to a common law tort.

67   It was held in *Ministry of Defence v Wheeler and Others* [1998] 1 All ER 790; [1998] 1 WLR 637; [1998] ICR 242; [1998] IRLR 23, CA, that any deduction for what was or would have been earned in the armed forces, and any deduction for failure to mitigate, should be carried out before the issue of loss of a chance is considered.

68   [1994] ICR 918; [1995] 2 All ER 449; [1994] IRLR 509, EAT. For calculating the chances of remaining in the job in a case of discriminatory dismissal, see *Vento v Chief Constable of West Yorkshire* [2002] EWCA Civ 1871.

In practice, cases of future loss of earnings most frequently arise where the allegation is of a discriminatory dismissal, and the claim may be combined with one of unfair dismissal. The principles governing compensation for loss of earnings in unfair dismissal are, with certain modifications, transferable to discrimination cases, and double compensation for the same element is not possible.[69] It should also be borne in mind that discrimination, perhaps especially in a case of harassment, may cause ill-health and thus pecuniary loss. Here the analogy with personal injury cases is closest.[70]

In most cases, pre-trial losses will be both modest and fairly easy to calculate, as the period of such losses is normally fairly short. The exception concerns cases where the losses potentially extend back to the date when the UK Government should have complied with a European Directive.[71] It is for this reason that the awards of compensation to pregnant women dismissed from the armed forces were so large[72] In most discrimination cases, these hypothetical questions will not be relevant, but the approach to what has been lost is of general application. It is simply that the contingencies are much less likely to arise, as the period in respect of which compensation is being assessed is so much less.

Just as in tort, expenses are recoverable, though these are likely to be modest. For example, the applicant may have undergone considerable expense in applying for a job or in travelling to an interview at which discrimination occurred.

(ii) *Injury to feelings*

It is clear that compensation for injury to feelings cannot be fixed with any degree of precision. In *Vento*, the Court of Appeal reviewed the case law, offered a guide for tribunals and considered when an appeal court should interfere with a tribunal's award.

Vento v Chief Constable of West Yorkshire Police [2002] EWCA Civ 1871

Ms Vento won her claim for sex discrimination following a series of incidents of bullying and ending in her dismissal for alleged dishonesty. The employment tribunal

---

69   *Sheriff v Klyne Tugs (Lowestoft) Ltd* [1999] IRLR 481, CA. Claiming discrimination may be advantageous. Unlike the present law of unfair dismissal, there is no qualification period (of one year) and no limit on compensation (at present, £52,600 under the ERA 1996, s 124. In 1998, the Government proposed to abolish this limit: *Fairness at Work*, Cm 3968, 1998, London: HMSO, para 3.5). Furthermore, compensation for injury to feelings is very limited in unfair dismissal cases. On the other hand, a dismissal may be unfair without the applicant being able to prove that it was discriminatory; there is no power under the discrimination legislation for the tribunal to order reinstatement, which in unfair dismissal law is an important, albeit rarely used, power; and unfair dismissal compensation includes a 'basic award' calculated on length of service which is not dependent upon measurable financial loss.

70   For the possibility of extending *Wilkinson v Downton* [1897] 2 QB 57 to harassment cases, see Mullinder, R, 'Racial harassment, sexual harassment, and the expressive function of law' (1998) 61 MLR 236.

71   It was held in *Emmott v Ministry of Social Welfare and AG* Case C-208/90 [1991] ECR I-4629; [1993] ICR 8; [1991] IRLR 387 that the limitation period for making a claim only started to run from the time that the Directive had been properly implemented in domestic law.

72   See *Ministry of Defence v Cannock* [1994] ICR 518; [1995] 2 All ER 449; [1994] IRLR 509, EAT; Arnull, A, 'EC law and the dismissal of pregnant servicewomen' [1995] 24 ILJ 215, and the Sex Discrimination Act 1975 (Application to Armed Forces, etc) Regulations 1994, SI 1994/3276.

found that she had 'been put through four traumatic years by the conduct of the respondent's officers'. It further found:

> that the respondent and his officers have throughout acted in a high-handed manner. First, they unreasonably condemned the applicant as dishonest. They raised questions about her private life, which had little or nothing to do with her conduct or capability as a police officer. They persisted in those matters throughout these proceedings until the appeal was lost. The respondent then made what we regard as a cynical offer of reinstatement principally designed to limit the financial damage to the respondent's resources. The apology from the respondent came very late in the day. There has been no apology from the five officers who are the subject of our second recommendation. The Deputy Chief Constable attended the hearing not having read our decision or that of the Employment Appeal Tribunal and, therefore, not really knowing for what he was apologising on behalf of the respondent. We characterise the respondent's attitude and that of his officers to this case as one of institutional denial, that is a refusal to see that supervising officers had throughout treated the applicant unreasonably, a refusal or inability to see that a view of the applicant's sexual morality had improperly coloured officers' judgments and a failure to ask the fundamental question as to why these things had happened.

For her non-pecuniary loss, the Court of Appeal awarded Ms Vento £18,000 for injury to feelings, £5,000 aggravated damages and £9,000 for psychiatric damage.

Mummery LJ:

[46] This is the first time for many years that the Court of Appeal has had the opportunity to consider the appropriate level of compensation for injury to feelings in discrimination cases. Some decisions in the Employment Tribunal and in the Appeal Tribunal have resulted in awards of substantial sums for injury to feelings, sometimes supplemented by compensation for psychiatric damage and aggravated damages. Cases were cited to the court in which Employment Tribunals had, as in this case, awarded compensation for injury to feelings (plus aggravated damages) larger than the damages separately awarded for psychiatric injury, and totalling well in excess of £20,000. The Court was shown the decision of an Employment Tribunal in a race discrimination case awarding the sum of £100,000 for injury to feelings, plus aggravated damages of £25,000: *Virdi v Commissioner of Police of the Metropolis* (8 December 2000, London Central ET, Case No: 2202774/98). (This pales into insignificance in comparison with the reported award in 1994 by a Californian jury of $7.1m to a legal secretary for sexual harassment, and even with the subsequent halving of that sum on appeal.)

[47] Compensation of the magnitude of £125,000 for non-pecuniary damage creates concern as to whether some recent tribunal awards in discrimination cases are in line with general levels of compensation recovered in other cases of non-pecuniary loss, such as general damages for personal injuries, malicious prosecution and defamation. In the interests of justice (social and individual), and of predictability of outcome and consistency of treatment of like cases (an important ingredient of justice) this Court should indicate to Employment Tribunals and practitioners general guidance on the proper level of award for injury to feelings and other forms of non-pecuniary damage. (See paras 65 – 68 below) ...

[50] It is self evident that the assessment of compensation for an injury or loss, which is neither physical nor financial, presents special problems for the judicial process, which aims to produce results objectively justified by evidence, reason and precedent. Subjective feelings of upset, frustration, worry, anxiety, mental

distress, fear, grief, anguish, humiliation, unhappiness, stress, depression and so on and the degree of their intensity are incapable of objective proof or of measurement in monetary terms. Translating hurt feelings into hard currency is bound to be an artificial exercise. As Dickson J said in *Andrews v Grand & Toy Alberta Ltd* (1978) 83 DLR (3d) 452 at pp 475–476, ... there is no medium of exchange or market for non-pecuniary losses and their monetary evaluation:

> ... is a philosophical and policy exercise more than a legal or logical one. The award must be fair and reasonable, fairness being gauged by earlier decisions; but the award must also of necessity be arbitrary or conventional. No money can provide true restitution.

[51] Although they are incapable of objective proof or measurement in monetary terms, hurt feelings are none the less real in human terms. The courts and tribunals have to do the best they can on the available material to make a sensible assessment, accepting that it is impossible to justify or explain a particular sum with the same kind of solid evidential foundation and persuasive practical reasoning available in the calculation of financial loss or compensation for bodily injury. In these circumstances an appellate body is not ... entitled to interfere with the assessment of the Employment Tribunal simply because it would have awarded more or less than the tribunal has done. It has to be established that the tribunal has acted on a wrong principle of law or has misapprehended the facts or made a wholly erroneous estimate of the loss suffered. Striking the right balance between awarding too much and too little is obviously not easy.

[52] As Smith J noted in *Prison Service v Johnson* [1997] ICR 275, [1997] IRLR 162 there were, in the first 20 years of the legislation against discrimination, very few reported cases on awards of damages for injury to feelings and they are now out of date. In *Alexander v Home Office* [1988] 2 All ER 118, [1988] ICR 685, the Court of Appeal increased an award for injury to feelings awarded for race discrimination by prison officers from £50 to £500. In the same year in *Northern Regional Health Authority v Noone* [1988] ICR 813, [1988] IRLR 195, the [Court of Appeal] ... awarded [£3,000] for injury to feelings in a case of a single act of race discrimination against a black woman doctor, who was not appointed to a position for which she applied. It should be noted that at that time the maximum amount of compensation that could be awarded for race discrimination was £7,500. [T]here is now no ceiling on the total amount recoverable for acts of sex and race discrimination.

[53] In *HM Prison Service v Johnson* Smith J reviewed the authorities on compensation for non-pecuniary loss and made a valuable summary of the general principles gathered from them. We would gratefully adopt that summary. Employment Tribunals should have it in mind when carrying out this challenging exercise. In her judgment on behalf of the Appeal Tribunal Smith J said at p 283B:

> (i) Awards for injury to feelings are compensatory. They should be just to both parties. They should compensate fully without punishing the tortfeasor. Feelings of indignation at the tortfeasor's conduct should not be allowed to inflate the award. (ii) Awards should not be too low, as that would diminish respect for the policy of the anti-discrimination legislation. Society has condemned discrimination and awards must ensure that it is seen to be wrong. On the other hand, awards should be restrained, as excessive awards could, to use the phrase of Sir Thomas Bingham MR, be seen as the way to 'untaxed riches'. (iii) Awards should bear some broad general similarity to the range of awards in personal injury cases. We do not think that this should be done by reference to any particular type of personal

injury award, rather to the whole range of such awards. (iv) In exercising that discretion in assessing a sum, tribunals should remind themselves of the value in everyday life of the sum they have in mind. This may be done by reference to purchasing power or by reference to earnings. (v) Finally, tribunals should bear in mind Sir Thomas Bingham's reference for the need for public respect for the level of awards made.

[54] The Appeal Tribunal in that case was concerned with a serious case of race discrimination suffered by a black auxiliary prison officer, who was the victim of a campaign of racial harassment and humiliation over a period of 18 months, involving elements of pure malice and victimisation on the part of his persecutors. In August 1995 the Employment Tribunal awarded him £21,000 for injury to feelings and £7,500 for aggravated damages. That was the largest reported award at that time. The appeal by the Prison Service against those awards was dismissed ...

[55] The Appeal Tribunal held that the award of £7,500 was not outside the bracket of reasonable awards. It was a very serious case, in which the treatment of the applicant had been appalling affecting both his work and home life, but not, apparently, inflicting any injury to health. The discrimination had been aggravated by the failure of the Prison Service to investigate his complaints.

[56] The general approach laid down in *Prison Service v Johnson* ... has been followed in three recent cases in the Appeal Tribunal, which provide useful illustrations of the range of awards of compensation to damages for feelings.

[57] In *Gbaja-Bianila v DHL International (UK) Ltd* [2000] ICR 730 (Lindsay J presiding), the Appeal Tribunal dismissed an appeal by the applicant, who contended that the award of £3,750 for injury to feelings was too low. No award for aggravated damages was made in that case. There was no evidence of high handed, malicious, insulting or oppressive conduct in respect of the acts of discrimination ... Relying on their experience and good sense the Employment Tribunal had reached a figure, which could not be said to be wholly erroneous. Reference to awards in other cases was only of value in giving a broad indication of the level of award.

[58] In *ICTS (UK) Ltd v Tchoula* ... the Appeal Tribunal ... allowed an appeal against an award of £27,000 in a race discrimination case brought by a security officer. The Employment Tribunal awarded £22,000 for injury to feelings and £5,000 for aggravated damages. The Appeal Tribunal considered that the total sum awarded was so excessive as to be in error of law. It was a relatively serious case, but fell within the lower category of awards. It was not a case of a campaign of discrimination. Having referred to the Guidelines of the Judicial Studies Board, the Appeal Tribunal reduced the sum awarded to an overall sum of £10,000.

[59] The most recent reported case is the decision of the Appeal Tribunal ... in *HM Prison Service v Salmon* [2001] IRLR 425. That was a serious case of sex discrimination brought by a woman police officer complaining of humiliating and degrading conduct, which was so serious that she had suffered psychiatric harm for which she received an award of £11,250. In addition, the sum of £20,000 for injury to feelings, including £5,000 aggravated damages, was awarded. The Appeal Tribunal dismissed the appeal of the Prison Service ... [and] did not consider that in that case there had been any vitiating double counting. ...

[61] At the end of the day this Court must first ask itself whether the award by the Employment Tribunal in this case was so excessive as to constitute an error of law. ... The totality of the award for non-pecuniary loss is seriously out of line

with the majority of those made and approved on appeal in reported Employment Appeal Tribunal cases. It is also seriously out of line with the guidelines compiled for the Judicial Studies Board and with the cases reported in the personal injury field where general damages have been awarded for pain, suffering, disability and loss of amenity. The total award of £74,000 for non-pecuniary loss is, for example, in excess of the JSB Guidelines for the award of general damages for moderate brain damage, involving epilepsy, for severe post-traumatic stress disorder having permanent effects and badly affecting all aspects of the life of the injured person, for loss of sight in one eye, with reduced vision in the remaining eye, and for total deafness and loss of speech. No reasonable person would think that that excess was a sensible result. The patent extravagance of the global sum is unjustifiable as an award of compensation ...

[62] The next question is what is the appropriate amount to award under this head? ...

[63] In our judgment, taking account of the level of awards undisturbed on recent appeals to the Appeal Tribunal and of the JSB Guidelines, the fair, reasonable and just award in this case for non-pecuniary loss is a total of £32,000, made up as to £18,000 for injury to feelings, £5,000 aggravated damages and £9,000 for psychiatric damage, which took the form of clinical depression and adjustment disorder lasting for 3 years ... We also bear in mind that there was no finding by the Employment Tribunal that the injury to Ms Vento's feelings would continue after the psychiatric disorder had passed. During the period of psychiatric disorder there must have been a significant degree of overlap with the injury to her feelings. ...

Guidance

[65] Employment Tribunals and those who practise in them might find it helpful if this Court were to identify three broad bands of compensation for injury to feelings, as distinct from compensation for psychiatric or similar personal injury:

(i)   The top band should normally be between £15,000 and £25,000. Sums in this range should be awarded in the most serious cases, such as where there has been a lengthy campaign of discriminatory harassment on the ground of sex or race. This case falls within that band. Only in the most exceptional case should an award of compensation for injury to feelings exceed £25,000.

(ii) The middle band of between £5,000 and £15,000 should be used for serious cases, which do not merit an award in the highest band.

(iii) Awards of between £500 and £5,000 are appropriate for less serious cases, such as where the act of discrimination is an isolated or one off occurrence. In general, awards of less than £500 are to be avoided altogether, as they risk being regarded as so low as not to be a proper recognition of injury to feelings.

[66] There is, of course, within each band considerable flexibility, allowing tribunals to fix what is considered to be fair, reasonable and just compensation in the particular circumstances of the case.

[67] The decision whether or not to award aggravated damages and, if so, in what amount must depend on the particular circumstances of the discrimination and on the way in which the complaint of discrimination has been handled.

[68] Common sense requires that regard should also be had to the overall magnitude of the sum total of the awards of compensation for non-pecuniary loss made under the various headings of injury to feelings, psychiatric damage and aggravated damage. In particular, double recovery should be avoided by taking

> appropriate account of the overlap between the individual heads of damage.
> The extent of overlap will depend on the facts of each particular case.

The guidance tells tribunals to categorise a case into one of three broad bands, with awards ranging from £500 to £25,000. There is no point appealing against a tribunal award unless it was made on a wrong principle of law, or the tribunal misapprehended the facts or made a wholly erroneous estimate of the loss suffered (para 51).

Compensation in *Orlando v Didcot Power Station Sports & Social Club*[73] was lower than might have been the case because the employer admitted discrimination, or 'pleaded guilty'. However, the fact that the employers do not admit discrimination is not in itself an element of aggravation.[74]

(iii)   Exemplary damages

At present, these may not be awarded in a discrimination case, despite the decision to the contrary in *City of Bradford Metropolitan Council v Arora*.[75] In a review of the general principles applicable to exemplary damages, the Court of Appeal held in *AB v South West Water Services Ltd*[76] that such damages can only be awarded in respect of torts where they were awardable before the 1964 decision of the House of Lords in *Rookes v Barnard*.[77] Subsequently, the EAT in *Deane v London Borough of Ealing*[78] accepted the inevitable, that such damages cannot be awarded in a discrimination case. It was further held, by the EAT, in *Ministry of Defence v Meredith*,[79] one of the armed services pregnancy cases, that EC law imposes no requirement that exemplary damages be available. Claims under the Equal Treatment Directive are analogous to those under the SDA 1975 and the same rule applies.

There is a clear argument that such damages are potentially appropriate in discrimination cases, an argument accepted by the Law Commission.[80] Such damages should be awardable where there is 'deliberate and outrageous disregard' of the complainant's rights, and where 'the other remedies awarded would be inadequate to punish the defendant'. An example given is where an employer ignores, and effectively connives in, a campaign of sexual or racial harassment.

---

73   [1996] IRLR 262, EAT.
74   *McConnell v Police Authority for Northern Ireland* [1997] IRLR 625, NICA, a case under the Fair Employment Act but governed by the same basic principles as to compensation.
75   [1991] 2 QB 507; [1991] 3 All ER 545; [1991] IRLR 165, CA.
76   [1993] QB 507; [1993] 1 All ER 609, CA. See also *Kuddus v Chief Constable of Leicestershire Constabulary* [2002] 2 AC 122, HL.
77   [1964] AC 1129; [1964] 1 All ER 367.
78   [1993] ICR 329; [1993] IRLR 209. See Rowland, D, 'Exemplary damages and racial discrimination' [1994] 23 ILJ 64. In *Kuddus v Chief Constable of Leicestershire Constabulary* [2002] 2 AC 122, HL, Lord Mackay said, *obiter* (at para 46): 'Exemplary damages would be available only if the [discrimination] legislation expressly authorises exemplary damages in relation to any particular breach.' (The case concerned the misfeasance in public office by a constable forging a crime-victim's withdrawal of compliant.)
79   [1995] IRLR 539, EAT.
80   *Aggravated, Exemplary and Restitutionary Damages*, Law Commission Report No 247, 1997, London: HMSO. This is a general survey into their appropriateness as tort remedies.

(iv)   Interest

Marshall (No 2)[81] held that, where applicable, interest must be included as an element of compensation. Both the SDA 1975 and the RRA 1976 were amended in the light of this decision.[82] Interest is normally payable on the injury to feelings element from the date of discrimination to the date of decision.[83] For other losses, the interest runs from a date *halfway* between discrimination and calculation date.[84] In addition, interest payable on awards of compensation from the date of the award, except that no interest need be paid if the award is paid in full within 14 days.[85]

(v)   Compensation for indirect discrimination

Both the SDA 1975 and RRA 1976 originally provided that, in the context of indirect discrimination: 'no award of damages shall be made if the respondent proves that the requirement or condition was not applied with the intention of treating the claimant unfavourably ....'[86] It was clearly arguable after the European Court of Justice (ECJ) ruling in *Marshall (No 2)*[87] that this restriction, which was designed to make compensation for indirect discrimination the exception rather than the rule, contravened European law. This view was accepted by some industrial tribunals, but of course could be utilised only in an action against an emanation of the State.[88] The approach of these tribunals now seems eminently justified in the light of *Draehmpaehl*,[89] where it was held that compensation may not be made to depend on proof of fault. The SDA 1975 was amended[90] (but not the RRA 1976) *so far as*

---

81   *Marshall v Southampton and South West Hampshire AHA (No 2)* Case C-271/91 [1993] IRLR 445, ECJ.

82   Sex Discrimination and Equal Pay (Remedies) Regulations1993, SI 1993/2798; Race Relations (Interest on Awards) Regulations 1994, SI 1994/1748.

83   Employment Tribunals (Interest on Awards in Discrimination Cases) Regulations 1996, SI 1996/2803, reg 6(1)(a). See *Derby Specialist Fabrication Ltd v Burton* [2001] IRLR 69, EAT.

84   *Ibid*, reg 6(1)(b). Exceptionally, tribunals may depart from this rule, for example, where the whole loss was incurred many years before the tribunal hearing; see *Ministry of Defence v Cannock* [1994] ICR 518; [1995] 2 All ER 449; [1994] IRLR 509, EAT.

85   *Ibid*, reg 8.

86   SDA 1975, s 66(3); RRA 1976, s 57(3). See, eg, *Orphanos v QMC* [1985] AC 761; [1985] 2 All ER 233; [1985] IRLR 359, HL.

87   *Marshall v Southampton and South West Hampshire AHA (No 2)* Case C-271/91 [1993] IRLR 445, ECJ. The decision in *Marshall* had been foreshadowed by that in *Von Colson and Kamann v Land Nordrhein-Westfalen* Case 14/83 [1984] ECR 1891; [1986] 2 CMLR 430, where the Court had held that the Equal Treatment Directive requires that any sanction must guarantee real and effective protection and must have a real deterrent effect, and that any award of compensation must be adequate to remedy the damage sustained. For commentaries on the effect of *Marshall*, see McColgan, A, 'Remedies for discrimination' [1994] 23 ILJ 226; Arnull, A, 'EC law and the dismissal of pregnant servicewomen' [1995] 24 ILJ 215.

88   This is discussed in Chapter 5, pp 108–14.

89   In *Draehmpaehl v Urania Immobilien Service ohg* Case C-180/95 [1997] IRLR 538, the Court held, first, that a Member State may not make an award of compensation in a sex discrimination case dependent on showing fault on the part of the employer; secondly, it is impermissible to place an upper limit of three months' salary where the applicant establishes that she would have been appointed but for the act of unlawful discrimination, but that such a limit is permissible where it is established that the applicant would not have been appointed. Such a limit may apply to any financial losses which are established, but is only permissible where the national law gives no better remedies for breaches of analogous provisions of domestic law. Finally, it was held unlawful to establish a limit on total compensation where there is more than one victim of discrimination in relation to the same recruitment exercise.

90   By the Sex Discrimination and Equal Pay (Miscellaneous Amendments) Regulations 1996, SI 1996/438, reg 2(2).

employment tribunals are concerned, with the introduction of s 65(1B), which provides, basically, the same test as in a direct discrimination case: it must be just and equitable to make an award of compensation. However, it is spelt out that the tribunal must be satisfied that the power to make a declaration or a recommendation (or both) are not in themselves an adequate remedy in the circumstances. The original restriction remains for county court hearings.

The same formula is used for employment tribunal cases under the Sexual Orientation, and Religion or Belief, Regulations 2003.[91] However, here there is no restriction for county court hearings. This has a lesser significance because the Regulations cover only employment and vocational training, for example, in a case of indirect discrimination arising against a university, in the field of vocational training. No such restriction exists under the DDA 1995.

For the RRA 1976, the original restriction, provided by s 57(3), remains unaffected by the Race Directive[92] and the consequent amendments. However, s 57(3) applies only to discrimination defined by s 1(1)(b) of the RRA 1976 and, as the Race Relations Act 1976 (Amendment) Regulations 2003[93] introduced a separate definition of indirect discrimination (inserted as s 1(1A)) for cases within the Race Directive's competence,[94] s 57(3) will only regulate 'residual' cases outside of the new definition, such as claim for indirect discrimination based purely on colour or nationality. For claims falling within the new definition, damages are not dependent on discriminatory intent. These claims fall under the guideline in s 56(1) that an employment tribunal must order remedies 'as it thinks just and equitable'. Unlike the other legislation, it is not spelt out that a declaration or recommendation (or both) must be inadequate for damages to be awarded. For the residual cases and others still covered by the restriction, the interpretation of the word 'intention' in these provisions has recently undergone a radical rethink.

JH Walker Ltd v Hussain [1996] IRLR 11; [1996] ICR 291, EAT

A complaint of indirect discrimination arose after 18 employees were disciplined for taking a day off work to celebrate Eid, a Muslim holy day, in breach of a new rule that non-statutory holidays would no longer be permitted during the company's busiest months – May, June and July.

The tribunal held that the requirement was not justifiable and awarded each applicant £1,000 compensation for injury to feelings.

The EAT dismissed the appeal.

Mummery J (p 15):

The burden of proof under s 57(3) [to show that the requirement or condition was not applied with the intention of treating the claimant unfavourably on the ground of race] is on the company.

'[I]ntention' in this context signifies the state of mind of a person who, at the time when he does the relevant act ...

---

91 Sexual Orientation, or Religion or Belief, Regulations 2003, reg 30(2), in force since 1 December and 2 December 2003, respectively.
92 Council Directive 2000/43/EC. This Directive, peculiarly, covers activities beyond employment, such as housing, services and education.
93 SI 2003/1626, in force since 19 July 2003.
94 See above, Chapter 10, pp 242–43.

(a)   *wants* to bring about the state of affairs which constitutes the prohibited act of unfavourable treatment on racial grounds; and

(b)   *knows* that the prohibited act will follow from his acts.

In our view, s 57(3) is not concerned with an inquiry into the motivation of a respondent, that is, the reason why he did what he did. It is concerned with the state of mind of the respondent in relation to the consequences of his acts.

[A] tribunal may infer that a person wants to produce certain consequences from the fact that he acted knowing what those consequences would be [for example, continuing to apply a requirement or condition after it had been declared unlawful], even though his reason or motive for persisting in the action was one of business efficiency.

The tribunal took account of the company's knowledge of the consequences of its acts and made an inference that it wanted to produce those consequences. The company knew that Eid was important to its Muslim employees, that they were the only employees affected by the application of the condition or requirement, and that they were required to work on that day ... The fact that the company's reason or motive in adopting or applying the holiday policy was to promote its business efficiency does not, in our view, either displace the company's knowledge of the consequences ... or prevent the Industrial Tribunal from inferring that the company wanted to produce a state of affairs in which the applicants were in fact treated unfavourably on racial grounds.[95]

The impact of this decision is unclear. Intentional indirect discrimination may be easier to establish in gender cases than in race cases. In such cases, indirectly discriminatory requirements often have an obvious, general and well-documented adverse impact, knowledge of which employers would be hard put to deny. This point is still relevant despite the change in the law, for the purpose of the requirement and the knowledge of its adverse impact will remain factors in the tribunal's determination of whether it is just and equitable to award compensation for indirect discrimination, and in the amount so awarded. The same may be true of race cases, but not so frequently. *Walker* could have been argued as a case of direct *religious* discrimination. However, the lack of a religious discrimination law at the time meant it could only be argued as an indirect discrimination case. It would be relatively easy for a tribunal which was so minded to distinguish the case and hold that no compensation was payable because of the employer's lack of knowledge of adverse impact.

Extension of compensation to indirect discrimination is extremely important. Its absence was based on a quasi-criminal notion that a requirement to pay compensation was only 'just' if the employer was in some way blameworthy.[96] Such an approach entirely loses sight of the functions of compensation, both as a deterrence mechanism and as an incentive to initiate legal action. While victims may sue in order to prevent the discrimination happening to others in the future, the absence of any financial incentive to bring an indirect discrimination case has surely contributed to its lack of

---

95   Likewise, in *London Underground Ltd v Edwards* [1995] ICR 574; [1995] IRLR 355, EAT, a gender case decided before the change in the law, it was held that compensation was payable for indirect discrimination as the employers were aware of the adverse impact of the new rostering arrangements, even though they had not been drawn up with the purpose of treating women unfavourably.

96   See the commentary on this issue in Chapter 10, pp 237–40.

use. While the change brought about by legislation and by *Walker v Hussain* will not transform the effectiveness of this area of the law, it was a very necessary step in that direction.

(c)   Recommendations

If it considers it just and equitable to do so, a tribunal may make 'a recommendation that the respondent take within a specified period action appearing to the tribunal to be practicable for the purpose of obviating or reducing the adverse effect on the complainant of any act of discrimination to which the complaint relates'.[97]

The drafting of this power is seriously defective. First, it is limited to making a recommendation affecting the complainant. Those in a similar position are untouched. This utterly fails to grasp that discrimination, by its very nature, may very well occur more than once, in similar or not-so-similar situations. There is no power even to recommend that the employer revises its hiring or promotion procedure. It would be possible to give tribunals power to recommend that employers consult with and take advice from the appropriate Commission in order to avoid the recurrence of discriminatory practices. Moreover, a recommendation cannot be made if the employee has another job, where any action by the defendant can have no effect *on that particular claimant*. The claimant may even have used evidence of discrimination against others as part of the case, but still no recommendation affecting those others or those like them may be made.[98] There is thus little scope for making recommendations in either recruitment or dismissal cases where the claimant either never has been, or is no longer, an employee of the defendant.[99]

The way in which the power has been interpreted has not helped. In *Noone v North West Thames RHA (No 2)*,[100] Dr Noone was not appointed for the post of consultant microbiologist on racial grounds. The industrial tribunal found in her favour and made a recommendation to the effect that the Health Authority dispense with the statutory procedure of advertising the next consultant microbiologist post, so the field would be narrowed, thus favouring Dr Noone. The Court of Appeal held this was too wide under the power given by s 56(1)(c) of the RRA 1976, because it 'set at nought' the statutory hiring procedure. Of course, this being the reason for the decision, it is arguable that the case is not of general application.

In *British Gas v Sharma*,[101] an industrial tribunal recommended that the claimant be promoted the next time a post (from which she had been wrongfully excluded) arose. The EAT held that this (a) amounted to positive discrimination and (b) as it was

---

97   SDA 1975, s 65(1)(c); RRA 1976, s 56(1)(c); Sexual Orientation Regulations 2003, or Religion or Belief, Regulations 2003, reg 30(1)(c); DDA 1996, s 8(2)(c) (due to be renumbered s 17A on 1 October 2004).

98   'It seems to be the case that the legislators contemplated the race and sex Commissions following up individual cases to deal with the wider implications, either by promotional work ... or by use of the formal investigation power.' Bourn, C and Whitmore, J, *Anti-Discrimination Law in Britain*, 3rd edn, 1996, London: Sweet & Maxwell, pp 263–64.

99   Fair Employment and Treatment Order 1998, Art 39(1)(d), permits the Northern Ireland Equality Commission to make a recommendation regarding a person *other than the complainant*.

100 [1988] IRLR 530, CA.

101 [1991] ICR 19; [1991] IRLR 101, EAT.

not known when such a vacancy would arise, it could not indicate a 'specified period', as required by s 56(1)(c) of the RRA 1976. As the purpose was reparation of previous discrimination, the second ground alone is preferable.

Finally, in *Irvine v Prestcold*,[102] the Court of Appeal held that a recommendation could not include an increase in wages (to compensate for lost promotion) as such matters should be accounted for by compensation.

The fact that the power is merely to recommend is typical of the timidity of UK employment law to the issue of remedies. The law will not specifically enforce a contract of employment and thus will not force an employer to hire an employee against his will. In the law of unfair dismissal, where the tribunal has power to 'order' reinstatement or re-engagement, failure to comply with such an 'order' merely leads to increased compensation. Breach of a court order is here not treated as contempt of court. The point is even clearer in the context of anti-discrimination legislation; the power is to *recommend*, not *issue an order*, and thus the remedy for failure to comply can be no more than increased compensation.[103]

(4) After the Tribunal Hearing

The impact of litigation is of course highly variable. Some claimants, both successful and unsuccessful, are victimised,[104] but even successful applicants who are not victimised may find it impossible to remain with their employer, and bringing a case may harm job prospects. The victimisation provisions may need strengthening, perhaps by making it a criminal offence or by setting a minimum amount of compensation, even though this would not transform the situation, both because the pressures which cause people to leave may be too subtle to fall foul of the law, and because it is asking a great deal of an applicant who has finished a law case to commence another shortly afterwards. The extension of remedies in appropriate cases to other similarly situated members of a group would assist in countering the current problem of the isolation and the individuation of victims' experiences.

The impact of litigation on employers is uncertain and largely unresearched, but the CRE has taken steps to utilise the outcome of individual litigation in a strategic manner.

'Life after the tribunal: the CRE and follow-up work' (1997) 76 EOR 13, pp 13–15:

There are basically two types of follow-up work. The first focuses on the individual respondent to ensure that it takes the necessary steps to prevent further breaches of the Race Relations Act, and ensure equality of opportunity ... The second type of follow-up takes a much broader perspective, extending beyond the individual firm to the relevant sector or class of organisation ... For example, following an Industrial Tribunal finding ... that the employer's failure to take prompt action to protect and support a black probation officer exposed to racism from clients was unlawful

---

102 [1981] ICR 777; [1981] IRLR 281, CA.

103 SDA 1975, s 65(4); RRA 1976, s 56(4); Sexual Orientation, or Religion or Belief, Regulations 2003, reg 30(3); DDA, 1995, s 8(5) (due to be renumbered s 17A on 1 October 2004). In one respect, discrimination claimants may be in a better position than their unfair dismissal counterparts, as even the increased award for refusing to comply with a reinstatement order is subject to a statutory maximum. See *O'Laoire v Jackel* [1990] ICR 197; [1991] IRLR 70, CA.

104 See above, Chapter 11, p 299.

discrimination, the [CRE] wrote to all probation services, local authorities and health authorities and trusts, giving advice on the decision and its implications for action.[105]

The letter also included the following four recommendations made by the tribunal:

- Clients expressing racist views about staff should receive prompt written advice making it clear that this behaviour is unacceptable.

- Clients objecting on racially prejudiced grounds to the allocation of their case to a particular officer should receive prompt written advice firmly rejecting their attempt to influence the choice of officer.

- Effective steps should be taken to safeguard the personal safety of officers at risk from racially prejudiced clients.

- Policies on racial equality should be specific in this regard ... and provide for the training of managers in this area.

Employers are not legally bound to collaborate with follow-up work, so why do they? ... [E]mployers realise 'that Industrial Tribunal cases are embarrassing and cost time and resources, they realise it makes business sense to prevent discriminatory practices happening in the first place' ... 'Progress has been most marked with public sector bodies such as local authorities and colleges and with some large national companies.' The most resistant employers ... have been medium sized and smaller firms in the private sector.

(5) Individual Remedies under the DDA 1995

The enforcement provisions and available remedies are effectively identical to those under the other discrimination legislation.[106] Two comments may be made. First, the highest awards for injury to feelings under the RRA 1976 and the SDA 1975 apply where there is clear evidence of hostility. To the extent that disability discrimination is due to ignorance, it may be surmised that awards may be somewhat lower.[107] On the other hand, awards for loss of future earnings may tend to be higher, especially where an employee becomes disabled and loses a job in consequence, for tribunals may need little convincing that another job may be hard to come by. Secondly, the assumption that employment tribunals are a suitable forum for resolution of these disputes can be questioned. The legislation would have provided an ideal opportunity at least to experiment with alternative forms of dispute resolution. If many such cases arise through ignorance, forcing the parties into the confrontation arena of a courtroom may be inappropriate. Such a forum imposes stresses and pressures on all applicants, but perhaps to an even greater extent where the applicant is disabled. In addition, monetary compensation seems even less appropriate here than in race and gender cases; many applicants might prefer an apology and a belated adjustment to the discriminatory practice. This is not to deny that there may be circumstances where none of these three points is true, where the publicity and formality of a tribunal hearing is entirely appropriate; what is being contended is that a different remedial route to which the parties might have opted should have been provided.

---

105 See *Jeffers v North Wales Probation Committee*, unreported, IT, Case 61385/93, see 31 DCLD 5.

106 But for the difficulties of establishing causation where the employer has failed to make a reasonable adjustment, see *Cosgrove v Caesar & Howie* [2003] All ER (D) 14 (Jan), EAT.

107 An award of £103,000 was made in *Kirker v British Sugar plc*, IT, unreported, Case 2601249/97, see 35 DCLD 1, upheld by the EAT: [1998] IRLR 624. The bulk of the compensation was for future loss of earnings, £3,500 being awarded for injury to feelings.

3   STRATEGIC ENFORCEMENT OF THE LEGISLATION

The Equal Opportunities Commission, the Commission for Racial Equality and the Disability Rights Commission[108] are the bodies charged both with enforcement of the legislation and with acting in various ways on behalf of their constituencies.[109] There are as of yet no bodies representing the sexual orientation or religion or belief legislation, although the SDA 1975 has been amended to bring discrimination on the ground of gender reassignment within the competence of the EOC.[110] The statutory duties which all three bodies have in common are to work towards the elimination of discrimination, to promote equality of opportunity and to keep the working of the legislation under review, a task which entails the making of reform proposals.[111] In addition, the CRE has the duty to: 'promote good relations between persons of different racial groups ....'[112] For this duty there is no EOC or DRC equivalent.[113]

The statutes define and limit the various powers vested in the Commissions. We have already looked at the power to issue Codes of Practice,[114] the duty to assist individuals to enforce the legislation,[115] the duty to take enforcement action in relation to pressure and instructions to discriminate,[116] and discriminatory advertising.[117] The main emphasis here is on the Commissions' power to conduct formal investigations. In addition, two further ways in which the Commissions may take legal action in their own name will be examined: the power to deal with persistent discrimination and the taking of judicial review proceedings.

(1)   How the Commissions Operate

The Commissions are quangos; they are nominally independent of the Government but are funded by Government money. A potential conflict of interest is immediately apparent. The Commissions may fund individual actions or formal investigations against the Government as an employer, and may seek judicial review against the Government. Not only are the Commissions funded by the Government; the Government 'appoints the Commissioners, approves additional Commissioners for formal investigations, approves the decision making arrangements internally, frequently sends in review teams, provides observers to sit in on chief executive appointments, and reviews the papers for Commission meetings'.[118] Some of the

---

108 Established by the Disability Rights Commission Act (DRCA) 1999.
109 The Government has proposed, in 2002, a single Discrimination Commission, representing all the legislation. See discussion below, p 567 *et al*.
110 SDA 1975, s 53(1)(ba), covering employment and vocational training only, reflecting the limited obligation under EC law.
111 SDA 1975, s 53; RRA 1976, s 43; DRCA 1999, s 2. The DRC in addition may encourage good practice: DRCA 1999, s 2(1)(c).
112 RRA 1976, s 43(1)(b).
113 For discussion of the structure and functions of the CRE, see McCrudden, C, Smith, D and Brown, C, *Racial Justice at Work: Enforcement of the Race Relations Act 1976 in Employment*, 1991, London: Policy Studies Institute, pp 49–56.
114 See above, pp 317–19 and for disability, p 464.
115 See above, p 528.
116 See above, p 538 and for disability, p 520.
117 See above, Chapter 13, p 375.
118 Bourn, C and Whitmore, J, *Anti-Discrimination Law in Britain*, 3rd edn, 1996, London: Sweet & Maxwell, p 291.

Commissioners are directly chosen by the government, others are nominated by the TUC or CBI. There is no necessity for prior experience in matters of discrimination or equal opportunity. The pattern of membership of the EOC and CRE is one-third employer, one-third union and one-third government[119] and has its genesis in the corporatist approach to industrial relations epitomised by the Labour Government of the 1970s. It assumes that all sides can work towards a consensus. There are two particular problems with this model: first, to assume that union representatives necessarily represent the interests of women and minority ethnic groups fails to appreciate the conflicts between different groups that may arise within unions and the role that unions have had in maintaining unequal structures; secondly, this approach conceptualises employment discrimination as an industrial relations issue, rather than as a human rights or civil liberties issue, underestimating the cost which the elimination of discriminatory practices may have for *both* sides of industry. Arguably, British industrial relations law and practice has frequently been hampered by a search for a non-existent consensus; the basis of the work of the Commissions may fall into the same trap. In America, the Equal Employment Opportunities Commission, which covers both race and gender discrimination, is a pressure group as well as a law enforcement agency. This is probably because powerful statutory agencies, such as the Federal Communications Commission and the Securities and Exchange Commission, are part of the American legal and administrative tradition. It has not been easy for the Commissions to develop a sense of identity and a high public profile. There has been internal tension between the legal/conflict approach to their duties and the consensus/bridge-building approach. The Commissions encourage employers to take a more proactive approach to equal opportunities and advise them how to do so; at the same time they may be involved with legal action against the same employers.

It is virtually impossible to know how far these somewhat theoretical points actually affect their everyday work.[120] Many staff are committed to a human rights/legal intervention approach and there have been many instances of the Commissions using the law extremely effectively. Many problems that have arisen have more to do with the law as drafted and interpreted than the structure and organisation of the Commissions.

(2)   Formal Investigations[121]

In most situations, the Commissions have no power to institute proceedings directly against an employer suspected of discrimination. The route laid down by the statutes is that of a formal investigation (FI)[122] which may lead to the issue of a non-discrimination notice (NDN).[123] The model for this remedial approach is health and safety law, where inspectors have power through a prohibition notice to order the immediate ceasing of a dangerous practice. The expert agency investigates the facts

---

119 The DRC is drawn from more sources, including the voluntary sector and journalism. See www.DRC-GB.org.
120 The Annual Reports of each Commission are a useful indicator of the balance of different types of work within the Commissions.
121 See McCrudden, C, Smith, D and Brown, C, *Racial Justice at Work: Enforcement of the Race Relations Act 1976 in Employment*, 1991, London: Policy Studies Institute, Chapters 3 and 4.
122 SDA 1975, ss 57–61; RRA 1976, ss 48–52; DRCA 1999, s 3 and Sched 3.
123 SDA 1975, ss 67–70; RRA 1976, ss 58–61; DRCA 1999, s 4 and Sched 3.

through an administrative process, and if it finds that unlawful behaviour has occurred, it has the power to order it to stop. The model has two perceived advantages: first, the courts are removed from the day-to-day task of determining whether discrimination has occurred; not only does this have procedural advantages, but it vests fact-finding in the hands of an expert agency presumed to be more sensitive to the subtleties and nuances of discriminatory behaviour; secondly, the remedy effectively extends beyond an individual complainant to embrace those who are also victims and those who might be in the future. The individualistic thrust which bedevils the English law of remedies is thereby sidestepped.

> **Applebey, G and Ellis, E, 'Formal investigations: the Commission for Racial Equality and the Equal Opportunities Commission as law enforcement agencies' [1984] PL 236, pp 273–75:**
>
> [F]ormal investigations provide the best remedy in five situations:
>
> (1) Cases of 'victimless' discrimination ... where discriminatory attitudes have existed for a long time and are well known so that, for example, women do not apply for jobs ... and no specific act of discrimination therefore occurs.
>
> (2) Situations where many people are affected, too many for the courts to handle, and where there would be a waste of resources if everyone had to pursue an individual claim.
>
> (3) Where the practices are very complicated and require the ascertainment of facts which are beyond the capacity and resources of an individual.
>
> (4) Where the individual who has been discriminated against is in fact a member of a clearly defined group and the Commission feels it essential to investigate further in the interests of the remaining members of the group.
>
> (5) Where references are made to the Commissions to investigate matters believed to be in the public interest.

To understand why this vision of an effective enforcement agency has been shattered is far from straightforward.

> *Hillingdon London BC v CRE* **[1982] IRLR 424; [1982] AC 779, HL**

All local authorities are obliged to house the homeless. Heathrow Airport lies within the boundary of Hillingdon Borough. Hillingdon Borough Council was obliged to house immigrants arriving at Heathrow and the council felt strongly that this should be a responsibility of national government. As a protest, a member of the council placed an immigrant family of Asian origin in a taxi and abandoned them outside the doors of the Foreign Office. Meanwhile, the council housed an immigrant family of English origin from Zimbabwe (at the time, Rhodesia). The Commission formed a belief that Hillingdon Council were acting in a discriminatory way when housing arrivals at Heathrow and so they decided to embark upon a formal investigation. However, the terms of reference stated that the Commission believed that the council were discriminating when offering accommodation to *the public, or a section of it*. The council sought certiorari to quash the CRE determination.

The House of Lords held: (1) s 49(4) provides that before the Commission can embark upon a 'named-person' formal investigation, they must undertake a 'preliminary inquiry'; (2) the purpose of the preliminary inquiry is to hear what the person named had to say in response to the Commission's accusations; (3) it follows that if the person named is to be given a genuine opportunity to answer, the Commission cannot 'throw the book at him'; thus, the accusations must be based upon a (reasonably formed) belief; (4) accordingly the scope of the Commission's investigatory power is limited to their belief; (5) as the terms of reference expressed a belief ('section of the public') wider than the Commission's actual belief ('arrivals at Heathrow'), the Commission had no power to conduct a formal investigation within the terms of reference, and their decision to do so would be quashed.

Lord Diplock (pp 427–30):

It is a condition precedent to every FI embarked upon by the Commission on their own initiative that terms of reference for the investigation should have been drawn up by them, and where the terms of reference are confined to the activities of named persons it is also, in my view, a condition precedent to the drawing up of any terms of reference for an investigation of this kind ... that the Commission should have formed the belief, and should so state in the terms of reference, that the named persons may have done or may be doing discriminatory acts ...

[T]he Commission's belief *as stated in the terms of reference* defines and limits the scope of the full investigation and thus of the information which the Commission may lawfully demand ... [F]airness demands that the statement in the terms of reference as to the kinds of acts which the Commission believe the persons named may have done or may be doing should not be expressed in any wider language than is justified by the genuine extent of the Commission's belief.

The purpose of the preliminary inquiry is to give the persons named in the terms of reference an opportunity of making written or oral representations or both, with regard to the proposal to embark upon a full investigation of unlawful acts of the kinds specified in the terms of reference ...

The right of a person to be heard in support of his objection to a proposal to embark upon an investigation of his activities cannot be exercised effectively unless that person is informed with reasonable specificity what are the kinds of acts to which the proposed investigation is to be directed and confined. The Commission cannot 'throw the book' at him; they cannot, without further particularisation of the kinds of acts of which he is suspected, tell him no more than that they believe that he may have done or may be doing *some* acts that are capable of amounting to unlawful discrimination ... if their real belief (which is a condition precedent to embarking upon a belief investigation at all) is confined to a belief that they may have done or may be doing only acts of one or more particular kinds ...

To entitle the Commission to embark upon the full investigation it is enough that there should be material before the Commission sufficient to raise in the minds of reasonable men, possessed of the experience of covert racial discrimination which has been acquired by the Commission, a suspicion that there may have been acts by the person named of racial discrimination of the kind which it is proposed to investigate.

If they are of opinion that, from individual acts which raise a suspicion that they may have been influenced by racial discrimination, an inference can be drawn that the persons doing those acts were also following a more general policy of racial discrimination, the Commission are entitled to draw up terms of reference wide enough to enable them to ascertain whether such inference is justified or not. But such is not the instant case; the Commission never did draw any inference of this kind, nor did they suspect the council of doing any acts of discrimination upon racial grounds except in relation to that particular section of the public which consisted of immigrant families newly arrived at Heathrow airport who claimed to be homeless.

Re Prestige Group plc [1984] IRLR 166; [1984] ICR 473; [1984] 1 WLR 335, HL

The Commission embarked upon a 'named-person' formal investigation into the employment practices of Prestige. The Commission had no prior suspicion that Prestige had acted in contravention of the RRA 1976 and no such belief was expressed in the terms of reference. Prestige challenged the investigation as being outside of the Commission's powers on the grounds that the Commission had no belief of wrongdoing prior to the investigation. It was held, applying *Hillingdon*, that s 49(4) provides that before the Commission can embark upon a formal investigation, they must have a (reasonable) belief that those named in the terms of reference have acted in contravention of the RRA 1976.

Lord Diplock (pp 168–70):

[T]he terms of reference [of the FI] contained no statement that the CRE believed that Prestige had committed acts of racial discrimination of any kind and the CRE, at the time when they gave notice to Prestige of the holding of the FI with those terms of reference, did not, in fact, believe that Prestige might have committed *any* [such] unlawful acts ...

In essence the contention of the CRE ... is that even if the CRE had no such belief when they started on the FI, any invalidity there might have been initially was cured by the subsequent formation by the CRE of such a belief during the course of the investigation, and that this was so notwithstanding that no notice of the formation of the belief was given to Prestige and that no revision was made of the terms of reference of the FI ...

[S]ections 49 and 50 disclose a clear dichotomy between a named-person investigation and an investigation ... which is not confined by its terms of reference to the activities of persons actually named in it. The crucial difference between these two types of FI is that in a general investigation, the Secretary of State, who is answerable to Parliament, retains control of any exercise by the CRE of coercive power to require persons to give oral information or to produce documents; whereas over a named-person investigation he has none. The discretion of the CRE, who are not answerable to Parliament, as to whether these coercive powers shall be exercised and, if so, how, is quite unfettered ...

In contrast to a named-person investigation, in which the terms of reference must confine it to 'activities' of persons named in them, the only limitation upon the subject matter of a general investigation is that it must be for a purpose connected with the carrying out of the duties of the CRE ...

[T]he nature [of a named-person investigation is] accusatory in the sense that it is directed to determining whether or not there is justification for pre-existing suspicions of the CRE that the person to whose activities the named-person investigation is confined [had committed unlawful acts] ...

From these two cases, it would seem that before a Commission can embark upon a 'named-person' formal investigation, it must: (a) have a reasonable belief or suspicion that the persons named have contravened the RRA 1976; (b) hold a 'preliminary inquiry' giving the named persons an opportunity to make representations in reply to the accusations; and (c) draw up terms of reference stating the actual belief of the CRE. Finally, the investigation cannot go beyond the scope of the terms of reference.

Nine other formal investigations by the CRE were abandoned following the *Prestige* decision.[124] Previously, the CRE considered that the RRA 1976 permitted them to make exploratory investigations, ie, formal investigations without any prior suspicion of discrimination. *Hillingdon* can be distinguished from *Prestige*: in *Hillingdon*, the CRE stated an incorrect belief in the terms of reference, whereas in *Prestige*, no belief was stated at all. Thus, the House of Lords were not bound to follow *Hillingdon* as precedent.

The key to these restrictive decisions lies in the drafting of s 49[125] of the RRA 1976. Section 49(1) provides that 'the Commission shall not embark upon a formal investigation unless the requirements of this section have been complied with'. Section 49(2) requires that the Commission draw up 'terms of reference'. Section 49(4) states that where the terms of reference are confined to persons named in them and the Commission propose to investigate any act made unlawful under the RRA 1976 which they believe that a 'named person' has done, they must inform that person of their belief and afford him the opportunity to make oral or written representations with regard to it. Section 49 appears to state, therefore, that before the Commission can embark upon a named-person investigation, they must have a 'belief' that a person named in the terms of reference has committed an act of unlawful discrimination. Moreover, according to principles of public law, that belief must be a reasonable one; in other words, there must be an objectively justifiable basis for it. However, it would be reasonable to assume that such an important requirement would have been more explicit. Section 49(4) *presumes* rather than states the requirement of a belief and it is usual practice for Parliament to attach the word 'reasonable' to belief or suspicion where it is intended. The truth is that sub-s (4) was inserted into s 49 in error. It was an amendment forced by Lord Hailsham and intended to be a new s 50.[126] If the amendment was made as Parliament intended, it would *not* have been a prerequisite to a formal investigation. However, prior to *Pepper v Hart*,[127] no court could use parliamentary debates as a source of statutory interpretation. Unfortunately, the problem exposed in *Hillingdon* and *Prestige* was not solved with the drafting of the DRCA 1999.[128]

In other, less important areas, the courts have made decisions favourable to the CRE. In *Home Office v Commission for Racial Equality*,[129] the CRE announced a 'general' formal investigation into the administration of immigration control. They purported to act under their power prescribed by s 43(1)(a) of the RRA 1976: 'to work towards the elimination of discrimination.' The Home Office challenged that, arguing that s 43(1)(a) covered only discrimination under the RRA 1976, and as that Act did not cover immigration, the CRE had no power to investigate it. Woolf J held that the CRE had no power to investigate immigration under s 43(1)(a). However, he found they did have such a power under s 43(1)(b) 'to promote good race relations generally'.[130]

---

124 Applebey, G and Ellis, E, ' Formal investigations: the Commission for Racial Equality and the Equal Opportunities Commission as law enforcement agencies' [1984] PL 236, at p 264.

125 The same formula is used in the SDA 1975, s 58.

126 See for instance HL Deb, 4 October 1976, Cols 1000–1008 and comments of Lord Denning MR in the Court of Appeal in *R v Commission for Racial Equality ex p Hillingdon LBC* [1982] QB 276, pp 285–286.

127 [1993] AC 593, HL.

128 For a discussion of FIs by the DRC, see below, pp 559–62.

129 [1982] QB 385; [1981] 1 All ER 1042; [1981] 2 WLR 703.

130 *Ibid*, at p 396B.

In *R v Commission for Racial Equality ex p Cotterell & Rothon*,[131] the Commission carried out a formal investigation into a firm of estate agents (C & R) and produced a report. During the investigations, the Commission interviewed C & R's clients. Later the Commission wrote to C & R informing them that, on the basis of their report, they were minded to issue a non-discrimination notice, but not before offering C & R an opportunity to make written and oral representations (as provided by s 58(5)). C & R sent written representations and instructed counsel to make oral representations. At the hearing, none of the Commission's witnesses were present. After the hearing the Commission went ahead and served the NDN. C & R argued that the hearing was not conducted in accordance with the rules of natural justice (as required by public law) because their counsel had no opportunity to cross-examine the witnesses. It sought an order of certiorari to quash the Commission's decision to issue the non-discrimination notice. It was held, in favour of the Commission, that the procedure is so near an administrative one, cross-examination is not necessary.[132]

In sum, these are difficulties and problems for the Commissions at each stage of the procedure:

(a) An NDN can only be issued if the Commission is satisfied, through an FI into the activities of a named person, that unlawful discrimination has occurred.[133] It follows that the judicial hamstringing of the FI procedure directly impacts upon the utility of NDNs.

(b) *Prestige* decides that there can be no general investigation into the activities of a named person. The EOC may not, for example, conduct a general investigation into whether a university is guilty of gender discrimination in its hiring practices. Only an 'accusatory' investigation is possible into the activities of a named person.[134] This decision should be reversed, enabling a formal investigation to occur without specific evidence of discriminatory activities. However, even were this to occur, the history of the Commissions' work would suggest that such investigations are most unlikely to form the centrepiece of their activities which was originally envisaged.

(c) To embark on a named-person investigation, there must be belief[135] that such person may have committed specific unlawful acts (*Hillingdon*), although *Prestige* held that *some* grounds for belief will be adequate. It seems both safe and sensible to assume that statistical evidence of gross disparity such as is relevant in individual cases would be sufficient to provide evidence of belief, but such information would need to be in the public domain to start with. There is no legal right in the Commission to obtain information in order to determine if adequate grounds for a belief in discrimination exist. The investigation may not be to see if there is such information: that would be a general investigation into the activities

---

131 [1980] 3 All ER 265.

132 *Ibid*, at p 270j.

133 SDA 1975, s 67; RRA 1976, s 58.

134 This contrasts with general investigations into an area of activity, such as entry into the profession of chartered accountancy, and equal opportunities at a shopping centre. The impact of a general investigation is purely persuasive; an NDN cannot result.

135 An example is the FI into the Crown Prosecution Service; the belief was based on an internal report on the Croydon branch which identified segregated teams. Available at www.cre.gov.uk.

of a named person, which is not permissible. One of the reasons for the courts' requiring the Commissions to show evidence of discrimination before embarking on a named-person investigation is that such an investigation carries with it considerable powers to obtain information from the person being investigated.

(d) The Commissions must give notice to the 'named person' that an investigation is contemplated, state what are the proposed terms of reference and offer an opportunity to make representations.[136] Legal representation is permissible at preliminary hearings, at which the employer may argue that the FI should not proceed or that the terms of reference should be modified. Such preliminary hearings have been expensive and lengthy, as employers have fought to prevent FIs from being started. Not only that, if, during the conduct of an FI, the Commission discovers evidence of discrimination not covered by the original terms of reference, it must draw up revised terms of reference and hold *another* preliminary hearing providing an opportunity for representations to be made on the revised terms of reference.

The Commissions must issue a formal report concerning the findings of an FI. If the evidence discloses that unlawful discrimination has occurred, or if there has been a finding of breach of the Equal Pay Act (EqPA) 1970, SDA 1975 or RRA 1976, the appropriate Commission may serve an NDN.[137] This requires the employer not to commit unlawful acts and, in appropriate cases, to inform both the Commission and other persons concerned what changes to practices and procedures have been made to prevent a recurrence of discrimination.[138] As with the conduct of an FI, there are detailed procedural requirements. The employer must be informed that an NDN is contemplated, on what grounds, and an opportunity to make representations offered.[139] If it is nonetheless issued, there may be an appeal within six weeks to an employment tribunal. It is provided that where it is considered that 'a requirement [of an NDN is] unreasonable because it is based upon an incorrect finding of fact or for any other reason, the court of tribunal shall quash the requirement'.[140] Moreover, the EAT has the power to rewrite the NDN as it thinks fit.

Commission for Racial Equality v Amari Plastics Ltd **[1982] IRLR 252, CA**[141]

The company appealed on the ground that the findings in the NDN were contrary to the weight of the evidence.

The EAT held that all facts forming the basis of the requirements in an NDN were open for consideration on an appeal under s 59 of the RRA 1976. The CRE argued that challenge should be permitted only to findings of fact which were relevant to the reasonableness of the Commission's requirements in the NDN, and hence which bore on such matters as the cost or feasibility of compliance with the requirements.

The court dismissed the CRE's appeal.

---

136 SDA 1975, s 58(3A); RRA 1976, s 49(4).
137 SDA 1975, s 67; RRA 1976, s 58.
138 SDA 1975, s 67(2), (3); RRA 1976, s 58(2), (3).
139 SDA 1975, s 67(5); RRA 1976, s 58(5).
140 SDA 1975, s 68; RRA 1976, s 59.
141 See also [1982] 1 QB 1194; [1982] 2 All ER 409.

Lord Denning MR (pp 254–55):

[O]n the wording of the statute, it seems to be that it is only on the appeal that the company can get a proper hearing. The appeal to the Industrial Tribunal is the first time that the company are able to put their case. It is the first time they can say that the findings of fact are wrong. It is the first time that they can be heard by an impartial tribunal ... The foundation of the whole NDN is those findings of fact already made by the Commission themselves.

This case shows that the machinery of the Act is extremely cumbersome. This case has taken four years already, from 1978 until now. It is still only at a stage in which further particulars have been ordered to be given by both sides. That will take some time. Then there is to be a hearing. Goodness knows when it will take place. The machinery is so elaborate and so cumbersome that it is in danger of grinding to a halt. I am very sorry for the Commission, but they have been caught up in a spider's web spun by Parliament, from which there is little hope of their escaping.

Griffiths LJ (pp 255–56):

There is no doubt that before an NDN is served, the Commission have carried out a searching inquisitorial inquiry to satisfy themselves of the truth of the facts upon which the notice is based and have given at least two and probably three opportunities to the person to put his case, either orally or in writing ... This is necessarily an expensive and time consuming process ... I can understand the frustration the Commissioners must feel if the Act requires that their findings of fact are liable to be reopened and reversed on appeal.

[T]he Commission submit that it cannot have been the intention of Parliament that the findings of fact at which they have so painstakingly arrived in the course of an FI should be reopened on appeal. They submit that Parliament has constituted them as the fact-finding body for the purpose of an anti-discrimination notice, subject only to the safeguard that if they do not conduct the investigation properly and fairly, it can be challenged by ... judicial review. If it were not for the plain wording of s 59(2), I should be most sympathetic to the Commission's argument ...

There is little doubt that the concept of an NDN is potentially very effective in requiring employers to revise procedures and thereby deal with discrimination at a structural level.[142]

Coussey, M, 'The effectiveness of strategic enforcement of the Race Relations Act 1976', in Hepple, B and Szyszczak, E (eds), *Discrimination: The Limits of Law*, 1992, London: Mansell, pp 38–39:

The strategic investigations carried out ... before *Prestige* ... were chosen with reference to the broad labour market position. It was decided to carry out a rolling programme of general inquiries into the extent of inequality in a number of representative industries located in areas of significant ethnic minority population. In this way it would be possible to build up a range of models, demonstrating in practical terms how discrimination operates ... [While many] aims were not fulfilled because many of

---

142 Eg, the NDN in relation to Dan-Air required them to cease banning men from employment as cabin staff, to change their recruitment practices, and to provide the EOC with information to enable the changes to be monitored: *Formal Investigation Report on the Recruitment and Selection Policy and Practice of Dan-Air Services Ltd*, 1986, Manchester: EOC. The NDN served on SOGAT 82, as well as requiring the provision of information to members and to the EOC, required recognition that seniority in the women's branch counted equally with seniority in the women's branch: *Formal Report: The Society of Graphic and Allied Trades*, 1987, Manchester: EOC.

the early strategic investigations had to be abandoned after the *Prestige* decision ... the experience gained was the basis for many of the recommendations in the Code of Practice ...

Many potentially discriminatory practices were identified. These included informal word-of-mouth recruitment ... and the application of geographical preferences ... Discriminatory selection criteria were also found, such as informal oral or written English tests which had little relation to the standards needed for the work ... Subjective criteria, acceptability criteria and stereotypical judgments were widespread ...

None of the companies involved in these pre-1984 investigations had taken steps to introduce equal opportunities polices. The discriminatory practices could flourish unchecked, as there were no records of the ethnic origins of applicants or employees. Ironically, in the absence of such data, it was difficult for the Commission to find sufficient evidence of discriminatory practices. The alternative was to rely on employers' records of reasons for rejection or their accounts of selection practices. Not surprisingly, the evidence gleaned from this was often too weak to justify the use of enforcement [a problem made worse by *Amari*].

It is all the more disappointing that the procedural barriers now provide serious disincentives to embarking on the long and expensive procedure that *might* lead to the issue of such a notice. At every stage, from the preliminary hearing, through the investigation, to the question of whether an NDN should be issued and in what form, employers have ample opportunity for challenging the Commissions and for delaying tactics. In consequence, the Commissions, badly stung by their experiences with the courts in the three cases above, have largely abandoned the FI, at least as the centrepiece of their strategy for enforcing the employment part of the legislation.[143] For reasons of tactics and reasons of resource, the preferred approach is now to deal with employers on a voluntary basis, using their expertise to conduct what becomes in effect a voluntary investigation.[144] Under such an approach, the legal technicalities become irrelevant, and undue delay is avoided, yet such a strategy, for all the evident advantages, is dependent on employer goodwill for its success.[145] An example is the agreement between the CRE and the Ministry of Defence to promote racial equality practices in the armed forces.[146] In return for abandoning the possibility of seeking an NDN, the CRE persuaded the Ministry to introduce detailed measures to recruit more ethnic minority servicemen and women, and to take steps to counter harassment. The agreement contains specific numerical targets for minority recruitment.[147]

Nevertheless, if the agreement is not adhered to, the only powers of the CRE are persuasive and political. There is a strong argument that the Commissions should have powers to seek and enter into legally binding undertakings, breach of which would give them power to go to court or tribunal, where victims of such discrimination would be entitled to be awarded compensation.

---

143 The point is less true of the non-employment parts of the legislation, but here the emphasis has been more on general investigations which do not have the capacity to lead to an NDN.
144 For discussion of the way in which the FI procedure changed following the judicial decisions, see *op cit*, McCrudden *et al*, fn 17, pp 78–85.
145 *Op cit*, McCrudden *et al*, fn 17, pp 94–95, 111–14.
146 See 'Partnership for equality: agreement between the CRE and the armed forces' (1998) 79 EOR 44.
147 For permissible affirmative action, see Chapter 18, p 571.

Coussey, M, 'The effectiveness of strategic enforcement of the Race Relations Act 1976', in Hepple, B and Szyszczak, E (eds), *Discrimination: The Limits of Law,* **1992, London: Mansell, pp 46–47:**

Experience in the United States suggests that employers begin to take voluntary action when they see it as to their advantage to do so. In order to create this perception, six conditions are necessary. First, the standard must be established by law. Where standards are not so established, employers will change or waive them for economic or professional reasons ... Arguably, the employment Code has such an authority and sets standards for carrying out certain employment practices, but these are not legally enforceable and so fail as regulatory standards.

The second condition for self-regulation is that there must be a vigorous enforcement programme, one in which there is significant risk of serious consequences to employers who flout the standards ...

The third condition is that the results achieved must be objectively measurable ...

The fourth condition is that the law should provide for liability to individuals, so that even where an organisation is carrying out equal opportunity programmes which may protect them from State regulatory action, an individual is free to litigate. This condition does apply in this country ...

The fifth condition is that employers should be better off after voluntary compliance. There must be a regulatory inspection, or other periodic reporting requirements, of voluntary affirmative action plans.

The final condition is that there must be sufficient and organised public concern. Given that there has never been an effective independent civil rights movement in Great Britain, arguably no such condition exists here.

Enforcement in Britain meets only one of these tests, that of private access to litigation.

(3) Disability Rights Commission and Formal Investigations

The Disability Rights Commission was established by the Disability Rights Commission Act (DRCA) 1999. It has similar functions and powers to the Commission for Racial Equality and the Equal Opportunities Commission.[148] As with the CRE and EOC, the Commission has powers to assist others in bringing claims.[149]

Disability Rights Commission Act 1999

Section 2 General functions

(1)   The Commission shall have the following duties—
    (a) to work towards the elimination of discrimination against disabled persons;
    (b) to promote the equalisation of opportunities for disabled persons;
    (c) to take such steps as it considers appropriate with a view to encouraging good practice in the treatment of disabled persons; and
    (d) to keep under review the working of the Disability Discrimination Act 1995 ... and this Act.

---

148 For a discussion on a single equality commission, see below, pp 567–70.
149 DRCA 1999, s 7.

(2)   The Commission may, for any purpose connected with the performance of its functions—

(a) make proposals or give other advice to any Minister of the Crown as to any aspect of the law or a proposed change to the law;

(b) make proposals or give other advice to any Government agency or other public authority as to the practical application of any law;

(c) undertake, or arrange for or support (whether financially or otherwise), the carrying out of research or the provision of advice or information.

Nothing in this subsection is to be regarded as limiting the Commission's powers.

(a)   Formal investigations

Disability Rights Commission Act 1999

Section 3

(1)   The Commission may decide to conduct a formal investigation for any purpose connected with the performance of its duties under section 2(1).

(2)   The Commission shall conduct a formal investigation if directed to do so by the Secretary of State for any such purpose.

Explanatory Notes:

A general investigation may be undertaken to find out what is happening in a particular sector of society or in relation to a particular kind of activity.

A named party investigation may confine the investigation to the activities of one or more named persons (individuals or organisations). This is the form of investigation which must be used if the DRC wants to investigate a case where it has reason to believe that a person has committed or is committing an unlawful act (see paragraph 3 of Schedule 3). For the purposes of a named party investigation, an unlawful act means discrimination which is made unlawful by Part II (employment) or Part III (access to goods, services, facilities and premises) of the DDA 1995 or any other unlawful act which may be prescribed by the Secretary of State in regulations. Among acts which might be considered for inclusion in regulations are acts breaching section 6 of the Human Rights Act 1998 which affect disabled persons.

A formal investigation may also be undertaken to monitor whether a person is complying with any requirements in a non-discrimination notice or in an action plan (see section 4), or with any undertakings in a statutory agreement (see section 5).

The Explanatory Notes envisage three types of investigation: a general investigation, and two types of 'named-person' investigation. Before the Commission can embark on any type of investigation, terms of reference must be drawn up and published accordingly. This is explained in Sched 3.

Disability Rights Commission Act 1999

Schedule 3, para 2

(1)   The Commission shall not take any steps in the conduct of a formal investigation until—

(a) terms of reference for the investigation have been drawn up; and

(b) notice of the holding of the investigation and the terms of reference has been served or published as required by sub-paragraph (3) or (4).

(2)   The terms of reference for the investigation shall be drawn up (and may be revised)—

    (a) if the investigation is held at the direction of the Secretary of State, by the Secretary of State after consulting the Commission; and

    (b) in any other case, by the Commission.

(3)   Where the terms of reference confine the investigation to activities of one or more named persons, notice of the holding of the investigation and the terms of reference shall be served on each of those persons.

(4)   Where the terms of reference do not confine the investigation to activities of one or more named persons, notice of the holding of the investigation and the terms of reference shall be published in such manner as appears to the Commission appropriate to bring it to the attention of persons likely to be affected by it.

The Commission is empowered to issue an NDN, in line with the powers of CRE and EOC. However, a power new to the DRC is that it may 'make an agreement in lieu of enforcement action'.

Disability Rights Commission Act 1999

Section 4 Non-discrimination notices

(1)   If in the course of a formal investigation the Commission is satisfied that a person has committed or is committing an unlawful act, it may serve on him a notice (referred to in this Act as a non-discrimination notice) which—

    (a) gives details of the unlawful act which the Commission has found that he has committed or is committing; and

    (b) requires him not to commit any further unlawful acts of the same kind (and, if the finding is that he is committing an unlawful act, to cease doing so).

(2)   The notice may include recommendations to the person concerned as to action which the Commission considers he could reasonably be expected to take with a view to complying with the requirement mentioned in subsection (1)(b).

(3)   The notice may require the person concerned—

    (a) to propose an adequate action plan ...

Section 5 Agreements in lieu of enforcement action

(1)   If the Commission has reason to believe that a person has committed or is committing an unlawful act, it may ... enter into an agreement in writing under this section with that person on the assumption that that belief is well founded (whether or not that person admits that he committed or is committing the act in question).

(2)   An agreement under this section is one by which—

    (a) the Commission undertakes not to take any relevant enforcement action in relation to the unlawful act in question; and

    (b) the person concerned undertakes—

        (i) not to commit any further unlawful acts of the same kind (and, where appropriate, to cease committing the unlawful act in question); and

        (ii) to take such action ... as may be specified in the agreement.

(3)   Those undertakings are binding on the parties to the agreement; but undertakings under subsection (2)(b) are enforceable by the Commission only as provided by subsection (8) ...

(8)   The Commission may apply to a county court or by summary application to the sheriff for an order under this subsection ... [if the other party fails to comply or

the Commission reasonably believes he intends not to comply, with the agreement].

A problem from the CRE/EOC legislation remains. It was held in *Prestige*[150] that the CRE must have a reasonable belief of unlawful behaviour before it could embark upon a named-person investigation. At the root of that decision was an error in the drafting of the RRA 1976, where a sub-section requiring a 'belief' in unlawful behaviour was mistakenly included in the section on the terms of reference.[151] The mistake was not repeated in the DRCA. However, the position has not been clarified significantly more than that.

Paragraph 3(1) of Sched 3 states: 'This paragraph applies where the Commission proposes to investigate in the course of a formal investigation (whether or not the investigation has already begun) whether (a) a person has committed an unlawful act ...' Paragraph 3(2) of Sched 3 provides that 'the Commission may not investigate' whether a person named in the terms of reference has committed an unlawful act unless (a) it has a reasonable belief, or (b) it is in the course of a formal investigation into compliance with a non-discrimination notice or agreement in lieu. So sub-para (a) suggests that at the *outset* of most FIs (that is, where there is no such notice or agreement), the Commission must have a reasonable belief of unlawful behaviour by those named. This perhaps contrasts with para 3(1), where the phrase in parenthesis 'whether or not the investigation has already begun' suggests that on the one hand, a formal named-person investigation may begin *without* a reasonable belief of unlawful behaviour; it the investigation *within* the FI that needs to be supported by a reasonable belief. But the question remains, what was the purpose of the formal named-person investigation in the first place? Formal investigations can only be made for a purpose connected with its duties under s 2(1),[152] such as promoting equalisation of opportunities and encouraging good practice. Logically, the Commission could embark upon a named-person formal investigation to 'encourage good practice' and during that investigation develop the reasonable belief that there has been unlawful behaviour.

The Explanatory Notes do little to confirm this. The Notes envisage two types of named-person formal investigation. One is to monitor compliance with an NDN or agreement in lieu. The other is to investigate 'the activities' of a named person. However, the only example given of this category is where the Commission has a reasonable belief of unlawful behaviour. It is possible to read the legislation in a way to support the Commission embarking upon, without reasonable belief in unlawful behaviour, a named-person formal investigation, but to avoid lengthy and expensive challenges, it would have been better to make this clear.

(4)   Persistent Discrimination

After an NDN has been issued, or following a tribunal finding of breach of the law, the Commissions have the power to seek a county court injunction at any time within five years if further acts of discrimination are likely to be committed.[153] After such an

---

150 *Commission for Racial Equality v Prestige Group* [1984] 1 WLR 335; [1984] ICR 473; [1984] IRLR 166, HL. See above, p 553.
151 See above, p 554.
152 See above.
153 SDA 1975, s 71; RRA 1976, s 62; DRCA 1999, s 6.

injunction is issued, further breaches are contempt of court, which could lead to severe sanctions.

(5)   Discriminatory Practices

In most discrimination cases, there will be an identified victim who must establish that a detriment has been suffered. Where there is no such victim, action may be taken by the appropriate Commission. A discriminatory practice is an indirectly discriminatory practice where there is no identifiable victim.[154] There is no power to take immediate action before an employment tribunal; the Commission can only act through an NDN, having first completed a formal investigation.

(6)   Judicial Review

It is specifically provided that the remedial structure of the legislation 'does not preclude the making of an order of *certiorari*, mandamus or prohibition'.[155] Thus, judicial review may be an alternative method of enforcing obligations under the legislation, assuming that the body charged with having behaved unlawfully is a public body. In *R v Secretary of State for Employment ex p Equal Opportunities Commission*,[156] the House of Lords held that the Commission had *locus standi* to allege the incompatibility with European law of the qualifying requirements to claim unfair dismissal or a redundancy payment. The basic requirement for such standing is that the applicant has sufficient interest in the matter, and, after this case, this is unlikely to be a hard task for the Commissions, given that they have a statutory function to work towards the elimination of discrimination. Furthermore, individuals may themselves seek judicial review of an unlawful policy, as in *Seymour-Smith*,[157] and in the cases where it was eventually conceded that the armed forces pregnancy policy was unlawful, two individual nurses and the EOC each sought judicial review.

---

154 SDA 1975, s 37; RRA 1976, s 28. The sections include the new definition of indirect discrimination, ie, 'provision, criterion or practice'. They do not apply to directly discriminatory practices.

155 SDA 1975, s 62(2); RRA 1976, s 53(2) (does not apply to certain Government appointments: ss 53(4) and 76); Sexual Orientation, or Religion or Belief, Regulations 2003 (in force since 1 December 2003 and 2 December 2003, respectively), reg 27(2); DDA 1995, Sched 3, para 2(1). Judicial review is not available if a conventional remedy (such as a claim in the county court) is available: *R v South Bank University ex p Coggeran* [2000] ICR 1342, CA.

156 [1995] 1 AC 1; [1994] ICR 317; [1994] 1 All ER 910; [1994] IRLR 176, HL.

157 *R v Secretary of State for Employment ex p Seymour-Smith* [1996] All ER (EC) 1; [1995] ICR 889; [1995] IRLR 464, CA; referred to the ECJ by the House of Lords [1997] 2 All ER 273; [1997] ICR 371; [1997] IRLR 315; Case C-167/97 [1999] All ER (EC) 97, ECJ; decided by HL [2000] 1 All ER 857, HL. See further, Chapter 10, pp 270 and 295.

(7) Duty Of Public Bodies under the RRA 1976[158]

Race Relations Act 1976

71 Specified authorities: general statutory duty

(1) Every body or other person specified in Schedule 1A or of a description falling within that Schedule shall, in carrying out its functions, have due regard to the need—

   (a) to eliminate unlawful racial discrimination; and

   (b) to promote equality of opportunity and good relations between persons of different racial groups.[159]

(2) The Secretary of State may by order impose, on such persons falling within Schedule 1A as he considers appropriate, such duties as he considers appropriate for the purpose of ensuring the better performance by those persons of their duties under subsection (1).

71C General statutory duty: codes of practice

(1) The Commission may issue codes of practice containing such practical guidance as the Commission think fit in relation to the performance by persons of duties imposed on them by virtue of subsections (1) and (2) of section 71.

71D General statutory duty: compliance notices

(1) If the Commission are satisfied that a person has failed to comply with, or is failing to comply with, any duty imposed by an order under section 71(2), the Commission may serve on that person a notice ('a compliance notice').

(2) A compliance notice shall require the person concerned—

   (a) to comply with the duty concerned; and

   (b) to inform the Commission, within 28 days of the date on which the notice is served, of the steps that the person has taken, or is taking, to comply with the duty.

(3) A compliance notice may also require the person concerned to furnish the Commission with such other written information as may be reasonably required by the notice in order to verify that the duty has been complied with.

(4) The notice may specify—

   (a) the time (no later than three months from the date on which the notice is served) at which any information is to be furnished to the Commission;

   (b) the manner and form in which any such information is to be so furnished.

---

158 Outside of England and Wales, the duties are not always confined to racial discrimination. The Scottish Parliament may (by the Scotland Act 1998, Pt II, Sched 5) impose anti-discrimination duties on local authorities; eg, Housing (Scotland) Act 2001, s 106, imposes an equal opportunities duty upon Scottish Ministers and local authorities and covers (in housing): 'the prevention, elimination or regulation of discrimination between persons on grounds of sex or marital status, on racial grounds, or on grounds of disability, age, sexual orientation, language or social origin, or of other personal attributes, including beliefs or opinions, such as religious beliefs or political opinions.' The Northern Ireland Act 1998, s 75(1) provided: 'A public authority shall in carrying out its functions relating to Northern Ireland have due regard to the need to promote equality of opportunity— (a) between persons of different religious belief, political opinion, racial group, age, marital status or sexual orientation; (b) between men and women generally; (c) between persons with a disability and persons without; and (d) between persons with dependants and persons without.'

159 The phrase 'equality of opportunity' does not apply to immigration and nationality functions: RRA 1976, s 71A.

(5)   A compliance notice shall not require a person to furnish information which the person could not be compelled to furnish in evidence in civil proceedings before the High Court or the Court of Session.

71E Enforcement of compliance notices

(1)   The Commission may apply to a designated county court or, in Scotland, a sheriff court for an order requiring a person falling within Schedule 1A to furnish any information required by a compliance notice if—

    (a)   the person fails to furnish the information to the Commission in accordance with the notice; or

    (b)   the Commission have reasonable cause to believe that the person does not intend to furnish the information.

(2)   If the Commission consider that a person has not, within three months of the date on which a compliance notice was served on that person, complied with any requirement of the notice for that person to comply with a duty imposed by an order under section 71(2), the Commission may apply to a designated county court or, in Scotland, a sheriff court for an order requiring the person to comply with the requirement of the notice.

(3)   If the court is satisfied that the application is well-founded, it may grant the order in the terms applied for or in more limited terms.

(4)   The sanctions in section 71D and this section shall be the only sanctions for breach of any duty imposed by an order under section 71(2), but without prejudice to the enforcement under section 57[160] or otherwise of any other provision of this Act (where the breach is also a contravention of that provision).

Section 71 was heavily amended by the Race Relations (Amendment) Act 2000.[161] This extended the duty from local authorities to some 60 bodies, specified in Sched 1A. Secondly, in addition to general duties, specific duties may now be specified by statutory instrument.[162] The third change is the power given to the CRE to issue codes of practice in these fields.[163] Finally, there is now a system of enforcement by 'compliance notices' underpinned, if necessary, by a court order.

The underlying duty to have 'due regard' to eliminating discrimination, promoting equality and good race relations remains the same.[164] In *R v Lewisham London BC ex p Shell UK Ltd*,[165] the council boycotted Shell products because of their continuing ties to South Africa. This was held to be unlawful, because one of the main objectives of the policy was to exert pressure on the company to pull out of South Africa. It was contended that such an outcome would result in improved race relations in Lewisham, but, as Shell had done nothing unlawful, it was held to be beyond the scope of s 71 to seek to persuade Shell to withdraw from South Africa. They could not use their powers under the section to punish a company which had

---

160 Claims under Pt III: 'Provision of goods, facilities and services.'
161 In force since 2 April 2001: see SI 2001/566, Art 2(1). For a commentary, see O'Cinneide, C, 'The Race Relations (Amendment) Act 2000' [2001] PL 220.
162 Section 71(2). See, eg, Race Relations Act 1976 (Statutory Duties) Order 2001, SI 2001/3458, requiring certain bodies to publish race equality schemes.
163 See 'Code of Practice on the duty to promote racial equality' (2002) London: CRE (ISBN 1 85442 430 0). For a commentary, see (2002) 102 EOR 28. The CRE has also issued four non-statutory codes in this field.
164 This provision mirrors one of the functions of the CRE and, as in that context, there is no gender equivalent.
165 [1988] 1 All ER 938, DC.

done nothing contrary to English law. Similarly, in *Wheeler v Leicester CC*,[166] the council was held to be acting beyond its powers in withdrawing use of a recreation ground for one year in order to punish a rugby club, three of whose members had chosen to tour South Africa. The club itself had done nothing wrong, its members for this purpose being private citizens, but both these cases make clear that the section does empower councils to have regard to the wider race relations implications of their decisions, even though on the facts their actions were lawful.

(8)   Reform

Lustgarten, L, 'Racial inequality and the limits of the law' (1986) 49 MLR 68, pp 72–73:

Discrimination law is hampered in several ways by individuation, but in none so important as the restrictions on the scope of remedies. These may be backward looking (compensation) or forward looking (changes in discriminatory polices and practices). Because all members of the minority group will have been identically affected by the discrimination, it is reasonable that all such persons adequately qualified and shown to be affected be accorded the same remedy as the individual who won his particular case. In the United States, this is accomplished by means of the class action, but there is nothing magical about this particular procedural device: it is quite conceivable that the representative action could be adapted to achieve the same result. The practical consequence is that an American employer adjudged to have discriminated will face a large bill for compensation to all those within the law. It therefore often becomes cheaper and easier to obey the law: the employer is forced to bear the true cost of his illegality because its effect is fully taken into account rather than measured only in relation to the individual who has had the courage, persistence and patience to bring an action. This cost-maximising deterrence is not possible under English law and its absence, by making discrimination cheap, virtually ensures the ineffectiveness of the rights approach.

It is worthwhile summarising the main criticisms of the current remedial structure. Formal investigations may only occur where there is specific suspicion of discrimination. An appeal against an NDN may re-open the whole factual premise on which it is based. An NDN cannot require particular changes as opposed to merely requiring discrimination to cease, as there is no power in the Commissions to accept legally binding undertakings as an alternative to the NDN procedure. The Commissions have very few powers to instigate proceedings in their name, such as where patterns and practices of discrimination have been identified, and to seek remedies on behalf of a group of similarly situated victims. While the law on compensatory damages has improved, there is no current power to award exemplary damages and the tribunal's power to make recommendations is feeble in the extreme. There is nothing which comes anywhere close to an injunctive power.

Furthermore, the two approaches of individual remedies and Commission enforcement have virtually no points of contact with each other. As a result, the advantages of the one system are unavailable to the other. For example, no award of compensation is payable to victims of compensation identified during the course of a

---

166 [1985] AC 1054; [1985] 2 All ER 105, HL.

formal investigation, and a recommendation may only concern the applicant, there being no power to extend its effects to similarly situated employees. This 'iron curtain' seriously weakens the enforcement arm of the legislation. The Commissions should be given a far greater role as regards individual enforcement, such as by representing in their own name a group of applicants, a power which might be especially useful in equal pay claims. At the same time, tribunals should have power to order that compensation be payable to other victims of similar discriminatory acts, and to require employers to post a plan concerning what steps employers will take in order to prevent a recurrence of such discrimination.

(a)   A single equality commission?

The Government proposed, in 2002, a single equality discrimination commission, representing all the legislation.[167] Whatever the merits of this proposal, there would be a risk of diluting the expertise and specialisms within the CRE and EOC. In Northern Ireland, the Fair Employment Commission, the EOC (NI), the CRE (NI) and the Disability Council (NI) have been merged to form one over-arching Equality Commission. However, the new commission continues work under the respective four separate regimes and functions alongside the new Northern Ireland Human Rights Commission. Parliament's Joint Committee on Human Rights, reporting principally on the case for a human rights commission, considered the possible arrangements for equality and human rights commissions.

Joint Committee on Human Rights: Sixth Report (2002–03) HL Paper 67-I, HC 489-I:

Options for the Institutional Arrangements for Equality and Human Rights

189. The Government has announced that it has come to a settled view on the establishment of a single equality body. We take that as our starting point, without expressing any view on whether that was the correct decision. In that context, we have concentrated upon four main options for equality and human rights institutional architecture—

— an Equality Commission confined to tackling unjustifiable discrimination and promoting equality of opportunity and no human rights commission;

— an Equality Commission that also has regard to other human rights relevant to its work in tackling unjustifiable discrimination and promoting equality of opportunity, but no separate human rights commission;

— two separate Equality and a Human Rights Commissions, however configured in relation to the two models for an equality body outlined above; and

— a single Human Rights and Equality Commission.

We consider the advantages and disadvantages of each model in turn.

An Equality Commission alone

190. ... No-one who has given evidence to us appears to support such a model. It does not provide an answer to the pressing needs we have identified above for a body to help create a culture of human rights.

---

167 See www.womenandequalityunit.gov.uk/equality_body/cons_doc.htm. The EU Commission Report on Equality Bodies is available at http://europa.eu.int/ comm/employment_social/fundamental_rights/publi/pubs_en.html.

An Equality Commission with a Human Rights Remit

191.   ... this option would not meet the pressing need that we have identified for a commission able effectively to protect and promote the wide range of civil and political, and economic and social, rights, beyond the right to equality. It could answer the stated needs of the current commissions for powers to tackle human rights violations in relation to the groups with which they are concerned. It would not, of itself, answer the need for a human rights commission—substantial areas of human rights would still have no independent body other than the courts and Parliament to promote and protect them. It is likely that the impact on the delivery of public services would be minimal.

Separate Equality and Human Rights Commissions

192.   Either of the above models could in theory be combined with a separate human rights commission, with responsibility for those areas that would still lie outside the remit of the single equality body.

193.   The main practical advantage we perceive in either of these arrangements is that it would free the two new bodies from the danger of being overwhelmed by the extent of their remits. The main practical disadvantage is really just the reverse of the same coin. We have noted above the very large degree of overlap in real life between the work of an anti-discrimination body and that of a human rights body. The degree of overlap between the missions of the two new bodies would mean there would have to be arrangements put in place in order to avoid inefficient duplication of effort or institutional rivalry, and to provide shared access to expertise and experience useful to both institutions. Such a model could also restrict or preclude shared use of services which could well be cost-effective, particularly in outreach and education, but also in legal advice and administrative support. Perhaps most importantly, there would not be a single gateway to help for citizens and other bodies (including employers and service providers) seeking advice and assistance with real life problems. We have no doubt that arrangements could be designed to overcome this divide, but it is not at all obvious to us that the practical advantages which might come from this institutional arrangement would outweigh the practical disadvantages it could produce.

194.   Combining a separate human rights commission focussing on Convention rights and other human rights but not expressly focussing on freestanding equality issues, with an equality body focussing on the equality issues including the new grounds, but which had no human rights remit, would have the theoretical advantage of clarity of mission for each. This is closest to the Northern Ireland model. We are not at all persuaded by the experience of that body that the division works in the interests of human rights. Nor are we convinced it would meet the stated needs of the anti-discrimination commissions for functions in relation to the Human Rights Act. If we were starting from the position where there were still to be three or more separate anti-discrimination commissions, or even a pre-existing single equality body, this would have appeared to be the neatest and simplest answer. But that is not our starting point any longer. It does not appear necessarily to be the most efficient answer to designing a human rights commission at the same time as one is designing a new equality body—indeed it could be open to accusations of creating a wasteful duplication of resources.

195.   The alternative dual institution model is one in which an equality body with express human rights functions has alongside it a human rights commission dealing with the residual human rights functions ... our main disquiet is that this

arrangement would leave the human rights body divorced from many of the mainstream concerns of citizens. We do not believe this would be to the advantage of either the priorities of the equality agenda or of a human rights culture. The greatest risk, we fear, is that the human rights body would be in danger of being depicted (not only outside Government circles) as the champion largely of the criminal, subversive, alien or just plain eccentric, and standing in opposition to the state and the interests of the majority of its citizens. People such as these share the human rights that protect us all, but there is a view, given vivid expression by a tabloid newspaper, that the Human Rights Act is—

> ... a charter for terrorists, violent criminals, drug dealers, ponces, assorted troublemakers and chancers.[168]

That perception is wrong. Human rights are for everyone.

196. The resulting equality body might in theory benefit from such an arrangement, being able to tackle the human rights violations suffered by the most vulnerable groups in society while being able to divest itself of some of the more challenging and controversial problems in reconciling conflicts and balancing rights. But under this arrangement the new equality body would relinquish much of the benefit of being able to claim that the rights it was promoting were the concern of all rather than the expression of sectoral interests.

197. The resulting human rights body could, in our view, also be quite seriously disadvantaged. Our case for a human rights commission depends on the need we have identified for the promotion of a culture of respect for human rights in public authorities and in society more generally. A human rights commission would be hampered in this mission if it was cut off from involvement in many of the day-to-day concerns of citizens going about their lives—concerns about, for example, their equal treatment at work, the care of their elderly parents or disabled children, their equal right to observe their religious practices and express their beliefs at work or at school, their equal access to education, and so forth.

A Human Rights and Equality Commission

198. ... This would overcome the disadvantages we identify above but, on the other hand, it would risk saddling a single commission with too wide a range of duties, functions and powers, and of blunting the cutting edge of a more specialised and focussed equality body.

199. Those who are sceptical of this integrated model fear it would lead to tension within the institution. It almost certainly would. But there will in any event be tensions between the six equality 'strands' within a single equality body, with or without human rights responsibilities. ...

200. It might reasonably be feared that an integrated body would simply have too much to do. Any new single equality body certainly faces a formidable challenge, though one which we should note that the Northern Ireland Equality Commission appears to have risen to (on a smaller scale) with some success. But we should also recognise that putting human rights in the mix will be a reconfiguration of, rather than a multiplication of, the challenge. The champions of each of the six equality 'strands' express fears that their concerns will be the most controversial, least recognised or least popular. There are also concerns that the priorities of the human rights agenda could swamp or marginalise those of the equality agenda within an integrated institution. In our view, reinforced by our study of integrated commissions elsewhere in the Commonwealth, the

168 Richard Littlejohn (2002) *The Sun*, 18 October.

risk lies the other way – it is more likely that human rights will receive less attention and resources. However, it is undeniable that a broad human rights remit would bring with it additional competing concerns to be reconciled with scarce resources. At the same time we should recognise that in practice, while some issues would clearly engage discrimination issues and others would clearly engage human rights questions, many would engage both – for example, an inquiry with an age focus with a human rights dimension or a human rights inquiry with a strong focus on race and religion and belief. The integrated commission may have the ability to adopt a more holistic approach than two separate bodies could, for example, to a situation engaging discrimination on grounds of age, systemic failure in services to people with a disability, and deprivations of fundamental rights ...

One Commission or Two?

202. The main disadvantage of creating two separate commissions, one dealing with equality and the other with the rest of the human rights agenda, is that it would create an institutional divide weakening the interdependence and indissolubility of human rights.

203. A powerful argument for bringing all strands of the human rights agenda into a single body is that this would strengthen the ability to promote a culture that respects the dignity, worth and human rights of everyone. Provided that this were done in a way that did not blunt the cutting edge of the specialised compliance work in tackling unjustifiable discrimination by means of monitoring and law enforcement, we consider that, on balance a single body would be the more desirable of the two options. However, the option of creating two separate bodies that has been used both in Northern Ireland and in the Republic of Ireland would be a viable alternative, provided that they were closely linked in their work.

CHAPTER 18

AFFIRMATIVE ACTION

1   DEFINITIONS OF AFFIRMATIVE ACTION

It has long been argued that the mere avoidance of discrimination carries with it little prospect of significant overall improvement in the socio-economic position of disadvantaged groups. For that reason, it is contended, more proactive measures are essential, aiming positively to redress such disadvantages, especially in the field of employment. Such action may be undertaken by employers and those concerned with employment, and in a more general sense, by the government. Affirmative action is, potentially, legally and politically controversial, especially when it raises the spectrum of a less well-qualified person being preferred for a job over a better qualified person. However, whether or not one considers this type of action to be appropriate or permissible, it is important to see that most affirmative action falls far short of such an ultimate step.

The definition of positive or affirmative action is potentially problematic. There are at least three interrelated types of objective. First, many policies are directed towards the identification of policies and practices which may disadvantage women and black people in the workplace. This is usually a major objective of workforce monitoring, but is really no more than taking action to ensure that there is no direct or indirect discrimination. Such steps are very important, but hardly merit being described as affirmative action. A second type of positive action concerns the organisation of work and the workplace. This category includes the development of policies to reconcile home and work, such as maternity and childcare policies, career break schemes, etc. Anti-harassment policies can also be classified under this heading, though there is clearly the additional element of the prevention of unlawful behaviour. To some extent, these issues are dealt with elsewhere, though they are frequently and properly included in a company equal opportunity policy. The third focus, often the source of the greatest controversy, is on positive action to overcome the fact that, in many jobs, black people and women are under-represented.[1] This may vary from outreach programmes designed to increase the number of applicants from members of groups perceived to be disadvantaged, through the provision of training designed to promote competition on a level playing field with white males, to programmes which take account of the actual numbers performing such jobs, whether in the form of aims or targets, or in the form of quotas whereby a particular proportion of jobs in a particular grade is reserved for women or black people. This final example might be referred to as reverse discrimination, as it permits the hiring of a person with fewer qualifications for the position than an unsuccessful candidate, and is principally unlawful under English and European law.

The above classification is not the only possible approach.

---

1   Logically, the same approach could be taken to the issue of the under-valuation of typically female jobs; it is purely for convenience that positive action in relation to that issue is considered (by job evaluation) in the chapter on equal pay: see pp 397–407.

McCrudden, C, 'Rethinking positive action' [1986] 15 ILJ 219, pp 223–25:

Five types[2] of action appear to come under the rubric of what positive action *might* include, not in the sense of what is legally permissible, but in the sense of how the term appears to be used in common parlance.

Eradicating discrimination ... Employers should be encouraged to consider it necessary to review regularly the steps taken to eradicate unlawful discrimination, assess the effectiveness of the steps taken, and consider what more needs to be done to achieve the objective ...

Facially neutral but purposefully inclusionary polices. Such policies seek to increase the proportion of members of the previously excluded or currently under-represented group ... Thus, for example, the status of being unemployed or living in a particular geographical area might be stipulated as a relevant condition ... with the knowledge that a greater proportion ... are members of the under-represented group than the majority group.

Outreach programmes ... Outreach programmes are designed to attract qualified candidates from the previously under-represented group. They do so in two ways: first, by bringing employment opportunities to the attention of members of the group who might not previously have been aware of them and encouraging them to apply ... second, by providing members of the under-represented group ... with training the better to equip them for competing when they do apply.

Preferential treatment in employment ... This ... involves a plan to reduce under-representation ... more directly ... by introducing what has sometimes been called reverse discrimination in favour of members of the group ... There may be different aspects of the employment relationship covered, with some programmes involving preferences only in hiring while others extend to promotion and redundancy. A second difference relates to whether race or gender is merely a relevant consideration among others (eg, where minority status is a positive factor to be considered in evaluating the applications of minority applicants) or whether it is the sole consideration (eg, where a predetermined number of new hires is reserved for qualified minority applicants).

Redefining 'merit'. This ... differs from the previous four in that it alters substantially the qualifications which are necessary to do the job by including race, gender or religion as a relevant 'qualification' in order to be able to do the job properly ... Positive action has been defended, for example, as a means of encouraging the recruitment of more social workers from minority groups ...

The fourth of these (preferential treatment in employment) covers a number of possibilities. The employer could prefer the minority (or under-represented), candidate from two equally qualified applicants (the 'tie-break'). The employer could go further and choose a lesser-qualified candidate from a minority group; this would be characterised as hiring by quotas. The employer may use these standards in hiring, promotion or redundancy.

---

2   See also McCrudden, C, 'The constitututionality of affirmative action in the United States: a note on *Adarand Constructors Inc v Pena*' (1996) 1 International Journal of Discrimination and the Law 369, where the author identifies 'at least' three types of affirmative action.

2 BRITISH LAW[3]

(1) Disability Discrimination

Unlike the other discrimination legislation, the Disability Discrimination Act (DDA) 1995 does not take a symmetrical approach. It affords protection only to those with disabilities.[4] As such, positive discrimination is lawful under the DDA 1995, but there is a constraint in the public sector. Section 7 of the Local Government and Housing Act (LGHA) 1989 requires that all local authority workers be appointed on 'merit'. Originally, s 7(2) provided an exception related to the Disabled Persons (Employment) Act 1944, which required that 3% of workers should be registered disabled. This allowed public sector employers to discriminate in favour of disabled persons. However, the DDA 1995 repealed s 7(2)[5] and replaced it with the general duty not to treat less favourably and to make reasonable adjustments.[6] The position now for local authorities is summarised by the Code of Practice.

> *Code of Practice for the Elimination of Discrimination in the Field of Employment Against Disabled People*[7]
>
> 4.66 The Disability Discrimination Act does not prevent posts being advertised as open only to disabled candidates. However, the requirement, for example, under Section 7 of the Local Government and Housing Act 1989 that every appointment to local authorities must be made on merit means that a post cannot be so advertised. Applications from disabled people can nevertheless be encouraged. However, this requirement to appoint 'on merit' does not exclude the duty under the 1995 Act to make adjustments so a disabled person's 'merit' must be assessed taking into account any such adjustments which would have to be made.

Finally, s 10 of the DDA 1995[8] allows for 'supported employment' for a particular group of disabled persons and for charities to confer benefits on any group of disabled persons.

(2) Sex, Race, Sexual Orientation and Religion or Belief

The legislation spells out certain forms of permissible positive action. It is vital to grasp that these are not the *only* steps that may be taken. Positive action is only unlawful if it results in an individual becoming the victim of unlawful discrimination. Most action under employer equal opportunity policies concerns general policies and practices which do not result in individual victims. Indeed, much of what is

---

3 See, 'Achieving equal opportunity through positive action' (1987) 14 EOR 13.
4 The other legislation can protect, men, whites, atheists and so on.
5 DDA 1995, s 70(4) and Sched 6. See Cunningham, I and James, P, 'The DDA – an early response from employers' (1989) 29 Industrial Relations Journal 304.
6 See now, LGHA 1989, s 7(f). Discussed briefly by Morison J in *Hillingdon LB v Morgan* EAT/1493/98 (unreported) available at www.employmentappeals.gov.uk.
7 *Code of Practice for the Elimination of Discrimination in the Field of Employment Against Disabled Persons or Persons Who Have Had a Disability*, 1996, London: HMSO. The Codes can be four at www.drc.org.uk; click on 'The law'.
8 To be renumbered s 18C from 1 October 2004: Disability Discrimination Act (Amendment) Regulations, 2003/1673, reg 11.

specifically spelled out in the legislation and the Codes of Practice as permissible may strictly speaking be legally unnecessary, but to do so is of importance symbolically and as an encouragement to the taking of voluntary action.

There are two types of permissible positive action under the legislation, one designed to encourage more of a protected group to apply for the job in question, and the other to equip members of such groups with the skills to enable them effectively to compete for such jobs.

(a)   Training and encouraging recruitment – Sex Discrimination Act 1975

Section 48 of the Sex Discrimination Act (SDA) 1975, covers employers or trade unions[9] giving training to *existing* workers or members, or positive encouragement in and beyond the workforce or membership to take up particular work. In addition, it allows trade unions (but not employers) to encourage women to become members. Section 47 covers *any person*[10] giving positive encouragement or training to women. The trigger in each case is under-representation, although, as we shall see, the definition varies in some cases.

47 Discriminatory training by certain bodies

(1)   Nothing in Parts II to IV shall render unlawful any act done in relation to particular work by [any person] in, or in connection with—

(a) affording women only, or men only, access to facilities for training which would help to fit them for that work, or

(b) encouraging women only, or men only, to take advantage of opportunities for doing that work,

where [it reasonably appears to that person] that at any time within the 12 months immediately preceding the doing of the act there were no persons of the sex in question doing that work in Great Britain, or the number of persons of that sex doing the work in Great Britain was comparatively small.

(2)   Where in relation to particular work [it reasonably appears to any person] that although the condition for the operation of subsection (1) is not met for the whole of Great Britain it is met for an area within Great Britain, nothing in Parts II to IV shall render unlawful any act done by [that person] in, or in connection with—

(a) affording persons who are of the sex in question, and who appear likely to take up that work in that area, access to facilities for training which would help to fit them for that work, or

(b) encouraging persons of that sex to take advantage of opportunities in the area for doing that work.

(3)   Nothing in Parts II to IV shall render unlawful any act done by [any person] in, or in connection with, affording persons access to facilities for training which would help to fit them for employment, where [it reasonably appears to that person] that those persons are in special need of training by reason of the period

---

9   This actually includes any worker, employer, trade, or professional, organisation. See the RRA 1976, s 12.

10   Section 47 is not confined to *accredited* training bodies, but a major exception, by s 47(4), is employers acting within s 6 ('discrimination against applicants and employees'; see p 317 *et al*, above), so s 47 does not apply to apprenticeships.

for which they have been discharging domestic or family responsibilities to the exclusion of regular full time employment.

The discrimination in relation to which this subsection applies may result from confining the training to persons who have been discharging domestic or family responsibilities, or from the way persons are selected for training, or both.

(4)   The preceding provisions of this section shall not apply in relation to any discrimination which is rendered unlawful by section 6.

48 Other discriminatory training etc

(1)   Nothing in Parts II to IV shall render unlawful any act done by an employer in relation to particular work in his employment, being an act done in, or in connection with—

(a) affording his female employees only, or his male employees only, access to facilities for training which would help to fit them for that work, or

(b) encouraging women only, or men only, to take advantage of opportunities for doing that work,

where at any time within the twelve months immediately preceding the doing of the act there were no persons of the sex in question among those doing that work or the number of persons of that sex doing the work was comparatively small.

(2)   Nothing in section 12 shall render unlawful any act done by an organisation to which that section applies in, or in connection with—

(a) affording female members of the organisation only, or male members of the organisation only, access to facilities for training which would help to fit them for holding a post of any kind in the organisation, or

(b) encouraging female members only, or male members only, to take advantage of opportunities for holding such posts in the organisation,

where at any time within the twelve months immediately preceding the doing of the act there were no persons of the sex in question among persons holding such posts in the organisation or the number of persons of that sex holding such posts was comparatively small.

(3)   Nothing in Parts II to IV shall render unlawful any act done by an organisation to which section 12 applies in, or in connection with, encouraging women only, or men only, to become members of the organisation where at any time within the twelve months immediately preceding the doing of the act there were no persons of the sex in question among those members or the number of persons of that sex among the members was comparatively small.

There are two possible triggers to these provisions: first, 'under-representation' and, secondly, 'domestic responsibilities'. Under both sections, the first trigger is that either no women, or a comparatively small number of women, are doing the work (or holding the post or membership in question) for a period of one year preceding the act. Under s 47, what matters is the numbers of women across the whole of Great Britain, or an area within Great Britain, are doing the kind of work in question. It makes no difference whether there is such under-representation in the employment of the particular employer. An enlightened employer may thus continue with such policies even after there is adequate representation at that particular enterprise.

Section 48 is different, focusing on the issue of whether there is under-representation among women doing the particular job for the particular employer.[11] There is no authority on the meaning in this context of 'comparatively small'.[12]

Secondly, permissible gender-specific training under s 47 can also be triggered where a person needs such special training, because of time she (or he) has devoted to domestic or family responsibilities to the exclusion of regular full-time employment (s 47(3)).

(b)   Other activities – Sex Discrimination Act 1975

Section 49 permits trade unions[13] to reserve, or create, seats on an elected body to 'secure a reasonable minimum number' of women on that body.

Sex Discrimination Act 1975

49 Trade union etc: elective bodies

(1)   If an organisation to which section 12 applies comprises a body the membership of which is wholly or mainly elected, nothing in section 12 shall render unlawful provision which ensures that a minimum number of persons of one sex are members of the body—

    (a) by reserving seats on the body for persons of that sex, or

    (b) by making extra seats on the body available (by election or co-option or otherwise) for persons of that sex on occasions when the number of persons of that sex in the other seats is below the minimum,

    where in the opinion of the organisation the provision is in the circumstances needed to secure a reasonable lower limit to the number of members of that sex serving on the body; and nothing in Parts II to IV shall render unlawful any act done in order to give effect to such a provision.

(2)   This section shall not be taken as making lawful—

    (a) discrimination in the arrangements for determining the persons entitled to vote in an election of members of the body, or otherwise to choose the persons to serve on the body, or

    (b) discrimination in any arrangements concerning membership of the organisation itself.

Finally, s 42A of the SDA 1975[14] allows arrangements 'adopted for the purpose of reducing inequality in the numbers of men and women elected, as candidates for the party'. This applies for elections to the UK, European and Scottish parliaments, as well as the Welsh Assembly and local government.

---

11 For discussion of the meaning of under-representation in the context of the Fair Employment (Northern Ireland) Act, see McCrudden, C, 'Affirmative action and fair participation: interpreting the Fair Employment Act 1989' [1992] 21 ILJ 170, pp 186–90.

12 See Sacks, V, 'Tackling discrimination positively', in Hepple, B and Szyszczak, E (eds), *Discrimination: The Limits of Law*, 1992, London: Mansell, pp 376–78.

13 This actually includes any worker-, employer-, trade-, or professional-organisation. See RRA 1976, s 12.

14 Inserted by the Sex Discrimination (Election Candidates) Act 2002, s 1. The provision will 'expire' at the end of 2015, unless renewed by statutory instrument: SD(EC)A 2002, s 3. See further, Chapter 12, pp 352–53.

(c)   Training and encouraging recruitment – Race Relations Act 1976

Section 37 of the Race Relations Act (RRA) 1976 parallels s 47 of the SDA 1975, except for two matters. First, when assessing under-representation, it is the *proportions*, not numbers, that must be compared.[15] Secondly, s 37 of the RRA 1976 does not provide a 'domestic responsibility' trigger. Section 38 of the RRA 1975 parallels s 48 of the SDA, except in two matters. As before, when assessing under-representation, it is the *proportions*, not numbers, that must be compared. Secondly, the pool for the comparison can be the workforce, or the employer's normal recruitment area. Section 38(2) defines under-representation thus:

(a)   that there are no persons of the racial group in question among those doing that work at that establishment; or

(b)   that the proportion of persons of that group among those doing that work at that establishment is small in comparison with the proportion of persons of that group—

   (i)   among all those employed by that employer there; or

   (ii) among the population of the area from which that employer normally recruits persons for work in his employment at that establishment.

The formulas may appear reasonable, but *Hughes v London Borough of Hackney*[16] revealed that, in practice, it may be difficult to prove under-representation by comparison with the recruitment area. The background to this case was that 9% of the council's gardeners were ethnic minority, in comparison to 37% of the borough's population, although only 58% of the council's recruits were from within the borough. The council advertised for two parks apprentices, stating:

Blacks and ethnic minorities are heavily under-represented in the Parks and Open Spaces Services. Where such conditions exist the RRA (section 38) allows an employer to establish extra training opportunities specifically for those groups. We would therefore warmly welcome applications from black and ethnic minority people for the two apprenticeships.

The applicant was rejected by a letter stating that 'you cannot be considered for these posts as they are only open to black and ethnic minority people as was indicated in the advertisement'. The industrial tribunal upheld his claim of unlawful discrimination for two reasons. First, to prove under-representation, the council compared the workers with the population of the *borough*, not, as required by s 38, the *normal recruitment area*. There was no evidence of where the remaining recruits came from or what percentage of that group were from minority ethnic groups. (The second reason was that s 38 did not extend to restricting job opportunities to particular groups.)[17]

---

15   This difference is based on the assumptions that 50% of Britain's population is female and evenly distributed. These assumptions cannot be made for the race relations legislation.

16   (1986) unreported, London Central Industrial Tribunal, see 7 EOR 27. Discussed by McCrudden, C, 'Rethinking positive action' [1986] 15 ILJ 219, pp 233–34.

17   This upholds the clear statutory policy of distinguishing between, on the one hand, positive action in the sense of encouraging people to apply for jobs and enabling them to be appropriately qualified for such jobs and, on the other hand, restricting jobs to members of one race or one gender or, by logical extension, requiring lower qualifications for women or black people.

Finally, s 35 of the RRA 1976 provides a defence: 'for any act done in affording persons of a particular racial group access to facilities or services to meet the special needs of persons of that group in regard to their education, training or welfare ...' This legitimises, for example, literacy campaigns targeted at immigrant groups, or assisting minority ethnic groups with housing or employment problems, assuming that the particular needs of the group targeted were sufficiently 'special'. Section 36 legitimises the provision of education or training to people not ordinarily resident in Great Britain and who do not intend to remain afterwards; language schools are the obvious example.

(d)   Training and encouraging recruitment – sexual orientation and religion or belief

Regulation 26 of the Employment Equality (Sexual Orientation) Regulations (the 'Sexual Orientation Regulations') 2003, and reg 25 of the Employment Equality (Religion or Belief) Regulations (the 'Religion or Belief Regulations') 2003 follow the scheme set out in ss 37 and 38 of the RRA 1976 or ss 47 and 48 of the SDA 1975, above. The difference is the trigger. Rather than under-representation, the Regulations state that training or encouragement may be given 'where it reasonably appears to the person doing the act that it prevents or compensates for disadvantages linked to sexual orientation [or religion or belief] suffered by persons doing that or likely to take up that work'.[18] The reason for the change given in the *pre-consultation* Explanatory Notes to the Sexual Orientation Regulations (but not the Religion or Belief Regulations) is the difficulty of obtaining statistics. These Explanatory Notes to both sets of Regulations suggest that 'disadvantage' could be under-representation or harassment.

(e)   The legislation generally

There is no question that training opportunities reserved for members of a particular protected group would, in the absence of these provisions, be unlawful. This is not necessarily true of other practices mentioned in the statutes. In particular, encouraging women to apply for a job does not entail discrimination against any individual man in the arrangements made for determining who is to be offered a job. It is thus permissible to state in advertisements that applications from women or black people will be particularly welcome because of under-representation. It may be lawful to adopt such a policy even where the specific under-representation provisions are not satisfied, but an employer would need to show that, despite the statement, there was no discrimination in the arrangements made for determining who should be employed. To make such a statement otherwise than in specific accord with the statutory provisions would be a high-risk strategy for an employer.

Other forms of acting to increase the number of applicants from the protected groups are also permissible, for example: advertising not only in traditional outlets but also in black newspapers; sending careers information specifically to schools with a substantial black population; and notifying employment agencies that applications from women or black people are particularly welcome. It is here hard to see that there

---

18 In the case of trade organisations, such as trade unions, 'holding such posts or likely to hold such posts'.

is any male or white victim of discrimination, especially if the targeting is not exclusively aimed at black or female recipients.[19] If male or white applicants have in the past predominated, taking action to increase the number of female or black applicants does not involve any less favourable treatment, and no requirement or condition, however widely that be interpreted, is imposed. Furthermore, it is only if the targeting is exclusively aimed that the statutory sections apply and thus need to be satisfied. Employers might wrongly be led to believe that the only permissible encouragement is that falling within the precise wording of the statute.

Section 48 of the SDA 1975 and s 38 of the RRA 1976, and the Regulations, apply similar principles to encouragement and training provided by employers in relation to work in their employment. This is of special significance in relation to career development, promotion, etc. If women or black people are under-represented in supervisory or management positions, it is lawful to run training courses to equip them for such positions, and specifically to encourage applications from members of these groups. The relevance and effectiveness of such policies depend on the reasons for the under-representation:

> There is a real risk that special training schemes will be set up to cater for ethnic minorities and women when the real problem is not that they lack training, but that there was a reluctance to appoint them to supervisory positions because of their race or sex. If the persons on such training schemes look to be already well qualified, the chances are that the organisation concerned has expected ethnic minority or women managers to be better qualified than whites or men ...[20]

By far the most important point concerning these provisions is that they are in all circumstances permissive rather than mandatory.[21] British employers are *never*[22] under a positive obligation to engage in any form of affirmative action, from the mildest forms of encouragement upwards. The provisions themselves are complex and ill-understood. Lack of detailed knowledge of the law may cause employers both to fear legal challenge and to under-estimate the scope of what is lawful. Many employers have implemented voluntary equal opportunities policies, but it is contended that these sections rarely have been central to such decisions.

(f) The 'symmetry problem'

The symmetrical nature of the legislation means that it protects men as well as women, white and black, straight and gay, Christian and Muslim,[23] even though protecting the former of each of these pairs is not its principal goal. The consequence is that an act to favour a principal protected group will *disfavour* another group. Once this produces a victim, it becomes unlawful as direct discrimination. This means that,

---

19 To take a different but parallel example, that Oxford and Cambridge universities might attempt to encourage more applicants from comprehensive schools certainly implies no discrimination against applicants from private schools.

20 Bourn, C and Whitmore, J, *Anti-Discrimination Law in Britain*, 3rd edn, 1996, London: Sweet & Maxwell, pp 146–47.

21 Cf the law on affirmative action which applies to Northern Ireland.

22 Under the DDA 1995, of course, there is a duty to make 'reasonable adjustments'.

23 The Religion or Belief Regulations 2003 should protect atheists as well. See further Chapter 6, pp 150–52.

save for the specified exceptions noted above, most affirmative action will be unlawful. The unforgiving nature of the legislation was emphasised in the next two cases.

Lambeth LBC v Commission For Racial Equality [1990] IRLR 231; [1990] ICR 768, CA

Balcombe LJ (at p 234):

It is undoubtedly the case that certain sections of the Act encourage positive action to meet the special needs of particular racial groups in certain defined fields, by providing that acts of discrimination that would otherwise be unlawful shall not be so if done for those purposes ...

Nevertheless, ... I am wholly unpersuaded that one of the two main purposes of the Act is to promote positive action to benefit racial groups. The purpose of the Act, as stated in its long title, is 'to make fresh provision with respect to discrimination, on racial grounds and relations between people of different racial groups,' and the substance of the operative Parts (I to IV) of the Act is to render acts of racial discrimination unlawful ...

However, I should make it clear ... I express no view of the case for or against positive action in favour of ethnic minorities in order to counter the effects of past discrimination; I confine my attention to the present meaning of the Act of 1976.

ACAS v Taylor EAT/788/97 (transcript)

The Advisory, Conciliation and Arbitration Service (ACAS) invited its staff to apply for 31 Senior Executive Officer (SEO) posts. This was a nationwide exercise and the first stage was for regional managers to rank the applicants. In Mr Taylor's region, four applicants, three of whom were male, were ranked 'B' grade. Mr Taylor was one of these. However, only the female was selected for interview. Nationally, eight out of eight of the 'B' grade females, and just six from 16 'B' grade males, were selected for interview. This selection procedure was influenced by the following guidance:

Please remember that more needs to be done to ensure the reality of the claim that ACAS is an equal opportunity employer. For example women make up only 17% of those at SEO level at present and ethnic minorities staff less than 1%. All staff should be considered on their merits as individuals. Where you have any doubts about the fairness of the Annual Reports you should not hesitate to take appropriate action.

The industrial tribunal found that Mr Taylor had been a victim of a policy of positive discrimination and as such had suffered direct sex discrimination. The Employment Appeal Tribunal (EAT) upheld that decision.

Morison J:

It seems to us that the guidance provisions to which we have referred should be reconsidered by ACAS. The sentence 'Please remember that more needs to be done to ensure the reality of the claim that ACAS is an equal opportunity employer' is readily capable of being misconstrued. Furthermore, it begs the question as to what is to be done and by whom. It seems to us that it would have been more appropriate and quite sufficient for the guidance to have reminded the line managers that ACAS was an equal opportunity employer and to draw attention to the fact that women and ethnic minorities staff at SEO level were poorly represented. Such poor representation was itself suggestive of potentially discriminatory practices in the past and the employers were entitled to draw that to the attention of those who had the responsibility for making decisions about promotions in the future. The way the guidance was composed seems to us to be capable of leading the unwary into positive discrimination.

The symmetry of the anti-discrimination principle denies discussion of the merits of any form of affirmative action. In *Hughes v Hackney LB*,[24] for example, a policy to increase the number of ethnic minorities doing a particular job did not prevail over the *individual's* right not to be discriminated against, that is, to be treated on the basis of merit. The reasoning in the leading case on the definition of direct discrimination, *James v Eastleigh BC*,[25] is based on the notion that good motive cannot be a defence to a claim of direct discrimination. While this is crucial as necessitating rejection of what might generally be regarded as bad motives, such as cost and customer preference, the decision treats all motives, good and bad, in the same condemnatory fashion. However, to entrust decisions as to the validity of motives to employment tribunals – or any courts – would itself be problematic. Such decisions would inevitably draw courts and tribunals into issues of great political sensitivity, as has happened in the USA. It is arguable that decisions as to the permissible scope of affirmative action are, so far as possible, more appropriately taken by legislatures than by the judiciary.

3   EC LAW

EC Treaty

Article 141(4)

With a view to ensuring full equality in practice between men and women in working life, the principle of equal treatment shall not prevent any Member State from maintaining or adopting measures providing for specific advantages in order to make it easier for the under-represented sex to pursue a vocational activity or to prevent or compensate for disadvantages in professional careers.

Equal Treatment Directive 76/207

Article 2

(4)   This Directive shall be without prejudice to measures to promote equal opportunity for men and women, in particular by removing existing inequalities which affect women's opportunities in the areas referred to in Article 1(1).[26]

---

24   (1986), unreported, London Central Industrial Tribunal, see 7 EOR 27. See further above, p 577, and discussed by McCrudden, C, 'Rethinking positive action' [1986] 15 ILJ 219, pp 233–34.

25   [1990] 2 AC 751; [1990] 2 All ER 607; [1990] IRLR 208, HL, discussed in Chapter 7, p 182.

26   That is, access to employment, vocational training and promotion, and working conditions. This is due to be replaced (by Art 2(8)) with a simple reference to the formula used in Art 141(4) of the EC Treaty (above); Equal Treatment (Amendment) Directive 2002/73/EC, Art 1, due to be implemented by 5 October 2005.

Race Directive 2000/43[27]

Article 5

With a view to ensuring full equality in practice, the principle of equal treatment shall not prevent any Member State from maintaining or adopting specific measures to prevent or compensate for disadvantages linked to racial or ethnic origin.

In addition to this legislation, there are other pronouncements indicating the policy of the law, and which have been used in the European Court of Justice (ECJ). The Declaration on Art 119(4) (now Art 141) of the EC Treaty, attached to the Treaty of Amsterdam, stated: 'When adopting the measures referred to in Article 119(4) of the Treaty ... Member States should, in the first instance, aim at improving the situation of women in working life.' The Council Recommendation (EEC) 84/635 (on the promotion of positive action for women)[28] stated: '... existing legal provisions on equal treatment, which are designed to afford rights to individuals, are inadequate for the elimination of all existing inequalities unless parallel action is taken by governments, both sides of industry and other bodies concerned, to counteract the prejudicial effects on women in employment which arise from social attitudes, behaviour and structures ...', and with reference to Art 2(4) of the Equal Treatment Directive recommended that Member States adopt a positive action policy designed, *inter alia*, to encourage: 'women candidates and the recruitment and promotion of women in sectors and professions, at levels where they are under-represented, particularly as regards positions of responsibility.'

European law grants the same primacy as English law to the principles of symmetry and the individual's right to be free of discrimination. It also resembles the British approach in that affirmative action is *permissible*, rather than mandatory. Until recently, the only pronouncements of the European Court in relation to positive action concerned the specific issues of pregnancy and maternity, areas which do not concern the question of the scope of permissible positive action in relation to recruitment. The following cases reveal – initially, in *Kalanke* – a deep-rooted judicial hostility at the European level to the very concept of affirmative action. Such hostility is especially apparent from the opinion of the Advocate General, whose philosophy was wholeheartedly endorsed in the much briefer judgment of the full Court. Subsequently though, and perhaps in response to the criticism of *Kalanke*, the ECJ has taken a less strict line and endorsed a number of affirmative action programmes. The case law so far has concerned only sex discrimination.

Kalanke v Freie Hansestadt Bremen Case C-450/93 [1995] IRLR 660; [1996] All ER (EC) 66; [1996] ICR 314, ECJ

The case, originating from Germany, concerned promotion to the position of section manager in the Parks Department. Where two candidates were equally qualified, the employers gave preference to the woman (the 'tie-break'). This implemented the

27 The Equal Treatment in Employment Directive 2000/28/EC, Art 7 (covering religion or belief, disability, age and sexual orientation) uses the same formula, qualified by Art 7(2) which provides: 'With regard to disabled persons, the principle of equal treatment shall be without prejudice to the right of Member States to maintain or adopt provisions on the protection of health and safety at work or to measures aimed at creating or maintaining provisions or facilities for safeguarding or promoting their integration into the working environment.'

28 OJ 1984 L331, p 34.

(regional) Bremen public service law, which required such preference where (a) the candidates were equally qualified and (b) where women were under-represented in the relevant post, defined as where women 'do not make up at least half the staff ... in the relevant personnel group ...'. The ECJ held that that this measure breached the Equal Treatment Directive.

Judgment (pp 667–68):

A national rule that, where men and women who are candidates for the same promotion are equally qualified, women are automatically to be given priority in sectors where they are under-represented, involves discrimination on grounds of sex.

...

[Article 2(4) of the Equal Treatment Directive] is specifically and exclusively designed to allow measures which, although discriminatory in appearance, are in fact intended to eliminate or reduce actual instances of inequality which may exist in the reality of social life ...

It thus permits national measures relating to access to employment, including promotion, which give a specific advantage to women with a view to improving their ability to compete in the labour market and to pursue a career on an equal footing with men.

Nevertheless, as a derogation from an individual right laid down in the directive, art 2(4) must be interpreted strictly (see *Johnston v Chief Constable of the RUC* ... (para 36)).[29]

National rules which guarantee women absolute and unconditional priority for appointment or promotion go beyond promoting equal opportunities and overstep the limits of the exception in Art 2(4) ...

Advocate General (pp 663–64):

To my mind, giving equal opportunities can only mean putting people in a position to attain equal results and hence restoring conditions of equality between members of the two sexes as regards starting points. In order to achieve such a result, it is obviously necessary to remove the existing barriers standing in the way of the attainment of equal opportunities between men and women ...

It seems to me to be all too obvious that the national legislation at issue in this case is not designed to guarantee equality as regards starting points. The very fact that two candidates of different sex have equivalent qualifications implies in fact by definition that the two candidates have had and continue to have equal opportunities; they are therefore on an equal footing at the starting block. By giving priority to women, the national legislation at issue therefore aims to achieve equality as regards the result or, better, fair job distribution simply in numerical terms between men and women. This does not seem to me to fall within either the scope or the rationale of Art 2(4) of the Directive ...

Article 2(4) ... does enable intervention by means of positive action, but ... only so as to raise the starting threshold of the disadvantaged category in order to secure an effective situation of equal opportunity. Positive action must therefore be directed at removing the obstacles preventing women from having equal opportunities by tackling, for example, educational guidance and vocational training. In contrast, positive action may not be directed towards guaranteeing women equal results from occupying a job, that is to say, at points of arrival, by way of compensating for historical discrimination. In sum, positive action may not be regarded, even less employed, as a means of remedying, through discriminatory measures, a situation of impaired equality in the past.[30]

Such systems are relatively commonplace in Germany and their lawfulness a matter of some political significance.[31] However, the operation of the system apparently left no room for leeway as under-representation was not merely a relevant factor; rather, if under-representation was established, and two candidates were held to be equally qualified, the law required automatic preference to be given to women, so, for example, a man repeatedly rejected on this basis would have no ground for complaint.[32] Furthermore:

> [the] target for women's representation in the public service chosen by the Bremen legislature was notably crude. Women may represent 50% of the population, but because of family responsibilities, women do not represent 50% of the economically active population. There was no attempt by Bremen to measure women's availability in the labour market or the proportionate numbers with qualifications for particular posts or grades. Thus, to give preference to women until they form 50% of each post and grade bore little relation to what the position would be in the absence of sex discrimination.[33]

The reaction to *Kalanke* was almost universal hostility, especially from the European Commission, which itself operated a scheme not unlike that which the European Court had condemned and thus had a vested interest in the issue. The Commission, in a communication sent to the European Parliament and the Council,[34] stated that the decision was only meant to condemn automatic quota systems which preventing the taking into account of individual circumstances. Unsurprisingly, the European Court had a second look at the issue.

Marschall v Land Nordrhein-Westfalen Case C-409/95, ECJ[35]

The rule under challenge here stated that where 'there are fewer women than men in the particular higher grade post in the career bracket, women are to be given priority for promotion in the event of equal suitability, competence and professional performance, unless reasons specific to an individual [male] candidate tilt the balance in his favour'. (This last phrase has become known as a 'savings clause'.) Advocate General Jacobs argued that no distinction could be drawn between this case and *Kalanke*. For the ECJ, however, the savings clause distinguished the case. It held that the rule was permissible.

Judgment (p 48):

> [E]ven where male and female candidates are equally qualified, male candidates tend to be promoted ... particularly because of prejudices and stereotypes concerning the role and capacities of women in working life and the fear, for example, that women

---

30 For comment, see Szyszczak, E, 'Positive action after *Kalanke*' (1996) 59 MLR 876.
31 See Shaw, J, 'Positive action for women in Germany: the use of legally binding quota systems', in Hepple, B and Szyszczak, E (eds), *Discrimination: The Limits of Law*, 1992, London: Mansell.
32 See (1996) 65 EOR 31.
33 *Ibid.*
34 COM(96) 88 final.
35 See also [1988] IRLR 39; [1998] CMLR 547; [1997] All ER (EC) 865.

will interrupt their working lives more frequently, that owing to household and family duties they will be less flexible in their working hours, or that they will be absent from work more frequently because of pregnancy, childbirth or breastfeeding.

For these reasons, the mere fact that a male candidate and a female candidate are equally qualified does not mean that they have the same chances.

It follows that a national rule, in terms of which, subject to the application of the saving clause, female candidates for promotion who are equally as qualified as the male candidates are to be treated preferentially in sectors where they are under-represented may fall within the scope of Art 2(4) if such a rule may counteract the prejudicial effects on female candidates of the attitudes and behaviour described above ...

[S]uch a national measure specifically favouring female candidates cannot guarantee absolute and unconditional priority for women in the event of a promotion without going beyond the limits of the exception laid down in [Art 2(4)] ...

[A] national rule which contains a saving clause does not exceed those limits if, in each individual case, it provides for male candidates who are equally as qualified as the female candidates a guarantee that the candidatures will be the subject of an objective assessment which will take account of all criteria specific to the individual candidates and will override the priority accorded to the female candidates where one or more of the criteria tilts the balance in favour of the male candidate.

'Limited positive discrimination allowed' (1998) 77 EOR 38, pp 39–40:

Positive action is the engine of progress for women in many Member States. Lacking a tradition of litigation by individuals to enforce the right not to be discriminated against such as has developed in the UK, women in countries such as Germany, Austria, the Netherlands and Scandinavia have focused on measures increasing group representation ... [R]ules mandating preferential treatment where women are under-represented are often the main way in which equal opportunities are implemented in practice ...

From a legal standpoint there is little to be said for this decision other than its outcome, though many will think that the outcome is all that really matters. The reasoning [in *Marschall*] is undistinguished. It is extremely difficult to see how this kind of positive discrimination can be said to fall within the scope of the derogation from the principle of non-discrimination allowed by Art 2(4) for 'measures to promote equal opportunity'. The ECJ refers to whether the rule 'is designed to promote quality of opportunity,' whether it is in fact 'intended to eliminate or reduce actual instances of equality.' The intention of the rule-maker, however, should have been of little weight; all positive discrimination measures are intended to reduce inequality, including the measure held unlawful in *Kalanke*. The relevant issue is not intent, but whether the rule properly falls within the description of a 'measure to promote equal opportunity' ...

Nor is there much of a basis for a principled distinction between *Marschall* and *Kalanke*. The North Rhine-Westphalia rules [permitted in *Marschall*] have all the heavy-handedness found in Bremen [prohibited in *Kalanke*], other than the vague savings clause allowing the preference in favour of women to be overridden in individual cases.

[O]peration of the rule does not require any prior assessment of how likely it is that women would be equally represented in the grade if there had been no discrimination by the employer. In many jobs, the proportion of women is a function of sex discrimination in education or vocational training, or of occupational choice by women, not of sex discrimination in recruitment by the employer. An employer can appoint 20% of all female applicants and 20% of all male applicants, but if there are 10 times as many men as women applying, there will be far fewer women than men in the post. Does this mean that women are 'under-represented' and should be given preferential treatment?

Re Badeck [2000] All ER (EC) 289; [2000] IRLR 432[36]

Here five particular systems (provided by German local legislation), designed to give equal access to public service posts, were challenged:

- *Flexible result quota*. Sectors and departments set binding targets. A woman will be preferred in any appointment if (a) she is equally qualified as the man, (b) it is necessary to achieve the target, and (c) there are no 'reasons of greater legal weight'. These 'reasons' favoured former employees, who left because for family reasons, employees who went part-time for family reasons, former temporary soldiers, seriously disabled persons, the long-term unemployed.

- *Academic flexible result quota*. Women were under-represented in the universities' temporary research assistants and academic assistants. These quotas worked as above, in that they reflected the proportion of women among respectively, graduates or students, in the particular discipline.

- *Strict training quota*. Where women were under-represented on training programmes, half of the places were reserved for women, if enough women applied. This, of course, attacks a cause of under-representation in the workplace.

- *Interview quota*. At least as many women as men, or all the women applicants, shall be called for interview for a job or training position. Those called must be suitably qualified for the job. If, for example, there are only three qualified women from seven applicants, then only three men can be called for interview, no matter how many qualified men apply. If, however, all the female applicants are qualified and called, then there is no limit on the number of qualified men who may be called.

- *Quota for collective bodies*. In making appointments to commissions, advisory boards, boards of directors and supervisory boards and other collective bodies, at least half the members should be women.

Before ruling that all five systems were permissible, the ECJ summarised the case law.

Judgment:

PRELIMINARY OBSERVATIONS

... 14. The interpretation of art 141(4) EC, [is] ... material to the outcome ... only if the court considers that art 2 precludes national legislation such as that at issue in the main proceedings.

15.   The court observes, next, that according to art 1(1) of the directive, its purpose is to put into effect in the member states the principle of equal treatment for men and women as regards, *inter alia*, access to employment, including promotion, and to training. That principle of equal treatment means that 'there shall be no

---

discrimination whatsoever on grounds of sex either directly or indirectly' (art 2(1)) ...

17. The court held in *Kalanke's* case that a national rule, to the effect that where equally qualified men and women are candidates for the same promotion, in sectors where there are fewer women than men at the level of the relevant post, women are automatically to be given priority, involves discrimination on grounds of sex ...

22. ... the court in *Marschall's* case (para 33) held that, unlike the rules at issue in *Kalanke's* case, a national rule which contains a saving clause does not exceed the limits of the exception in art 2(4) of the directive if, in each individual case, it provides, for male candidates who are as qualified as the female candidates, a guarantee that the candidatures will be the subject of an objective assessment which will take account of all criteria specific to the individual candidates and will override the priority accorded to female candidates, where one or more of those criteria tilt the balance in favour of a male candidate.

23. It follows that a measure which is intended to give priority in promotion to women in sectors of the public service where they are underrepresented must be regarded as compatible with Community law if it does not automatically and unconditionally give priority to women when women and men are equally qualified, and the candidatures are the subject of an objective assessment which takes account of the specific personal situations of all candidates.

24. It is for the national court to determine whether those conditions are fulfilled on the basis of an examination of the scope of the provision at issue.

25. However, under the case law the court has jurisdiction to supply the national court with an interpretation of Community law on all such points as may enable that court to determine that issue of compatibility for the purposes of the case before it ...

[*The first system*]

38. ... art 2(1) and (4) of the directive does not preclude a national rule which, in sectors of the public service where women are underrepresented, gives priority, where male and female candidates have equal qualifications, to female candidates where that proves necessary for ensuring compliance with the objectives of the women's advancement plan, if no reasons of greater legal weight are opposed, provided that that rule guarantees that candidatures are the subject of an objective assessment which takes account of the specific personal situations of all candidates ...

[*The second system*]

42. As the Advocate General observes in para 39 of his opinion, the special system for the academic sector, at issue in the main proceedings, does not fix an absolute ceiling but fixes one by reference to the number of persons who have received appropriate training, which amounts to using an actual fact as a quantitative criterion for giving preference to women.

43. It follows that the existence of such a special system for the academic sector encounters no specific objection from the point of view of Community law ...

[*The third system*]

49. ... when the [system] was adopted the legislature of the Land of Hesse considered that:

Despite the requirement enshrined in the Basic Law of equal rights for women and men and the prohibition of discrimination on grounds of sex in

Article 3 of the Basic Law, in social reality women continue to be disadvantaged compared with men and that, despite formal legal equality, in particular in employment, [women] do not have equal access to qualified ... positions.

That was regarded by the legislature of Hesse as an intolerable injustice in the light of the recent but consistent development of the marked educational success of young women compared to young men. ...

51.   That intention does not, however, necessarily entail total inflexibility. Paragraph 7(2) clearly provides that if, despite appropriate measures for drawing the attention of women to the training places available, there are not enough applications from women, it is possible for more than half of those places to be taken by men. ...

53.   Since the quota applies only to training places for which the state does not have a monopoly, and therefore concerns training for which places are also available in the private sector, no male candidate is definitively excluded from training. ...

54.   The measures provided for are thus measures which are intended to eliminate the causes of women's reduced opportunities of access to employment and careers, and moreover consist of measures regarding vocational orientation and training. Such measures are therefore among the measures authorised by art 2(4) of the directive, which are intended to improve the ability of women to compete on the labour market and to pursue a career on an equal footing with men.

[*The fourth system*]

... 58. The applicants ... consider that art 2(1) and (4) of the directive precludes such a rule. In their view, this is direct discrimination within the meaning of art 2(1) of the directive, which is not covered by the exception in art 2(4).

59.   The Land Attorney considers that the provision at issue in the main proceedings constitutes a strict quota, in that it concerns the number of women who are to be called to interview. In a case where not all the male and female candidates can be called for interview, the provision prescribes that at least as many women as men must be. In those circumstances, men may be disadvantaged and hence discriminated against on grounds of their sex. ...

60.   As the Advocate General observes in para 41 of his opinion, the provision ... does not imply an attempt to achieve a final result appointment or promotion but affords women who are qualified additional opportunities to facilitate their entry into working life and their career.

61.   Next, ... that provision, although laying down rules on the number of interviews to be given to women, also provides ... only qualified candidates ... are to be called to interview.

62.   This is consequently a provision which, by guaranteeing, where candidates have equal qualifications, that women who are qualified are called to interview, is intended to promote equal opportunity for men and women within the meaning of art 2(4) of the directive.

[*The fifth system*]

65.   It ... is not compulsory, in that it is a non-mandatory provision which recognises that many bodies are established by legislative provisions and that full implementation of the requirement of equal membership of women on those bodies would, in any event, require an amendment to the relevant law. Moreover, it does not apply to offices for which elections are held. Finally, since the provision is not mandatory it permits, to some extent, other criteria to be taken into account.

66. ... art 2(1) and (4) of the directive does not preclude a national rule relating to the composition of employees' representative bodies and administrative and supervisory bodies which recommends that the legislative provisions adopted for its implementation take into account the objective that at least half the members of those bodies must be women.[37]

67. In view of the foregoing, there is no need to rule on the interpretation of art 141(4) EC.

Here, the ECJ followed the 'savings clause' doctrine from *Kalanke* and *Marschall*. The last three systems had no savings clause as such, but the ECJ highlighted features that meant that each was not 'absolute' or 'mandatory'. The *interview quota* also fell into the acceptable category, identified in *Kalanke*, of removing obstacles to women attaining equal opportunity.

Abrahamsson and Anderson v Fogelqvist Case C-407/98 [2000] IRLR 732[38]

In the Swedish university sector, just 10% of professors were women. In response, legislation was passed to the effect that a woman possessing sufficient qualifications for the post *must* be chosen in preference to a male candidate who would otherwise have been chosen, provided that the difference between their qualifications was not so great that the appointment would be contrary to the requirement of objectivity in the making of appointments. There are two features to this system. First, it is mandatory, with no 'savings clause'. Secondly, a *lesser-* (rather than just *equally-*) qualified candidate could be selected. The ECJ held that this legislation breached the Equal Treatment Directive, but in answer to a further question stated (in para 62) that it would be permissible if it was not mandatory.

Judgment:

50 As regards the selection procedure, ... it does not appear from the relevant Swedish legislation that assessment of the qualifications of candidates by reference to the requirements of the vacant post is based on clear and unambiguous criteria such as to prevent or compensate for disadvantages in the professional career of members of the under-represented sex.

51 On the contrary, under that legislation, a candidate for a public post belonging to the under-represented sex and possessing sufficient qualifications for that post must be chosen in preference to a candidate of the opposite sex who would otherwise have been appointed, where that measure is necessary for a candidate belonging to the under-represented sex to be appointed.

52 It follows that the legislation at issue in the main proceedings automatically grants preference to candidates belonging to the under-represented sex, provided that they are sufficiently qualified, subject only to the proviso that the difference between the merits of the candidates of each sex is not so great as to result in a breach of the requirement of objectivity in making appointments.

53 The scope and effect of that condition cannot be precisely determined, with the result that the selection of a candidate from among those who are sufficiently qualified is ultimately based on the mere fact of belonging to the under-represented sex, and that this is so even if the merits of the candidate so selected are inferior to those of a candidate of the opposite sex. Moreover, candidatures are not subjected to an objective assessment taking account of the specific

---

37 The Advocate General had taken the opposite view on the fifth system.
38 See Numhauser-Henning, A, 'Swedish sex equality law before the ECJ' [2001] 30 ILJ 121.

personal situations of all the candidates. It follows that such a method of selection is not such as to be permitted by Article 2(4) of the Directive.

54   In those circumstances, it is necessary to determine whether legislation such as that at issue in the main proceedings is justified by Article 141(4) EC.

55   In that connection, it is enough to point out that, even though Article 141(4) EC allows the Member States to maintain or adopt measures providing for special advantages intended to prevent or compensate for disadvantages in professional careers in order to ensure full equality between men and women in professional life, it cannot be inferred from this that it allows a selection method of the kind at issue in the main proceedings which appears, on any view, to be disproportionate to the aim pursued. ...

62   ... Article 2(1) and (4) of the Directive does not preclude a rule of national case-law under which a candidate belonging to the under-represented sex may be granted preference over a competitor of the opposite sex, provided that the candidates possess equivalent or substantially equivalent merits, where the candidatures are subjected to an objective assessment which takes account of the specific personal situations of all the candidates.

In *Lommers*,[39] the ECJ held that Art 2 of the Equal Treatment Directive did: 'not preclude a scheme set up by a Minister to tackle extensive under-representation of women within his Ministry under which, in a context characterised by a proven insufficiency of proper, affordable care facilities, a limited number of subsidised nursery places made available by the Ministry to its staff is reserved for female officials alone whilst male officials may have access to them only in cases of emergency, to be determined by the employer. That is so, however, only in so far, in particular, as the said exception in favour of male officials is construed as allowing those of them who take care of their children by themselves to have access to that nursery places scheme on the same conditions as female officials.' Again, the 'savings clause' (the exception for lone male parents) is central to that decision.

It is clear from these cases that the ECJ has abandoned its 'strict' interpretation taken in *Kalanke*. From *Marschall and Badeck*, three requirements emerge for affirmative action to be lawful. First, there must be under-representation in the particular sector, department or profession. Secondly, the woman being preferred must be *equally* qualified to the man.[40] Thirdly, there must be 'savings clause'. This third ingredient is what the ECJ used to distinguish *Kalanke*, even though, as pointed out above, in *Marschall* it was 'vague'. The practical impact is highly dependent on when two people can properly be regarded as equally qualified. In the wide range of jobs where personal factors play a part in a hiring decision, it will not be difficult to justify a conclusion that there was no equality. It may be, however, that in Germany, candidates were sometimes treated as equally qualified to trigger the operation of the tie-break provision. In *Marschall*, the ECJ noted that: 'a man would tend to be appointed over an equally qualified woman ... because he is likely to be older and to have had longer service ...' In Britain, the experience of the respective candidates would normally feature as one of the qualifications for the job. If such qualifications prove unnecessary, they may be challenged as indirect discrimination.

---

39   *Lommers v Minister Van Landbouw, Natuurbeheer en Visserij* Case C-476/99 [2002] IRLR 430.

40   *Quaere* did the ECJ in *Abrahamson*, by suggesting that the candidates could possess 'substantially equivalent merits', imply it is permissible to give priority to a *lesser*-qualified candidate? (Case C-407/98 [2000] IRLR 732, at para 62 (see above). Emphasis supplied.)

4   US LAW[41]

In the USA, public sector affirmative action programmes are measured by the constitutional right to equal protection under the law. In *Metro Broadcasting v FCC*,[42] the challenged programmes were designed to encourage participation by racial minorities in the broadcasting industry. The purpose was *not* to compensate for past discrimination, but to promote diversification in programming. The Supreme Court held that as it served an 'important governmental objective', it was constitutional. However, in *Adarand Constructors v Pena*, the Court went back on this, holding that to be constitutional, an affirmative action programme had to be 'narrowly tailored' to serve a *compelling* governmental objective. In other words, it should be subjected to a 'strict scrutiny'. *Adarand* represents the current approach to affirmative action in the US. This was confirmed in the recent 'University of Michigan' cases, *Grutter* and *Gratz*.

Adarand Constructors v Pena 515 US 200 (1995) United States Supreme Court[43]

The Small Business Act[44] provided that not less than 5% per annum of all Government contracts should be awarded to certified small business concerns owned and controlled by socially and economically disadvantaged individuals.[45] A certified company was awarded a sub-contract, despite an uncertified company (Adarand) offering a lower bid. Adarand claimed that the statute discriminates on the basis of race in violation of the Federal Government's obligation, under the Fifth Amendment, not to deny anyone equal protection of the laws. The Supreme Court remanded the

---

41 See generally Eskridge Jr, W and Frickey, P, *Cases and Materials on Legislation, Statutes and the Creation of Public Policy*, 1995, St Paul: West Publishing, pp 67–87; White, JB, 'What's wrong with our talk about race? On history, particularity, and affirmative action' (2002) 100(7) Michigan Law Review 1927; Kamp, AR, 'The missing jurisprudence of merit' (2002) 11(2/3) Boston University Public Interest Law Journal 141; Cunningham, C, Loury, G and Skrentny, J, 'Passing strict scrutiny: using social science to design affirmative action programs' (2002) 90(4) Georgetown Law Journal 835; Edwards, J, *When Race Counts: The Morality of Racial Preference in Britain and America*, 1995, London: Routledge; Abram, M, 'Affirmative action: fair shakers and social engineers' (1986) 99 Harv L Rev 1312; Goldman, A, *Justice and Reverse Discrimination*, 1979, Princeton: Princeton UP; Merritt, D and Reskin, B, 'Sex, race and credentials: the truth about affirmative action in law faculty hiring' (1997) 97 Columbia L Rev 199; Duncan, M, 'The future of affirmative action: a jurisprudential/legal critique' (1982) 17 Harv CR CL LR 503; Rutherglen, G and Ortiz, D, 'Affirmative action under the Constitution and Title VII: from confusion to convergence' (1988) 35 UCLA L Rev 467; Rosenfeld, M, 'Affirmative action, justice and equalities: a philosophical and constitutional appraisal' (1985) Ohio State LJ 845.

42 *Metro Broadcasting v Federal Communications Commission* (1990) 497 US 547, 111 L Ed 2d 445, 110 S Ct 2997.

43 See also 115 S Ct 2097, 132 L Ed 2d 158. See Hasnas, J, 'Equal opportunity, affirmative action, and the anti-discrimination principle: the philosophical basis for the legal prohibition of discrimination' (2002) 71(2) Fordham Law Review 423; Anderson, E, 'Integration, affirmative action, and strict scrutiny' (2002) 77(5) New York University Law Review 1195; Weeden, D, 'Creating race-neutral diversity in federal procurement in a post-*Adarand* world' (2002) 23(4) Whittier Law Review 951; Baynes, L, 'Life After *Adarand*: what happened to the Metro Broadcasting diversity rationale for minority telecommunications ownership' (1999/2000) 33 University of Michigan Journal of Law Reform 87; McCrudden, C, *op cit*, fn 2.

44 72 Stat 384, as amended, 15 USC § 631.

45 Defined respectively as: 'those who have been subjected to racial or ethnic prejudice or cultural bias because of their identity as a member of a group without regard to their individual qualities' (*ibid*, s 8(a)(5), 15 USC § 637(a)(5)), or 'those socially disadvantaged individuals whose ability to compete in the free enterprise system has been impaired due to diminished capital and credit opportunities as compared to others in the same business area who are not socially disadvantaged' (*ibid*, s 8(a)(6)(A), 15 USC § 637(a)(6)(A)).

case to be reviewed under 'strict scrutiny'. Thomas J offered a more political, rather than technical, explanation.

Justice Thomas (at 240–41):

That these programs may have been motivated, in part, by good intentions cannot provide refuge from the principle that under our Constitution, the government may not make distinctions on the basis of race. As far as the Constitution is concerned, it is irrelevant whether a government's racial classifications are drawn by those who wish to oppress a race or by those who have a sincere desire to help those thought to be disadvantaged. There can be no doubt that the paternalism that appears to lie at the heart of this program is at war with the principle of inherent equality that underlies and infuses our Constitution. See Declaration of Independence ('We hold these truths to be self-evident, that all men are created equal, that they are endowed by their Creator with certain unalienable Rights, that among these are Life, Liberty, and the pursuit of Happiness').

These programs not only raise grave constitutional questions, they also undermine the moral basis of the equal protection principle. Purchased at the price of immeasurable human suffering, the equal protection principle reflects our Nation's understanding that such classifications ultimately have a destructive impact on the individual and our society. ... [T]here can be no doubt that racial paternalism and its unintended consequences can be as poisonous and pernicious as any other form of discrimination. So-called 'benign' discrimination teaches many that because of chronic and apparently immutable handicaps, minorities cannot compete with them without their patronizing indulgence. Inevitably, such programs engender attitudes of superiority or, alternatively, provoke resentment among those who believe that they have been wronged by the government's use of race. These programs stamp minorities with a badge of inferiority and may cause them to develop dependencies or to adopt an attitude that they are 'entitled' to preferences. ...

In my mind, government-sponsored racial discrimination based on benign prejudice is just as noxious as discrimination inspired by malicious prejudice. In each instance, it is racial discrimination, plain and simple.

Grutter v Bollinger (2003) 123 S Ct 2325, United States Supreme Court[46]

The University of Michigan's Law School included in its admissions policy the School's commitment to diversity, which was to contribute to the Law School's character and the legal profession. It made special reference to African-American, Hispanic and Native-American students, who otherwise may not be included in meaningful numbers. Accordingly, the School admitted a 'critical mass' of under-represented minority students. Quotas were not used. A majority (5:4) held the policy to be lawful. On the same day, the Court handed down a judgment[47] rejecting, by a majority of 6:3, the University's College of Literature, Science and the Arts policy of awarding each under-represented minority student 20% of the necessary admission

46 See also 156 L Ed 2d 304; 2003 US LEXIS 4800; 71 USLW 4498; 2003 Cal Daily Op Service 5378; 16 Fla L Weekly Fed S 367.
47 *Gratz v Bollinger* (2003) 123 S Ct 2411; 156 L Ed 2d 257; 2003 US LEXIS 4801; 71 USLW 4480; 91 Fair Empl Prac Cas (BNA) 1803; 84 Empl Prac Dec (CCH) P41,416; 2003 Cal Daily Op Service 5362; 16 Fla L Weekly Fed S 387.

points. In both cases, the Court applied Powell J's 'touchstone' judgment in *Regents of The University of California v Bakke*.[48]

Justice O'Connor (Part IIA):

Justice Powell began by stating that 'the guarantee of equal protection cannot mean one thing when applied to one individual and something else when applied to a person of another color. If both are not accorded the same protection, then it is not equal', *Bakke*, 438 US, at 289–90. In Justice Powell's view, when governmental decisions 'touch upon an individual's race or ethnic background, he is entitled to a judicial determination that the burden he is asked to bear on that basis is precisely tailored to serve a compelling governmental interest', *ibid*, at 299. Under this exacting standard, only one of the interests asserted by the university survived Justice Powell's scrutiny.

First, Justice Powell rejected an interest in 'reducing the historic deficit of traditionally disfavored minorities in medical schools and in the medical profession' as an unlawful interest in racial balancing, *ibid*, at 306–07. Second, Justice Powell rejected an interest in remedying societal discrimination because such measures would risk placing unnecessary burdens on innocent third parties 'who bear no responsibility for whatever harm the beneficiaries of the special admissions program are thought to have suffered', *ibid*, at 310. Third, Justice Powell rejected an interest in 'increasing the number of physicians who will practice in communities currently undeserved', concluding that even if such an interest could be compelling in some circumstances the program under review was not 'geared to promote that goal', *ibid*, at 306, 310.

Justice Powell approved the university's use of race to further only one interest: 'the attainment of a diverse student body', *ibid*, at 311. With the important proviso that 'constitutional limitations protecting individual rights may not be disregarded', Justice Powell grounded his analysis in the academic freedom that 'long has been viewed as a special concern of the First Amendment', *ibid*, at 312, 314. Justice Powell emphasized that nothing less than the 'nation's future depends upon leaders trained through wide exposure' to the ideas and mores of students as diverse as this Nation of many peoples', *ibid*, at 313 ... In seeking the 'right to select those students who will contribute the most to the 'robust exchange of ideas', a university seeks 'to achieve a goal that is of paramount importance in the fulfillment of its mission' 438 US, at 313. Both 'tradition and experience lend support to the view that the contribution of diversity is substantial', *ibid*.

Justice Powell was, however, careful to emphasize that in his view race 'is only one element in a range of factors a university properly may consider in attaining the goal of a heterogeneous student body', *ibid*, at 314. For Justice Powell, 'it is not an interest in simple ethnic diversity, in which a specified percentage of the student body is in effect guaranteed to be members of selected ethnic groups', that can justify the use of race, *ibid*, at 315. Rather, 'the diversity that furthers a compelling state interest encompasses a far broader array of qualifications and characteristics of which racial or ethnic origin is but a single though important element', *ibid* ...

Part IIIA

... The Law School's educational judgment that such diversity is essential to its educational mission is one to which we defer. The Law School's assessment that

---

48   438 US 265; 98 S Ct 2733; 57 L Ed 2d 750; 1978 US LEXIS 5; 17 Fair Empl Prac Cas (BNA) 1000; 17 Empl Prac Dec (CCH) P8402 (medical School's policy of reserving 16 out of 100 places for minority students held to be unlawful).

diversity will, in fact, yield educational benefits is substantiated by respondents and their *amici*. Our scrutiny of the interest asserted by the Law School is no less strict for taking into account complex educational judgments in an area that lies primarily within the expertise of the university. Our holding today is in keeping with our tradition of giving a degree of deference to a university's academic decisions, within constitutionally prescribed limits ...

These benefits are substantial. As the District Court emphasized, the Law School's admissions policy promotes 'cross-racial understanding', helps to break down racial stereotypes, and 'enables [students] to better understand persons of different races' ... These benefits are 'important and laudable' because 'classroom discussion is livelier, more spirited, and simply more enlightening and interesting' when the students have 'the greatest possible variety of backgrounds'.

The Law School's claim of a compelling interest is further bolstered by its *amici*, who point to the educational benefits that flow from student body diversity. In addition to the expert studies and reports entered into evidence at trial, numerous studies show that student body diversity promotes learning outcomes, and 'better prepares students for an increasingly diverse workforce and society, and better prepares them as professionals' ...

These benefits are not theoretical but real, as major American businesses have made clear that the skills needed in today's increasingly global marketplace can only be developed through exposure to widely diverse people, cultures, ideas, and viewpoints. ... Brief for General Motors Corp as *Amicus Curiae* 3–4.

5   EQUAL OPPORTUNITIES IN PRACTICE

It has been argued that affirmative action is widespread in the USA for four main reasons: (a) the public availability of the requisite statistics; (b) the potential imposition of extremely high damages; (c) the powerful position of the Equal Employment Opportunities Commission in conciliating and monitoring out-of-court settlements; and (d) the power and willingness of the courts to impose positive action orders in response to 'egregious' discrimination by the employer.[49] None of these four criteria apply to the current British situation. Why, then, should any British employer seek to engage in positive action? Most large employers have, in recent years, introduced equal opportunities policies. These may include communicating to employees the steps which are necessary to avoid breach of anti-discrimination law, the use of voluntary measures to increase female and black representation in the workplace[50] and, in much rarer cases, the use of numerical targets by which such increases may be judged.

The motivations for such policies are variable and not always clear. There is no doubt that, especially in the public sector, some employers have manifested an altruistic desire to attract more women and black people, such motivation not being primarily concerned with increasing the operational effectiveness of the employing enterprise. Other explanations are more functional: employers have sought to

---

49   See *Sheet Metal Workers v EEOC* (1986) 478 US 421, *United States v Paradise* (1987) 480 US 149. Atkins, S and Hoggett, B, *Women and the Law*, 1984, Oxford: Martin Robertson, p 55.

50   Many such policies also deal with discrimination on other grounds, such as sexual orientation and disability. Discussion of their operation in these areas will be found in the appropriate chapter.

improve the quality of their workforce by seeking to attract and retain highly qualified female employees, partly in response to a perceived shortage of skilled labour. While for such enterprises issues of race have taken a back seat, image factors may mean that they cannot be entirely ignored.

Jenkins, R, 'Equal opportunity in the private sector: the limits of voluntarism', in Jenkins, R and Solomos, J (eds), *Racism and Equal Opportunity Policies in the 1980s*, 1987, Cambridge: CUP, pp 113–15:

[T]here are at least seven factors which may lie behind the initial organisational decision to adopt an [equal opportunities] policy ...

In the first place, an EO policy may represent a straightforward response to a 'race' problem, such as, for example, pressure from the Commission for Racial Equality, an unfavourable [legal] decision, or a 'race'-related industrial relations problem. Second, the formulation and implementation of an EO policy may be an attempt at a pre-emptive strike, to prevent [such] difficulties ... happening in the future ... Third, such an initiative may be nothing more than a public relations strategy, aimed at improving the organisation's standing in the eyes of a particular constituency, be that its employees, its customers, or its paymasters. Looked at together, these three factors may be categorised as *defensive* or *reactive*. Impressionistic evidence leads one to believe that, certainly in the private sector, they are among the most characteristic reasons for EO policy formulation and implementation.

Coming now to the public sector in particular, a fourth factor which may underlie EO initiatives – one which is not unrelated to the public relations strategy discussed above – is the *political* appeal of such a problem. This is particularly the case in local government and especially in those cities with a concentration of the black vote ...

A fifth reason relates to the fact that the equal opportunity issue has become part of the professionalising rhetoric of personnel management specialists, an integral component of the profession's claim to the custodianship of employment policy and legal issues ... There are two dimensions of the professional personnel model of 'best practice' ...: one, it offers a *technical* rationale for formal 'rational' employment procedures, that is, in this manner the best possible recruits are selected and the optimum utility derived from manpower resources; and two, it is also a *moral* rationale, that is, that such an approach serves to ensure the fairness of the process ...[51]

Related to this is a sixth factor: the use to which individuals ... can put an EO policy in their personal mobility strategies within or between organisations ...

[The final factor] is the impact of *external* organisational policy. This can take three forms. The first is found in multinational organisations; here one may find policy

---

51   Thus, eg, the Equal Opportunities Commission Code of Practice, paras 34–35, states that an 'equal opportunities policy will ensure the effective use of human resources in the best interests of both the organisation and its employees. It is a commitment by the employer to the development and use of employment procedures and practices which do not discriminate on grounds of sex or marriage and which provide genuine equality of opportunity for all employees ... An equal opportunities policy must be seen to have the active support of management at the highest level. To ensure that the policy is fully effective, the following procedure is recommended:
   (a) the policy should be clearly stated and, where appropriate, included in a collective agreement;
   (b) overall responsibility for implementing the policy should rest with senior management;
   (c) the policy should be made known to all employees and, where reasonably practicable, to all job applicants'.

imperatives and even, in some cases, the *minutiae* of policy and procedural detail ...
being imported by an American or European controlling organisation and imposed on
its UK subsidiaries ... Second, policy may be formulated by management in the UK,
although more with an eye to satisfying the requirements of top management
elsewhere ... Third, even in wholly UK-owned organisations, policy may be
developed centrally at a senior corporate level and passed down to, or imposed upon,
subsidiary organisations ...

At the one extreme there are those organisations who express a public commitment to
'equal opportunity', in their job advertisements for example, but make no further
moves towards the operationalisation of such a commitment ... At the other end of the
spectrum, however, there are highly elaborate policies which include a wide variety of
topics from training, promotion and recruitment, to the provision of special facilities
for particular minority groups, to systems for the detailed ethnic and gender
monitoring of the workforce.

INDEX

remedies 548
remuneration 75
risk assessment.................... 499
reoccurring conditions........ 479–83, 489
sensory impairments................ 471
small businesses............ 489, 516–17
social model of disability 466, 478–79
statutory interpretation.... 466–73, 495–97
stereotyping 77–78
transport 514
unemployment...................... 77
United States........ 463, 469–70, 473
vicarious liability 490
victimisation 490, 492, 507–08, 519
vocational training................. 519

Disability Rights
  Commission 131, 515, 520
  assistance from.................. 528–29
  compensation 566–67
  discriminatory practices 563
  employment tribunals............ 528–29
  enforcement of
    anti-discrimination
    legislation 521, 549, 559–63
  establishment of 559
  functions 559–60
  injunctions...................... 562–63
  investigations, formal 559–62, 566–67
  named party investigations 560
  non-discrimination notices.... 560–63, 566
  persistent discrimination 562–63
  reform 566–67
  suspicion or belief of
    discrimination............. 561–62, 566
  terms of reference................ 560–61
  undertakings, need for binding 566

Disciplinary or grievance procedure.... 531

Discovery 416–19

Disfigurements 478–79

Dismissal
  See also Unfair dismissal 323–25
  adverse impact 270–73
  age discrimination 167–68
  compensation 384, 537
  constructive dismissal............ 323–25
  equal pay........................ 384
  pregnancy and childbirth 196–209, 213
  racial harassment.................. 230
  sex discrimination 323
  sexual harassment 229–31
  sexual orientation.......... 321, 323, 327
  statistics 270–73

Diversity..................... 4, 26–27, 91

Domestic life
  See Home

Domestic violence.................... 375

Dress
  anti-discrimination legislation 177
  codes........................... 177–82
  comparisons 177–82
  direct discrimination 177–82
  health and safety 290
  image 177–78
  justification 179
  less favourable treatment 177–82
  Northern Ireland 179
  Prison Service 355
  race............................. 290
  religion.......................... 290
  school uniforms 144–46, 184
  sex discrimination 177–82, 355
  sexual harassment 72–73
  stereotyping 177–79

EC law
  See also Equal treatment
  Acquired Rights Directive 120
  adverse impact 269–71
  affirmative action............... 581–90
  age discrimination 164, 167
  burden of proof 188–91, 247–48,
                                269, 273–74
  collective agreements............. 432–33
  compensation.............. 347, 434–36,
                                543–44
  difference, meaning of
    considerable 269–71
  direct race discrimination 169
  direct effect
    directives 109–12, 113
    EC Treaty 109
    horizontal.............. 109, 110, 113
    vertical 109, 110
  directives......................... 132
  disability discrimination 218, 461, 516,
                                518–19
  EC Treaty....................... 108–09
  emanations of the State 110–11
  employment 325, 327–28
  enforcement..................... 113–14
  equal pay 114, 379, 381–85, 276,
                                280, 401–02, 431–36,
                                438, 441–49, 452–53
  equality clauses 431
  free movement of workers 141–42
  gender reassignment 152–58, 162, 341
  genuine material factors... 410–11, 417–18,
                                421–22
  genuine occupational
    requirements 328–30, 338,
                                341–43, 345–48
  housing 371
  indirect discrimination 242–43, 543–44
  indirect effect..................... 111–12